Java™ Bible

Java™ Bible

Aaron Walsh and John Fronckowiak

IDG Books Worldwide, Inc.
An International Data Group Company

Foster City, CA ✦ Chicago, IL ✦ Indianapolis, IN ✦ New York, NY

Java™ Bible

Published by
IDG Books Worldwide, Inc.
An International Data Group Company
919 E. Hillsdale Blvd., Suite 400
Foster City, CA 94404
www.idgbooks.com (IDG Books Worldwide Web site)

Library of Congress Catalog Card No.: 97-070946

ISBN: 0-7645-8030-2

Printed in the United States of America

10 9 8 7 6 5 4 3 2 1

1B/QV/QV/ZY/FC

Distributed in the United States by IDG Books Worldwide, Inc.

Distributed by Macmillan Canada for Canada; by Transworld Publishers Limited in the United Kingdom; by IDG Norge Books for Norway; by IDG Sweden Books for Sweden; by Woodslane Pty. Ltd. for Australia; by Woodslane New Zealand Ltd. for New Zealand; by Addison Wesley Longman Singapore Pte Ltd. for Singapore, Malaysia, Thailand, Indonesia, and Korea; by Distribuidora Norma S.A.-Colombia for Colombia; by Intersoft for South Africa; by International Thomson Publishing for Germany, Austria, and Switzerland; by Toppan Company Ltd. for Japan; by Distribuidora Cuspide for Argentina; by Livraria Cultura for Brazil; by Ediciencia S.A. for Ecuador; by Ediciones ZETA S.C.R. Ltda. for Peru; by WS Computer Publishing Corporation, Inc., for the Philippines; by Unalis Corporation for Taiwan; by Contemporanea de Ediciones for Venezuela; by Computer Book & Magazine Store for Puerto Rico; by Express Computer Distributors for the Caribbean and West Indies. Authorized Sales Agent: Anthony Rudkin Associates for the Middle East and North Africa.

For general information on IDG Books Worldwide's books in the U.S., please call our Consumer Customer Service department at 800-762-2974. For reseller information, including discounts and premium sales, please call our Reseller Customer Service department at 800-434-3422.

For information on where to purchase IDG Books Worldwide's books outside the U.S., please contact our International Sales department at 650-655-3200 or fax 650-655-3297.

For information on foreign language translations, please contact our Foreign & Subsidiary Rights department at 650-655-3021 or fax 650-655-3281.

For sales inquiries and special prices for bulk quantities, please contact our Sales department at 650-655-3200 or write to the address above.

For information on using IDG Books Worldwide's books in the classroom or for ordering examination copies, please contact our Educational Sales department at 800-434-2086.

For press review copies, author interviews, or other publicity information, please contact our Public Relations department at 650-655-3000 or fax 650-655-3299.

For authorization to photocopy items for corporate, personal, or educational use, please contact Copyright Clearance Center, 222 Rosewood Drive, Danvers, MA 01923, or fax 978-750-4470.

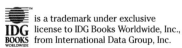

is a trademark under exclusive license to IDG Books Worldwide, Inc., from International Data Group, Inc.

ABOUT IDG BOOKS WORLDWIDE

Welcome to the world of IDG Books Worldwide.

IDG Books Worldwide, Inc., is a subsidiary of International Data Group, the world's largest publisher of computer-related information and the leading global provider of information services on information technology. IDG was founded more than 25 years ago and now employs more than 8,500 people worldwide. IDG publishes more than 275 computer publications in over 75 countries (see listing below). More than 60 million people read one or more IDG publications each month.

Launched in 1990, IDG Books Worldwide is today the #1 publisher of best-selling computer books in the United States. We are proud to have received eight awards from the Computer Press Association in recognition of editorial excellence and three from *Computer Currents'* First Annual Readers' Choice Awards. Our best-selling *...For Dummies*® series has more than 30 million copies in print with translations in 30 languages. IDG Books Worldwide, through a joint venture with IDG's Hi-Tech Beijing, became the first U.S. publisher to publish a computer book in the People's Republic of China. In record time, IDG Books Worldwide has become the first choice for millions of readers around the world who want to learn how to better manage their businesses.

Our mission is simple: Every one of our books is designed to bring extra value and skill-building instructions to the reader. Our books are written by experts who understand and care about our readers. The knowledge base of our editorial staff comes from years of experience in publishing, education, and journalism — experience we use to produce books for the '90s. In short, we care about books, so we attract the best people. We devote special attention to details such as audience, interior design, use of icons, and illustrations. And because we use an efficient process of authoring, editing, and desktop publishing our books electronically, we can spend more time ensuring superior content and spend less time on the technicalities of making books.

You can count on our commitment to deliver high-quality books at competitive prices on topics you want to read about. At IDG Books Worldwide, we continue in the IDG tradition of delivering quality for more than 25 years. You'll find no better book on a subject than one from IDG Books Worldwide.

John Kilcullen
CEO
IDG Books Worldwide, Inc.

Steven Berkowitz
President and Publisher
IDG Books Worldwide, Inc.

Eighth Annual Computer Press Awards ≥1992

Ninth Annual Computer Press Awards ≥1993

Tenth Annual Computer Press Awards ≥1994

Eleventh Annual Computer Press Awards ≥1995

IDG Books Worldwide, Inc., is a subsidiary of International Data Group, the world's largest publisher of computer-related information and the leading global provider of information services on information technology. International Data Group publishes over 275 computer publications in over 75 countries. Sixty million people read one or more International Data Group publications each month. International Data Group's publications include: **ARGENTINA:** Buyer's Guide, Computerworld Argentina, PC World Argentina; **AUSTRALIA:** Australian Macworld, Australian PC World, Australian Reseller News, Computerworld, IT Casebook, Network World, Publish, Webmaster; **AUSTRIA:** Computerwelt Osterreich, Networks Austria, PC Tip Austria; **BANGLADESH:** PC World Bangladesh; **BELARUS:** PC World Belarus; **BELGIUM:** Data News; **BRAZIL:** Annuário de Informática, Computerworld, Connections, Macworld, PC Player, PC World, Publish, Reseller News, Supergamepower; **BULGARIA:** Computerworld Bulgaria, Network World Bulgaria, PC & MacWorld Bulgaria; **CANADA:** CIO Canada, Client/Server World, ComputerWorld Canada, InfoWorld Canada, NetworkWorld Canada, WebWorld; **CHILE:** Computerworld Chile, PC World Chile; **COLOMBIA:** Computerworld Colombia, PC World Colombia; **COSTA RICA:** PC World Centro America; **THE CZECH AND SLOVAK REPUBLICS:** Computerworld Czechoslovakia, Macworld Czech Republic, PC World Czechoslovakia; **DENMARK:** Communications World Danmark, Computerworld Danmark, Macworld Danmark, PC World Danmark, Techworld Denmark; **DOMINICAN REPUBLIC:** PC World Republica Dominicana; **ECUADOR:** PC World Ecuador; **EGYPT:** Computerworld Middle East, PC World Middle East; **EL SALVADOR:** PC World Centro America; **FINLAND:** MikroPC, Tietoverkko, Tietovikko; **FRANCE:** Distributique, Hebdo, Info PC, Le Monde Informatique, Macworld, Reseaux & Telecoms, WebMaster France; **GERMANY:** Computer Partner, Computerwoche, Computerwoche Extra, Computerwoche FOCUS, Global Online, Macwelt, PC Welt; **GREECE:** Amiga Computing, GamePro Greece, Multimedia World; **GUATEMALA:** PC World Centro America; **HONDURAS:** PC World Centro America; **HONG KONG:** Computerworld Hong Kong, PC World Hong Kong, Publish in Asia; **HUNGARY:** ABCD CD-ROM, Computerworld Szamitastechnika, Interneto online Magazine, PC World Hungary, PC-X Magazin Hungary; **ICELAND:** Tolvuheimur PC World Island; **INDIA:** Information Communications World, Information Systems Computerworld, PC World India, Publish in Asia; **INDONESIA:** InfoKomputer PC World, Komputek Computerworld, Publish in Asia; **IRELAND:** ComputerScope, PC Live!; **ISRAEL:** Macworld Israel, People & Computers/Computerworld; **ITALY:** Computerworld Italia, Macworld Italia, Networking Italia, PC World Italia; **JAPAN:** DTP World, Macworld Japan, Nikkei Personal Computing, OS/2 World Japan, SunWorld Japan, Windows NT World, Windows World Japan; **KENYA:** PC World East African; **KOREA:** Hi-Tech Information, Macworld Korea, PC World Korea; **MACEDONIA:** PC World Macedonia; **MALAYSIA:** Computerworld Malaysia, PC World Malaysia, Publish in Asia; **MALTA:** PC World Malta; **MEXICO:** Computerworld Mexico, PC World Mexico; **MYANMAR:** PC World Myanmar; **NETHERLANDS:** Computer! Totaal, LAN Internetworking Magazine, LAN World Buyers Guide, Macworld Netherlands, Net, WebWereld; **NEW ZEALAND:** Absolute Beginners Guide and Plain & Simple Series, Computer Buyer, Computer Industry Directory, Computerworld New Zealand, MTB, Network World, PC World New Zealand; **NICARAGUA:** PC World Centro America; **NORWAY:** Computerworld Norge, CW Rapport, Datamagasinet, Financial Rapport, Kursguide Norge, Macworld Norge, Multimediaworld Norge, PC World Ekspress Norge, PC World Nettverk, PC World Norge, PC World ProduktGuide Norge; **PAKISTAN:** Computerworld Pakistan; **PANAMA:** PC World Panama; **PEOPLE'S REPUBLIC OF CHINA:** China Computer Users, China Computerworld, China InfoWorld, China Telecom World Weekly, Computer & Communication, Electronic Design China, Electronics Today, Electronics Weekly, Game Software, PC World China, Popular Computer Week, Software Weekly, Software World, Telecom World; **PERU:** Computerworld Peru, PC World Profesional Peru, PC World SoHo Peru; **PHILIPPINES:** Click!, Computerworld Philippines, PC World Philippines, Publish in Asia; **POLAND:** Computerworld Poland, Computerworld Special Report Poland, Cyber, Macworld Poland, Networld Poland, PC World Komputer; **PORTUGAL:** Cerebro/PC World, Computerworld/Correio Informático, Dealer World Portugal, Mac*In/PC*In Portugal, Multimedia World; **PUERTO RICO:** PC World Puerto Rico; **ROMANIA:** Computerworld Romania, PC World Romania, Telecom Romania; **RUSSIA:** Computerworld Russia, Mir PK, Publish, Seti; **SINGAPORE:** Computerworld Singapore, PC World Singapore, Publish in Asia; **SLOVENIA:** Monitor; **SOUTH AFRICA:** Computing SA, Network World SA, Software World SA; **SPAIN:** Communicaciones World España, Computerworld España, Dealer World España, Macworld España, PC World España; **SRI LANKA:** Infolink PC World; **SWEDEN:** CAP&Design, Computer Sweden, Corporate Computing Sweden, Internetworld Sweden, it.branschen, Macworld Sweden, MaxiData Sweden, MikroDatorn, Natverk & Kommunikation, PC World Sweden, PCaktiv, Windows World Sweden; **SWITZERLAND:** Computerworld Schweiz, Macworld Schweiz, PCtip; **TAIWAN:** Computerworld Taiwan, Macworld Taiwan, NEW ViSiON/Publish, PC World Taiwan, Windows World Taiwan; **THAILAND:** Publish in Asia, Thai Computerworld; **TURKEY:** Computerworld Turkiye, Macworld Turkiye, Network World Turkiye, PC World Turkiye; **UKRAINE:** Computerworld Kiev, Multimedia World Ukraine, PC World Ukraine; **UNITED KINGDOM:** Acorn User UK, Amiga Action UK, Amiga Computing UK, Apple Talk UK, Computing, Macworld, Parents and Computers UK, PC Advisor, PC Home, PSX Pro, The WEB; **UNITED STATES:** Cable in the Classroom, CIO Magazine, Computerworld, DOS World, Federal Computer Week, GamePro Magazine, InfoWorld, I-Way, Macworld, Network World, PC Games, PC World, Publish, Video Event, THE WEB Magazine, and WebMaster; online webzines: JavaWorld, NetscapeWorld, and SunWorld Online; **URUGUAY:** InfoWorld Uruguay; **VENEZUELA:** Computerworld Venezuela, PC World Venezuela; and **VIETNAM:** PC World Vietnam.   3/24/97

Credits

Acquisitions Editor
John Osborn

Development Editors
Matt Lusher
Heidi Steele

Technical Editor
Rich Burridge

Copy Editors
Tim Borek
Tracy Brown
Barry Childs-Helton
Mary Ann Faughnan
Suki Gear
Nate Holdread
Michael D. Welch

Project Coordinator
Tom Debolski

**Graphics and
Production Specialists**
Linda Marousek
Hector Mendoza
Christopher Pimentel
Andreas Schueller

Quality Control Specialists
Mick Arellano
Mark Schumann

Cover Design
Murder By Design

Proofreader
Mary C. Barnack

Indexer
Liz Cunningham

About the Authors

Aaron Walsh of Boston, Massachusetts, is President and CEO of Mantis Development Corporation, an Internet development and consulting firm. He has been building state-of-the-art software for 14 years and was an early convert to the Java programming language. He is author of *Java For Dummies* (IDG Books Worldwide) and *Foundations of Java Programming for the World Wide Web* (IDG Books Worldwide). He can be reached at aaron@mantiscorp.com.

John W. Fronckowiak is president and founder of IDC Consulting, Inc., which specializes in Internet/intranet consulting, application development, and network consulting. He has extensive experience with database application development, client-server networking, Internet and intranet presence development, application development, and project management.

John's previous writing experience includes *COBOL For Dummies Quick Reference*, and *Building an Intranet For Dummies* from IDG Books Worldwide.

John lives in East Amherst, New York, with his wife Diane and their cat Eiffel. John can be reached at john@idcc.net.

To my nephew Dane, with love. — Aaron Walsh

For my family. — John Fronckowiak

Preface

Welcome to *Java Bible*, a book designed to teach programmers how to develop dynamic, distributed Web content using the Java language. Although experience with C or C++ is helpful, it's not required. Not only is this book a comprehensive reference for the Java language, it actually teaches you how to create and deploy dynamic software products using the most exciting programming language ever!

Unlike many programming books that get placed on the bottom shelf of your bookcase, this one is different: *Java Bible* is designed to be both a guide and a reference. As you learn the ropes of Java, you'll appreciate the attention given in each chapter, teaching you the ins and outs of the language and the issues you'll face along the way. Once you're comfortable programming in Java, this book takes on an entirely different appeal.

As a comprehensive reference to the massive Java language, *Java Bible* is packed with information necessary to refine your programming skills. Specifically, you'll find it rich with source code examples, Application programming interface (API) tables, hints, tips, and warnings that are meant for the experienced Java programmer. As a result, you'll find yourself turning to this book long after it has helped you become a master Java developer.

What You'll Need

The only thing you'll need to become an experienced Java programmer is this book and a computer capable of running the Java Development Kit (JDK). The CD-ROM provided contains all the tools you'll need to write, compile, test, and debug all levels of Java program. Specifically, it comes with the JDK for the following supported platforms: Windows 95/NT, Sun Solaris, and the Macintosh.

Additionally, the CD-ROM is packed with more than 100 applets, their complete source code (graciously contributed by scores of Java developers from around the world), and online tutorials. This alone is reason enough to clear off a space on your desk for this book/disc combo. But that's just the beginning. You'll also find back issues of *JavaWorld*, IDG Books' Web-based magazine for Java developers, containing "living" articles in HTML format. Here you'll find a raft of in-depth Java articles, applets, and their source code written by professional Java developers.

Use or Lose It: How to Use This Book

The only way to learn a programming language is to use it! And that's exactly what this book is designed to do: get you up and running with Java. Although the text itself is meant to be read, the examples in it are meant to be used.

Of course, as you get more experienced with Java, you'll outgrow the introductory programs provided in the text. That's why the listings become more complicated the deeper you get into it, and why such a wide range of real, working applets and their source code have been provided on CD-ROM. Think of this book and the CD-ROM as inseparable, and use them both.

Feel free to jump around from part to part or chapter to chapter as you see fit. If you've already dabbled in the Java language and know how to write and compile programs, there's absolutely no need to do it all over again. Instead, you might want to take a peek at the tables, tips, warnings, and other reference materials provided for the experienced programmer.

As you read this book, you'll notice we "flip-flop" between the UNIX and Windows styles when it comes to entering commands on the command line (see "Command-line entries" later in this preface) or discussing the JDK and a general sense. Because Java is a cross-platform technology, we attempt to give equal play to both platforms. Because the majority of the book was written on a Windows system, you'll notice that the text and examples tend to favor that platform. Whether you're a Windows user or a UNIX user, however, you should realize that any platform-specific material presented in the text must be adapted to the particular machine you are using. Once you are comfortable doing so, the material discussed in this book will be easily applied to the platform you use.

The Many Versions of Java

This book provides information on all three available versions of the Java platform: JDK 1.0, JDK 1.1, and JDK 1.2, which was still in beta 2 during final review of this manuscript. As this book went to press, Sun released beta 3 of JDK 1.2, and a beta 4 and final product release were yet to come.

We faced a difficult choice in deciding whether to publish the *Java Bible* today or to wait for the JDK 1.2 final release. We have chosen the former course because the JDK 1.2 changes of greatest importance to readers of this book are either complete or well-specified, and because we suspect most of you want to know about these now rather than later. For those developing applications with Java 1.1, this book covers a number of classes that are in final release, but are not yet integrated with the Java JDK 1.2. The most important of these are the new JFC 1.1 classes and Swingset components for creating cross-platform graphical user interfaces (GUIs).

Let's face it; Java is a moving target. We will do our best to keep you informed of new developments at http://www.idgbooks.com. We also encourage you to periodically check the JavaSoft Web site (http://java.sun.com) for news of JDK 1.1 maintenance releases and 1.2 betas. And of course, JavaWorld (http://www.JavaWorld.com) is the place to look for in-depth technical updates and breaking Java news.

Part I: Introducing Java

Part I is the foundation for the entire book. This part introduces the Java programming language and its concepts. You gain an understanding of how the Java programming language was developed and why Java has become all the rage with Web-based application developers. You are introduced to object-oriented programming concepts and design methodologies. After that introduction, you learn how to apply its techniques to building your own Java applications and Web-based applets.

This part also introduces the tools that comprise Sun's Java Development Toolkit (JDK) — the tools you use to create your own Java programs.

Part II: Getting Up to Speed

In this part, you walk through the process of designing, developing, testing, and debugging your first Java application. You learn how to design your applications to function as both standalone applications and Web-based applets. You also are introduced to the debugging tools provided with the Java Development Toolkit, and you learn how to use the Java debugger to stomp those annoying bugs. This part shows you how to modify your Java applications and applets to accept and use the parameters specified by command-line arguments. By the time you finish this part, you'll know how to use the Web to find and borrow Java applications and objects that can get your applications up and running even faster!

Part III: Programming Elements and Techniques

This part introduces the brass tacks of the Java programming language. Beginning with the basic concepts of tokens, types, and values, the chapters explore all the nooks and crannies of Java. You are introduced to the language basics such as defining and using variables, controlling program flow, creating your own classes, and handling exceptions. All the standard Java packages and classes — including strings, arrays, streams, and threads — are reviewed in detail. Finally, this part shows you how to weave your Java applications into Web pages and how to package your Java applications efficiently, using Java Archive (JAR) files for fast Web access.

Part IV: Abstract Windowing Toolkit

This part introduces the Abstract Windowing Toolkit. Although the AWT is being replaced by the Java Foundation Classes (JFC) in JDK 1.2, understanding the AWT will help you support older Java applications and give you a solid foundation for understanding the JFC. This part shows you how to add graphics, fonts, windows, and user-interface controls — such as buttons, list boxes, combo boxes, menus, and sliders — to your own Java applications. Each AWT object described also includes a complete reference for you to use when you develop your own applications.

This part includes a step-by-step guide to the development of the JavaDraw application — a basic graphic-drawing application. You'll learn how to use the AWT classes to design and implement your application. To get you ready to move to the latest and greatest Java Development Kit — version 1.2 — this part introduces the powerful newcomers to JDK 1.2: the Java Foundation Classes and the new user interface classes included in them, nicknamed Swing. A detailed review of each interface component in the Swing classes demonstrates why these classes are poised to replace the Abstract Windowing Toolkit for Java-based user-interface development.

Part V: Advanced Java

This section introduces you to some advanced topics that outline exciting Java capabilities and directions. In this part you learn how to implement and use *JavaBeans*, standalone components that can be used by other applications, including the Java applications you create. Java also provides complete support for networking and database connectivity. These chapters also discuss adding network connectivity to your Java applications, and how to use the Java Database Classes (JDBC) to add database support. Finally, this part reviews the support provided by Java for multimedia applications.

Conventions

As you go through this book, there are a few elements you'll find in nearly every chapter. These are conventions established to help make the text easy to read and consistent from start to finish.

Source code

Any time you encounter source code, it will be in a special font; this applies to code listings as well as code fragments. This way, it's easy to identify code throughout the book. Whether in a fragment or a numbered listing, code in the text appears in the following style:

```
import java.net.*;
public class GetAddresses {
    public static void main(String[] argv) {
        InetAddress ia;
        try {
            ia = InetAddress.getLocalHost();
            System.out.println("Local host: " + ia);
            ia = InetAddress.getByName(null);
            System.out.println("Null host: " + ia);
            ia = InetAddress.getByName("www.idgbooks.com");
            System.out.println("IDG host: " + ia);
        } catch(UnknownHostException e) {
            System.out.println(e);
        }
    }
}
```

Code elements that appear in the running text — such as the names of objects, classes, variables, methods, and the like — are also shown in the code font (for example, the JComponent class or the toCharArray() method), as are the file and folder names and Web URLs.

Command-line entries

Any time a command-line entry appears in the book, it will reside on its own line and in the code style to distinguish it from the rest of the text. Although the majority of command-line examples are in the Microsoft Windows format, many are in the UNIX format. In most cases, the precise format doesn't matter, since you're able to use the command for your particular platform as long as you follow the format conventions for it. Many times, command-line entries are generic enough to be used "as is," regardless of the platform you're running; therefore, the command-line prompt is identified with a greater-than symbol (>), as in the following example:

```
> javac myprogram.java
```

Icons

A number of special icons appear throughout the book to call your attention to topics of special relevance and interest.

The CD-ROM icon identifies materials provided on (you guessed it) the CD-ROM that accompanies this book. For details on the contents of the CD-ROM, see Appendix B.

The Note icon is used to bring your attention to things you might otherwise be tempted to highlight with a fluorescent marker.

The Tip icon is used to point out a tip or technique that will save you time, effort, money, or all three!

The Warning icon is used to alert you to potential problems that might wreak havoc on your Java programs. Throughout the text, this icon pinpoints bugs, errors, oversights, gaffes, and anything else that may disrupt your Java programs.

JDK 1.1 and 1.2 icons point out specific parts of Java that have changed since JDK 1.0 was released. Although much of the basic Java syntax has been maintained since the initial release, which enables us to cover most topics from a common standpoint, it's worth highlighting important changes in JDK 1.1 and JDK 1.2.

A note on our examples in the text

This book's cover tells you that two authors collaborated in writing this book. Most chapters, however, were written by one author or the other, drawing upon individual experience. Thus we've used first-person-singular constructions in many of the examples and opinions ("I recommend," "in my experience," and so forth). We hope this convention helps maintain the book's personal tone. But do remember two of us are out there—so the use of *I* may change from chapter to chapter.

Acknowledgments

From Aaron Walsh:

I'd like to give special thanks to the many people who made this book possible, especially to my co-author, John Fronckowiak, for all his fine work and great help. I'd also like to thank the small army of writers and developers who have contributed their time and effort to the charge, especially Paul Kinnucan, Doug Schwartz, Piroz Mohseni, Bernard Van Haecke, Arthur Griffith, and Charley Cleveland; and to Rich Burridge, who, as technical editor of this book, kept us all on track.

In addition, I'd like to extend great thanks to Barbara Mikolajczak of Mantis Development Corporation, for finding and capturing most of the Web sites sprinkled throughout this book, and for building the CD-ROM that comes with it; to Lisa Sontag for her help with permissions for those Web sites; and to Heidi Steele, whose developmental editing contributed so much to the quality of the book. And finally, special thanks to the good folks at IDG Books Worldwide without whom this book would never have seen the light of day — especially John Osborn, Matt Lusher, Barry Childs-Helton, Lenora Chin-Sell, and Jake Mason.

From John Fronckowiak:

I would like to thank everyone that helped make this book possible: my wife, Diane, for helping me work through the day-to-day ups and downs while helping to keep me focused on my larger goals; and my family — Mom, Dad, Kim, Mike, Marie, Mom S., Alicia, and Becky — for understanding and supporting my desire to write. I'd also like to send special thanks to Studio B Productions, Inc. for presenting me with the opportunity to work on this project — David Rogelberg, who believed in me and my abilities; and Brian Gill, who provided an immeasurable amount of assistance in working through the many details of this project I could never handle on my own, and many words of encouragement. Thanks to John Osborn, who believed that I could offer something to this project, and Matt Lusher, who helped immensely in running the marathon this book presented! Finally, thanks to my cat, Eiffel, and Quaker parrot, Elmo, for providing companionship and many loud meows and squawks!

Contents at a Glance

Contents

Part V: Advanced Java 839

Chapter 26: JavaBeans 841

Chapter 27: Networking 871

Introducing Java

Part I provides a foundation for the entire book. In this part you are introduced to the Java programming language and its concepts. You gain an understanding of how the Java programming language was developed and why Java has become all the rage with Web-based application developers. Before you begin programming with Java, it's useful to understand the object-oriented programming concepts and design methodologies introduced in this part. Object-oriented programming requires a different way of thinking from that used with traditional programming languages (such as C). Following your introduction to object-oriented programming, these chapters show you how to apply their techniques to building your own Java applications and Web-based applets.

In addition to exploring Java technology, this part introduces the tools that comprise Sun's Java Development Toolkit (JDK) — the tools you use to create your own Java programs. You'll also learn how to get the latest Java JDK installed on Solaris, Windows 95, and Windows NT platforms.

An Overview of Java

What is Java? This entire book is devoted to answering that question. Java is the most important advance in programming technology of the past decade; it promises a whole new programming paradigm of portability and robust object-oriented capabilities. By the time you finish this book, you will have learned Java in all its glory. If you're new to programming, this will be a whole new world for you; if you're already a developer but don't know Java, you'll most likely be convinced to switch to Java as a primary programming language. But before you toss your old development environment out the window, perhaps an introduction to Java is in order. After all, Java is an entirely new technology, with many facets that work together to get the job done.

Java Environment

Following is a brief rundown of Java's main features. You'll find more detailed information on these in subsequent chapters of this book.

Java language

The Java *language* is an object-oriented programming language developed by James Gosling of Sun Microsystems. Although its roots are in C++, it is a completely new software development language. Unlike C++, it is entirely object-oriented and designed expressly with distributed, platform-independent environments in mind. The Java language is designed to create executable content, such as applets, applications, and handlers. In fact, Sun's HotJava Web browser, the first Java-savvy browser, is an application written entirely in the Java language.

A Brief History of Java

Sun Microsystems developed the Java programming language in 1991 as part of a research project that sought to create software for consumer electronic devices such as television sets, television set-top boxes, and VCRs. Java's primary goal at that time was to be small, fast, efficient, and easily portable to a wide range of hardware devices. Pursuing that goal has made Java the general-purpose programming language it is today.

Java was used in several projects by Sun, but it really was invisible until the release of the HotJava browser in 1994. Sun wrote HotJava quickly to demonstrate the prowess of Java as a language for the Internet, and to show the complexity of possible applications that could be developed.

The first Java Development Kits were released shortly afterward. Version 1.0 of the JDK included tools for developing applets and applications for Sun Solaris 2.3, Windows NT, Windows 95, and Macintosh. Shortly after the first JDK release, Java took the world by storm — and it hasn't stopped making news since!

Java runtime environment

Once you have written an applet, application, or handler in the Java language, it's up to the runtime environment to execute the code. The Java *runtime environment*, also called the Java *architecture*, is made up of the Java language and the Java Virtual Machine, which together provide the means to execute Java code. The Java runtime environment is portable and platform-neutral; it is the basis of Java's distributed computing capabilities, and it will eventually be available for most popular personal computing platforms.

Currently, the Java runtime environment is available to end users through Sun's HotJava browser, Netscape Communications Corp.'s Netscape Navigator browser, and Microsoft's Internet Explorer.

Java tools

The tools Java uses provide developers with everything they need to begin creating Java code. They include the Java compiler, interpreter, documentation, debugger, and class libraries from which you build actual Java programs (applets, applications, and handlers). In addition, the HotJava browser and Applet Viewer provide a runtime system for executing Java code.

Java applets

Java *applets* are pieces of executable Java code that are embedded in an HTML document using the `<APPLET>` tag. When a Java-capable browser accesses such a page, it automatically downloads the executable code pointed to by the special tag. When the code arrives, the Java runtime environment executes it within the browser.

Applets are different from applications because they are derived from a special class of Java code (the Applet class) and rely on a Java-enabled environment, such as the HotJava browser, in which to execute.

Java applications

Standalone software applications written in the Java language are known as Java *applications*. They can be executed outside of a Java-enabled environment (such as the HotJava browser or Applet Viewer). In fact, the HotJava browser itself is actually a standalone Java application.

Java handlers

Java *handlers* are special pieces of Java code that process incoming information and convert it into an object that the Java environment can use.

In essence, handlers provide the Java environment with a mechanism for dynamically learning how to deal with incoming data. For example, while connected to the World Wide Web, your Java-savvy browser may come across data that it doesn't inherently know how to display. First-generation browsers would either pass the data off to a helper application or would be incapable of displaying the data at all; the Java-savvy browser dynamically learns to display the data through the assistance of a handler that the data identifies. (In this case, the handler would be downloaded to the browser and executed, giving the browser the ability to display the previously unknown data.)

Java supports two types of handlers, protocol handlers and content handlers. *Protocol handlers* extend HotJava's knowledge of (you guessed it) protocols. If the browser comes upon a protocol it doesn't understand, it can dynamically learn the protocol by simply downloading and executing the associated protocol handler, assuming one exists.

Content handlers, on the other hand, extend HotJava's knowledge of (surprise, surprise) content. The combined power of protocol and content handlers is truly incredible; a Java-capable browser can learn as it goes, eliminating the need for costly upgrades and the difficulties of maintaining the kitchen sink when it comes to content and protocols.

Java Virtual Machine (the JVM)

The Java Virtual Machine (JVM) is a specification to which you must write Java code. All Java code is compiled for use on this non-existent machine, which is actually a set of specifications for how the code should be generated during the program compilation process. Writing code that runs under the Java Virtual Machine helps ensure platform independence. To guarantee true platform independence, though, your application must include no code native to a particular platform, and depend on no native methods of that or any other platform. Truly platform-independent code that is entirely Java can be certified by Sun as 100% Pure Java.

You really won't deal directly with the Virtual Machine when writing Java programs, unless of course, you're porting it to a new platform. But even that is unlikely, because the Virtual Machine has already been ported to the Sun Solaris, Windows NT, Windows 95, Windows 3.1, and Apple Macintosh, BeOS, OpenVMS, FreeBSD, IRIX, NEXTStep, OS/390, OS/400, RiscOS, VxWorks, SunOS, AIX, BSDI, Digital Unix, HP 3000, Linux, NetBSD, OpenBSD, OSF/1, SCO, UnixWare, AmigaOS, DG/US, EPOC 16, HP-UX, MachTen, NetWare, OS/2, Reliant Unix, Solaris, and UXP/DS at the time of writing. The Microsoft Windows 95, NT 4.0, and Sun Solaris Java Virtual Machine are directly provided by Sun. Many Java-enabled browsers, such as Netscape Communicator and Internet Explorer, provide their own Java Virtual Machine implementations. This is an important point for developers, since the Java Virtual Machines supported in your favorite Web browser may not include support for the latest Java features. It took Netscape almost six months after the release of Java Version 1.1 to include its complete support in Netscape Communicator, and due to legal wrangling, Internet Explorer's Java Virtual Machine still doesn't support all of the Java 1.1 features.

Understanding Java

Now that you know more about Java, it's time to go beyond the concepts and to get to know the entire Java environment—the Java language, runtime environment, and tools—on a deeper level. And what better way to start than with the technology at the center of it all?

The Java technology consists of three entities:

✦ The language itself

✦ A runtime environment

✦ A set of tools

At the core of everything is the programming language formerly known as Oak. Without the language itself (now known simply as Java), the runtime environment and tools would have no purpose. And so it only makes sense that more often than not, when people speak casually of Java, they are referring to the programming language.

But what makes the language so revolutionary? Haven't we been introduced to a number of programming-language "revolutions" over the years, each of which failed in one way or another to measure up to the hype surrounding them? In the software-development industry we're accustomed to new languages that promise to change the way we program, become the next level of software development, make our jobs easier, and advance the state of the art. So why get in a tizzy about Java? What's so great about it that this time we should believe the hype and bother to learn a new paradigm at the expense of time and money?

These are all valid questions, many of which will only be answered as the language itself enters the mainstream. For now, Java is effectively brand spanking new. Yes, it has been under development for more than six years, but it's only now seeing the light of day. So what's all the buzz about? What makes Java special? To find out, we can start with a rousing marketing message coming directly from Sun.

A Mouthful of Java

Java: A simple, object-oriented, distributed, interpreted, robust, secure, architecture-neutral, portable, high-performance, multithreaded, and dynamic language. —Sun's definition of Java

That's quite a mouthful of buzzwords, especially considering that just about every one of them is a goal in the forefront of modern software development. Rather than simply accepting this definition and moving on, let's see how the Java language embodies these qualities.

Simple

Programming isn't simple, no matter how you look at it. Even the most rudimentary programming languages such as BASIC are far too complex to expect an average computer user to sit down in front of one and whip up a functional software product. No, the general public will never think Java is simple. Those buzzwords listed in the Sun definition are enough to send tingles of fear up and down a nonprogrammer's spine. But what about those of us who develop software for a living or hack around just to keep ourselves amused?

Well, to programmers, the Java language indeed appears simple. Not overly simple, mind you, but simple enough to get going without having to spend time learning a completely new language. For starters, Java is designed to be as close to C++ as possible, to ensure that today's massive base of C++ programmers can migrate easily to the new language. Because Java has its roots in C++, anyone already familiar with C++ will get up to speed with Java in no time.

People who now program in C need more time getting into the Java frame of mind. Java is an object-oriented language through and through; C isn't. Procedural programmers must first learn to think in terms of objects and methods.

Not only that, but procedural programmers altogether unfamiliar with C syntax (do we have any Pascalites in the room?) will have to come up to speed with both object-oriented programming *and* the syntax of the Java language.

Although C++ programmers have an advantage right off the bat, C programmers need only familiarize themselves with the object-oriented approach to software development before plunging right in. And the others? Well, it's a bit more work than learning a new syntax.

Luckily, Java is simpler to learn than C++, because Java developers intentionally removed much of the difficulty programmers encountered with the earlier programming language. Indeed, Java was built to be easier to learn and use than C++; as a result, it does give up some of the power found in C++. However, the C++ features that Java omits are not used as often as one might think, and often they lead to overly complex software design and difficulties in maintaining code.

Specifically, *operator overloading*, *multiple inheritance*, and *extensive automatic coercion* have been omitted (although *method overloading* is supported). Some C++ programmers may be clutching their chests and breathing quick, shallow gasps of air at this very moment. But until they regain control of their lungs and vocal cords, you'd be hard-pressed to figure out whether it's from joy or shock.

Hey, you can't please everyone all the time, and Java doesn't try to. By eliminating what it believed to be the worst of C++ — for better or worse — the Java team stripped away much of the complexity of the language. Score one for simplicity.

While eliminating complexity, the Java team introduced *garbage collection* to further simplify the language. Although this makes the internal Java system more complex overall, it takes the burden of memory management off the programmer. Not only is software easier to write, thanks to the fact that memory management comes "for free," but bugs related to memory are dramatically reduced. Score two for simplicity.

Java support is currently built in to the most popular Web browsers, Netscape Communicator and Microsoft Internet Explorer 4.0.

Object-oriented

If the Java language is at all complex, it is because the language is entirely object-oriented. To the uninitiated, *object-oriented* equals fear. But to those who are comfortable with thinking in terms of objects, it equals bliss. If you haven't already given object-oriented software development a shot, or have abandoned earlier efforts to learn this new paradigm out of sheer frustration, now is the time to take up the challenge. You won't be sorry.

The premise of *object-oriented programming (OOP)* is simple: every programming task is considered in terms of objects and their relationships. Think of it as similar to the challenge of building a sculpture out of Lego bricks. Procedural programming techniques are like hand-crafting each brick when it is needed — which takes an inordinate amount of time and effort on the programmer's part. Each brick requires considerable attention to how it looks, feels, and fits into the larger work.

Object-oriented programming puts the focus on the larger work itself, on what the final sculpture should be. Rather than creating a hand-crafted brick for each part of the whole, the object-oriented approach relies on a generic form of a Lego brick, from which all other such bricks are derived. You save the time and effort of hand-crafting individual bricks; you simply use the generic brick as a template and build on that (see Figure 1-1). The template gives you all the basic properties, and you customize it to fit your needs. The result is a dramatic increase in productivity and reusability.

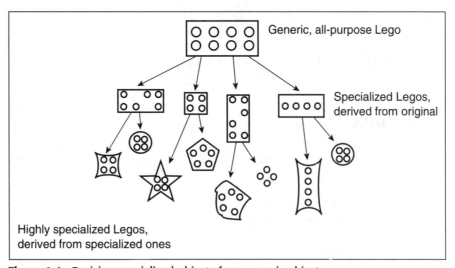

Figure 1-1: Deriving specialized objects from generic objects

For instance, if you derived a special-purpose brick from the generic brick as you worked on (say) the hands of a sculpture, you'd only need to tweak each piece of Lego a bit more to get it to look like a finger. Heck, they all look and act about the same; they just need a little bit of customizing here and there. Why fashion a different type of brick for each of the ten fingers? Simply customize your basic template to look like a finger, and then derive the rest of the fingers from that. You could then derive the toes of your sculpture from the fingers you've created (they're just stubby little fingers anyway). No sense crafting those little fellas from scratch, no sir.

When all is said and done, you've put more attention and work into the sculpture as a whole than into the individual bricks. And the biggest benefit? The next time you need to create a Lego sculpture—even though it may differ in form and function from your previous one—the bulk of the real work is already done. You simply derive the new sculpture from your existing one, tweaking it here and there to customize it as needed. Sure, this is a simplified view of object-oriented programming, but the basic approach is the essence of working with objects.

In the object-oriented world, you focus primarily on the design of your bricks (objects) and on the operations that go along with it (methods). If you have done a good enough job of defining the basic, all-purpose piece of Lego (and have not been all thumbs about it, to stretch this analogy even further), you can then derive all special-purpose pieces of Lego from it.

The object-oriented functions of Java are essentially those of C++. Although current C++ programmers will feel right at home, those without object-oriented experience will need to spend a little time getting comfortable with this terminology and its associated concepts. To help jump-start the process, we'll explore object-oriented programming in more detail in Chapter 2.

Although C is not an object-oriented language, it forms the basis for C++. Because Java is rooted in C++, Java code will look very familiar to C programmers, as far as the syntax of the language is concerned.

Distributed

Java is built with network communications in mind; these communication features are thrown in for free. It has a comprehensive library of routines for dealing with network protocols such as the Transmission Control Protocol/Internet Protocol (TCP/IP), the Hypertext Transfer Protocol (HTTP), and the File Transfer Protocol (FTP). As a result, Java applications can open and access objects across the Internet with the same ease that programmers normally expect when accessing a local file system.

This is another dramatic advantage over C and C++. You don't have to worry about implementing the details of networks yourself; Java comes with everything needed for truly distributed computing. A good example of this is the HotJava browser which, thanks to the Java language, understands how to access and handle objects over the World Wide Web. Most other programming languages require you to either write these networking layers yourself or purchase a library of networked code for this purpose; Java provides these capabilities from the start.

The Future of Java Security—Java Protected Domains

The future of Java security will introduce Java Protected Domains. This is a Java security component that has its scope defined by a set of objects that are accessible by a principal. A *principal* is an entity that has accountability—in other words, it is an object for which authorizations can be granted and revoked. A prime example of a Java Protected Domain is the Java Sandbox itself. With the Java Sandbox—in which all code is considered untrusted, therefore restricted—file and network access are tightly controlled. Java Protected Domains are distinct; they may only interact with each other through trusted code, or through explicit permissions. Java Protected Domains can be controlled on a user and application basis.

Interpreted

The Java language is *interpreted*. In other words, an interpreter must be available for each hardware architecture and operating system on which you want to run Java applications. Traditionally, interpreted programs are not converted into machine code, as compiled programs are. Instead, they remain in a human-readable form, which an interpreter executes line by line.

Software developers often cringe at the thought of using interpreted language for "serious" programming projects. Interpreted languages are notorious for being slow in comparison to their compiled brethren and often draw heat for that reason alone.

Through the innovative use of its Virtual Machine, however, Java overcomes many of the speed issues that bog down other interpreted languages. Java code actually goes through a compile process that outputs what is known as Java *bytecode*. Java bytecode is machine-independent, conforming to the Java Virtual Machine's specifications, and you can run it on any system that supports the Java environment. This code is at an intermediate stage, not fully compiled, but close enough to actual machine code that the interpretation process takes much less time than it would otherwise.

To further reduce the overhead of interpretation, Java implements *multithreading* (which permits programs to juggle several tasks at once) and handles interpretation efficiently in the background. Compiling Java code to an intermediate stage—and then interpreting it in the background through threads—results in much faster interpretation and gives Java a significant speed boost over traditional interpreted languages.

Note

The Java Virtual Machine is not really a machine at all! It's a set of specifications that define how Java bytecode is to be handled on a given computer system. Java programs can execute on any computer that has a virtual machine present. Currently, the Virtual Machine exists for Sun Solaris, Windows NT, Windows 95, Windows 3.1, and Apple Macintosh, BeOS, OpenVMS, FreeBSD, IRIX, NEXTStep, OS/390, OS/400, RiscOS, VxWorks, SunOS, AIX, BSDI, Digital Unix, HP 3000, Linux, NetBSD, OpenBSD, OSF/1, SCO, Unixware, AmigaOS, DG/US, EPOC 16, HP-UX, MachTen, NetWare, OS/2, Reliant Unix, Solaris, and UXP/DS.

Robust

Reliability is extremely important to software developers, especially professionals whose reputation and careers are on the line for the products we create. It behooves us, therefore, to create robust programs that are unlikely to fail under unknown or adverse conditions. Although this goal may sound obvious, many languages (C in particular) are a long way from providing developers with the tools needed for developing robust programs.

The C language, for example, is very relaxed in terms of type checking, resulting in programming errors that fall through the cracks, only to surface later—and often at the most inopportune moments. C++ is a much more strongly typed language, but because it is rooted in the C language, it fails to catch a number of bugs during compile time. Not so with Java.

Java requires declarations, ensuring that the data types passed to a routine are exactly the data types the routine requires. Furthermore, Java doesn't allow automatic casting of data types, as C and C++ do; the programmer must explicitly write casts. By forcing the programmer to do so, Java drastically reduces the likelihood that slippery logic errors will be introduced into your code.

The most significant difference between Java and C/C++ is the use of a pointer model that prohibits overwriting memory and corrupting data. Instead of pointer arithmetic, Java supports true arrays on which subscript (boundary) checking is enforced. Since a programmer can't mistakenly overwrite data or access an array element out of bounds, the language eliminates the possibility of these common bugs. The result is a very robust development system that frees the programmer from such concerns.

Java, unlike C/C++, eliminates entirely the support for true pointers.

Secure

Any time network access happens, security concerns become a big issue. Security has always been a worry, even on the local level before networks became so popular. Now that executable content is available, imagine the Trojan horses that might hide the most horrible viruses and interlopers come to invade our privacy. After all, what better way to get into a user's computer system than through the front door? Because applets are automatically downloaded and executed, they'd never know what hit 'em, right?

Not so. The Java team designed Java for networked and distributed environments from the onset, and it addressed the issue of security from the very beginning. Security is a critical part of the Java environment. Java allows you to create virus-free, tamper-free systems, thanks to the number of security checks it performs before a piece of code can be executed.

First of all, pointers and memory allocation are removed during compile time. By blocking memory allocation and memory access until runtime, Java prevents programmers from assuming memory locations in advance and "jumping" into memory.

Second, the interpreter verifies all bytecodes before they are executed, as shown in Figure 1-2. If the code isn't valid Java code, it won't execute. Deviant code is blocked before it can become a problem. Such things as illegal access to memory space, violation of access privileges, illegal class access, and illegal data conversions are not permitted. As a result, a potential virus has no way of gaining access to data structures, objects, or memory locations.

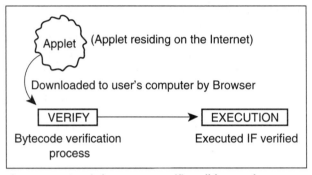

Figure 1-2: Java's interpreter verifies all bytecode.

And finally, all Java applets are treated as untrusted code executing in a trusted environment. This means that all applets downloaded from the Web are restricted in what they can do once they reach your machine. Even after passing the bytecode-verification process, applets are prohibited from accessing files on your computer. Nor can they make network connections outside of the Web server they came from. This prevents applets from accessing Web resources other than those available on the site from which they were downloaded. As an added security measure, applets are prohibited from executing any code (such as external code libraries and applications) that cannot be verified in the same way that an applet itself is. Figure 1-3 illustrates this.

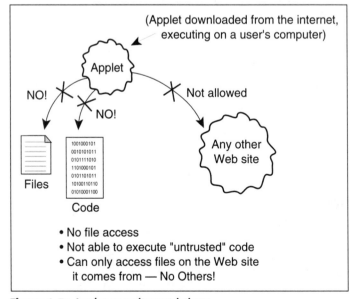

Figure 1-3: Applet security restrictions

However, we all know that every security measure employed by Java is nothing more than a juicy enticement to the world of virus authors and thrill-seeking hackers. Although Java shouldn't be possible to infiltrate, someone will surely find a way. And, as certainly as a security hole will be found and exploited, it will be immediately sealed by the Java team. JavaSoft works in close conjunction with the security team at Princeton University to find and fix Java security problems. Such is the cat and mouse game of security in our modern world. Stay tuned.

Note

Sun is currently investigating a variety of security models for future Java releases, including the use of encryption and authentication devices, in the hope of relaxing restrictions applied to applets. The goal is to allow developers to create *trusted* applets—applets guaranteed to be free of malicious intent or capabilities. For detailed information regarding current and future Java security models, visit Sun's Java home page at http://www.javasoft.com/.

Architecture-neutral

Because Sun designed Java to support distributed applications over computer networks, you can use it with a variety of CPU and operating-system architectures. To achieve this design goal, a Java compiler produces architecture-neutral object files, or Java *bytecode*, from the Java source code you write. Assuming that the Java runtime environment exists on the client-system end, the resulting bytecode executes regardless of platform.

This architecture works, not only for networks, but also for standard software distribution. With Java you can create a single executable that can be run on any computer that has the Java runtime environment, as shown in Figure 1-4.

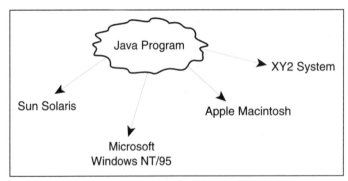

Figure 1-4: Java is architecture-neutral (platform-independent).

Such platform independence is possible thanks to a compiler that generates bytecode instructions that are completely independent of any specific computer architecture. As a result, Java programs can be executed on any computer since the bytecodes they are composed of may be dynamically translated into native machine code by any Java runtime environment.

The Java Runtime Environment

The Java runtime environment is actually an interpreter that converts architecture-neutral Java bytecode files into native machine code that can be executed. A Java runtime environment is typically installed on end-user systems when the user installs a Java-savvy Web browser such as Netscape Navigator or Internet Explorer. Although this is the most popular way to get a Java runtime environment up and running, it's only useful for running Java applets embedded in Web pages. To run full-blown Java applications, you must install a Java runtime environment that operates independent of Web browsers. This is easy enough, since Sun's Java Development Toolkit (JDK)—and most Java development tools, for that matter—come with a standalone Java runtime environment.

Because Java runtime environments are merely Java bytecode interpreters that conform to the Java Virtual Machine (JVM), vendors are free to produce their own. (It's worth noting that people often use the terms *Java runtime environment* and *Java Virtual Machine* interchangeably because the Java runtime environment is an implementation based on the JVM specification.) In fact, it's only a matter of time before all major operating system vendors, such as Microsoft and Apple, build Java runtime environments directly into the operating system. When they do, users won't have to bother installing a runtime environment themselves; Java will be supported at the operating-system level!

Portable

Assuming the Java runtime environment is present on a given computer, Java bytecode will execute properly. Thanks to its architecture-neutral capabilities, the Java system is highly portable.

One part of the portability equation is Java's representation of data types. C and C++, although touted as being highly portable, are hampered by being implementation-dependent. That is, the size of primitive data types, and the arithmetic performed on them, changes from system to system. An int (integer data type) on one system isn't necessarily the same size as an int on another. As a result, ease of portability suffers.

In Java, however, primitive data-type sizes and the behavior of arithmetic on these types are explicitly specified. For example, int is always a signed 32-bit integer value, and float is always a 32-bit floating-point number conforming to the Institute of Electrical and Electronics Engineers' IEEE 754 specifications. When you use primitive data types in Java, their representation and arithmetic behavior are consistent from system to system.

The Java class libraries include portable interfaces for each platform on which the runtime environment is available. For example, an abstract Windows class and implementations of it are available for Sun Solaris, Windows, and the Macintosh. When using these graphics interfaces, Java automatically loads the appropriate platform-specific interfaces for the current machine.

Finally, the entire Java system itself is portable. The current compiler is written in Java (although it was originally written in C) and the runtime is written in ANSI C, with a clean portability boundary. The Java system can therefore be ported to just about any computing environment, the most popular of which (Sun Solaris, Windows, and Macintosh) are already available or currently under development.

High-performance

Java performance is impressive for an interpreted language, mostly because of the development of just-in-time (JIT) compilers that optimize the bytecodes on the fly. According to Sun, Java programs execute at speeds "nearly indistinguishable" from native C/C++ programs.

Although interpreting bytecodes is faster than interpreting raw programming languages, since they are already in an intermediate stage, the Java architecture is also designed to reduce overhead during runtime. Additionally, threads are incorporated into the language, which further enhances the overall perceived speed of Java executables.

Note

Although Java's performance is impressive when compared to other interpreted languages, many developers are concerned that it is still too slow to use where raw speed is a factor. Some accounts have Java programs running anywhere from 10 to 30 times slower than their C/C++ counterparts. While this debate heats up, Sun is working to improve the overall speed of Java programs. Future releases of Java are likely to include an optimized compiler and a faster runtime environment.

In addition, several leading software tool vendors, such as Borland, Symantec, Microsoft, and Metrowerks, have developed just-in-time (JIT) compilers that convert Java bytecodes into native machine code before execution. As a result of JIT compilers, browser vendors can now greatly increase the speed of Java applet execution. In fact, the latest versions of both Netscape Navigator and Microsoft's Internet Explorer utilize JIT compiler technology, making non-JIT Java-savvy browsers look slow by comparison. By the time you read this, a number of just-in-time compilers should be available for speed-conscious developers.

HotSpot Virtual Machine

With the release of the Java SDK 2.0 in earlier 1998, a new and faster virtual machine is promised—Java HotSpot Virtual Machine. HotSpot VM gets its name from the fourth-generation bytecode interpreter technology JavaSoft acquired when it purchased Animorphic Systems. HotSpot VM achieves faster speeds by enabling the VM to look for loops and dynamically compile the bytecode into machine code. The VM also will look for repetitive method calls that can be dynamically integrated into the application and "inlined" for faster execution. The HotSpot Virtual Machine promises application execution speed similar to C and C++ applications.

Multithreaded

Multithreading is a major feature of Java, giving executables the ability to maintain several threads of execution at one time. Not to be confused with *multitasking*, the capability of an operating system to run more than one program at once, *multithreading* permits applications to juggle several tasks at once.

For instance, in a nonthreaded environment, only one line of execution exists for programs. Typically, an *event loop* is used to keep track of the particular task at hand. This loop identifies which task is to be executed (such as refreshing the contents of a window, tracking user input, or printing a document), and passes it off to the appropriate routine(s). Once the task is handled, another can begin. Because only one task at a time can be handled, the system must wait until the current task has been completed before handling a new one.

Although programming languages such as C and C++ allow the developer to implement multithreading, it takes a considerable amount of effort compared to Java, which implements threading synchronization directly. Based on C.A.R. Hoare's widely used monitor and condition-variable paradigm, Java supports multithreading in a clean and robust implementation.

So what can you do with threads? Just about anything, really; you can assign each line of execution to a thread and synchronize that thread with other threads as needed. They can dramatically improve interaction with users, handling multiple requests at once. With threads, real-time response times are possible.

A good example of threads in action is the garbage collection feature of the Java language. This facility is a low-priority thread which runs in the background as other tasks are executing. It monitors objects and all references to them, disposing of them when they are no longer in use. Because this process is controlled by a thread running in the background, other threads go on undisturbed.

Another powerful example of multithreading would be a program that supports simultaneous input, output, and user interaction, such as taking real-time audio input from a microphone while synchronizing it with a video image being played on the screen. In this case, such a system could match incoming audio to the lips of computer-generated characters in real time. Such a computer karaoke program would take all the difficulty out of singing in sync with a video image, always the most embarrassing part of the party piece. (On second thought, is there any part of karaoke that isn't embarrassing?)

Okay, this is pretty demanding. Although it's not likely that you could develop such a program using Java today, future versions of the language may be fast enough to keep up. Nonetheless, it's a valid example of threads handling different parts of a program.

For the power of multithreading to be fully realized, however, the systems on which Java code is executed must also support threads. Because true preemptive multitasking and multithreading are at the foundation of all modern operating system developments, in the near future most platforms will be up to par. For the time being, Java's multithreading capabilities are limited by the underlying architectures of the systems on which it executes.

Dynamic

Fundamentally, distributed computing environments must be dynamic. Java was designed to adapt in a constantly evolving environment. It is capable of incorporating new functionality, regardless of where that functionality comes from—the local computer system, local and wide area networks, and the Internet are all potential contributors.

In object-oriented C++ environments, as in most programming environments, developers don't write every line of code themselves. Instead, they rely on a wide array of class libraries to extend the functionality of their programs. If a developer needs to add support for a particular feature, such as the ability to play moving videos, he or she simply links in new class libraries that can handle the job.

Sometimes, these libraries are distributed in ways the developer can't control, such as with an operating system or windowing environment. In these cases, updates to libraries might reach the customer before a developer has the chance to recompile the program using them. When a customer is running an old version of the developer's product, and it attempts to dynamically link in an updated library such as this, there is the potential for real problems. Since the program hasn't been recompiled to handle the updated class library, it will likely break.

If the developer had the ability to simply recompile the program with the updated library, and then get it into customers' hands in time, everything would be fine. In this regard, the object-oriented goal of C++ falls short of the mark.

Contrast these limitations of C++ with Java, which is capable of dynamically linking in new class libraries, methods, and instance variables at runtime, without fear of breaking the system. Java can also determine the type of a class at runtime through a query, making it possible to either dynamically link in new classes or abort the mission altogether depending on the results of such queries. These capabilities give Java programs a level of flexibility when executing not possible with most other programming languages.

Java in a Nutshell

It's clear that the Java language is an extremely sophisticated and powerful new entry into the world of programming. It's also clear that the language is a perfect fit for the World Wide Web. But what's not so clear is where Java will be in a year or two.

Yes, it started off with tremendous momentum. The Web world is all wound up over its potential, and for good reason. Just the first few Java applets to hit the Web were impressive enough, beyond anything the Web had to offer by itself, and reams of even more impressive work have surfaced, and continue to do so, since the language moved from release to release. The fact that Java itself was used to create the HotJava browser proves the language is capable of more than applets; it can also be used for full-blown applications.

But will it survive and become the next great programming language? Will it ever equal or overthrow C++ in terms of industry acceptance? Although this remains to be seen, the Java language is clearly positioned for such a steady and successful rise to the top. For starters, it is based on technology that the next generation of software programs will require. Like it or not, we're moving into a networked world where distributed computing will become the norm.

Java has everything it takes to make the transition from desktop to network-based computing a smooth one. It was built specifically for that, and it's clearly up to the task. However, the professional software development industry is slow to change and Java might not have had such a brilliant chance were it not easily learned by C++ programmers and had it not maintained compatibility with both C and C++.

The ability to use C and C++ within Java is very important. C++ succeeded where Objective C did not because it was backward-compatible with the volumes of C code that programmers had spent years developing. Companies have a lot of time and effort represented in old code, not to mention money, and so it's to Java's benefit that it can coexist with existing C/C++ source code.

Heavy hitters in the technology world have already jumped feet-first into Java. Borland, Symantec, Metrowerks, Macromedia, Microsoft, Mitsubishi Electric, Fuji, Xerox, Andersen Consulting, U.S. Postal Service, NASA, Novell, Sybase, Oracle, and scores of others are already working with Java. But more importantly, Java is fast becoming a must-have technology in the latest crop of Web browsers.

Perhaps more important is integration of Java into all the popular Web browsers— including Netscape Communicator and Microsoft Internet Explorer. Thanks to this development, Java will be seen and used by more people in a shorter period of time than any other programming language, ever.

In order for Java to become the next *de facto* development language, it will have to do all this and more. It's nearly impossible to shift an entire industry to a new standard just because an up-and-coming technology holds such promise. Java is new, brand new, and will have to deliver on all its promises before it stands a chance of taking over the programming world. But, if early indicators are any sign of things to come, hold on tight. A revolution is in the air and sweeping out into the ether.

Java Versus C/C++

Java was developed to address the inadequacies of C++; perhaps now is the best time to take a look at the differences between it and the C/C++ languages.

First, remember that Java is closer to C++ than to C. It's a fully object-oriented language, while C is not. C++ maintained a backward compatibility with C, and in doing so sacrificed the possibility of becoming a full-fledged object-oriented language.

Sure, C++ is more than capable in terms of object-oriented development, there's no denying that. Many believe that C++ is the be-all-and-end-all of programming languages and staunchly defend its position in the object-oriented programming world. But there are just as many, if not more, who feel it falls short of being a true object-oriented language. In fact, that's exactly what prompted the development of Java; C++ just didn't cut it.

While the years-old debate over C++ and its viability as an OOP language rages, which I'm not eager to get into here, let's take a look at what Java does differently than C/C++.

Data types

Java omits three key data types that C/C++ supports: *pointers*, *unions*, and *structs*.

Pointers

Conventional wisdom insists that C and/C++ programmers must become proficient in the use of pointers if they are to master these languages. Although pointers are no problem once you've spent the time learning how to use them and become comfortable with the nuances of their implementation, beginners often struggle greatly with them. Despite these difficulties, mastering the use of pointers made it possible for C/C++ programmers to directly access memory locations and infiltrate the innards of data structures.

Significantly, Java does away with pointers entirely, passing all arrays and objects by reference without the use of the pointer type at all. As a result, memory locations can't be infiltrated as they could (and often are) with C/C++. The lack of a pointer type makes it impossible for a program to accidentally, or intentionally, overwrite data at a location in memory. This makes for a much more secure and bug-free development experience, because the whole pointer-management process is eliminated.

Unions and structs

Both union and struct data types are omitted from the Java language, immediately raising the question, *How can this be good?*

Although these types do not exist, the Java language provides similar functionality within the framework of an object. For example, a typical C/C++ struct needed to define the various fields of a book record used in an inventory control program might look something like this:

```
struct Book {
    char title[TITLESIZE]; /* book name (ex. "Java Bible") */
    int pubCode;
     /* code to identify publisher (ex. 3435 = IDG) */
    char authFirst[NAMESIZE];
     /* author's lastFirst nName (ex. "WalshAaron") */
    long isbnCode; /* ISBN book code */
    int quantity;  /* number of books in stock */
    double msrp;  /* manufacturer's suggested retail price */
    double (*calc_price)(double, double);
     /* price at time of purchase*/
};
```

Aside from the fact that this is a simple example, whereas lots of additional information might be included in a real implementation, the above structure is very typical of those found in many C/C++ implementations. The last line, in particular, is worth looking at:

```
double (*calc_price)(double, double);
```

This line of code is actually a pointer to a function. When the structure for a book is allocated and initialized, the programmer must supply one of these, as defined in the struct declaration. In our example, the calc_price function takes two doubles as arguments and returns a double that is the computed sale price of the book. Such a calc_price function might look like this:

```
double calc_price (double msrp, double discount) {
/* calculate and return price based on discount percentage: */
return (msrp - (msrp*discount));
};
```

Here we have a struct that lays out the various fields to be used and a function that is used to calculate the sale prices, based on whatever the current discount percentage is. When a book record is allocated and initialized, the function pointer goes along with it:

```
main(){
struct Book FoundJava = {
 "Java Bible", /* title */
 3435,       /* code to identify book's publisher */
 "Walsh",    /* author's last name */
 4367758,    /* ISBN code */
 100,       /* number in stock */
 49.95,     /* manufacturer's suggested retail price */
 calc_price /* pointer to the function calc_price */
 };
}
```

Now, suppose the book was being sold at a discount of 15 percent. In C, the following line of code would perform the calculation and output the sale price:

```
printf("price = %f\n", FoundJava.calc_price (FoundJava.mspr,
    0.15));
```

This is all well and good, but what happens in Java, where structs don't exist?

In Java, classes perform all the functionality of unions and structs, making those data types obsolete. In addition, classes in Java allow the programmer to write cleaner code that combines the object (the Book layout) and methods (the routines that operate on the object; calc_price, in this case) in one unit, while providing a mechanism for keeping certain information private.

For instance, many fields of the book record shouldn't be available to routines other than those that have an absolute need to modify their content. With C, any field in the Book structure can be easily accessed and changed. This might seem like a good idea at first, but in reality, only certain pieces of code should have access to this private information. This is exactly what Java provides, as shown in Listings 1-1 and 1-2:

Listing 1-1: **The Book class definition**

```
class Book {
   String title;
   int pubCode;
   String authLast;
   long isbnCode;
   int quantity;
```

```
private double msrp;
double calc_price (double discount) {
  return (msrp - (msrp*discount));
  /* notice that this function is part of the class definition
     itself, and is not an external function, as with C */
}
```

Listing 1-2: **The Book class constructor**

```
Book(String a_title, int a_code, String a_auth, long a_isbn,
int a_quant, double a_msrp) {
  title = a_title;
  pubCode = a_code;
  authLast = a_auth;
  isbnCode = a_isbn;
  quantity = a_quant;
  msrp = a_msrp;
  }
}
```

What we have here is the same basic concept of a structure and the `calc_price` function, yet all bundled up into a single object. The `Book` class, the code template from which an object can be created when executed, not only describes all the data but also the routine `calc_price` previously residing outside the structure. Here, the routine is part of the object, an inherent part of the class. As such, it references the data element `msrp` directly to perform the calculation.

Classes and methods

In Java, as with other OOP languages, we have declared what is known as a *class* (`Book`) and the *method* (`calc_price`) that goes along with it. You can think of a class as a template for creating objects, where an object is a variable created from a given class. Classes can include both data, known as *instance variables,* and the routines that operate on that data, known as *methods*. In the `Book` class example we've been working with, both data and methods are included in the declaration.

In addition to declaring a number of standard instance variables (`title`, `pubCode`, `authLast`, `isbnCode`, `quantity`), one has been declared private. Since `msrp` is a private instance variable of the `Book` class, it can only be accessed by objects created from the original `Book` class. This prevents `msrp` from being accessed or modified without proper cause; it keeps this data safe and private, available only to those methods that should have access to it.

We've also included a second method that has the same name as the class itself (Book). Methods having the same name as the class they are part of are known as *constructors*, and they are invoked when a new object is created from that class. When put into action, a new Book object is instantiated from the class we created:

```
class MyClass {
   public static void main(String args[]) {
      Book FoundJava = new Book("Java Bible", 3435,
         "Walsh", 4367758, 100, 49.95);
      System.out.println("price = " +
      FoundJava.calc_price(0.15));
   }
}
```

What we have with Java is functionally equivalent to what we had with structs and a separate calc_price routine, yet it's all within one easy-to-use chunk of code—the Book class!

Additionally, we've been able to create code that prevents unauthorized use of instance variables. This is easily seen in our example, as we can calculate the price of a book without having to access msrp directly. The calc_price method has access to the private msrp instance variable and performs the calculation for us without our having to reference this data directly. We simply feed the calc_price method a discount percentage and it does the rest.

No matter how many different Book objects are instantiated, we only need to pass a discount amount to the calc_price method for each. We don't have to bother accessing this value directly and are freed of the responsibility of keeping track of variables such as these. We let the object take care of itself, as it should.

Operators

As you'll see in Chapter 13, Java supports almost all operators found in C, and the Java operators have the same precedence and associativity as their C counterparts. In addition, Java introduces several new operators:

```
+
```

```
>>>
```

& and |

```
instanceof
```

+

Although + may appear to be the arithmetic addition operator, when applied to strings it is actually a concatenation operator. As you'll learn in Chapter 15, Java strings are objects that may be joined together (concatenated) with the + operator.

Note

Although it might appear that having two operators of the same name implies operator overloading, Java doesn't support overloading of operators as C++ does. The arithmetic + and string concatenation + operators are two completely different operators, each operating on its own data types.

>>>

In Java, the >>> operator performs a right shift with sign extension. All integer values in Java are signed values. As a result, Java introduces a >>> operator that performs a right shift while treating the value on which it is operating as an unsigned value: bits are shifted right with zero sign extension.

& and |

Although the & and | operators perform bitwise operations when applied to integral values (& performs a bitwise AND, | performs a bitwise OR), it's another story when these operators are applied to boolean values. Unlike C/C++, where boolean values may be treated as integral values, Java Booleans are actually objects that resolve to true or false. As a result, when these two operators are applied to boolean values, logical operations are performed (& performs a logical AND, | performs a logical OR).

Java's logical & and | operators always evaluate both operands. They don't "short-circuit" when the result is known after evaluating only the left operand (as their C/C++ counterparts do). In cases where you want a short-circuit logical evaluation, use the && and || operators.

Note

Since pointers are not implemented in Java, the & (dereference) operator from C/C++ isn't supported. For that matter, neither is the * (reference) operator.

instanceof

Java's instanceof operator is used to determine if an object was created from a specific class (objects and classes are explained in Chapter 4). Use of the instanceof operator is shown in Appendix B, the Java Language Reference.

Note

Although the instanceof operator may conjure up fond memories of a similar sounding operator found in C/C++, Java doesn't support sizeof. You'll also note that, unlike C/C++, Java doesn't support the comma operator to combine two expressions into one, except in a very limited fashion in the conditional portion of for loops, as discussed in Chapter 12.

Command-line arguments

Command-line arguments are those arguments sent to an application program when it is invoked from, you guessed it, the command line. For instance, when you are at the DOS prompt in a DOS environment, you execute a program by typing the name of the program:

```
c:\>crunch
```

In this example, the program named `crunch` would be executed. We've simply typed the program name at the command prompt and pressed Enter. The program, if available, is executed. Let's say, for illustrative purposes, that `crunch` takes two files and compresses them into a single file. How do we specify which files to compress and the name of the file that would result? Since we didn't provide command-line arguments above, `crunch` might prompt us for the names of each when it is executed:

```
First File to crunch: fileone
Second File to crunch: filetwo
Compress and save as: mycrunch
```

This is fairly straightforward, since `crunch` prompted us for the name of each file to compress and the name of the file to save the compressed files into. Here, we'd expect the file `mycrunch` to contain our crunched files, when all is said and done.

But what if we didn't want to bother with these prompts and knew right from the beginning what files to compress? If `crunch` supported command-line arguments, we could supply these names at the same time as we execute the program:

```
c:\>crunch fileone filetwo mycrunch
```

Upon executing, `crunch` would see that the file names had been specified as command-line arguments and bypass the prompt altogether. The result would be the same as if we had manually entered the names at each prompt, although the use of command-line arguments makes the process a little faster, since we don't have to bother typing these three file names upon executing.

Some programs expect all user input to come directly from the command line at execution time and don't bother to prompt you for information if it has been omitted from the command line. These programs simply return an error message, if even that, to let you know they were unable to complete the job successfully.

So how does a program such as `crunch` get these command-line arguments and make use of them? In C/C++, the operating system passes them directly to the program through the use of argument variables:

argc—specifies the number of arguments appearing on the command line

argv—a pointer to an array of strings containing the arguments

In C/C++, the operating system passes the entire command line as arguments to the program, including the name of the program itself. In our example, then, the first argument in the `argv` parameter would be `crunch`. But Java is a little different; in Java, only one parameter is passed to the executable:

> `args`—an array of strings that contain the arguments

The `args` parameter is simply an array containing the command-line arguments. Rather than bothering with two parameters, as C/C++ does, Java only needs this one.

But how does the Java program know how many parameters are included, since only an array is passed, without the benefit of an `argc` parameter? It's simple; arrays in Java include a `length` variable that can be used to extract the number of arguments in the array itself, eliminating the need for an `argc` parameter:

```
args.length;. /* retrieve the number of elements
                  in the args array */
```

Another difference between Java and C/C++ command-line arguments is seen in the content of the argument array. Where the C/C++ `argv` parameter contains the name of the program itself, such as `crunch`, Java's `args` parameter contains only the command-line arguments (such as `fileone`, `filetwo`, and `mycrunch`, in our `crunch` example). In Java, the name of the application being invoked is the same as the name of the initial class executed where the main method is defined. (It is possible for several classes to contain a main method.) As a result, Java already knows the name of the program being executed and doesn't need to be told this explicitly, as it does with C/C++. The Java runtime environment just passes along the command-line arguments, and that's enough.

Strings

In C/C++, strings are really nothing more than a null-terminated (/n) array of characters. But in Java, they are first-class objects. Actually, two classes exist for strings, `String` and `StringBuffer`. Java strings offer four main advantages over C/C++ strings:

- ✦ Consistency: As objects, the manner in which strings are obtained and their elements accessed is consistent across all strings and all systems.

- ✦ Predictability: Java strings function predictably every time, thanks to well-defined programming interfaces for both the `String` and `StringBuffer` classes.

- ✦ Reliability: `String` and `StringBuffer` classes perform extensive testing for boundary conditions at runtime, catching errors before they become a real problem.

- ✦ Localization of text: Strings consist of Unicode characters, which makes localization of text transparent.

Java strings are covered in more detail in Chapter 14, but for now it's worth noting that strings have always caused difficulty for C/C++ programmers. Because strings are such an important part of any programming language, Java makes it possible to use them to their fullest extent without the difficulties often encountered with C/C++.

Note

The Java `String` class is used to represent strings that will not change. `StringBuffer`, on the other hand, is specifically for strings that will change during the course of program execution.

Comments

Java supports both C and C++ style comments, in addition to an altogether new comment syntax. Here's a brief example of the three types of comments you can use in Java:

```
int i; /* this is the ANSI-C style comment */
int i; // and this is the C++ style, limited to one line of text
int i; /** And here's a completely new comment syntax! Notice
that this comment begins with a slash and two asterisk characters
and can span many lines, just as with ANSI-C comments. But
what's the difference, besides the extra asterisk at the
beginning of this comment? */
```

Although Java supports both C and C++ comments, it also introduces a special type of comment that does just what any comment does. It tells the compiler (or interpreter) to ignore everything inside the comment, since it's only there to help people make sense of the code.

Besides functioning as a regular comment, this new comment serves a special purpose—*automatic documentation generation*. That's right—documentation generated automatically from comments. This documentation is created as a series of HTML files that not only help document your programs, but also show the hierarchy of your code in relation to the larger system of Java classes! (See Figure 1-5.) And since it's in the HTML format, you can hypertext-jump through this documentation just as you would any other Web page. All thanks to an odd-looking comment.

This special type of comment, formally known as a *Doc Comment*, is often found at the beginning of class and method definitions to assist in the creation of code documentation. In addition, Doc Comments can be applied to variables.

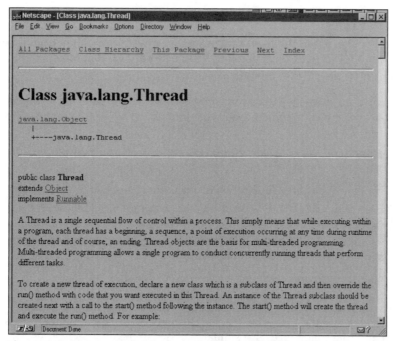

Figure 1-5: Documentation automatically generated from a Doc Comment, showing this class in relation to others in the system

With Doc Comments, you use /** to indicate that what comes between it and the closing */ should be treated as documentation when encountered by the javadoc tool. (javadoc is one of the many tools that come with Sun's Java Development Toolkit.) You can embed special documentation tags (*Doc Tags*), which begin with the @ character, within Doc Comments to further extend the automatic document generation performed by javadoc:

```
/**
 * A bogus class definition whose only purpose is to show
 * the format of Doc Comments and Doc Tags in action:
 * @version    1.0 6 Nov 1997
 * @author     Aaron E. Walsh
 */
class BogusClass {
...
}
```

When run through the javadoc tool, the above comment would generate documentation with an associated version and author entries. Doc Comments and Doc Tags can be a great help when you're documenting software developed with Java. For details on using Doc Comments, point your browser to http://java.sun.com/docs/codeconv/CodeConventions.doc4.html.

Odds 'n' ends

Although we've discussed the most obvious areas where Java differs from C and C++, there are a few other things you'll want to be aware of when making the transition to Java:

✦ Through a mechanism known as *varargs*, C and C++ provide for a variable number of arguments to be passed to a function. This is not supported with Java.

✦ Although goto is a reserved word in Java, it is not implemented or supported.

✦ Boolean data types are true literals in Java, not a representation of the integers 0 and 1, as they are in C and C++. Java boolean data types, therefore, cannot be typecast into integers.

✦ #define and #include (preprocessor mechanisms) are not available in Java, although they are available in C and C++.

✦ Java does not provide enumerated types.

These odds and ends, and those detailed previously, sum up the differences between the Java and the C/C++ languages. However, there are a number of areas where Java and these languages are similar.

To make the transition from either C or C++ relatively easy, Java maintains a lot of the look and feel of those languages. For instance, the style of Java programs (such as the use of whitespace, comments, and grouping of code) is much the same as in C and C++. Just as with C/C++, whitespace and comments (with the exception of Doc Comments) are ignored by Java altogether and are only used to make code more readable to human beings. For instance, the example Book class we created earlier could just have easily been written without whitespace and comments:

```
class Book {String title;int pubCode;String authLast;long
isbnCode;int quantity;private double msrp;double calc_price
(double discount) {return (msrp-(msrp*discount));} Book(String
a_title, int a_code, String a_auth, long a_isbn, int a_quant,
double
a_msrp){title=a_title;pubCode=a_code;authLast=a_auth;isbnCode =
a_isbn; quantity=a_quant; msrp=a_msrp;}}
```

Although this makes for ugly reading to you and me, Java doesn't care. For that matter, neither does C or C++. White space and comments simply make the code more understandable and prettier to look at for our sake.

Another thing you'll notice immediately about Java, which it shares with C/C++, is case sensitivity. Case matters, so you have to pay special attention to exactly how you mix and match upper- and lowercase letters in class, method, and variable names. For instance, the variable myJavaThing is not the same as MyJavaThing.

And while we're on the subject, it's worth noting that classes are typically capitalized, but methods and objects are not. This is merely a convention of Java (one also seen in C++), so you can in fact do whatever you want when it comes to capitalization. However, in the interest of code readability and maintenance, it's better to stick to the conventional way of doing things.

C/C++ programmers will also find comfort in the way Java code is arranged. As with C/C++, you usually indent statements to reflect their hierarchy within a block of code, and you balance curly braces ({ }) to show the nesting of functions.

With Java, you make your code more readable by using curly braces to separate blocks of code and semicolons to separate statements. These conventions should be familiar to C/C++ programmers.

These factors, taken together, make the Java language enough like C++ in both syntax and the implementation of object-oriented devices (such as classes, methods, objects, and inheritance) that C++ programmers will have little problem leaping feet first into it.

C programmers, on the other hand, must first become comfortable with the entire object-oriented approach to software development—which we discuss in detail in Chapter 2.

Summary

Java technology consists of the Java language, a runtime environment, and a set of tools. The language is simple, object-oriented, distributed, interpreted, robust, secure, architecture-neutral, portable, multithreaded, dynamic, and capable of high performance.

  ✦ Java, like C++, is object-oriented, and it is similar to C++ in syntax and style. However, it also offers significant improvements. It replaces pointers, unions, and structs with code that prevents unauthorized use of instance variables. It uses operators, significantly improved command-line arguments, and more consistent, predictable, and reliable strings. It also supports an entirely new type of comment.

  ✦ C++ and Java are similar in a number of significant ways, such as case sensitivity, the arrangement of code, and ways of implementing OOP devices such as classes and methods.

✦   ✦   ✦

Object-Oriented Programming and Terminology

Because Java is an object-oriented programming (OOP) language, it only makes sense for us to take time to find out what that means. Programmers experienced with object-oriented concepts and terminology may choose to skim this chapter and refresh their memories, or to skip it altogether, depending on their comfort level with the topic. Others will want to devote some serious time to the following material. In it are the keys to fully unlocking Java's potential, for without a solid understanding of object-oriented programming, making sense of this new language is next to impossible.

If you are new to object-oriented programming, you may become overwhelmed by the end of this chapter. Hyperventilation is understandable, if not expected, because so many of the concepts found in the object-oriented world run counter to the way you're normally taught to program. If you're new to OOP, I'd suggest taking a moment to search the Web for Java-related information, such as is available at Sun's JavaSoft site, Gamelan, or JARS, followed by a quick trip to your local library or bookstore. By all means, proceed with this book, but while you're at it, take the time to learn more about object-oriented programming. This type of programming is a very different approach to software development than most of us have experienced before. We've probably spent a great amount of time learning procedural programming languages such as Pascal and C, which are not object-oriented, and that makes it extremely difficult for us to think of software development from this new perspective.

Despite the fact that object-oriented programming is nearly 30 years old, originating with the Simula67 language introduced in 1967, the term *object-oriented programming* has been misused and misunderstood since it was first coined, and it continues to be a source of confusion even today.

Several schools of thought exist regarding what OOP is and what constitutes a "real" object-oriented programming language—these are the result of programmers trying to make sense of and establish a standard way of defining such things. In fact, in professional software engineering circles the term *object-oriented programming* represents only one portion of a much larger software development process. In this sense, OOP refers to the actual implementation in code that comes after the processes of *object-oriented analysis* (OOA) and *object-oriented design* (OOD) have been completed.

Although object-oriented concepts and terminology aren't very difficult to learn on a superficial level, it takes time for the principles to sink in, to settle, to become a natural part of our thinking. Because of this, some observers claim that learning the object-oriented approach is overly difficult and not worth the effort. Such thinking is a shame, because the potential benefits are tremendous. Anything worth learning usually takes a bit of effort, and OOP is no exception.

But fear not—I won't attempt to turn you into a master of the art of object-oriented programming, nor will I introduce highly technical concepts and terminology here. And I only briefly discuss OOP as a part of object-oriented analysis and object-oriented design; a number of books dedicate themselves entirely to these subjects. Instead, I attempt to give you a clear understanding of OOP as it relates to the task at hand—learning Java. As you'll soon see, the rewards are great and the effort is relatively small, once you understand the basic concepts we're about to explore.

So What Shall We Look at in This Chapter?

How are objects created? How are messages sent? How does encapsulation work? These are some of the questions this chapter answers. Objects, messages, and encapsulation are just a few of the terms covered here. As we proceed from term to term, concept to concept, I'll try to maintain a vein of continuity—a theme of learning:

1. After talking about objects, I'll plunge directly into *abstraction*, a way of thinking that's crucial to our ability to properly define objects.

2. Abstraction is followed by a look at the state and behavior of an object, known in Java terminology as *variables* and *methods*.

3. After exploring the internal workings of objects, I take a closer look at *encapsulation*, the interface each object has, and the messages objects send to each other.

4. Next, I'll ease into *modularity*, which lets us change the internal variables of an object, and *classification*, which lets us define the external properties of objects.

5. Finally, I'll take a look at *inheritance*—a powerful OOP capability that lets you use existing objects to construct new ones.

Keep in mind that the concepts we'll cover are not unique to Java; they are fundamental to the practice of object-oriented software development. However, although the concepts are the same, the actual terms vary among languages. For instance, in Java, the behavior of an object is implemented using *methods*, while C++ calls them *member functions*.

Because this book focuses on Java, I present all object-oriented terms and concepts to you as they are formally known in the Java language. And because I suspect that the majority of people reading this have had experience with C and/or C++, I point out similarities between Java's object-oriented implementation and those languages as much as possible.

Object-Oriented Terminology

Superficially, *object-oriented* means nothing more than looking at the world in terms of objects. In life, we are surrounded by objects: clothes, dishes, appliances, pets, cars, bikes, computers, friends, neighbors, and so on (see Figure 2-1).

Figure 2-1: In life, we are surrounded by objects.

Each of these objects has traits that we use to identify them. For instance, my cat is a black shorthair with a white crest on his chest. Harley can further be identified by his green eyes and the extra two toes he has on each paw (that's right, seven toes per paw—it looks a little funny, but doesn't seem to bother him).

Harley is also incessantly hungry, no matter how often I feed the little fellow. The fact that he's hungry helps identify him. When a friend drops by for lunch, it's not uncommon for me to say, "Keep your eyes on your sandwich, or the hungry one will get to it." By saying "the hungry one," I've identified Harley as opposed to Bennett, the other cat likely to be rubbing up against my guest's leg.

While I'm at it, allow me to identify the Bennett object as well. Bennett is the yin to Harley's yang: She's pure white, has blue eyes and the softest fur I've ever known a cat to have. She's sweet and gentle, whereas Harley's a holy terror. Bennett prefers to snuggle up and sleep on my chest while the hungry one holds the rest of the house hostage in search of food.

Interesting, perhaps, but what do my cats have to do with object-oriented programming?

What I've done is identify two objects according to what they look like and how they act. How about another rousing example?

I live in a city, so two more objects I deal with every day are the subway train and/or taxicab I take to work. The subway train object is underground, about 200 feet long, and holds about 100 people in each of its four sections. It is slow, noisy, and not very comfortable, but is relatively inexpensive to ride to work. A taxicab, on the other hand, is about 12 feet long, runs above ground on four wheels, holds only me and the driver, and is fast, quiet, and comfortable by comparison. Unfortunately, the cost of a taxi ride to the office is about ten times that of the train.

Fascinating, huh? Well, not really, but the point is that I'm able to easily identify objects by their traits. In object-oriented programming, the object is essential. It is the focus of the entire process, and the cause for much confusion among procedural programmers. Procedural programmers are accustomed to writing procedures that act upon data. They write functions that manipulate and produce data. They do not think in terms of objects because they don't need to. But in object-oriented programming, the object is at the heart of everything.

Object-oriented programmers look at the world in terms of objects. They see how objects look, how they act, and how they interact with other objects. When developing software, they create entities in code known as *objects*. These code objects contain traits, just as their real-world counterparts do.

As with real-life objects, programming objects contain details that list their characteristics. The object Harley, for instance, could contain the following details:

✦ Black, short hair

✦ White crest on his chest

✦ Green eyes

✦ Four legs

✦ Seven toes per paw

✦ Always hungry

✦ Eats Whiskas Seaside Supper

✦ Sleeps on the bed

✦ Jumps from couch to table

✦ Scratches the curtains . . .

Clearly, this list could go on forever—the number of his whiskers, his length, shape, medical history, and so on. What we have to do is *abstract* the data we think will be relevant.

Just as the preceding list enables us to identify the object Harley, software objects contain details that define how they appear, what knowledge they contain, and how they behave. The purpose of software objects is to combine data (regarding appearance and knowledge) and behavior into a nifty package, just as objects in the real world do.

Software objects have special names for these traits: *state* and *behavior*. We will consider this distinction in a moment, but let's first turn to the need for abstraction.

Abstraction

"Everything essential and nothing more" is about the cleanest definition of *abstraction* I can think of. Consider Harley. His essential functions are eating, sleeping, and creating chaos; everything else is merely a detail that gets those functions done.

Humans are great at abstraction; as Figure 2-2 illustrates, it's something we do naturally. When I hop in the driver's seat of my car, I don't think about the power train, axle, tires, radiator, engine, fan belt, and all the other things that make it possible for me to drive. Heck no, I think about the essential function of the car— to get me from A to B—as I whip down the back streets and open roads of Boston.

Not having to consider the finer details of its inner workings enables me to concentrate on the tasks at hand—driving and keeping my eyes peeled for traffic cops. Abstraction enables me to focus on the essential and ignore the nonessential. It frees me to think of the bigger picture.

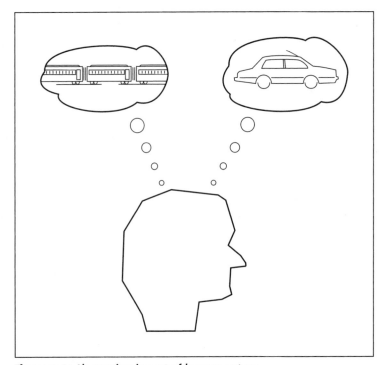

Figure 2-2: Abstraction is part of human nature.

When creating software objects, we must apply this principle of abstraction. We must consider what the essence of each object is and not think at all about the details of implementation or other elements that distract from the process.

Even though we do it in the course of our everyday lives, abstraction can be difficult to do consciously if we're accustomed to thinking in terms of procedural programming. But without abstraction, our objects will be stuffed full of data and behavior that doesn't really belong there. Ideally, during the process of abstraction, we don't even consider implementation. We focus on the objects involved in solving a problem and their relation to one another long before the details of coding become important. Indeed, software objects enable us to more closely model problems, because problems are made up of either real or conceptual objects.

We must first identify the essential functions of the object, and then select only the data relevant to those functions. In Harley's case, he has three distinct functions: eating, sleeping, and creating mayhem. Accordingly, I can abstract details essential to those functions and reject the rest:

✦ Always hungry

✦ Eats Whiskas Seaside Supper

✦ Sleeps on the bed

✦ Jumps from couch to table

✦ Scratches the curtains

In this way, we can easily identify objects by their traits, as illustrated in Figure 2-3.

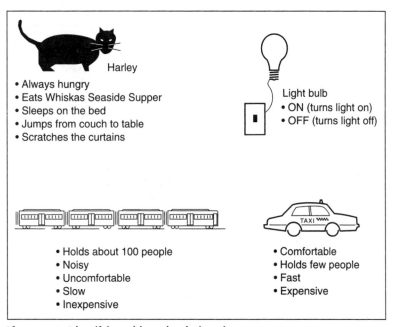

Figure 2-3: Identifying objects by their traits

Combining state and behavior

A key concept of object-oriented programming is the capability to represent both data and the functions that operate on that data in one software bundle known as an *object*. By placing all data and the functions that operate on it inside a bundle of code, we create something unique. The data and functions that make up a software object are known as *state* and *behavior*.

Looking at the essential details of Harley, for example, both state and behavior emerge. But it's not just Harley we need to consider; every object contains state and behavior:

✦ *State* is what the object knows or looks like. In the case of a cat object, the state is its fur color and texture, eye color, breed, personality, and so on.

✦ *Behavior*, on the other hand, is how the object acts. Meowing, scratching, rubbing, begging for food, and the like are examples of behavior.

Although an object's state and behavior change over time, together they form the identity of that object, as you can see in Figure 2-4.

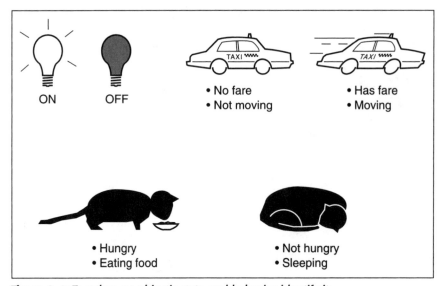

Figure 2-4: Together, an object's state and behavior identify it.

Objects contain only state and behavior that are appropriate for them. For instance, a cat object doesn't have any need to understand how much to charge for every mile it travels, as a taxicab object does. The cat object contains only those things that apply to a cat, while the taxicab object contains only those things that apply to a taxicab. They are *self-contained.*

Figure 2-5 shows a generic way to illustrate objects. This representation is intentionally amorphous—a blob of information containing *state* on the inside surrounded by *behavior*. Although a number of techniques are possible for illustrating objects, I chose this one because it is clean, simple, and easy to understand. The idea is that state is hidden from the outside world, something only the object itself can change. An object's behavior, in fact, is the only thing that can alter that object's state. In this sense, state is protected.

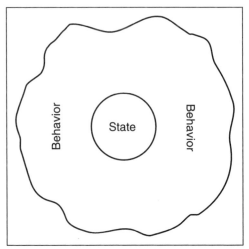

Figure 2-5: State is hidden from the rest of the world; only the behavior of the object can change it.

For instance, if Harley is hungry, only when he eats will the feeling of hunger subside. Yes, his ability to get food depends on other factors too, but in the final analysis, it's his behavior that changes his state. If he doesn't eat, he'll stay hungry. If he eats, the state of hunger is changed into a state of comfort. From an OOP perspective, only Harley can change his state.

Variables and methods

In Java, an object's state consists of *variables*, while behavior is implemented as functions called *methods* (see Figure 2-6). The combination of variables and methods together maintains state and behavior. The idea of variables and methods is nothing new, although you're probably accustomed to referring to functions rather than methods. The only thing new here is how the two are combined into a single object.

Procedural programmers are used to writing functions that sit out in the open, to be called upon whenever needed, whereas object-oriented programmers embed those functions inside objects. Say, for example, you were to write a procedural program in any language that modeled the behavior of Harley. After you got over the shock of being asked to write a program simulating my cat, you'd probably start by spending a few moments thinking about him.

You know he has fur and that it's of a specific color. You also know he has four legs, each having a paw with seven toes. (Some of you may think this is the mark of the devil, and after living with this little monster for the past few years, so do I—but that's another story.)

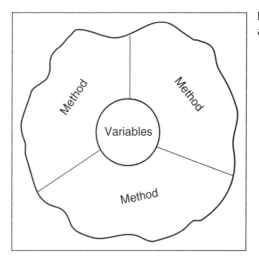

Figure 2-6: An object consists of variables and methods.

After thinking about it for a while, you'd realize that only some of the possible variables really apply to the simulation. Variables such as `hungry`, `thirsty`, `awake`, `asleep`, and the like are more closely related to Harley's behavior than are the purely physical ones. You might write them down on a piece of paper or type them into your computer.

In fact, you'd probably start coding right off the bat, perhaps beginning with the global variables that apply to Harley. Maybe you'd combine them into a structure for the sake of convenience, maybe not. You'd then consider the things in Harley's life that affect this data. For instance, when he's hungry, he eats. After he eats, he becomes sleepy and eventually finds a warm spot to snooze while his food digests. Upon waking, he has a burst of energy and burns up the food by running around the house, leaping from chair to couch to kitchen table like a lunatic — at which point he becomes hungry again. Come to think of it, that's *all* Harley ever does. . . .

In a procedural world, you would write a bunch of functions (the equivalent of object methods) that could be called from anywhere as needed, including `Eat()`, `Sleep()`, and `GoCrazy()`, each capable of altering the global data or data passed in when called. In effect, you would be creating each procedure in Harley's life that applies to this simulation. In the end, you would have a bunch of data (either globals, structures, or a combination of the two) and a bunch of functions. You'd also have an event loop of some sort that runs continually, calling functions such as `Eat()` as specific events are encountered or when conditions such as `Hungry=TRUE` trigger such actions.

In an object-oriented approach, we spend a whole lot less time writing code and a whole lot more time defining the objects themselves. We think about Harley in terms of an object, attempting to model our code after him as closely as possible. In this sense, he isn't a collection of data and routines residing in different files. As Figure 2-7 demonstrates, we create an object containing all variables and methods having to do with him.

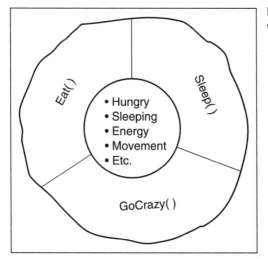

Figure 2-7: We define the object's variables and methods.

OOP is therefore unlike procedural programming, where data can be accessed and modified by any function. Instead, data residing inside an object is surrounded by the methods of that object, protected from direct manipulation.

In Java, methods consist of three parts:

✦ The name of the object to receive the message

✦ The name of the method to execute

✦ Optional parameters required by the method

In the case of my troublesome feline, the name of the object is

```
Harley
```

the name of the method to execute is

```
eat
```

and the parameter required by the method is

```
catfood
```

Taken all together, Harley's method would be invoked as follows:

```
Harley.eat(catfood);
```

The preceding is known as *dot notation*, and it is similar to how a C programmer would access an element in a struct. A period, or *dot*, is used to separate the object (appearing to the left) from the method and any parameters it may require. Here, when the object Harley receives the message eat catfood, his eat method is invoked with `catfood` as a parameter. In Java, as with other object-oriented languages, dot notation is the standard mechanism for executing methods inside objects.

As mentioned previously, only the methods of an object can change that object's data. This powerful concept is called *encapsulation,* and it is central to object-oriented programming.

Encapsulation (information hiding)

The idea of hiding data inside an object, making it unavailable to anything but that object's methods, is known as *encapsulation* (also called *information hiding*). Encapsulation extends to the implementation of methods themselves, meaning that the details of an object's inner workings are never available to anything but the object itself.

Encapsulation is very powerful because it permits objects to operate completely independently of each other as discrete, self-contained bundles of data and code. The only way to access information in an object is through its methods; these form an *interface* (see the next section) that remains consistent to the world outside of the object.

But encapsulation doesn't apply only to data; it also pertains to the implementation details of the methods themselves, without concern for other objects (and frequently comes into play as such routines are optimized, updated to fix bugs, or rewritten altogether). Because objects have an interface through which they communicate, the underlying data and implementation details are hidden and protected. Thanks to encapsulation, both data and implementation can change without breaking the system. In fact, entire objects can be replaced with new objects, assuming the interface is the same.

Encapsulation prevents objects from becoming dependent on each other's inner details, because otherwise small changes could cause tremendous damage to the overall system. Bug fixes, code optimization, and entire code rewrites are possible because of encapsulation.

Think of encapsulation in terms of your computer. When you upgrade the hard drive, RAM, or the CPU, you don't have to worry about how upgrading affects your ability to interact with your system. Sure, it will have more storage capacity, be able to run more programs at the same time, and be faster; that's why you upgraded. But you don't depend on the internals of your computer to interact with it. You can swap these out as needed without disturbing other parts of the system and causing your computer to come to a grinding halt. This is the power of encapsulation; the internal details of objects are hidden so that their underlying implementation can change without breaking the system.

Encapsulation makes it possible for you to treat objects like discrete "black boxes." Each object performs a specific function, and you don't have to be concerned about internal implementation. Conceptually, information goes in one end of a black box and comes out the other. We don't know or care what's going on inside; we only know what we can put into the box and what it will give back. You can see this process in Figure 2-8.

Figure 2-8: Encapsulation enables objects to be treated like discrete "black boxes."

We can string together any number of black boxes, each performing a specific task, to build as large and complex a system as we need. And, thanks to encapsulation, we can even tinker with the internals of any black box without crashing the works. Better yet, we can replace whole black boxes with better black boxes as they are developed. The entire system is modular, much like the internals of the computer itself, as illustrated in Figure 2-9.

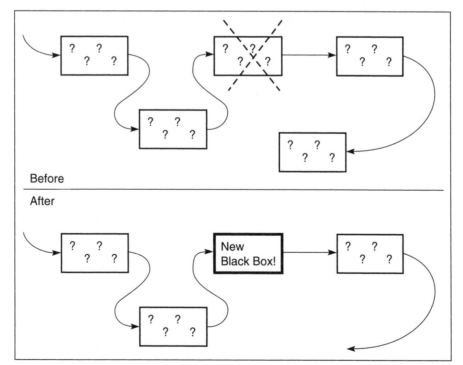

Figure 2-9: Encapsulation enables us to change and string together individual objects with a great deal of freedom.

Interfaces

Software objects are complex on the inside, just as their real-world counterparts are. On the outside, however, software objects are uncomplicated. They provide a simple interface to their data and behavior, through which other objects can interact with them. Think for a moment of a television set. Inside, it's a mess of electrical components: a picture tube, one or more speakers, and all kinds of stuff I have no idea how to deal with. But thanks to my remote control, I don't need to know anything about the complex innards to enjoy using it.

My remote control is the interface to my television, enabling me to communicate with it. I can turn it off or on, change channels, turn the volume up or down, and even adjust the picture's horizontal and vertical holds, tint, and hue (fancy remote, huh?). With the remote control, which is itself an object (for which the buttons are the interface), I am able to get functionality from my television without messing around with the guts of the system.

Objects interact with each other through similar interfaces all the time. One object produces a response in reaction to the messages it gets from another object. This is just like my cat. Opening a can of cat food and putting it in front of Harley's face triggers specific behavior. Objects send messages to each other, setting off behavior, as shown in Figure 2-10. Using dot notation, as explained in the "Variables and methods" section earlier in this chapter, a good deal of the Java code you write involves sending messages to objects.

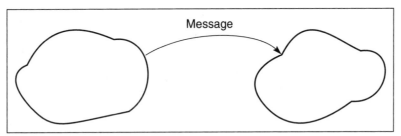

Figure 2-10: Objects trigger behavior between each other by sending messages.

Messages: Objects communicating with objects

With a software program full of objects, each only able to access and modify its own data through its own methods, how does anything ever get done? After all, it does begin to sound as if we have a bunch of well-defined entities that are very lonely in the world, capable of interacting only with themselves. A highly introspective, if not entirely isolated, group of software objects, yes?

No. Objects aren't ships lost at sea, out of radio contact. They have the ability to send messages to each other, thereby triggering the execution of methods inside each other, as Figure 2-11 demonstrates.

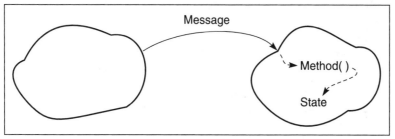

Figure 2-11: A message sent from one object to another triggers a method inside the target object.

Think of a microwave oven. In and of itself, your microwave doesn't do much but sit there waiting to be called into action. When you want to heat up some food, you put the food inside and close the door. You then send the microwave a message, such as "Heat for two minutes at full power," by pressing the appropriate buttons on the front. Because you're using the interface provided with the microwave—the buttons on the front—your message is understood and carried out.

You must send messages in accordance with the interface of an object or your message won't be understood. For instance, you might try using your television's remote control on the microwave and send the message "Change to Channel 25 and turn up the volume," but you'll wait an awfully long time before Homer Simpson appears!

In object-oriented programming, objects are constantly communicating with each other through a complex web of messages, as illustrated in Figure 2-12. Not only are the messages sent by objects able to trigger the execution of methods inside other objects, they can also contain parameters that those methods require.

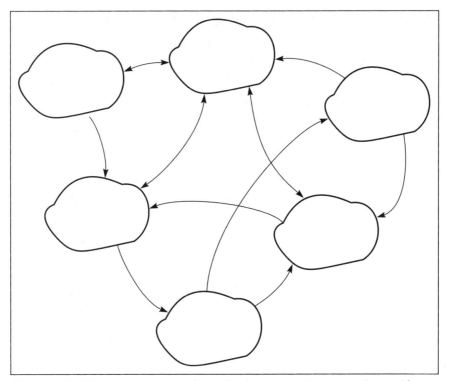

Figure 2-12: Objects weave a complex web of messages to communicate with each other.

Following our television analogy, sending the message "Change station to Channel 25" to the television object might look something like this in Java code:

```
Television.changeStation(25);
```

The television object, `Television`, receives the message `changeStation` with `25` as a parameter. The period, or dot, separating the object and message is intentional. In most object-oriented languages, as with Java, the object receiving the message is on the left and the message is on the right. The dot sits between the object and the message, with no spaces, and in effect says, "Send the message on my right to the object on my left."

In our example, keep in mind that messages contain the name of the method to execute. When the object `Television` receives a message such as the one illustrated, it looks inside itself for a method named `changeStation`. If such a method exists, it is executed, with a value of `25` as the parameter.

The beautiful thing about messages is that they are generic, in the sense that any object can send a message to any other object, even if they exist in different programs or on entirely different computer systems. Objects existing on the Internet halfway around the world can send and receive messages to or from any other objects over the Internet. This is the capability that makes distributed objects possible, and you will see it more and more as software programs begin to "live" on networks.

Modularity

We have seen that objects contain both variables and methods, that they are encapsulated, and that they can send messages to each other through interfaces. Because data and behavior are neatly packaged inside objects, and because the only way to access data is through the interface defined by the methods, you can change the internal workings of an object without breaking the rest of the system. The result is a major benefit to the software developer: *modularity*.

Modularity is based on discrete programming objects, which you can change without affecting the system as a whole, and it is greatly enhanced by encapsulation. You develop and maintain each object's source code independently of other objects, and the only way to access and change information inside an object is through methods. This represents true code modularity.

Not only can you change the implementation details of an object without affecting any other part of the system, but you can replace or rewrite entire objects from the ground up, as long as the interface doesn't change or inheritance isn't abused in the method.

Think of it in terms of electrical wiring. Each wire in an electrical system is connected to the others in a predefined way: It has an interface. These interfaces differ (wall sockets, adapters, surge protectors, and so on), but each piece of wiring has one. Additionally, each wire is designed to fit perfectly within the context of the system as a whole. It is created with a special purpose in mind, reflected in its length, material, and type of interface.

When a wire breaks or begins to corrode and to perish, an electrician comes to the rescue. He or she locates the piece of the system causing the problem and replaces it with another. No muss, no fuss. Assuming our electrician has the wire needed, it's replaced then and there. One wire is removed and another put in its place. Because the interface for the wires is consistent, the process is simple and painless.

Our electrician doesn't have to worry about creating a wire from scratch; he or she can rely on one having been created specifically for the job. This is the beauty of modularity, be it in electrical wiring or software development: You can yank out one part and put in another without bringing down the whole system (see Figure 2-13).

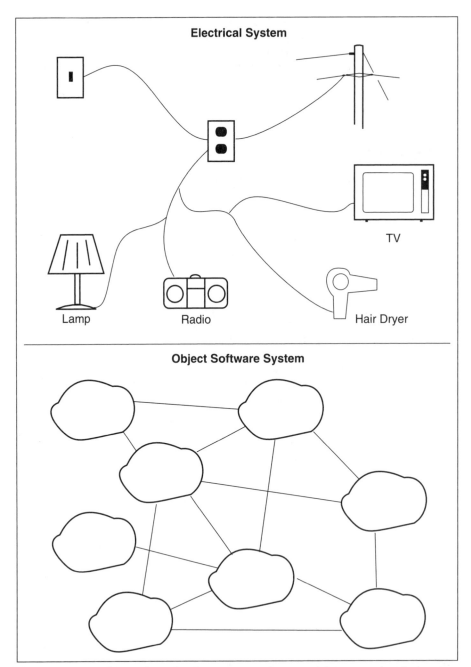

Figure 2-13: An object-oriented software system is as modular as an electrical system in a house.

Classification

Classification, grouping things according to how they look and act, is another key concept in object-oriented programming. In the real world, everything is classified. We put things into classes to help us better understand and remember what their general properties are. Cadillacs are in the automobile class, ferns are in the Filicales class, trout are in the Salmonidae class, and we are in the Homo sapiens class.

In object-oriented programming we classify things as well, specifically objects. We group them into classes according to their characteristics. Classes and objects go hand in hand and are so similar that programmers often use the two terms interchangeably. You'll find a distinct difference between them, however.

Classes are the blueprints, the source-code templates from which *objects* are created. You can see this in Figure 2-14. These blueprints contain all of the programming code describing state and behavior. They contain all the variables and methods an object will possess.

When we think of objects, we tend to think of conceptual entities that contain both state and behavior and are able to communicate by way of messages. In fact, an object cannot exist without a class that first defines the variables, methods, and interfaces that the object will have. Each and every object is created, or *instantiated*, from a class.

It might help to think of objects and classes in terms of C structs and variables derived from those structs. A *struct* defines a group of data types, from which a programmer can create any number of variables (memory permitting, of course). For example, the following C struct defines a basic `Point` structure:

```
struct Point {
   int h; /* horizontal coordinate */
   int v; /* vertical coordinate */
};
```

This struct could be regarded as a class; it's the template from which new Point variables are created:

```
Point myPt, anotherPoint, yetAnother; /* just making my Points!
*/
```

In this example, we've created three different variables, all having the same structure. We have, in essence, created objects from a template. This is exactly the purpose that classes serve; they are templates from which objects are created.

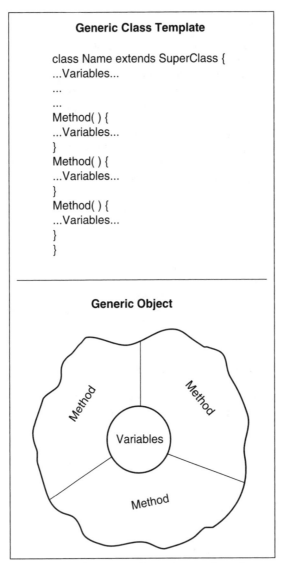

Figure 2-14: Classes are the code templates from which objects are created.

Classes, however, don't just define data types. They also define methods, giving the object its behavior and an interface through which that object communicates with other objects. In Java, a class definition has the following form:

```
class name {
    . . . instance variables . . .
    . . . method declarations . . .
}
```

Although you can declare your methods first and the instance variables last, it's good coding practice to follow the preceding model. The Java keyword class begins the definition for a class. You provide the class with a name (such as Point). The variables and methods of the class are enclosed in the curly braces ({ }) that begin and end the class definition block.

Let's take a look at the structure of Point, this time written as a Java class. The variables representing horizontal and vertical would be the same, but we might also want to include a method for setting these variables and one each for retrieving the value of these variables:

```
class Point {
   private int h; /* horizontal coordinate */
   private int v; /* vertical coordinate */
   public void setPoint (int newH, int newV) {
         h = newH;
         v = newV;
   }
   public int getH() {
      return (h);
   }
   public int getV() {
      return (v);
   }
}
```

Now, this certainly has a lot more meat than the C struct we created, and for good reason. The Point class contains three methods: setPoint() to set the horizontal and vertical integer variables; getH() to retrieve the horizontal variable; and getV() to retrieve the vertical variable. Fair enough, but what's going on with the keywords private and public?

Private versus public

Remember that objects have the capability to encapsulate, or hide, their data. No need exists for other objects to access the variables of a Point object directly, thus they are both declared as private when we create our class. The only way to set or retrieve this data is through a Point object's public methods, which any other object can do by simply sending a message. Which leads me to the issue of *instantiation*, the act of creating an object from a class.

Note

Java provides four levels of access control: public, protected, private, and friendly. Each of these is discussed in Chapter 7, "Getting Started: HelloWorld Application and HelloWorld Applet," and Chapter 13, "Classes, Interfaces, and Packages."

Instantiation

Until we create an object from our new class, nothing is really going on. Before we can work with an object, we must instantiate one:

```
Point myPt = new Point(); /* instantiate myPoint object */
```

The preceding line of code creates an object named myPt from the Point class we created earlier; in other words, it creates an *instance* of the Point object. The new operator followed by Point() creates an object of class Point in memory, to which the myPt variable now refers. The new Point() part is necessary because the new operator is required to instantiate an object from a class. Following new is what's known as a *constructor*, a special method that *initializes* an object (gives value to it at the beginning of its lifetime). The combination of the new operator and the Point() constructor effectively creates (in memory) and initializes the object to which myPt now refers.

Now, let's suppose we want to do something with the object we've just created. How about setting the horizontal and vertical coordinates, and then, just for fun, we can retrieve and copy them into local variables:

```
myPt.setPoint(145,124); /* set the h and v variables */
int theHorizontal = myPt.getH(); /* get myPt h value, and assign
                                    to a variable */
int theVertical = myPt.getV(); /* get myPt v value, and assign to
                                  a variable */
```

So, what we have done in this set of examples should be pretty clear by now:

1. We created a class named Point, which had instance variables h and v and three methods: one to set the variables; the other two to retrieve them.

2. We then instantiated an object, myPt, of class Point.

3. We set the instance variables of our new object, and then retrieved each and assigned it to a local variable (theHorizontal was set to 145 while theVertical was set to 124).

Although this is a relatively simple example of creating and using a class in Java, it should help to put the concepts of objects and classes into the proper perspective. Later in this book you'll create much more substantial classes, from which sophisticated objects will be brought to life. And thanks to another powerful OOP concept, inheritance, you'll be able to draw life from existing classes. If this sounds like a trailer for the movie *Dawn of the Living Dead*, read on.

Inheritance

It's time we got to the real meat of the matter of OOP: *inheritance*. Inheritance is arguably the most powerful feature of any object-oriented language, as it makes it possible to reuse code as never before.

When we speak of classes and classification, we mean things that can be grouped together in accordance with specific traits. Harley is a member of the Felis class, you and I are members of the Homo sapiens class, and so on. But what's the real advantage to classification in software programming?

Inheritance, my Homo sapiens friend.

Once a class has been created, the general, all-purpose state and behavior for all objects to be derived from that class are defined. For example, suppose I create a class called `TimePiece`. `TimePiece` is an abstraction of the concept of keeping track of time. In it, I have a variable called `Time` (surprise, surprise). I also have two methods, one to set the time (`SetTime`), and one to display it (`DisplayTime`). These are set out in Figure 2-15.

```
class TimePiece extends Object {
   int Time;

public void SetTime (int NewTime) {
   Time = NewTime;
}
public void ShowTime( ) {
   System.out.println (Time);
}
}
```

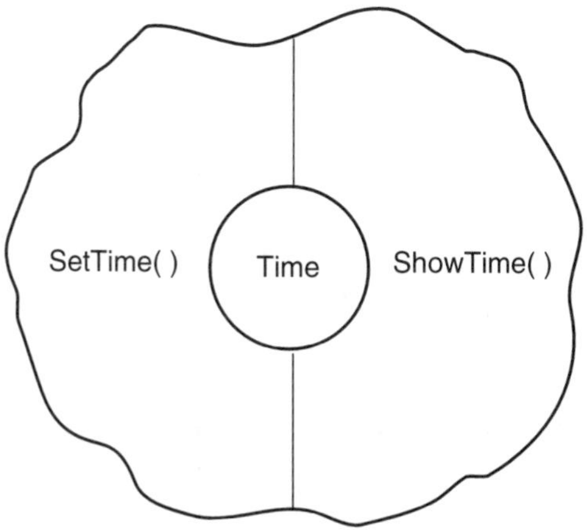

Figure 2-15: Class TimePiece, showing its variable and methods

This is all well and good, but what's important to understand is that all objects I create using `TimePiece` will have a `Time` variable and `SetTime`/`DisplayTime` methods. This means I can create a bunch of different `TimePiece` objects, such as a wristwatch, alarm clock, or grandfather clock, and each inherits the traits of the `TimePiece` class. This means I don't have to write new methods for each type of clock I create, as shown in Figure 2-16.

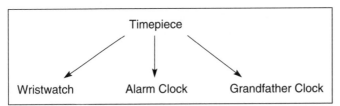

Figure 2-16: All objects of the class TimePiece inherit its variables and methods.

Suppose that I recognize the need for an alarm as well. I could add an alarm method to the `TimePiece` class, and each new object created using `TimePiece` would then come with an alarm. Or, I could simply use `TimePiece` as the basis for an entirely new class, which I'll call `TimeAlarmPiece`.

While this new class automatically inherits the variables and methods of `TimePiece`, I can add entirely new variables and methods to it as I wish. Thanks to inheritance, I can create an entirely new subclass of `TimePiece` that has all the traits of its superclass, plus whatever capabilities I add. You can see the relationship between subclass and superclass in Figure 2-17.

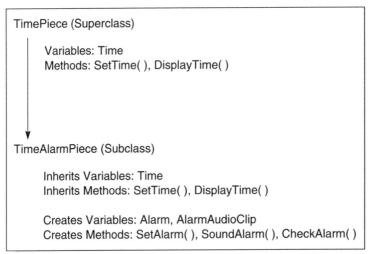

Figure 2-17: Creating a subclass makes TimePiece a superclass.

Reusable code

This capability to reuse existing code to create new objects is a profound feature of OOP; the only new code I have to write is that needed for the alarm. The TimePiece code comes for free; I'm reusing it to create an entirely new class that understands alarms.

The result is a dramatic increase in proficiency; the new class is up and running in a fraction of the time it would take to write it from scratch. And, to further dramatize the power of inheritance, I can use the new TimeAlarmPiece class to create any number of objects that require both time and an alarm. Any object instantiated from the TimeAlarmPiece class automatically knows how to deal with both time and alarms.

To add even more drama to the concept of inheritance, we'll take it one step further and extend the TimeAlarmPiece class to create an entirely new class capable of dealing with time, alarms, and mathematical calculations. That's right, we can create a subclass of the TimeAlarmPiece subclass and get all the time and alarm traits for free. We need only add code to handle calculations, and *voilà*, we have a class from which we can create a wristwatch that tells the time, sets and sounds an alarm, and calculates the excessive cost of our electricity bill.

Class hierarchy/inheritance tree

As a class is extended through subclassing, the resulting objects become more and more specialized.

A *class hierarchy*, or *inheritance tree*, refers to the family of classes that result from the act of subclassing. At the top level, the class is generic; it becomes more specialized as it goes down. A class hierarchy often resembles the roots of a tree, with offshoots at many levels, as shown in Figure 2-18.

Warning!

Because object-oriented programming lends itself so beautifully to the concept of inheritance, things can quickly grow out of control if you give subclasses to a class without considerable thought. It is very difficult to determine precisely which aspects of state and behavior the class should have, and which should be added only into subclasses.

Without foresight and proper design considerations, object-oriented systems can run rampant, like multiplying bacteria in a warm petri dish. It's for these reasons that the practice of object-oriented analysis (OOA) and object-oriented design (OOD) have become as important to serious software development as object-oriented programming itself.

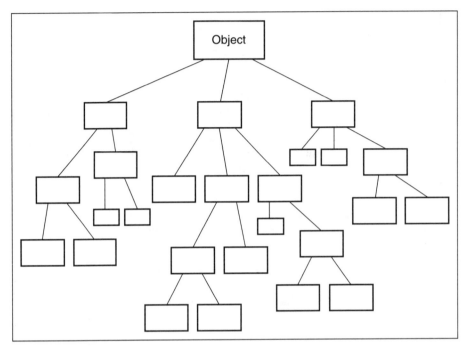

Figure 2-18: A class hierarchy

Object-Oriented Analysis and Object-Oriented Design

"In OOA, we seek to model the world by identifying the classes and objects that form the vocabulary of the problem domain; and in OOD, we invent the abstractions and mechanisms that provide the behavior that this model requires."—Grady Booch

It is very easy to become entangled in object-oriented programming because of the technology's flexible nature. For this reason, professional software engineers such as Grady Booch and James Rumbaugh are attempting to establish a standard way of applying object-oriented techniques to software development.

Object-oriented analysis (OOA) and object-oriented design (OOD) ensure that object-oriented programming is done with foresight and in the best way possible for each problem we attempt to resolve. Programming comes only after a thorough analysis of the problem and the careful design of a solution.

Notation method

One aspect of OOA/OOD is having a *notation method*. A notation method provides a way for us to map out a program on paper, whiteboard, or other media before committing it to code. It serves much the same purpose as flowcharts do for procedural programming—it gives us a visual idea of how everything works without the need for actual code.

Once we have decided how we want to subdivide our classes and objects (variables, methods, and interfaces), a notation method lets us represent them and their often complex relationships with other objects. The Booch Method is one popular notation method, although it is only one of many.

I won't assert that you need to adopt object-oriented analysis and object-oriented design methodologies in order to learn OOP. That's simply not the case. In fact, you can begin programming in Java without even learning object-oriented programming, if you really want to. But in reality, you're much better off learning about object-oriented analysis and object-oriented design while learning the language. You may find them of no use to you at this point, or exceptionally helpful. It depends on what you want to do with Java and how you plan to use the language. Either way, it's worth checking out as you get deeper into Java programming. A great place to learn more about object-oriented programming is at Ricardo Devis's Object-Oriented Page at `http://www.well.com/user/ritchie/oo.html`. It contains a number of links to sites all over the Web that focus on object-oriented programming and methodologies.

Summary

Object-oriented programming (OOP) is the foundation of the Java programming language. You need to understand the concepts of OOP before you jump into Java.

- ✦ OOP is based on a few key concepts: abstraction, states, behavior, variables, methods, and encapsulation (information hiding).
- ✦ OOP uses object interfaces to communicate with the outside world.
- ✦ Inheritance is one of the most powerful features of object-oriented programming—because it enables you to reuse your code.
- ✦ Object-oriented programming is just the tip of the iceberg—object-oriented analysis (OOA) and object-oriented design (OOD) techniques help you create and manage your object-oriented development projects.

✦　　　✦　　　✦

Applet Design Basics

Before diving in and writing your first Java applet, it's important to first consider the design of applets. By "design," I not only mean the overall design—how it looks, what it does, how it interacts with the webber, and so forth—but also the internal organization of the source code needed to create the applet in the first place.

Although discussing design concepts before covering the language may seem akin to putting the cart before the horse, in truth it's not as off-the-wall as you might at first think. Since many programmers are likely to be up and running with Java in no time, there's no telling whether they'll bother to read the various chapters in this book before cranking out functional applets and putting them on the Web for the world to see and use.

So, I'm discussing design issues here rather than at the end of the book, with the hope that if you take the time to skim this chapter before reading on, much of it will sink in and stick with you along the way. If you're whipping out applets within 24 hours of picking up this book, as many experienced C and C++ programmers will be doing, be sure to consider the design guidelines presented here, even if you don't need to read every chapter that follows.

And, aside from the practical issue of catching you before you surf off into the sunset with Java and browser in tow, there's another reason for discussing design basics here: Because I won't discuss implementation details at all, I can paint an overall portrait—in broad strokes—of the things you'll learn by reading the rest of this book.

In the coming chapters, you'll read in detail about the various features of the Java language and learn how to create your own executable Web content. By covering each major topic in a separate chapter, I hope to get right to the meat (artichoke heart, if you're a vegetarian) of each feature. I've laid out the book in a linear fashion, proceeding from topic to topic as you might encounter them were you to explore the language on your own with little more than a vague idea of what it held in store.

If you didn't get an overview in this chapter first, a significant and unreasonable burden would land squarely on your shoulders: To understand each of the basic design issues before releasing an applet upon our global village, you'd have to read the entire book from front to back!

To ease this burden, this chapter gives you a "sneak peek" at topics and issues well in advance of actually exploring them. You'll gain a better understanding of what applets can and cannot do, what they should and shouldn't do, and what you can expect as challenges to your programming prowess. By taking the time here and now to consider applet design, you might save your forehead the pain of being beaten against the keyboard out of frustration later on.

Get Started by Walking Away from the Computer

Today, with midnight hacking in vogue, sleepless nights at the keyboard an honorable living, and cutting every conceivable corner to get products to market on schedule being the mantra of many software companies, taking time to put ideas on paper may seem a bit old-fashioned. But no matter how you slice it, sketching out your programs in advance will save you a great deal of time in the long run (see Figure 3-1).

And I'm not talking flowcharts here. I am merely suggesting that the time you take to step away from the keyboard and place your ideas on that flat white stuff you had consigned to the garbage can of history will more than pay for itself when it comes to implementation. If you're an experienced programmer, chances are you already follow a design process for projects before even beginning to code. And if you're new to programming, it's a good habit to get into.

Since Java is an object-oriented programming (OOP) language, your programs will consist of objects that interact with each other. As you learned in Chapter 2, objects can be easily represented on paper as "amorphous blobs that do something."

By taking the time to work out the "blobs" and how they interact with one another on paper, you'll save yourself a good deal of wasted implementation effort. Much like the master artist who sketches renditions of a masterpiece before—and even during its creation—you'll have an opportunity to refine your programs on an abstract level before committing to a single line of code.

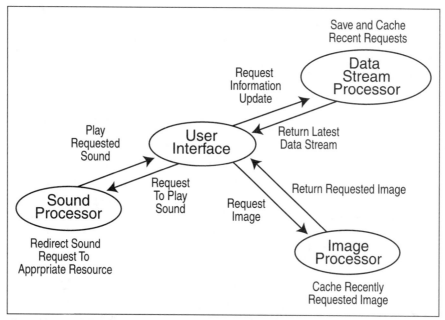

Figure 3-1: Taking the time to sketch out the design of your applet and the relationships of its objects can save time down the road.

Once you begin to code, you're essentially strapping yourself into a straitjacket; your initial attempt may not turn out to be the best solution after all, and it might even strangle your good intentions in the end. Without sketching the program in advance, you'll barrel ahead and almost certainly make a mess of the code, since you won't give adequate time to considering the various classes you'll be coding and the objects they give birth to. Certainly, the most simple of programs won't be an issue, but try and implement larger applets off the cuff, and you'll find yourself looking at a mighty unattractive spaghetti dinner of code, when all is said and done.

Sketching a user interface

Aside from sketching your applet objects and their relationship with each other, it's also crucial to put on paper the user interface (UI) your applet will require. Notice I didn't say *graphical* user interface (GUI), which tends to be limited to windowing elements (buttons, scroll bars, windows, dialogs, and the like). Instead, I'm referring to the interface at large: Precisely what will the webber experience when he or she encounters your applet?

This is all-encompassing, and not limited to windowing elements. Everything a person will see or hear when using your applet is part of the UI. And yes, I do mean hear. Since applets can play sound with as little as one line of code, you must consider what audio yours will support (if any) and how that fits in with the rest of the program.

Again, there's no need to whip out a slide rule and sweat out the exact details. You need only sketch the UI your applet will support to get a better idea of how it will look and sound to those who use it. Rather than waste time coding elements that you might later reorganize or omit altogether, you should work through the UI of an applet before committing to a single line of code.

As a general rule, I prefer to sketch the UI before anything else is done. Typically, I let an idea for a program rattle around for a while, thinking through the details of what it should look like and how it should act. Once I've roughed it out in my head for a few days, or longer, I then begin to sketch out the user interface.

Invariably, I discover things I've left out or want to drop that I would never have noticed in a purely mental design. If you go straight to code relying only on loosely organized thoughts, you will likely start in the wrong direction and waste a great deal of time. Instead, it pays to take the UI ideas you're considering out of your mind and place them on paper. Once there, you can tweak, massage, and rework them as much as necessary, since this is an iterative process (and one that you might spend a lot of time with if you're anything like me).

Once I'm satisfied with the UI, I sketch out the various objects the program needs. This may take several attempts or be a quick and surprisingly easy process. Whatever the case, before I begin so much as a line of code, I know a great deal about what my program will ultimately look like and what code I have to write to get it there.

Contrast this approach with diving into code head-first like a manic surfer on the beach at Maui who can't wait to get into the water (which, I admit, I sometimes do when overcome with excitement for a particular project). Despite my best efforts and the most honest intentions, I'm almost never satisfied with programs I develop in this manner, and I often spend a great deal of time trying to get them right. The code may look and act as it's supposed to on the surface, but under the covers is another matter altogether.

The programs you create without taking the time to think things through will be much less elegant, and even downright ugly, when compared to their well-considered counterparts. Worse still, they're typically inflexible and much more difficult to maintain than they should be. Except in cases where the program is a "one-off" effort (made for a special purpose that won't require an upgrade, and won't find itself in the hands of customers), you'll eventually need to rewrite most, if not all, of the code to bring it up to snuff.

Unless you're writing such disposable programs, do yourself a tremendous favor and spend the necessary "up-front" time placing your ideas on paper and working through the overall design of your projects before committing to code. You won't be sorry.

Giving the Webber Control

When designing your applets, it's a good idea to remember that every person who encounters them will have a different opinion about what is and isn't cool. Although a thumping background soundtrack and spinning disco balls on a Web page may seem like the ultimate multimedia experience to you, not everyone will agree.

Whenever you choose to add nifty features such as looping soundtracks (audio that plays continuously by starting over when the end is reached), loud sounds, and animation, you need to give users a way to turn off the ones they don't like. For example, the webber might turn off an animation by clicking it, stop a looping soundtrack by clicking a button, or mute all audio sources at once by clicking another button.

Exactly how you give the user control is your business. Sometimes buttons aren't possible, and so you might consider a less obvious interface element, such as a check box or simply a mouse click. However you do it, give visitors a choice and let them know how to control the various elements of your applet. After all, webbers aren't likely to come back if they're annoyed by your creative use of Java.

Mouse control

There are two aspects to consider with regard to the mouse control: single or double clicks, and single or multiple buttons.

Single clicks

For most applets, the mouse is the primary control mechanism. You can easily determine if it has been clicked, released, moved, or even been clicked and dragged without first being released. In contrast, you can't easily determine if a double-click has occurred.

Java doesn't support double-clicking, so you'll have to write your own code to calculate the time between each click and determine if such an event has occurred. Although writing such code isn't difficult, it's a bad idea. The Web is, by design, a single-click navigation system. Not only will use of double-clicking confuse the webber, but it breaks with the tradition of the Web.

As a result, you should design your applet around single clicks, and unless it's absolutely necessary, eliminate double clicks altogether.

On the CD-ROM

If you must have support for double clicks in your applet, look in the *JavaWorld* Topical Index in the JavaWorld archive provided on the accompanying CD-ROM, under Tips and Tricks. There you'll find information in double-click support.

Single button

Java originally supported only a one-button mouse. Since JDK 1.1, Java has supported up to three mouse buttons, enabling more sophisticated mouse control. This might sound like a good feature to add to your Java programs, but you'll find it's not always a good idea.

If you design your applet to understand and respond to specific mouse buttons, you'll be cutting a large population of Web users out of the loop. Instead, use the keyboard to modify a mouse click. For example, when the mouse is clicked and no keys are pressed, treat it as a standard mouse event. When the mouse is clicked and the Shift key is pressed, treat it as you would a special mouse button. Of course, you're not limited to the Shift key when it comes to modifying mouse clicks, but there are a few things you should be aware of when incorporating keyboard control into your applet.

Keyboard control

Because Java doesn't allow you to write applets that support a multibutton mouse, you may rely on the keyboard to signal special webber input. In this way, you can react to different combinations of keyboard and mouse down events.

When using the keyboard to modify a mouse click, it's a good idea to limit the keys you support to the Shift and Ctrl keys. These are available on almost every personal computer, and are used by standard software programs to modify mouse clicks. The concept of Shift-clicking or Ctrl-clicking is familiar to the majority of personal computer users, and these keyboard-mouse combinations can make your applet easier to use.

Avoid obtuse keyboard modifiers, and only use those that might help the webber remember what key to press when clicking the mouse. Suppose, for example, that you write a video game that uses the mouse to control a submarine. Clicking the mouse alone might launch a torpedo, while clicking the mouse while holding down the *P* key might activate the periscope.

Stop when stopped!

When a Web page is accessed with a Java-savvy browser, all applets embedded in that page are told to "start." At this point, applets load the sounds and graphics they need (if any) and do their stuff.

When the Web page is left, either by the webber navigating to another page or the browser being quit altogether, all applets in the page are told to "stop." It is here that you'll bring your applet activity to a screeching halt. However, this process isn't handled for you automatically.

The programmer is responsible for stopping any sounds that are currently playing, for bringing animation to a standstill, and halting all threads in their applet. Rarely, if ever, does an applet have a good reason to continue along its merry way when the page it is embedded in has been exited. By ceasing all activity upon receiving the "stop" message, your applets become well-behaved and courteous inhabitants of the Web pages in which they are embedded.

Flexibility through applet parameters

If you've looked at the HTML code many applets are embedded in, you may have noticed the word *PARAM* used inside the <APPLET> tag. The PARAM attribute lets applets receive data through HTML code, which allows Web page authors to configure applets for their specific needs without actually dealing with Java code (that's our job!).

Applets that utilize parameters are much more flexible than those that don't. Instead of creating several slightly different versions of the same applet, you can use the PARAM attribute to customize a single applet. By responding to parameters embedded in the HTML code, an applet can behave uniquely in different pages.

Bandwidth Considerations

Because Java makes creating Web pages with sophisticated animation and sounds a snap, those new to the language often tend to lose themselves in the excitement. Iceberg-sized images and audio clips abound on the high seas of the Web. And while this may be just fine for the developer who has access to the Web via a T1 line or cable connection, the equivalent of an ocean liner, the rest of the world isn't so fortunate; creaky wooden rafts and pontoon boats are the norm.

Since bandwidth is a major issue with the majority of webbers, you must consider the lowest-common denominator. Although you might try to convince yourself that 28.8 Kbps is the norm, with ISDN and cable modem access not far behind, many folks today surf the Web at speeds of 14.4 Kbps or less. Sure, the technophiles are working with all the latest gadgets, but the masses . . . well, that's a completely different story. To offer your applets to everyone without penalizing those with slower access takes extra effort and means you should assume the average access speed is no higher than 28.8 Kbps, with a large percentage of folks on the Web still dog-paddling along at 14.4 Kbps and even 9600 bps!

Battling bandwidth bottlenecks

Although applets themselves are quite small, and come across the wire in no time, the graphics and audio files they often utilize are tremendous by comparison. To prevent serious bottlenecks when downloading these files over the network, there are several things you can do to decrease transmission time.

Sound files

Java only supports Sun's *.au* format for sound files, which uses *μ*Law (pronounced *mu-law*) encoding. Thus, if you intend to use sound files, you'll have to convert your existing audio files to this 8-bit, 8kHz, single-channel (mono) format.

Sun users can create sounds in the *.au* format using the *audiotool* application. Windows users can use the GoldWave utility supplied on the CD-ROM that comes with this book to create and export sounds in this format.

Although the *.au* format creates files that are smaller in size than other formats, the sound quality isn't the best. As a result, you may find yourself fiddling with various sound editing functions in an attempt to eliminate the hiss you'll hear when converting higher-quality sounds to this format.

In order to reduce the size of sound files as much as possible, you'll only want to keep the absolutely essential portions of it around. Cut out any preceding or trailing silence, although you may be tempted to keep it.

Since cutting out every second of preceding and trailing silences tends to make sounds begin and end abruptly, many programmers figure keeping a second or two of "dead space" on either end of the sound clip is worth the extra download time. However, you can achieve the same results by applying a "fade in" effect to the beginning of the sound, and a "fade out" effect at the end. These two effects give nice, smooth transitions instead of abrupt starts and stops. Not only is the sound more professional and appealing, but you'll trim off a bit of the download time in the process.

Sound loops

Sound is such an effective way to grab attention and add impact to an applet that many first-timers overuse it. Rather than playing a large number of audio clips, consider whether looping would be a reasonable alternative. When you loop a sound file, it will repeat itself continuously until you tell it to stop.

The result can be quite powerful, especially if the sound clip you loop is subtle. Instead of bombarding the visitor with sound after sound, sucking up valuable network bandwidth in the process, consider this option. You'll be happy to know that you can play any number of sounds at once, meaning you don't have to stop a sound loop in order to play another sound clip. All sounds you play at the same time will be mixed together, allowing for a rich audio production with minimal effort on your part.

In order to accommodate the demands of media-hungry developers, JavaSoft has announced an "extension" to the core Java API, and it should be available for download by the time you read this. The Media API, discussed in more detail in Chapter 30, gives applets and applications much more capability in terms of the sounds and images they may use. However, the Media API isn't built into the core Java API at the moment; it's a separate library of Java classes that you can't guarantee will be available on every user's system. Refer to Chapter 30 for more details regarding the Media API and other forthcoming APIs that will extend the core capabilities of Java.

Images and colors

Java supports the use of *GIF* (*graphics interchange format*) and *JPEG* (*Joint Photographic Experts Group*) images, meaning that it gives you a nice and easy mechanism for retrieving these images from the Web and displaying them in your applet. Java also supports a 24-bit color model, which allows the programmer to define and use more than 16 million different colors for use in drawing primitive graphics (lines, rectangles, ovals, polygons, and so forth) and fonts.

Although the use of color applied to primitive graphics doesn't negatively affect bandwidth, images do. Since the JPEG format is supported, you can utilize 24-bit color images within your applets. With GIF you're currently limited to a palette of 256 colors. This is a limitation of the GIF file format, not Java, although 24-bit GIF files will soon be possible through an enhancement of this popular type of graphic.

Image palette reduction

Regardless of which format you use, graphic images suck up bandwidth. To reduce the amount of time it takes an image to travel across the wire, you must cut down the amount of data used to represent it. Luckily, the most popular graphics programs on the market (Adobe Photoshop, CorelDraw!, Fractal Design Painter, and others such as the Paint Shop Pro shareware program) allow us to cut file sizes by reducing the amount of colors used to display an image.

Rather than using a full palette of 256 colors, you may find that only a small number are necessary to represent the image. By removing unused colors from the palette, you conserve storage space and decrease download times. And you can further reduce the palette by forcing colors close to one another to map to a certain value. For example, rather than having 16 different shades of gray in an image, you might reduce the palette to support only three shades. This technique applies to all colors, meaning you can reduce the entire palette of an image to significantly reduce its size.

Certainly, there is a trade-off between the quality of the image and overall storage size. However, you (or the graphic artist responsible for Web artwork at your site) can typically reduce the palette considerably without adversely affecting the image quality (see Figures 3-2 and 3-3).

Figure 3-2: Reducing the palette of colors can significantly reduce the storage size of an image. This image contains several hundred colors, and requires 200KB of disk space.

Figure 3-3: After palette reduction, this image contains only 40 colors and takes up less than 100KB of disk space. Can you tell the difference?

GIF versus JPEG

When using images, you'll eventually need to decide upon a format to support. Java supports both CompuServe GIF and JPEG formats in your applets, but there are a number of factors that may make one preferable over the other. Start by taking a look at the GIF format.

You'll find several benefits with GIF images. For starters, every graphics-based Web browser supports inline GIF images; webbers won't need an external helper application to view them. In addition, the GIF format is highly efficient and has built-in compression that produces relatively small file sizes for images that lend itself to this format. Finally, GIF images support transparency and interlacing, which can greatly enhance the visual appeal of your applet.

JPEG images, on the other hand, can contain more than 256 colors, and can be compressed to a higher degree than GIF when a large number of colors are involved. The JPEG format currently doesn't support transparency or interlacing.

Transparency

Transparency allows the graphic artist to specify any color in an image as "transparent." When the image is rendered on the screen, this color isn't shown. Instead, whatever is underneath it shows through (typically the background color, although other images may be drawn underneath, as well).

Without transparency, images are displayed using all colors in the palette, including the background color of the image. As a result, they may appear quite unattractive under certain circumstances—unless the color of these portions matches exactly the underlying background (see Figure 3-4). Therefore, the GIF format is the only choice for images that must have a "see-through" portion.

Figure 3-4: Transparency allows us to specify a color in an image as "see-through." The image at the top of this figure uses transparency to appear as a natural part of this page, while the one underneath it does not.

Interlacing

Interlacing, another feature supported by the GIF format, allows images to be incrementally drawn on the screen as they come across the wire. Rather than appearing only after the entire image is transmitted, interlaced images appear on the screen a little at a time as they are transmitted over the network.

The effect is similar to watching a Polaroid photograph develop before your eyes; you have an idea of what the image is before it is completely downloaded, and see it materialize on the page over time. If you give webbers something to watch as the image becomes clearer, they aren't as likely to abort the process and go elsewhere. Instead, many will stick around and watch these images appear.

GIF and JPEG: the bottom line

Since the GIF format supports both transparency and interlacing, in addition to being the default format for Web graphics, you'll more often than not find it a better choice for your applets than JPEG.

However, GIF images are currently limited to 256 (8-bit) colors. The JPEG format, on the other hand, supports over 16 million (24-bit) different colors. In cases where you absolutely must have more than 256 colors in an image, you'll have to use the JPEG format.

JPEG images are compressed using a lossy compression algorithm, allowing you to specify a trade-off between image quality and storage size. When you use high levels of compression, these images lose information (hence the term *lossy*). Future versions of the JPEG format may include support for transparency and interlacing, although at the moment neither are available.

A new version of the JPEG format, called *JPEG Progressive Download* (fondly known as "Progressive JPEG"), is similar in nature to an interlaced GIF. As these images come across the wire, they are displayed incrementally. At first they look blurry, but become sharper and more defined as the image data is downloaded, until finally the entire image is clearly visible. Unfortunately, this new JPEG format is not yet supported by Java. However, future versions of Java are expected to support it.

Although you might think the choice of formats is clear—use GIF in most situations and turn to JPEG only when you need more than 256 colors—you ought to take into consideration that some releases of Java for Windows dither ALL graphics to 256 colors before displaying them! This is because supporting more than 256 colors on Windows-based machines proved too time consuming for the first release of the Java Developer's Kit (JDK). So, even if you use JPEG images, their beauty will be lost on webbers who have Windows systems, until the JDK is updated.

If you can do it, you're better off using GIF images. Since a large number of webbers won't be able to see the difference anyway, there's no sense wasting bandwidth with high-resolution JPEG images, unless you have no choice.

As a general rule of thumb, you should keep the total amount of material that has to download for each Web page (text, graphics, sound files, and so on) under 250K. If you have a large number of graphics and are above 250K in total Web page material, you should consider using the JPEG format, simply to gain the highest degree of compression possible. Since images with more than 100 colors tend to compress more efficiently in the JPEG format than they do with GIF, first target images with the most colors for JPEG compression.

If you still have too much data to download, consider reducing the overall amount of material on the page. You can also reduce the dimensions of the images, cropping out excess material altogether. And, of course, you can always use the

JPEG format with the highest degree of compression for all your images. Just be aware that you'll lose both the transparency and interlacing features available with the GIF format.

Finally, there is the user's equipment to consider. The majority of webbers can't see more than 256 colors on their screen anyway. In fact, a large number of systems connected to the Web can't even display that many. For some, the upper limit is 16 colors or less!

Although I wouldn't spend a great deal of time attempting to accommodate systems at the lowest end, I highly recommend that you assume the majority of webbers can only see up to 256. And so, the choice between JPEG and GIF becomes even easier.

Webber System Considerations

In addition to considering bandwidth, you must also consider the variety of systems your applets will run on once they become available to a global population. Just as most webbers lack ultrafast connections to the Web, they're often surfing with systems that are remarkably less powerful than those we use to develop applets. As a result, you must develop applets to run on a wide variety of systems, from entry-level boxes to silicon-heavy hot rods.

In addition to raw computing horsepower, you must also consider the wide range of video displays your applets will be viewed on. In short, you must design your applets to run on just about every system out there, or risk alienating those whose systems aren't up to your personal standards. This means eliminating excessive processing and media consumed by your applets, and streamlining them in ways that you might not consider necessary based on your own computer setup.

To do this, you have to think in terms of absolute efficiency from the get-go, cutting out every unnecessary bit and byte of code and media (sounds and images) possible, and testing the results as you go along on a variety of low-end computer systems.

Images and colors

When using colors for rendering primitive graphics (such as lines, rectangles, ovals, and polygons), stick to the predefined colors supplied by Java. Although you can define your own colors, with over 16 million options, it's a bad idea to assume the webber will ever see them. Because most webbers only have 256 colors on their systems, and some only 16, a color you define will usually be converted to the closest match or dithered down to accommodate their less capable monitors. Your efforts will be lost on all but those who happen to use systems like yours. To be safe, use the built-in colors and only define others when absolutely necessary.

Color matching

To complicate matters, you can't guarantee that an image or color will be consistent across multiple platforms. Colors on a Windows machine won't necessarily look the same as those on a Sun machine, and will look different once again on a Macintosh. As more platforms become Java-savvy, the disparity will grow.

To combat this problem, stick to minimal palettes and built-in colors. Don't spend too much time trying to get an image or color "just right" until you've had a chance to view it on a variety of platforms. The time you spend tweaking an image or color may well be wasted, since few webbers will have exactly the same system and display setup as you.

Instead, go for attractive and clean images. Avoid subtle hue shifts, fine lines in special colors, custom palettes, and the like. Before you spend too much time refining an image or creating custom colors for your primitives, take a look at it from a different perspective: Put what you have on the Web, and view it with as many different systems and browsers as possible. If you don't have access to a particular platform, ask a friend who does to give his or her opinion. The earlier in the development process you do this, the better off you'll be.

Animation

The most eye-catching thing an applet can do is animate images and graphics. When things move around the screen, you can't help but look at them. Unfortunately, you must also be aware of the diversity of systems your animations will be run on.

Animation takes horsepower, and if you've spent time honing an animation to look ideal on your system, you can guarantee it won't appear that way to everyone else. What happens when an animation created on a high-end workstation is run on an entry-level personal computer? Digital roadkill, that's what.

In such cases, the animation may be considerably slower than you'd expect. As a result, it loses its appeal to those with less capable systems; low-end webbers won't find it nearly as fascinating or slick as those using high-performance systems.

Interestingly enough, the exact opposite can happen when an animation is developed specifically for low-end systems. The developer might have spent considerable time and effort making the animation as fast as possible on a low-end development system, but when it's executed on a much faster machine it runs the risk of being so fast that it can't be appreciated—or even seen!

To reduce the risk on both fronts, you must assume that your applets will be run on a wide range of systems. Some will be blazing fast, perhaps souped up with multiple processors, while others will be painfully slow by comparison.

Don't despair! There's no need to throw yourself over the nearest cliff. Just hang on for a few more minutes; as you'll soon see, there are a few things you can do to create animations that execute smoothly in all cases.

Frame rate support

First, always assume your applets will run on machines that are considerably faster than yours. Although you may have a top-of-the-line system today, tomorrow it will be old news. In particular, if you are to prepare for tomorrow's fastest machines, you need to exercise control over how fast the individual frames in an animation are drawn. Although you might think that no delay between frames is ideal, nothing could be further from the truth.

With no delay between frames, the animation will run at breakneck speed. It might seem perfect on your machine, but on faster computers it may become a blur roughly equivalent to the Hale-Bopp Comet seen through the windshield of a moving car on a foggy night. Inserting a delay between each frame, however, gives our eyes a moment to actually see the various stages of animation; you effectively apply the breaks a wee bit between frames, giving our feeble eyeballs just enough time to focus on the current frame before advancing to the next one in the series.

Unfortunately, a problem arises when you control the frame rate with only faster systems in mind. Suppose, for example, that you've inserted a half-second delay between every frame in an animation. This is fine when running on fast machines, preventing blur, but when run on low-end systems, it could be a tremendous detriment to the animation.

The problem is that on slower machines, the frame rate is already slow enough for the frames to be painfully visible, so why add another half-second delay? In practice, you might need to eliminate the artificial delay altogether to compensate for this.

Rather than inserting a delay between every frame, you need only ensure that a specific amount of time has passed between the previous frame and the one about to be drawn. If the machine is incredibly fast, you'll want to delay the process a bit, but if the machine is incredibly slow, you'll want to draw the next frame as quickly as possible.

Although this may sound like a lot of work, you'll be happy to know that it's pretty easy to do. You simply enter a loop that does nothing but check to see if it's time to draw, and exit the loop when enough time has passed between the last frame being drawn and the current one. Following is pseudo-code (not the real McCoy, merely a rough idea having no direct relationship to a specific programming language) for just such a timing device, which would take place just before each frame is drawn:

```
while (timepassed < framerate) {
  update timepassed variable
    ... do nothing else but loop while waiting ...
}
... draw the current frame ...
timepassed = 0; // reset timer
```

Reduce overhead

The technique of controlling frame rate should only be coupled with a serious effort to reduce any overhead that might occur within your animations. The easiest way to do this when animating a series of images is to reduce the storage size of each image, as discussed in "Bandwidth Considerations" earlier in this chapter.

If the images in an animation are massive in size, low-end machines will barely be able to keep up with it. Likewise, low-end machines might not be up to the task if the calculations required to derive the next frame in a computer-generated animation (in other words, not animating a series of images, but generating each frame on the fly) require a great degree of computational power. Although high-end systems won't have a problem keeping up with each frame of the animation, and may even require an artificial delay between each, many low-end systems will be left in the dust.

In order to allow low-end machines in on the fun, it's a good idea to streamline all parts of your animations. When animating images, you can reduce the storage size of each one by reducing the color palettes, as described earlier, and by restricting the overall dimensions of each image. When generating animation frames on the fly, you should give considerable attention to making the frame generation algorithm as tight and efficient as possible. And in both cases, you should use *threads* to prevent processing bottlenecks from monopolizing the central processing unit (CPU).

Threads are a powerful, complex feature of many modern operating systems, and Java allows us to tap into them with relative ease. Threads give us the capability to run many different tasks concurrently, without forcing us to keep track of the state of each task (that is, we can set up threaded objects that run independent of our main program, without our having to write terribly complicated code to manage everything that's going on). For details on using threads in your Java programs, see Chapter 14.

To further reduce overhead, you can decrease the download time of individual images used in an animation by placing all of them in one image file. If you do this, the user downloads a single "animation strip" containing all of the images instead of a number of different images, each of which requires a separate HTTP network connection. The images are transmitted across the wire more efficiently and without the overhead of multiple connections. To use this method, you draw the appropriate portion of the animation strip on the screen rather than drawing a number of different images one after another. And instead of loading each individual image into memory, the single file is loaded into memory.

Processing bottlenecks

Depending on what your applets do, they may or may not suck up a considerable amount of system resources. For those that are computationally intensive or manage a large number of images, it's important to reduce potential bottlenecks. Any time one task blocks others, such as when your applet uses input/output streams or performs complex computations, you should implement the tasks as threads.

Threads are dealt with fully in Chapter 14, but suffice it to say here that they allow multiple tasks to occur at once when multiple central processing units (CPUs) are available, or are so interwoven with one another that they appear to be happening at the same time even on systems that have only one processor. And, since a time-consuming task running in a thread can yield to other threads, you can eliminate processing bottlenecks; each task gets a crack at the CPU without requiring the current task to be completed in entirety.

"Processing . . . please wait"

At times when your applet is immersed in a particularly time-consuming activity (such as retrieving large chunks of data from a file, or performing complex calculations), it's a good idea to let the webber know what's going on. If too much time passes before the applet somehow informs the Web surfer that things are going along as planned, they may assume the program isn't working properly, or simply become impatient and abandon your Web page altogether.

There are a number of ways to indicate to the webber that your applet is involved in a time-consuming task. You can display a message, such as "Processing . . . Please Wait," either in the applet itself or on the status bar portion of the browser. (If you want to display a message in the status bar, however, keep in mind that not every browser on the market may have one, and, for those that do, remember that webbers are free to hide them from view entirely!)

A more subtle approach is to change some aspect of the applet to visually indicate that activity is taking place. A small animation showing sand pouring through an hourglass might be appropriate, or perhaps a blinking "WORKING" image would do the trick. You might even consider a subtle sound loop or play a sound clip of a voice saying, "please wait." Whichever way you do it, it's a good idea to let users know they'll have to be patient.

If the process is particularly long, you should consider altering the message occasionally. If the same message appears for a long period of time, webbers might think the system is hung or not working properly. If the message alternates, the frame rate changes, or the rate of an animation alters as time passes, they'll be less likely to think something is wrong and abandon ship.

Fonts

When using fonts to display text, you'll need to be careful about which ones you choose. Since you can't be sure what fonts are installed on the various machines your applet will be executed on, it's important to determine if a font you want to use is available to all systems before attempting to use it. If you try to use a font that isn't installed on everyone's computer, a font substitution will take place that might ruin the visual effect you had planned.

It's simple, and recommended, to find out what fonts are installed. However, you don't have to bother if you're using the widely installed Times Roman and Courier fonts.

File Access and Network Connections

The majority of applets you create will require external data stored in a file (such as images, audio clips, and so on), which must be located on the Web. Because of the security restrictions imposed by current browser implementations, applets fetched from the Net can't access local files, so any files an applet accesses must be stored on the *same* Web server that the applet itself resides on.

Save yourself the frustration of trying to access local files, or files located anywhere but on the server where the applet itself resides, as it would be an exercise in futility. Since applets simply aren't allowed to touch files residing anywhere outside of the server on which they themselves come from, it's hopeless to even try to access files on the user's machine or other Web servers.

Although future versions of Java/browser combinations are expected to support local and remote file access, for now you'll have to design your applets to retrieve files from their own server. However, the same isn't true for *uniform resource locator* (URL) connections. Your applets can open any valid URL and have the browser automatically load the page (see Chapter 15 for details).

These restrictions on Java applets do not apply to Java applications. Applications can access files on the user's local system, or from anywhere on the Web (assuming, of course, that they can make a connection to the Web server on which such files are located).

Testing locally, releasing globally

Although your applets can't load files located on the webber's own computer, or on a server other than the one they come from, you can do the majority of development and testing on your local system.

Rather than going through the process of uploading each revision of your applet to the Web and testing it from afar, you can write and test your applets locally, assuming the data files they require are also local. If an applet's directory layout on your local computer system is the same as the one on the server the applet will be uploaded onto, and if all of the files the applet requires are present and in the same relative directories, you can greatly streamline the development process.

In this case, you can write and test applets locally and merely upload them to the server when you are ready to test them in a networked environment. Of course, you'll want to test them extensively after you've placed them on the Web. However, developing and testing locally can still save you a great deal of time.

Other Considerations

There are a number of other design issues to consider when developing applets. For starters, you must assume that your programs will be accessed by a global community.

A universal language

Since not everyone in the world speaks your language (except, perhaps, the language of love—but that's another story altogether), try to minimize the amount of text you use. If possible, use images and icons to convey meaning rather than words. In many cases, of course, text is required and you'll have no choice. But when you do have a choice, opt for images rather than words.

You should also consider the concept your images convey. Even though images are often more easily understood than words, just because you're using them doesn't mean the concept they convey is universal. In cases where your applet must be understood by a diverse audience, it's a good idea to have the graphic artist creating the artwork used in your applet consult with a multilingual specialist or agency beforehand.

Avoid language and images that could be construed as racist, sexist, or culturally insensitive. What may be appropriate to you might be offensive to others.

Layout managers

Because applets can be run on a variety of platforms, it can be a bit difficult to ensure that your graphical elements will always appear in the proper positions on the screen. If you attempt to explicitly position elements (buttons, scroll bars, pop-up menus, drawing and painting areas, for example) at exact locations on the screen, you're flirting with disaster. The system of coordinates on your computer won't map exactly to others, so your neat and tidy layout may become an ugly mess (or even impossible to use) on other platforms.

To overcome this difficulty, Java utilizes *layout managers*, which are dealt with in detail in Chapter 21. With layout managers, you don't place elements on the screen using explicit coordinates. Instead, the *order* in which you add them, and the layout manager associated with such elements, dictates where they'll be placed. When your applet is displayed, the layout manager positions the elements in their proper places, regardless of what platform the applet is executed on. Furthermore, when the webber resizes the applet, the layout manager takes care of repositioning each element accordingly. By using Java's layout managers, you can ensure your applet's user interface will look and act as it should across a wide array of platforms.

Inter-applet communications

In many cases, a single applet won't be appropriate for your needs. For example, you might require applet activity in one part of a Web page to be coordinated with activity in another part of the page. You might also need to have standard Web content appear between the two areas, preventing you from creating one big applet that spans the entire page.

Rather than creating one giant applet, it may be easier and more appropriate to create two. Since applets in a Web page can send each other messages, they can effectively "talk" to each other. In fact, you can have any number of applets in a Web page, all communicating with one another (see Chapter 15).

Dual-purpose programs

At times, you'll develop Java programs that will be deployed both in applet and application form. There may be differences between the two, but portions may be exactly the same. When this is the case, you don't have to develop both programs separately. Instead, you can write one body of code that can be executed as both an applet and an application, as illustrated in Chapter 18. Doing so saves the time and effort of managing two different versions of essentially the same program, and ensures that consistency and code integrity exists between the two.

Managing Source Code

When it comes time to implement your applet, you'll have to carefully consider the code you will write in addition to the design issues discussed earlier in this chapter. Although much of the time and effort you spend will go into the overall design of the applet and the objects that will make it possible, eventually you'll have to get down to the nitty-gritty and write the actual source code. When programming in Java, there are number of things you can do to make the process go as smoothly as possible.

Only one class to a source file

As you learned in Chapter 2, objects are created using code templates known as *classes*. When creating a large number of classes, you should consider placing each in its own source code file.

By separating classes into their own source files, the concept of programming in terms of objects is strongly reinforced. Classes in separate files can only interact with others in a well-defined manner, meaning you won't be tempted to take shortcuts that might compromise the integrity of your code.

When you compile an applet or application whose classes exist in multiple source files, each is automatically compiled in turn. You don't have to worry about compiling every source file on your own, making the separation that much easier.

For many smaller applets and applications, saving each class in a separate source code file may be more hassle than it's worth. When you are beginning to program in Java, as with any language, it helps to start out with small programs and work your way to more complex ones as your understanding grows.

When you place all classes in the same source file, be sure to remember that each class should be written as its own island and have no knowledge of the innards of other classes. Even if classes aren't physically separate, their implementation should be independent from that of others. Later, when your programs become more complex, you may choose to separate classes into their own files.

Tip Keep in mind as you set forth on your Java programming adventure that each source code file can only contain *one* public class. If you attempt to place more than one public class inside a single source code file, the Java compiler will refuse to compile the file!

Document, document, document

As with most programming languages, it's highly recommended that you document your programs as they are written, using code comments. Document? Comments?! Yep. But before you jam that index finger down your throat in an attempt to clear your now queasy stomach, hear me out.

Although many programmers tend to gloss over source code documentation, or avoid it altogether, it's an important part of the process. So important, in fact, that Java provides a special comment that is used to generate documentation files in HTML format—complete with hyperlinks—directly from source code. By making the process of documentation so easy, Java encourages even the most hasty programmers to properly comment their code.

Thanks to Java's special Doc Comments, which look almost exactly like the standard C comments (with exception of an added asterisk), creating code documentation is a cinch. In addition to making your source code easier to understand when it comes time to enhance or maintain the work you've done, you can use Doc Comments to produce lovely HTML documentation that you would otherwise have had to create by hand. Thanks to Doc Comments, a single effort on your part (and a simple one at that) produces two extremely useful forms of code documentation. You can't beat that, can you?

Variable names

When you're using variables, it's important to choose clear and understandable names for them. Just as with source-level documentation using comments, some programmers tend to choose terse, if not entirely cryptic, variable names.

Reading and maintaining such code is more difficult than it should be, and it can be especially frustrating and time consuming for people other than the original programmer. Even in cases where you'll be the only one to see the code, it's a wise idea to use descriptive variable names. As time passes, you'll find reading the code a pleasure because it remains readily understandable.

In Java, variable names can be any length, so you're not restricted in how many characters you can use. Employ as many as you feel necessary to ensure that the names make sense.

Of course, some variables don't merit distinguished names. Take, for example, variables used to control the iteration of loops and other control-flow structures. Typically, single-character names (such as *i* or *x*) are just fine, since experienced programmers recognize such variables as being specific to the loop. In these cases, using a descriptive variable name (such as *loopCounter* or *iterationCount*) buys little, if any, value and may even make the code more difficult to read by cluttering an otherwise clean implementation.

 Since different types of variables serve different purposes in your programs, be sure to follow the recommended naming conventions when it comes to actually giving your variables identifying names. Chapter 9 describes the conventions for *identifiers* (names given to variables, classes, and methods).

Altering variables

In Java, there is no such thing as a "global" variable. Instead, objects contain variables, which other objects may or may not be able to directly alter depending on how access to the variable is specified. (You specify access using *access specifiers*, which are known formally as *field modifiers*. Access specifiers are discussed in detail in Chapter 9.)

As a general rule, however, objects should assume no knowledge whatsoever of the details of other objects in a program. This means that an object shouldn't be able to directly access another object's variables, regardless of how access to such variables is specified. Instead, the object should politely request that the other object access its own variables and return the result or modify the value it holds.

For example, if object *A* wants to retrieve a variable inside object *B*, it should ask *B* for the variable. Likewise, if object *A* wants to change the value of a variable in object *B*, it should ask object *B* to alter its own variable. This way, your objects won't have intimate knowledge of one another, and you can easily replace or update one without affecting the others. You accomplish such behavior by using *accessor methods*, which are nothing more than methods used to retrieve and/or alter the value of an object's variable. Thanks to accessor methods, the objects in your Java programs are much more modular in nature, letting you easily update or alter them in the future without worrying about "breaking" hard-coded dependencies among objects. You'll learn more about accessor methods in Chapter 9.

Avoiding native code

Although Java allows programmers to use non-Java, or native, source code (such as C code), you should always rewrite the code in standard Java if possible.

In order to make a clean transition to Java, you shouldn't try to use your existing non-Java source code unless absolutely necessary. Instead, you should take the time to rewrite that code in Java to avoid potentially compromising the object-oriented nature of your programs.

Aside from the fact that it's good practice to use pure Java code in your programs, only C may be integrated at this time (unless you use the *Java Native Interface*—JNI). And so you shouldn't even consider using code in other languages. If however, you rely on existing C code that simply can't be rewritten in Java, you can integrate this native code into your Java programs. If you do so, however, be forewarned—you'll likely spend the majority of your bug-fixing time inside the native code you introduce into your programs!

Peeking under the covers

One of the best ways to learn how to program in Java is to look at the work of others. That's why we've included a CD-ROM full of applets and their source code with this book.

In addition to looking at the source code for these applets, you should spend some time looking at the source code provided with Java itself. The JDK, which provides all the tools you'll need to write your own Java programs, gives us a great deal of code to examine.

Along with the JDK's own applets, which are also available on the enclosed CD-ROM, thousands of lines of Java code are used to implement the standard class libraries you'll use to write your own programs. In particular, the JDK class source files provide an excellent insight into the Java language. They illustrate every aspect of the Java language, and are documented with source code comments. Don't be afraid to peek under the covers; you'll see how the Java team at Sun writes Java code, and learn a great deal in the process.

Packages

Once you've written a fair amount of Java code, you'll be faced with the challenge of managing it. You'll eventually want to reuse classes you've written, and organize your growing base of code for future reuse.

In Java you can easily organize classes into *packages* (discussed in Chapter 11). You can think of packages as collections of classes that allow you to efficiently organize and reuse existing Java code.

The Java system comes with a number of packages all ready for you to use. These packages contain a large number of pre-built classes written by the JavaSoft team at Sun, many of which you'll use in your own programs.

Summary

Before diving in and writing your first Java applet, it's important to first consider the design of applets. By "design," I mean not only the overall design—how it looks, what it does, how it interacts with the webber, and so forth—but also the internal organization of the source code needed to create the applet in the first place.

✦ Remember that every person who encounters your applets will have a different opinion as to what is and isn't cool.

✦ Because Java makes creating Web pages with sophisticated animation and sounds a snap, people who are new to the language often tend to lose themselves in the excitement. Iceberg-sized images and audio clips abound on the high seas of the Web. And while this may be just fine for the developer who has access to the Web via a T1 line or cable connection, the equivalent of an ocean liner, the rest of the world isn't so fortunate; creaky wooden rafts and pontoon boats are the norm.

✦ Along with bandwidth concerns, you must consider the variety of systems your applets will run on once they become available to a global population. Just as most webbers lack ultrafast connections to the Web, they're often surfing with systems that are remarkably less powerful than those we use to develop applets. As a result, you must develop applets to run on a wide variety of systems, from entry-level boxes to silicon-heavy hot rods.

✦ The majority of applets you create will require external data stored in a file (such as images, audio clips, and so on), which must be located on the Web. Because of the security restrictions imposed by current browser implementations, applets fetched from the Net can't access local files, so any files an applet accesses must be stored on the *same* Web server that the applet itself resides on.

✦ When designing your Java applications you should have only one class to a source file; add as much documentation as possible; use understandable variable names; provide methods to manipulate object variables; and avoid using any native code.

✦   ✦   ✦

Installing and Configuring the Java Development Kit

To develop applets and applications in Java, you must first install Sun's *Java Development Kit* (JDK) on your computer. The JDK contains everything you need to begin creating Java programs. This chapter explains how to get, install, and configure the most recent release of the JDK for Solaris, Windows 95, Windows NT, and Macintosh computer systems. In addition, this chapter briefly looks at each of the tools in the JDK.

Getting the JDK

JDK 1.2 was unavailable as this book went to press, but can be downloaded directly from Sun's JavaSoft Web site—the official Java support site—at `http://java.sun.com`. In both cases, you'll find JDK 1.2 for the Solaris and Windows 95/NT development machines, as well as older versions of the JDK for these systems and Apple Macintosh computers (at the time this book was written, only JDK 1.02 was available for the Mac!). Sun's JavaSoft division (a Sun-owned company focused entirely on Java development) regularly releases new versions of Java and Java development tools at this site. Other third-party ports are also available through Sun's JavaSoft support site.

On the CD-ROM

JDK release 1.1.5 is included on the CD-ROM that comes with this book. Unless a more current version is now available, you can save the time and effort of downloading JDK by installing it directly from the CD-ROM (see Appendix B).

Dodson Green

The Java Developer Connection (JDC)

One of the most important Web sites Java developers should get into the habit of visiting is the Java Developer Connection (JDC), located at `http://java.sun.com/nav/developer/index.html`.

According to Sun, the company ultimately responsible for Java, the JDC is for individual developers. Sun states, "JDC is a free service offering online training, a searchable bug database, product discounts, feature articles, and more. JDC also features online discussion forums with industry luminaries like James Gosling, among others."

Personally, I try to spend as much time as I can at the JDC. At the time this book was being written, the JDC was just getting started, but already offered tons of useful information and source code. One of my favorite JDC areas to visit is the "DukeDollars" page, which allows members to post Java-related technical questions and answer those already posted.

To ask a question in this area, you must decide how many "DukeDollars" it's worth to you (every member gets 10 free DukeDollars to start), and then be willing to give away that amount when someone supplies a satisfying answer. Conversely, you can make off like a bandit by answering questions posted to this forum, which has allowed some developers to amass a staggering number of DukeDollars over time. The online trading of DukeDollars here is fast and furious, and you'll walk away a winner by simply drinking in the technical questions and answers that fuel this mini economy on the JDC.

Of course, you have to register to become a member of the JDC site, but once you do, you'll find links to early releases of Java software, online training courses, source code, and technology briefings. If you're serious about programming in Java, this is one site you should immediately visit and then bookmark in your browser.

Once you've located the JDK for your platform, download it to your local computer (or copy it from the enclosed CD-ROM if you don't want to waste time and money online). This may take some time, depending on the speed of your Internet connection, so you might seriously consider using the JDK provided on the CD-ROM instead. In fact, the only reason you should bother downloading the JDK from the Web is if the version online is significantly more current than the one provided on disc.

Note   Chances are pretty high that you've already got your hands on the most current JDK. The CD-ROM contains JDK version 1.1.5. To find out more about the versions of JDK, version 1.1.5, go to the JavaSoft Website at either `http://java.sun.com` or `http://www.javasoft.com` (either URL gets you there).

Regardless of whether you download the JDK from the Web, you can always download the full-blown JDK documentation supplied online, since that's not part of the JDK. JDK documentation is provided in several popular formats, including Adobe's Portable Document Format (PDF), Adobe Postscript (PS), plain old-fashioned HTML (my personal favorite), and even WinHelp format (for Windows users), all of which you can find at http://java.sun.com/products/jdk/1.1/, or at the Documentation Web site, http://java.sun.com/products/jdk/1.1/docs/index.html.

Expanding the JDK Archive

Whether you download the JDK from the Web or simply copy it to your computer from the enclosed CD-ROM, you'll first have to decompress the archive it comes in before you can actually use it. Both the Solaris and Windows 95/NT versions of the JDK are self-extracting archives, making them relatively easy to decompress and install.

Subsequent discussions assume you're working with JDK 1.2; if you've got 1.1.5, simply adjust for the differences in file and directory names.

You expand the Windows 95/NT self-extracting archive with a double-click:

1. Ensure that the JDK archive file is at the root level of your primary drive (usually C:\).

2. Double-click the JDK archive file to start the extraction process.

You expand the Solaris self-extracting archive from the command line. This is also a straightforward process, and one you're likely familiar with if you've dealt with self-extracting archives before:

1. First this command to change the JDK archive file into an executable file:

```
chmod a+x jdk1.2-solaris2-sparc.bin
```

2. Then type this command to extract the JDK files:

```
./jdk1.2-solaris2-sparc.bin
```

You can expand the Solaris JDK archive anywhere on your Solaris machine.

Once the JDK archive has been expanded, a Java directory similar to the one shown in Figure 4-1 is created. This directory contains a number of subdirectories, tools, and files, which together make up the Java Development Kit. Each of the Java tools (see Table 4-1) are actually executable programs. (To learn more about the tools supplied with the JDK, see "Using Java Tools" later in this chapter).

Figure 4-1: Upon installing the JDK, a java directory is created on your computer containing the various tools and files necessary to develop Java programs.

Table 4-1 Java Tools	
Tool	**Description**
appletviewer	The standalone *Applet Viewer*, which allows applets to execute without the use of a Java-savvy browser.
jar	The *Java archive tool*, which combines multiple files into a single, Java Archive format (JAR) file.
Java	The *interpreter*, which executes Java bytecode.
Javac	The *compiler*, which converts Java source code into bytecode.
Javadoc	The *documentation generator*, which can create files from source code.
Javah	The *native method C file generator*, which creates C-header and source files for native methods.
Javakey	The *Java digital key tool*, which generates a digital signature for JAR files.
Javap	The *disassembler*, which disassembles Java bytecode and outputs the result in a human-readable form.
Jdb	The *debugger*, a text-based tool for debugging Java programs on the command line.
Jre	The *runtime interpreter*, which you can use to run Java applications. This tool is similar to the java tool, but it is intended primarily for end users who do not require all the development-related options available with the java tool.
Native2ascii	The *native code page tool*, which converts nonUnicode Latin-1 (source code or property) files to Unicode Latin-1.

Tool	Description
Rmic	The *remote method invocation compiler*, which generates stub and skeleton class files for Java objects implementing the java.rmi.Remote interface.
Rmiregistry	The *remote object registry tool*, which starts a remote object registry on a specified port. The remote object registry is a bootstrap naming service used by RMI servers.
Serialver	The *serial version tool*, which returns the serialVersionUID for one or more classes.

Warning

Once you've installed the JDK, all of Java's own class libraries are placed inside the JDK lib directory (a subdirectory of the main directory into which the JDK is extracted), and are compressed into an archive named classes.zip. Whatever you do, *never* decompress the classes.zip archive! This archive is used to keep the suite of Java class files well organized and easily accessible, meaning you should leave the archive intact; if you decompress it, the Java tools won't have a clue where to find the class files, and so will give you serious grief in return.

While the classes.zip archive is strictly hands-off, the class *source code* archive, src.zip, is another matter altogether. You can unzip (decompress) these Java source code files to take a look at how their corresponding class files in classes.zip were created, and then place them wherever you like. While the source code files aren't necessary since the classes.zip archive has everything you'll need, they're nice to keep around if only to take an occasional peek at how Sun's own engineers created the library of classes you'll use regularly from within your own Java programs.

On the CD-ROM

A Windows ZIP utility, WinZip 6.3, is provided on the enclosed CD-ROM. You can use this wonderfully powerful piece of shareware to create your own ZIP archives, or to decompress those you come across in your travels (such as the scr.zip archive described here). See Appendix B, "What's on the CD-ROM," to find out more about WinZip 6.3 and the other useful utilities provided on disc.

Setting Up Your Java Environment

After you've installed the JDK, you must ensure that two environment variables, PATH and CLASSPATH, are set properly. The correct settings for both variables hinge on *where* you install the JDK onto your computer.

The PATH environment variable specifies where the operating system looks for executable files when you don't supply the full directory path leading to the file you'd like to execute. To use the JDK, you must either change an existing PATH environment variable or specify a brand new PATH environment variable, both of which you do differently under Solaris, Windows 95, and Windows NT.

The CLASSPATH environment variable specifies where the Java tools look for class files when you don't supply a full directory path manually. (The class files could be the suite of class files contained in the classes.zip archive discussed earlier, or even your own library of class files if you happen to create enough classes to merit placing them in a library package of your own making.) Since the process of setting the CLASSPATH environment variable varies from platform to platform, I'll explain how to go about setting CLASSPATH for Solaris, Windows 95, and Windows NT at the same time that you set the PATH environment variable.

Solaris

Solaris users typically set environment variables in the startup file for the shell you use. Since most Solaris users do this through either a variation of the sh shell or the csh shell, I'll include a brief description of each here. In both cases, assume that the JDK has been installed into a directory called jdk1.2. If this isn't the case, you'll have to substitute the actual directory name you placed the JDK into anytime a directory named jdk1.2 appears below.

Note

If you install the JDK in the default location the installer provides, /usr/local/ jdk1.2/bin, you don't need to set the CLASSPATH environment variable at all! The JDK tools automatically append .:/usr/local/jdk1.2/classes:/usr/local/ jdk1.2/lib/classes.zip to the CLASSPATH setting each time a tool is run. If you create your own library of class files, however, you should create an appropriate CLASSPATH setting to allow the JDK tools to find them.

To modify the setting of your PATH environment variable and to set the CLASSPATH environment variable in your .cshrc file (for csh shell variants), insert these lines:

```
set path=(/usr/local/jdk.1.2/bin $path)
set CLASSPATH=(/usr/local/jdk1.2/classes:
/usr/local/jdk1.2/lib/classes.zip)
```

Once you've made these changes, you should force the operating system to reread your .cshrc file by entering this command:

```
source ~/.cshrc
```

To modify the setting of your PATH environment variable and to set the CLASSPATH environment variable in your .profile file (for sh shell variants), insert these lines:

```
PATH=($path:/usr/local/jdk1.2/bin) export PATH
CLASSPATH=(/usr/local/jdk1.2/classes:
/usr/local/jdk1.2/lib/classes.zip) export CLASSPATH
```

Once you've made these changes, you should force the operating system to reread your .profile file by entering this command:

```
. ~/.profile
```

Windows 95

Windows 95 users set environment variables in the `autoexec.bat` file, which is typically found on the root level of the primary hard drive (such as `C:\`). Since many Windows 95 users don't have an `autoexec.bat` file, you might have to create one manually using a text editor (`autoexec.bat` is simply a text file with the `.bat` extension). If this is the case, be sure that you name the file exactly, and be certain to place it on the root level of your hard drive. If you don't, Windows won't bother loading this file at startup, and the environment variables you specify here won't have a chance to become "active."

To modify the setting of your `PATH` environment variable and to set the `CLASSPATH` environment variable in your `autoexec.bat` file, append these lines:

```
set PATH=%PATH%;C:\jdk1.2\bin
set CLASSPATH=C:\jdk1.2\classes;C:\jdk1.2\lib\classes.zip
```

As with the Solaris instructions above, I'm assuming that the JDK has been installed into a directory called `jdk1.2`. If this isn't the case, you'll have to substitute the actual directory name you placed the JDK into where the directory name `jdk1.2` appears above.

Once you've made these changes, you must either restart your computer or manually force the operating system to reread your `autoexec.bat` file by entering this command:

```
\autoexec
```

Windows NT

Unlike Windows 95 users, who access environment variables by way of editing the `autoexec.bat` file, Windows NT users have the luxury of using the System program in the Control Panel. Simply open the Control Panel, double-click the System program, and then enter the following lines:

```
set path=%path%;C:\jdk1.2\bin
set CLASSPATH=C:\jdk1.2\classes;C:\jdk1.2\lib\classes.zip
```

You might notice that these two lines of text are exactly the same as those used for Windows 95, and for good reason: Windows NT and Windows 95 are similar in how they deal with environment variables. Perhaps the most significant difference lies in how you enter them. While Windows NT uses the System program, Windows 95 users have to edit an `autoexec.bat` file. Either way, the environment variables are loaded at startup time.

Once you've made these changes in the System program, you can either click the Done button, at which point you must restart you computer for the changes to take effect, or you can force Windows NT to reload your environment variables on the spot by clicking the Apply button. (If you click Done, you must reboot before Windows NT will recognize your changes—clicking Apply is a faster, more convenient way to accomplish the same thing.)

Testing the JDK Installation

After you've installed the JDK, you should test the installation. To do this, simply change to one of the demo subdirectories in your new java directory (which is named `jdk1.2` by default, although you may have specified a different name at installation) and run the Applet Viewer program on an associated HTML file.

For instance, to run the Tic-Tac-Toe demonstration applet from a Windows installation, start by changing to that directory:

```
cd C:\jdk1.2\demo\TicTacToe
```

Note that JDK files on Sun installations have the same path as on Windows installations, although Windows uses backslashes (\) to separate directories, whereas Sun systems use slashes (/). To move to the same directory on a Sun system, type this line:

```
cd jdk1.2/demo/TicTacToe
```

Inside each demo directory, such as `TicTacToe`, there is an HTML file that contains the `<APPLET>` tag to execute that demonstration applet. In this case, as with most of the demos included with the JDK, the HTML file is named `example1.html`. Once you're in the `TicTacToe` directory, run the Applet Viewer program (`appletviewer`) with that HTML file:

```
appletviewer example1.html
```

If everything was installed properly, you should now be playing a game of tic-tac-toe, as illustrated in Figure 4-2. If not, see the "Installation Troubleshooting for Solaris" or "Installation Troubleshooting for Windows 95 and Windows NT" sidebar for help.

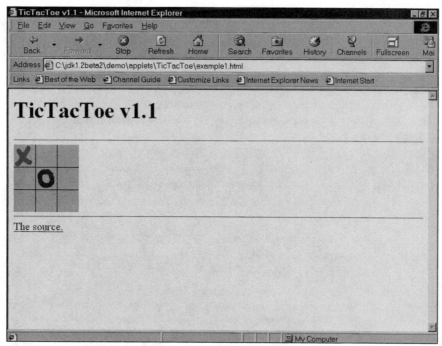

Figure 4-2: Java Tic-Tac-Toe, one of the many demo applets supplied with the JDK.

Note

If you've installed the most current version of the JDK (version 1.2.*x* at the time of this writing), you will likely notice that many of the demo directories provided with the toolkit contain additional directories named 1.0.2 and 1.1.5. This allows us to see how the same applet is written using different versions of the JDK. Remember, JDK 1.0 was first out of the gate, and eventually matured to 1.0.2 before a new "major" version of the language arrived. That first major upgrade, version 1.1, itself matured to version 1.1.*x* before yet another "major" upgrade came along: 1.2. Today, JDK version 1.2 has matured to version 1.2.*x*, and will soon be outdated by an even newer version—JDK 2.0. Since each major version of the language brings with it major changes in how Java programs are written, the good folks at Sun decided to include all past versions of the demos they've written that are included with the JDK. As a result, you can execute each of the earlier "major" versions of these demos, and also take a look at the source code to see how that version of the language was used to create the program.

Installation Troubleshooting for Solaris

The following troubleshooting information is taken from Sun's most current JDK installation documentation.

✦ If you get the error message "The download file appears to be corrupted" when you attempt to extract the JDK, delete the file and download a new copy. The JDK installation script does a checksum to ensure that the archive was not corrupted during the download.

✦ If you get the fatal error message "Exception in thread NULL" when running `java`, `javac`, or `appletviewer`, check the `CLASSPATH` environment variable. It may list the classes directory from an older JDK release. You can either unset the `CLASSPATH` variable, or set it to include only the latest version of the JDK class library.

If this suggestion does not resolve the problem, consult the installation documentation that came with the JDK release. You can also refer to the Java "Frequently Asked Questions" documentation available at the JDC.

✦ If you get the error message "Could not read properties file" or "Invalid JAVA_HOME" when running one of the JDK tools, such as `appletviewer`, it may mean that your `JAVA_HOME` environment variable is not set properly. Normally, you need not worry about setting `JAVA_HOME`. However, some Java IDEs set the `JAVA_HOME` variable to a value that won't allow you to run the JDK tools. Use the `echo` command to see if your `JAVA_HOME` value has been set:

```
echo $JAVA_HOME
```

If the `echo` command returns a value for `JAVA_HOME`, make a note of the setting (in case you want to restore it later), and then try unsetting it and see if you can run the JDK tools. Use the `unsetenv` command to unset the `JAVA_HOME` environment variable:

```
unsetenv JAVA_HOME
```

If you still cannot run the JDK tools after unsetting `JAVA_HOME`, try setting `JAVA_HOME` to the absolute path of the `jdk1.2` directory that was created when you installed the JDK. For example, if you install JDK 1.2, and the directory `jdk1.2` has the path `/usr/local/jdk1.2`, try setting `JAVA_HOME` as follows:

```
setenv JAVA_HOME /usr/local/jdk1.2
```

As long as you have not disturbed the `bin` and `lib` directories that are immediately below the `jdk1.2` directory, you should be able to run the JDK tools.

Installation Troubleshooting for Windows 95 and Windows NT

The following troubleshooting information is taken from Sun's most current JDK installation documentation.

✦ If you see either the error message "net.socketException: errno = 10047" or "Unsupported version of Windows Socket API," check which TCP/IP drivers you have installed. The Applet Viewer tool supports only the Microsoft TCP/IP drivers included with Windows 95. If you are using third-party drivers, such as Trumpet Winsock, you'll need to change over to the native Microsoft TCP/IP drivers if you want to load applets over the network.

If the Applet Viewer tool does not load applets, dismiss it and enter the following set commands in the same DOS command window as you invoked Applet Viewer:

```
set HOMEDRIVE=c:
set HOMEPATH=\
```

Restart the Applet Viewer tool in the same DOS command window. If you still cannot load applets, enter the following set command in the DOS command window:

```
set HOME=c:\
```

Again, restart the Applet Viewer tool in the same DOS command window. If you still cannot load applets, enter the following java tool command line in the DOS command window:

```
java -verbose sun.applet.AppletViewer
```

The java tool lists the classes that are being loaded. From this output, you can determine which class the Applet Viewer is trying to load and where it's trying to load it from. Check to make sure that the class exists and is not corrupted.

✦ If you get the fatal error message "Exception in thread NULL" when running `java`, `javac`, or `appetviewer`, check the `CLASSPATH` environment variable. It may list the classes directory from an older JDK release. You can either unset the `CLASSPATH` variable, or set it to include only the latest version of the JDK class library.

If this suggestion does not resolve the problem, consult the installation documentation that came with the JDK release. You can also refer to the Java "Frequently Asked Questions" documentation available at the JDC.

✦ If you cannot close the Applet Viewer tool's copyright window, move the launch bar to the side of the desktop to allow access to the copyright window's Accept and Reject buttons.

(continued)

(continued)

✦ If you get the error message "Could not read properties file" when running one of the JDK tools, such as appletviewer, or "Invalid JAVA_HOME", it may mean that your JAVA_HOME environment variable is not set properly. Normally, you need not worry about setting JAVA_HOME. However, some Java IDEs set the JAVA_HOME variable to a value that won't allow you to run the JDK tools. Use the echo command to see if your JAVA_HOME value has been set:

```
% echo %JAVA_HOME%
```

If the echo command returns "ECHO is on" or "ECHO is off", the JAVA_HOME environment variable has not been set. If the echo command returns a value for JAVA_HOME, make a note of the setting (in case you want to restore it later), then try unsetting it and see if you can run the JDK tools. Use the following set command to unset the JAVA_HOME environment variable:

```
set JAVA_HOME=
```

If you still cannot run the JDK tools after unsetting JAVA_HOME, try setting JAVA_HOME to the absolute path of the jdk1.2 directory that was created when you installed the JDK. For example, if you install JDK 1.2, and the directory jdk1.2 has the path /usr/local/jdk1.2, try setting JAVA_HOME as follows:

```
set JAVA_HOME=C:\jdk1.2
```

As long as you have not disturbed the bin and lib directories that are immediately below the jdk1.2 directory, you should be able to run the JDK tools.

Using Java Tools

Using the Java environment means you'll have to learn each of the tools outlined in Table 4-1 earlier in this chapter. Perhaps the three most common tools are the compiler (javac), the interpreter (java), and the Applet Viewer (appletviewer). With these three tools and a source code editor, you'll be able to write, test, and debug Java applications and applets.

Java source-code files contain, not surprisingly, the actual Java code you write. These are text files, and you can create them with any text editor or word processor capable of saving files in ASCII text format. As long as you save your source files in ASCII text format with a .java extension, you'll be fine. The following are examples of valid Java source filenames: HelloWorld.java; MyProgram.java; CoolGame.java.

If you omit the .java extension, or if the file is in any format other than ASCII text, the compiler will generate an error message.

Table 4-2 lists the tools with their proper usage syntax. To help make sense of these, we'll step through the process of writing a small application called *HelloWorld*. Although the details of *HelloWorld* (both application and applet versions of the program) are covered in Chapter 7, we'll use it here to illustrate the use of the Java tools.

Table 4-2 Using Java Tools	
Tool	**Syntax[1]**
`appletviewer`	`appletviewer [-debug]` *html_file*[2]
`java`	`java [-options]` *class* (see Table 4-4 for options)
`javac`	`javac [-option]` *file.java* (see Table 4-3 for options)
`javadoc`	`javadoc [-classpath` *path*`][-d` *directory*`][-verbose]` *file.java* | *packagename*
`javah`	`javah [-classpath` *path*`][-verbose][-stubs][-o` *outputfilename*`] [-d directory] classes`
`javap`	`javap [-v][-c][-p][-h][-verify][-classpath` *path*`][-l] class`
`jdb`	`jdb [java` *options*`] [ host` *hostname*`] [-password` *password*`]` *classname*

[1] Bracketed [] items are optional.

[2] Italicized items are used as parameter placeholders.

Since the actual source code isn't important for the following examples, assume that you have already entered the entire program in a text editor. You would save what you've written in ASCII text format (just plain text) in a file with the `.java` extension:

```
HelloWorldTest.java
```

Ignoring the issue of how your development environment directories should be structured (more on that later), assume that you have saved your `HelloWorldTest.java` program in an appropriate directory on your hard drive. Because the source code needs to be compiled before it can be executed, the next step is to do just that.

Compiling

You can run the Java compiler, `javac`, with a wide array of options (see Table 4-3). This is the basic syntax of `javac`:

```
javac [options] file.java
```

<table>
<tr><td colspan="2" align="center">Table 4-3
***javac* Compiler Options**</td></tr>
<tr><td>*Option*</td><td>*Description*</td></tr>
<tr>
<td>`-classpath` *path*</td>
<td>Specifies where `javac` looks for classes that are referenced in the source code being compiled. Classes can be located in directories in the path, or inside `ZIP` archives in the path.

This option overrides the path specified in the `CLASSPATH` environment variable. You can specify more than one directory in the path. (On UNIX systems, use a colon to separate the lists of directories; on Windows systems, use a semicolon.)

The basic form for *path*, in UNIX format, is:

`.:path1:path2:path3`

You should always include the default class directory and ZIP file in your `classpath` option, as in the following Windows example:

`javac -classpath C:\myclasses;C:\jdk1.2\`
`classes;C:\jdk1.2\lib\class.zip HelloWorld.java`

A period in the path specifies the current working directory, as in the following Solaris example, which searches the current directory for a class before any other directory:

`javac -classpath .:/home/classes:/export/`
`classes HelloWorld.java`</td>
</tr>
<tr>
<td>`-d` *directory*</td>
<td>Specifies the root directory where `javac` places the compiled class files. By default, `javac` places compiled class files in the same directory as the source files.

Use this option when you want a class file to be saved into a directory other than the one containing the source code file. For example:

`javac -d /home/javaapps/stuff HelloWorld.java`

Here, the resulting `HelloWorld.class` is not saved in the same directory as the source code file `HelloWorld.java`. Instead, `javac` saves `HelloWorld.class` in the `/home/javaapps/stuff` directory.</td>
</tr>
</table>

Option	Description
-depend	Recursively compiles any class files on which the currently compiling file depends. The compiler does not recursively descend to every leaf. Once it encounters an up-to-date file on a branch, it ceases descending that branch. For example: `javac -depend HelloWorld.java`
-encoding *name*	Specifies the source file encoding name. If this option is not specified, then the platform default converter is used. The encodings are used by the `native2ascii` native code page tool. Java can support multiple character sets, making internationalization of your Java applications complete. Using the encoding flag, you can specify the native character encoding used in your application.
-g	Adds debugging information to the class files that `javac` generates. Debugging tables contain information about variables, methods, and line numbers. By default, only line numbers are generated, unless you specify the `-O` (optimize) option. For example: `Javac -g HelloWorld.java`
-J*java_option*	Passes the string `java_option` to `java`, the Java interpreter. The string cannot contain any spaces. If you want to send multiple strings, use multiple `-J` options. This option is particularly useful for adjusting the compiler's execution environment or memory usage. For example, the following `javac` command has `java` fire up `jdb` to initiate a debugging session: `Javac -Jdebug HelloWorld.java`
-nowarn	Suppresses the generation and display of warnings errors. For example: `Javac -nowarn HelloWorld.java`
-O	Optimizes the code by inlining static, final, and private methods when possible. As a result, code often executes faster. The resulting class files, however, are often larger. If you use this option and the `-g` (debug) option at the same time, `javac` does not add line numbers to the resulting class files. For example: `Javac -O HelloWorld.java`
-verbose	Displays additional information about the source files being complied and about any classes being loaded. For example: `Javac -verbose HelloWorld.java`

We just want to compile the source file without any options, so you could simply execute the compiler with the name of our source code file. The following example shows how to compile your program without any options (the > indicates a command line prompt):

```
> javac HelloWorldTest.java
```

Any syntax errors or bugs caught by the compiler would immediately follow, although you can assume there are none in this example. If all goes well, the compiler will convert the human-readable source code into machine-readable bytecode. The compiler creates a bytecode file for each class declared in our program. This is in the same directory as our source file, since you didn't specify a different one using the -d option. Since your HelloWorld.java source file declares only one class, HelloWorld, the compiler creates the following file:

```
HelloWorld.class
```

In this binary file is the bytecode generated by the compiler for the class HelloWorld declared in your program. If there were other classes declared in your program, the compiler would create a new file to contain the bytecode of each. For instance, supposing your program declared three classes (HelloWorld, GoodbyeWorld, and SpinWorld), a bytecode file for each would have been created by the compiler (HelloWorld.class, GoodbyeWorld.class, and SpinWorld.class).

At this point, the source code has been converted to bytecode and can be executed by the interpreter (java, see the next section). You've simply used the compiler "as is," without specifying any of the options it understands. For a description of each option, see Table 4-3.

Executing applications with the interpreter

Once the bytecode for your application has been generated by the compiler, it can be executed. This is simple enough in the case of actual applications, since all you have to do is run the java interpreter and provide it with the bytecode file:

```
> java HelloWorld
```

Notice that you didn't supply the .class extension for the HelloWorld bytecode file. Although the interpreter requires the file to have such an extension, you don't need to provide it. In fact, an error would be reported if you did. For instance, suppose you did this:

```
> java HelloWorld.class
```

Since each bytecode file contains one class having the same name as the file itself (the only difference being the .class extension of the bytecode file), the interpreter would attempt to locate and execute a class named HelloWorld.class instead of HelloWorld. In this case, the interpreter would report the following error:

```
> Can't find class HelloWorld/class
```

Note that there are actually four ways to run your Java programs:

✦ The java command invokes the interpreter with a console window.

✦ The java_g command is the same as java but includes extra debugging information.

✦ The javaw command invokes the interpreter without a console window.

✦ The javaw_g command is the same as javaw but includes extra debugging information.

Don't forget that the compiler, javac, requires you to include the filename with its .java extension, while the interpreter, java, wants only the base name of the bytecode file, without the .class extension.

You can use the interpreter with a number of options, many the same as those the compiler supports. These options are listed in Table 4-4.

Table 4-4 *java* Interpreter Options	
Options	**Description**
CLASSPATH	This is not a command-line option; it is an environment variable that you can set to tell Java where to find classes (or classes in ZIP archives). Having the same parameters as the -classpath option, you only have to set this environment variable once.
	The following is the basic form, in UNIX format:
	.:path[:optional paths]
	Windows users should use semicolons to separate path listings. Once set, the CLASSPATH environment variable can be overridden with the -classpath option (see -classpath).

(continued)

Table 4-4 *(continued)*	
Options	**Description**
-classpath *path*	Specifies where java looks for class files to execute. Classes can be located in directories in the path, or inside ZIP archives in the path.
	This option overrides the path specified in the CLASSPATH environment variable. You can specify more than one directory in the path. (On UNIX systems, use a colon to separate the lists of directories; on Windows systems, use a semicolon.)
	The basic form for *path*, in UNIX format, is:
	`.:path1:path2:path3`
	You should always include the default class directory and ZIP file in your classpath option, as in the following Windows example:
	`Java -classpath C:\myclasses;C:\jdk1.2\` `classes;C:\jdk1.2\lib\class.zip HelloWorld`
	A period in the path specifies the current working directory, as in the following Solaris example, which searches the current directory for a class before any other directory:
	`Java -classpath .:/home/classes:/export/` `classes HelloWorld`
-cs, -checksource	Compares the modification time of the class bytecode files to their corresponding source code files. When a source code file has been modified more recently than its bytecode file, the source is recompiled and the new bytecode file is used.
-debug	Attaches jdb, the Java debugger, to the java session. When this option is used, java displays a password on the command line that you must use when the debugging session starts.
-D*propertyname* =*newValue*	Defines a property value, where *propertyName* is the name of the property to change and *newValue* is the new value for that property. You can specify any number of -D options on the command line.
-help	Displays information on how to use java.

Options	Description
-ms *size*[k | m]	Specifies the initial size, in bytes, of the memory allocation pool (the garbage collection heap). The minimum value for *size* is 1000, which is the default size.
	You can specify a value in kilobytes (K) or megabytes (MB) rather than bytes by appending a *k* or *m* character, respectively.
-mx *size*[k | m]	The maximum size, in bytes, of the memory allocation pool (the garbage collection heap). The minimum value for *size* is 1000. The default value is 16MB.
	You can specify a value in kilobytes or megabytes rather than bytes by appending a *k* or *m* character, respectively.
-noasyncgc	Turns off the asynchronous garbage collector, prohibiting garbage collection unless it is explicitly invoked or the program runs out of memory. By default, the garbage collector runs as an asynchronous thread, in parallel with other threads in your program.
-noclassgc	Turns off garbage collection of classes. By default, java reclaims the space of unused classes.
-noverify	Bypasses the bytecode-verification phase of the classes it loads. Use this option only when running code you know is safe (in other words, virus-free and having no malicious behavior).
-oss *size*	The maximum size, in bytes, of the stack for Java code in threads. (Java threads maintain two stacks, one for Java code and the other for C code.) The minimum value for *size* is 1000. The default value is 400K.
	Threads that are spawned during the execution of the program have the same stack size for Java code.
	You can specify a value in kilobytes or megabytes rather than bytes by appending a *k* or *m* character, respectively.
-prof [*file*]	Starts with profiling turned on and saves the profiling information in *file*. By default, the information is stored in java.prof in the current directory.

(continued)

Options	Description
-ss *size*	The maximum size, in bytes, of the stack for C code in threads. (Java threads maintain two stacks, one for Java code and the other for C code.) The minimum value for *size* is 1000. The default value is 128K.
	Threads that are spawned during the execution of the program have the same stack size for C code.
	You can specify a value in kilobytes or megabytes rather than bytes by appending a *k* or *m* character, respectively.
-t	Turns on tracing of instructions. This option is valid only with `java_g`.
-v, -verbose	Displays a message every time a class is loaded.
-verbosegc	Displays a message anytime the automatic garbage collector frees memory.
-verify	Runs the bytecode verifier on all classes that are loaded into the interpreter.
-verifyremote	Runs the bytecode verifier on all classes that are loaded by a class loader. This is the default, so you don't have to explicitly turn this option on.

Table 4-4 (continued) — header row

Executing applets with the Applet Viewer

Java applications are full-blown applications that are executed outside a Java-savvy browser. Unlike applets, which run inside a browser environment, applications need only the runtime environment to execute. Applets, on the other hand, require the help of a browser.

Since firing up a browser each time you want to test an applet can be time-consuming—and even impossible on some systems, because of memory constraints—you may prefer to use the Applet Viewer tool included with the JDK. This tool, shown running a demo applet in Figure 4-3, executes your applets without the aid of a browser, ameliorating the time and memory issues that come with launching a browser or keeping one running while developing your programs.

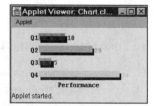

Figure 4-3: Applet Viewer, one of the many JDK tools, provides a fast, effective way to test your Java applets.

Keep in mind that applets are called into action through the ⟨APPLET⟩ tag in an HTML file, regardless of whether you use the Applet Viewer or a browser to execute them. This means you'll need to write a small HTML file for each applet in order to run them.

While not difficult, the details of doing this are covered in Chapter 7, so I won't bother going through the steps here. Assume you've written an HTML file for your HelloWorld program. Furthermore, assume you've rewritten the application in the form of an applet (also detailed in the Chapter 7) and have already compiled it.

Assuming you have your applet bytecode file and HTML file already prepared, you can test it with the Applet Viewer:

```
> appletviewer HelloWorldTest.html
```

The Applet Viewer opens the supplied HTML file, which can be named anything you wish; it looks for the ⟨APPLET⟩ tag specifying your program and executes it. This process is quite speedy when compared with launching a Java-savvy browser, so I'd recommend using the Applet Viewer during development instead of a browser.

If you followed the instructions in "Testing the JDK Installation" earlier in this chapter, you've actually used the Applet Viewer program already to execute the Tic-Tac-Toe applet. The syntax is about as simple as you can get, although you may wish to use the debug option:

```
> appletviewer -debug HelloWorldTest.html
```

Summary

In order to develop applets and applications in Java, you must first install the Java Development Kit on your computer.

✦ If you don't use the JDK provided on the CD-ROM, you must get the most recent release of Sun's JDK from its Web site (`http://java.sun.com`). You can also download the documentation and complete source code of the JDK libraries from this site.

✦ You will find that the JDK includes a number of Java tools, including an Applet Viewer (`appletviewer`), an interpreter (`java`), a compiler (`javac`), and a debugger (`jdb`). There are also a number of Java environment variables that need to be set before you can properly run your Java applications.

✦ Once installed, you'll need to set your path environment variable to include the JDK tools directory and the `CLASSPATH` environment variable to include the default class directory and `classes.zip` file.

✦ You can then test the JDK by running various demo applets, with the help of several troubleshooting hints.

✦   ✦   ✦

Getting Up to Speed

Now that you have an understanding of Java and its place in application development, you're ready to start developing your own applications. In this part, you walk through the process of designing, developing, testing, and debugging your first Java application. You learn how to design your applications to function as both standalone applications and Web-based applets.

It's almost impossible to develop a bug-free application from scratch — so to help with the development of your application, these chapters show you how to use the debugging tools provided with the Java Development Toolkit. You learn how to use the Java debugger to stomp out those annoying bugs.

Adding flexibility to your Java applications can really enhance their use. This part will show you how to modify your Java applications and applets to accept and use the parameters specified by command-line arguments. Command-line arguments can supply dynamic information that can change each time your application is run.

Finally, you'll learn how to use the Web as your greatest application-development tool. You've undoubtedly heard others ask *Why reinvent the wheel?* and you need not reinvent the Web, either. By the time you finish this part, you'll know how to use the Web to find and borrow Java applications and objects that can get your applications up and running even faster!

Getting Started: HelloWorld Application and HelloWorld Applet

In this chapter, we take a closer look at the difference between Java applications and Java applets by writing the infamous HelloWorld program. Here, you examine the source code for both the application and applet version of HelloWorld as you get to know the structure and purpose of both types of Java programs. You also execute each to better understand how they differ from a runtime standpoint.

Application Versus Applet

The two fundamental forms of Java programs are the application and the applet. We refer to Java programs that are capable of being executed outside the context of a browser as *applications*. The primary difference between applications and applets is their purpose. Java applications are just like others we're familiar with, although they require the presence of the Java runtime environment to be executed, as do applets. Unlike applets, however, Java applications aren't meant to exist on the Internet and be executed as World Wide Web content. They are, instead, full-blown applications that exist and are executed on users' local computer systems, as would a spreadsheet or word processor.

Applets, on the other hand, are designed to live on the network and be executed as part of a Web page. That's why they're referred to as *executable content*; although they are imbedded in Web pages, just as standard content is, they are really software programs and can be executed as such.

Applets require a Java-savvy browser such as Netscape Navigator (version 2.0 or later) or Microsoft's Internet Explorer (version 3.0 or later) because they must be downloaded from the network and, in essence, be given to the Java runtime environment to be executed.

Because of their different purposes, applications and applets are structured differently, both in terms of their code and in how they are ultimately executed. To examine these differences, we'll walk step-by-step through the process of creating a HelloWorld application and applet.

HelloWorld is a simple program, with little practical purpose other than to illustrate the structure and syntax of real Java code and the process of compiling and executing such code. When executed, the program does nothing more than output `Hello World!` to the screen. Because the application version is a little less complex in terms of code and execution than the applet version, let's start with that.

HelloWorld Application

Before we get into the nitty-gritty, be aware that Java programs, both applications and applets, are executed by the interpreter. They are not standalone, because they require the presence of the Java runtime environment.

In setting up the HelloWorld application, we shall go through the following steps:

1. Set up a directory structure to store our code, including a master directory and subdirectories.
2. Enter and saving the source code.
3. Compile the source code.
4. Execute the application, passing the bytecode file created during the compilation process to the Java interpreter to output to our screen.

Application directory structure

Before you begin writing a Java program, it's a good idea to set up a directory structure to store your code. In most instances, you'll create a new directory for each program, so I recommend a master directory in which all these subdirectories will reside. The location and name you choose for your master directory is up to you. I chose to name my master directory `aewcode`, and created it inside the main `java` directory for the sake of convenience.

Inside my master `aewcode` directory, I created a subdirectory called `Hello`, in which the source code and compiled classes for my HelloWorld program are kept, as can be seen in Figure 5-1. For the following example, I assume you have also created a `Hello` directory inside your master directory.

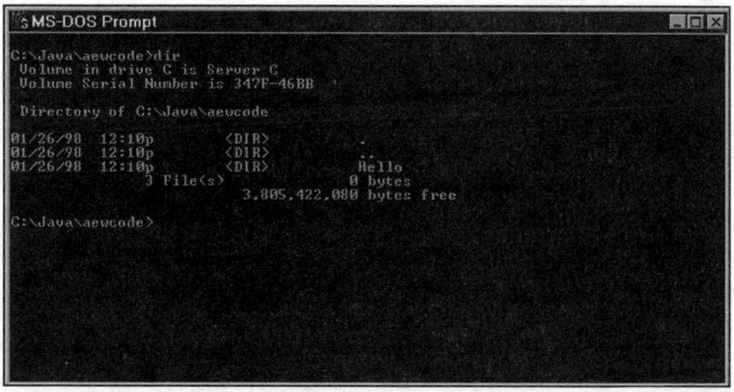

Figure 5-1: Creating a hierarchy of directories for your HelloWorld program

How you create a directory depends entirely on the platform you use. Windows users can create directories in the Windows environment using their mouse, or by issuing the `mkdir` command at the DOS prompt. Sun users can also use the `mkdir` command. Macintosh users, however, don't have a command line at which to enter such commands. They must select the New Folder item (using their mouse or the keyboard equivalent for this item) located under the File menu while inside the Finder.

Entering and saving the source

Using a text editor, enter the following source code and save it as a plain ASCII text file named `HelloWorldApp.java` inside your `Hello` directory. Don't forget to include the `.java` extension, or the compiler won't be able to see it!

```
class HelloWorld {
  public static void main (String args[]) {
    System.out.println("Hello World!");
  }
}
```

Did you notice that the name of the class, `HelloWorld`, isn't exactly the same as the name of the file in which it is saved? This is because we didn't specify the class as being a public class. If we had, the name of the source code file would have to be the same as the public class it contains. In this case, the source code file would be named `HelloWorld.java` to reflect the public `HelloWorld` class it defines. However, because our class isn't public, the filename can be anything we like. For details on public classes, see the section "Access modifiers" in this chapter or refer to Chapter 11.

Class declaration

Before actually compiling the program, we'll walk through each line of code to get a better feel for the Java language—beginning with the first line:

```
class HelloWorld {
```

This line declares a new class, `HelloWorld`, the body of which begins following the opening curly brace (`{`). The closing brace (`}`) on the last line of our source code signifies the end of the class, which is the blueprint from which `HelloWorld` objects will be instantiated.

Keep in mind that Java is an object-oriented language, where the fundamental building blocks are objects. In fact, everything in Java is an object; the language doesn't support global functions or global variables. This means that everything emanates from an object template, formally known as a class. What we are doing here is creating a class, the blueprint for an object. The class includes all the code for state (data) and behavior (methods), although in this example we only have methods and no explicitly declared data.

All classes are derived from, or are *subclassed*, from existing classes. In the case of our `HelloWorld` class, we do not explicitly state of which class it is a subclass. When no *superclass* (a class from which a class is derived) is specified, the default is assumed to be class `Object`. Although we could have explicitly specified that `HelloWorld` is a subclass of `Object`, as shown below, there's no need to do so.

```
class HelloWorld extends Object {
```

In the above example, we use the keyword `extends` to specify `HelloWorld` as a subclass of `Object`, although our original implementation does the same thing by default. When we rewrite `HelloWorld` as an applet, we'll actually subclass the `Applet` class. In this case, we must explicitly extend the `Applet` class, as you'll see later. Let's move on with our application for now.

Method declaration

The second line declares the `main()` method, and takes a string parameter, which will contain any command-line arguments provided when the application is executed. Let's take a look at the implementation of the first line of code, or *method signature*, for the `main()` method:

```
public static void main (String args[])
```

Just as with C and C++, a `main()` function must be included in a Java application; without it, the interpreter would have no idea where to begin executing. And just as with C/C++, Java applications can be executed with command-line arguments. The arguments for Java are passed to the program through the string parameter, `args[]`.

Although you must include the string `args[]` parameter in your `main()` method signature, you are under no obligation to use it. We ignore the `args[]` parameter in this example, because we have no need to use command-line arguments. While comman-line arguments are covered in more detail in Chapter 7, it's worth noting here that the `args[]` parameter is itself an object. It's an object of type `String`, a class defined to handle storage and manipulation of strings. However, we do nothing with the `args[]` object in `HelloWorld`, and so let's press on and take a closer look at the `main()` method itself.

Of most interest are the keywords preceding `main()`, specifically `public`, `static`, and `void`. As with C/C++, `void` simply means this method does not return any data. If it did, the data type it returned would be written in place of it. Straight-forward enough, but what about the keywords `public` and `static`?

Access modifiers

The keyword `public` is an access modifier. It specifies that the `main()` method can be called by any object. This means the `main()` method is openly available to other objects and is not in any way restricted.

Java supports four access modifiers (`public`, `private`, `protected`, and the implicit "friendly") that can be applied to both methods and variables, giving the programmer control over method and variable accessibility to other objects.

Access modifiers are used to control the visibility (accessibility) of variables and objects by other objects in a program. By applying one of the three access modifier keywords (`public`, `private`, or `protected`) to classes, variables, or methods, you can control the capability of other objects to use them. To apply an access modifier, include the appropriate keyword when declaring the variable, class, or method:

```
private int   miles;  // specifies a private variable
public void main (String args[]) { } // public main() method
protected class HelloWorld { } // protected HelloWorld class
```

Although access control is discussed in more detail in Chapters 9 and 11, you should always consider to what extent the variables, classes, and methods in your programs will be accessible to other parts of your program. With this in mind, consider the various level of controls provided through access specifiers.

public

Methods and variables specified as public are accessible from any method, regardless of the package to which the method's class belongs. Packages are used to organize Java classes, and are described in detail in Chapter 11. Classes can also be specified as public, making them available to other classes in other packages. In fact, Java requires that every applet source file (in other words, any class that extends the `Applet` class) contain a public class. However, only one public class is permitted in a source file.

private

Variables and methods specified as private are accessible only from inside their own class and aren't available to methods in any other class (including subclasses). Unlike the `public` specifier, `private` cannot be applied to classes.

Because early versions of Java supported private classes, some of the older source code you may encounter on the Web might actually specify classes as private. Attempting to compile such code using the current release of the Java compiler, however, will result in an error. To remedy the problem, simply remove the `private` keyword wherever it is applied to classes.

protected

Variables and methods specified as `protected` are accessible only from inside their class or subclasses of their class (subclasses can even override protected methods and variables). As such, the `protected` specifier is preferred to `private` in cases where you want subclasses to have access to variables and methods, but require tighter access restrictions than the `public` specifier provides. It can't, however, be applied to classes.

<blank>

If you don't specify an access modifier for methods and variables, Java treats them as "friendly" members, having limited public accessibility. Such methods and variables are accessible to other classes in the same package, but not classes in other packages. If you don't explicitly specify a class as being public, it will (by default) be available only within the package it is declared in (see Chapter 11).

static

The keyword `static` specifies the `main()` method as a static method (more commonly known as a class method). Just as with access modifiers, the `static` modifier can be applied to both variables and methods. When applied, `static` indicates that the method or variable can be accessed without first requiring that an object of the class they are part of be instantiated (see the sidebar "Class Versus Instance"). If the keyword `static` is not explicitly applied to a method or variable, it is automatically considered to be an instance method or variable.

Accessing an object's variables and methods

The final line in our HelloWorld program is the one that does all the work, at least as far as displaying the words "Hello World!" are concerned.

```
System.out.println("Hello World!");
```

What we've done is send the string "Hello World!" to the System class for output (in this case, standard output [STDOUT], typically the terminal or monitor). Because all variables and methods in the System class are static, there is no need for us to instantiate an object of this class prior to referencing variables and methods, as we have done (again, see the sidebar, "Class Versus Instance"). But what's going on with the two dots?

Periods, or dots, are used to access an object's variables and methods. The syntax is similar to how you'd access struct elements in C and C++. Suppose you wanted to directly access the horizontal variable of the Point class we talked about earlier in Chapter 2. Although, in this example, we declared both the horizontal and vertical variables as private, if they had been declared public the following would have done the trick:

```
int x = myPoint.h; /* access and assign myPoint's h variable
                      to x */
```

Class Versus Instance

In Java, class variables and methods can be either class or instance members of the class in which they are declared, as indicated by the presence or absence of the static modifier. For example, the main() method of HelloWorld is a static method. If the keyword static were not part of the method signature, such as in the following example, main() would instead be considered an instance method of the class HelloWorld:

```
public void main (String args [])
```

Static methods and variables are associated with the class rather than with an instance of the class and are also known as *class variables* or *class methods*. This is a fitting name, because each class variable and class method occurs once per class; instance methods and variables occur once per instance of a class. The difference between class and instance members is significant, especially when it comes to variables.

By occurring only once per instance of a class, class members are shared by all objects created from a class. That is, all objects created from a given class share the class variables and class methods defined in that class. Instance variables and instance methods, on the other hand, are created anew each time an object is created.

Class members can therefore be considered global to a class, even though true global variables aren't supported in Java. When an object changes the value of a class variable, all objects instantiated from that same class see the result. Because of this, class variables are often used to share data intended to be common to all objects created from a particular class.

To refer to instance methods and variables, an object must first be instantiated from that class, after which it can access the methods and variables from the instance. With static methods and variables, however, there is no need to instantiate an object before referring to these class members.

(continued)

(continued)

The use of a static method is seen in HelloWorld, as we call upon the `System` class to output a string of characters without first instantiating an object of that class.

```
System.out.println("Hello World!");
```

`System.out` refers to the `out` variable in the `System` class. We didn't instantiate the `System` class, yet we are able to directly refer to the `out` variable. Because the `System` class declares `out` as a static variable, we can access it directly without the need for instantiation. If `out` were not declared as a static variable, we would have to instantiate an object from the `System` class before accessing it.

When the `System` class is loaded into an application, the Java interpreter automatically creates `out` and all other static variables in that class. Because `out` has been created, the instance method `println()` can be sent to it, as we have done—`println()` is an instance method of `out`. Java enables the programmer to cascade together references to static and instance methods and variables, as we have done in HelloWorld.

In the `System` class, discussed in detail in Chapter 12, one of the variables is `out`. The `out` variable is itself an object, of which `println()` is a method. So, what we've done in the last line of HelloWorld code is access the `System` class's `out` variable, executing its `println()` method, passing our "Hello World!" string as a parameter.

Compiling the source code

You're now ready to compile the source code, assuming you have typed it in and saved it as an ASCII text file with the name `HelloWorldApp.java`. Going on that assumption, and also that the directory in which you've saved the source file is named `Hello`, you would now run the `javac` compiler:

```
Hello> javac HelloWorldApp.java
```

Assuming your file didn't contain typing errors, it should compile just fine. If not, the compiler will spit out a line or more showing you where the error was found (see Figure 5-2).

If this is the case, open your file and compare it carefully to the following source code:

```
class HelloWorld {
  public static void main (String args[]) {
    System.out.println("Hello World!");
  }
}
```

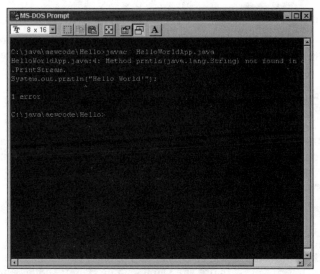

Figure 5-2: If your file contains errors, the compiler will spit out a line or more showing you where they were found.

Be sure all the curly brackets ({ }) are included and check your spelling. Fix any problems, save the file, and try again. When the contents of your text file exactly matches the HelloWorld source code shown here, you should have no problem compiling.

You'll know the compiler is successful when no error messages are reported. Assuming you're in the Hello directory, where your source file is also located, the following is typical of a successful compilation (where Hello> is the prompt):

```
Hello> javac HelloWorldApp.java
Hello>
```

Because no errors were reported here, the compiler was able to convert the source file into a binary bytecode file called HelloWorld.class. For every class the compiler comes across in a source file, it creates a bytecode file of the same name. Check the directory to see if a bytecode file was indeed created. Your Hello directory should now contain two files: HelloWorldApp.java and HelloWorld.class.

Once you have successfully compiled the source code, which results in a binary bytecode file being generated in the same directory, it's time to run the program.

Executing the application

When you execute a Java application, you're executing bytecode. Therefore, you must pass the bytecode file created during the compilation process to the Java interpreter:

```
Hello> java HelloWorld
```

Notice we do not include the .class extension. The interpreter assumes you passed it just the filename of the class. If you give it the .class extension as well, it thinks it's looking for a class named HelloWorld.class and comes up empty-handed. If you make this mistake, or do it intentionally just for kicks, an error message such as the following will be generated:

```
"Can't find class HelloWorld/class"
```

Also, notice that we have provided the interpreter with exactly the same upper- and lowercase formatting of the class name. This is no mistake, because Java is case-sensitive. The HelloWorld class is not the same as a helloworld class, nor as a helloWorld version. Sure, you and I might recognize them as the same, but Java sees each as different. Be sure to provide the interpreter with the precisely formatted name of the bytecode file, which should also be an exact replica of the compiled HelloWorld class.

Assuming you enter the class name exactly, the bytecode file will be loaded by the interpreter and the main() method will be executed. When the line of code containing System.out.println() is reached, "Hello World!" is sent to STDOUT, which is the computer screen by default, as shown in Figure 5-3.

Figure 5-3: If you have successfully executed the bytecode, "Hello World!" is output.

Congratulations! You've just written, compiled, and executed your first Java application. Sure, it's no Microsoft killer, but that'll come in time. In the meantime, let's take a look at our HelloWorld program written and executed as an applet.

HelloWorld Applet

Remember: while an application is executed using the Java interpreter and without any need whatsoever for a Java-savvy browser, applets are executed from within a Java-savvy browser.

Because of this, applets are a little more complicated to get up and running than applications. Not much, mind you, but a little. For starters, you have to create an HTML file (a Web page) that references the applet. And you also have to add a few more lines of code to let the Java compiler and runtime system know these programs are applets and not applications. But once you get the hang of it, you'll find that these are really easy steps. Let's start by taking a look at the directory structure for our HelloWorld applet.

Applet directory structure

Just as with an application, you'll need to create a directory to hold the source code file, compiled bytecode file, and HTML file for your applet. For this project, I created a `HelloApplet` directory right alongside the `Hello` directory created for the application version. Now, directories for both the applet and application version reside in my master `aewcode` directory, as can be seen in Figure 5-4. Of course, the directory structure you choose is completely up to you.

Figure 5-4: Directories for both the applet and application version of HelloWorld should now reside in your master directory.

Entering and saving the source

As you did with the application version of this program, you'll need to type the following source code and save it in your HelloApplet directory. Because the class we are defining here is called HelloWorldApplet, you should name the source code file HelloWorldApplet.java. And, just as before, be sure to include the .java extension when naming the file.

```java
import java.applet.*;
import java.awt.Graphics;
public class HelloWorldApplet extends java.applet.Applet {
   public void init() {
      resize(200,150);
   }
   public void paint(Graphics g) {
      g.drawString("Hello World!",50,100);
   }
}
```

Once you have entered this code, it must be saved in a plain ASCII text file named HelloWorldApplet.java. If the class you are defining in an applet does not have the same name as the text file in which you save it, the compiler spits out an error message. This is because the class for our applet is defined as being public, meaning the source code file in which it resides must have the same name.

Suppose, for example, you entered the above code exactly as shown but saved the file as HelloWorldStuff.java instead. The compiler would abort the mission and give you the following error message:

```
"Warning: Public class HelloWorldApplet must be defined in a file
called "HelloWorldApplet.java"
```

However, if you enter the code exactly as shown and save it in an ASCII text file named HelloWorldApplet.java you'll be all set. At this point, the applet is ready to be compiled. But before we do that, let's take a look at the new code our applet requires.

Import

Right off the bat, our applet uses two lines of code not seen in the application version:

```java
import java.applet.*;
import java.awt.Graphics;
```

These are very similar to the #include feature found in C/C++. Here, we are importing classes into our applet, methods of which our applet will utilize. The classes are from two different packages supplied with Java: the *applet package* and the *Abstract Windowing Toolkit* (AWT). For more information on packages, see Chapter 11; for more information on the AWT, see Part IV.

Take another look at the first line of import code:

```
import java.applet.*;
```

This `import` statement tells the compiler to include all classes in the `java.applet` package. This is done with the asterisk (*) character, or *wildcard*. Contrast this with the second line of code:

```
import java.awt.Graphics;
```

This line imports only the `Graphics` class from the AWT package. Here, the class we want to include — `Graphics` — is explicitly stated. Together, these two lines will provide our applet with the functionality every applet requires, as we'll soon see.

Class declaration

Unlike the application, the class declaration for our applet is much more involved:

```
public class HelloWorldApplet extends java.applet.Applet {
```

We specify the `HelloWorldApplet` class as being public, an access modifier indicating this class is available to all other objects regardless of the packages of which they may be part. We also explicitly state that this applet subclasses another. By extending the class `Applet` (`java.applet.Applet`) found in the applet package, the `HelloWorldApplet` class inherits the data and behavior in `Applet`. Because it is a subclass of the `Applet` class, `HelloWorldApplet` can be considered a more specialized version of it.

Contrast this with the application, which does not explicitly extend an existing class. By not specifying a particular class, `HelloWorld` became, by default, a subclass of `Object`. Here, however, we need to inherit the properties of the previously imported `Applet` class . All applets must extend this class, and so this code is essential here and in any other applet you'll create. The *inheritance tree*—also known as a *class hierarchy*—for `HelloWorldApplet` is shown in Figure 5-5.

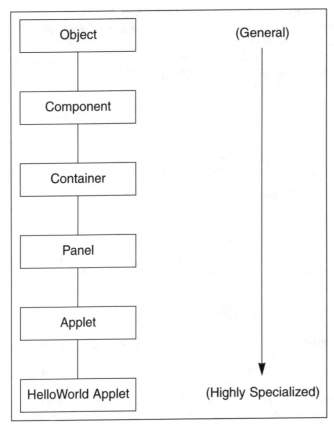

Figure 5-5: The inheritance tree for HelloWorldApplet

Method declaration/overriding

At a minimum, most applets will declare two methods: `init()` and `paint()`. These methods already exist in the `Applet` class extended by all applets, including our `HelloWorldApplet` subclass. As a result, `HelloWorldApplet` overrides them. By declaring a method in our class with the same name as one in a superclass, we replace the superclass's method with our own. Hence we override the `init()` and `paint()` originally declared in the `Applet` class with our specialized version of these methods. Let's take a closer look at them.

The first method we override, `init()`, takes no parameters, returns nothing, and is declared public. In fact, the only thing we do here is instruct the browser window to resize itself to 200 pixels wide and 150 pixels high. The method used to do this, `resize()`, is part of the `Applet` class. Because we have imported this class, we can use its methods:

```
public void init() {
  resize(200,150);
}
```

The second method we override is paint(), a method which is used by the applet to draw on the screen. Similar to init(), the paint() method is public and returns nothing. It does, however, take one parameter: a Graphics object. When called, paint() is passed an object of class Graphics. It uses this object, invoking the drawString() method contained in it, to draw our "Hello World!" string in the browser window at the location 50,100.

Unlike the System.out.println() code used in our application to output to STDOUT, applets use paint() to output to the browser window:

```
public void paint(Graphics g) {
    g.drawString("Hello World!",50,100);
}
```

The methods we've overridden are quite simple, as you can see, having only one line of executable code each. And thanks to Java's automatic garbage collection, we don't have to worry about disposing of memory or objects; we simply enter the code and let the Java runtime environment take care of these memory-management issues.

Compiling

Java applets are compiled exactly as their application counterparts. If you've typed the code precisely as shown and saved it in a file named HelloWorldApplet.java, you should have no problem compiling your new applet. Enter the following at the command line (where HelloApplet> is the prompt indicating you're inside the directory containing the source file):

```
HelloApplet> javac HelloWorldApplet.java
```

If the compiler is successful, a binary bytecode file named HelloWorldApplet.class will be created in the same directory as your source file. If not, double-check your source code against the listing above and try again.

Executing the applet

Unlike applications, Java applets cannot be executed directly with the interpreter. If you try, the interpreter will tell you it can't find the main() method required for all applications. That's no surprise, because we never declared main():

```
HelloApplet> java HelloWorldApplet
"In class HelloWorldApplet: void main(String argv[]) is
undefined"
```

To execute an applet, we must first create an HTML file that explicitly references it, using the <APPLET> tag, and then open that file with a Java-savvy browser. Luckily, this is fairly easy.

Creating an HTML file

Using the same text editor as you did to create your source code files, create a new file and enter the following:

```
<HTML>
<HEAD>
<TITLE> Hello World Applet Test </TITLE>
</HEAD>
<BODY>
Here is our applet:
<APPLET CODE="HelloWorldApplet.class" WIDTH=200 HEIGHT=150>
</APPLET>
</BODY>
</HTML>
```

When done, save this as a plain ASCII text file with the name `TestApplet.html` in the same directory as your new source and bytecode files. You can choose any name you want, but I'll use this name when referring to the HTML file.

All the HTML code you see here is standard, plain, vanilla stuff, with the exception of the following line:

```
<APPLET CODE="HelloWorldApplet.class" WIDTH=200 HEIGHT=150>
```

This is the line of HTML that tells a Java-savvy browser about our applet. The bytecode file is listed in quotes, as it's the compiled code that the browser will load and execute. Notice that the entire class name and the `.class` extension is required. If `.class` is omitted, the applet may not be found (depending on how the browser you're using deals with `<APPLET>` tags). To be safe, and ensure that every Java-savvy browser out there can find your applet, be sure to include the `.class` extension. Also, the class name must match that generated by the compiler exactly (see the section called "HTML case sensitivity" later in this chapter).

Because our applet is being executed locally, and because it exists in the same directory as the HTML file, there is no need to specify anything more than the name of the applet class file. However, if our applet was in a different directory than the HTML file or on the Web, we would need to provide additional information (see Chapter 7 for details).

WIDTH and HEIGHT

These two attributes of the `<APPLET>` tag, both of which are required, instruct the browser to create a display canvas of these dimensions when first loading the applet. The canvas is where your applet will be displayed in the browser, and can be controlled from within the applet itself using the `resize()` method.

For our purposes, the WIDTH and HEIGHT attributes are the same as those used in our applet's resize() method, called in init(). We could have two different sets of values, although the resize() method is called after the HTML file is parsed, effectively overriding the dimensions provided in HTML. By supplying the same dimensions in HTML as we have in our source code, the canvas remains the same size when the applet is loaded by the browser as when it was actually executed.

HTML case sensitivity

With the exception of the class name, which must be written exactly and in the same case format as the bytecode file generated by the compiler, the <APPLET> tag is not case-sensitive. That means you can write everything in this tag in upper, lower, or even mixed case. I've used uppercase for readability, although you should feel free to do as you wish.

For instance, either of the following three lines of HTML code would be fine:

```
<APPLET CODE="HelloWorldApplet.class" WIDTH=200 HEIGHT=150>
<applet code="HelloWorldApplet.class" width=200 height=150>
<Applet Code="HelloWorldApplet.class" Width=200 Height=150>
```

Executing the applet

Because an applet must be executed through a Java-savvy browser or similar environment, such as the Applet Viewer tool supplied with the Java Developer's Kit (JDK), we need only load our HTML file with one to see the results. However, it may not be terribly convenient to repeatedly launch a full-blown browser (or run it continuously) during the course of development. For this reason, I recommend using the Applet Viewer program provided with the JDK.

In practice, Applet Viewer is just as effective, yet executes faster and uses much less memory. To execute your program with this program, simply provide it with your HTML file:

```
HelloApplet> appletviewer TestApplet.html
```

Notice that the entire filename is included, even the .html extension. This is because Applet Viewer expects the entire filename and will generate an error message if it can't locate the file you give it. However, if everything is in order, it will create a window and execute HelloWorldApplet in it. This is demonstrated in Figure 5-6.

Figure 5-6: If everything is in order, Applet Viewer will create a window and execute HelloWorldApplet.

Although the Applet Viewer will execute any applets it finds in an HTML file, it won't display anything else. If you want to see the page as it will look to the world when placed on the Web (with text, graphics, hyperlinks, and anything else that's part of the page, but isn't generated by an applet) you need to use a Java-savvy browser such as Netscape's or Microsoft's latest beauties.

Living on the Web

Of course, in reality, your applets will be on a World Wide Web server waiting to be executed when visitors load your pages with a Java-savvy browser. In this case, the HTML file you create may specify the URLs of remote applets it expects to execute (see the CODEBASE discussion in Chapter 7).

In Chapter 6 we'll expand on the HelloWorld applet, adding sound and graphics. This new version of HelloWorld will exist on the Web, and so we'll also update our source code to better handle life in cyberspace.

JAR Files

Just as you can use a glass jar to can your tomatoes and peaches, *Java Archive* (JAR) files can be used to can your Java packages. JAR files store Java packages, classes, and resources in a compressed form. Because it takes time to download information over the Internet, if you can cram more information into less space, things will run faster. When adding applets to your HTML files, the ⟨ARCHIVE⟩ tag is used to specify a JAR file. Chapter 11 reviews the process of creating JAR files in detail.

Onward and upward

Although the HelloWorld application and applet aren't much to look at, they have helped us better understand the Java language and development environment. In fact, you've actually created two platform-independent programs, one of which, the applet, is capable of living on the Web. Not bad, considering it only took a handful of code.

In Chapter 6 we'll build upon this to get a better understanding of how to debug Java programs. We'll also upload the final applet to the Web, accessing it from there, instead of from our hard drive. And so, it's onward and upward with HelloWorld, but it's goodbye for now.

Summary

In this chapter we examined these topics:

✦ Creating Java applications and applets, using a basic HelloWorld example

✦ Executing Java applications

✦ Using the HTML <APPLET> tag to include a Java applet on your Web page

✦ Executing Java applets using your Web browser

✦   ✦   ✦

Extending, Enhancing, Debugging, and Uploading

In This Chapter

Determining when to
extend or enhance
existing Java classes
or develop your own

A step-by-step guide
to extending the
`HelloWorldApplet`
class

How to create
and document
your classes

Debugging and
testing your Java
applications and
applets

Having completed the simplistic HelloWorld examples,
it's time to improve on the work we've started. In this
chapter, we'll add an image and soundtrack to the HelloWorld
applet. In doing so, we'll see how classes are extended
(subclassed) in Java and get to know the debugging process.
Finally, we'll learn how to upload our new creations onto the
Web, for the world to admire.

Let's first consider a question you'll ask yourself often when
using Java: *Enhance or extend?*

To Enhance or Extend?

When you develop software in any object-oriented
programming (OOP) language, you'll often ask yourself
whether the task or program at hand should enhance existing
classes or extend them to create more specialized subclasses.
In large programs, you'll often do both.

To *enhance* an existing class means to add new variables or
methods to that class. To *extend* a class means you create a
subclass that will contain new variables or methods while the
superclass itself remains untouched. That is, you add your
variables and/or methods to the subclass (perhaps even
overriding methods in the superclass) to get the behavior you
want, without changing a line of code in the superclass.

Whether to enhance or extend depends a great deal on what it is you want to do. To make this decision, you need to have a clear understanding of the class itself. You need to ask yourself two basic questions:

1. Does the class have the essential data and behavior I need, and would it be easy to add to it?

2. Does the new functionality I want to add apply to all instances of the class, or just some?

If the functionality you want to add applies to the entire class (in other words, all instances require such functionality) and is easy to fit in with the class's existing data and behavior, then it's a good candidate for enhancing. If it lacks much of the data or functionality you require, or the new functionality only applies to some of the instances of the class, it may be easier to extend it by creating a new subclass.

Be very cautious when attempting to enhance a class. What you are actually doing is rewriting it. Therefore, you must take great care not to alter the interface it currently supports for interacting with other objects, lest you "break" the class. If you change the way in which it interacts with other objects, either by substantially changing its variables and/or methods, the integrity of the class will be compromised and any programs or classes relying on it will suffer.

While the decision to enhance or extend is made on a case-by-case basis, you'd do well to consider extending a class whenever possible. This, after all, is one of the key reasons OOP is so powerful. You don't have to go in and rewrite functions and data structures every time you need new functionality. You can simply create a subclass, inheriting all the data and behavior of the superclass, and add any specialized data and behavior without worry.

We can accomplish our task—adding sound and graphics to the HelloWorld applet we created in the previous chapter—by either enhancing or extending the `HelloWorldApplet` class. However, to help us become more comfortable with the concept of extending a superclass to inherit its state and behavior, we'll concentrate on extending `HelloWorldApplet`. As we go through the example, you'll see the new code that would have to be added to this class, were we not to extend it.

Extending the HelloWorldApplet class

Because we're going to extend the class, we need to create a new ASCII text file for the source code in Listing 6-1, which will then be compiled and executed. Create a new file using whatever text editor you prefer, enter the source code, and then save it in the same directory as `HelloWorldApplet`.

Listing 6-1: **MediaHelloWorld.java source code**

```
import java.applet.*;
import java.awt.*;
/**
* MediaHelloWorld applet, an extension of the HelloWorld
applet.
* Displays "Hello World!" string in applet canvas while a
* background audio track plays and an image follows the mouse
* around.
*
* @author Aaron E. Walsh
* @version 1.0, 12 Jan 98
*/
public class MediaHelloWorld extends HelloWorldApplet {
Image  myImage;
AudioClip  myAudio;
int  horizontal, vertical;
boolean  SoundOn = true;

  public void init() {
    super.init();
    myImage=getImage(getCodeBase(), "images/world.gif");
    myAudio=getAudioClip(getCodeBase(), "audio/hello.au");
  }

public void paint(Graphics g) {
  if (myImage !=3D null) {   /* only draw if the variable
contains
                                   data! */
      g.drawImage(myImage, horizontal, vertical, this);
    }
  super.paint(g);
}

  public void start() {
    myAudio.loop();
  }

  public void stop() {
    myAudio.stop();
  }

  public boolean mouseDown(java.awt.Event event, int x, int y)
{
    if (SoundOn) {
      myAudio.loop();
      SoundOn = false;
    }
```

(continued)

Listing 6-1 *(continued)*

```
   else {
     myAudio.stop();
     SoundOn = true;
   }
 return true;
 }

 public boolean mouseMove(java.awt.Event event, int x, int y)
{
   horizontal=x;
   vertical=y;
   repaint();
   return true;
 }
}
```

Name your new file MediaHelloWorld.java. Be sure to include the .java extension or the compiler won't be able to find it.

Because MediaHelloWorld extends our HelloWorld applet, the javac compiler must be able to access the HelloWorldApplet class in order to successfully compile MediaHelloWorld. This is why I've suggested that you place your MediaHelloWorld.java source code file in the same directory as HelloWorldApplet. However, as long as it's in the class path (specified by the CLASSPATH environment variable or using the classpath compiler option), any applet you create can extend HelloWorldApplet. See Chapter 4 for details on how to properly configure classpath for your system.

At this point, you should also create two new directories inside the same directory as your source code: audio and images. The audio directory will contain the sound file, and images will hold the GIF file used in this example. To make things easier, you can simply copy these directories and files from the CD-ROM included with this book. Refer to Appendix C for the details about where these are located.

Java versions prior to version 1.2 only support Sun's AU (µlaw) audio format. If you're using an earlier version of Java, you have to save sound files as 8-bit µlaw, 8KHz, with only one channel. To convert existing sound files to the AU format, use the audio tool application if you're a Sun workstation user, or the shareware program GoldWave on the enclosed CD-ROM if you're a Windows user. To save a sound file in the AU format using GoldWave, use the File-Export command.

JDK 1.2 includes a number of audio enhancements, including a new sound engine and support for audio in applications as well as applets. Java Sound now supports the AIFF, AU, and WAV audio file formats. It also supports these MIDI-based song file formats: TYPE 0 MIDI, TYPE 1 MIDI, and RMF. Java sound can render 8-bit or 16-bit audio data in mono or stereo, with sample rates from 8KHz to 48KHz.

The source code in Listing 6-1 is bug-free, meaning it should compile without a hitch, assuming it resides in the same directory as the `HelloWorldApplet` class (`HelloWorldApplet.class`) or as the source file (`HelloWorldApplet.java`). When the Java compiler is run on your new source file, it will look for `HelloWorldApplet.class`, because that class is extended. If it can't locate `HelloWorldApplet.class`, the compiler will look for the `HelloWorldApplet.java` source file and compile it, if it's available. If successful, the compiler will create a new class named `MediaHelloWorld.class`.

If the compiler insists that it can't find the `HelloWorldApplet` class, be sure that it (or the `HelloWorldApplet.java` source code file) is inside the same directory as your new `MediaHelloWorld.java` file. If it's not, or isn't in the class path at all, the compiler won't be able to find it.

If you're sure the file is in the correct place, and the compiler still can't find it, double-check the `CLASSPATH` environment variable to ensure that you set it properly.

Make sure that your `CLASSPATH` environment variable not only points to Java's `classes.zip` archive, which contains all the standard class files, but also includes the "current directory." In Windows, you do this by supplying a period and semicolon, followed by the full path leading to the .zip archive (`.;C:\java\lib\classes.zip`). With UNIX systems, you use a period and colon to specify the current directory (`.:/java/lib/classes.zip`).

If both `HelloWorldApplet.class` and its source, `HelloWorldApplet.java`, are missing, the compiler will tell you so:

```
MediaHelloWorld.java:11: Superclass HelloWorldApplet of class
    MediaHelloWorld not found.
public class MediaHelloWorld extends HelloWorldApplet {
                                     ^
1 error
```

A class, such as `HelloWorldApplet.class`, will be accessible to your Java programs if it resides in the same directory as the program itself (or the source code you intend to compile). It will also be accessible if it resides in the directory specified by the `CLASSPATH` environment variable. If you develop a class that's likely to be used by more than one program, make sure that you place it in the directory specified by `CLASSPATH`, so that it's universally accessible to all Java programs that might need it.

Stepping Through the Code

In this section, we'll step through each new part of the source code shown in
Listing 6-1 to give you a better idea of what each new variable and method does.
In the process, we'll get a better feel for how subclasses communicate with their
superclass through use of the `super` object.

Importing classes

To begin with, let's take a look at the classes our new program imports:

```
import java.applet.*;
import java.awt.*;
```

These two lines of code are very similar to those found in `HelloWorldApplet.
java`. Because we're creating an applet, we need to import the base `Applet` class.
This is accomplished with the first import statement, which every applet must
include.

In addition to the basic applet functionality our program requires, the `Applet` class
also provides the `AudioClip` interface we'll use to load and play a sound track.

The second import statement, however, is slightly different from its
`HelloWorldApplet.java` counterpart. Here, we instruct the compiler to
import classes in the `awt` package, not just the `Graphics` class imported in
`HelloWorldApplet`. Because this applet requires additional classes found in `awt`,
specifically those that deal with the `Image` object, we import all classes in the
`awt` package.

With these two lines of code, all of the classes our applet relies on are imported
into the program. If we had required additional classes, we could have imported
them in precisely the same way as we imported the `Applet` and `awt` classes.

Documentation comments

Following the import command is a special comment, created to help developers
generate documentation:

```
/**
 * MediaHelloWorld applet, an extension of the HelloWorld
applet.
 * Displays "Hello World!" string in applet canvas while a
 * background audio track plays and an image follows the mouse
 * around.
 *
 * @author Aaron E. Walsh
 * @version 1.0, 1 Jan 98
 */
```

This comment looks and acts in a similar way to the standard C comment, although an extra asterisk (*) is added to the beginning and special variables are included.

Inside a document comment, the @ character specifies special variables that are used when generating documentation with the javadoc tool. In this example, the author and applet version have been specified.

You can place document comments before any class or method declaration to serve as standard human-readable comments ignored by the compiler. In addition, you can use comments to help automate the document-creation process and take some of this burden from the programmer.

Class declaration

The MediaHelloWorld class declaration follows the documentation comment. Unlike our original HelloWorld applet, which extended the Applet class, MediaHelloWorld extends the HelloWorldApplet class:

```
public class MediaHelloWorld extends HelloWorldApplet {..}
```

By extending the HelloWorldApplet class, MediaHelloWorld inherits all data and behavior in that class. Although there isn't much to inherit — only the capability to output "Hello World!" — you'll soon see how powerful this ability to subclass an existing class is. And because we've inherited all the traits of HelloWorldApplet, we automatically get the functionality found in class Applet.

Variables

Next, the variables used in MediaHelloWorld are declared. Although these variables could have been declared anywhere inside the body of our class (with the exception of inside a method declaration), as long as they appeared before first being used, I've placed them here for easy reading:

```
Image  myImage;
AudioClip  myAudio;
int  horizontal, vertical;
boolean  SoundOn = true;
```

The most significant variables are those that will actually hold our graphic and sound data: myImage and myAudio. The others aren't nearly as interesting, but are every bit as necessary. The horizontal and vertical integer objects will hold the mouse coordinates, because our image will be drawn wherever the mouse moves. In addition, a boolean object SoundOn is declared and set to true. This variable keeps track of whether or not the sound clip should be played; it's necessary because a mouse click in our applet toggles the audio off and on.

Methods

Six common methods are often overridden when you create your own applets. They are init(), getCodeBase(), paint(), start(), stop(), mouseDown(), and mouseMove(). Let's take a close look at the function of each of these methods.

init()

MediaWorldApplet overrides six methods, beginning with init(), which all applets override:

```
public void init() {
    super.init();
    myImage=getImage(getCodeBase(), "images/world.gif");
    myAudio=getAudioClip(getCodeBase(), "audio/hello.au");
}
```

However, this init() method is quite different than the one we created for HelloWorldApplet. In that one, we simply resized the applet canvas in which our "Hello World!" string was to be drawn. Here, things are quite different. Although MediaWorldApplet does, in fact, resize the applet canvas, it does so by invoking the init() method in its superclass:

```
super.init();
```

By executing the init() method of MediaWorldApplet's superclass, as this line of code does, HelloWorldApplet's init() is called! Sure, the only thing it does is resize the applet canvas, but the point is that we were able to execute the init() method of the superclass without having to duplicate code. It's not a drastic saving in code in this example, but it could be tremendous in others.

Note

Although Sun's Applet Viewer supports the resizing of the applet canvas, there's no guarantee that every Java-savvy Web browser will do the same. As a result, you shouldn't rely on resize() working correctly when it's called. However, every <APPLET> tag is required to include both a HEIGHT and WIDTH attribute. Every Java-savvy browser will use the values supplied through these attributes to automatically set the size of an applet's canvas when it is first executed.

It doesn't matter how much or how little code we're saving in this example—it could be millions of lines or just one—the end result is that our new applet doesn't have to duplicate effort. We inherit the variables and methods we've already created in HelloWorldApplet, and we can access them from our new class thanks to the super object. As you can see in the paint() method, we don't even have to bother rewriting the code that outputs "Hello World!." (For an explanation of super, see the "Odds 'n' Ends" section at the end of this chapter.)

You should note that in Java, two special keywords, `this` and `super`, are used to refer to the current object (`this`), and its superclass (`super`). Because you'll make regular use of `this` and `super` in your Java programs, they are described in the "Odds 'n' Ends" section later in this chapter, and explained in detail in Chapter 11.

The next two lines in `init()` retrieve the image and audio data and place it in the appropriate objects. Actually, the data isn't loaded at this time! Only when an image is drawn, or a sound file played, does the download take place. After all, why load the data if it never gets used?

getCodeBase()

The two methods `getImage()` and `getAudioClip()` are courtesy of classes imported into our program. They both rely on another method, `getCodeBase()`, also made possible thanks to the imported `Applet` class (see the "Getting to Base" sidebar).

Getting to Base

Many applets use external data (such as graphic images and audio files) that may be stored outside of the directory in which the applet resides, so there must be a way to tell the applet where these files are. This is quite easy, thanks to two methods implemented in the `Applet` class: `getCodeBase()` and `getDocumentBase()`. Both methods return a URL object, which is used to tell the applet where the external data files reside:

`public URL getCodeBase()` returns the "base" URL for the applet itself. Use this method if your external data files are stored relative to the actual applet, not the HTML document it is embedded in.

`public URL getDocumentBase()` returns the URL for the actual document in which the applet is embedded. Use this method if your external data files are stored relative to the HTML document.

These methods are extremely useful because they enable your applet to locate files relative to itself or to the HTML document in which it is embedded. They work in both local and networked environments, so it doesn't matter if your applet is executed from your hard drive or the World Wide Web. Thanks to `getCodeBase()` and `getDocumentBase()`, your applet will be able to find the files it needs regardless of where it is executed, assuming these files are located relative to the class when using `getCodeBase()`, or to the HTML document when using `getDocumentBase()`.

Later in this chapter, you'll upload the compiled `MediaWorldApplet` class and associated audio and image files to your Web server. And because we use `getCodeBase()` to reference these files, Java will be able to locate them as easily as when the applet is executed locally.

paint()

Next, we override the paint() method:

```
public void paint(Graphics g) {
   if (myImage !=3D null) {   // only draw if the variable
contains data!
        g.drawImage(myImage, horizontal, vertical, this);
      }
   super.paint(g);
}
```

This implementation uses drawImage() to draw the graphic at the specified horizontal and vertical position on the applet canvas. These variables set the location of the mouse and are set in the mouseMove() method overridden later in the program. Of particular interest, however, is the parameter this, which refers to the current object.

The drawImage() method, described in detail in Chapter 17, takes as its last argument an ImageObserver object. Image observers are responsible for keeping track of images as they are loaded, a process which can take a long time when loading over a network. However, because applets themselves can act as ImageObserver objects, you don't have to instantiate them yourself in most cases.

Instead, you can pass a reference to the applet using the keyword this. Because this refers to the current object, which is the applet itself, you can get by without bothering to instantiate an ImageObserver object. (For a detailed explanation of this, see the "Odds 'n' Ends" section later in this chapter.)

After drawing the image, we call the paint() method of our superclass with the line:

```
super.paint(g);
```

This outputs "Hello World!" to the applet canvas, just as it did in class HelloWorldApplet, where it was declared. Because "Hello World!" is output after we draw the image, it appears over the image itself. If you want the image to be drawn over the text, simply reverse the order of these two lines.

start() and stop()

Although the init() and paint() methods should be familiar to you by now, the remaining code overrides several methods that HelloWorldApplet did not. The first two, start() and stop(), are used to begin and end our audio sound track, which is referenced by myAudio after init() is called.

When the applet is begun, start() is called. It is here that we execute the loop() method declared in the AudioClip class. When the applet is terminated (this occurs when the user unloads the Web page in which the applet is embedded), stop() is invoked. It is here that we execute the stop() method for AudioClip, which interrupts the looping sound track:

```
public void start() {
   myAudio.loop();
}

public void stop() {
   myAudio.stop();
}
```

These two methods are commonly overridden by applets, because they provide a mechanism for applets to begin and end their activities in response to the user loading and unloading the Web page in which the applet is embedded. For more information on start() and stop() and the three additional methods often overridden by applets, see "Fundamental applet methods" in the "Odds 'n' Ends" section at the end of this chapter.

mouseDown() and mouseMove()

Until now, our program has only overridden methods that are called when the applet is first executed or terminated. (The init(), paint(), and start() methods are called when the applet is executed; stop() is an example of a method that is automatically called when the document containing the applet is unloaded.) We haven't, at this point, established a mechanism to interact with the user.

The final two methods we override do just that. By overriding mouseDown() and mouseMove(), declared in the Component class (java.awt.Component, to be exact, imported as part of the entire awt package), we give our applet the ability to respond to the user's mouse activity:

```
public boolean mouseDown(java.awt.Event event, int x, int y) {
   if (SoundOn) {
      myAudio.loop();
      SoundOn = false;
   }
   else {
      myAudio.stop();
      SoundOn = true;
      }
   return true;
}

public boolean mouseMove(java.awt.Event event, int x, int y) {
   horizontal=x;
   vertical=y;
   repaint();
   return true;
}
```

Both methods have the same parameter list and return a boolean, sharing the same basic method signature:

```
public boolean methodname (Event evt, int x, int y) { ... }
```

`Event` is a class that encapsulates events from the local Graphical User Interface (GUI) platform, such as mouse and keyboard characteristics. The x and y parameters of each method specify the horizontal and vertical coordinates of the mouse at the time the method is invoked. Both methods must return `true` if the event is handled appropriately, meaning it should not be passed along for further processing. Because the buck stops with us, we return `true` in each case to prevent a parent component from also executing its `mouseDown()` and `mouseMove()` methods.

In `mouseDown()`, we do nothing whatsoever with the parameters passed to us. Instead, we simply determine whether the audio track should be started or stopped, based on the `SoundOn` variable, and act accordingly. It is here that we toggle the value of `SoundOn`, allowing the user to start and stop the soundtrack by clicking the mouse in the applet canvas.

Our implementation of `mouseMove()`, however, does use a portion of the parameter list. Although we ignore `Event`, x and y are used to set our horizontal and vertical variables. These two variables specify the coordinates where our image is drawn. Because we want the image to "follow" the mouse around, we immediately call `repaint()` to ensure our `paint()` method is called each time the mouse moves. The result is shown, frozen in time, in Figure 6-1.

Figure 6-1: MediaHelloWorld, residing locally, as executed by Applet Viewer

And that's MediaHelloWorld in its entirety. Before we begin the debugging process, you may want to run the program and tinker with the code. Because the code we've stepped through here is bug-free, it should compile and execute without a hitch. Of course, you'll have to create a new HTML file to execute first.

I strongly recommend developing and testing your applets using Applet Viewer initially, moving on to a Java-savvy Web browser when you've worked out all the kinks. Applet Viewer is fast, takes up less memory, and doesn't cache applets as a Web browser might. As a result, you can guarantee that Applet Viewer will load your applet class fresh every time it is executed.

If you use a Web browser that happens to cache files by default, as Netscape Navigator does, you'll have to flush the cache or quit the browser and start anew each time you want to execute a freshly compiled class. In fact, many programmers who use Netscape Navigator exclusively can't understand why their applet won't work as expected, even after substantial changes to the source code. Most of the time it's because their particular Java-savvy browser is running an old, cached version of their applet instead of the freshly compiled one!

Creating the HTML file

Just as you created an HTML document for the HelloWorld applet, you must create one for MediaHelloWorld. Simply create a plain ASCII text file with the following contents, and save it inside the directory in which your compiled MediaHelloWorld class resides:

```
<HTML>
<HEAD>
<TITLE> MediaHelloWorld Applet Test </TITLE>
</HEAD>
<BODY>
Here is our MediaHelloWorld applet:
<APPLET CODE=MediaHelloWorld.class height=150 width=200>
</APPLET>
</BODY>
</HTML>
```

After you've saved the above HTML code as a text file, you're ready to execute the applet embedded in it. For the purpose of this section and the next, I'll assume you've named the HTML file `TestMediaHello.html`. If you use this name, you simply enter the following command line to execute the applet using the Applet Viewer program:

```
appletviewer TestMediaHello.html
```

This, of course, assumes the HTML file is located locally. You can also use Applet Viewer to execute applets on the Web by providing a URL to the HTML document, instead of its name:

```
appletviewer
http://www.mantiscorp.com/books/java/found/TestMediaHello.html
```

This will come in handy when you want to test pages after you've placed them on the Internet, as described in "Making Applets Live on the Web" later in this chapter. If you're anxious to get on the Web, feel free to jump ahead.

Botching the Code

Code that compiles perfectly doesn't help you understand the debugging features of Java, however, so let's screw it up a bit. The source code in Listing 6-2 is a version of `MediaHelloWorld` (originally found in Listing 6-1) with a slippery little problem that will give us a good opportunity to work with the Java debugger.

Listing 6-2: **A buggy version of MediaHelloWorld.java**

```
import java.applet.*;
import java.awt.*;

public class MediaHelloWorld extends HelloWorldApplet {
Image   myImage;
AudioClip  myAudio;
int   horizontal, vertical;
boolean   SoundOn = true;

  public void init() {
    super.init();
    myImage=getImage(getCodeBase(), "images/world.gif");
    myAudio=getAudioClip(getCodeBase(), "audio/hello.au");
  }

public void paint(Graphics g) {
  if (myImage !=3D null) {   /* only draw if the variable
contains
                                  data! */
    g.drawImage(myImage, horizontal, vertical, this);
  }
  super.paint(g);
}

  public void start() {
    myAudio.loop();
  }

  public void stop() {
    myAudio.stop();
  }

  public boolean mouseDown(java.awt.Event event, int x, int y)
{
    if (SoundOn) {
      myAudio.loop();
      SoundOn = false;
    }
    else {
```

```
            myAudio.stop();
            SoundOn = true;
         }
      return true;
      }

   public boolean mouseMove(java.awt.Event event, int x, int y)
   {
         horizontal=x;
         vertical=x;
         repaint();
         return true;
      }
   }
```

Can you see the error in Listing 6-2? How about if you compare it to Listing 6-1? Because the entire body of code for this applet is relatively short and clean, you can probably spot the error immediately. But if you can't find it right off the bat, here's a clue: When executed, the image doesn't follow the cursor around as it once did. Specifically, when you move the mouse, the image isn't painted on the screen at the same coordinates as the cursor.

On the CD-ROM

The source code for both HelloWorld and MediaHelloWorld are provided on the CD-ROM included with this book, as are all source code examples. If you want to save yourself the effort of typing, simply refer to Appendix C for details on where these files are located. Open them with any text editor and then save them to your local hard drive.

The bug I've introduced to this code is really just an oversight, something you might do when tired or rushed to finish a program. And, unless you go through the code line by line, it's tough to find, because the compiler doesn't know there's a problem. But there is one, and it's in the mouseMove() method:

```
public boolean mouseMove(java.awt.Event event, int x, int y) {
    horizontal=x;
    vertical=x;    // here's the little bugger...
    repaint();
    return true;
}
```

Instead of setting the vertical variable to y, as it should be, I've set it to x. Sure, we don't need a debugger to find this; with a little effort we'd find it ourselves. After all, with such a short code listing, where could it hide? But it will serve our purpose and give us a chance to use the debugger, in preparation for times when we can't hunt down a bug just by scanning through the source code.

Be warned

If I've sounded like a Java zealot so far, it's because I absolutely love the language and what it's done and will do for network-centric computing. But as much as I love Java, I hate the debugger that comes with the JDK (intensely, with the white-hot intensity of a thousand fiery orbs in the sky). Alas, Sun — the company that blessed us with the Java language — also bestowed upon us the jdb debugger.

The jdb debugger is about as bare-boned as you can get. It is, in fact, written in Java just as the HotJava browser is. But what makes it unbearable isn't the fact that it's entirely command-line based (something DOS and UNIX programmers won't mind at all), or that it lacks the ability to set conditional breakpoints (such as, "break when x exceeds 100"). No, I can live with these things. What I can't bear is how terribly unstable the debugger can be at times.

So why would I tell you to use the jdb? So you can share my pain? No. In fact, I suggest you don't use it, if at all possible. If you're serious about debugging, or plan to make extensive use of Java, you shouldn't rely on the JDK alone. Instead, I'd highly recommend a full-fledged Java development environment from a company that specializes in development tools. Borland, Symantec, and Metrowerks all have superior Java development environments that will free you from the shackles of the JDK's limited toolset.

Perhaps you'll become fast friends with jdb and drop me a few lines of flamemail to tell me how wrong I was to deride this virtuous tool. Fire away: aaron@ mantiscorp.com. I hope that's the case, truly, but in my experience and that of everyone I've dealt with who uses the jdb, you're more likely to join our "Programmers Who Love Java but Hate the JDB Support Group" than to defend it.

And there's another reason I've decided to include this section. Over time, I've gathered a few tips and warnings that, if followed, can bring some stability to the product, which you'll find throughout the remainder of this chapter. Because you may indeed need to use the jdb from time to time, employing these suggestions can make your experience more rewarding.

But enough with the warnings already; on with the show . . .

Stages in debugging your code

After you insert the bug and recompile the code, you have to follow several steps to properly find that annoying bug:

1. Invoke the jdb debugger.

2. Get the applet running.

3. Issue debugging commands.

4. Start your search.

5. Check the source code.

6. Resume program execution.

If there's still a problem:

1. Step through the code.

2. Clean your house.

Recompile the source code

To run through this exercise, you don't need to bother entering the source code from scratch. Instead, just change the one line in `mouseMove()` that introduces the bug we'll be tracking:

```
vertical=x;
```

Once you've slipped this change into your code, you'll need to recompile it. But you need to do more than just a straight compile; you need to instruct the compiler to include line numbers and information about local variables when it generates a class file. By default, the `javac` compiler only generates line numbers. To generate information about local variables, you must use the `-g` option when compiling:

```
> javac -g MediaHelloWorld.java
```

By invoking this option, you'll be able to see the local variables and their values when debugging. And, because we need to inspect the variables our program uses to see what's happening, this option is a necessity.

Invoke the jdb debugger

As with the other JDK tools, the jdb debugger is entirely text-based, controlled by issuing commands on the command line. UNIX developers will recognize it as being very similar in nature to the dbx or gdb debuggers often used on that platform.

When invoked, the jdb actually starts the Java interpreter and "attaches" itself to it. As a result, you can supply jdb with any of the options the interpreter itself can handle: jdb simply passes such options over to the Java interpreter. In addition, you can execute the Applet Viewer in a debugger mode, which will invoke the jdb for you. This is the option we'll use, because our program is an applet and needs to be debugged as such:

```
appletviewer -debug TestMediaHello.html
```

If all goes according to plan, the debugger will be invoked and you'll be staring at a command-line prompt, from which you can enter jdb commands. If, however, you see something similar to the error message shown in Figure 6-2, you'll have to ensure that a connection to the Internet has been established and try again. In this case, simply connect as you usually do when surfing the Web with a browser, and then return to the command line and issue the above command again.

Figure 6-2: The *jdb* requires that you first establish a connection to the Internet before it will execute.

Issue debugging commands

Once invoked, the jdb waits around for a command. For a list of the commands it understands, enter **help** (or **?**) or refer to Table 6-1. The first command we'll issue is run, to get the applet running.

Table 6-1 jdb Options and Commands	
Options[1]	**Description**
-host hostname	Sets the name of the host machine of the interpreter session you want to debug.
-password password	"Attaches" the jdb to the current interpreter session, which must have been invoked with the -debug option, causing it to generate a password. Without this password, the debugger won't be able to attach to the interpreter.
Commands	
!!	When used, these two characters are replaced by the text of the previous command. When followed by additional text, that text is appended to the end of the previous command.
catch [exception classname]	Sets a breakpoint for the specified exception; whenever the exception is thrown, jdb will break. Displays all exceptions currently being caught, if one isn't specified (see ignore).
classes	Prints a list of all loaded classes.
clear [class:line]	Removes breakpoint for a specified line in the class. Displays all current breakpoints (along with line numbers), if one isn't specified.
cont	Resumes program execution.

Commands

down [number]	Moves down a number of frames in the current thread's call stack (stack frame). The default is one frame (see up).
dump object	Prints the instance variables of a given object. Objects may be specified by their hexadecimal IDs or by their names.
	Note: When a class you'd like to dump isn't loaded, you must provide its full name (such as `java.awt.Button`). When a class is already loaded, however, you can specify a partial name (such as `Button`).
exit (or quit)	Terminates the current jdb session.
gc	Forces garbage collection (reclaims unused objects, freeing memory).
help (or ?)	Displays a list of commands the debugger understands, along with a brief description of each.
ignore exception classname	Turns off the catch mechanism for the specified exception, preventing it from being treated as a breakpoint (by default, exceptions that aren't caught are treated as a nonrecoverable breakpoints).
list [line number]	Lists the specified line of code (and several before and after it), or the current thread's stack frame if no line number is provided (see use).
load	Loads the specified class.
locals	Displays locals variables for the current stack frame.
	Note: Code must be compiled using `-g` option
memory	Displays amount of memory being used by the current program.
methods classname	Prints all methods for the specified class.
next	Steps one line — steps over calls.
print object	Prints a Java object, calling that object's toString() method in order to properly format the output. You can print objects by specifying their IDs or names.
	Note: When a class you'd like to print isn't loaded, you must provide its full name (such as `java.awt.Button`). When a class is already loaded, however, you can specify a partial name (such as `Button`).
resume [threads]	Resumes execution of the specified thread(s); resumes or suspends threads if none are specified (see suspend).

JDK 1.2

(continued)

Table 6-1 (continued)

Commands

run [classname] [arguments]	Executes the main() method in the specified class. Any arguments specified—which can be any of those supported by the java interpreter—are passed to the class.
step	Executes the current line of code, and then stops program execution.
stepi	Executes the current instruction.
stop [at classname:line] [in classname.method]	Sets a breakpoint at the class's specified line of code or for the specified method. Displays all breakpoints, if neither are supplied.
suspend [threads]	Suspends the specified thread(s), or all threads if none are specified (see resume).
thread thread	Sets the current thread.
threadgroup groupname	Sets the current thread group.
threadgroups	Lists all thread groups in the current debugger session.
threads [threadgroups]	Lists the current threads in the default thread group, if a thread group is specified.
up [number]	Moves up a number of frames in the current thread's call stack (stack frame). The default is one frame (see down).
use [path]	Sets the path jdb will use to locate source files (the default is the path specified by classpath). If no path is specified, it outputs the path.
where [thread] [all]	Prints the stack of a specific thread (or the current thread, if one isn't specified). Prints the stack trace for all threads when the all option is specified.
wherei [threadid] [all]	For PC platforms only. Prints the stack of a specific thread—providing PC-specific information.

[1] When a class file is specified when jdb is invoked, any of the Java interpreter options may be supplied. However, when "attaching" to an existing interpreter session, only these two options are available.

Get the applet running

At this point, our applet isn't actually running. Applet Viewer simply invoked the debugger with the class file embedded in the HTML file we passed to it. The first thing you'll want to do is get the applet running:

```
> run
```

Once executed, this command puts our applet into motion as expected. In a few seconds, you'll hear the soundtrack and see the image appear. Just to make sure everything is working as normal, and to prepare for our debugging session, move the cursor around as you normally would. As you can see, the image doesn't appear where it should. Now, it's time to find out why.

Start your search

Of course, you already know why the image doesn't appear where it should, but pretend for just a moment that you don't have any idea. The first thing you need to do is consider where the problem is occurring. Naturally, you'll want to see what's going on in the method that paints the image to the screen. After all, this is the place where the rubber hits the road; where the image is actually slapped up on the screen.

Use the methods command

Assuming you forgot the exact spelling of the `paint()` method (work with me here), or weren't sure of exactly what methods were in the program to begin with (and so didn't know where to begin looking for suspicious behavior), you could get a listing of each by issuing the `methods` command:

```
> methods MediaHelloWorld
```

The results are shown in Figure 6-3, and they give you a good idea of where to start the debugging process. Oh, yes, it is indeed the `paint()` method that we want to look inside while the program is running. And it's spelled p-a-i-n-t. Imagine that. Let's set a breakpoint for this method:

```
> stop in MediaHelloWorld.paint
```

Figure 6-3: Use the methods command for a listing of the methods in a class.

Once set, you'll need to force your applet to invoke the method. The debugger will just sit around and wait until this method is invoked, at which point it will stop the program execution entirely. To invoke the `paint()` method, you need only switch to Applet Viewer (perhaps moving your mouse to trigger the method).

The jdb supports two types of breakpoints: method and line number. In this case, we only want to break when `paint()` is called. Later, we'll set a breakpoint at a specific line number. Keep in mind that the commands for each differ slightly:

```
stop in class.method    (sets breakpoint for method)
stop at class:line      (sets breakpoint at line number)
```

Check the source code

Once the breakpoint is reached, the applet will seem to "freeze." The sound will stop playing, and the image will no longer move. This is because the debugger has suspended all activity, and is now waiting for another command. At this point, we'll want to take a look at the source code within the debugger and see exactly where execution was stopped:

```
> list
```

Once executed, the `list` command shows you precisely where the debugger has stopped the flow of program execution. Not only is the method listed, but an arrow points to the line of code that will be executed next (see Figure 6-4). If you don't see the code listing, you may have to specify the path to your source file:

```
> use
```

Figure 6-4: After listing the source code for the current breakpoint, print out the variables you want to inspect.

The use command

If you issue the use command by itself, it displays the path list that jdb uses to find source files. By default, the class path is used. However, if the directory containing your source file isn't included, you won't be able to list the source code at all! In this case, you must supply the path to the file (use <path list>):

```
> use C:\java\aewcode\HelloApplet
```

Assuming the source file is available, the list command will spit out the code (with line numbers) surrounding the breakpoint.

The print command

At this point, you can see that the drawImage() method is about to be invoked. But are the horizontal and vertical values being provided to it valid? There's only one way to find out:

```
> print horizontal
> print vertical
```

The print command outputs the value of the item you provide to it. You'll use this command to inspect the value of classes, objects, and variables. You can either specify the name of these items, as we have, or the hexadecimal number that is used to uniquely identify an object running in the debugger.

In our case, printing out these variables reveals that they are exactly the same (see Figure 6-4). Coincidence? Perhaps. Enter the cont command to resume execution, move your cursor over a different part of the applet, and print out these values again. Hmmm . . . looks like we're on to something.

The dump command

Use the dump command to find out the names and IDs of the methods and variables for a class, along with the superclass and any interfaces it may implement:

```
dump MediaHelloWorld
```

Clear the breakpoint

Perhaps we should take a look at the method that calls this one? But first, clear the breakpoint that you've already set. If you don't, each time you return to Applet Viewer it will attempt to refresh the display by calling the paint() method, triggering the breakpoint each time.

First, execute the `clear` command without any parameters. This will give you a listing of all the current breakpoints, of which there will only be one. Using this information, clear the breakpoint by specifying the name of the method and the line number:

```
> clear   (get a listing of all breakpoints)
> clear MediaHelloWorld:28 (clear breakpoint using method:line form)
```

Resume program execution

Once the breakpoint has been cleared, issue the `cont` command to resume program execution. Once program execution has resumed, set a breakpoint for the `mouseMove()` method:

```
> cont
> stop in MediaHelloWorld.mouseMove
```

After setting the breakpoint, invoke it by moving the mouse inside the running applet. This triggers the `mouseMove()` method and grinds program execution to a halt once again as the debugger waits for your command. List the code, as usual, and then take a peek at the values of the local variables, using the `locals` command:

```
> list
> locals
```

At this point, we know the x and y values are valid — they're coming into the `mouseMove()` method set to different values, as seen in Figure 6-5 (unlike our horizontal and vertical variables, which always have the same value). Of course, local variables are only available if you've recompiled your source code using the `-g` option. If you didn't, you'll have to exit the debugger, recompile with `-g` on, and try again. (See "Debugging Tips and Warnings" later in this chapter before exiting the debugger!)

Figure 6-5: Use the `locals` command to inspect the value of variables in a method.

If there's still a problem . . .

But suppose you didn't realize the improper variable assignment, even though it's obvious by looking at the code listing. Hey, it can happen. A few weeks of long nights and non-stop pressure to get a product out the door can do strange things to your eyes and mind. You might look straight at the error, but still get the message that "everything looks just fine here." One way to find errors is to walk through your code while it's running, one line at a time: See the "Stepping Lightly" sidebar next for more information on intelligently walking through your code.

Stepping Lightly

When stepping though code, it's possible that you may lose your "place" in the program. Thanks to threading, many things are going on at once in a Java program, and a thread may have a shot at executing during the time you're stepping from one line to the next. In this case, you won't be able to see the source code or print variables for your method!

What you must do is return the debugger to your method, so you'll have access to your source and variables. To do so, you must first find out where you are:

```
> where
```

The `where` command displays a stack trace for the current thread. The frame of the stack you are currently in is displayed on the `jdb` command line in square brackets:

```
AWT-Callback-Win32[1]
```

In the above example, the current thread is AWT-Callback-Win32 and the frame is 1. However, if you're in a frame other than the one containing your method, you won't be able to do much of anything. In that case, you must use the `up` or `down` commands to ensure the `jdb` command line is at the same frame as the one containing your method. This process is shown in Figure 6-6.

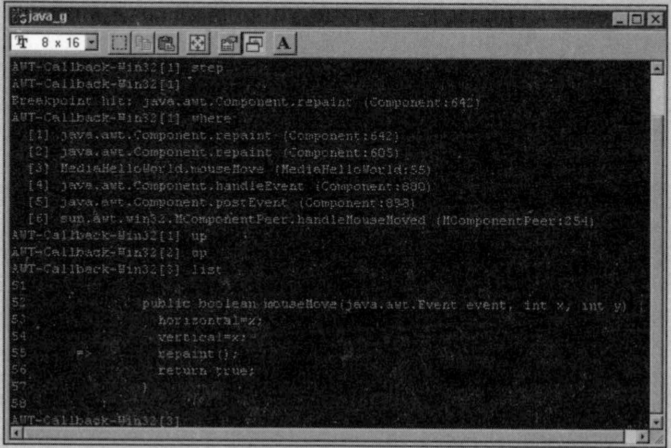

Figure 6-6: Use the `where` command, along with up and down, to ensure you are in the correct stack frame.

Single-step through the code

In this case, it's time to single-step through the two lines of code that assign values to the horizontal and vertical variables:

```
> step
> step
```

Of course, you can also set a breakpoint for the line following these two, and then issue the `cont` command. This is particularly useful when a number of lines must be executed, and you don't want to step though them one at a time:

```
> stop at MediaHelloWorld:55
> cont
```

Inspect the local variables

Now, inspect the local variables to see if x or y have magically changed. If they're in order, check to see if the assignment to your horizontal and vertical variables actually took place:

```
> locals
> print horizontal
> print vertical
```

A-ha! The x and y local variables are fine, but the assignment never took place. What's this? Have you mistakenly assigned x to both horizontal and vertical? Impossible! Rub your eyes again, if you like, but the results will look the same every time this method is invoked: you've found the bug! (See Figure 6-7.)

Figure 6-7: After stepping through the two lines of assignment code and inspecting the results, our bug becomes clearly visible.

Cleaning house

Having tracked down your first bug using jdb, you'll want to clear any remaining breakpoints and continue program execution before exiting altogether. Although you shouldn't have to bother, in theory, you'll be in for a rude surprise if you don't. About half the time I tried to exit the debugger without clearing each breakpoint and resuming program execution, it resulted in a crash. Save yourself the headache:

```
> clear                  (lists the current breakpoints)
> clear class:55
> clear class:53
> cont
> exit
```

Of course, once program execution has resumed, you can quit the applet by closing the Applet Viewer itself. Alternately, you can issue jdb's exit or quit commands to terminate the debugging session. But either way you do it, be sure to clear all breakpoints and resume program execution beforehand (see Figure 6-8).

Figure 6-8: Be sure to clear all breakpoints and continue program execution before exiting the debugger.

Debugging Tips and Warnings

In the course of working with the jdb debugger, there are a few words of caution I'd like to put forth. If the crashes that brought an untimely close to many of my debugging sessions don't plague you, you won't have to worry about taking these extra precautions. However, if you're having problems working with jdb, the following suggestions might be just the trick.

Disable sound and graphics

Whenever possible, comment out the line(s) of source code that play sound clips. Then do the same for code that displays images, and recompile. Unless playing audio or painting to the screen are integral to your debugging session, you're only making jdb's job more difficult than it needs to be.

For example, you didn't need to hear the audio snippet in the previous debugging session. By commenting out the lines of code that dealt with playing audio, you've taken a burden off the debugger and the runtime system. The same goes for painting graphics in many cases; if it's not directly related to the bug you're tracking down, comment it out!

Quit programs you don't need

Debugging is a delicate process, as you'll soon find out. There's no reason to have programs in the background sucking away much-needed resources, especially when it comes to memory. Quit every program you don't really need to have running; this will free up memory and the CPU for the debugger and your program.

Don't try to copy/paste in the DOS box

Windows users may be tempted to save time by not typing jdb commands, but using the Copy and Paste toolbar buttons supplied in the DOS box instead. After all, why type something when you can paste it in?

Don't try it.

Every time I paste a command into the debugger, the puppy seizes up, as if asked to recite poetry in public. Sometimes, but not always, pressing the Escape key followed by Enter brings it back to life.

The jdb supports the !! command, which takes some of the repetition out of typing commands (see Table 6-1). Although not as flexible as copy/paste, it won't lock up the debugger.

Clear breakpoints and resume program

You can exit a debugging session in one of two ways: issue the exit (or quit) command to jdb, or allow the program to terminate naturally (for applets, this means closing the Applet Viewer window). However you chose to exit the session, be sure to first clear all breakpoints and resume program execution using the cont command! (See Figure 6-8 earlier in this chapter.)

Even though it shouldn't make a bit of difference if breakpoints are set or the program is suspended, my computer has gone up in smoke on many occasions when exiting the debugger under such conditions. Clearing breakpoints and resuming program execution prior to an exit, however, seems to do the trick.

Making Applets Live on the Web

Once you've created an applet, the chances are pretty good that you'll want to make it available to the entire Web population. To do this, you must upload the various files that make up the applet to a Web site and test it, to make sure nothing breaks in the process.

Uploading applets to a Web site assumes you have the authority, and tools (such as an FTP tool), to do so. If the site to which you want to add the applet is maintained by someone other than yourself, you'll have to obtain permission and perhaps even get the access passwords, if you plan to upload the materials yourself. If you don't already have such authority, you'll have to arrange for it, or provide the applet and the various files it uses to someone who will eventually perform the upload.

Web server directory layout

If this is the first time Java is being used at a site, a directory structure will need to be created to hold your compiled Java classes and associated files (such as the audio and graphics files used in our latest version of `HelloWorld`). This is pretty straightforward because the directories you create on the Web will be similar to those you created locally.

Create a directory structure

First, you'll need to create a directory on the Web server to store your HTML file. For this example, why not use the same name as the directory on your local hard drive?

Although any name will do, I'll assume you use `HelloApplet`. Inside this directory you must create two additional directories: `images` and `audio`. These will hold the graphic and sound files your applet requires. Because the directory and filenames are hard-coded in our applet, we don't have the option of using any other names; the names you use on the Web must exactly match those used locally.

When a Java-savvy browser comes upon an HTML file containing an `<APPLET>` tag, it looks inside the same directory as the HTML file for the specified class file (`MediaHelloWorld.class` in this case), unless told to look elsewhere. If the browser finds the class file specified in the `<APPLET>` tag, it downloads that file onto the local computer and hands it off to the Java runtime environment for execution.

Note

Although it's possible to specify a different directory location for the class file by using an optional `<APPLET>` tag attribute (the `CODEBASE` attribute, illustrated in Chapter 7), for now we'll assume it's located in the same directory as the HTML file that calls for it.

Relative support

When executed, our MediaHelloWorld applet loads the image and audio files it requires. Because we've used the method `getCodeBase()` to reference these files, the browser looks for them relative to the `Applet` class file itself. That is, the browser looks inside the directory in which it found the compiled class for the two directories we specified in our applet, `images` and `audio`, expecting to find the files `world.gif` and `hello.au`. If available, each file is downloaded over the Internet and onto the user's local computer.

If we had used `getDocumentBase()` instead of `getCodeBase()` in each `getImage()` method, the browser would expect these files to be located relative to the HTML document, rather than relative to the class file. (See the sidebar "Getting to Base" earlier in this chapter.)

Because our `<APPLET>` tag doesn't specify a unique location for the class file, it is expected, by default, to be inside the same directory as the HTML file. As a result, it really doesn't matter if we use `getCodeBase()` or `getDocumentBase()`; the audio and graphic files our applet uses will be located relative to the HTML document in either case, unless we utilize the optional `CODEBASE <APPLET>` attribute to specify a different location for the class file (refer to Chapter 7 for an example).

Uploading the files

Once you've created the required directories, it's time to upload the various files that comprise our applet onto the Web server. You can do this easily using an FTP tool, although if you happen to administer your own Web server, you probably don't have to bother with FTP at all. In this case, simply move the files on your Web server by network or removable media (tape, floppy disk, and so on). Regardless of how you get the files to the Web server, make sure each is placed in its appropriate directory.

The HTML file should be located one directory level above the `audio` and `images` directories, along with the compiled MediaHelloWorld applet class files. Because our applet actually extends `HelloWorldApplet`, the compiled class file for `HelloWorldApplet` must also be uploaded into the same directory as the `MediaHelloWorld` class. In fact, you have to place every class file your applet uses, with the exception of those that come with the Java runtime environment (the `Applet` and `awt` classes, for instance), on the Web server in the same directory. If you don't, your applet won't be able to execute!

After the HTML and all applet classes have been uploaded to the Web server, upload the audio and graphic files into their appropriate directories. The `world.gif` file should be placed in the `images` directory, while `hello.au` must be located in the `audio` directory. For a graphical representation of where each file is located, see Figure 6-9.

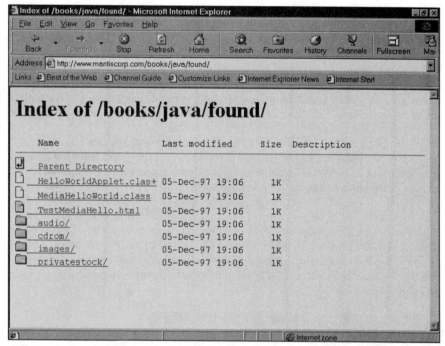

Figure 6-9: When uploading applets to the Web, be sure to use the same directory structure found on your local system.

When uploading files to your Web server, be sure their names remain intact. Many FTP programs impose the DOS filename restriction of eight characters for the name and only three characters for the extension, automatically chopping off the others! As a result, `MediaHelloWorld.class` might become `MediaHel.cla`.

If this happens, rename the files before terminating your FTP session. And don't forget to supply the proper mix of uppercase and lowercase characters (`MediaHelloWorld.class` is *not* the same as `mediahelloworld.class`!)

Testing the applet

When all the files have been uploaded into their appropriate directories, it's time to test the applet. Simply access the HTML file on the Web server with your Java-savvy browser by loading its URL. Or, if you prefer, do it with Applet Viewer. Applet Viewer can execute applets on the Web, as long as you provide a URL to the page like this:

```
appletviewer
http://www.mantiscorp.com/books/java/found/TestMediaHello.html
```

In the above example, Applet Viewer will connect to the Web page and execute any applets it finds. If a connection isn't already established to the Internet, it will attempt to establish one. Of course, Applet Viewer doesn't display anything but applets, so you won't see any HTML, as you would using a Java-savvy browser.

However, because Applet Viewer is fast and easy to use, I prefer to use it first. If the applet works as expected using Applet Viewer, I then test it with a Java-savvy browser, such as Netscape Navigator. But however you do it, be sure to test your applets once you've placed them on the Web.

If all goes well, you'll be greeted by the same "Hello World!" text string that appeared when the applet was executed locally. And, in a few moments (give or take a few more moments, depending on the speed of your connection), the image will be downloaded from the World Wide Web and also appear (see Figure 6-10). At about the same time, the sound track will finish downloading and begin to play.

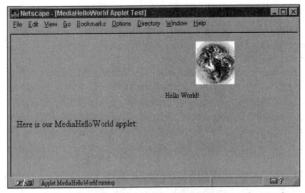

Figure 6-10: MediaHelloWorld, now living on the Web, is accessible to the world.

If it does, the world's your oyster! If it doesn't, consider some of the problems outlined in the sidebar "If Your Applet Fails to Load."

If Your Applet Fails to Load

If your applet fails to load, there are a few things to consider. First, make sure your files are all uploaded and in their proper directories. If the browser can't locate the compiled class specified in the HTML file, the applet will fail to execute. Also, if the image and sound files are missing or in the wrong place, the applet will fail to execute as it should. For instance, if the graphic file is in the wrong place or missing altogether, you won't see it. And if the audio file can't be found, you won't hear a background track at all.

If all the files are on the Web server and in their proper directories, check to see that each filename is spelled exactly as it is on your local hard drive. Because some FTP tools take the liberty of appending extensions to files during the upload process, or truncating long names, you may have to rename the file once it is on the Web. And be sure to check the case of each filename — a browser won't be able to find `MediaHelloWorld.class` if it appears on the Web site as `mediahelloworld.class`.

Also, make certain the files were successfully uploaded. Although a filename might appear on your Web server, that doesn't mean the entire file was successfully transferred. To be certain, compare the file sizes of each upload to those on your local machine. While it's normal for file sizes to be off by a few kilobytes either way, if the difference between your local and uploaded file sizes is significant, you'll have to try again. In this case, delete the file from the Web server and upload it from scratch.

Between each attempt to rectify an applet problem, it's a good idea to quit your browser and launch anew (or manually force the page containing your applet to reload from scratch). This way, you can be certain that the browser is loading a fresh copy of the applet instead of opening a cached copy from your hard disk.

Getting complex and flexible

The applet you have just created and deployed on the World Wide Web would be considered complex to software developers who don't program in Java. After all, it's an example of dynamic Web content featuring text, graphics, and audio. But as you know, the real complexity is taken care of by Java, allowing you to concentrate on the behavior of your applet without getting bogged down with the details of writing graphics and audio routines. Even the ability to locate and utilize resources such as image and audio files on the network is taken care of by the rich Java classes that have already been written for you, meaning you don't have to write a line of this code yourself. You simply import the classes you need from those there for the taking.

But what if you want your applet to be a bit more flexible than it would be if you hard-coded the names and locations of files? After all, to change the name or directory location of the audio or image file, you must actually change the code of the applet itself, recompile it, then upload the resulting class once again. Wouldn't it be nice if there was a mechanism for supplying your applet with information directly from the HTML document, such as specifying filenames and locations? Wouldn't this greatly increase the flexibility of your applets? That's exactly what the folks at Sun thought, and so they created the notion of "applet attributes." We'll explore these and application command-line parameters in the next chapter.

Odds 'n' Ends

Before we come to a close, a few areas deserve a bit more attention. Specifically, you should be aware of the this and super variables that are commonly found in Java programs. And, in addition, you should know the fundamental methods all applets support.

this and *super*

In order to allow convenient access to the current object and its superclass, Java provides two special variables: this (references the current object) and super (references the object's superclass). You can use these variables, discussed in detail in Chapter 14, anywhere in the body of a class.

You can also use this to invoke the current object's constructor, although typically you don't use it to invoke methods, because the method name alone will do the trick:

```
this([parameterList]); // invoke current object's constructor
this.methodName(); // functional equivalent to methodName();
Meanwhile, super is typically used to invoke a method or
constructor in the superclass:
super.methodName();  // invoke superclass method
super([parameterList]); // invoke superclass constructor
```

Fundamental applet methods

Every Java applet inherits five key methods from the applet class: init(), start(), stop(), paint(), and destroy(). These methods give applets the ability to respond to major events, such as when a Web page containing the applet is viewed or left by the user.

Following is the basic structure of an applet, including these five methods. Although the init() method must be overridden, the remaining four do not necessarily need to be. If your applet has no use for one of them, simply ignore it (that is, don't bother to override it). The applet structure looks like this:

```
public class AnyApplet extends java.applet.Applet {
```

```
. . .
public void init() { . . . }
public void start() { . . . }
public void stop() { . . . }
public void paint(Graphics g) { . . . }
public void destroy() { . . . }
. . .
}
```

Although you can probably guess what each of these methods should do if you choose to override them, Table 6-2 gives a brief explanation of each one.

Table 6-2 An Applet's Five Basic Methods	
Method	**Description**
init()	Override this method to initialize the applet each time it's loaded or reloaded. At the very least, this is where most applets call the resize() method to set the size of their canvas.
start()	Override this method to begin actual applet execution, as when the page containing the applet is loaded or reloaded by the user.
stop()	Override this method to terminate applet execution when the user leaves the Web page containing the applet or quits the browser.
paint (Graphics g)	Override this method if you wish to display text or images on the applet canvas. This method is called every time the applet's display needs to be drawn (in other words, when the applet first becomes visible to the user, when it's scrolled, or when the applet itself requests to be repainted).
destroy()	Override this method if you need to do a final clean-up in preparation for unloading.

As stated earlier, not every applet is obligated to override all five methods. The most simple applets, such as our original HelloWorld applet, need only implement init() and possibly paint(). However, most applets are more complex. Those that change their visual appearance, or interact with the user, for example, will likely override start() and stop() as well.

Such is the case with the MediaHelloWorld applet detailed in this chapter. A sound clip is played continuously once start() is executed and it stops playing when stop() is called. You'll notice, however, that we don't bother to override destroy(), as we do everything necessary to "clean up" in our stop() method, which is called before destroy(). Applets that must release resources they access upon executing, however, can rely on destroy() as a final step in bringing their applet to a successful close.

Summary

It is very simple to add images and soundtracks to Java applets. Once you've considered whether your applet should be enhanced or extended, it's merely a matter of implementing the code that will do the work. Compiling the code is easy — just as you saw in the previous chapter.

✦ If you plan to debug your Java programs, you'll have to recompile them with the -g option. This option ensures you'll be able to view local variables, something you won't want to be without in a debugging session.

✦ You can use the jdb tool (although I would strongly suggest investing in a professional development environment for the robust debugging tools alone) to debug your Java applications.

✦   ✦   ✦

Command-Line Arguments and Applet Tag Attributes

Until now, the Java programs we've written have been very inflexible. That is to say, the data these programs use is hard-coded and can't be changed, except by a programmer.

The original HelloWorld application will always output the words "Hello World!" to the screen, until the program has been altered by the programmer to say something else. And the MediaHelloWorld applet you created in the previous chapter will always use the same audio and image files until it is rewritten to use others. In both cases, the programs require fiddling around with the source code and must be recompiled before changes to the data they use can be put into effect.

Need for Flexibility

In some cases, this lack of flexibility may be exactly what you want. Perhaps there is a portion of the data your program uses that you want never to change unless the program itself is updated. Such is the case with copyright notices and developer credits, which remain constant throughout the life of a particular software version release.

However, more often than not, the data your programs use will change regularly.

In the case of an application, you may well want your program to act in a certain way, depending upon what input is provided by the user at the time of execution. For this, you have the option of using Java *command-line arguments*. With command-line arguments, you can specify any number of parameters to the application at the time it is executed.

If you're a C/C++ programmer with experience developing programs executed from the command line, the notion of command-line parameters will come as no surprise. If not, the following chapter will be of particular interest.

But how does this affect applets? These little devils live on the Web, and are downloaded into your computer by the browser. Why would you need to provide parameters to an applet, and how would you do such a thing, even if you wanted to?

To help answer these questions, consider for a moment the environment in which an applet exists on the Web. Think about the Web server, and why applets have become so popular. Until Java came along, the Web was a very static environment that, for the most part, merely connected people to information. Thanks to Java, our Web sites can now support executable content: Distributed multimedia and true interaction with the user are a reality. Web pages have become dynamic, alive.

But why have flexible applets?

From a practical standpoint, the answer lies in the Web server. Unless the directory structure of your Web site never changes, and the files your applet relies on are always in the same place, applet flexibility is a tremendous advantage when it comes to maintaining a site. Most Web sites grow continually, with new content being added on a regular basis. If the data files your applet requires are hard-coded, as ours have been, maintaining a Web site becomes a nightmare.

If you think of the Web server as a giant, universally accessible hard drive, it may help drive home the point that you're more likely than not to be reorganizing files and directories regularly. How many times have you moved files and directories around on your local hard drive to keep it organized? This will eventually become necessary on your Web server, if it isn't already. And if you have to update source code, recompile it, and then upload the result for each applet at your site merely to reflect changes in the server directory layout, you'll certainly appreciate the ability to pass parameters to applets.

Couple ease of maintenance with an ability to create very robust applets that can be customized without touching the applet or applet source code, and you have extremely compelling reasons to build flexible applets. And, thanks to *applet attributes*, your applets can be as flexible as you choose.

Let's take a look at how command-line arguments are handled by Java applications, and then move on to applets and the use of applet attributes. Of course, most of you will have only passing interest in developing applications. Creating applets is by far the most popular use of Java, and so you may be tempted to jump ahead to the section covering applet attributes. If this is the case, I suggest that you at least skim through the first section regarding application command-line arguments and then give special attention to the section on String objects. Regardless of whether you develop Java applications or applets, you'll be dealing with the String class.

Java Command-Line Arguments

Java command-line arguments are arguments that are passed to a Java application when it is invoked from the command line. If you created the HelloWorld application discussed in Chapter 5, you're already familiar with executing Java applications at the command line:

```
c:\> java HelloWorld
```

Here, no command-line arguments are passed to the HelloWorld application. And for good reason: HelloWorld, as we wrote it, doesn't know what to do with command-line arguments. If we provided them, nothing would happen.

Although you are free to pass any number of command-line arguments to a Java application, it's up to the application to make use of them. If an application hasn't been written to handle command-line arguments, it will execute as it normally would and ignore the arguments altogether.

Supporting command-line arguments

So, how do you write a Java program capable of handling command-line arguments? If you're a C/C++ programmer, you probably have a pretty good idea. If not, don't worry; supporting command-line arguments is easy. All arguments are passed to your application through an array of strings in the main() method. You simply take them out of the array, and do with them as you wish. This is the signature of a typical main() method in Java:

```
public static void main (String args[]) { ... }
```

Programmers who have worked with C/C++ command-line arguments are already familiar with the concept of receiving parameters through the main() function. In Java, however, there are a few differences in how the commands are passed to an application that affect how they are processed.

In Java, executable routines such as main() are known as *methods*. In C, such routines are referred to as *functions* or *procedures*. And, just to confuse you, in C++, they are referred to as *member functions* as well as *methods*.

Java command-line arguments versus C/C++

Command-line arguments in Java differ from their C and C++ counterparts in two major ways: number and type. C/C++ uses two variables to pass arguments to applications; Java uses only one, and the data type of the variable containing the parameters is not the same.

Number of argument variables

With C and C++, the operating system passes command-line arguments directly to the program using two *argument variables*:

✦ `argc`: the number of arguments appearing on the command line

✦ `argv`: a pointer to an array of strings containing the arguments

In Java, only one argument variable is used:

✦ `args`: an array of strings that contain the command-line arguments

Since the variable used to store command-line arguments in Java is an array of `String` objects, there is no need for a second variable to hold the number of arguments. By simply referencing the `length` instance variable of the array, you can find the number of command-line arguments:

```
args.length; /* get number of command-line arguments */
```

Because each element in the `args` array is a command-line argument, the length of the array is equal to the total number of command-line arguments the user provided when executing the application. By referencing the number of elements in the array, as shown above, your Java applications will know exactly how many command-line arguments were provided when executed. This eliminates the need for a second variable to keep track of how many command-line arguments were provided.

Argument variable type

In addition to eliminating the need for a variable to hold the number of command-line arguments passed to your application, Java differs from C and C++ in the data type used to hold these arguments. In C/C++, this variable is a *pointer* to an array of strings. In Java, it's simply an array of `String` objects; you don't have to dereference a pointer and then deal with an array to get to the arguments.

In Java, you deal directly with the array. To access a command-line argument, you only need to access a particular element in the `args` array. Suppose, for instance, that you wanted to get the third command-line argument provided by the user. Since all array indexing begins with 0 (zero; just as with C/C++), this would do the trick:

```
String theArg;  /* variable to hold argument */
theArg = args[2]; /* retrieve third argument */
```

If you're already comfortable using C or C++, this approach makes plenty of sense. If not, you're probably wondering why in the world we're using an index of 2 in order to retrieve the third value in the array! While it may be confusing at first, once you commit this indexing convention to memory (or carve it in your mousepad), you'll have no problem dealing with this "off by one" situation.

In C, C++, and Java, the individual elements in an array are accessed by supplying an index, or *subscript*, to the element in its position in that array. In the example above, we've provided a subscript of 2 in an attempt to retrieve the third element, or member, of the `args` array. Because array indexing begins with 0 in these programming languages (and not 1, as you might expect), we need to subtract 1 from our subscript value before attempting to use it. Since we want item 3 in the array, we come up with a subscript value of 2. Perhaps the following will help you commit this to memory:

```
String theArg;    /* variable to hold argument */
theArg = args[0]; /* retrieve first argument */
theArg = args[1]; /* retrieve second argument */
theArg = args[2]; /* retrieve third argument */
theArg = args[3]; /* retrieve fourth argument */
theArg = args[4]; /* retrieve fifth argument */
```

Note

In this example, I assume at least five elements are in the array. If there were fewer than five elements, this code would be attempting to access an element that does not exist. In this case, our subscript would be out of the legal range and would cause the runtime system to throw an `ArrayIndexOutOfBoundsException` exception. See the discussion on applets later in this chapter for details on exceptions, or refer to Chapter 10, "Language Fundamentals."

It's considered bad programming style to use explicit numbers as subscripts to arrays (as we've been doing), so array elements are usually accessed with an integer index variable. Keep in mind that the index variable must be one less than the element you wish to retrieve. To keep confusion to a minimum, it's a good idea to initialize this variable to zero (0) and use the following "off by one" method when changing its value:

```
String  theArg; /* variable to hold argument */
int  i=0; /* index variable, initialized to zero */

theArg = args[i]; /* retrieve first argument */
i = 5 - 1; /* prepare index to retrieve 5th element in array
*/
theArg = args[i]; /* retrieve fifth argument */
```

Although subtracting 1 from the value of the index you want to access (five in this case) might seem like extra work, doing so will help you become comfortable with the idea that the array subscript is always one less than the element you want to retrieve. After using this "off by one" method for a while, you'll have no need for it: The technique will become second nature. If you want to access the fifth element in an array, you'll automatically use an array subscript of 4.

Tip

It may help to mentally repeat "off by one" to yourself every time you think of arrays. But be warned: While this method will almost certainly guarantee that you subtract 1 from your subscript values, it may have disastrous consequences in your personal life. Without getting into such details, let's just say you'll come up one short in just about everything you do. Shopping, paying bills, and having children will never be the same again.

Argument variable contents

Aside from the number of variables and their data type, yet another difference exists between Java and C/C++ command-line argument variables: the contents of the argument array. In C and C++, the command-line argument array variable contains the name of the program that is executed, in addition to the command-line arguments:

```
c:\> HelloWorld howdy doodie
```

In this C/C++ example, the array variable would contain all three strings on the command line: `HelloWorld`, `howdy`, and `doodie`. In Java, this array consists only of command-line arguments:

```
c:\> java HelloWorld howdy doodie
```

Upon execution, only `howdy` and `doodie` would be in the `args` array. Only the actual command-line arguments would be passed to your program by the runtime system. There is no need for your program to receive the name of the application, since it's always the same as the name of the class where the `main()` method is defined. In this example, `main()` would have been defined in class `HelloWorld`.

Java strings are first-class objects

As you now know, all elements in a Java command-line argument array are strings. Perhaps you've noticed that the word *string* often begins with a capital S when we talk about Java, yet also appears in lowercase from time to time and whenever we're talking about the C and C++ languages. Why is this?

Java strings are defined in the `String` class; when we instantiate and use them, we're dealing with `String` objects. Anytime we're talking about the `String` class or `String` objects, the S is capitalized. If we're just talking about strings in general, without any specific reference to the class or object, the S is in lowercase. But when it comes to C and C++, there are no built-in `String` classes or objects. Here, we're always dealing with the generic concept of strings, not a formal class or object that is identified by an uppercase S.

In C/C++, a string is nothing more than an array of null-terminated characters. As a result, C/C++ strings don't have well-defined behavior or mechanisms for manipulating them. A common problem with C/C++ strings is that it's very easy to overrun their array boundaries.

Since no error-checking is performed with C/C++ strings, there is no way to be certain if the subscript you provide is out of range. Suppose you were dealing with a C string 15 characters in length, but forgot that array indexing begins at zero. By accessing an element in the array using a subscript value of 15, you'd actually be attempting to access the sixteenth element. But you might not realize it, since it's possible in C/C++ to reference any location in memory! A value would be returned, and you might go merrily along your way none the wiser.

Now, suppose you later tried to change the value you had just referenced. In that case, you'd be hip-deep in trouble. You're not changing the string, as you think, but altering some unknown memory location by mistake. You would be lucky to get out alive, and your program runs the risk of crashing. When reading and writing to data in such a situation, you're dealing with garbage values at best and running the risk of corrupting your data. But with Java, this won't happen.

Java strings behave predictably

With Java strings, you're dealing with first-class objects that have a number of methods created specifically for retrieving and setting data. To prevent problems like the one I just described from sneaking up on the unsuspecting programmer, bounds-checking is performed at compile and run time.

If you explicitly exceed the value of an array directly in your code, the compiler will catch the mistake and let you know. If the index can't be checked at that time, as is often the case, the runtime environment will catch any out-of-range values. Unlike C/C++, you'll know immediately where the problem is and have an opportunity to fix it.

With C/C++, you make a small sacrifice to the beta-test gods and pray each night to the software testing cycle that any such errors are caught before the product ships. Okay, to be fair, there are tools that help find these problems during the development stage, but you have to use them. With Java, it's all taken care of within the environment itself.

Java provides two classes for dealing with strings: String and StringBuffer. String is used for strings that will not change, while StringBuffer is a class for dealing with strings that may be changed. Since we don't alter the command-line arguments in our applications, this chapter focuses on the String class. For details on both String and StringBuffer, refer to Chapter 12.

Note   You should also note that both the `String` and `StringBuffer` classes are part of the `java.lang` package. A package is a group of related classes. For details on packages, refer to Chapter 11.

Java Command-Line Argument Conventions

The Java language adheres to UNIX conventions for command-line arguments, defining three different types:

✦ Word arguments

✦ Arguments that require arguments

✦ Flags

You should be sure to adhere to the conventions listed in the next three sections when dealing with command-line arguments.

Word arguments

Word arguments, such as -verbose, must be specified precisely on the command line. As a result, -ver would not be valid if you wanted to invoke the -verbose option: only -verbose would work!

Typically, your program will test to see if a particular word argument has been specified, and set a flag accordingly:

```
if (argument.equals("-verbose")){
  verbose = true;  // turn the verbose flag (verb) "on"
}
```

In this case, we've tested for the -verbose word argument and set the verb flag accordingly.

Arguments that require arguments

In many cases, you'll want to use arguments that are followed by some type of information (that is, more than just the argument itself is necessary). You might, for example, want to use a command-line argument such as -file to redirect output of the program into a file. The -file option alone, however, isn't enough. A filename must also be supplied.

In this case, you need to read in the filename following the -file argument. That is, you must parse the command line to retrieve the additional information:

```
if (argument.equals("-file")) {
  if (nextarg < args.length)
    filename = args[nextarg++]; // set the "filename" variable
  else
    System.err.println("-file must be followed by a filename!");
}
```

In this example, we test to see whether the user actually supplied an argument following -file. If so, it's retrieved and assigned to a variable. If not, a message is output to the user telling him or her how to use this argument.

Flags

Single-character codes used to modify the behavior of a program are known as *flags*. You might, for example, want to supply a help option in your program. In this case, you would use the -? flag. Of course, you could also implement a -help word argument. In fact, you might want to use both.

Typically, flags can be specified separately and in any order. For example, either -?, -z, or -z -? work just fine. In addition, flags can typically be concatenated and specified in any order. Thus -z? and -?z are also hunky-dory.

Other conventions

In addition to the conventions described in the three previous sections, there are a few others that you should be aware of when developing Java applications:

✦ You can assume the user will precede all options, flags, or series of flags with the dash character (-).

✦ The names of files your program will use (operate on) are typically the last argument on the command line.

✦ Your application should output a usage statement whenever a command-line argument can't be recognized; it should have the following form:

```
usage: application_name [ optional_args ] required_args
```

Using Command-Line Arguments in the HelloWorld Application

Now that you are comfortable with the concept of command-line arguments, it's time to put what you've learned to good use. We'll start by enhancing HelloWorld to accept and process the most basic command-line argument, and then walk through a generic command-line parser that you can customize for your own specific purposes.

Enhancing the HelloWorld application

When it comes to enhancing our existing HelloWorld application, there really isn't much to work with. The program was only a few lines of Java code that output "Hello World!" when executed. Since there isn't a lot of code to integrate with support for command-line arguments, this will seem like a major overhaul. But, in reality, we're only adding very rudimentary command-line argument support for the moment.

As always, we'll choose a new name for our program, since it's a very different program than the one we created several chapters ago. The real reason we're adding support for command-line arguments (aside from the pulse-pounding adrenaline rush) is to make our program more flexible by being able to process information supplied by the user at the time of execution. For this reason, we'll call our new program FlexibleHelloWorld (see Listing 7-1).

Listing 7-1: **FlexibleHelloWorld.java source code**

```
/**
 * FlexibleHelloWorld.java
 *
 * "Flexible" HelloWorld application. Uses command-line
 * arguments as part of the standard "Hello" output to user.
 *
 * @author Aaron E. Walsh
 * @version 1.0, 17 Jan 98
 */

class FlexibleHelloWorld {

  public static void main (String args[]) {
    int argCount, i=0;
    String theArg;
```

```
argCount =  args.length;
System.out.println("Total number of arguments: " +
  argCount);

while (i < argCount) {
  theArg =  args[i];
  i = i+1;
  System.out.print(i + ":" + theArg );
  System.out.println("...Hello " + theArg + "!");
}
}
}
```

Note

Did you notice that the name of the class, `FlexibleHelloWorld`, isn't exactly the same as the name of the file it is saved in? This is because we didn't specify the class as being a public class. If we had, the name of the source code file would have to be the same as the public class it contains. In this case, the source code file would be named `FlexibleHelloWorld.java` to reflect the public `FlexibleHelloWorld` class it defines. However, since the class isn't public, the file name can be anything we'd like. For details on public classes, see Chapter 11.

By this point, you should be comfortable with the process of creating and compiling a new Java program. Assuming you've entered the source code exactly as it appears in Listing 7-1, it will compile without a problem. With that done, let's step through the code that you may not be familiar with. That is, the code dealing with command-line arguments:

```
public static void main (String args[]) {..}
```

Although you've seen the `main()` method signature several times before, now you're seeing it with new eyes. In particular, the `args` parameter stands out. And for good reason: It's the array that contains all command-line arguments received by our program. It's easy to see that we're dealing with an array, and not just one string, thanks to the brackets (`[]`) that appear immediately after the variable name.

Following this method signature (which happens to be the only method in the program) are the variables our program uses when processing the arguments:

```
int argCount, i=0;
String theArg;
```

The first two variables, argCount and i, are integers. You'll notice that i is initialized to zero, while argCount isn't initialized at all. The i variable is used as a subscript for accessing elements in the args array, and so I've taken the liberty of initializing it to the index value for the first element. This technique was described earlier, and ensures we begin accessing array elements at the very beginning. By initializing it here, we don't have to worry about setting its value later.

We don't have to bother initializing argCount, however, since the first line of code sets this variable equal to the total number of elements in the array:

```
argCount =  args.length;
```

Here, we've used the array instance variable length to determine how many command-line arguments were passed into our application. We then output this value to the screen with the following line:

```
System.out.println("Total number of arguments: " + argCount);
```

The last portion of code is a while loop, in which each argument in the args array is retrieved in succession and output along with its position in the array:

```
while (i < argCount) {
   theArg =  args[i];
   i = i+1;
   System.out.print(i + ":" + theArg );
   System.out.println("...Hello " + theArg + "!");
}
```

Executing with command-line arguments

When executed, this program outputs the number of command-line arguments supplied at the time of execution and then drops into the while loop. Once in the loop, each element in the args array at index value i is retrieved and output, as shown in Figure 7-1.

The four lines of code inside the loop were chosen to illustrate the "off by one" problem discussed earlier. Experienced programmers would likely have written the loop with only two lines of code in the body:

```
while (i < argCount) {
   theArg =  args[i++];
   System.out.println(i + ":" + theArg + "...Hello " +
      theArg + "!");
}
```

This loop is functionally the same as our original one, yet takes half as many lines of code. You'll notice in both cases that our array subscript, i, is increased by one inside the body of the loop. Of particular interest is where this increment takes place: after the array element has been retrieved, yet before it is output to the screen. This is due to the "off by one" situation we've been dealing with all along.

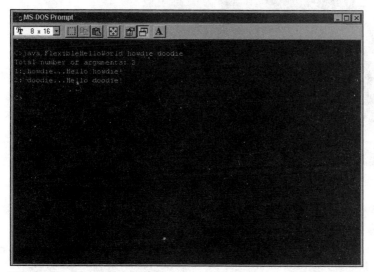

Figure 7-1: When in the while loop, each element in the args array is retrieved and output.

Coming into the loop for the first time, our subscript i is 0 (zero). Using an index value of 0 ensures that we retrieve the first element in the array. However, we want to tell the user that we've received the first command-line argument, not the zero item! So, we bump up the index value by one before using it, to tell the user what argument we've processed.

In doing so, we've dealt with the "off by one" situation, while also incrementing the index to ensure that the next element in the array is retrieved as we repeat the loop. If we incremented the index after the output statement, as shown in the following code snippet, we'd be off by one (see Figure 7-2):

```
while (i < argCount) {
   theArg =  args[i];
   System.out.print(i + ":" + theArg );
   System.out.println("...Hello " + theArg + "!");
   i = i+1; /* RESULTS IN THE ABOVE OUTPUT BEING OFF BY ONE! */
}
```

Figure 7-2: By incrementing our counter after the print statements, our output appears "off by one," even though it is correct: The user would prefer to see the numbering begin at one, not zero.

However, we could have incremented the index inside the conditional portion of the `while` statement, as long as we subtracted one from it when retrieving elements in the array:

```
while (i++ < argCount) {
   theArg =  args[i-1];
   System.out.print(i + ":" + theArg );
   System.out.println("...Hello " + theArg + "!");
}
```

Many programmers prefer this style of code; it's very clear, going into the loop, where the index is incremented and by how much. And, since there is only one line of code that accesses the array, we don't have to spend much mental energy keeping track of what's going on.

But suppose we forgot to subtract one from the index in that line of code? Thanks to Java's runtime bounds-checking facilities, you'd know the first time the program was executed. In this case, the runtime system throws an `ArrayIndexOutOfBoundsException` exception, as shown in Figure 7-3.

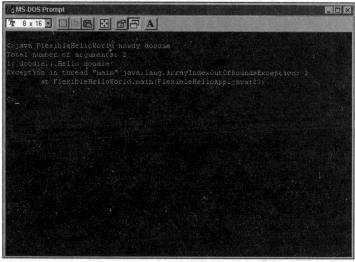

Figure 7-3: The runtime system throws an ArrayIndexOutOfBoundsException exception if the index in the code is out of the legal range.

Spaces and quotations

In each of the preceding examples, we've supplied two command-line arguments: howdy and doodie. I stuck to these two arguments throughout the examples in order to make the output in each case consistent and easy to follow. However, any number of arguments could have been provided. Since the system interprets the space character as a separator for command-line arguments, we can feed our program as many arguments as we'd like, as long as each is separated by a space.

But what if you need to supply a space as part of the argument itself? In this case, you would need to use quotation marks on the command line. Any text surrounded by quotation marks is treated as a single argument, as illustrated in Figure 7-4.

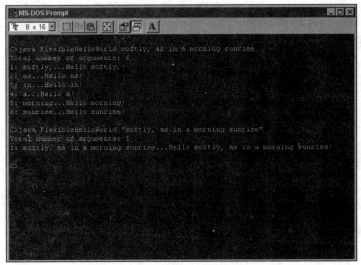

Figure 7-4: Text surrounded by quotation marks is treated as a single argument.

Parsing arguments

Our FlexibleHelloWorld application is an extremely simple program. It accepts command-line arguments and outputs them in the order they were supplied. Sure, it also outputs the total number of arguments supplied, and uses the arguments as part of the `Hello` output, but as far as real functionality goes, the program is just about worthless.

Many programs that accept command-line arguments do so to allow the user a degree of control over some aspect of execution. Such is the case with UNIX and DOS utility programs. Take, for instance, the utility program that displays files in a directory. In DOS, the `dir` program is used, while UNIX users rely on `ls`. In both cases, the user can supply command-line arguments along with the program that affect the way in which files are listed.

Since a number of different arguments can be provided, the program must somehow find out which one(s) the user is supplying. To complicate matters, these arguments can be supplied in any order. Because it's entirely up to the program to figure out which commands were used and act accordingly, the program must parse the command line.

To help you parse command-line arguments in your own Java applications, you can use a generic command-line parser (see Listing 7-2) as the basis for your own work. This skeleton program accepts command-line arguments of each type: a word argument (`-verbose`), an argument that requires an argument (`-out`, which must be followed by the name of a file to be used for output), and several flags (?, x, y, and z). In addition, this program requires a file name (an input file). If the program is invoked without the proper arguments, a usage statement is output in accordance with command-line argument conventions. (See the "Other conventions" section earlier in this chapter.)

**Listing 7-2: ParseSkeleton .java, a generic command-line\
argument parser**

```
/*
A generic command-line argument parser. (you must first
understand Java strings, arrays, and loops before this code
will make complete sense).
*/
class ParseSkeleton {

    public static void main(String args[]) {

        String command = ""; /* to hold each command-line argument
as
                              they are processed */
        boolean verbose = false; // initialize verbose flag to
false
        boolean xFlag= true, yFlag= true, zFlag = true; /* a few
                                flags, initialized to false
*/
        String outputfile = ""; /* variable to recieve -out
                             argument's argument */
        int i = 0; // a little variable to control our while
loop...

        /* -- Parse all command-line arguments via a while loop --
*/
        while (i < args.length && args[i].startsWith("-")) {
          command = args[i++];

          /* --- Parse Word Arguments --- */
          if (command.equals("-verbose")) {
              verbose = true;
          }

          /* --- Parse Arguments That Require Arguments --- */
          else  if (command.equals("-out")) {
              if (i < args.length) {
                outputfile = args[i++];
              } else {
                System.err.println("The -out argument must be
followed
```

(continued)

Listing 7-2 *(continued)*

```
                    by an output file name!");
        }
    }

    /* --- Parse Flags --- */
    else {
        char flag; // a temporary variable to process flags
        for (int loop = 1; loop < command.length(); loop++) {
            flag = command.charAt(loop);
            switch (flag) {
                case '?':
System.out.println(" --------- HELP --------
  -");
System.out.println("Help? You want help? Try calling 911...");
System.out.println("Ring...");
System.out.println("        Ring...");
System.out.println("                Ring...");
System.out.println("Sorry, all operators are taking a coffee
  break. Try again
  later.");
System.out.println(" ------------------- ");
break;
case 'x':
xFlag = true;
if (verbose) System.out.println("The x option has been
  specified.");
break;
case 'y':
yFlag = true;
if (verbose) System.out.println("The y option has been
  specified.");
break;
case 'z':
zFlag = true;
if (verbose) System.out.println("The z option has been
  specified.");
break;
default:
System.err.println(flag + " is not a valid option!");
break;
                }
            }
        }
    }

/* -- The final verdict? -- */
if (i == args.length) {
System.err.println("Usage: ParseSkeleton  [-verbose] [-?xyz]
  [-out outputFile] inputFile");
}
else if (verbose) {
```

```
System.out.println("Input file = " + args[i++]);
System.out.println("Output file = " + outputfile);
      }
   }
}
```

The following is the usage statement for the program:

```
Usage: ParseSkeleton   [-verbose] [-?xyz] [-out outputFile]
      inputFile
```

Although the arguments inside brackets ([ ]) are optional, the filename argument is required. If you don't include a filename argument when executing this program, the usage statement will be displayed. Figure 7-5 shows this output, in addition to the output produced when the program is executed properly.

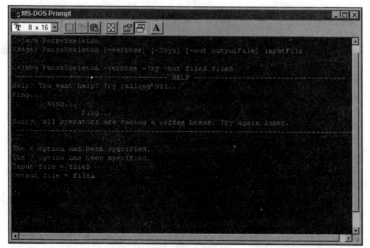

Figure 7-5: ParseSkeleton is executed initially without command-line arguments and then again with several arguments specified on the command line.

The ParseSkeleton.java program makes use of the Array, String, and System classes. If you find this code difficult to understand, you might consider turning ahead to Chapter 12 and Chapter 13 for detailed information on these classes before attempting to integrate this program with your own.

Applet Attributes

Now that you're comfortable with receiving and processing command-line arguments within Java applications, chances are your attention wants to turn to the applet. After all, most of you will be dealing with applets, and many may never bother with applications beyond what we cover in this book. But how is information passed to an applet?

While it's pretty obvious that command-line arguments are supplied on the command line at the time of execution, an applet is downloaded from the Web and passed to the Java runtime environment for execution. At first glance, there doesn't seem to be a mechanism for supplying applets with user-defined information, as there is with applications. But there is, and it's an elegant one: applet attributes.

What are applet attributes?

Applet attributes are specified in the `<APPLET>` HTML tag, and provide information that either the browser, the Java runtime system, or the applet itself will use to execute properly. The `HEIGHT` and `WIDTH` items specified in all the HTML documents we've created so far are actually applet attributes, just as the name of the class file we specify for `CODE` is:

```
<APPLET CODE="MediaHelloWorld.class" WIDTH=200 HEIGHT=150>
```

At a minimum, these three attributes must be included in the `<APPLET>` tag. They are required, whereas the majority of applet attributes are optional.

Tip   The identifiers used to specify applet tags (such as `CODE`, `HEIGHT`, and `WIDTH`) are not case-sensitive. They can be in uppercase, lowercase, or a mixture of both. For the sake of readability, however, it's a good idea to use uppercase. The values you provide for these attributes, such as `MediaHelloWorld.class` in the above example, are another matter. Be certain to use the proper case: `MediaHelloWorld.class` is not the same as `MEDIAHELLOWORLD.CLASS`!

The following code illustrates the basic structure of the `<APPLET>` tag:

```
<APPLET standard-attributes>
applet-parameters
alternate-context
</APPLET>
```

Until now, we've only specified standard applet attributes. And of these standard attributes, we've only used the three that are required: `CODE`, `HEIGHT`, and `WIDTH`.

There are a number of optional applet attributes. Although they are optional, they are still considered part of the standard suite. Table 7-1 details all required attributes, while Table 7-2 describes the optional ones.

<table>
<tr><td colspan="2" align="center">**Table 7-1**
Required Applet Attributes</td></tr>
<tr><td>*Attribute*</td><td>*Description*</td></tr>
<tr><td>CODE</td><td>Specifies the name of the class file (applet), which must be a subclass of <code>java.awt.Applet</code>.</td></tr>
<tr><td>WIDTH</td><td>Specifies the initial width of your applet in pixels.</td></tr>
<tr><td>HEIGHT</td><td>Specifies the initial height of your applet in pixels.</td></tr>
</table>

To use an optional attribute, you simply include its name and an associated value within the ⟨APPLET⟩ start tag. The start tag begins with ⟨APPLET and ends with a closing angle bracket (⟩). You can supply optional attributes after the required ones, as long as they are inside the closing angle bracket:

```
<APPLET CODE="MediaHelloWorld.class" WIDTH=200 HEIGHT=150
    ALIGN=top>
```

<table>
<tr><td colspan="2" align="center">**Table 7-2**
Optional Applet Attributes</td></tr>
<tr><td>*Attribute*</td><td>*Description*</td></tr>
<tr><td>ALIGN</td><td>Specifies where your applet is placed on the page in respect to the text around it. It can have one of the following nine alignments: <code>left</code>, <code>right</code>, <code>top</code>, <code>texttop</code>, <code>middle</code>, <code>absmiddle</code>, <code>baseline</code>, <code>bottom</code>, and <code>absbottom</code>.</td></tr>
<tr><td>ALT</td><td>Specifies alternate text to be displayed by text-only browsers.</td></tr>
<tr><td>CODEBASE</td><td>Specifies the base URL for your applet. The applet itself must be located relative to this URL. If CODEBASE isn't specified, the URL of the HTML document in which the applet is embedded is used.</td></tr>
<tr><td>HSPACE</td><td>Specifies the horizontal space surrounding your applet. The value you specify for HSPACE is used only when the ALIGN attribute is set to <code>left</code> or <code>right</code>.</td></tr>
<tr><td>NAME</td><td>Specifies the symbolic name of your applet, allowing other applets embedded in the same page to locate your applet by name.</td></tr>
</table>

(continued)

	Table 7-2 *(continued)*

Attribute	Description
VSPACE	Specifies the vertical space surrounding your applet. The value you specify for VSPACE is used only when the ALIGN attribute is set to left or right.
ARCHIVE	Specifies one or more archives (for example, JAR files) that will be pre-loaded. Classes are loaded using an instance of the AppletClassLoader with the CODEBASE specified. JAR files are discussed in more detail in Chapter 15, "Weaving Applets into Web Pages."
OBJECT	Specifies the name of a class that contains a serialized version of an applet. When a serialized applet is loaded, its init() method is not invoked, but its start() method will be. An applet must have either the OBJECT or CODE attribute specified.

Note

Although Applet Viewer will resize itself in response to an applet invoking the resize() method, not all browsers will do so. Netscape Navigator, for example, sets the size of an applet to the values specified in HTML by the WIDTH and HEIGHT attributes and ignores calls to resize() altogether!

As a result, you shouldn't rely on the resize() method to work as you'd expect. Instead, rely on the WIDTH and HEIGHT attributes that are required in all <APPLET> tags.

Here, we've added the optional ALIGN attribute, specifying a value of top. When the browser loads this applet, the top of it will be aligned to the surrounding text (see Figure 7-6). Had we specified bottom, the bottom of applet would have been aligned to the surrounding text, as shown in Figure 7-7.

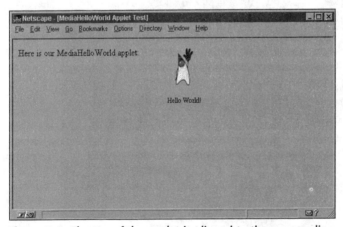

Figure 7-6: The top of the applet is aligned to the surrounding text, using the ALIGN attribute and specifying a value of *top*.

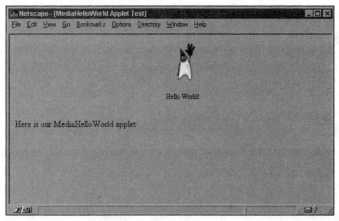

Figure 7-7: The bottom of the applet is aligned to the surrounding text by specifying a value of *bottom*.

It's worth noting that the start tag can extend over several lines, even though we've managed to cram it onto a single line. As long as the opening and closing angle brackets are present, the start tag can span as many lines as needed:

```
<APPLET CODE="MediaHelloWorld.class"
WIDTH=200
HEIGHT=150
ALIGN=top>
```

Attributes can appear in any order, although it's a good idea to place the required three immediately following the word APPLET.

The following is functionally equivalent to the start tag above, but more difficult to read because you expect the required attributes to appear first and in a certain order:

```
<APPLET
ALIGN=top WIDTH=200
CODE="MediaHelloWorld.class"
HEIGHT=150>
```

You might have noticed that I didn't include the </APPLET> end tag in these examples. It is certainly required! I omitted it simply so we could focus exclusively on the start tag. Without it, the browser would consider everything following the start tag to the end of your HTML document as part of the <APPLET> body. An example of proper usage follows:

```
<APPLET CODE="MediaHelloWorld.class"
WIDTH=200
HEIGHT=150
ALIGN=top>
</APPLET>
```

Similarity to command-line arguments

Applet attributes are similar in nature to command-line arguments in that they provide an easy way to allocate the applet with information. However, the standard suite of attributes won't allow you to pass special information to your applet for processing. It merely allows you to set the various attributes needed by the browser or Java runtime system to execute your applet.

Take, for instance, the CODE attribute. Your applet doesn't do anything with it, or with any other standard attribute for that matter. CODE simply tells the browser what file to download and hand off to the runtime system; it means nothing to your applet.

In this sense, you can think of standard attributes as special settings that the browser and runtime system use to execute your applet according to your specifications. And while it's true that methods do exist that allow your applet to retrieve the values for some of these attributes (such as getCodeBase(), which returns the base URL for your applet), you can't use any of the standard attributes to pass special information to your applet.

If your applet is to be flexible—able to receive and process input—there must be a mechanism for passing information to it. Thankfully, there is.

Applet "parameter" attributes

In order to pass information to your applet, such as the URL of a file on the Web or a text string to display when executed, you'll need to use an attribute designed for just such a purpose. Specifically, you'll have to use an *applet parameter attribute*, more commonly known simply as an *applet parameter*.

Applet parameters follow the <APPLET> start tag, yet come before the </APPLET> end tag. They appear as a pair of name and value attributes inside a <PARAM> tag:

```
<PARAM NAME=hello VALUE="Hello World!">
```

In this example, the parameter called hello is specified as having the value "Hello World!". In order to retrieve this value from within an applet, we must use the getParameter() method defined in the Applet class:

```
String  helloStr = getParameter ("hello");
```

Here, we've declared a String variable, helloStr, into which we've received the value of the hello parameter. After this line of code is executed, helloStr will contain the string "Hello World!". Of course, we could have just as easily declared the variable on one line and retrieved the parameter on another:

```
String  helloStr; /* declare the variable first */
helloStr = getParameter ("hello"); /* and then get the
parameter */
```

Functionally, these two approaches are equivalent. Yet in both cases, we're assuming an applet parameter specifying a value for hello exists in the HTML document. We're expecting something like this:

```
<APPLET CODE="MediaHelloWorld.class" WIDTH=90 HEIGHT=50
ALIGN=top>
<PARAM NAME=hello VALUE="Hello World!">
</APPLET>
```

This HTML code clearly specifies a hello parameter with the value of "Hello World!". But what if the second line of code didn't exist? What if you forgot to include it when creating the HTML document, yet included the code in your applet to retrieve a hello parameter. In this case, your helloStr variable would be set to null, since the getParameter() method would fail to find the hello parameter and return null instead of a valid string.

It's a good idea to test for null values when processing applet parameters and act accordingly. In some cases, such as with the code I'll present here, you may provide default values to allow your applet to continue executing where it would otherwise fail to run properly.

As with the identifiers used to specify attributes (CODE, HEIGHT, WIDTH, PARAM NAME, VALUE, and so on), you can use either uppercase or lowercase letters when associating a value with the PARAM NAME. As you can see, I've supplied the word *hello* in all lowercase characters. I could just as easily have used all capital letters (*HELLO*), or a combination of both (*Hello*).

Since the getParameter() method isn't case-sensitive, it really doesn't matter how we name an applet parameter. The Java code getParameter("hello") will find and return the value associated with hello, HELLO, or even Hello. However, to make your HTML code easier to read, it's a good idea to use uppercase letters for the attribute identifiers (CODE, HEIGHT, and so on) and lowercase for the actual parameter (such as hello in our example).

Be extremely cautious when entering the attributes of your applet tag! Specifically, make sure when you enclose items that you only use one set of quote marks. For example, the following is fine:

```
<PARAM NAME=hello VALUE="Howdy">
```

While this is not:

```
<PARAM NAME=hello VALUE=" Howdy"">
```

Warning

The parameter value in this code, Howdy, has an extra closing quote. No big deal, right? Wrong! The current version of Applet Viewer will just wait around forever for another closing quote, even if you didn't bother to write a corresponding getParameter() method. Other browsers may crash as well, or simply be unable to parse the HTML correctly. Picky, picky . . .

All applet parameters are strings

Because the getParameter() method always returns a String object, all applet parameters—even numeric parameters—come to you in the form of a string. This is extremely important to realize, since you must first convert the string to an actual number if you want to use it as such!

Suppose, for instance, that you want to specify an applet parameter that controls how often a while loop is executed. Your HTML parameter tag might look like this:

```
<PARAM NAME=loop VALUE=5>
```

This is just fine. However, the Java source code that you might be tempted to write to retrieve this parameter might look like this:

```
int  loop = getParameter ("loop");
```

At first, this might look fine as well. But it's not. Since the getParameter() method returns a string, not an int, the compiler will choke when it gets to this line of code and generate a "type mismatch" error.

In order to properly retrieve this value, you must receive the parameter as a string and then convert it into an int. There are two ways you can do this:

```
String loopString = getParameter("loop");
int loop = Integer.valueOf(loopString).intValue();
```

The first line retrieves the loop parameter in string form, as it should. The second line makes use of the Integer class, a special class known as a *type wrapper*.

In Java, numbers (int, long, float, and double data types) are not actually objects. Since most of the Java utility classes require objects, such numbers must somehow be converted into objects before they can be used. A direct conversion, or *cast*, isn't possible. As a result, we "wrap" the number inside an object using type wrapper classes. (For details on wrapper classes, see Chapter 12.)

In the second line of this code, we've used the Integer class to convert loopString into an Integer object. We then invoke the intValue() method, which returns the value of this Integer as an int. It may seem a bit complicated, but it's necessary.

Note

The `valueOf()` method requires a valid string, one that can be used to create an `Integer` object initialized to an `int` value. If the string it receives can't be treated as an `int`, an exception—`NumberFormatException`—is thrown. For details on exceptions, see Chapter 10, "Language Fundamentals".

As an alternative, we could have used the `parseInt()` method without having to explicitly create a new `Integer` object:

```
String loopString = getParameter("loop");
int loop = Integer.parseInt(loopString);
```

Assuming `loopString` represents an integer, `parseInt()` will return the value of that integer. If the `String` object passed to `parseInt()` can't be treated as an `int`, the method will throw an exception, just as `valueOf()` would.

When specifying an integer parameter in your HTML file, you either surround the value in quotes, as you would a string, or leave the quotes off, as we did earlier. As far as your applet is concerned, the following two lines of HTML code are functionally the same:

```
<PARAM NAME=loop VALUE=5>
<PARAM NAME=loop VALUE="5">
```

Alternate applet context

Now that you're familiar with applet attributes and parameters, we come to the part of the `<APPLET>` tag known as the *alternate applet context*. This allows you to include any type of HTML code between the last applet parameter and the `</APPLET>` end tag. It is displayed by browsers that are not Java-savvy, and won't be visible to users viewing the document with a browser that is capable of dealing with Java applets.

Alternate applet context can contain any type of HTML code you wish, such as text or tags, or both. This is an example of text-only applet context:

```
<APPLET CODE="MediaHelloWorld.class" WIDTH=90 HEIGHT=50
    ALIGN=top>
<PARAM NAME=hello VALUE="Hello World!">
...This page requires a Java-savvy browser: GET ONE!
</APPLET>
```

The line immediately preceding the `</APPLET>` end tag will appear as standard HTML text to a browser that doesn't support Java, as shown in Figure 7-8.

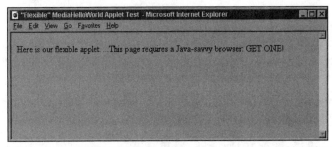

Figure 7-8: Alternate applet context can contain any type of HTML code you wish; it will appear as standard HTML would.

You're free to include any type of HTML code to be used as alternate applet context. In the next piece of code, I've added a simple hypertext link that will bring users to Sun's Java home page when they click the words "GET ONE!":

```
<APPLET CODE="MediaHelloWorld.class" WIDTH=90 HEIGHT=50
    ALIGN=top>
<PARAM NAME=hello VALUE="Hello World!">
...This page requires a Java-savvy browser:
<A HREF="http://www.javasoft.com">GET ONE!</A>
</APPLET>
```

Of course, you're not limited to text. You could just as easily display a graphic using the <IMG> tag, or a combination of both text and graphics. What you provide as alternate applet context depends on how you want your page to look to users who don't use a Java-savvy browser.

Tip

In most cases it's a good idea to include alternate applet context when creating your HTML pages, even if it's nothing more than a "You need a Java browser to see this page!" message. If you don't, those users who view your pages using a browser that doesn't support Java will have no idea that they are missing out on something.

Using Applet Attributes in MediaHelloWorld

Now that we're comfortable with applet attributes, especially the special-purpose PARAM attribute, it's time to create a flexible version of the MediaHelloWorld applet created in Chapter 6. While there are many ways to customize an application, we'll extend MediaHelloWorld by allowing it to receive input through parameter attributes.

The source code in Listing 7-3 adds great flexibility beyond the MediaHelloWorld applet it subclasses. For this reason, we'll call this new program FlexibleMediaHello. Unlike its predecessor, FlexibleMediaHello does not rely on hard-coded filenames when it comes to displaying a graphic image and playing a background sound track, since these may be supplied as applet parameters. If these parameters are omitted from the HTML file in which our applet is embedded, FlexibleMediaHello uses defaults that are defined in the program itself.

Listing 7-3: **FlexibleMediaHello.java source code**

```java
/**
 * FlexibleMediaHello.java
 *
 * "Flexible" extension of the HelloWorld applet.
 * Displays "Hello World!" string in applet canvas while a
 * background audio track plays and an image follows the mouse
 * around.
 * "Flexible" due to the ability to accept <PARAM> applet
 * attributes specified within the <APPLET> tag, allowing URLs to
 * audio and image files to be used in the HTML document that
 * references this applet.
 *
 * @author Aaron E. Walsh
 * @version 1.0, 17 Jan 98
 */

import java.applet.*;
import java.awt.*;
import java.net.URL;
import java.net.MalformedURLException;

public class FlexibleMediaHello extends HelloWorldApplet {

  String  helloString;
  Image   myImage;
  AudioClip  myAudio;
  int  horizontal, vertical;
  boolean  SoundOn = true;

  public void init() {

    /* GET THE APPLET PARAMETERS: */
    helloString = getParameter ("hello");
    String  imageString = getParameter ("image");
    String  audioString = getParameter ("sound");

    /* GET FILES USING PARAMETERS: */
    if (imageString==null) {
      myImage=getImage(getCodeBase(), "images/world.gif");
    }
    else {
      URL imageURL=null;
      try {
        imageURL = new URL(imageString);
      }catch (MalformedURLException e) { ; }
    myImage=getImage(imageURL);
    }

    if (audioString==null) {
      myAudio=getAudioClip(getCodeBase(), "audio/hello.au");
```

(continued)

Listing 7-3 *(continued)*

```
    }
    else {
      URL audioURL=null;
      try {
        audioURL= new URL(audioString);
      }catch (MalformedURLException e) { ; }
      myAudio=getAudioClip(audioURL);
    }
}


public void paint(Graphics g) {

    if (myImage != null) {
      g.drawImage(myImage, horizontal, vertical, this);
    }

    if (helloString==null) {
      super.paint(g);
    } else {
      g.drawString(helloString,50,100);
    }
}
public void start() {
    myAudio.loop();
}

public void stop() {
    myAudio.stop();
}

public boolean mouseDown(java.awt.Event event, int x, int y) {
    if (SoundOn) {
      myAudio.loop();
      SoundOn = false;
    }
    else {
      myAudio.stop();
      SoundOn = true;
    }
    return true;
}

public boolean mouseMove(java.awt.Event event, int x, int y) {
    horizontal=x;
    vertical=y;
    repaint();
    return true;
}
}
```

Note

Unlike our FlexibleHelloWorld application, we've defined the applet version of this program to be public. More precisely, the class declaration of the applet shown in Listing 7-3, FlexibleMediaHello, has been declared public. As a result, the file containing the source code for this program must have the same name: `FlexibleMediaHello.java`. (For details on public classes, see Chapter 11.) In addition, FlexibleMediaHello is no longer hard-coded to output "Hello World!" in the `paint()` method; it will display whatever text is associated with the `hello` parameter supplied in the `<APPLET>` tag. If this parameter is omitted, it calls upon its superclass, `MediaHelloWorld`, to perform the `paint()` operation. Because `MediaHelloWorld` calls upon its own superclass when `paint()` is invoked, the `paint()` method we created in our original HelloWorldApplet program is used! As a result, "Hello World!" will be output to the screen (see Figure 7-9).

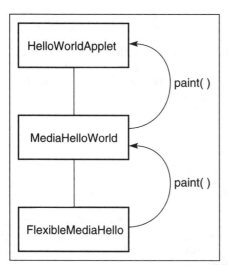

Figure 7-9: Using the *super* keyword, our program can now invoke the paint() method of its superclass, which itself invokes the paint() method of its own superclass!

At this point, the source code for FlexibleMediaHello should make sense to you. It may be a little more complex than what we've dealt with so far, but there are only two elements that should cause you to raise an eyebrow: uniform resource locators (URLs) and exceptions.

URLs and exceptions

Our original HelloWorldApplet program used a sound and image file, both located relative to the applet itself. We have since augmented the program to make it more flexible (see Listing 7-3); it now has the ability to retrieve these files, as specified by a URL. To provide our applet with this capability, we imported the class that deals with URLs:

```
import java.net.URL;
```

However, to allow our program to form a URL from a `String` object, we also had to handle exceptions that might arise in the process. Although exceptions are discussed in detail in Chapter 10, for now you can think of them as general-purpose error handling mechanisms. In order to deal with the possible exceptions that might occur when creating URLs, we included the following `import` statement:

```
import java.net.MalformedURLException;
```

Both of these classes could have been included in your program using one line:

```
import java.net.*
```

The asterisk is treated as a wild card, meaning all classes in the network package will be available to your program, instead of any specific one.

Understanding the code

The most significant changes to our original code are in the `init()` method. It is here that we retrieve and process the applet parameters that our program now supports: `hello`, `image`, and `sound`. This code shows you how these parameters might be specified:

```
<PARAM NAME=hello VALUE="Hickory, dickory, doc.">
<PARAM NAME=image
VALUE="http://www.anywhere.com/images/picasso.gif">
<PARAM NAME=sound

VALUE="http://www.anywhere.com/audio/milesdavis.au"">
```

Due to security restrictions imposed by Java, applets can only load URLs that point to resources located on the host on which the applet itself resides. As a result, the URLs I've just specified are only valid when the FlexibleMediaHello applet is executed from Mantis Development Corp.'s Web site. This means that any Web page that references this applet must either reside on this host, or use the `CODEBASE` applet attribute to point to it. For more details on the `CODEBASE` applet attribute, refer to Chapter 15.

The changes to the `init()` method are substantial, although easy to understand if you walk through them step by step. The first three lines of code do nothing more than load the applet parameters:

```
helloString = getParameter ("hello");
String  imageString = getParameter ("image");
String  audioString = getParameter ("sound");
```

The first line sets the variable `helloString` equal to the value associated with the `hello` applet parameter specified in our HTML file. Unlike the next two lines, which declare the variables `imageString` and `audioString` on the same line as their assignment statements, the `helloString` variable is declared outside the scope of `init()`.

As such, it is available to all methods in the class, not just `init()`. Since we only need `imageString` and `audioString` long enough to create a URL object from each, we declared these variables on the spot. Thanks to Java's automatic garbage collection, the memory associated with these variables is released once the `init()` method has executed.

Most programmers are accustomed to declaring all variables before the first line of executable code. In C, the compiler would choke because the executable line of code `helloString = getParameter ("hello");` appears before the string variables are declared. With Java (and C++) you can declare a variable where it is needed, just as we have done.

Once we've retrieved the parameters, they are processed. We begin with the `image` parameter, using the `imageString` variable that now contains the value associated with this parameter:

```
if (imageString==null) {
    myImage=getImage(getCodeBase(), "images/world.gif");
}
else {
  URL imageURL=null;
  try {
     imageURL = new URL(imageString);
  }catch (MalformedURLException e) { ; }
myImage=getImage(imageURL);
}
```

First, we check to see if the HTML document did indeed specify an `image` parameter. If the parameter isn't specified, `imageString` will be null. In this case, we use the same line of code found in `MediaHelloWorld` as a default.

If an `image` parameter was specified in the HTML document, we attempt to build a URL from it. First, we declare a URL variable, and set it to null:

```
URL  imageURL=null;
```

Once the variable exists, we use a special *try-catch* clause to form what is known as an *exception handler*. We "try" to form the URL, and if the operation fails we "catch" the error:

```
try {
  imageURL = new URL(imageString);
}catch (MalformedURLException e) { ; }
```

However, you'll notice that we don't actually do anything if an error occurs. Rather than add complexity to the code, we ignore it entirely. This is intentional, since we'll deal with exceptions in Chapter 10. For this chapter, you need only know that any error-handling code would appear in the braces, where now only a semicolon exists.

Regardless of the outcome from our exception handler, we next attempt to load the image from the resulting URL:

```
myImage=getImage(imageURL);
```

In an actual production environment, you'd handle any exceptions and ensure the URL was valid before attempting to use it. For details on how this is done, refer to Chapter 10. At the moment, we're not concerned with making this applet bullet-proof; we're mainly concerned with processing parameters.

Note

You may have noticed that our code contains two versions of the getImage() and getAudioClip() methods. In procedural programming languages such as C, the compiler wouldn't permit two versions of the same function to exist. Yet in Java and C++ it is not only possible but is a vital part of the language: Methods in a class can share the same name as long as the parameter list is different. This is a feature known as *overloading*, which is supported by most object-oriented programming languages.

After processing the image parameter, we process the sound parameter, following the same steps. When our init() method is complete, we've retrieved all three parameters and processed two of them. With that done, the remaining code is nearly identical to that of our original HelloWorldApplet program. The only place where the code differs is in the paint() method:

```
public void paint(Graphics g) {
if (myImage != null) {
    g.drawImage(myImage, horizontal, vertical, this);
    }

  if (helloString==null) {
    super.paint(g);
  }
  else {
    g.drawString(helloString,50,100);
  }
}
```

Here, we draw the image at the horizontal and vertical coordinates set in our mouseMove() method, just as we did in HelloWorldApplet. However, we also test helloString to determine if a hello applet parameter was supplied in our HTML document. If this parameter was omitted, our helloString is null. In this case, we invoke the paint() method of FlexibleMediaHello's superclass. If not, we output the value supplied with the hello parameter.

Writing the HTML document

The next piece of code supplies all the applet parameters in the HTML document. FlexibleMediaHello will use each one during execution. You should keep in mind, however, that applets are only able to access files residing on the same Web site from which they come. This security restriction, discussed in Chapter 15, means the following HTML example will work only when the applet itself resides on the Mantis Development Corp.'s Web server or on your local computer. Of course, you're free to change the image and sound URLs to point to files on your own server.

When an applet doesn't reside on the Web, however, it's treated as a "trusted" program. As a result, your Web browser isn't as paranoid: Local applets are allowed to access files residing on the Web without concern for what server these files are coming from. This means you'll be able to hear and see the files the following HTML document points to, if it and the applet are located on your hard drive (or CD-ROM, as the case may be):

```
<HTML>
<HEAD>
<TITLE> "Flexible" MediaHelloWorld Applet Test </TITLE>
</HEAD>
<BODY>

Here is our flexible applet:

<APPLET CODE="FlexibleMediaHello.class"
WIDTH=200 HEIGHT=150
ALIGN=top>
<PARAM NAME=hello VALUE="Hello! How are you?">
<PARAM NAME=image
VALUE="http://www.mantiscorp.com/images/mdchomebutton.gif">
<PARAM NAME=sound
VALUE="http://www.mantiscorp.com/java/classes/audio/welcomeIntr
o.au">
...This page requires a Java-savvy browser:
<A HREF="http://www.javasoft.com">GET ONE!</A>
</APPLET>
</BODY>
</HTML>
```

This use of applet parameters is illustrated in Figure 7-10. If the sound and image files pointed to by the URL exist on the same host as the applet itself, they are utilized.

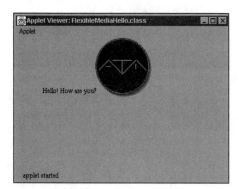

Figure 7-10: FlexibleMediaHello, no longer bound to hard-coded values, displaying an image pulled off the Web

The CODEBASE Attribute Saves Time

Using the CODEBASE attribute, HTML documents can utilize applets residing anywhere on the Web. Suppose, for example, that the following CODEBASE attribute were included in the HTML file:

```
CODEBASE="http://www.mantiscorp.com/java/applets/FlexibleMediaHel
    lo/"
```

In this case, the applet specified by the CODE attribute would be coming from the Mantis Development Corp.'s Web server. As a result, the files pointed to by the image and sound URLs would also have to be located on this server.

Also note that, even though the image and sound files appear to be loaded in our init() method, this isn't the case. Only when the image is first drawn is it downloaded to the user's computer, and the sound file isn't downloaded until it's first played. This saves time and processing power in the event that you reference an audio or graphics file that isn't used. Why bother downloading a file if it isn't actually used?

Applets that make use of parameters are tightly coupled to the HTML file in which the parameters are supplied. As a result, you must consider the HTML file as you design your program. You must consider not only the parameters that your applet will use, but what each should be named and how they should be organized.

Applet usage guide

Some applets require a great number of parameters to be specified in the HTML document, making it a chore to recall which parameter does what. It's a good idea to provide a usage guide with your applets that specifies how the parameters are to be used. In this guide, you should group similar parameters. This will reduce any confusion that may result when someone else attempts to configure an HTML document that references your applet. Following is a sample usage guide for FlexibleMediaHello:

```
<APPLET CODE="FlexibleMediaHello.class" WIDTH=200 HEIGHT=150>
<PARAM NAME=hello VALUE="Hello! How are you?">
<PARAM NAME=image
    VALUE="http://www.mantiscorp.com/images/earth.gif">
<PARAM NAME=sound
    VALUE="http://www.mantiscorp.com/audio/welcome.au">
...This page requires a Java-savvy browser:
<A HREF="http://www.javasoft.com">GET ONE!</A>
</APPLET>
```

FlexibleMediaHello is a simple applet that takes three parameters:

✦ hello: A string that is output as text on the Web page. The default for this parameter is "Hello World!".

✦ image: A URL pointing to a GIF or JPEG graphics file that will follow the mouse cursor around as it's moved in the applet. The default for this parameter is not a URL, but a GIF file named world.gif, which is assumed to be located in an images directory relative to the applet itself.

✦ sound: A URL pointing to a AU format sound file that will play continuously once the applet is loaded. The default for this parameter is not a URL, but an .*au* file named hello.au, which is assumed to be located in an audio directory relative to the applet itself.

If one of these three parameters is omitted, the defaults are used. The HTML file shown next omits all three parameters, relying on the default values our applet provides for each:

```
<HTML>
<HEAD>
<TITLE> "Flexible" MediaHelloWorld Applet Test </TITLE>
</HEAD>
<BODY>
```

Here is our flexible applet:

```
<APPLET CODE="FlexibleMediaHello.class" WIDTH=200 HEIGHT=150>
...This page requires a Java-savvy browser:
<A HREF="http://www.javasoft.com">GET ONE!</A>
</APPLET>
</BODY>
</HTML>
```

Summary

With Java, we can write two very different types of programs: applications and applets. In this chapter you learned how to prepare you Java applications and applets for the ever changing world out there. Things to remember when writing dynamic applications and applets include:

✦ Java command-line arguments are arguments that are passed to a Java application when it is invoked from the command line.

✦ Where applications are stand-alone programs that reside in and are executed on a local environment, applets live on the Web and are downloaded by a Java-savvy browser before they are executed.

✦ By necessity, and due to their very nature, applications and applets are further distinguished by the manner in which you can pass information to each prior to execution.

✦ Applications accept arguments on the command line, much like C/C++ programs, while applets accept special attributes supplied in the `<APPLET>` HTML tag. By taking advantage of these mechanisms, we're able to develop robust, powerful, and fully customizable Java programs.

✦   ✦   ✦

Surfing the Web for Java Source Code

✦   ✦   ✦   ✦

In This Chapter

Finding cool Java
applets — ready to
use in your own
applications — on
the Web

Surfing up some cool
Java development
resources on the Web

Using Internet search
engines to find Java
applets

Making sure you
give the proper credit
for code you've
borrowed

✦   ✦   ✦   ✦

Although the CD-ROM included with this book contains a hefty number of applets and their source code, including those supplied with the original and current Java Development Kit (JDK 1.02 and JDK 1.1.5), you'll probably want even more. Perhaps you need an example not provided with the JDK, want to see how a particular feature is coded, or are simply interested in the latest Java developments. Whatever the case, you'll be happy to know that a great deal of Java source code is available directly on the World Wide Web.

A surprising number of Java developers have made their source code public on the Web, providing a large repository of Java code that's there for the taking. More often than not, the source code is provided as a link on the applet page itself, so you can see the applet in action and download the source code then and there if you need it. In fact, Java programming has become so popular that several sites have been established as a resource for developers looking for code.

Table 8-1 lists a few places to visit when looking for Java source code. These Web-based Java developer resources are broken up into three main categories:

- ✦ Code repositories
- ✦ Support areas
- ✦ Electronic magazines

Although most sites provide some degree of coverage in all three categories, they are strongest in the category listed in the table.

Table 8-1
Java Developer Resources

Name	Category	Address (URL)	Description
Mantis Java Links	Code repository	`http://www.mantiscorp.com/java/`	A master page providing Java links to all sites mentioned in this book and up-to-date links and source code for each applet provided on the CD-ROM with this book (and many that weren't available at press time). Includes links to source code repositories and other Java resources on the Web beyond those listed here.
Gamelan	Code repository	`http://www.gamelan.com/`	A comprehensive Java applet and source code repository. It includes the ability to search for specific files at the site.
JARS	Code repository	`http://www.jars.com/`	A code repository with a twist: a rating system! Here you'll find links to top-rated applets, as rated by a large panel of judges.
Sun's Java Site	Support area	`http://www.javasoft.com/`	This is Sun Microsystems' official Java site. It includes Sun's latest Java tools, documentation, and source code examples.
Java Language Newsgroup	Support area	`news:comp.lang.java`	The "official" Java language newsgroup. Here you'll find answers to Java problems of all levels, source snippets, links to Java sites, and heated debates about the Java language.
Digital Espresso	Support area	`http://www.mentorsoft.com/DE/`	A well-organized summary of the Java Language Newsgroup (`news:comp.lang.java`). If you don't want to wade through the sometimes overwhelming newsgroup, this is the place to visit.
Java FAQ Archives	Support area	`http://www-net.com/java/faq/`	Do you have a question about Java? Chances are, you'll find the answer in one of the many Java-specific frequently asked questions (FAQ) documents archived here.
IDG's *JavaWorld*	Electronic magazine	`http://www.Javaworld.com/`	A Web-based magazine dedicated to to Java development.

Table 8-2 suggests a number of search engines you might use if you can't find the code you need on the sites listed in Table 8-1. Although the majority of search engines are more or less the same, in that they index pages on the World Wide Web, many have areas dedicated to Java. One of the engines, Alta Vista, allows you to do an actual search by class name for applets embedded into Web pages (see "Alta Vista" later in this chapter).

Between the online Java resources and the large number of search engines to choose from, you could spend the better part of your waking hours trolling through the thousands of Java links out there. Whatever your needs, you're likely to find the source code you're looking for and much, much more along the way.

Fire up your browser and dig in!

Table 8-2 World Wide Web Search Engines	
Engine Name	Web Address (URL)
SEARCH.COM	http://www.search.com/
Lycos	http://www.lycos.com/
WebCrawler	http://webcrawler.com/
Internet Search	http://home.netscape.com/home/internet-search.html
InfoSeek	http://www.infoseek.com/
Yahoo!	http://www.yahoo.com/
World Wide Web Worm	http://www.cs.colorado.edu/home/mcbryan/WWWW.html
Alta Vista	http://www.altavista.digital.com/
DejaNews	http://www.dejanews.com/

Java Developer Resources

With Java-powered pages spreading like wildfire—thanks to hundreds of thousands of Java developers scattered around the world—the demand for comprehensive developer support has gone through the roof. In response to this need, a number of sites dedicated to assisting Java developers have emerged.

Although it's difficult to pigeonhole these sites, they can, more or less, be distinguished by the resource(s) they provide. Three significant categories become apparent: code repositories, support areas, and electronic magazines. These aren't hard-and-fast categories, however, since many of the sites you can visit feature a bit of all three!

Depending on what you're looking for, you'll find yourself visiting certain sites more than others. For example, if you're looking for source code, hit the code repositories first. If you're looking for support resources, such as tools, newsgroups, or FAQs, hit the support areas first. If you want instructional resources in the form of articles and tutorials, hit the electronic magazines first. If your first shot draws a blank, visit the others in that category. If you still don't find what you're looking for, try resources listed in another category. Eventually you'll find what you're looking for.

Just because you're looking for source code, for instance, is no reason to ignore the support areas. You'll find that most support areas also provide some amount of source code, and vice versa. Likewise, the source code you're looking for may wind up being discussed in detail in an online article in one of the electronic magazines. It's hard to know exactly where the information you're looking for will surface, but starting in the category that best matches your needs is a wise move.

Depending on your needs, you may find yourself hitting sites in all three categories during your quest for Java. If these fail to produce what you're looking for, you can always turn to the search engines. Personally, we tend to use search engines as a last resort, and only after making the rounds of my tried-and-true Java sites. Since what we're looking for is usually located at one or more of the sites listed in Table 8-1, we usually turn to the search engines only after coming up empty-handed.

Tip
For fast access to these sites, add them to your browser bookmarks (also called *hotlinks* or *favorites*). If you don't want to bother keeping track of the links—some of these addresses may change over time—or if you would like a current list of the best resources as they emerge, bookmark the Mantis Java Links site (`http://www.mantiscorp.com/java/`). Here you'll find all of the links mentioned in this book, including developer resources and search engines, updated regularly and categorized for easy access.

Code repositories

If you're looking to get your hands on a specific piece of source code, either to plug into what you're doing or to learn how to do something in particular in Java, a code repository is the first place to hit.

Mantis Java Links

The code repository established for this book, Mantis Java Links, is a repository in the purest sense of the word (see Figure 8-1). Here the applets and their source code physically reside on one Web server and are maintained by a team of Webmasters dedicated to this site alone. The applets and source code you'll find here are an extension of those found on the CD-ROM that accompanied this book; you can think of this site as a Web-based "upgrade" to the CD-ROM. Not only are all the applets found on the CD-ROM at this site, many more have been added.

Figure 8-1: You can think of the Mantis Java Links code repository as a Web-based upgrade to this book's CD-ROM.

As a self-contained code repository, all Mantis Java Links applets and source code reside on the Mantis Development Corporation server. Because they're located and managed at a single site, these links are not dependent on external resources. This is a controlled approach to maintaining a code repository, since you don't have to click a hyperlink and jump to the applet author's site to view the applet or retrieve the source code. As a result, the authors of the applet are free to rearrange their Web pages (or entire site!) without fear of "breaking" the Mantis Java Links site. Since external links are not provided, applet authors don't have to worry about maintaining the applet once it has been placed in this repository.

Gamelan

Gamelan is perhaps the best known, most used, and most comprehensive code repository on the Web, and it is a favorite among Java developers. Rather than maintaining applets and source code on its own Web server, Gamelan provides links to external pages maintained by the applets' authors. Although this might not sound like a "true" repository, in the traditional sense of being a single storage area, it really is. If you think of the Web as being a seamless network of storage devices, a repository is any site that maintains links to resources that span the network.

And maintain links it does! Gamelan offers links to hundreds of applets and source code (see Figure 8-2). But it doesn't stop there; Gamelan is a place where Java developers can register themselves as resources. Later, when someone searches for a particular piece of code using Gamelan's private search engine, the author's profile is made available along with any matching applets.

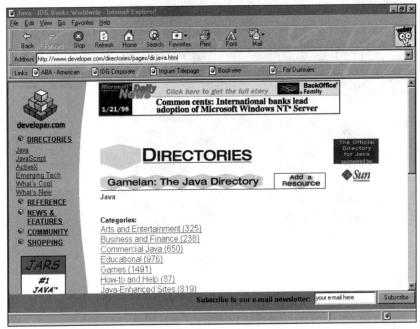

Figure 8-2: Gamelan is the mother of all code repositories.

Gamelan is also a wonderful place to find anything related to Java, not just source code. You'll find links to applets, source code, electronic magazines, developers, newsgroups, support areas, and everything else having to do with Java. In addition to being a wonderfully rich storehouse of Java-related links, Gamelan has categorized its contents nicely, allowing developers to browse for code according to functionality rather than forcing them to rely on the search engine provided.

Java Applet Rating Service (JARS)

Where Gamelan is a code repository of impressive proportions, the Java Applet Rating System (JARS) intentionally pares down its offering by rating the applets it references. Although JARS provides hyperlinks to external Java-powered pages, it ranks the applets in these pages according to the average score it receives by a large panel of judges. When you look at the "JARS Top 1%" list of applets, you know you're dealing with the cream of the crop (see Figure 8-3).

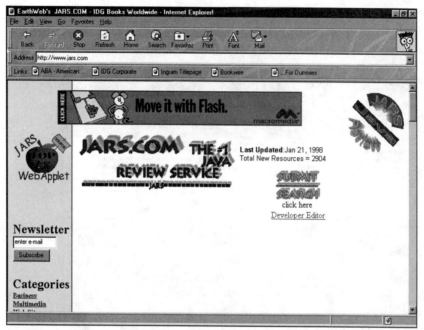

Figure 8-3: JARS applets are ranked by a large panel of judges using a "best of breed" approach to categorizing the applets.

Support areas

Support areas, unlike code repositories, attempt to provide you with the tools and information you'll need as a developer. They may also provide source code, but that's not their focus. Instead, you're more likely to find Java development tools, documentation, technical support, frequently asked questions (FAQ), and other information that is extremely valuable to programmers.

The most obvious Java support area is Sun's own Java site, JavaSoft. This is the official home of Java, available at `http://java.sun.com/`. Here you'll find all supported versions of the Java Developer's Kit, extensive documentation, frequently asked questions, source code samples, and links to other Java resources.

Another area of support is the Java newsgroups. There are now a number of Java-language newsgroups, including these:

comp.lang.java.advocacy	comp.lang.java.announce
comp.lang.java.api	comp.lang.java.misc
comp.lang.java.programmer	comp.lang.java.security
comp.lang.java.setup	comp.lang.java.tech

Here you'll not only find tons of questions and answers running the gamut of Java issues, but you'll also find links to source code and other Java resources (see Figure 8-4).

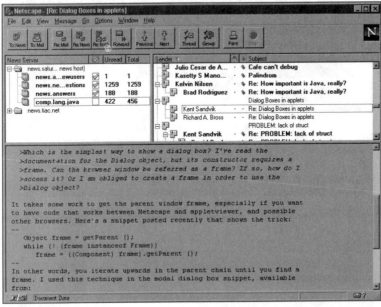

Figure 8-4: The Java newsgroups are chock-full of text-based conversations between Java developers; these messages often contain source-code snippets and links to other Java resources.

They're great places to visit if you're having a problem and need help, or have a useful nugget of Java code in which you think others might be interested.

Unfortunately, the Java newsgroups have become so popular recently that they're regularly flooded with scores of new questions every day, most of which go unanswered. As a result, you'll spend a lot of time wading through messages to find the piece of information for which you're looking. In the process, you can learn a lot about Java, but it can be frustrating if you're pressed for time.

Worse, a lot of tripe finds its way into the discussions. Since they are not monitored (led in a general direction), discussions that contribute little or nothing to the Java programming community often surface. If you have the time, it can be a real hoot to follow the messages and flames that abound on these newsgroups, and pick up some real Java gems along the way. If you don't have much time, or aren't in the mood to explore, you'll probably just find yourself knee-deep in Java drivel.

If you need to find the answer to a question that you think might have been posted to a Java newsgroup, but don't have the time or patience to filter through all the messages, take heart: Digital Espresso comes to the rescue. Digital Espresso is a standard Web site, not a newsgroup, that distills the best of the Java language newsgroups into a well-organized set of pages, as shown in Figure 8-5. This is especially nice if you don't have a newsgroup reader or access to a newsgroup server. Fire up your ol' Web browser and take a sip of Digital Espresso. It's just the thing for frazzled nerves.

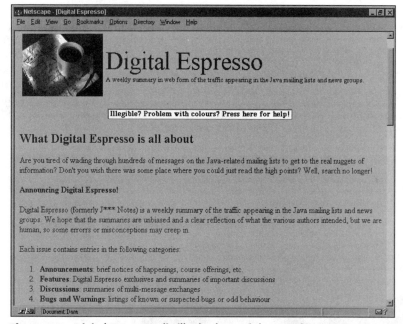

Figure 8-5: Digital Espresso distills the best of the Java language newsgroups into a well-organized set of Web pages.

In addition, many search engines allow you to search through newsgroup messages, meaning that you can bypass the newsgroup entirely by searching for what you need through the engine, rather than manually. If you're interested in saving time, check out DejaNews at `http://www.dejanews.com`. The DejaNews Web site is a search engine dedicated to newsgroups, and well worth a visit if you haven't been there before.

Note

When it comes to the Java newsgroup, become part of the solution and not the problem: Look high and low for the answer to your question rather than simply posting it to the group right off the bat. There are far too many unanswered questions on the newsgroup, probably because most of the answers to these questions have been posted time and time again! With a little research, most of the folks posting questions could find the answer elsewhere (even by looking farther back in the newsgroup, in the "digests" of questions answered in the past) and save the group from being further saturated with unanswered queries.

If newsgroups aren't your style, you can turn to any number of sites popping up on the Web to help answer Java questions. After a trip or two to Mantis, Gamelan, and JARS, you'll have found more Java links than you probably dreamed were possible. But perhaps you're a cut-and-dry, no-nonsense type of person. You may have a bunch of questions and no time to hunt down the answers. Time is of the essence, and you just don't seem to have any. Clearly, you need to take a vacation. But until then, you can visit the Java FAQ Archives.

The Java FAQ Archives could be considered a FAQ repository; it's dedicated to documents answering frequently asked questions. If you have a question, and it's been asked enough times by other folks, it will likely have made its way into a FAQ document. Since they are nothing more than text documents, you can download FAQs to your local computer and then use them anytime you have a question. If you don't want to spend a lot of time scanning through FAQ documents, you can always use a text-search tool (such as that of your word processor) or any "find" utility that allows you to search the contents of files.

There are a number of FAQs out there related to Java, and there's no better place to get to them all than the Java FAQ Archives (see Figure 8-6). You'll find Java-related FAQs of all stripes and colors here, and it's worth visiting them from time to time if you like to stay current.

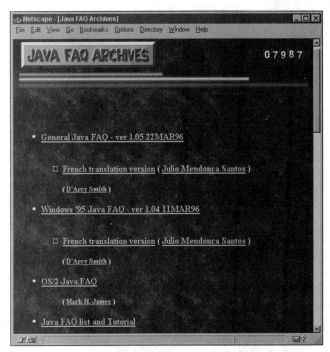

Figure 8-6: The Java FAQ Archives site is dedicated to Java-related FAQ documents.

Electronic magazines

A new breed of Java resource has emerged on the Web. Electronic magazines, or *e-zines,* are sprouting up at every turn. Much like traditional magazines, e-zines contain articles written to inform you about something. In the case of Java e-zines, that "something" is . . . drum roll . . . Java!

A lot of e-zines are out there, but relatively few are dedicated to Java. This will change over time, as more publishers migrate to the Web. I'm talking about professional publishers here, a small minority when compared to the millions of folks out there who happen to publish information on the Web, in between their full-time jobs and weekend outings.

With professional e-zines, you can expect consistent, well-written information to be published on a regular basis. The others aren't usually as reliable, well thought out, or comprehensive. However, they are often much more creative, irreverent, exciting, and visceral. Since they're not tied to a corporate culture or required to conform to standards or regulations that might otherwise be imposed on a professional publisher, independent e-zines are the free spirits of publishing.

Unfortunately, they have a much more difficult time attracting professionals to contribute articles. When it comes to Java, this means the caliber of content in independent e-zines tends to pale in comparison to their professional brethren. I suspect this will change in time, however, as more and more developers become fluent in Java and are willing to contribute to independent e-zines.

Until then, you can turn to JavaWorld. This online magazine, published by IDG Books Worldwide (the same company that published the book you're now reading) is a wonderful piece of work. So wonderful, in fact, that we've included on the CD-ROM all the back issues of JavaWorld available at the time this book went to press.

JavaWorld (`http://www.JavaWorld.com`) is packed with detailed articles written expressly for Java developers (see Figure 8-7). Here, you'll not only read about the technology, you'll see it working right then and there. With a click of your mouse, you'll see the entire source code listing, ready to copy/paste into your own programs, or save to disk for later. It's one of my all-time favorite Java resources, and one you shouldn't ignore.

Figure 8-7: JavaWorld is packed with detailed articles written expressly for Java developers.

Search Engines

When standard Java resources don't deliver, it's time to turn to search engines. More often than not, we turn to these only as a last resort, since the plethora of Java resources just discussed usually turns up whatever we're looking for. In the rare occasion that I come up empty-handed, I call in the Mounties.

Actually, using a search engine is more like calling in the dogs; bloodhounds, to be precise. Search engines typically employ a technology known as a *spider*, or agent, which scours the Web tirelessly, looking for new pages and information day and night. (If you're wondering why I used the analogy of "calling in the dogs," rather than spiders, just think about it; if you were lost in the woods, cold, hungry and near death, which would you prefer the authorities send in to find you? A dog or a spider?)

Spiders return information to the search engine in the form of hyperlinks, along with some details about the information itself. Using this data, the search engine provides an "index" (actually a gigantic database) of the Web, which you can query. If, for example, you search for the keyword *applet*, the search engine will return all the occurrences of *applet* in the database, along with a brief description of each. If a particular description sounds interesting, you can click on that item to visit the actual site.

The problem with this approach is that you will receive a vast quantity of information if you don't qualify your search. Instead of searching for a general term such as *applet,* you should supply specific details about what you are actually looking for (such as *ticker tape applet, Java games,* and the like). But even in this case, you're going to get back a large number of matches. To see whether these are really what you want, you'll have to visit each one. This is why we rarely use search engines; we'd rather spend the time prowling around newsgroups and code repositories.

Luckily, the best search engines also categorize their index for you. Rather than visiting all the links returned by a query, you can see all those that fall within a specified category. Yahoo!, for example, features a Java category that contains only links to valid Java sites (see Figure 8-8). As a result, you won't be off on a wild goose chase; Yahoo! chases the geese for you.

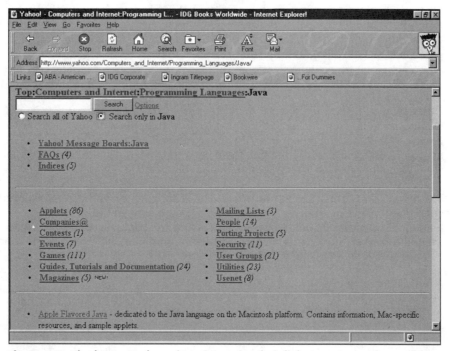

Figure 8-8: The best search engines categorize their links to save you from wild goose chases.

Tip

Many search engines allow you to search newsgroups. If time is of the essence, and you don't want to waste time sifting through the messages in a newsgroup, you can use a search engine instead. We don't mind searching through newsgroups manually, since we usually find three or four useful pieces of information having nothing to do with our original quest in the process. If you're interested in saving time, check out DejaNews at `http://www.dejanews.com`. The DejaNews Web site is a search engine dedicated to newsgroups; it's well worth a visit if you haven't been there before.

Alta Vista

Although the best search engines are similar in their capabilities, one alone demands special attention. Digital Equipment Corporation's Alta Vista search engine claims to be the fastest and most comprehensive. But really, don't they all?

The most impressive part of Alta Vista isn't how big or fast it is. That's not much of a help when it comes to finding Java on the Web, since you have to sift through all the sites manually unless they're categorized for you. What makes Alta Vista worth mentioning is a unique feature it offers when searching for applets.

Where other search engines simply return all matches to the word *applet* wherever it occurs in a document, Alta Vista lets you search for the name of the applet class file itself. You can actually search inside the `<APPLET>` tag! If you wanted, for example, to find all the pages that had an applet named *LivingLinks* embedded in them, you could do just that (see Figure 8-9). Using Alta Vista, you'd simply precede the name of the applet with *applet:* as follows:

```
applet:LivingLinks
```

Other search engines, in contrast, would return *every* page that had the word *LivingLinks* in it, even if they had nothing to do with applets or Java. Rather than having to separate the wheat from the chaff yourself, so to speak, Alta Vista does it for you. This is particularly helpful if you need to track down a particular applet or are looking for one that has a certain functionality.

If you don't know the name of the applet you're looking for, you can take a pretty good guess. Since most programmers tend to name classes based on their functionality, a few reasonable guesses would do the trick. For example, If you wanted to find an applet that performed texture mapping on 3D wire-frame models, you might try the following variations:

```
applet:texture
applet:map
applet:3-D
applet:wireframe
applet:wire
applet:model
```

On the CD-ROM

LivingLinks is a powerful applet that brings Web pages to life with animation, special effects, sounds, music, and multiple hyperlink capabilities. It's highly configurable, thanks to the rich set of PARAM settings it understands, and Java programmers can extend it by using "effect" plug-ins. The LivingLinks applet is provided on the enclosed CD-ROM, along with the LivingLinks Software Developer's Toolkit (LivingLinks SDK), should you want to create your own special effects.

Figure 8-9: Alta Vista allows you to search for applets embedded in Web pages; it looks inside the <APPLET> tag.

Although you'd have to manually visit each site Alta Vista returns to see whether the applets did what you wanted, at least you'd know they all contain applets. With other engines, performing a search with these keywords will return zillions of pages of information having nothing to do with Java applets.

Note

Clearly, the example I've used here is fictional. A 3D texture-mapping applet is way too cool to live in obscurity; as soon as one becomes available, every Java resource will have a link to it. If you happen upon one before the general Java public does, drop me a note at aaron@mantiscorp.com. (It'll be our little secret.)

Don't think for moment, however, that Alta Vista will be the only ticket in town for this show. By the time you read this, or shortly after, I'd bet most of the other search engines add the same capability. Searching for applets by name, inside the <APPLET> tag itself, is a useful feature. It won't be long before they all have it.

In fact, I'll rub my crystal ball a little harder. I'll bet $1.50 that in less than a year, one of the search engines out there will unveil the ability to search for applets based on *what they do*, not just their names. What!? How's that possible? Ahhh . . . now I've got your attention, eh? Check out the "Peering into the Crystal Ball" sidebar (coming up) for a peek into the future.

Peering into the Crystal Ball

All applets have the ability to implement the `getAppletInfo()` and `getParameter Info()` methods, which programmers use to return detailed information about the applet. When the `getAppletInfo()` applet is invoked, it returns a string containing the author of the applet. Typically, applet authors return a string containing their name, the name of the applet, and the applet version. However, authors can provide anything they like, as long as it's in a `String` object.

The `getParameterInfo()` method, on the other hand, returns details about the parameters that the applet understands. This method, according to Sun Microsystems, can be used as the basis of a tool designed to set parameters graphically. Come to think of it, typing in applet parameters really is a pain. Wouldn't it be much more fun and effective to use sliders, pop-up menus, and text entry boxes? You bet— wouldn't it be great to see the applet respond immediately, as you change the parameter, instead of having to save the HTML code and reload? Absolutely!

With these two methods in the back of your mind, it doesn't take long before the idea of another one, or better yet, an extension to `getAppletInfo()`, surfaces. How about a `String` object that is used to describe the applet in layman's terms? When taken all together, a search engine's spider could easily invoke the appropriate methods to find out the complete functionality of an applet. Not just a description, mind you, but all the parameters with which the applet knows how to deal.

In fact, an addition to these methods really isn't needed at all. The `getParameterInfo()` method already allows the applet author to provide a description of each parameter it supports. This alone is enough! All it takes is a spider smart enough to query the applets it encounters and to store that information in the search engine database for you to query.

No problem. I give it a year, tops, before a search engine is announced with just such a feature. In fact, just to be safe, I'll e-mail this sidebar to all the ones listed here. Hey, a dollar fifty is a dollar fifty.

Also new to JDK 1.1 is the reflection API. *Reflection* allows a Java class to look inside itself. The `java.lang.Class` class has been enhanced to include methods which now return the fields, methods, and constructors defined by a class. The `java.lang.reflect` package defines the `Field`, `Method`, and `Constructor` classes that are returned by the reflection methods. Reflection allows your applications to obtain complete and detailed information about any class during runtime. The most prevalent use of reflection is with JavaBeans, which is discussed in more detail in Chapter 6. For further information about class reflection, consult the Reflection Web page on the JavaSoft Web site at `http://java.sun.com/products/jdk/1.1/docs/guide/reflection/index.html`.

Do the Right Thing

When you do find a piece of source code that fits your needs, you should give the person who wrote it some degree of credit. You might drop him or her an e-mail, as a personal thank-you for freely supplying something you need. Of course, how you use the source code greatly influences what type of credit you give the person who wrote it.

If you only use it to see how something is done, as a sort of detailed documentation, then a personal "thank-you" e-mail message may be fine. But what if you actually incorporate the source code into your own program, meaning that you're putting someone's personal effort into your own work?

Electronic mail and Web page footnotes

If you actually use somebody's source code, why not give the person credit in your applet?

Some folks give credit by providing a note at the bottom of the page in which they've used the other programmer's source code. In this case, the note might read something like "Special thanks to J. Doe, Benjamin Spock, and Dr. Kevorkian." Others might go so far as to specify precisely what functionality the other programmer contributed, and even provide a link to his or her home page though standard HTML.

Applet-based credit

The manner in which you credit someone really depends on how much you value the person's effort, how critical it is to your program, and whether you can provide thanks on the Web page their work is part of. Non-personal sites (such as your company's home page) might be prohibited from including a line of thanks at the bottom of a page containing such an applet. If the site is your own, or you have authority over what the site is comprised of, you really aren't prohibited from providing a word of thanks directly on the Web page in which the applet appears. But with many commercial sites (and similar ones such as government, company, and network sites), you might not be able to include credit directly on the Web page because of organization policy. What then?

Again, it comes back to how much or how little the contribution means to you and your program. How do you really want to say thank you? A personal "thank-you" e-mail might be just fine, but if you want to include credit to a programmer who really helped you out, you'll find a way, even if the site your applet appears on is prohibited from displaying an explicit "Thanks to J. Doe" directly on its page. In these cases, you can include thanks in the applet itself, if the program lends itself to such a thing.

Say, for instance, the applet is a Web-based video game. You might include a scrolling list of credits in the game introduction splash screen, at the end of each game played, or somewhere in the online documentation. In this case, you've included credit in a way that doesn't alter the look of a Web page, yet manages to extend a word of thanks to those who helped you when you were in a pinch.

On the CD-ROM

For an example of scrolling text, take a look at any one of the "ticker tape" applets provided on the CD-ROM. Although these applets are generally used to display a scrolling message on the screen, you can use the source code in any way you see fit. In this case, simply copy the source code that performed the scrolling text functionality and use it as a method (or perhaps even a class) in your own program.

In fact, this is the reason so many different applets have been provided on CD-ROM. Not only will examining the source code show you how to get the most out of Java, you can use them as the basis for your own programs.

If displaying credits directly in the applet itself isn't possible, you can alternately display them on the status bar of the browser itself. This is generally the area you'll see messages such as "Connecting to host . . . Please wait," and a general progress report on what's going on with the browser (such as what percentage of the page transfer is complete, what state the applet is in, and so on).

To display text on the browser's status bar, simply call the following method with the message you want displayed:

```
showStatus("Special thanks to Tiny Tim for all his help...");
```

That's it! This showStatus() method, defined in java.applet.Applet, shows the string you pass to it in the status portion of the browser (see Figure 8-10). Actually, this method is described in Sun's application programming interface (API) documentation as one to "show a status message in the applet's context." Most Java-savvy browsers respond to the method by displaying whatever string you pass to it directly on the status area, although future browsers may handle it differently. (Browsers are free to handle this method however they'd like, and aren't even required to have a status area in the first place!)

To that end, another showStatus() method is defined in the java.applet.AppletContext class. Here, the API documentation is even more terse, describing the method in four words: "Shows a status string." This method is usually cascaded with the getAppletContext() method (defined in java.applet.Applet), which returns an AppletContext object:

```
getAppletContext().showStatus("Howdy!");
```

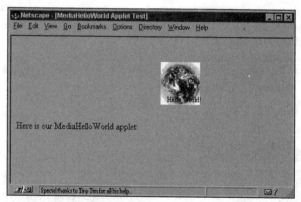

Figure 8-10: With showStatus() you can output text messages
to the status area of a browser window, which is typically
located in the lower-left corner, as shown here.

Note

The applet context allows an applet to control its environment, which is typically
the browser or the Applet Viewer.

In both cases, Netscape Navigator and Microsoft's Internet Explorer display the
string parameter you pass to it in their status area. Although other browsers may
deal with this call differently, Navigator originally set the precedence for how
showStatus() should be handled, since it was the first Java-savvy browser to hit
the ether. Many developers already rely on this method to display a message in the
status bar of the browser, and so it's unlikely that a browser would do anything
differently when showStatus() is invoked. Although the status area may be
located in different areas, depending on the browser itself, it's unlikely that it
would ignore the call and refuse to output a message to the status area.

HTML comment tags

If the applet you're creating doesn't lend itself to an embedded credit, and if you're
prohibited from including thanks in the applet's documentation, there's still hope:
HTML comment tags. Using HTML comment tags to give credit is about as
unobtrusive and clean a way as you'll find, outside of actually dropping the
contributor a personal e-mail. You can include anything you want in an HTML
comment tag, and it will never be seen by casual webbers unless they explicitly
choose to view the HTML source code of your page. Because Java programmers
often peek at the HTML source code for pages with embedded applets, your note
of thanks won't go unnoticed. In fact, it will be seen by that group of people most
likely to understand and appreciate it.

The following is an example of placing credit inside an HTML document. After the applet is specified with the ⟨APPLET⟩ tag, a ⟨!⟩ tag (comment tag) containing a word of thanks is included:

```
<APPLET = "CoolApplet.class" HEIGHT = 200 WIDTH = 300>
<! This applet was written by me, with special thanks to
J. Doe for graciously providing the widget functionality.>
```

Give As Good As You Get

If you've used source code provided by others, either something from the CD-ROM included with this book or code you found on the Web, consider going one step further and placing your own code on the Web in return.

All you have to do is provide a hyperlink to the source code file somewhere in the page that contains your applet; it's that simple. For an example of how this is usually done, take a look at any of the applets provided on the CD-ROM that comes with this book. Each of these pages contains a hyperlink to the applet source code, allowing one-click access.

Once you've made your source code available, get the word out! Register your applet with Gamelan and sign yourself up as a contributor on their site. Stop by the Mantis Java Links page, and take a look at the other code repositories with which you can register your applet.

If you've developed an applet that you think would be of interest to fellow developers, register it with the Mantis Java Links site or drop our Webmasters an e-mail at webmaster@mantiscorp.com.

Don't be shy! There's a good chance your applet and source code could wind up on the CD-ROM to be included with this book when it's revised, as well as on our Web-based update.

By placing your code on the Web, you're doing a great service to existing Java developers and those just learning the language. Scores of people are looking for source samples of all levels of complexity and you stand a good chance of helping somebody out by making yours freely available.

This is also a good idea from the perspective of the World Wide Web community in general. The Web has become a place where businesses attempt to extract a profit in one way or another, sometimes at the expense of good taste and ethics. It has also become tainted by some folks who have no apparent restraint or responsibility for what they spew out into our community. In both cases, the spirit of the Internet and World Wide Web has suffered.

By putting some of your own intellectual property out on the Web, you are taking another step towards preserving it and the Internet as a universal conduit for give and take, fostering the notion of a truly global village.

Summary

A great deal of Java source code is available directly on the World Wide Web. With the number of Java-powered pages spreading like wildfire, thanks to hundreds of thousands of Java developers scattered around the world, the demand for comprehensive developer support has gone through the roof. In response to this need, a number of sites dedicated to assisting Java developers have emerged.

✦ If you're looking to get your hands on a specific piece of source code, either to plug into what you're doing or to learn how to do something in particular in Java, a code repository is the first place to hit.

✦ Support areas attempt to provide you with the tools and information you'll need as a developer. You're likely to find Java development tools, documentation, technical support, and frequently asked questions (FAQs).

✦ A new breed of Java resource has emerged on the Web. Much like traditional magazines, e-zines contain articles written to inform you all about Java.

✦ When standard Java resources don't deliver, it's time to turn to search engines. More often than not, I turn to these only as a last resort, since the plethora of Java resources just discussed usually turns up whatever I'm looking for.

✦ When you do find a piece of source code that fits your needs, you should give some degree of credit to the person who wrote it.

✦   ✦   ✦

Programming Elements and Techniques

This part introduces the brass tacks of the Java programming language. Beginning with the basic concepts of tokens, types, and values, the chapters explore all the nooks and crannies of Java. Part III will be an ideal reference to use as you create your own applications.

These chapters show you how to do language basics such as defining and using variables, controlling program flow, creating your own classes, and handling exceptions — demonstrating that Java is more than just a programming language. Much of the beauty of the Java language is in its packages — predesigned classes available for your use in your own applications. The chapters introduce you to all the standard Java packages and classes, including strings, arrays, streams, and threads.

Finally, this part shows you how to weave your Java applications into Web pages — introducing you to the HTML programming that's required, and showing how to have your Web browser communicate with your applications. You also learn how to package your Java applications efficiently, using Java Archive (JAR) files for fast Web access.

Tokens, Types, and Values

In This Chapter

Getting down to
the basics of the
Java programming
language

Attaining an overview
of types and values
provided by Java

Using the built-in
language operators
and methods

Understanding how
to use objects,
methods, and
references to objects

At some time or other, you're going to need detailed information on exactly how to use the Java language. If you've made it this far, you're probably ready for the hard stuff. At this point, you need more than concepts, examples, and step-by-step explanations of different facets of the language. You need the nuts and bolts of the language, detailed syntax, brass tacks.

Brass Tacks

Don't worry, you're not alone. Everyone learning a new programming language must, sooner or later, learn proper syntax. Even language experts must learn the syntax for each language in their repertoire. Depending on your personal tastes, the following chapter will be either exciting and revealing, or dry and painful. Some folks absolutely love learning the details of new programming languages, while others might prefer having root-canal work done instead. Either way, this chapter must be dealt with.

As you read, your eyes are guaranteed to glaze over at some point. What you're about to experience is a solid case of information overload; this chapter is packed with details. However, there's no need to try and memorize everything you read. This is an excellent chapter to skim though and come back to, time after time, as needed. Eventually, you will absorb a large portion of it as you continue along the path to Java enlightenment. And what you don't remember will be waiting right here, in case you need a refresher or forget exactly how a particular syntax is supposed to be written.

This chapter was distilled from Sun's official Java Language Specification document. For thrill seekers and language lovers, I'd suggest taking a peek at that. You'll find it loaded with more information than you can imagine—it's an essential guide to becoming a Java language expert. But for now, you can warm up for that tome by concentrating on this chapter.

Let's begin by examining how the lines of code you write are broken into pieces, or *tokens*, by the compiler.

Note

The Java Language Specification is available through the documentation section of JavaSoft's Web site: `http://java.sun.com`.

Tokens

Java is a tokenized language: The lines of code that you write are translated by the compiler into discrete elements known as *tokens*. Working from left to right, the compiler discards all comments and whitespace (blank spaces and similar meaningless characters). What remains is separated into one of five possible tokens:

- ✦ Keywords
- ✦ Identifiers
- ✦ Literals
- ✦ Separators
- ✦ Operators

In order to fully understand the Java language, it's important to have a solid grasp of each of these five tokens. Of course, you don't have to memorize this section in one pass, or even memorize it at all. However, you'll find it beneficial to understand the purpose of each type of token now. You can always return later for details, as needed. Let's begin by looking at keywords.

Note

Java programs are written to the Unicode character encoding standard, which is a superset of the ASCII character set. Unicode expands the number of bits used to represent characters to 16, whereas ASCII uses only eight. Unicode also provides characters for many non-Latin languages, which ASCII does not.

Despite these differences, you need not concern yourself with finding a Unicode text editor! As long as your Java programs are stored in ASCII text format, the compiler can do its job. For details on the Unicode standard, see "The Unicode Standard: Worldwide Character Encoding" at `http://unicode.org` or use FTP to connect to `ftp://unicode.org`.

Keywords

Keywords are character sequences formed by ASCII letters that are reserved by the Java language for special purposes. You cannot use them for anything other than their intended purpose. For instance, you can't give a class, method, or variable the same name as a keyword.

Table 9-1 contains all the reserved keywords for the 1.0 release of Java, although a few aren't actually used by the language. The keywords goto, byvalue, cast, const, future, generic, inner, outer, operator, rest, and var are all reserved, even though they're not used. They may be used in a future release of the language.

You should note that although true and false look as though they might be keywords, they are not. Technically, true and false are boolean literals.

Tip

Since there are a large number of keywords, chances are you won't remember most of them. As a result, you may accidentally use a keyword without realizing you are doing so. If the compiler doesn't stop you, this may lead to unexpected problems with that code. If this happens, check to see whether you're using a keyword as an identifier. This can only happen if the identifier in question is a sequence of all lowercase letters, however, since keywords are never uppercase and do not contain numbers.

Table 9-1 Java Keywords			
abstract	boolean	break	byte
case	cast	catch	chars
class	const	continue	default
do	double	else	extends
final	finally	float	for
future	generic	goto	if
implements	import	inner	instanceof
int	interface	long	native
new	null	operator	outer
package	private	protected	public
rest	return	short	static
super	switch	synchronized	this
throw	throws	transient	try
var	void	volatile	while

Class modifier keywords

A subset of Java keywords, known as *access specifiers*, are used to control the access that objects have to classes, methods, and variables. You can apply the Class Modifier access specifiers listed in Table 9-2 to classes and interfaces to define the extent to which other objects can access that class or interface. (Interfaces are discussed later in this chapter, and in more detail in Chapter 11.)

	Table 9-2
	Class Modifier Keywords

Class Modifier	Description
<blank>	When no class modifier is specified, the class or interface is accessible to objects within the current package.
public	Specifies that the class or interface is accessible to objects outside the package it is part of. Only one public class is permitted per source code file, and that file must have the same name as the class and a .java extension (for example, HelloWorldApplet.java).
final	Specifies that the class or interface cannot be subclassed. The String class, for example, is final. As a result, you can't create a String subclass.
abstract	Specifies that the class or interface contains abstract methods (methods having no actual implementation), or that it isn't directly implemented.

The following is the syntax for class modifiers. Note that items in square brackets ([]) are optional:

```
ClassModifier class name [extends superclass] [implements
interfaces] {
    . . .
    . . .
}
```

For instance, suppose we don't want our HelloWorldApplet to be subclassed. We can do this easily using the keyword final, a modifier that prevents the class from being subclassed:

```
final class HelloWorldApplet extends java.applet.Applet {
    . . .
    . . .
}
```

What if we want to allow subclassing? Better yet, we might also want to allow other objects outside the `HelloWorldApplet.class` source code file to access this class:

```
public class HelloWorldApplet extends java.applet.Applet {
    ...
    ...
    }
```

In this case, it can be subclassed. Since it's public, `HelloWorldApplet` can be used by any other Java program. If we hadn't specified a class modifier, the class would have been available only within the package it was part of (see Chapter 11 for information on packages):

```
class HelloWorldApplet extends java.applet.Applet {
    ...
    ...
    }
```

Method modifier and field modifier keywords

Two other sets of access specifiers, Method Modifiers and Field Modifiers, also let you control the access that objects have to methods and variables.

Method modifiers

The Method Modifier access specifiers listed in Table 9-3 can be applied to methods. Field Modifiers are applied to class or method variables, which are also known as *fields*. They are the same as Method Modifiers, with the exception of `abstract`, `synchronized`, and `native` (variables cannot be defined as abstract, synchronized, or native).

Table 9-3
Method Modifier Keywords

Method Modifier	Description
<blank>	When no access modifier is specified, the method or variable is accessible only within the current package.
abstract	Specifies that implementation for the method will be supplied by a subclass.
public	Specifies that the method or variable is accessible outside its class.
private	Specifies that the method or variable is only accessible to other methods inside its own class.
protected	Specifies that the method or variable is accessible to subclasses, and also to the package in which it is defined.

(continued)

	Table 9-3 *(continued)*	
Method Modifier	**Description**	
private protected	Specifies that the method or variable is accessible only within its class and subclasses. A subclass can access variables it inherits, but not directly through an instance of the superclass.	
final	Specifies that the method cannot be overridden, or that the value of a variable won't change.	
static	Specifies that the method can be invoked without first instantiating an object, and can only access static variables. Static variables are shared by all objects; only one copy is available to all instances.	
synchronized	Used with threads; specifies that the method will be locked when executed by a thread, preventing another thread from invoking it until it is unlocked upon exit by the first thread. (See Chapter 14.)	
native	Specifies that the method is actually a code stub written in another language, such as C.	

This is the syntax for method modifiers:

```
MethodModifiers returnType name (argumentType1 argument1, ...) {
    ...
    ...
    }
```

For instance, if we didn't want any methods other than those defined in our HelloWorldApplet class to have access to the paint() method, we would use the following:

```
private void paint (Graphics g) {
    ...
    ...
    }
```

However, since we *do* want to grant methods outside the HelloWorldApplet class access to paint(), we declare it as public:

```
public void paint (Graphics g) {
    ...
    ...
    }
```

If we hadn't specified a method modifier at all, the `paint()` method would have been available only to methods within the package it was part of (see Chapter 11):

```
void paint (Graphics g) {
    ...
    ...
    }
```

Field modifiers

When you apply access modifiers to variables, you should use this syntax:

```
FieldModifer   type name;
```

For instance, the integer `horizontal` and `vertical` variables we defined in `HelloWorldApplet` could have been restricted to only methods in that class:

```
private int   horizontal, vertical;
```

And we could have just as easily made them available to methods outside the `HelloWorldApplet` class:

```
public int   horizontal, vertical;
```

However, we didn't specify an access modifier for these two variables (or any other `HelloWorldApplet` variables). As a result, they are available to all methods in the same package:

```
int   horizontal, vertical;
```

Keep in mind that field modifiers are the same as method modifiers, with this exception: `abstract`, `synchronized`, and `native` are not supported.

Identifiers

An *identifier* is a sequence of Unicode characters that you use to name a class, method, or variable. Identifiers can be of any length, and they can contain both letters and digits. However, they must begin with a letter, not a digit. You can use any name you can think of for an identifier, provided it doesn't begin with a digit and is not the same as a keyword. Because identifiers are Unicode, they can even include non-Latin letters and digits.

As a general rule, you should use uppercase letters in your identifiers only if they help improve readability. Identifiers that are all uppercase can make your code difficult to read, and they may reduce the impact capital letters should have for emphasis. There is an exception to this rule, however (isn't there always?): Variables declared as final should be *entirely* in uppercase characters. Final variables can't be altered once declared, and are used to represent constant values (constants) in Java. For more details on final variables, see Chapter 11.

Also, you should avoid the use of the underscore character (_), except when it appears between two words as a way to improve readability. See Table 9-4 for examples of legal and illegal use of identifiers, as well as those you should avoid, even though they may be legal.

Table 9-4
Examples of Legal and Illegal Identifiers

Legal	Illegal	Legal but Not Recommended
i	if	IF
dollar	1dollar	_dollar
speed	5speed	SPEED
customerLastName	customer-last-name	customerlastname
leapYear	leap-year	leapyear
minutes_In_365_Days	365Days	MinutesIn365DAYS
monthlyIncome	monthly Income	$monthlyIncome

Tables 9-5 and 9-6 contain the range of Unicode characters that comprise the digits and letters you can use to form an identifier. Each table contains raw Unicode characters; they begin with \u and are followed by four hexadecimal digits. When you use raw Unicode characters (as opposed to actual characters, as shown in Table 9-4), Java converts them into the actual characters they represent.

Table 9-5
Unicode Digits

Point Code Range	Description
\u0030–\u0039	ISO-LATIN-1 digits (0–9)
\u0660–\u0669	Arabic-Indic digits
\u06f0–\u06f9	Eastern Arabic-Indic digits

Point Code Range	Description
\u0966–\u096f	Devanagari digits
\u09e6–\u09ef	Bengali digits
\u0a66–\u0a6f	Gurmukhi digits
\u0ae6–\u0aef	Gujarati digits
\u0b66–\u0b6f	Oriya digits
\u0be7–\u0bef	Tamil digits
\u0c66–\u0c6f	Telugu digits
\u0ce6–\u0cef	Kannada digits
\u0d66–\u0d6f	Malayalam digits
\u0e50–\u0e59	Thai digits
\u0ed0–\u0ed9	Lao digits
\u1040–\u1049	Tibetan digits

Table 9-6
Unicode Letters

Point Code Range	Description
\u0024	$ (dollar sign—for historical reasons)
\u005f	_ (underscore—for historical reasons)
\u0041–\u005a	Latin capital letters (A–Z)
\u0061–\u007a	Latin small letters (a–z)
\u00c0–\u00d6	Various Latin letters with diacritics
\u00d8–\u00f6	Various Latin letters with diacritics
\u00f8–\u00ff	Various Latin letters with diacritics
u0100–\u1fff	Other non-CJK1 alphabets and symbols
\u3040–\u318f	Hiragana, Katakana, Bopomofo, and Hangul
\u3300–\u337f	CJK squared words
\u3400–\u3d2d	Korean Hangul Symbols
\u4e00–\u9fff	Han (Chinese, Japanese, Korean)
\uf900–\ufaff	Han compatibility

With the introduction of JDK 1.1, the Unicode 2.0 standard has been adopted. The Unicode 2.0 standard contains 38,885 distinct characters and covers the major written languages of America, Europe, Middle East, Africa, India, Asia, and Pacifica. For more information on Unicode and the Unicode standard, visit the Unicode Consortium at `http://www.unicode.org`

Identifiers are considered the same only if they have an identical Unicode code point for every letter or digit. For instance, the single letters Latin capital *A* (\u0041), Latin small *a* (\u0061), Greek capital *A* (\u0391), and Cyrillic small *a* (\u0430) each have a distinct code point and therefore would not be considered identical.

Literals

Literals are explicit values, such as `18345` or `"Hello World!"`, that are specified directly in your Java code. Java supports three categories of literals:

✦ Those that are numbers (integer and floating-point literals)

✦ Boolean literals (`true` and `false`)

✦ Those that are composed of characters (character literals and string literals)

You use literals to specify values for variables, or to place explicit values directly in your source code. For instance, in the following line of code, 135 is a numeric literal used to initialize an integer variable:

```
int myInteger = 135;
```

We can also assign a boolean literal, either `true` or `false`, to boolean variables:

```
boolean myFlag = true;
```

You can also use literals to control the flow of program execution, as we've done here with the integer literal 15 and the boolean literal `false`:

```
while (x < 15) {
   ...
}
while (myFlag != false) {
   ...
}
```

And, as you may recall from our "Hello World!" programs, you can also use literals as arguments to methods. In our application, we used the string literal `"Hello World!"` to communicate with the user:

```
System.out.println("Hello World!");
```

In the applet version of Hello World, we used a string literal and two integer literals to position output at an exact location on the screen:

```
g.drawString("Hello World!",50,100);
```

As with keywords and identifiers, you've been using literals all along in previous chapters. But now that you've been formally introduced to them, let's take a closer look at each type of literal in the Java language.

Numbers

Java supports two types of numeric literals:

✦ Integer literals

✦ Floating-point literals

Integers are numbers that do not have a decimal point, while floating-point numbers do. Following are a few integer numbers: 545, 43, 7632, 4367, 2346, and 57. And here are some floating-point numbers: 545.00456, 43.3535, .76326464, 4367.26, 2346.00, and 5.7.

Integer literals

The most common literal is the integer literal. Using ASCII characters, integer literals may be expressed in three different ways:

✦ Decimal (base 10)

✦ Hexadecimal (base 16)

✦ Octal (base 8)

The legal positive and negative ranges for each notation are shown in Tables 9-7, 9-8, 9-9, and 9-10 in the next three sections.

Note

An integer literal is considered to be of type int unless it is suffixed with an upper- or lowercase "L" (L or l). For instance, 15 is an integer literal of type int, while 15L and 15l are both integer literals of type long.

Decimal literals

Decimal literals represent positive integer values, and consist of an initial digit ranging from 1 to 9, which may be followed by one or more digits ranging from 0 to 9, such as: 935, 467L, 534643, 63036, 2, and 2L.

The legal ranges of decimal literals are expressed in Table 9-7.

Table 9-7
Legal Ranges of Decimal Literals in Java

Literal	Legal Range
Max Positive (2^31 - 1) int	2147483647
Max Negative (-2^31) int	n/a
Max Positive (2^63 - 1) long	9223372036854775807L
Max Negative (-2^63) long	n/a

Hexadecimal literals

Hexadecimal literals represent a positive, zero, or negative number. They consist of a leading 0x or 0X, followed by one or more hexadecimal digits. The hexadecimal representation of decimal digits is shown in Table 9-8. Hexadecimal digits 10–15 aren't represented by digits, but are instead represented by the letters *A* through *F* (or by *a* through *f*— these letters can be either uppercase or lowercase).

Java's Forbidden Numbers

The largest negative `int` (-2147483648, or -2^{31}) can't be represented in Java as a decimal literal! Since the literal `-2147483648` is tokenized as the unary operator "`-`" followed by the decimal literal value of 2147483648, the compiler generates an error (2147483648 exceeds the legal maximum value for decimal integer literals, as shown in Table 9-7). You should represent this value in hexadecimal notation (0x80000000).

Similarly, a compile-time error is generated if a decimal literal of type `long` is larger than 2^{63}-1. This means the largest negative `long` can't be represented as a decimal literal, because `-9223372036854775808L` is tokenized as the unary operator "`-`" followed by a decimal literal value of 9223372036854775808L. Because `9223372036854775808L` is not a valid decimal long-integer literal, an error is generated. On the off chance that you need to represent this value, use the hexadecimal literal 0x8000000000000000L instead.

Table 9-8
Hexadecimal Digit Representation

Decimal	Hexadecimal
1	0x1 or 0X1
2	0x2 or 0X2
3	0x3 or 0X3
4	0x4 or 0X4
5	0x5 or 0X5
6	0x6 or 0X6
7	0x7 or 0X7
8	0x8 or 0X8
9	0x9 or 0X9
10	0xA, 0XA, 0xa, or 0Xa
11	0xB, 0XB, 0xb, or 0Xb
12	0xC, 0XC, 0xc, or 0Xc
13	0xD, 0XD, 0xd, or 0Xd
14	0xE, 0XE, 0xe, or 0Xe
15	0xF, 0XF, 0xf, or 0Xf

The legal ranges of hexadecimal literals are expressed in Table 9-9.

Table 9-9
Legal Ranges of Hexadecimal Literals in Java

Literal	Legal Range
Max Positive (2^31 - 1) int	0x7fffffff
Max Negative (-2^31) int	0x80000000
Max Positive (2^63 - 1) long	0x7fffffffffffffffL
Max Negative (-2^63) long	0x8000000000000000L

Here are some examples of hexadecimal literals: 0xA887, 0X20C15E0, 0xFFFA9B12, 0x5AD6, 0x63036, 0X2, and 0x2L.

Octal literals

Octal literals also represent a positive, zero, or negative number. They consist of a leading 0 (zero), optionally followed by one or more digits in the range 0 through 7, like this: 0235, 05323434, 0000, 035674L, and 000235.

The legal ranges of octal literals are expressed in Table 9-10.

Table 9-10 Legal Ranges of Octal Literals in Java	
Literal	*Legal Range*
Max Positive (2^31 - 1) int	017777777777
Max Negative (-2^31) int	020000000000
Max Positive (2^63 - 1) long	0777777777777777777777L
Max Negative (-2^63) long	0400000000000000000000L

Floating-point literals

Floating-point literals represent numbers with decimal values. A floating-point literal is composed of five parts:

✦ A whole number
✦ A decimal point
✦ A fractional part
✦ An exponent
✦ A type suffix

Floating-point literals must have at least one digit, which may appear in either the whole number or the fractional part of the number. They must also have either a decimal point or an exponent, although all other parts are optional.

The exponent, if one exists, is represented in scientific notation by the letter E (or e), which may be followed by a signed integer.

Note

A floating-point literal is considered to be of type double unless it is suffixed with an F or f, in which case it's of type float. For instance, 15.35 (as well as 15.35D and 15.35d) is a floating-point literal of type double, while 15.35F and 15.35f are both floating-point literals of type float.

Tip

The float type is used to represent single precision floating-point numbers, whereas the double type represents numbers as double precision values. If your calculations need to be exceptionally accurate, be sure to specify floating-point numbers as type double. Examples of floating-point literals of type double include these: 3e1, 5.34, 5.34d, 2., .366, and 3e-6. Floating-point literals of type float include these others: 3e1f, 5.34F, 5.34f, 2.f, .366F, and 3.03e+6f.

Boolean literals

In Java, boolean literals are of type boolean, and can have one of two possible values: true or false. Java's boolean literals are actual *literals*, not strings, and can't be converted into string literals (see "String literals" later in this chapter). Nor are they integer values of zero and one, as booleans in C and C++ are.

Character literals

An addition to the numeric and boolean literals described in the preceding sections, Java supports literals that are composed of characters. These can be:

✦ An individual character (character literal)

✦ A number of characters in a string (string literals)

Character literals are expressed as a single character, or an escape sequence beginning with the backslash character enclosed in single quotes (' \ '). The escape sequence permits non-graphic characters to be represented, in addition to the single quote (') character and the backslash (\) character themselves.

Character literals are 16-bit integer values. Following are a few examples of valid character literals: a, A, z, Z, '\t', '\b', '\u12d', '\\'.

Table 9-11 shows the character literal escape codes for each escape sequence, as well as what they represent.

Table 9-11		
Character Literal Escape Codes		
Escape Sequence	**Unicode Escape Code**	**What It Represents**
\b	\u0008	backspace (BS)
\t	\u0009	horizontal tab (HT)
\n	\u000a	linefeed (LF)
\f	\u000c	form feed (FF)
\r	\u000d	carriage return (CR)

(continued)

Table 9-11 (continued)

Escape Sequence	Unicode Escape Code	What It Represents
\"	\u0022	double quote (")
\'	\u0027	single quote (')
\\	\u005c	backslash (\)
\?	\u0034	question mark (?)

Note

Unicode escapes are processed very early on in the compilation of Java code. For instance, if you were to use a character literal escape sequence of \u000a (for linefeed), Java would see the \u000a Unicode escape and translate it into an actual linefeed on the spot, even before realizing that it is part of a character literal escape sequence! This linefeed is then further reduced to a line terminator, blowing your character literal out of the water. The same thing happens when \u000d is encountered. As a result, you should use '\n' for a character literal linefeed and '\r' for a carriage return.

String literals

String literals are comprised of zero (0) or more characters enclosed in double quotes (" "), and may use the same escape sequences as character literals. Table 9-12 shows examples of valid string literals.

Table 9-12
Examples of Valid String Literals

Literal	String Type
"Hello World!"	basic string
"Are you looking at me?"	your basic string, with an attitude
""	an empty string
"\""	a string containing only a double quote (")
"This string is " +	three strings treated as
"too long to fit "" +	an expression using the
"on one line!"	+ operator

Note   If your string literal contains a line separator (such as a carriage return or linefeed) between the opening and closing double quotes (" "), the compiler generates an error. If necessary, you can use the string concatenation operator, +, to break your string into smaller pieces, as shown in Table 9-12.

Separators

Separators are characters used to group and arrange Java source code. They let you organize your code into a form the compiler understands. The following characters are valid Java separators:

```
(   )    {   }     [   ]     ;     ,     .
```

You've already seen all of these used in some way or other. For instance, the while loop used in Chapter 7 makes use of the ( ) and { } separators:

```
while (x <15) {
   ...
}
```

Perhaps you've used a for loop? If so, you've also used the ; separator:

```
for (x=0; x<100; x++) {
   ...
}
```

You've even used the ; and . separators in one line of code, along with the ( ) separators:

```
System.out.println("Hello World!");
```

And how about the comma (,) separator? We use that, and the ( ) and ; separators in every method that has more than one argument:

```
g.drawImage(myImage, horizontal, vertical, this);
```

Finally, we've dealt with arrays. As a result, we've already used the [] separators:

```
theArg =  args[i];
```

Operators

Operators are individual characters and combinations of characters used to perform calculations. Table 9-13 lists all of the Java operators, current as of JDK 1.2. Chapter 10 provides a detailed overview of these operators, including precedence and associativity.

Table 9-13 Java Operators							
=	>	<	!	~	?	:	==
<=	>=	!=	&&	||	++	−	+
-	F	/	&	|	^	%	<<
>	>>	+=	−=	*=	/=	&=	|=
^=	%=	<<=	>=	>>=			

Types and Values

In this section, we shall look at two more important elements of Java syntax, types and values.

Types

Types are used to identify the information stored in variables and returned by methods (on those occasions when a method does in fact return data when called). The information stored in a variable or returned by a method is known as the *value* of the variable or return. In essence, you create variables that have a certain type. The type, in turn, determines what values can be stored in the variable. The same is true for method return types: You define what information will be returned by specifying a return type. As a result, only values conforming to the type can be returned.

Because Java is a *strongly typed* language, you're prevented from making common programming mistakes seen with *loosely typed* languages. Passing incorrect data types as parameters to a method, treating return values in a manner inconsistent with their type, and unwittingly casting data values from one type to another are all prevented thanks to Java's strong adherence to data typing.

Java supports four distinct categories of data types:

   ✦ Primitive types
   ✦ Class types
   ✦ Interface types
   ✦ Array types

Every variable in a Java program has an associated data type, often called its *compile-time type* because the compiler can always determine the type before the program is executed.

Values

Java also supports two kinds of data values:

✦ Primitive values

✦ References

These values can be stored in variables, passed to methods as arguments, returned as values, and operated upon. In this section, we'll take a look at the types and values that are supported by the Java language.

Primitive values

Primitive values are indivisible, meaning they can't be reduced any further. They don't share state with other primitive values. A variable defined as having a primitive compile-time type always holds a value of that exact primitive type. Such a value is not shared in any way with any other variable, so the value of the variable can be changed only by operations using that variable.

Values stored in a variable must be compatible with the compile-time type of that variable. That is, you can't define a variable of type `int` and then attempt to store a string in it.

References

References are pointers to dynamically allocated objects (here we mean the concept of pointing to something in memory, not actual pointers of the kind found in C/C++; Java doesn't support such pointers). These objects are composed of primitive values, and are sometimes called *composite data types* for that reason.

The rest of this chapter is dedicated to Java's data types and values. To help organize this material, we'll explore these in the context of primitive types and references. Let's begin with primitives.

Primitive types and values

Primitive types, also known as *simple* or *basic* types, are the fundamental data types of Java. They are defined the same way in all implementations of the language, regardless of platform, making them more portable than primitive data types of other languages, such as C and C++. When you use primitive data types in Java, their representation and arithmetic behavior are consistent from system to system.

Primitives are named by one of the reserved keywords listed in Table 9-14, and fall into one of three categories:

✦ Arithmetic (integral or floating-point)

✦ Boolean

✦ Character

	Table 9-14	
	Primitive Data Types	
Type	**Category**	**Values**
byte	integral arithmetic	8-bit signed two's complement integers
short	integral arithmetic	16-bit signed two's complement integers
int	integral arithmetic	32-bit signed two's complement integers
long	integral arithmetic	64-bit signed two's complement integers
float	floating-point arithmetic	32-bit IEEE 754 floating-point numbers
double	floating-point arithmetic	64-bit IEEE 754 floating-point numbers
char	character	16-bit Unicode characters
boolean	boolean	true and false

The values that a primitive variable can contain depend upon the data type of that variable. It's interesting to note, however, that you can't treat primitive types as objects. Instead, you have to place them in what's known as an *object wrapper* before passing them as arguments to most methods. In addition to allowing you to embed primitive types in objects, type wrapper classes (discussed in detail in Chapter 12) also contain MIN_VALUE and MAX_VALUE class variables for easy access to the upper and lower range of values permitted for each type.

Integral arithmetic type and values

The primitive integral data types—byte, short, int, and long—are used to perform integer arithmetic. These types do not support numbers with decimals. The char data type is compatible with integral types because it supports 16-bit unsigned integer values, which are used to represent a Unicode code point.

Ranges and casts

Table 9-15 shows the legal range for each integral type. Although the char type is not represented in this table, any integral value may be cast to a type char, while any character may be cast to any of the integral types. And, not surprisingly, any integral value may be cast to any other arithmetic type.

Table 9-15
Legal Value Ranges for Integral Types

Type	Legal Range
byte	-128 to 127, inclusive
short	-32768 to 32767, inclusive
int	-2147483648 to 2147483647, inclusive
long	-9223372036854775808 to 9223372036854775807, inclusive

Note

Although integral types can be cast to a char type and vice versa, the same cannot be said for boolean types. It is illegal to attempt a cast between integrals and booleans.

Operands

Table 9-16 includes the various operators that Java provides for performing integral operations.

Table 9-16
Java Operators for Integral Operations

Type	Operators
equality operators	= and !=
relational operators	<, <=, >, and >=
unary operators	+ and -
additive and multiplicative operators	+, -, *, /, and %
prefix and postfix increment/decrement operators	++ and --
signed and unsigned shift operators	<<, >>, and >>>
unary bitwise logical negation operator	~
bitwise logical operators	&, |, and ^

Widening

If an operation is performed on integrals, it is considered an integer operation, provided that both operands are of the integral type. However, if one of the operands is of type long, the operation is performed using 64-bit precision. In this case, all operands that are not also of type long are first widened (as if a cast was performed) to type long, and the result is of type long as well (assuming the operation wasn't meant to return a boolean, in which case a boolean type is returned).

If none of the operands are of type `long`, the operation is performed using 32-bit precision. In this case, all operands that are not of type `int` are first widened to type `int` and the result is also of type `int` (once again, assuming the operation wasn't meant to return a boolean, in which case the `boolean` type is returned).

Although the built-in integral operators widen their operands to perform 32-bit or 64-bit precision operations, values of integral type are not automatically widened when used as arguments in method calls. You can write individual methods to do so, but the calling process does not automatically perform widening.

Exceptions

If the right-hand operand to an integer divide operator (/) or integer remainder operator (%) is zero, Java throws an `ArithmeticException`. Some programmers may recognize this as the ol' "divide by zero" error, which everyone encounters at some time or another. However, this is the only way for an exception to be generated by an operator on integral types.

Floating-point arithmetic types and values

The primitive floating-point data types—`float` and `double`—are used to perform single precision 32-bit and double precision 64-bit format operations, respectively, on values that conform to the Institute of Electrical and Electronics Engineers' IEEE 754 standard. Unlike integrals, floating-point data types support numbers with decimals. Their values can be positive, zero, or negative.

For detailed information on the IEEE 754 specification, refer to the publication "IEEE Standard for Binary Floating-point Arithmetic," ANSI/IEEE Std. 754-1985 (IEEE, New York).

Ranges and casts

Table 9-17 shows the legal range for `float` and `double` data types. As with integrals, any floating-point value may be cast to a type `char`, while any character may be cast to any floating-point type. In addition, any floating-point value may be cast to any other arithmetic type.

Table 9-17
Legal Value Ranges for Floating-Point Types

Type	Legal Range (Arranged from Smallest to Largest)
float	negative infinity, negative finite values, negative zero, positive zero, positive finite values, and positive infinity
double	negative infinity, negative finite values, negative zero, positive zero, positive finite values, and positive infinity

And, just as with integrals, it is illegal to attempt a cast between floating-point types and the `boolean` type. Booleans can only hold `true` or `false` values, and can't be cast into other data types.

Finite non-zero values

Finite non-zero values of type `float` are of the following form:

```
s(m x 2e)
```

where s is +1 or -1, m is a positive integer less than 2^{24}, and e is an integer between −149 and 104, inclusive.)

Don't be confused by the ^ appearing in this section (as in 2^{24}). In this case, it's used to indicated a value "raised to the power of" another value. This isn't Java code, mind you, but simply a mathematical notation appearing in regular text.

In contrast, Java's ^ operator has two different meanings, depending on the operands involved. When used with integral operands, a bitwise exclusive OR (XOR) operation is performed. With boolean operands, however, a logical exclusive OR (XOR) operation is performed, where the result is either `true` or `false`.

Finite non-zero values of type `double` are also of the form:

```
s(m. 2e )
```

where s is +1 or -1, m is a positive integer less than 2^{53}, and e is an integer between −1045 and 1000, inclusive.

NaN: Not-a-Number

Floating-point data types support a special value known as Not-a-Number (NaN). NaN is used to represent the result of operations where an actual number isn't produced. Most operations that have NaN as an operand will produce NaN as a result.

The presence of NaN can produce unexpected results when dealing with floating-point data types. Since NaN is unordered, the result of a $<$, $<=$, $>$, $>=$, or $==$ comparison between a NaN and another value is always `false`. In fact, $==$ always produces `false` when both operands are NaN. However, the result of a $!=$ comparison with a NaN is always `true`, even if both operands are NaN.

Operands

Table 9-18 lists the various operators that Java provides for performing floating-point operations.

Table 9-18
Java Operators for Floating-Point Operations

Operation	Operators
basic equality operations	= and !=
relational operations	<, <=, >, and >=
unary operations	+ and -
additive and multiplicative operations	+, -, *, /, and %
prefix and postfix increment/decrement operations	++ and -

Operations

If an operation is performed on floating-point data types, it's considered a floating-point operation if both operands are of the floating-point type. An operation is also considered a floating-point operation if one of the operands is a floating-point type and one is an integral data type.

If one of the operands is of type double, the operation is performed using 64-bit floating-point arithmetic. In this case, any operand that is not also a double is first cast to type double and the result is of type double (assuming the operation wasn't meant to return a boolean, in which case a boolean type is returned). If none of the operands are of type double, the operation is performed using 32-bit floating-point arithmetic. If this is the case, all operands that are not float are first cast to type float and the result, if not boolean, is of type float.

Note

All operations on floating-point numbers behave exactly as specified by the IEEE 754 standard.

Rounding

In Java, floating-point arithmetic is performed as if every floating-point operator rounds its floating-point result to the result precision. Inexact results are rounded to the nearest representable value, in accordance with the IEEE 754 "round to nearest" mode. For instance, if two representable values are equally distant from the true mathematical result of the operation, Java returns the value whose least-significant bit is zero (0).

Note

Similarly, Java rounds towards zero when floating-point values are cast to integers.

Exceptions

In Java, floating-point arithmetic will not generate an exception. Any operation that overflows will produce a signed infinity value, so there's no need to throw an overflow exception (see Chapter 10 for details on exceptions). Likewise, when an operation underflows, a signed zero is produced. If an operation produces a result that has no mathematically definite value, NaN is produced. Since these are all valid results, no exceptions are generated.

Character types and values

In Java, the `char` type is used to store a Unicode character value. While Unicode values are two bytes in size, you don't have to do anything special when assigning values to Java `char` types. Their internal representation is not of concern to you, and, in fact, you can't even tell what size a `char` type is (Java doesn't support the `sizeof` operation popular with C/C++).

Java `char` types are unsigned. As such, if a `char` is cast to another type (such as a `byte` or `short`) the result may be a negative value.

Boolean types and values

Java's `boolean` data type represents a 1-bit logical quantity with only two possible values: `true` and `false`.

Casts

No casts are defined for booleans, although an integer can be converted to a boolean following the convention of the C programming language. Suppose we have an integer, x. Since C treats 0 as false and every non-zero value as true, we can use the expression `x!=0` to convert x into a boolean.

Likewise, a boolean value b is converted to a zero/one integer value using the expression `b?1:0`. However, there are no explicit casts on booleans. You cannot, for instance, convert a `boolean` type to a floating-point data type or `String` object.

Operands

Operations defined on booleans appear in Table 9-19.

<table>
<tr><td colspan="2" align="center">Table 9-19
Java Operators for Boolean Operations</td></tr>
<tr><td>*Operation*</td><td>*Operators*</td></tr>
<tr><td>relational operations</td><td>== and !=</td></tr>
<tr><td>logical operations</td><td>!, &, |, and ^</td></tr>
<tr><td>short-circuit logical operations</td><td>&& and ||</td></tr>
</table>

Note

The `if`, `while`, `do`, and `for` statements all rely on boolean truth values to control the flow of program execution. Likewise, the conditional ? : operator uses boolean truth values to determine which subexpression is selected.

Reference types and values

In Java, there are two kinds of dynamically allocated objects:

✦ Class instances

✦ Arrays

These non-primitive types are commonly known as *reference types*, since they are dealt with using the address of the object or array rather than the actual value of the object or array itself. The address, or reference, of an object or array is what's stored in variables and passed as an argument to methods. In contrast, primitive types are handled by value: Actual values are stored in variables and passed as arguments to methods. This makes for two very distinct types in Java:

✦ Primitive

✦ Reference

Since arrays are covered in detail in Chapter 12, this section focuses more on the nature of objects. While arrays are treated a lot like objects, they are unique beasts. As such, special attention is given to them later in this book. Feel free to skip ahead for details on arrays if you'd like, or read on to learn more about objects.

Creating objects

Objects are created, or instantiated, from class definitions using the new keyword:

```
new ClassName(); // instantiates an object from class
```

When a constructor is used in the instantiation of an object, parameters are often required:

```
new ClassName(param1, param2, param3, ...);
```

Typically, the objects you create are assigned to a variable. To do this, you must declare the variable as being of the same data type as the class itself (or of a data type compatible with the class):

```
ClassName myObject = new ClassName(); // set variable equal to
  new object
```

Accessing methods

Methods in an object are invoked by sending that object a message using dot notation. The message you send is actually the name (and parameter list, if parameters are required) for the method to invoke:

```
myObject.methodName(); // invoke method requiring no parameters
myObject.methodName(param1, param2, param3, ...); // parameters
    are required
```

Variables in an object may (or may not, depending on implementation) be available using dot notation. Typically, variables are accessible only though special accessor methods:

```
myObject.variableName; // direct access
myObject.getVariableMethod(); // access via method
```

Class variables may be directly accessed without having to first instantiate an object, if they are declared as static, by providing the name of the class in dot notation:

```
ClassName.classVariable; // class variable access without
    instantiation
```

Likewise, static class methods may be accessed without first requiring object instantiation:

```
className.classMethod(); // class method access without
    instantiation
```

For information about static variables and methods, see Chapters 5 and 11.

Object references

Whenever you assign an object to a variable or pass an object as a parameter to a method or class, it is done by reference. That is, instead of the object itself, the address of the object is used. As a result, dealing with objects is very different from dealing with primitive types.

Note

Variables of interface types can contain references to objects that implement that interface. For details on interfaces, see Chapter 11.

Copying objects

Perhaps the most obvious difference between objects and primitives is seen with the = assignment operator. With primitive types, this operator is used to store a value in a variable. With objects, however, it stores the reference instead of the value.

For example, consider the following:

```
objectVariable1 = objectVariable2;
```

In this example, we don't copy `objectVariable2` into `objectVariable1`. Instead, `objectVariable1` now merely references (or points to) `objectVariable2`. Whenever `objectVariable2` is altered, `objectVariable1` sees the result. This is very different from actually copying an object's value, because both variables point to the same instance instead of each maintaining a separate copy.

To copy the value of an object into another, you can use either the `copy()` or `clone()` method:

```
objectVariable1.copy(objectVariable2); // copy objectVariable2
  into objectVariable1
objectVariable1 = objectVariable2.clone(); // clone object
```

When using `copy()`, both objects are instances of the same class. The value of all instance variables of the object you pass as an argument to `copy()` are copied into the instance variables of the object on the left side of the dot notation. If an instance variable contains the reference to an object, only the reference is copied, not the object itself.

With `clone()`, a new instance is created and the value of all instance variables of the current object are copied into the new one. Just as with `copy()`, if an instance variable contains the reference to an object, only the reference is copied (not the object itself). If the two objects aren't of the same type, you must perform a cast:

```
objectVariable1 = (objectVariable1) objectVariable2.clone();
```

Note

Not all objects support `copy()` and `clone()`. When they are supported, you may need to cast objects from one type to another in order to carry out the method. Casting objects is possible as long as the object you're casting is related (by inheritance) to the object it's being cast to. This means you can only cast an object to an instance of its superclass or subclass. To perform the cast, enclose the name of the class you are casting the object to in parentheses:

```
(ClassName) theObject;
```

When a cast is performed, a new instance of the specified class is created, which has the contents of the object. The original object isn't altered, and can be used exactly as it was before the cast was performed.

In addition to explicit casts, variables can contain references to objects whose runtime type can be converted to the variable's compile-time type through assignment conversion.

Testing for equality

Dealing with objects by reference rather than by value also affects the way in which the objects are tested for equality. With primitive types, the == operator is used for this. With objects, however, this operator only tests the references to objects for equality. As a result, the following does not tell you if the two objects are equal:

```
objectVariable1 == objectVariable2; // test references for
    equality
```

While this will tell you if two variables refer to the same thing, it doesn't compare the contents of what each points to. In order to find out if the objects themselves are equal, you must use the equals() method:

```
objectVariable1.equals(objectVariable2); // test value of
objects for equality
```

Null references

The null reference is used to specify an object that has no instance. We can set objects to null, and test them to see if they are null or an actual instance:

```
anyObject = null; // set an object to null
if (anyObject = = null) { // test for null
    . . .
}
```

Determining an object's class

Every object that isn't an array is an instance of a class. An object's class is often called its *runtime type*. You can find out what class an object was created from by cascading the getClass() and getName() methods, as follows:

```
anyObject.getClass().getName();
    // retrieve the class name (returns a string)
```

Since cascading these two methods returns a String object, you'll often assign the object to a string variable for future use:

```
String theClassName = anyObject.getClass().getName();
```

The getClass() method is defined in the Object class (java.lang.Object), from which all classes are derived. Since every Java class is ultimately a descendant of the Object class, the variables and methods defined in this class are available to every object (see Table 9-20). As a result, we can send any object the getClass() message in order to invoke that method and retrieve the class it was instantiated from.

Table 9-20
Class java.lang.Object

Method	Signature	Description
Object	public Object()	Creates a new object.
clone	protected Object clone() throws CloneNot SupportedException	Creates a clone of the object.
equals	public boolean equals (Object obj)	Compares two objects for equality, returning true if they are equal, false if not.
finalize	protected void finalize() throws Throwable	Code to execute when this object is garbage-collected.
getClass	public final Class getClass()	Returns the class of this object.
hashCode	public int hashCode()	Returns the hash code for this object.
notify	public final void notify()	Notifies a single waiting thread that another thread's condition has changed (can only be called from within a synchronized method or block of code).
notifyAll	public final void notifyAll()	Notifies all waiting threads that a condition has changed (can only be called from within a synchronized method or block of code).
toString	public String toString()	Returns a string representing the value of this object. Subclasses should override this method.
wait	public final void wait(long timeout) throws InterruptedException	Causes a thread to wait for a notification, or until the specified timeout value expires (can only be called from within a synchronized method or block of code).
wait	public final void wait(long timeout, int nanos) throws InterruptedException	A more precise wait method (can only be called from within a synchronized method or block of code).
wait	public final void wait() throws InterruptedException	Causes a thread to wait indefinitely until notified (can only be called from within a synchronized method or block of code).

The getName() method is defined in the Class class (java.lang.Class), which contains the runtime representations of classes. Since every Java object is an instance of some class, the methods in Table 9-21 can be invoked when combined with the getClass() method, as we've done.

<table>
<tr><td colspan="3" align="center">Table 9-21
Class java.lang.Class</td></tr>
<tr><td>Method</td><td>Signature</td><td>Description</td></tr>
<tr><td>forName</td><td>public static Class forName(String className) throws ClassNotFoundException</td><td>Returns runtime class descriptor for this class.</td></tr>
<tr><td>getClassLoader</td><td>public ClassLoader getClassLoader()</td><td>Returns the class loader of this class. Returns null if a class loader isn't used by the class.</td></tr>
<tr><td>getInterfaces</td><td>public Class[] getInterfaces()</td><td>Returns the interfaces implemented by this class (an array of length zero [0] is returned if no interfaces are implemented).</td></tr>
<tr><td>getName</td><td>public String getName() getSuperclass()</td><td>Returns the name of this class.</td></tr>
<tr><td>getSuperclass</td><td>public Class</td><td>Returns the superclass of this class.</td></tr>
<tr><td>isInterface</td><td>public boolean isInterface()</td><td>Returns true or false, indicating whether the class is an interface or not.</td></tr>
<tr><td>newInstance</td><td>public Object newInstance() throws InstantiationException, IllegalAccessException</td><td>Creates a new instance of this class.</td></tr>
<tr><td>toString</td><td>public String toString()</td><td>Returns the name of this class or interface, with the word class prepended to classes and the word interface prepended to interfaces.</td></tr>
</table>

At times, you'll want to know what class an object was created from. To do this, you can use the `instanceof` operator, by providing the object to the left of the operator and the class name to the right:

```
anyObject instanceof ClassName
```

The boolean value of `true` is returned if the object is an instance of the specified class, otherwise `false` is returned.

```
if (theObject instanceof ClassName) {   // returns true if of
same class
}
```

Standard default values

In Java programs, every variable has a default value. If you don't initialize a variable when it's first created, the default for that variable type is automatically provided in accordance with Table 9-22.

Tip

Although Java automatically initializes variables to their standard default values, it's poor programming style to rely on this process. These automatic default values are required to guarantee portability of Java code, at considerable expense to the compiler. The compiler must locate all variables that are used by your program before a value is provided for them. Do the compiler a favor, and supply a value (either through initialization or later in the program) for each variable before it is used.

Table 9-22 Default Values for Types	
Type	*Default*
byte	zero: (byte)0
short	zero: (short)0
int	zero: 0
long	zero: 0L
float	positive zero: 0.0f
double	positive zero: 0.0d
char	null character: '\u0000'
boolean	false
reference	null

Summary

This chapter reviewed the core of the Java language. Each of the elements described are essential to understand before you begin to develop your own Java applications. Before you continue make sure that you understand these key concepts presented in this chapter:

✦ Java is a tokenized language: The lines of code that you write are translated by the compiler into discrete elements known as *tokens*. Working from left to right, the compiler discards all comments and whitespace. What remains is separated into one of five possible tokens: keywords, identifiers, literals, separators, operators.

✦ Keywords are character sequences formed by ASCII letters that are reserved by the Java language for special purposes. You cannot use them for anything other than their intended purpose.

✦ An *identifier* is a sequence of Unicode characters that you use to name a class, method, or variable. Identifiers can be of any length, and they can contain both letters and digits. However, they must begin with a letter, not a digit. You can use any name you can think of for an identifier, provided it doesn't begin with a digit and is not the same as a keyword. Because identifiers are Unicode, they can even include non-Latin letters and digits.

✦ Literals are explicit values, such as `18345` or `"Hello World!"`, that are specified directly in your Java code. Java supports three categories of literals: Those that are numbers (integer and floating-point literals), boolean literals (`true` and `false`), and those that are composed of characters (character literals and string literals).

✦ Types are used to identify the information stored in variables and returned by methods (on those occasions when a method does in fact return data when called). The information stored in a variable or returned by a method is known as the *value* of the variable or return. In essence, you create variables that have a certain type.

✦   ✦   ✦

Language Fundamentals

In this chapter, we'll continue to explore the fundamental elements of the Java language. We'll begin with a look at variables and see how to declare, initialize, and use them in our programs.

From there, we'll proceed to expressions, and learn how these statements are used to perform calculations and store values in variables. Since expressions make use of operators, we'll explore in more detail the Java operators introduced in the previous chapter.

Next, we'll see how the control of program execution is directed with Java's control-flow statements. We'll discuss branching statements and loops, and see how they are used to control the way in which our programs are executed.

Finally, we'll cover Java's general-purpose error processing mechanism, using what are known as *exceptions*. By learning to use them, we can create robust and reliable Java programs.

Variables

Variables are used to store values in Java, something we've been doing all along without much ado. Once a value is stored in a variable, we can use it for any number of purposes.

One such purpose is to represent an object's state, as discussed in Chapter 2. Since the value stored in a variable can be altered, the state of an object can also be altered by changing the value of its variables.

Variables are also used to perform calculations, control the flow of program execution, and effect the overall state of a program. They are a fundamental part of programming languages; without them we'd be hard pressed to develop software.

Declaring variables

To use a variable, you first have to declare it. A variable declaration consists of two parts:

✦ A data type: This determines the legal range of values a variable may contain, what operations may be applied to the variable, and how such operations are performed.

✦ An identifier: An identifier is used to associate a name with a variable:

```
type identifier [, identifier];
```

Any number of variables can be declared on a single line, each of the same type, as long as each identifier's name is unique and separated from the others by a comma. A semicolon is used to signal the end of a variable declaration.

Here, we declare an integer variable and give it the name horizontal:

```
int horizontal;
```

And here we declare several integer variables, all on the same line:

```
int horizontal, vertical, x, y, z, months, years, days,
ageInDays;
```

However, we could have broken the above declaration into a number of declarations:

```
int horizontal;
int vertical;
int x;
int y;
int z;
int months;
int years;
int days;
int ageInDays;
```

How you declare your variables depends mainly on personal taste, although most programmers would have chosen the first example for ease of readability. You aren't required to place all variable names on the same line, as I did in the example, however. You can spread them over several lines, if you want, as long as the last variable name is immediately followed by a semicolon:

```
int horizontal,
    vertical,
    x,
    y,
    z,
```

```
       months,
       years,
       days,
       ageInDays;
```

In fact, you can group variable names over several lines, in any way you see fit:

```
int horizontal, vertical,
    x, y, z,
    months, years, days,
    ageInDays;
```

Variable types

As you learned in the previous chapter, Java data types fall into two major categories: *primitives* and *references* to objects.

Primitive variables

Your programs will likely use a large number of different primitive variables. Any variable that you declare of type byte, short, int, long, float, double, char, or boolean is a primitive variable. The following are examples of variable declarations for each primitive type:

```
byte x;
short daysInMonth;
int counter;
long bacteriaCount;
float accountBalance;
double exactBalance;
char middleInitial;
boolean quit;
```

Reference variables

Reference variables are used to store references, or pointers, to objects. (Keep in mind that we're not referring to pointers such as those used in C and C++ here, but simply the concept of pointing to an object in memory.) These objects can be class instances, class instances that implement interfaces, or arrays.

Note

An *interface* is a collection of methods that are not implemented in code; interfaces are explained in detail in Chapter 11.

Following are examples of reference variable declarations for each category of objects (class instances, instances that implement interfaces, and arrays):

```
int highScores[]; /* array of integers */
```

Initializing and storing values in variables

Once a variable has been declared, a value may be stored in it. This may be done either at the time a variable is declared — a process known as *initialization* — or anytime after it has been declared. In either case, any value assigned to a variable must be of the same type as the variable itself.

These are examples of variables being initialized at the time of declaration:

```
byte x = 2;
short daysInMonth = 31;
int counter = 1043;
long bacteriaCount = 12239493;
float accountBalance = 533.35;
double exactBalance = 464.3243003;
char middleInitial = 'E';
boolean quit = false;
String helloString = "Hello World!";
AudioClip music = getAudioClip(getCodeBase(), "audio/hello.au");
```

In each of the above examples, a value consistent with the variable's data type is assigned to it at the time of declaration. These variables have been initialized. From the moment they are created, they contain a value. You'll notice, however, that there is no example of an array being initialized.

Array initialization

In the case of arrays, each element may contain a value. If we declare an array having a dozen integer elements, it can hold 12 different integers.

An array is typically initialized in two steps. First, we declare the number of elements it will have. Then each element in the array is individually initialized, or set to a value (usually zero). Here is an example of how we would initialize our array of integers:

```
int highScores[] = new int[12];      /* declare array of 12
   integers */
for (short i=0; i < 12; i++) {
   highScores[i] = 0; /* initialize each array element to zero */
}
```

As you can see, the for loop used above also contains a variable declaration. We declare an index, i, that is used to access each element in the array. Before using i, we initialize it to zero (0), since the first element in every array is at position zero (arrays in Java are zero-based, just as C/C++ arrays are). Each time through the loop, the ith element in the array is initialized to zero. After 12 iterations, each element in the array has been initialized to zero.

Tip

Arrays can be declared and initialized in a single step, instead of in two steps as shown here. For details, see Chapter 12.

Variable scope

Every variable has an associated *scope*—the extent to which it can be used. The scope of a variable begins immediately where it is declared, and ends with the closing brace (}) of the block of code in which it is declared. You can access a variable only within its scope. If you attempt to access a variable outside its scope, the compiler generates an error.

For instance, the scope of the variables declared in our MediaHelloWorld applet in Listing 10-1 is the class definition itself. The variables myImage, myAudio, horizontal, vertical, and SoundOn are all declared immediately following the class signature, and can therefore be accessed inside the scope of that class. This means that any of the class methods can access these variables. And, as you can see, each of the methods accesses at least one class variable.

Listing 10-1: **Declaring Variables in the MediaHelloWorld applet**

```
public class MediaHelloWorld extends HelloWorldApplet {
Image  myImage;
AudioClip  myAudio;
int  horizontal, vertical;
boolean  SoundOn = true;
public void init() {
  super.init();
  myImage=getImage(getCodeBase(), "images/world.gif");
  myAudio=getAudioClip(getCodeBase(), "audio/hello.au");
}
public void paint(Graphics g)
{
  if (myImage != null)
{  // only draw if the variable contains data!
      g.drawImage(myImage, horizontal, vertical, this);
      }
  super.paint(g);
}

public void start()
{
  myAudio.loop();
}

public void stop()
{
```

(continued)

Listing 10-1 *(continued)*

```
    myAudio.stop();
  }
public boolean mouseDown(java.awt.Event event, int x, int y) {
  if (SoundOn) {
    myAudio.loop();
    SoundOn = false;
  }
  else {
    myAudio.stop();
    SoundOn = true;
  }
  return true;
}
public boolean mouseMove(java.awt.Event event, int x, int y) {
  horizontal=x;
  vertical=y;
  repaint();
  return true;
}
} /* the variable scope ends here! */
```

However, suppose the `horizontal` and `vertical` integers were declared in the `paint()` method instead of in the class itself. If this were the case, the scope of these variables would be the `paint()` method only. Any attempt to access these variables outside `paint()` would generate an error, since they can't be accessed outside of their scope:

```
public void paint(Graphics g) {
  int horizontal=100, vertical=50; /* declared inside the
    method */
  g.drawImage(myImage, horizontal, vertical, this); /* so this
    is fine */
  super.paint(g);
} /* the scope of horizontal and vertical ends here! */
public boolean mouseMove(java.awt.Event event, int x, int y) {
  horizontal=x; /* ILLEGAL - attempt to access outside of
    scope! */
  vertical=y; /* ILLEGAL - attempt to access outside of
    scope! */
  repaint();
  return true;
}
```

A special situation can occur in which a variable is *hidden* by the declaration of another variable with the same name. This happens if the second variable declaration happens within a sub-block of code residing in the original variable's scope. For instance, suppose we declared our `horizontal` and `vertical` variables immediately following the class signature, as in Listing 10-1. Clearly, the scope of these variables would be the entire class itself.

However, if we also declared `horizontal` and `vertical` integer variables inside the `paint()` method, the original ones would be hidden from that method. In this case, any reference to `horizontal` or `vertical` inside `paint()` would refer to the variables declared in that method, instead of to the class variables of the same name:

```
int horizontal, vertical;  /* original variable declaration */
public void paint(Graphics g) {
   int horizontal=100, vertical=50; /* method variables of same
   name */
   g.drawImage(myImage, horizontal, vertical, this); /* refers to
   paint() method variables, not those declared earlier */
   super.paint(g);
} /* the scope of paint() horizontal and vertical ends here! */
public boolean mouseMove (java.awt.Event event, int x, int y) {
   horizontal=x; /* refers to original variable */
   vertical=y; /* refers to original variable */
   repaint();
   return true;
}
```

Expressions

Expressions are statements that, when executed, result in a value. When programming, we use expressions all the time, sometimes without even realizing it. Java expressions are similar in syntax to those of C and C++. The following are examples of Java expressions:

```
65 + 5 /* produces a value of 70 */
(i < 10) /* produces true or false, (depending on the value of
   i) */
5 * 100 /* produces 500 */
x = 25 - 5; /* subtracts five from 25, then places the result
   (20) in the x variable */
(35*5) - 4 /* produces 171 (multiples 35 and 5, then subtracts
   4) */
```

Expressions are typically composed of several smaller expressions, or subexpressions, connected by operators. For instance, consider the following lines of code:

```
int x = 100, y;
y = (x/4) + 3;
```

The first line of code, where our variables are declared, actually contains an expression in the assignment of 100 to the x variable. The integer literal 100 is an expression, albeit a simple one. When the compiler looks at this line, it sees something like "evaluate the expression to the right of the assignment operator, =, and place its value in the variable on the left." Since the expression is the integer literal 100, it evaluates to 100 and is then stored in the x variable. Pretty simple, yet it's an expression.

Now take a look at the next line. The complete expression would be:

```
y = (x/4) + 3;
```

However, this expression is made up of several subexpressions. You might recognize one right off the bat:

```
x/4
```

While you'd be correct, there are even subexpressions inside this simple statement! The x variable is a subexpression that evaluates to 100, and the integer literal 4 is another subexpression that evaluates to 4. After each of these is evaluated and the division operation is performed, the result is 25. To this, the value 3 is added, yet another subexpression! And finally, the entire value (28) is placed inside the y variable. As you can see, there are many levels of expressions, even in what appear to be simple statements.

Operators

Since Java expressions are typically several subexpressions linked together by operators, it's important to understand exactly how operators work. Java supports both unary and binary operators. Unary operators are those that act on a single operand, while binary operators act on two operands.

The following is an expression using the unary postfix increment operator. As you can see, it requires only one operand (x, in this case):

```
x++;
```

And here is the functional equivalent of the above using the binary addition operator:

```
x = x + 1;
```

In this case, the binary addition operator acts on two operands (x and 1). Once the right-hand side of the assignment operator is evaluated, the result is stored in the x variable on the left.

These two expressions do the same thing; they both increase the value of x by one. However, we've used a different operator in each case. In the first example, the unary operator ++ was used. In the second example, the binary addition operator + was used.

Operator precedence

Expressions are evaluated from left to right, according to the *precedence* of the operators in the expression—that is, the rules that determine which operators are executed first. By following a precedence order, Java guarantees that a particular expression will produce the same results every time it is executed. For instance, take into consideration the following expression:

```
x = 15 + 3 * 2 - 14;
```

Without a precedence order, which subexpression is evaluated first? Should it be 15 + 3, 3 * 2, or 2 – 14? For that matter, once the first subexpression is evaluated, which is next? Clearly, the value of the expression changes, depending on the order in which its subexpressions are evaluated.

If we couldn't rely on the order in which operations were performed, it would make our programs about as consistent as the New York City subway system. Luckily, Java operators are arranged and executed in order of precedence. Table 10-1 lists all Java operators according to their precedence order. You'll see that I've placed parentheses first in this table. They aren't really an operator, since they don't perform an operation on data types, but they appear in the table nonetheless to emphasize that they're given top priority during evaluation (see "Forcing order" later in this chapter).

Table 10-1
Java Operator Precedence

Precedence	Associativity	Operator	Description
First	N/A	( )	parentheses (forcing order)
Second	R-to-L	++	pre/post increment (unary)
	R-to-L	- -	pre/post decrement (unary)
	R-to-L	!	logical complement (unary)
	R-to-L	~	unary bitwise logical negation
	R-to-L	+	addition (unary)
	R-to-L	– (className)	subtraction (unary) cast object to class type

(continued)

Table 10-1 *(continued)*

Precedence	Associativity	Operator	Description
Third	L-to-R	* / %	multiplication, division, and remainder
Fourth	L-to-R	+ -	addition and subtraction
Fifth	L-to-R	<<	shift left
	L-to-R	>>	shift right (sign extension)
	L-to-R	>>>	right shift (zero extension)
Sixth	L-to-R	< <=	"less than" and "less than or equal to"
	L-to-R	> >=	"greater than" and "greater than or equal to"
	L-to-R	instanceof	"is the object an instance of this class?"
Seventh	L-to-R	==	equality
	L-to-R	!=	non-equality (not equal)
Eighth	L-to-R	&	bitwise AND, boolean AND
Ninth	L-to-R	^	bitwise EXCLUSIVE OR (XOR), boolean EXCLUSIVE OR (XOR)
Tenth	L-to-R	|	bitwise OR, boolean OR
Eleventh	L-to-R	&&	AND (boolean conditional "short-circuit")
Twelfth	L-to-R	||	OR (boolean conditional "short-circuit")
Thirteenth	R-to-L	? :	ternary conditional
Fourteenth	R-to-L	=	assignment
Last	R-to-L	*= /= %= += -= <<= >= >>>= &= ^= |=	assignment (and operation)

Since all operations are performed according to the precedence of the operators involved, Java expressions are evaluated in a predictable manner. Operations whose operators have the highest precedence are performed first, with lower precedence operators following in sequence. When operations of the same precedence occur within the same expression, they are processed according to operator associativity.

Note

When two operations of the same precedence are encountered, which is performed first? It all depends on the order, or *associativity*, specified for the operators involved. An operator's associativity determines whether it is evaluated from right to left (R-to-L) or left to right (L-to-R). See the next section, "Forcing order," to learn how to bypass an operator's natural associativity.

Now, let's return to our example:

```
x = 15 + 3 * 2 - 14;
```

Thanks to operator precedence, we can see that it evaluates in a very specific order. The middle operation (3 * 2) is performed first, and then the next two operations are carried out from left to right:

3 * 2	produces 6, which is used in the next operation
15 + 6	produces 21, which is used in the final operation
21 - 14	produces 7, which is stored in the variable x

Forcing order

If the natural order of evaluation isn't desired, you can use parentheses to control the order of evaluation. For instance, suppose you wanted the subexpression 2 - 14 to be evaluated first. You could ensure this by placing it inside parentheses:

```
x = 15 + 3 * (2 - 14);
```

In this case, the following steps are taken when the expression is evaluated:

2 - 14	produces –12, which is used in the next operation
3 * -12	produces –36, which is used in the final operation
15 + -36	produces –21, which is stored in the variable x

Since multiplication operators have precedence over arithmetic ones, this operation is performed after the subexpression inside parentheses. However, we could have added another pair of parentheses to force the multiplication operation to take place last:

```
x = (15 + 3) * (2 - 14);
```

In this case, the subexpressions inside the parentheses are of the same precedence. As a result, they are carried out from left to right. The steps are:

15 + 3	produces 18, which is used in the final operation
2 - 14	produces –12, which is used in the final operation
18 * -12	produces –216, which is stored in the variable x

And, of course, parentheses can be nested. We could, for example, group these three subexpressions by surrounding them with parentheses and add another subexpression to the mix. Here are a few examples, each producing a different data type:

```
x = ((15 + 3) * (2 - 14)) + 1;      /* produces an integer value */
x = ((15 + 3) * (2 - 14)) + 1.2;    /* produces a floating-point
                                       value */
x = ((15 + 3) * (2 - 14)) > 1;      /* produces a boolean value */
```

Types of operators

The types of operators that can be used in an operation depend on the data type of the operands involved. For instance, the operators used in an integer operation are different from those used in a boolean operation.

Integer operators

The operators used in integer operations are listed in Table 10-2. The result of an integer operation depends on the data type of the operands involved.

Table 10-2 **Arithmetic Operators**			
Type	**Operator**	**Operation**	**Notes**
Unary	-	negation	
	~	bitwise complement	
	++	increment	postfix and prefix
	--	decrement	postfix and prefix
	abs()	absolute value	usage: a = abs(3);
Binary	+	addition	
	+=	addition	(a=a+b) is equivalent to (a+=b)
	-	subtraction	
	-=	subtraction	(a=a-b) is equivalent to (a-=b)
	*	multiplication	
	*=	multiplication	(a=a*b) is equivalent to (a*=b)
	/	division	rounds toward zero; division by zero throws ArithmeticException
	/=	division	(a=a/b) is equivalent to (a/=b)

Type	Operator	Operation	Notes
	%	modulo	%0 throws `ArithmeticException`
	%=	modulo	(a=a%b) is equivalent to (a%=b)
	>>=	right shift (propagate sign)	(a=a>>b) is equivalent to (a>>=b)
	<<	left shift	
	>	right shift	sign is propagated
	>>>	zero-fill right shift	pads with zeros on left
	max()	maximum value of range	usage: i = max(x,y);
	min()	minimum value of range	usage: i = min(x,y);

For instance, if both operands in an integer operation are `int` data types, the result will be an `int`. If one operand is an `int` and the other a `long`, the result will be a `long`. However, regardless of the operands involved, an integer operation will always produce either an `int` or a `long` value. This is true even in cases where the operands are `byte`, `short`, or `char` data types.

As mentioned in the previous chapter, an `ArithmeticException` is thrown if an attempt is made to divide an integer by zero (0). The same holds true for modulo arithmetic: `ArithmeticException` is thrown whenever %0 is encountered.

Tip If the result of an integer operation overflows (that is, it is beyond the legal range of the result type), it will be reduced by modulo arithmetic. It is important, therefore, to ensure that your variables are capable of storing the range of values that might be returned when assigning the result of operations to variables.

Floating-point operators

Operations on floating-point numbers behave much the same as those on integers, using the same operands (see Table 10-2). If both operands in an operation are of type `float`, the result is also of type `float`. If one of the operands is of type `double`, the result will be of type `double`.

However, there are a few slight differences between integer and floating-point operations. For example, when the unary increment (++) or decrement (--) operators are used with a floating-point operand, the value of 1.0 is added to the operand (when applied to integers, the value of 1 is added).

Another difference occurs with the modulo (%) operator. When applied to integers (such as 10%4), the remainder of the division operation, 10/4, is returned as an integer (2). When the modulo operator is applied to a floating-point number, the remainder of the division operation is returned as a floating-point value.

Floating-point operations will never generate an ArithmeticException error, however, as explained in the previous chapter. Instead, a special value, NaN (Not-a-Number), is used to represent the result of operations that don't return a number.

Note

The presence of a NaN can produce unexpected results when dealing with floating-point data types. Since NaN is unordered, the result of a <, <=, >, >=, or == comparison between a NaN and another value is always false. In fact, == always produces false when both operands are NaN. On the other hand, the result of a != comparison with a NaN is always true, even if both operands are NaN.

Boolean operators

When an operation involves the use of a boolean operator, the result of that operation will return a boolean value of either true or false. This is the case even if the operands are not of the boolean data type, as the following code snippet shows:

```
int x = 3; // declare integer variable initialized to 3
boolean myBoolean; // declare boolean variable
myBoolean = x < 10; // a boolean expression
```

Since the expression x<10 uses the "less than" boolean operator, it returns a boolean value which we store in the variable myBoolean. In this example, myBoolean would be set to true, since x is indeed less than 10.

Table 10-3 contains the boolean operators supported by Java.

Table 10-3
Boolean Operators

Type	Operator	Operation	Notes
Unary	!	negation	
Binary	&	logical AND	evaluate both operands
	&=	logical AND	(a=a&b) is equivalent to (a&=b)
	|	logical OR	evaluate both operands
	|=	logical OR	(a=a|b) is equivalent to (a|=b)
	^	logical XOR	evaluate both operands
	^=	logical XOR	(a=a^b) is equivalent to (a^=b)
	&&	logical AND	short-circuit evaluation of operands
	||	logical OR	short-circuit evaluation of operands
	>	greater than	
	<	less than	

Type	Operator	Operation	Notes
	>=	greater than or equal to	
	<=	less than or equal to	
	==	equality	
	!=	inequality	
Ternary	?:	if, then	`(if a, then b)` is equivalent to `(a?:b)`

String operators

As you know, strings in Java are actually `String` objects. If the arithmetic addition operator (+) is used when one (or both) of the operands is of type `string`, the operation is considered a string concatenation. If only one of the operands is of type `string`, the other operand is converted into a string before the concatenation is carried out.

When a nonstring operand is converted to a string, the process is carried out according to the compile-time type of the operand.

If the value of the operand is null, then the literal string null is used. If the value is other than null, the `toString()` method of the operand is invoked. This method returns a reference value of type `string`, which is used (unless this value is null, in which case the literal string null is used). Since the class `Object` defines a `toString()` method, this method is always available when dealing with objects, even if the operand itself doesn't implement a `toString()` method.

If the operand is of the primitive integral type, it's converted into a string representing the value in decimal notation. If the value of the operand is negative, the string is preceded by a minus sign. If the value is nonzero, the first digit is nonzero. If the value is zero, the single digit 0 is produced.

If the operand is of type `char`, it's converted to a string containing the single character of the `char`.

If the operand is of type `boolean`, it's converted into a string containing the boolean's value (either the literal string "true" or the literal string "false").

Array operators

When operations are performed on arrays, they return the value of a specific element in that array. However, unlike the data types we've been dealing with thus far, an array must be allocated using the new operator before it can be assigned to a variable:

```
int a[] = new int[15];
```

In the preceding example, an array of 15 integer elements is created and assigned to the variable a. Once this operation has taken place, we can store and retrieve values in the array elements using the following syntax:

```
arrayVariable[expression]
```

For instance, each of the following lines of code accesses the same element in our array:

```
int x = 5, y = 2, z = 10; /* initialize a few integer
                               variables */
a[10] = 82569; /* store 82569 in 11th element */
a[z] = 4370; /* store 4370 in 11th element */
a[x*y] = 111791; /* store 111791 in 11th element */
a[x+5] = 592; /* store 592 in 11th element */
int i;
i = a[10]; /* retrieve 11th element */
i = a[x+5]; /* retrieve 11th element */
i = a[100/z+1] /* retrieve 11th element */
i = a[a.length - 5]; /* retrieve 11th element */
```

In the last example, we used the instance variable length in the expression. Since a.length returns the number of elements in the array, this is a valid expression.

Note

Since Java arrays are zero-based, like C/C++ arrays, using the subscript 10 as we do here actually accesses the 11th element. For details on zero-based array access, see Chapter 12.

If, in any case, an array index is negative or greater than the number of elements in the array minus one (14, in our example), an ArrayIndexOutOfBoundsException is thrown. Continuing with our previous example, the following operations would cause an out-of-bounds exception:

```
a[x+z]; /* expression evaluates to 15, an illegal index value */
a[x*x]; /* expression evaluates to 25, an illegal index value */
a[a.length]; /* expression evaluates to 15, an illegal index
                 value */
```

Array index values can be of `byte`, `short`, `int`, or even `char` types. However, array indexes of type `long` are not permitted. In order to use a `long`, it must be cast into the `int` type, as the following example shows:

```
long myLong = 10;
a[myLong]; // illegal, since array indexes can't be of type long
a[(int) myLong]; // legal, since the long is cast into an int
```

Note

Keep in mind that array indexing begins at zero, as explained in Chapter 7. In this example, as with all arrays, the first element is accessed with an index value of zero: `a[0]`. Since we have 15 elements in this particular array (from index 0 to 14), the last element is referenced with an index value of 14: `a[14]`. For details on arrays, see Chapter 12.

Object operators

In Java, a special operator exists that allows you to determine whether an object is an instance of a particular class, subclass, or interface. Using the `instanceof` binary operator, you can test objects to compare them against a specific class or interface type:

```
if (theObject instanceof ClassName) {
}
```

Control-Flow Statements

In order to direct the flow of program execution, Java supports several control-flow statements. These are similar to their C and C++ counterparts, so they look and act as you would expect if you're already familiar with one (or both) of these languages. We'll take a look at each, beginning with the popular `if` statement.

if statements

Java supports two types of `if` statements, both of which require the use of a boolean expression. This is the syntax for the most basic `if` statement:

```
if (boolean expression) {
    ...
}
```

Depending on the value of the boolean expression, the body of the `if` statement may or may not be executed. If the expression evaluates to `true`, the body is executed. If the expression evaluates to `false`, the body of code is skipped.

Take, for example, the following if statement:

```
if (x < 10) {
  System.out.println ("The if block is being executed.");
  System.out.println ("And the value of x is: " + x);
}
```

When the preceding statement is encountered, this boolean expression is evaluated:

```
x < 10
```

The body of code following the if statement executes only in cases where x is less than 10. If x is equal to (or greater than) 10, the block of code is skipped and program execution continues immediately after the closing brace (}).

Note

This form of control flow is often called an if-then statement, since it follows the logic of "if the expression is true, then execute this body of code."

The second form of if statement makes use of the keyword else, directing program execution along one of two distinct routes:

```
if (boolean expression) {
  ...
}
else {
  ...
}
```

If the boolean value evaluates to true, the block of code immediately following is executed. If the expression evaluates to false, the else block is executed.

Note

This form of control flow is often called an if-then-else statement, since it follows the logic of "if the expression is true, then execute this body of code, or else execute this one."

Our previous example looks like this, using the if-then-else statement:

```
if (x < 10) {
  System.out.println ("The if block is being executed.");
  System.out.println ("And the value of x is: " + x);
}
else {
  System.out.println ("The else block is being executed.");
  System.out.println ("And the value of x is: " + x);
}
```

At any given time, only one of the above blocks of code will be executed. At no time will both be executed, since the value of the boolean expression directs flow of execution in only one of two possible directions, not both.

You can use the `else-if` construct to add another aspect of control to the `if` statement:

```
if (boolean expression) {
  ...
}
else if (boolean expression) {
  ...
}
else {
  ...
}
```

Applying this to our previous example, we can exercise more precise control over the flow of program execution:

```
if (x < 10) {
  System.out.println ("The if block is being executed.");
  System.out.println ("And the value of x is: " + x);
}
else if (x == 15) {
  System.out.println ("The else-if block is being executed.");
  System.out.println ("And the value of x MUST be 15!");
}
else {
  System.out.println ("The else block is being executed.");
  System.out.println ("And the value of x is: " + x);
}
```

Note Unlike `if` statements in C, Java `if` statement expressions must return a boolean value. In C, a value of 0 (zero) is treated as false and a value of 1 is treated as true. This is not the case with Java, where only boolean expressions can be used in an `if` statement.

switch statement

The `switch` statement is similar in nature to the `if-then-else` statement, although it makes the programmer's job a lot easier when a number of `else` clauses are needed:

```
switch (expression) {
  case Constant1:
    ...
    break;
```

```
case Constant2:
   ...
break;
case Constant3:
   ...
break;
.
.
.
default:
   ...
break;
}
```

Upon entering a switch statement, the expression is evaluated.

The data type of the expression must be either char, byte, short, or int. Boolean expressions aren't allowed, although they are used in all other control-flow mechanisms.

The value of the expression is then converted to the int type, as are all the case constants. Beginning with the first case statement, the value of the expression is compared to the value of the case constant. If the two values are equal, any code following the colon is executed, until the break statement is reached. If the expression doesn't match the case constant, it is compared to the next one. This process continues until the default case is reached, at which point the code for this case is executed.

When a case is executed, the break statement is used to stop the flow of execution. When a break statement is reached, execution stops immediately and resumes after the closing brace (}) of the switch body. Since execution terminates when the first break is encountered, the default case will only be executed if no match is found between the value of the switch expression and all other cases.

The switch statement is particularly useful when a number of cases exist. If you were to try and write more than half a dozen else clauses in an if-else statement, you'd find the process more than a bit tedious. It would be even more difficult to read the code, since if-else statements containing more than a handful of clauses are typically messy when compared with a switch statement of the same length. With a switch statement, lengthy code is clean and easy to read by comparison. You can use as many cases as you need, without making a mess of the code. And, if none of the cases match the value of your expression, you can rely on the default case being executed.

Warning

Be certain to end each case with a break statement. If you don't, all cases following the matching one will be tested as well! This is an undesirable condition known as *fall-through*, which you can avoid by matching a break statement with every case.

Loops

Control-flow statements include a number of loops:

- ✦ while **loops**
- ✦ do-while **loops**
- ✦ for **loops**

while and do-while loops

Java while and do-while loops are identical to those in C:

```
while (boolean expression) {
   ...
}
do {
   ...
} while (boolean expression);
```

In the while loop, the boolean expression is evaluated. The value of this expression determines whether or not the body of the loop is executed. If the expression evaluates to true, the loop is executed. If expression value is false, it does not execute. Each time through the body of the while loop, the expression is re-evaluated. The loop continues until the expression evaluates to false:

```
int x = 0;
while (x++ < 10) {
   System.out.println ("The while loop is being executed.");
   System.out.println ("And the value of x is: " + x);
}
```

In the preceding example, the body of the loop continues executing as long as x is less than 10. Since we increment the value of x by one (x++) in the expression itself, the loop is executed 10 times.

Note that the increment could also have taken place in the body of the loop itself, as follows:

```
while (x < 10) {
   x++;
   System.out.println ("The while loop is being executed.");
   System.out.println ("And the value of x is: " + x);
}
```

With the `do-while` loop, the body of the loop executes once before the expression is ever evaluated. This ensures that your loop code is executed at least once, regardless of how the expression evaluates:

```
do {
  System.out.println ("The while loop is being executed.");
  System.out.println ("And the value of x is: " + x);
} while (x++ < 10);
```

As with the `while` loop, we could have incremented our expression inside the loop body, rather than inside the expression:

```
do {
  System.out.println ("The while loop is being executed.");
  System.out.println ("And the value of x is: " + x);
  x++;
} while (x < 10);
```

The `while` loop is by far the most popular of the two, although the `do-while` loop has the advantage of executing your code at least once, no matter what the expression evaluates to.

Tip   Be sure to change your expression value either inside the body of the `while` or `do-while` loop, or in the expression itself. If the value never changes, the expression always remains true and the loop executes indefinitely!

for loop

The `for` loop repeats program execution as controlled through a series of expressions, terminating when a certain condition is no longer met. It continues looping until the specified boolean condition evaluates to `false`, at which point the loop is broken and execution resumes after the loop body:

```
for (expression; booleanExpression; expression) {
  ...
}
```

The first expression initializes the loop variable. The second is a boolean expression that specifies the condition that must be met in order for the loop body to be executed. The third and final expression specifies how the loop variable is to change each time through the loop.

Consider the following example:

```
int x;
for (x=0; x<10; x++) {
  System.out.println ("The for loop is being executed.");
  System.out.println ("And the value of x is: " + x);
}
```

The first expression, x=0, sets our loop variable to zero. The loop executes until the second expression, x<10, evaluates to `true`. And the final expression, x++, increments our loop variable by one every time through the loop.

Unlike C, Java supports the declaration of loop variables inside the initialization portion of the loop statement:

```
for (int x=0; x<10; x++) {
   System.out.println ("The for loop is being executed.");
   System.out.println ("And the value of x is: " + x);
}
```

In this case, the scope of the loop variable is the loop itself. You're free to access x, as long as you do so in the body of the `for` loop. However, you can't use x outside the closing loop brace (}), since access outside the loop is beyond the scope of this variable.

break and continue statements

In addition to the `if`, `switch`, `while`, and `do-while` control-flow constructs, Java supports two additional statements: `break` and `continue`. These are considered "jump" statements, because they allow the flow of program execution to branch out in directions not seen with the standard control-flow statements we've already discussed.

As you've seen, the `switch` statement makes use of the `break` statement to terminate a specific case's execution. However, those `break` statements were used without labels. Both `break` and `continue` can be used with an optional label that specifies exactly where the execution will be transferred. Without a label, `break` and `continue` behave exactly as they do in C.

Take a look at the following example of a labeled `break` statement in a `switch` occurring in a `while` loop:

```
int x=0;
enterLoop:
while (x++<10) {
System.out.println ("Inside the while loop, iteration:" + x);
   switch (x) {
      case 0:  System.out.println ("Inside switch, x equals: " +
                                   x);
      break;
      case 1:  System.out.println ("Inside switch, x equals: " +
                                   x);
      break;
      case 2:  System.out.println ("Inside switch, x equals: " +
                                   x);
      break;
```

```
        default:
          if (x==5) {
            System.out.println ("Break out of switch, and while loop
                                 too!");
            break enterLoop; /* break to enterLoop label */
          }
          break;
      }
    System.out.println ("Out of switch, back in while loop.");
  }
```

Each time through the `while` loop, the `switch` statement is encountered. Up until the time x is equal to 5, standard `break` statements are used to break out of the `switch` statement and back into the `while` loop. However, when x is equal to 5, the following line of code is executed:

```
break enterLoop
```

When this happens, not only does the break occur for the `switch` statement, but also for the entire `while` loop! If this labeled break were not present, the `while` loop would execute ten times. However, it only executes five times, since the labeled break kicks the flow of control out of both the `switch` and `while` loop.

While the `break` statement is used to break out of the loop, a labeled `continue` statement redirects it to the label itself.

Unlike `break`, the labeled `continue` statement transfers control of program execution to the iteration following the label:

```
int x=0;
enterLoop:
while (x++<5) {
System.out.println ("Inside the while loop, iteration: " + x);
  for (int i=0; i<10;i++) {
    System.out.println ("Inside the for loop, iteration: " +
      i);
    if (i == 5) {
      System.out.println ("Transferring flow out of for
        loop!");
      continue enterLoop; /* jump to enterLoop label when i
                             is 5 */
    }
  }
System.out.println ("Out of for loop, back in while.");
}
```

Here, we've created a `for` loop inside a `while` loop. Each time through the `while` loop, the `for` loop is executed until i equals 5, at which point program execution jumps out of the `for` loop and goes to the first statement inside the `while` loop:

```
System.out.println ("Inside the while loop, iteration: " + x);
```

When this happens, the final output line in our `while` loop isn't executed, since the flow of execution has been rerouted to its beginning. However, if we hadn't included a label, the `break` statement alone would have rerouted the execution to the first line of code following the `for` loop. In that case, the final output line would have been executed.

Note

In Java, there are actually four jump statements:

✦   `break`

✦   `continue`

✦   `return`

✦   `throw`

The `return` statement is used to return program execution to the caller of a code segment, such as when a method has been invoked. At any point in the method, a `return` statement can return the flow of control back to the caller of that method.

The `throw` statement is used to signal a runtime exception, as described below, which interrupts the flow of program execution while a hander is sought to deal with that exception.

Exceptions

Java features a general-purpose error processing system known as an *exception mechanism*. The exception mechanism is composed of two parts: throwing exceptions and catching them. To throw an exception means to signal an error, while to catch one is to trap and handle an error that has been thrown. While new to C programmers, exceptions provide a uniform approach to signaling and processing errors, removing much of the burden of traditional error processing.

Note

The term *exception* is short for "exceptional event." Exceptional events are those that disrupt the normal flow of program execution. C++ programmers will find Java's exception mechanism very similar to that of C++, and will be throwing and catching exceptions in no time. If you're a C programmer, you'll find learning to use Java's exception mechanism well worth the effort.

In languages other than Java, such as C, each function is responsible for signaling success or failure during its execution. In many cases, this is done by returning an integer value that the caller can test. Typically, if the return value of a function is zero, the function has been executed without error. If a nonzero value is returned instead, an error may have occurred during execution.

However, not all routines return error codes, and those that do don't necessarily report errors in the same way. Some may return an error code, others might return a null value, and still others might set a global error variable. Such inconsistencies place a substantial burden on the programmer, who must learn the error-reporting mechanism employed by each routine and write the appropriate code to test for such errors.

As a result, many programmers save time by testing only for errors generated by critical routines, not bothering with the others. In some cases, the programmer may not fully understand the routine in question and handle errors incorrectly. In both cases, the integrity of the program suffers and error checking becomes a nuisance, if not a nightmare.

Using exceptions, Java provides developers with a consistent and relatively simple mechanism for signaling and dealing with errors. Exceptions provide methods with a way to stop program execution when an error is encountered, while allowing the method to notify its caller that a problem has occurred. If the caller chooses, it may ignore, or "duck" the exception, in which case the exception is passed down the call stack until it is dealt with. However, exceptions only allow you to temporarily pass the buck when an error is encountered, since you must deal with it eventually.

Call stack

A *call stack* is nothing more than the sequence of methods that have been invoked. For instance, if a method named drawShape() calls another method named drawCircle(), we'd have a pretty simple call stack, as shown in Figure 10-1. Here, we can see that drawShape() called the drawCircle() method. The drawShape() method is said to be at the "bottom" of the stack, while drawCircle() is at the "top."

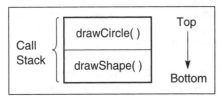

Figure 10-1: A very simple call stack, having only two method calls

However, `drawCircle()` might invoke another method named `draw()`. This would then sit at the top of the call stack. And `draw()` might call another method, named `paint()`, as the call stack continued to grow. If an exception occurred in `paint()`, it could possibly be ignored by every method. As a result, the exception would be passed all the way down the call stack, as illustrated in Figure 10-2.

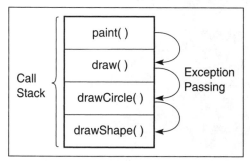

Figure 10-2: An exception is passed down the call stack until it's handled by a method.

If an exception isn't handled by a method, it's passed down the call stack to the method below it. If none of the methods in the call stack catch the exception by the time it reaches the bottom, and the method at the bottom doesn't catch it either, the program is aborted!

Somewhere along the way, the exception has to be caught and dealt with. If it isn't, the program is aborted. If you attempt to write a Java program that would result in such a situation, the compiler warns you about it.

In the last rendition of our HelloWorld applet, FlexibleMediaHello, we were forced to catch the exception that might have resulted when converting strings into URLs. Since the compiler recognized that the `URL()` method had the potential to throw an error (such as when the method is passed an invalid string), it refused to compile our program until we wrote an exception handler to catch such errors. In Java, all non-runtime exceptions must be caught or declared, as described below. If they are not, the compiler spits out an error message (see Figure 10-3) and refuses to compile the program.

Figure 10-3: If a non-runtime exception is not caught or declared, Java throws out an error message.

If the compiler realizes that a non-runtime error hasn't been properly handled, it refuses to compile the code. When this is the case, you must either catch or declare the exception (see the section "Catch or declare: It's the law," later in this chapter).

Throwing exceptions

Before an exception can be caught, it must be thrown. Exceptions can be thrown by any Java code: Your own code, code in the packages that come with the Java development environment, or code in packages written by others. Even the Java runtime system can throw exceptions that your programs must catch.

When an exception is thrown, the Java runtime system receives a signal that an error has been generated. Exceptions are thrown to flag errors, which is something you would do in your own programs to notify the system that an error has occurred. As soon as an exception is thrown, the runtime system searches for the matching catch clause to handle it.

Exceptions are thrown using the following Java syntax:

```
throw new AnyExceptionObject();
```

Regardless of what code raises an exception, it's always done using the throw statement. It takes a single argument: a *throwable object*. Throwable objects are instances of any subclass of the Throwable class defined in the java.lang package. In our example above, we instantiated a throwable object:

```
new AnyExceptionObject(); /* instantiate a throwable object */
```

If you attempt to throw an object that isn't throwable, the compiler emits an error message and refuses to complete the compilation process. Most exception objects you'll encounter are derived from either the `Exception` class, the `RuntimeException` class, or the `Error` class. Each of these classes is a subclass of `Throwable` (`java.lang.Throwable`), and therefore produces objects (or is extended by other classes) that are considered throwable.

Consider for a moment the following method declaration:

```
public static int myDivide(int x, int y) throws
ArithmeticException {
   if (y==0)
     throw new ArithmeticException();
   else
     return (x/y);
}
```

In the method signature we declare this method as being capable of throwing `ArithmeticException`:

```
   throws ArithmeticException
```

The Java language requires that methods either catch or declare all non-runtime exceptions they can throw. With the line above, we declare that our `myDivide()` method throws the `ArithmeticException`, satisfying this requirement.

In cases where you wish to define your own methods, you simply create a new class that is a subclass of `Exception`. Here is the same program, but using a custom exception:

```
class MyOwnException extends Exception {
}
public static int myDivide(int x, int y) throws MyOwnException
{
   if (y==0)
     throw new MyOwnException();
   else
     return (x/y);
}
```

However, throwing exceptions is only half the battle. In order to write effective Java programs, you must be able to catch exceptions as well.

For detailed information on creating your own exceptions, refer to the Java Language Tutorial. This step-by-step guide to learning the Java language is available in the documentation section of the JavaSoft Web site: `http://java.sun.com/docs/books/tutorial/index.html`.

Catching exceptions

When an exception is thrown, the Java runtime system immediately stops the current flow of program execution and looks for an exception handler to catch it. Searching backward through the call stack (refer to Figure 10-2), a corresponding handler is sought starting with the method where the error occurred.

The search continues down the call stack until a method containing an appropriate exception handler is found. The first handler encountered that has the same type as the thrown object is the one chosen to deal with the exception.

If the exception travels all the way down the call stack with no handler catching it, the program aborts execution. Typically, an error message is output to the terminal display in such cases. This, of course, assumes the exception is a runtime exception that can't be seen by the compiler.

Dividing a number by a variable that happens to be zero, accessing an array element using an index value (subscript) that is beyond the legal range, accessing null objects, and similar dynamic activities produce runtime exceptions that aren't recognized at compile time. As a result, the compiler can't force you to catch such exceptions, since it doesn't even realize they exist. And, in cases where a runtime exception propagates to the bottom of the call stack, your program is aborted.

try-catch clause

In order to catch an exception, you must write an exception handler using the try-catch clause. For instance, suppose we wanted to use the original myDivide() method created earlier. In order to catch the exception that might result, we'd write the following try-catch clause:

```
try {
   int y = myDivide(10,0);
} catch (ArithmeticException e) {
    System.out.println("Whoops - There it is!");
}
```

try block

The first part of a try-catch clause, the try block, encloses those statements that may throw an exception. Here is the syntax of a typical try block:

```
try {
   ...
   /* statements capable of throwing an exception */
   ...
}
```

The only code in our example capable of throwing an exception is the `myDivide()` method. However, you can include in the `try` block any number of legal Java statements that have the potential to throw an exception. As you can see, we intentionally supply `myDivide()` with parameters that will cause an exception to be thrown. Specifically, the second integer passed to the method is zero.

If we had additional lines of code following `myDivide(10,0)`, they wouldn't be executed. Instead, `myDivide()` would throw an exception that would immediately stop program execution at that point, which would then drop into the `catch` portion of the `try-catch` clause.

catch block

Following the `try` block are one or more `catch` blocks that you can use to trap and process exceptions. This is the `catch` block syntax:

```
catch (ThrowableClassName variable) {
   ...
}
```

Although we only supplied one `catch` block in the `myDivide()` exception handler, any number could have been provided. However, since the `myDivide()` method throws only one exception, we have to catch that one. In our example, we merely output a line of text to prove that our exception was indeed caught. In the case of multiple catches, the `try-catch` clause has this syntax:

```
try {
   ...
} catch (ThrowableClassName variable) {
   ...
} catch (ThrowableClassName variable) {
   ...
} catch (ThrowableClassName variable) {
   ...
} catch (ThrowableClassName variable) {
   ...
}
```

For instance, suppose `myDivide()` was capable of throwing two different exceptions. In this case, we would provide a `catch` block for each of the possible exceptions:

```
try {
  int y = myDivide(10,0);
} catch (ArithmeticException e) {
    System.out.println("Have caught an ArithmeticException.");
} catch (MyOwnException e) {
    System.out.println("Have caught MyOwnException.");
}
```

The exception that is thrown is compared to the argument for each `catch` block in order (the `catch` argument can be an object or an interface type). When a match is found, that `catch` block is executed. If no match is found, the exception propagates down the call stack, where it is compared against potential exception handlers until a match is found. And, as always, if no match is found, the program is aborted.

You can access the instance variables and methods of exceptions, just as for any other object. With this in mind, you can invoke the exception's `getMessage()` method to get information on the exception—`getMessage()` is a method defined in the `Throwable` class:

```
System.out.println(e.getMessage());
```

The `Throwable` class also implements several methods for dealing with the call stack when an exception occurs (such as `printStackTrace()`, which outputs the call stack to the display). The `Throwable` subclass that you, or anyone else, creates can implement additional methods and instance variables. To find out what methods an exception implements, look at its class and superclass definitions.

finally block

Unlike C++, Java's `try-catch` clause supports the use of an optional `finally` block. If defined, this is guaranteed to execute, regardless of whether or not an exception is thrown. As a result, you can use it to perform any necessary clean-up operation (closing files and streams, releasing system resources, and so on) that your methods require before the flow of control is transferred to another part of the program. This is the syntax of the `finally` block:

```
finally {
  ...
  /* statements here are executed before control transfers */
  ...
}
```

In the context of our `myDivide()` example, a `finally` block might look like this:

```
try {
int y = myDivide(10,0);
} catch (ArithmeticException e) {
   System.out.println("Have caught an ArithmeticException.");
} catch (MyOwnException e) {
   System.out.println("Have caught MyOwnException.");
} finally {
   System.out.println("cleaning up...");
   // do any clean-up work here
}
```

Upon executing the `finally` block, control is transferred out of the `try-catch` clause. Typically, whatever event caused the `try` statement to terminate (fall-through; the execution of a `break`, `continue`, or `return` statement; or the propagation of an exception) dictates where the flow of control will resume.

The `finally` block could also execute a jump statement. This would cause another unconditional control transfer outside its block, or cause another uncaught exception to be thrown. In either case, the original jump statement is abandoned, and the new unconditional control transfer (or exception) is processed.

All jump statements (`break`, `continue`, `return`, and `throw`) transfer control unconditionally. Whenever one causes control to bypass a `finally` block, the control transfer pauses while the `finally` part is executed, and continues if the `finally` part finishes normally.

Catch or declare: It's the law

Java requires that methods either catch or declare all non-runtime exceptions that can be thrown within the method's scope. This means that if a method chooses not to catch an exception, it must declare that it can throw it.

Sometimes, it's not a good idea to catch exceptions. For example, if you catch an exception deep down in the call stack, you might not know how or why your method is being called. What would you do with the exception, once caught?

Since you don't know enough about what caused your method to be called, you might not be able to adequately handle the exception. In that case, it would be better to pass the exception back down the call stack: You should declare the exception rather than catch it.

To declare an exception, simply add the `throw` statement to your method signature, followed by the exception name. To declare more than one exception, separate each name by a comma.

Suppose, for example, we wanted to define a new method that calls the `myDivide()` method we created earlier. Instead of implementing an exception handler for `myDivide()` in our new method, we can declare the potential exceptions in order to pass them down the call stack:

```
public void myMath() throws ArithmeticException, MyOwnException
{
   ...
}
```

Tip　Some programmers realize that it takes a lot less time to declare an exception than it does to write an appropriate exception handler, and are often tempted to simply pass the buck rather than deal with it. As a general rule, this is a bad idea. However, there are times when it is appropriate to declare an exception rather than handle it. For a detailed discussion of this topic, see "Handling Errors Using Exceptions" in the Java Language Tutorial (available on the JavaSoft Web site at `http://java.sun.com/docs/books/tutorial/index.html`), specifically the section named "Runtime Exceptions — The Controversy."

Finally

In this chapter, as in the last one, we've covered the fundamentals of Java programming. Between the two, we've dealt with the "nuts and bolts" of the language. As a programmer, you'll be using these elements on a regular basis. Without them, you won't be able to write Java software.

As with the last chapter, there's no pressing need to memorize all the material presented here. Simply return when you need a refresher. With time, you'll become comfortable with each of the subjects we've covered.

At some point, you may have questions or issues regarding a specific facet or nuance of the language. In that case, you can always turn to the Java Language Specification. This document covers all aspects of the language in considerable detail. You can find it on Sun's JavaSoft Web site: `http://java.sun.com/docs/books/jls/`.

Summary

Well, this chapter gave you more of the puzzle pieces you need to start building your own Java applications. With the knowledge you have gained in this chapter and Chapter 9, you should be well on your way to creating simple applications using Java. Key points to remember about this chapter include:

✦ Variables are used to store values in Java. When a value is stored in a variable, you can use it for a wide range of purposes. One such purpose is to represent an object's state. Variables are also used to perform calculations, control the flow of program execution, and effect the overall state of a program. They are a fundamental part of programming languages; without them we'd be hard pressed to develop software.

✦ Any variable that you declare of type `byte`, `short`, `int`, `long`, `float`, `double`, `char`, or `boolean` is a primitive variable. Reference variables are used to store references, or pointers, to objects (which can be class instances, class instances that implement interfaces, or arrays).

✦ Expressions are statements that result in a value when executed. When programming, we use expressions all the time, sometimes without even realizing it. Java expressions are similar in syntax to those of C and C++.

✦ The types of operators that can be used in an operation depend on the data type of the operands involved. For instance, the operators used in an integer operation are different from those used in a boolean operation.

✦ In order to direct the flow of program execution, Java supports several control-flow statements. These are similar to their C and C++ counterparts, so they look and act as you would expect if you're already familiar with one (or both) of these languages. Control-flow statements include: `if`, `switch`, `while/do`, `for`, and `break/continue`.

✦ Java features a general-purpose error processing system known as an *exception mechanism*. The exception mechanism is composed of two parts: throwing exceptions and catching them. To throw an exception means to signal an error, while to catch one is to trap and handle an error that has been thrown. While new to C programmers, exceptions provide a uniform approach to signaling and processing errors, removing much of the burden of traditional error processing.

✦ ✦ ✦

Classes, Interfaces, and Packages

In order to write Java programs, you must be able to create and manage objects. As you know, objects are instantiations of classes, which you can think of as the code templates or blueprints for objects.

In this chapter, we get into the nitty-gritty of Java classes. In order to really understand how to create and use them, we also discuss interfaces. You can think of interfaces as classes whose methods are not actually implemented. Interfaces allow our Java programs to gain the advantages of multiple inheritance without becoming weighed down by the complexity that goes along with true multiple inheritance.

Lastly, we see how classes and interfaces can be organized into packages. Packages allow us to group classes and interfaces together as we see fit, helping to manage what might otherwise become overwhelming, allowing us to create well-organized repositories of Java code.

Classes

You can think of classes as templates, or blueprints, from which objects are created. As such, we often think of classes as data types. When objects are created or instantiated from the same class, they are considered to be of the same type.

Note

All objects are an instance of a class. The class that an object is instantiated from determines the type of that object. If two objects are instantiated from the same class, they are considered to be of the same type. To find out whether an object is instantiated from a particular class, use the instanceof operator discussed in the two previous chapters.

When writing Java programs, we use a number of classes that are supplied with the Java development environment. We might also use classes written by fellow developers, and we will certainly create our own. In fact, if you've been following the examples presented in the preceding chapters, you've already created several classes based on the HelloWorld program introduced in Chapter 5.

In order to create a class, we must declare it and code the body of the class:

```
class declaration {
    ...
    /* class body (typically variables and methods) */
    ...
}
```

Although this is an over-simplified example, it helps us see the two parts of a class implementation clearly. The class declaration specifies such things as the name of the class, what type of access other objects will have to it, and what superclasses (and interfaces) it inherits state and behavior from.

However, the real meat of the class is in its body. This is where the specific state and behavior of the class are defined, through the implementation of variables and methods. Before getting into the class body, let's take a closer look at the class declaration.

Tip

In Java, only one public class declaration is allowed in each source file (you'll learn about public classes later). You can, however, have any number of nonpublic classes in one file. Although this is technically possible, it's not recommended. It's best to create a separate source file for each class and use the package mechanism, discussed in detail at the end of this chapter, to organize and use them.

Class Declaration

The class declaration, which is followed by a block of code known as the *class body*, probably isn't new to you at this point. Yet the exact syntax of the class declaration demands another look:

```
[modifiers] class ClassName [extends superClass] [implements
interfaces]
```

As you can see, three elements in the class declaration, those in brackets ([ ]), are optional. You can declare a class by simply providing the keyword class, followed by a name, as shown in the next piece of code. Here we have declared SimpleClass, an example of the simplest class signature you can declare:

```
class SimpleClass(){
}
```

Even so, you'll need to learn and use each of the optional portions of the declaration in order to get the most out of Java. Let's take a look at them individually.

Tip

The class name you specify must be a valid identifier (see Chapter 9 for information on Java identifiers). Although you can begin your class names with a lowercase letter, the convention is to begin them with a capital letter. Variables, on the other hand, typically begin with a lowercase letter.

Modifiers

Class modifiers declare whether a class is abstract, final, or public. If an access modifier such as `final` or `public` isn't specified, the class is abstract.

abstract

The `abstract` modifier specifies a class that has at least one abstract method in it. An abstract method is one that has no implementation (see "Abstract classes and methods" later in this chapter for details).

The purpose of having an abstract class is to allow it to declare methods, yet leave them unimplemented. As such, the subclasses of an abstract class are required to provide implementation for the abstract methods.

You should declare a class as `abstract` when you know that its subclasses will implement a certain method differently. Take, for instance, a method such as `draw()`. In a drawing program, several of the program's classes (such as `Circle`, `Rectangle`, `Triangle`, and others) will implement a `draw()` method, but each will implement it differently. It makes sense in this case to declare the parent class as `abstract`, allowing all subclasses to implement the abstract methods declared in the parent classes they wish:

```
abstract class MyGraphics {
    . . .
}
```

In the preceding example, only the class declaration is shown. To be a complete and valid class implementation, we'd also need to declare at least one abstract method such as `draw()`. Since we're concentrating only on the class declaration here, I've omitted the abstract method declaration.

Note

If you declare a class as `abstract`, at least one of the methods in that class must also be abstract. The compiler kicks out an error message and refuses to compile an abstract class that has no abstract methods in it.

final

The final modifier specifies a class that can have no subclasses. Declaring a class as final ensures that any objects instantiated from it are not created from a subclass that might introduce new and inconsistent properties. Since final classes can't be subclassed, additional variables and methods can't be added, and more importantly, methods can't be overridden and implemented differently from the way the author of the class intended.

For example, Java's String class (see Chapter 12) is a final class. Whenever you use a string, you're dealing with an object that is instantiated directly from the String class, as defined in the java.lang package. As a final class, you can be certain you're always dealing with objects defined in the String class, not something that is defined by a subclass of the String class.

To specify a final class, use the keyword final just before the keyword class. For example, the String class defined in java.lang.String is declared as follows:

```
public final class String {
    . . .
}
```

As you can see, the final modifier is preceded by yet another modifier: public. The public modifier, discussed next, specifies the scope of the String class; it specifies what other objects can access it. The public and associated modifiers are sometimes called *access modifiers*; they specify the access for a class.

 Since it doesn't make sense for a class to be both final and abstract, don't bother trying it! When a class is abstract, it leaves implementation of certain methods up to its subclasses. However, because a final class can't be subclassed, the two can't coexist. The compiler generates an error any time an attempt is made to declare a class as both abstract and final.

public

The public modifier specifies that a class can be used by objects outside the current package (see the "Packages" section later in this chapter). By default, when no access modifier is specified, classes can only be used within the package in which they are declared.

For example, the String class is declared public because other classes and objects outside its package, such as classes and methods in your programs, need to have access to it. Thus, Java's String class is declared as public:

```
public final class String {
    . . .
}
```

Tip When specifying a class as `public`, you should provide the `public` keyword first in the declaration, as shown here. If your public classes also happen to be final or abstract, be sure these words come after `public`. Although you don't have to follow this convention, doing so will make your class declarations consistent with Sun's and those of your fellow developers.

Superclass

Arguably, the most powerful feature of any object-oriented programming (OOP) language is the ability to reuse existing code through inheritance. For instance, rather than writing a class from scratch, we can benefit greatly by inheriting the variables and methods defined in another class that has the basic properties we require. When we do this, we create what's known as a *subclass* of the original class. The class we inherit from is known as the *superclass*. This relationship, described in detail in Chapter 2, is illustrated in Figure 11-1.

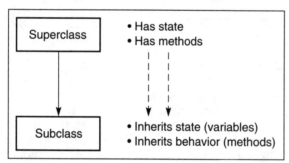

Figure 11-1: A subclass descends from a superclass, inheriting the state (variables) and behavior (methods) of that superclass.

In Java, all classes are descendants of the `Object` class. The `Object` class is at the top of the inheritance tree, or class hierarchy, as illustrated in Figure 11-2. Every other class, either directly or indirectly, subclasses the `Object` class. Even those classes at the bottom of the hierarchy are descendants of the `Object` class; they subclass any class which, through a long chain of subclasses, can eventually be traced back to the top of the tree.

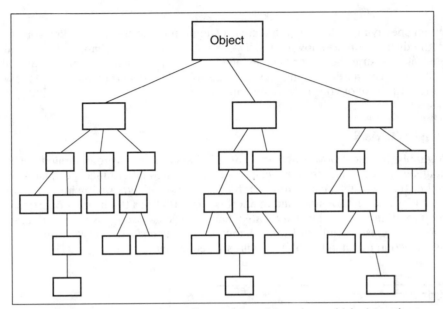

Figure 11-2: All classes are descendants of the Object class, which sits at the top of the Java class hierarchy.

Note

If it helps, you can think of the class hierarchy as a family tree for objects. In this sense, Object is the great, great, great, great, great (well, you get the picture) grandparent of all other objects. The further down the inheritance tree, or class hierarchy, a class is defined, the more specialized it is. Classes at the top of the hierarchy are more general, with more specific state and behavior being added with every subclass.

As you now know, almost any class can be subclassed as long as it's not specified as final. The process of subclassing is a natural and powerful feature of Java, allowing your classes to inherit functionality that you would otherwise have to write yourself.

In order to inherit properties from an existing class, that class must be explicitly specified using the extends keyword. In Java parlance, our subclass is said to "extend a superclass." As you've seen in earlier chapters, our applet version of "Hello World!" inherited a great deal of functionality by simply extending the Applet class:

```
public class HelloWorldApplet extends java.applet.Applet {
    ...
}
```

In this case, we specified `java.applet.Applet`; the `Applet` class is defined in the `java.applet` package. However, if the `Applet` class wasn't part of a package, we would have used the following syntax:

```
public class HelloWorldApplet extends Applet {
    ...
}
```

In this case, the `Applet` class is expected to reside in the same directory as the `HelloWorldApplet` class itself. Since a package wasn't specified (such as `java.applet`), the Java compiler doesn't have a clue where to look for the superclass. As a result, it expects to find the class inside the same directory as the program itself.

If you don't explicitly extend a class, the compiler assumes the superclass to be `Object`. For instance, consider the following class declaration, which omits the `extends` keyword and a superclass altogether:

```
public class MyClassName {
    ...
}
```

This is functionally equivalent to:

```
public class MyClassName extends Object {
    ...
}
```

Of course, you don't have to explicitly extend the `Object` class as just shown. The compiler does it for you whenever you leave the "extends" portion blank in a class declaration.

Classes and interfaces

In addition to specifying a superclass, you can specify one or more interfaces in your class declaration. An *interface*, discussed in more detail later in this chapter, declares a set of constants and methods but doesn't actually *implement* any of the methods. Similar to an abstract class, an interface requires other classes to provide the implementation for its methods; it does not provide them itself.

However, with an abstract class, only one of the methods in it is required to be abstract. The remaining methods can be fully functional, meaning your class inherits the functionality of all methods except the ones defined as abstract. With an interface, none of the methods are implemented, leaving this responsibility up to the classes that use it.

When a class implements an interface, it must provide implementations for all of the methods declared in that interface. And, unlike the act of subclassing an abstract class, a class can implement any number of interfaces. In other words, Java supports only single inheritance (meaning you can't subclass more than one class), whereas you can implement any number of interfaces to achieve a result similar to the multiple inheritance found in C++.

To implement an interface, declare your class as usual with the keyword `implements` followed by the name of the interface. The `implements` clause should come after the `extends` clause, if one exists, or immediately following the class name otherwise:

```
class Triangle extends MyGraphics implements Brushes {
  ...
  /* each method declared in Brushes must be implemented here */
  ...
}
```

The preceding example illustrates the declaration of a class named `Triangle`, which is a subclass of `MyGraphics`, and implements the `Brushes` interface. Since `Triangle` specifies the use of the `Brushes` interface, it must also override and implement each of the methods declared in that interface.

Following is the same example, this time without explicitly specifying a superclass:

```
class Triangle implements Brushes {
  ...
  /* each method declared in Brushes must be implemented here */
  ...
}
```

In this case, `Triangle` is a direct descendant of the `Object` class; it is said to be a subclass of `Object`. However, it specifies the same interface and so must provide the implementation for each of `Brushes`' methods.

In the case of multiple interfaces, a comma is used to separate the names of the interfaces:

```
class Triangle implements Brushes, Paints, Surfaces {
  ...
  /* every method in Brushes, Paints, and Surfaces must
     be implemented in Triangle */
  ...
}
```

And, just as with a single interface, the `Triangle` class must implement the methods of each one it specifies. In this case, `Triangle` must implement all the methods declared in `Brushes`, `Paints`, and `Surfaces`.

On the CD-ROM

For a hands-on example of using interfaces, see the "LivingLinks Software Developers Kit" provided on the CD-ROM. LivingLinks is a multipurpose animation applet that supports special-effects plug-ins. To create your own LivingLinks special-effects plug-ins, you must also use the "Effect" interface provided with the SDK. This ensures that each plug-in implements the methods required by the LivingLinks applet. Check out the various LivingLinks special-effects source-code examples provided on disc to see how easy it is to use interfaces.

Class Body

So far, we've only discussed the class declaration. However, the real meat of a class is found in its body. It is here that the variables and methods of a class are declared and defined, bringing it to life with variables (state) and methods (behavior).

Variables

In Java classes, there are two types of variables:

✦ *Non-member variables*: These are not associated with the class (such as local variables used in methods and variables used as parameters for methods).

✦ *Member variables*: These are directly associated with the class and objects made from it.

Non-member variables

Variables that are part of a method parameter list, or that are declared inside a class method, are *not* considered member variables (see "Methods" later in this chapter). Although they may be critical to the object, they aren't considered part of the object's formal state.

Member variables

All member variables are declared within the body of the class, not inside a method or as a parameter to a method. Member variables come in two flavors:

✦ Class variables

✦ Instance variables

Following is a summary of the possible member variable declarations (items in square brackets are optional):

```
[accessSpecifier] [static] [final] [transient] [volatile] type
variablename
```

Note

Transient is meant to specify variables that are not part of the persistent state of the class, it is used to indicate a field that is not part of an object's persistent state and needs to be serialized with the object. Volatile specifies a variable whose value is vulnerable to thread access (and is therefore read from memory each time it is used, and stored to memory after each occasion, to ensure data integrity. (See Chapter 14 for information about threads.)

The keyword that has the most significant impact on the behavior of variables is static, which specifies that a variable is either a class variable or an instance variable.

Access Control

Java supports five levels of access for variables and methods:

- ✦ Private
- ✦ Private protected
- ✦ Protected
- ✦ Public
- ✦ Friendly (if left unspecified)

Table 11-1 gives a breakdown of the access level each specifier provides.

A check mark in the first column indicates that the class in which the variable or method is declared has access to use the variable or call the method.

A check mark in the second column indicates that subclasses of the class (regardless of which package they are in) have access to the variable or method.

A check mark in the third column indicates that classes in the same package (regardless of their parentage) as the class in which the variable or method is declared have access.

A check mark in the fourth column indicates that all classes have access to the variable or method.

For an example of each specifier, as applied to both variables and methods, refer to the Java Language Tutorial (specifically, "Controlling Access to a Class's Variables" and "Controlling Access to a Class's Methods," both of which are under the section entitled "Creating Your Own Class"). This step-by-step guide to learning the Java language is available on Sun's Java Web site: http://sun.java.com.

Table 11-1
Variable and Method Access Specifiers

Specifier	Class	Subclass	Package	World
private	✓			
private protected	✓	✓		
protected	✓	✓	✓	
public	✓	✓	✓	✓
\<blank\> ("friendly")	✓		✓	

For details on controlling access to member variables, be sure to read the previous sidebar entitled "Access Control" before moving on to methods. In the meantime, we'll focus on the difference between class variables and instance variables.

Class variables occur only once per class, no matter how many instances of that class are created. Memory for class variables is allocated by the Java runtime system the first time a class is encountered, and only then.

In contrast, instance variables are allocated once for every instance of a class. Whenever an instance of a class is created, the system allocates memory for all instance variables in that class. In essence, class variables are shared by all instances of a class while each object gets its own copy of instance variables. So, how are class variables distinguished from instance variables? With the keyword static, as the following example illustrates:

```
class Bogus {
    static int myClassVar; // declare class variable of type int
    int myInstanceVar; // declare instance variable of type int
    ...
    /* Method Declarations would follow... */
    ...
}
```

When the keyword static precedes the data type in a variable declaration, that variable becomes a class variable. In this example, memory for myClassVar is allocated only once, regardless of how many instances of class Bogus are created. In contrast, myInstanceVar is created anew each time an instance of Bogus is created.

As a result, the variable myClassVar is the same, no matter what object of type Bogus accesses it. For example, suppose the value 3 were stored in myClassVar. Every time this variable was retrieved, regardless of when or how, it would contain 3 in all cases (at least until a value other than 3 was stored in it). When a class variable is altered (that is, changing myClassVar to 15) , all instances of that class see the change. It can be said that all instances of a particular class share the same class variables.

Since all the instances of a particular class share the static variables that are declared in that class, these variables can be referenced directly without requiring that an object first be instantiated. For example, to access the static variable declared in our `Bogus` class, we can simply do the following:

```
int i = Bogus.myClassVar; // set i equal to the class variable
```

As you can see, we've accessed the class variable directly and assigned it to `i` without first having to instantiate a `Bogus` object using the new operator. While this may seem new to you, in truth we've been dealing with class variables all along. Remember outputting data via `System.out.println()`? Since `out` is a static variable declared in the `System` class, we don't have to bother creating an instance of that class before accessing this variable. Instead, we conveniently access the `out` class variable directly.

Note

System's `out` class variable is a `PrintStream` object, which implements the `println()` method. All along we've been invoking this method, without concern for exactly what it is or how it does what it does. To learn more about the `System` class, its `out` class variable, and `PrintStream`s, see Chapter 13.

In contrast, because a new `myInstanceVar` variable is created with each instantiation, each `Bogus` object has its own copy. This means the value of `myInstanceVar` is different from object to object; each has its own copy of the variable, unlike `myClassVar`, which is shared by all. You have to access an instance variable through an instance of the class:

```
Bogus freshBogus = new Bogus(); // create an instance of Bogus
   // set i equal to an instance variable:
int i = freshBogus.myInstanceVar;
```

Here we've created a `Bogus` object, through which we access the instance variable `myInstanceVar`. In this case, the instance variable was available directly. In some cases, however, instance variables may be declared private. If this is the case, the only way to access them is through an object's methods. Such data hiding is vital to an object-oriented language such as Java, as it prevents direct access to the internal representation of an object and enforces a "black box" approach to software development (see Chapter 2 for details).

Constant variables (final variables)

Regardless of whether a variable is a class or instance variable, it can also be declared as final. A variable that has been declared as final can never be changed once a value is assigned to it. You can think of final variables as constants: Once they're set, they can't be altered. As such, they can be used like #define statements are in C/C++. (Remember, Java doesn't support #define statements, so this is the closest you'll get!) Attempting to alter the value of a final variable is illegal, and invokes an error message from the compiler.

While all other variables in Java should begin with a lowercase letter, final variables are different. By convention, constant names in Java are spelled in all capital letters. Thus, you might declare the value of pi using a constant as follows:

```
final double PI = 3.14159265359;
```

Class variables are often used to declare constants that all objects of that class will share. It's more efficient to use a static (class) variable than an instance variable in this case; memory is only allocated once. To declare a class variable as a constant, simply precede the static keyword with final (by convention, Java constant names are uppercase):

```
final static double PI = 3.14159265359;E
```

Before the JDK 1.1, whenever a final was declared it was immediately required to be initialized—otherwise a compilation error would result. Now finals can be declared without being initialized. Once they are assigned a value though, they cannot be changed. This allows you to now create calculated constants, which cannot be changed once they have been assigned a value. This is a subtle, but useful, change to the Java programming language.

Retrieving and setting member variables

As you know, your member variables can be retrieved and set directly, using the dot notation:

```
Bogus freshBogus = new Bogus(); // create an instance of Bogus
freshBogus.myInstanceVar = 1827; /* set variable using dot
                                    notation */
int i = freshBogus.myInstanceVar; // retrieve using dot notation
```

Or set using methods defined for doing just that:

```
Bogus freshBogus = new Bogus(); // create an instance of Bogus
freshBogus.setIt(1827); // set variable using setIt() method
int i = freshBogus.getIt(); // retrieve using getIt() method
```

Of course, the preceding example assumes that the two methods, setIt() and getIt(), are defined in the body of the Bogus class, for the purpose of setting and retrieving the myInstanceVar variable. The only way to know if a method exists for setting or retrieving an object's value is to read the documentation or source code of the class.

Setting and retrieving class variables

In the previous examples, the class's instance variable was accessed. This is apparent by looking at the name of the variable (myInstance), and, more importantly, by the fact that we had to instantiate a Bogus object in order to get to the instance variable. In the case of class variables, however, we don't have to bother creating an object:

```
Bogus.myClassVar = 111791; // set class variable w/o
instantiation
int i = Bogus.myClassVar; // retrieve w/o instantiation
```

As you can see, we can get and set a class variable without bothering to instantiate an object. However, we can also access class variables through objects, just as we do instance variables:

```
Bogus freshBogus = new Bogus(); // create an instance of Bogus
  // set class variable using dot notation:
freshBogus.myClassVar = 111791;
int i = freshBogus.myClassVar; // retrieve using dot notation
  // set variable using setClassVar() method:
freshBogus.setClassVar(111791);
  // retrieve using getClassVar() method:
int i = freshBogus.getClassVar();
```

Tip If you access class variables through an object, as shown here, you'll get the same results as if you accessed them directly with the class name and dot notation, as illustrated in the first example. To make your programs easier to read, and less confusing ("Am I dealing with a class or instance variable here?"), it's a good idea to avoid accessing class variables through objects.

Member variable scope

Member variables can be referenced anywhere in the body of your class, even inside methods, as discussed in Chapter 10. As you may remember, however, a member variable is "hidden" when a variable of the same name is declared inside a method. For details on variable scope, refer to Chapter 10.

Shadowed variables

An interesting situation, known as variable shadowing, occurs when a subclass declares a member variable having the same name as a member variable in its superclass. As you might recall, this situation is known as *overriding* if methods are involved; when we're dealing with variables, it's called *shadowing*.

Consider, if you will, the following class declaration, which subclasses the Bogus class we've been dealing with so far:

```
class UltraBogus extends Bogus {
  double myInstanceVar; /* shadows myInstanceVar in
                         class Bogus */
  int    good, bad, ugly; /* UltraBogus instance variables */
}
```

As you can see, although a myInstanceVar variable is declared in UltraBogus, it is not of the same data type as the one in Bogus (this is a double, whereas Bogus declared an int). Nonetheless, it shadows the myInstanceVar variable declared in Bogus.

Any reference to myInstanceVar in the context of UltraBogus (whether in the class body or through an object) refers to the one declared in UltraBogus. After all, how would Java know which one you're talking about unless it automatically uses one or the other? It wouldn't, so it chooses the variable declared in the subclass over the one in the superclass. In order to access the Bogus variable of the same name, you have to use the super keyword (see the next section).

this and super variables

In Java, two special keywords, this and super, are used to refer to an object and its superclass. Although we'll see more about this and super later when we talk about methods, they are worth getting to know now.

this

Whenever we're dealing with member variables in the body of a class, we refer to them by name. Take a look at the following code, which declares two classes (ShowDown and HighNoon):

```
class ShowDown {
  final static  int SHERIFF = 50000; // constant class variable
}

public class HighNoon extends ShowDown {
  int good=20, bad=125, ugly=53256; // a few instance variables
  final static int SHERIFF = 100; // constant class variable
  static String welcome = "Have a pleasant stay."; //class
variable
  static String warning = "Get outta town!"; //class variable
  public static void main (String args[]) {
    System.out.println("It's a showdown...");
    HighNoon test = new HighNoon(); // instantiate object
    test.Encounter(); // invoke Encounter() method
  }

  void Encounter() {
    System.out.println("Anything greater than " + SHERIFF +
                    " is out.");
    SizeUp(good);
    SizeUp(bad);
    SizeUp(ugly);
  }

  void SizeUp(int dude) {
    System.out.print(dude + ":");
    if (dude > SHERIFF) {  // is it bigger than SHERIFF?
```

```
        System.out.println(warning); // Yes? Run 'em out of town
      }
    else {
        System.out.println(welcome); // No? welcome to
numberville!
      }
   }
}
```

In this example, our use of variables is pretty straightforward. We declare them, then use them. Since we're only referring to variables within the scope of HighNoon, there's no problem. Although you might not realize it, the this variable is implied each time we use a variable. Since this is a reference to the current instance of an object, HighNoon in this case, we could have explicitly specified so in our code:

```
class ShowDown {
  final static  int SHERIFF = 50000; // constant class variable
}

public class HighNoon extends ShowDown {
  int  good=20, bad=125, ugly=53256; // a few instance variables
  final static int SHERIFF = 100; // constant class variable
  static String welcome = "Have a pleasant stay."; /*class
                                              variable */
  static String warning = "Get outta town!"; //class variable
  public static void main (String args[]) {
    System.out.println("It's a showdown...");
    HighNoon test = new HighNoon(); // instantiate object
    this.test.Encounter(); // invoke Encounter() method
  }

  void Encounter() {
    System.out.println("Anything greater than " + this.SHERIFF +
                       " is out.");
    SizeUp(this.good);
    SizeUp(this.bad);
    SizeUp(this.ugly);
  }

  void SizeUp(int dude) {
    System.out.print(dude + ":");
    if (dude > this.SHERIFF) {  // is it bigger than SHERIFF?
      System.out.println(this.warning);/* Yes? Run 'em out of
                                        town! */
    }
    else {
      System.out.println(this.welcome); /* No? Welcome to
                                        numberville */
    }
  }
}
```

In each of the variable references shown, with the exception of the parameter dude, we're saying, "Give me the variable declared in this class." In either case, the program produces the same results when executed (see Figure 11-3).

Figure 11-3: The this keyword is used to reference the current object.

Note

Since all variables in a class are implicitly preceded with this, you aren't required to explicitly use it in your code. However, feel free to use it to clarify your code when dealing with shadowed and hidden variables and overridden methods.

The this variable is used to reference an object's instance variables, or pass the object as a parameter to a method (more on that later).

Although it's not necessary to explicitly use this in our example program, it comes in handy when you need to access a member variable that has been hidden by a method (in other words, when a local method variable of the same name exists). For example, suppose our Encounter() method were to hide one (or more) of the member variables:

```
void Encounter() {
   int ugly = 23;//declared here hides member variable of same
name
   System.out.println("Anything greater than " + this.SHERIFF +
                   " is out.");
   SizeUp(good);
   SizeUp(bad);
   SizeUp(ugly); // <- refers to the "ugly" method variable
declared above!
}
```

In this case, we need a way to refer to the member variable, as opposed to the one declared inside `Encounter()`. And thanks to `this`, we can do that (pardon the play on words):

```
void Encounter() {
  int ugly = 23; // declared in method, hiding member
  SizeUp(good);
  SizeUp(bad);
  SizeUp(this.ugly);  // now refers to the member variable!
}
```

Since `this` refers to the object, the preceding example uses the member variable instead of the local one declared in `Encounter()`. You might recall our `MediaHelloWorld` `paint()` method, which also made use of the variable `this`:

```
public void paint(Graphics g) {
  g.drawImage(myImage, horizontal, vertical, this);
  super.paint(g);
}
```

Here we needed to provide the `drawImage()` method with four parameters: an image, the horizontal and vertical coordinates, and an `ImageObserver` object. An `ImageObserver` object receives information about an image as it is being constructed, such as when it is being downloaded from the Web. Since our program didn't explicitly create an `ImageObserver` object, we simply passed it a reference to our `MediaHelloWorld` class using `this`. (We were able to pass a reference to `MediaHelloWorld` because all applets are able to act as `ImageObserver` objects—if applets didn't have this ability, passing `this` would have caused the compiler to choke.)

super

Another special Java variable is `super`, which refers to the parent class, or superclass, of an object. This is useful in many cases, such as in `MediaHelloWorld`'s `paint()` method shown in the previous section. Since we wanted to pass some of the responsibility for drawing to the `MediaHelloWorld`'s superclass, we used the keyword `super` to invoke that class's `paint()` method:

```
super.paint(g);
```

While this is an example of using `super` to invoke methods in an object's parent class, it's also helpful when you need to access a member variable in a superclass that has been shadowed by a variable in the subclass.

Suppose, for example, that we wanted to use the `SHERIFF` variable declared in `ShowDown` rather than the one declared in `HighNoon`. All we'd have to do is replace references to `SHERIFF` or `this.SHERIFF` with:

```
super.SHERIFF
```

If we did this with the two lines of code in HighNoon that reference the SHERIFF variable, the output of the program would be radically different. Rather than comparing numbers to 100, as SHERIFF is defined in HighNoon, they would be compared to 60000, as defined in ShowDown. As a result, all the numbers would pass the test, as shown in Figure 11-4.

Figure 11-4: Using the super keyword allows you to access variables and methods that reside in the superclass.

Methods

Variables are used to maintain an object's state; *methods* provide the behavior. For those of you who are new to object-oriented programming, you can think of a method as a function. However, unlike procedural programming where functions sit out in the open (or, more accurately, are organized into files) to be called upon at any point, a method is encapsulated inside the class in which it is defined, along with the variables of that class.

Warning

In Java, every method must reside inside a class declaration. If you create a method outside the body of a class declaration, the code will not compile.

Together, a class's variables and methods give objects their state and behavior. The bulk of Java programming is spent creating methods, just as the bulk of most software implementation efforts is spent writing functions. It's these code routines that really form the meat of a program, with variables (data) being used to keep track of state.

Declaring methods

To create a method, you must write a method declaration and then implement the body of it. At the least, a method is made up of

✦ A return type

✦ The method name

✦ A method body

You can see these three elements in this code:

```
returnType name() {
  ...
  /* method body */
  ...
}
```

The preceding example is a simple skeleton of a method declaration, which has many optional parts. In the following method declaration summary, each of the items in square brackets is optional:

```
[accessSpecifier] [static] [abstract] [final] [native]
[synchronized] returnValue methodname ([paramlist]) [throws
exceptionsList]
```

Note

At a minimum, a method declaration must include a return type and a name for the method. Beyond that, each option allows you to control how your method will act and to what extent it may be used. As with variables, Java supports five distinct access levels for methods (see the "Access Control" sidebar earlier in this chapter, for details).

As you've seen in our HighNoon example, the return type specified in the method declaration doesn't have to be an actual data type. In the case where a method does not return a data type, you must specify void as the return type:

```
void SizeUp(int dude) {  // void specifies method returns no
data
  ...
}
```

However, if the method does return a value, you must specify that data type in the method declaration. Following are several variations of the SizeUp() method, each returning a different data type:

```
int SizeUp(int dude) {  // specifies that method returns an int
  ...
  return (anInt); // an int value must be returned!
}

boolean SizeUp(int dude) {  // returns a boolean
```

```
      ...
      return (aBoolean); // a boolean value must be returned!
   }

   double SizeUp(int dude) {  // returns a double
      ...
      return (aDouble); // a double value must be returned!
   }

   String SizeUp(int dude) {  // returns a String
      ...
      return (aString); // a String value must be returned!
   }
```

As you can see, when a return type is specified in the method declaration, a value of that data type must be returned. When a `return` statement is executed, control transfers out of the method and back to the caller of that method. Before the transfer of control is complete, the data being returned is placed on the stack, where the calling method can retrieve it.

Note

Any Java data type can be returned by a method. Data types in the Java language fall into two categories:

✦ *Primitive types*: These comprise a single value and include integer and floating-point numbers, boolean values, and single characters (such as a, b, and c).

✦ *Composite types* (also known as *reference types*): These comprise multiple values and include classes, interfaces, strings, and arrays.

For instance, if `SizeUp()` were to return an `int` data type, a call to it might look something like this:

```
int x;
x = SizeUp(235); // call SizeUp, set x to whatever it returns
```

Since the `return` statement terminates the execution of a method, it is often the last line of code in the body of a method (although it may occur elsewhere in the body). There follow two ways in which `SizeUp()` might return a value:

```
boolean SizeUp(int dude) {
   boolean beenWarned; // declare a variable to hold return value
   System.out.print(dude + ":");
   if (dude > SHERIFF) {
     System.out.println(warning);
     beenWarned = true; // set variable to true
   }
   else {
     System.out.println(welcome);
     beenWarned = false; // set variable to false
   }
 return (beenWarned);
}
```

In the preceding example, we declared a boolean variable to hold a value which changes, depending on what happens inside the body of the method that is eventually returned. However, we could have also used the following technique:

```
boolean SizeUp(int dude) {
  System.out.print(dude + ":");
  if (dude > SHERIFF) {
    System.out.println(warning);
    return (true); // return true
  }
  else {
    System.out.println(welcome);
    return (false); // return false
  }
}
```

Although these two code snippets are functionally the same, the latter can be confusing to follow since more than one `return` statement is present. For ease of reading, it's best to use a variable to hold and manipulate the value to be returned, and only use one `return` statement whenever possible.

Note

Even though a `return` statement is required if the method declaration specifies a return type, the value returned doesn't have to be what you might consider a "valid" value. For instance, when a string return type is specified, a value of null can be returned. Likewise, zero (0) and negative values can be returned for integral data types. Although you must return a data type if one is declared, any value in the legal range for that type is acceptable.

The data type a method returns must match the data type in the method declaration. As a case in point, in the two examples we are considering the data type declared is a `boolean`, so we can't return anything but a boolean value. To return an `int`, `float`, `string`, or anything other than a `boolean` would result in a compiler error.

However, when returning an object, that object's class must either be the same as the class specified in the method declaration or a subclass of it. If a method returns an interface, the object returned must implement that interface.

Overloading methods

When choosing a name for your method, any valid Java identifier will do. However, if you choose the same name as another method in the class, you'll have to supply a different parameter list to differentiate between the two. Having more than one method with the same name is known as *method overloading*, and it is permissible only so long as the parameter list for each method is unique.

Suppose we wanted to create a few variations of our `SizeUp()` method. In C, we'd create a unique name for each function: `SizeUp()`, `SizeUpArray()`, `SizeUpCompare()`, and so on. In Java, however, we can overload the `SizeUp()` method by simply providing a different parameter list for each one:

```
void SizeUp(int dude) {
...
}

void SizeUp(int dude[]) {
...
}

void SizeUp(int dude, int dude2) {
...
}
```

Since each of these method declarations has a different set of parameters, they can all be included in the same class file. When one of them is called, Java checks the type and number of parameters and invokes the appropriate method.

Note

Overloading is *not* the same as overriding! When overloading a method, you create more than one method with the same name (each having a distinct parameter list) in a class. When overriding a method, you create a method in a class that has the same name and parameter list as a method in the superclass. In this way, the method in the superclass is overridden by the one in your class. For instance, when we declared a paint() method in our FlexibleMediaHello program, we were overriding the paint() method declared in its superclass. However, we can always use the super variable to execute the method in the superclass:

```
super.paint();
```

Class and instance methods

Just as there are class variables and instance variables, there are class methods and instance methods. By default, all methods are instance methods, unless one is specified as a class method using the static keyword:

```
static void SizeUp(int dude) {
...
}
```

As with class variables, class methods are shared by all objects instantiated via that class. And, just as with class variables, they can be used at any time without first instantiating an object of that class. An example of this is seen in the Math class, where all variables and methods are declared static. You can use any of Math's methods without first creating an object of that class:

```
int maxOfTwoNumbers = Math.max(x,y); // returns maximum of x
and y
double myRandomNumber = Math.random(); // returns random number
double mySine = Math.sin(45.56); /* returns trigonometric sine
of
                            the angle passed in */
```

Tip

The Math class is part of the java.lang package, and has a large number of mathematical methods you may find useful. Before writing your own mathematics methods, check the Math class first to see if the work has already been done for you.

Aside from this convenience, class methods operate on class variables. In contrast, an instance method operates on instance variables: When an instance method accesses an instance variable, it is accessing the one for that particular object. Since each object shares the same class variables, it makes sense to declare methods as static if they operate on class variables, or have no need to operate on instances of a class.

final methods

The final keyword can be used to declare a final method. Final methods can't be overridden by subclasses. If you have a method that should never be overridden, declare it as final:

```
final void SizeUp(int dude) {
  ...
}
```

Method constructors

A *constructor* is a method that has the same name as the class in which it is declared. The purpose of a constructor is to provide a way for new objects to be initialized in a special way. If a constructor isn't provided, as in the case of HighNoon, an object of that class can still be created. However, we would have to set the good, bad, and ugly variables manually, if they weren't already initialized. And we also had to invoke the Encounter() method explicitly.

If a constructor had been provided, the variables could have been automatically initialized. In fact, a constructor can even call methods:

```
HighNoon (int a, int b, int c) {
  good = a; // initialize good to value of a
  bad = b; // initialize bad to value of b
  ugly = c; // initialize ugly to value of c
  Encounter(); // now invoke the Encounter() method!
}
```

Now, rather than having to rely on the internal initialization of these variables, we can provide our own values when creating a new HighNoon object:

```
    // instantiate using constructor:
HighNoon test = new HighNoon(15, 25, 460);
```

When our new HighNoon object is created, the constructor is called. Not only are the good, bad, and ugly instance variables set to the values we specify, but the Encounter() method is automatically invoked, saving us from doing it explicitly.

Just as with regular methods, constructors can be overloaded. We can create as many constructors as needed, provided they each have a unique parameter list. And if you ever need to invoke one constructor from within another, you can do so using the this variable.

For example, suppose we create another HighNoon constructor that takes an array as a parameter. Rather than set the variables and call Encounter() here as well, we can simply invoke the original HighNoon constructor and let it do all the work:

```
HighNoon (int dudeArray[]) {
    // using "this" to invoke original constructor:
  this(dudeArray[0],dudeArray[1],dudeArray[2]);
  }
```

Tip

As with standard methods, you can invoke a constructor in the class's superclass using the super keyword.

finalize() method

While a constructor method initializes an object, a finalize() method may be created that is used to help optimize the disposing of an object. It is called just before Java's automatic garbage collection mechanism reclaims an unused object, allowing your object to close any files or streams it has opened, and perform similar housekeeping tasks:

```
finalize() {
  ...
  }
```

When an object is no longer used, meaning there are no longer references to it, it is marked for garbage collection. Unfortunately, you have no guarantee of exactly when an object will be garbage collected or if your finalize() method will ever be called!

As a result, you should only use a finalize() method to optimize the disposing of your object. But you should never depend on it to be executed, and your programs should never rely on it to work properly. Use finalize() methods for optimization of your code *only*, if at all, and you'll save yourself a great deal of anxiety—since Java's garbage collector isn't guaranteed to invoke this method, mission-critical code shouldn't be placed in finalize().

It's interesting to note that you can manually invoke an object's finalize() method just as you would call any other method. However, calling this method does not force garbage collection for that object. Instead, you can force garbage collection for the entire program using this System method:

```
System.gc();
```

You can also invoke the finalize() method for all recently released objects by calling this System method:

```
System.runFinalization();
```

These methods are particularly useful if a Java program is being run with the garbage collector disabled. This is done by invoking an application at the command line with the -noasynchgc flag, as follows:

```
c> java -noasynchgc ProgramName
```

Method exceptions

As you learned in the previous chapter, methods can throw exceptions. In order to do so, the method declaration must list each exception that the method can throw:

```
public static int myDivide(int x, int y) throws
ArithmeticException {
   if (y==0)
     throw new ArithmeticException();
   else
     return (x/y);
}
```

If more than one exception may be thrown, they are listed one after another and separated by commas.

Abstract classes and methods

Java supports both abstract classes and abstract methods, which are similar in nature to interfaces. As you know from our earlier discussion, interfaces declare a set of constants and methods but don't actually implement any of the methods. The class that implements an interface is responsible for providing the implementation for each of its methods.

With an abstract class, only one of the methods it declares is required to be abstract. The remaining methods can be fully functional, meaning the subclass inherits the functional methods but must provide the implementation for those that are abstract. For example, we might have declared our ShowDown class as abstract, in addition to one or more of the methods in that class, as shown here:

```
public abstract class ShowDown {
   int aVar; // an instance variable
```

```
public abstract void Encounter(); // abstract method
public abstract void SizeUp(int dude); // abstract method
void aRegularMethod() {  // a standard method, not abstract
  ... // implementation here...
}
}
```

In this case, an object of type ShowDown could never be instantiated. As an abstract class, it can only be subclassed. And whenever subclassed, the two abstract methods, Encounter() and SizeUp(), must be implemented by the subclass.

An abstract class is a nice intermediate between a standard class and an interface. Since it can actually implement methods, it is useful when a class must be created that needs to rely on the subclass for the implementation of one or more methods. Other than containing abstract methods, and the fact that an object can't be created directly from them since one or more of the methods are empty, abstract classes behave like standard classes.

Inner Classes

New in the JDK 1.1 is the concept of *inner classes*. Inner classes are primarily used for defining simple helper classes, which are intended to be used for a specific function in a particular place in a Java program. Inner classes are not for use as top-level, general-purpose classes. With inner classes, you can define these specific-use classes right where they are utilized—helping to make your application more understandable. There are three different types of inner classes: nested top-level classes, member classes, and local classes. There is also a fourth type of inner class—an anonymous class—which is actually an extension of the local class type. OK, so that's great. You know the different types of inner classes, but what does it actually all mean? Well, let's review each of the inner class types in detail. For even more information about inner classes, visit the Inner Classes Specification Web page on the JavaSoft Web site at http://java.sun.com/products/jdk/1.1/docs/guide/innerclasses/index.html.

Nested top-level classes and interfaces

A nested class is just what it sounds like—a class within another class. Nested top-level classes must be declared as static, and they can only be nested within other top-level classes; the same applies. You define a nested class like this:

```
public class TopClass {
  public static class NestedClass {
    ...
  }
  ...
}
```

As you can see, you can now define classes within other classes. Why would you want to do this? Well, if the nested class is only used within the top class, defining it as a nested class makes it clear that this is the only place this class is used.

Tip

Nested classes can be nested to any depth, which just means that you can keep nesting classes as many times as you want! Don't go too crazy with this capability—nesting your classes too deep can make your code nearly impossible to understand. I recommend that you only nest classes one level deep, unless you have a compelling reason to do otherwise.

Member classes

Nested classes are defined within top-level classes. Because they are essentially static classes, however, they really aren't any different from top-level classes. Member classes are different though, because they aren't declared as static. Member classes are truly members of the containing class; they are defined in the same manner as nested classes, except the static option is omitted. Member classes can be defined as public, protected, or private. Methods of a member class can access the fields or methods of enclosing classes—even private fields and methods.

Warning

There are two important restrictions to remember when using member classes:

+ They cannot have the same name as any containing class or package.

+ They cannot contain any static fields, members, or classes.

Local classes

Local classes are classes defined within a block of code. They are only visible within the block of code in which they are defined. Local classes are analogous to local variables—they are defined just where they are used. There are two important features of local classes:

+ They are only visible in the block of code where they have been defined.

+ They can use any final local variable or method parameters in the block of code where they are defined.

JDK 1.1

The most common use of local classes is with event listeners and the new AWT model found in the JDK 1.1. I discuss the Abstract Windowing Toolkit in Part IV.

A local class is defined as follows:

```
public class TopClass {
  public void methodA {
    class LocalClass {
      . . .
```

```
        }
      ...
    }
    ...
  }
```

This is a trivial example of a local class. I have omitted the class bodies for simplicity. As illustrated in this example, the LocalClass class is only visible within the methodA method. LocalClass can access any methods and fields of the TopClass class.

Warning

Like member classes, local classes cannot contain any static fields, methods, or classes.

Anonymous classes

Finally, the last type of inner classes are *anonymous classes*—a special case of local classes. The main difference between local and anonymous classes is that anonymous classes are shy—they don't have any name. So, how can a class without a name be useful and used? Let's take a closer look at how an anonymous class is defined:

```
class A {
  AnonymousClass method1 {
    return new AnonymousClass() {
      int i = 0;
      public int increment() { return(i++); };
      public int decrement() { return(i-); };
    };
  };
}
```

In this example, method1 creates and returns the anonymous class—AnonymousClass. Anonymous classes are created by calling following a class body definition after the new command. In this case, an anonymous class is created that defines two methods, increment() and decrement().

Another important feature of anonymous classes is their use as instance initializers, which are similar to static initializers found in the 1.0 JDK. An *instance initializer* is simply a block of code that is embedded inside a class definition. Here is an example of an instance initializer:

```
class A {
  // Example of an instance initializer…
  int[] array1 = new int[5]; { for(int i=0; i<5; i++)
                                 array1[i] = i * 100; }
}
```

Instance initializers are executed in the order they appear. They are run after any superclass constructors, but before the constructor of the current class.

When should you use an anonymous class over a local class? Well, if your class fits any of these descriptions, it might be appropriate:

✦ Only one instance of the class is ever used.

✦ The class is used immediately after it's defined.

✦ The class is small.

✦ Naming the class doesn't make your code easier to understand.

There are four important restrictions to keep in mind when you're using anonymous classes:

✦ Anonymous classes can't have constructors.

✦ Anonymous classes cannot define any static fields, methods, or classes.

✦ Anonymous classes cannot be public, private, protected, or static.

✦ You can only ever create one instance of an anonymous class.

Reflection

JDK 1.2

Also new to JDK 1.1/1.2 is the reflection API. *Reflection* allows a Java class to look inside itself. The `java.lang.Class` class has been enhanced to include methods that now return the fields, methods, and constructors defined by a class. The `java.lang.reflect` package defines the `Field`, `Method`, and `Constructor` classes that are returned by the reflection methods. Reflection allows your applications to obtain complete and detailed information about any class during runtime. The most prevalent use of reflection is with JavaBeans, which is discussed in more detail in Chapter 28. For further information about class reflection, consult the Reflection Web page on the JavaSoft Web site at `http://java.sun.com/products/jdk/1.1/docs/reflection/index.html`.

JDK 1.2

In JDK 1.2, a `Field`, `Method`, or `Constructor` object may be explicitly flagged as suppressing default Java language access control. When the reflective object is used, this flag—a new instance field—is consulted as part of access checking. If the flag is true, access checks are disabled and the requested operation proceeds; otherwise, normal access checks are performed as in JDK 1.1. The flag is false by default in a reflected member or constructor. Thus, in JDK 1.2 each concrete reflected class (`Field`, `Method` and `Constructor`) extends a new base class, `AccessibleObject`.

Interfaces

By this point in the chapter, you're probably pretty comfortable with the concept of an interface. After all, you've seen how to declare interfaces in a class using the implements keyword. And you've seen how to declare abstract classes and abstract methods, which are similar in nature to an interface.

You might also realize that an interface is an entirely abstract class; not a single method declared in an interface can be implemented by the interface. All methods in an interface must be implemented by the class that claims to use them. (Refer to the "Classes and Interfaces" section earlier in this chapter to see how your classes can claim to use an interface.)

And so it's time to see how an interface is created. Let's begin by looking at the declaration syntax for an interface. Following is the syntax for declaring an interface (items in square brackets are optional):

```
[public] interface name [extends interface1, interface2, ...] {
   ...
}
```

As you can see, an interface can extend any number of other interfaces. And, if you recall, a class can extend any number of interfaces. This allows for an extremely powerful capability, similar to multiple inheritance found in C++.

In an interface, all variables are automatically treated as public, static, and final. You can explicitly specify each, if you want, but it really doesn't matter. However, you aren't allowed to use anything other than public, static, and final variables. If you were to specify a variable as protected, for instance, the compiler would generate an error.

The same is true for an interface's methods, which are automatically treated as public and abstract. You can explicitly declare your interface methods as public and abstract, but it really doesn't matter since the system will do it for you automatically. However, just try to specify a private method, and see what the compiler has to say about it!

Consider for a moment our ShowDown class, rewritten as an interface:

```
public interface ShowDown {
   int SHERIFF = 60000; // all variables are public, static, &
                                                       final
   void Encounter();  // all methods are public and abstract
   void SizeUp(int dude); //  all methods are public and
abstract
   }
```

You'll notice that I didn't bother to declare the constant variable SHERIFF as being final and static, as I did when ShowDown was implemented as a standard class earlier in this chapter. I didn't have to because it's automatically treated as public, static, and final when implemented as an interface. The same goes for ShowDown's methods. There's no need to declare them as public because they already are when implemented as an interface. And since each method is also abstract, we're relying on the subclass to do the implementation—don't even bother with the body of methods declared in an interface.

We only need to provide the name and parameter list of interface methods. The curly braces ({}) of the body block aren't even needed. In fact, if you included them, the compiler would generate an error, regardless of whether or not you actually provided code for the body:

```
void SizeUp(int dude){  // illegal! Can't include braces!
}
```

With interfaces, you need to remove the method block entirely and replace it with a semicolon, as follows:

```
void SizeUp(int dude); // this is fine
```

Even though all the variables and methods in an interface are implicitly prefixed with access specifiers and modifiers, the same is not true with the interface declaration itself. If you don't specify your interface as being public, Java doesn't automatically make it public. Instead, the scope of your interface is "friendly," making it available only in the package in which it is created. As a result, you may want to explicitly declare a package for your interfaces (see the next section, "Packages," for more details):

```
package numberville; // make part of numberville package

interface ShowDown { /* not public; making class available
                        only to the numberville package */
  int SHERIFF = 60000;
  void Encounter();
  void SizeUp(int dude);
}
```

Note

Since all variables in an interface are automatically considered public, static, and final (whether or not you supply the keywords yourself), be sure to initialize them. If you don't, the compiler tells you to get your act together. Save yourself the embarrassment, and initialize all interface variables before the compiler has a chance to give off attitude.

Packages

After writing a few Java programs and creating a number of classes in the process, you'll probably find yourself wanting to reuse some of the classes in new projects. And this is exactly what you're supposed to do: Why rewrite when you can reuse?

To make it easier to reuse code and organize classes, Java supports a mechanism called *packages*. Packages allow classes to be grouped according to their purpose, much like you might group files inside a directory on your computer's hard drive.

Actually, you're already familiar with packages on a basic level; we've been importing them for use with our HelloWorld programs in previous chapters. However, to really make use of them, we need to explore packages in more detail. First we'll learn how to fully use existing packages. Then we'll see how to create and manage our own packages.

Although I refer to packages in terms of classes, they can also contain interfaces. Rather than having to say "classes and interfaces" every time I talk about packages, I'll simply use the term *classes*, with the understanding that interfaces are implied.

Using packages

As you know, packages are used to organize and categorize classes. In fact, the Java Developer's Kit (JDK) comes with eight packages that contain the Java Application Programmer's Interface (API) classes, and one that contains Sun's debugging tool classes (see Table 11-2).

Table 11-2 **Standard Java Packages**	
API Packages	**Description**
`java.applet`	Applet classes and interfaces
`java.awt`	Abstract Windowing Toolkit (AWT) classes and interfaces
`java.awt.image`	(Subpackage of AWT) Bitmap image classes and interfaces
`java.awt.peer`	(Subpackage of AWT) Platform-specific AWT classes and interfaces (such as Windows, Sun, and Macintosh)
`java.io`	Input/Output classes and interfaces
`java.lang`	Core Java language classes and interfaces
`java.net`	Network classes and interfaces

(continued)

Table 11-2 (continued)	
API Packages	**Description**
java.util	Utility classes and interfaces
Other Packages	**Description**
sun.tools.debug	Debugging classes and interfaces

Note At the time this book went to print, the Macintosh JDK did not include a debugger or Sun's debugging classes.

Importing packages

There are a few ways to access classes that are in packages. The most basic method is to import a package in the beginning of your programs, as we did in our FlexibleMediaHello applet. In this case, you simply provide the import statement(s) before any other code in your program. (It's okay if they come after comments and white space such as character returns and linefeeds):

```
import java.applet.*;
import java.awt.*;
import java.net.URL;
import java.net.MalformedURLException;
```

As you can see, we have imported four packages (or, more precisely, the public classes of four packages) using two different techniques. In the first two lines of code, we used the asterisk (*) to effectively tell the compiler to "Give me access to all of the public classes in this package":

```
import java.applet.*; // import all public classes in
  java.applet package
import java.awt.*; // import all public classes in java.awt
  package
```

In the second two lines, we explicitly state the name of the public classes to import:

```
  // import URL class in the java.net package:
import java.net.URL;
    // import MalformedURLException class in the java.net
        package:

import java.net.MalformedURLException;
```

A Note About Importing Public Classes

You can only import the public classes in a package, and only those public classes that are directly part of that package. You can't, for example, import the java.awt subpackages, java.awt.image and java.awt.peer, using the following import statement:

```
import java.awt.*; // import public classes in java.awt, but not
    subpackages!
```

This example imports only the public classes that are directly part of the java.awt package. If you want to import the classes in a subpackage, you have to specify each subpackage explicitly:

```
import java.awt.image.*;  // import public classes in image
subpackage of java.awt
import java.awt.peer.*; // import public classes in peer
    subpackage of java.awt
```

We could just as easily have used the asterisk to import all the classes in the java.net package, instead of specifying the specific classes, as we just did:

```
import java.net.*; // import all public classes in the entire
    java.net package
```

Although you might initially think this is excessive, since we only use the URL and MalformedURLException classes, it's really not. Even though it seems that the entire java.net class is imported, in truth, only those classes that are used in the program are imported; Java links in classes only when they are actually used.

Although I could have used asterisk notation to import all public classes in the java.net package (import java.net.*), I explicitly specified the URL and MalformedURLException classes to make it clear to the reader of this program what portions of the java.net package are used. In general, it's better programming style to explicitly import the classes you use in a program (as I've done with URL and MalformedURLException) rather than using the asterisk approach. Clearly identifying the classes you import in this way makes it much easier for others to maintain your code; they won't have to search through your program to find out which classes in a package you use.

Any time you want to use a class, you need to import the package it is part of (or reference it explicitly in your code, as described shortly). However, you don't need to import the java.lang package; these classes are fundamental to Java and are automatically imported regardless of whether you explicitly import them or not.

Explicit class references in imported packages

Once a package has been imported, the public classes in it can be used as often as desired in your code. This is all well and good, but what if you only need to use a class once? In this case, you can explicitly reference the class, without having to import the package it is part of. For example, suppose we didn't want to bother importing the URL class in our earlier example. If we precede all references to URL with the java.net package, we wouldn't have to:

```
java.net.URL imageURL=null; // explicitly reference to declare
    variable...
try {
    imageURL = new java.net.URL(imageString); // and once again
        in the code
} catch (MalformedURLException e) { ; }
```

Since we've explicitly specified the java.net package immediately before the URL class name, Java knows exactly what package the URL class is part of. And, as a result, we don't have to import the java.net package at all. Contrast the preceding code snippet with how it was written originally:

```
import java.net.URL;  // import the URL class
URL  imageURL=null;
try {
    imageURL = new URL(imageString);
} catch (MalformedURLException e) { ; }
```

If it weren't for the fact that the URL class name is pretty descriptive, we wouldn't have any idea where it comes from just looking at the implementation: You can't tell that URL is part of the java.net package by merely looking at the code. This is a downside to importing packages; you can't easily see where a class is coming from by looking at the code alone. Instead, you have to have an understanding of what classes are in each package and make an educated guess whenever a class name appears in code.

Unless you have a large number of references to a particular class in a program, it's often more helpful to precede the class with its package rather than import that package. In fact, our FlexibleMediaHello program would be more readable in general if we discarded all of the import statements and explicitly referenced the entire package each time a class is used. However, there is a trade-off between readability and ease of coding. It's much easier to simply type "URL" than it is to type "java.net.URL." As result, you may prefer to import packages, rather than reference them explicitly.

Naming conflicts

One of the main benefits of explicitly referencing packages, apart from the clarity of code produced as a result, is the fact that class names won't conflict, as they could when using an import statement. At some point, you're going to create a class with the same name as one that exists in another class. For example, how many understandable yet unique identifiers can you come up with for a Sort class?

Suppose, for a moment, that your Sort class is part of a package called utilityPackage. Now, what if you imported that package and another one that happens to also have a class named Sort?

```
import utilityPackage; // contains your Sort class
import anyOtherPackage; // also contains a Sort class
Sort mySort = new Sort(); // which Sort class is instantiated?
```

As you can see, we've got a problem here. Which Sort class is instantiated when this code is executed? Since that can't be determined, the compiler kicks out an error and refuses to compile the code. You can avoid this, however, by using an explicit class reference directly in the code:

```
utilityPackage.Sort mySort = new utilityPackage.Sort();
```

Here we resolved any potential conflict by explicitly declaring the package name along with the class. There will be no confusion to a person reading your code, or when the compiler tries to create a Sort object. It's clear just by looking at the code that the object we're talking about comes from utilityPackage.

Package levels

Package names are arranged in levels, with each level separated from the next with a period. Consider, for example, the java.applet package. It's comprised of two levels: The first level is java and the second is applet. The java.awt.image package, on the other hand, is made up of three levels, with image being the third level.

When you create your own packages, it's up to you to decide upon the names and number of levels. However, creating your own package isn't as simple as merely dreaming up a nifty package name. Packages are directly related to the directory structure containing the classes they're composed of—when you create your own packages, you do so based on the directory layout containing the classes to be included in these packages.

Creating packages

It's easy to create your own packages, something you'll almost certainly want to do at some time or another. To create a package (that is, to add a class to a package), simply use the following statement as the first line of code in your source code file:

```
package packageName;
```

Suppose, for example, we wanted to create a new package called numberville to organize all the classes that might be used to simulate a bunch of numbers living together in harmony. (Hey, even numbers need a home!) We could easily do this by placing the following statement in every class file that we wanted to be part of the package:

```
package numberville;
```

For instance, our ShowDown superclass would look like this:

```
package numberville; // make ShowDown part of numberville package
class ShowDown {
   ...
   }
```

The HighNoon class file would look like this:

```
package numberville; // make HighNoon part of numberville package
public class HighNoon extends ShowDown {

   ... /*  member variables */
   void Encounter() {
      ...
   }

   void SizeUp(int dude) {
      ...
   }
}
```

Now, whenever we need to use the HighNoon or ShowDown classes, we need only import the numberville package or explicitly specify it when creating a HighNoon or ShowDown object. Furthermore, we could continue to create classes that operate on numbers, as these two classes do, and easily add them to the numberville package using only one line of code:

```
package numberville; // make this class part of numberville
   package
```

Be sure to place your `package` statements first, before all other statements in your program. A `package` statement should come before all other code, including `import` statements.

Unique names

The naming convention used when creating packages is designed to provide unique packages that can be made universally available without causing a name conflict. Any packages that you create, and that will be made available outside your organization, should use your organization's Internet domain name in reverse order to ensure a unique name.

For example, if I wanted to make an animation package available to the world, I'd use my company's `mantiscorp.com` domain name in reverse when creating the package:

```
COM.mantiscorp.animation; // this package is unique
```

As you can see, the first portion of a unique name must be in uppercase letters. The remainder of the name should be in lowercase letters, with only the classes having a capital letter. For example, suppose we needed to specify a `Sprite` class in the previous package:

```
COM.mantiscorp.animation.Sprite;
```

Due to the naming convention of unique packages, we can immediately tell that animation comes from the `mantiscorp.com` domain. And since only classes begin with a capital letter (with the exception of the first level in a unique name, in which all letters are capitalized), we know right off the bat that `Sprite` is a class and not another level of the package.

JAR Files

Just as you can use a glass jar to can your tomatoes and peaches, you can use JAR (Java Archive) files to can your Java packages. JAR files store Java packages, classes, and resources in a compressed form. It takes time to download information over the Internet, so if you can cram more information into less space, things will run faster. When adding applets to your HTML files, you use the `<ARCHIVE>` tag to specify a JAR file. A more complete discussion on the `<ARCHIVE>` tag and adding Java applets to your HTML can be found in Chapter 17. For now, I review how to create JAR files.

If you've used any file-zipping utility, you should feel quite at home when creating JAR files. You use the `jar.exe` tool to create a JAR file. If you want to create one that contains the `COM.mantiscorp.animation` package, simply execute this command from the directory that contains the package:

```
jar cvf mantiscorp *
```

The * causes all the files in the current directory to be added to the JAR file. The `c`, `v`, and `f` are command-line options, and they are detailed in Table 11-3.

Table 11-3
JAR Tool Command-Line Options

Option	Description
c	Creates a new or empty archive.
T	Lists the contents of the JAR file.
x [file]	Extracts all files, or just the filenames specified.
f [jar-file]	Specifies the name of the JAR file to work with. Without the f option, output will be sent to standard output.
V	Generates verbose output.

Summary

This chapter introduced the concept of creating and using objects in your Java applications. This is the final big puzzle piece required to start developing your own Java applications. The upcoming chapters will continue to take a closer look at fundamentals required to develop your own Java applications. Key concepts to remember about this chapter include:

✦ Classes are templates, or blueprints, from which objects are created. As such, we often think of classes as data types. When objects are created or instantiated from the same class, they are considered to be of the same type. All objects are an instance of a class. The class that an object is instantiated from determines the type of that object. If two objects are instantiated from the same class, they are considered to be of the same type.

✦ All member variables are declared within the body of the class, not inside a method or as a parameter to a method. They are used to maintain the state of an object.

✦ While variables are used to maintain an object's state, methods provide the behavior. For those of you who are new to object-oriented programming, you can think of a method as a function. However, unlike procedural programming where functions sit out in the open (or, more accurately, are organized into files) to be called upon at any point, a method is encapsulated inside the class in which it is defined, along with the variables of that class.

✦ An interface is an entirely abstract class; not a single method declared in an interface can be implemented by the interface. All methods in an interface must be implemented by the class that claims to use them.

✦ To make it easier to reuse code and organize classes, Java supports a mechanism called *packages*. Packages allow classes to be grouped according to their purpose, much like you might group files inside a directory on your computer hard drive.

✦ It's easy to create your own packages, something you'll almost certainly want to do at some time or another. To create a package (that is, to add a class to a package), simply use the `package` statement as the first line of code in your source code file.

✦ JAR files store Java packages, classes, and resources in a compressed form. It takes time to download information over the Internet, so if you can cram more information into less space, things will run faster. When adding applets to your HTML files, you use the `<ARCHIVE>` tag to specify a JAR file.

✦   ✦   ✦

Strings and Arrays

By now you know that in Java strings aren't merely arrays of characters; they're first-class objects (meaning they can't be subclassed). In fact, Java offers two classes for dealing with strings: `String` and `StringBuffer`.

In this chapter, we'll learn about the `String` and `StringBuffer` classes, and find out what it means to be a first-class object. We'll also take a closer look at arrays, which are also first-class objects, and their loosely related relatives, `Vector` and `Hashtable`.

As you'll soon see, Java provides several ways to store, retrieve, and utilize data. In the next chapter, we'll take a look at streams, which give us an abstract ability to read and write to a flowing buffer of data. However, streams are often overkill for many programming tasks, and so we need to look at easier ways of storing and retrieving data.

With the `String` and `StringBuffer` classes, we can create objects that utilize character data. With arrays, we can store and retrieve any type of data we'd like in each element, even other arrays. However, since we create arrays with an explicit dimension, there's no way of extending their size when we run out of elements. As a result, we turn to the `Vector` class, which provides us with growable arrays.

Once the concept of arrays has been covered in detail, we'll take a look at the `Hashtable` class. Here, we'll see how to create objects in which we can store values that are retrieved through a key, rather than an index. In addition, we'll see how the `Stack` class extends `Hashtable` to implement this familiar data structure.

And, since `Vector`, `Hashtable`, and `Stack` are all part of the `java.util` package, we'll take this opportunity to explore that package as well. We'll see how our strings can be tokenized using `StringTokenizer`, allowing us to break these objects into their discrete pieces. Finally, we'll look at the purely utilitarian classes found in this package, specifically `Date`, `Calendar`, `TimeZone`, `Random`, and the `ResourceBundle` classes.

But, before we get too far ahead of ourselves, let's pull back and take a closer look at the `String` and `StringBuffer` classes.

Strings (java.lang.String)

As we learned in Chapter 7, Java strings aren't like the ones we're accustomed to in C and C++. In those languages, strings are simply a null-terminated array of characters. Java strings, however, are actually objects defined by the `String` class. As a result, they feature a number of methods that are used to access (and, in the case of `StringBuffer` objects, manipulate) their contents.

Additionally, bounds checking is performed on Java strings at both compile and runtime. If we attempt to access portions of a string outside the legal bounds, an exception is thrown, which we can catch and handle (see Chapter 10 for details on exceptions).

C and C++ strings, in contrast, don't support such well-defined behavior. In these languages, it's quite easy to overrun the boundaries of the array in which our characters are stored. Sometimes, the error is immediately apparent, sometimes it's not.

At best, we manage to identify the problem early in the development cycle and fix it. At worst, the problem slips through our bug-hunting efforts and makes its way to the customer and surfaces sporadically, perhaps causing the program to behave unexpectedly, or even crash.

Since the program's behavior is normal for the most part, it can be difficult to track down and eliminate the programming error. Often, the problem can be traced to an improper use of strings, such as overshooting the string array boundary and accessing data in memory, rather than the contents of the array.

Since no error checking is performed with C/C++ strings, we're free to go right past the end of the array. Of course, we don't do this intentionally, but it tends to happen from time to time. Unfortunately, the result is often a slippery bug that doesn't rear its ugly-buggish head consistently. Such errors are extremely tough to track down.

Java strings are first-class objects

With Java, strings are first-class objects that support a well-defined set of methods, as shown in Table 12-1. Using these methods, our relationship with strings becomes one of trust and reliance, as opposed to the paranoia C and C++ programmers sometimes develop after a few bad string experiences.

Table 12-1
java.lang.String

Constructor	Signature	Description
String	public String()	Constructs a new, empty string.
String	public String (String value)	Constructs a new string that is a copy of the specified string.
String	public String (Char value)	Constructs a new string whose initial value is the specified array of characters.
String	public String (char value[], int offset, int count)	Constructs a new string whose initial value is the specified subarray of characters. The length of the string will be count characters, beginning at offset within the specified character array.
String	public String (byte ascii[], int hibyte, int offset, int count) count characters starting at offset within the string	Constructs a new string whose initial value is the specified subarray of bytes. The high-byte of each character can be specified, although it is usually 0. The length of the string will be the specified character array.
String	public String (byte[] ascii, int hibyte)	Constructs a new string whose value is the specified array of bytes. The byte array will be transformed into Unicode chars using hibyte as the upper byte of each character.
String	public String (StringBuffer buffer)	Constructs a new string whose value is the current contents of the given string buffer.
length	public int length()	Returns the length of the string. The length of the string is equal to the number of 16-bit Unicode characters in it.
charAt	public char charAt(int index)	Returns the character at the specified index (index values range from 0 to length() - 1).

(continued)

Table 12-1 *(continued)*

Constructor	Signature	Description
`getChars`	`public void getChars(int scrBegin, int scrEnd, char dst[], int dstBegin)`	Copies characters from this string into the specified character array. The characters of the substring (as defined by `scrBegin` and `scrEnd`) are copied into the array, starting at the array's `dstBegin` location.
`getBytes`	`public void getBytes(int srcBegin, int srcEnd, byte dst[], int dstBegin)`	Copies characters from this string into the specified byte array. Copies the characters of the substring (as defined by `scrBegin` and `scrEnd`) into the byte array starting at array's `dstBegin` location.
`equals`	`public boolean equals(Object anObject)`	Compares this string to the specified object. Returns `true` if they are equal (have the same length and the same characters in the same sequence).
`equals IgnoreCase`	`public boolean equalsIgnoreCase (String anotherString)`	Compares this string to another object. Returns `true` if the object is equal to this string; that is, has the same length and the same characters in the same sequence. Uppercase characters are folded to lower-case before they are compared.
`compareTo`	`public int compareTo (String anotherString)`	Compares this string to another specified string. Returns an integer that is less than, equal to, or greater than zero. The integer's value depends on whether this string is less than, equal to, or greater than the `anotherString`.
`regionMatches`	`public boolean regionMatches (int toffset, String other, int ooffset, int len)`	Determines whether a region of this string matches the specified region of the specified string.
`regionMatches`	`public boolean regionMatches (boolean ignoreCase, int toffset, String other, int ooffset, int len)`	Determines whether a region of this string matches the specified region of the specified string. If the boolean `ignoreCase` is `true`, uppercase characters are considered equivalent to lowercase letters.

Constructor	Signature	Description
startsWith	public boolean startsWith (String prefix, int toffset)	Determines whether this string starts with some prefix, starting at toffset.
startsWith	public boolean startsWith (String prefix)	Determines whether this string starts with some prefix.
endsWith	public boolean endsWith(String suffix)	Determines whether the string ends with some suffix.
hashCode	public int hashCode()	Returns a hash code for this string. This is a large number composed of the character values in the string.
indexOf	public int indexOf(int ch)	Returns the index within this string of the first occurrence of the specified character. This method returns −1 if the index is not found.
indexOf	public int indexOf(int ch, int fromIndex)	Returns the index within this string of the first occurrence of the specified character, starting the search at fromIndex. This method returns −1 if the index is not found.
lastIndexOf	public int LastIndexOf(int ch)	Returns the index within this string of the last occurrence of the specified character. The string is searched backwards, starting at the last character. This method returns −1 if the index is not found.
lastIndexOf	public int lastIndexOf(int ch, int fromIndex)	Returns the index within this string of the last occurrence of the specified character. The string is searched backwards, starting at fromIndex. This method returns −1 if the index is not found.
substring	public String substring(int beginIndex, int endIndex)	Returns the substring of this string. The substring is specified by a beginIndex (inclusive) and the end of the string.
replace	public String replace(char oldChar, char newChar)	Converts this string by replacing all occurrences of oldString with newString).
toLowerCase	public String toLowerCase()	Converts all the characters in this string to lowercase.

(continued)

Table 12-1 *(continued)*

Constructor	Signature	Description
toUpperCase	public String toUpperCase()	Converts all the characters in this string to uppercase.
trim	public String trim()	Trims leading and trailing white space from this string.
toString	public String toString()	Converts a character array to a String object.
toCharArray	public char[] toCharArray(	Converts this String object into a character array.
valueOf	public static String valueOf (Object obj)	Returns a string that represents the string value of the object. The object may choose how to represent itself by implementing the toString method.
valueOf	public static String valueOf (char data[])	Returns a string that is equivalent to the specified character array. Uses the original array as the body of the string (in other words, it doesn't copy it to a new array).
valueOf	public static String valueOf (char data[], int offset, int count)	Returns a string that is equivalent to the specified character array.
copyValueOf	public static String copyValueOf (char data[], int offset, int count)	Returns a string that is equivalent to the specified character array. It creates a new array and copies the characters into it.
copyValueOf	public static String copyValueOf (char data[])	Returns a string that is equivalent to the specified character array. It creates a new array and copies the characters into it.
valueOf	public static String valueOf (boolean b)	Returns a String object that represents the state of the specified boolean.
valueOf	public static String valueOf (char c)	Returns a String object that contains a single character.

Constructor	Signature	Description
valueOf	public static String valueOf (int I)	Returns a String object that represents the value of the specified int.
valueOf	public static String valueOf (long l)	Returns a String object that represents the value of the specified long.
valueOf	public static String valueOf (float f)	Returns a String object that represents the value of the specified float.
valueOf	public static String valueOf (double d)	Returns a String object that represents the value of the specified double.
intern	public String Intern()	Returns a string that is equal to this string, but is guaranteed to be from the unique string pool.

With first-class objects, you can only use the String class to create new String objects, as we've been doing all along. But since String is a final class, we can't create our own subclasses:

```
class MyStrings extends String { // ILLEGAL!
    . . .
}
```

If we try to extend String, as shown, the compiler spits out a "Can't subclass Final Objects" message and refuses to go on. Of course, we're still free to use the String class to create String objects. We've been doing that all along. However, attempting to create a subclass of String is forbidden.

String versus StringBuffer

As you're now aware, Java provides two distinct string classes: String and StringBuffer. The String class is used to create String objects which are immutable; their contents can't be altered once characters have been stored in them. StringBuffer, on the other hand, is specifically for strings that are mutable, or able to be changed even after characters have been stored in them. We'll get to StringBuffer in a moment, but for now, let's take a closer look at the String class.

Note

In Java, the `char` data type is twice the size C/C++ developers might expect. Instead of being 8 bits, the Java `char` is a 16-bit unsigned type, capable of holding tens of thousands of values associated with Unicode characters. However, if you are using standard ASCII or Latin-1 characters, there is no way to tell the difference between Java `char` values and their C/C++ counterparts. Due to `char`'s 16-bit size, the byte is actually the smallest of all integral data types in Java, weighing in at a lean 8 bits.

Suppose we created a `String` object and then tried to change its value later in the program:

```
String myString = "There once was a mouse from Nantucket";
myString = "Hickory, Dickory, Dock"; // legal?
```

Is this legal? Sure it is, even though you might think otherwise. In this case, we're not attempting to alter the contents of the string; that is, we're not trying to change the individual characters in the `String` object. Instead, we're storing a brand new set of characters into it, which is perfectly legal. The original string is replaced entirely by "Hickory, Dickory, Dock"—the whole string is replaced, lock, stock, and barrel.

However, if we attempted to change the individual characters in a `String` object, we'd be in for a rude awakening:

```
String myString = "There once was a mouse from Nantucket";
myString[0] = 'Z'; // ILLEGAL!
```

In this example, we're trying to treat the Java `String` object as we would a standard C/C++ string. However, when it attempted to set the first character in the `String` array to the character "Z", the compiler screamed bloody murder:

```
StringTest.java:8: [] can only be applied to arrays. It can't
be applied to java.lang.String.
   myString[0] = "Z";
            ^
1 error
```

We've been told in no uncertain terms that a `String` object isn't an array (we'll get to arrays later), and so we'd better not treat it as such. "No problem," you might think to yourself, "I'll just use the handy `setCharAt()` method defined in `StringBuffer`." But:

```
myString.setCharAt(0,'Z') ; // ILLEGAL!
```

A fine thought, except for the fact that the compiler will clutch its heart and gasp for air as you try to manhandle an immutable `String` object. Remember, you can't change the contents of a `String` object, only `StringBuffer` objects. And, since `setChar()` isn't defined in the `String` class, you can't use it.

As you can see from the methods listed in Table 12-1, you can find out a lot about `String` objects, but you can't change their contents. The closest you can get is to blow away the entire string representation and replace it with another, as we did earlier. But, no matter how hard you try, you can't twiddle the contents of a `String` object.

Creating strings

Although our programs have been giving birth to `String` objects all along, the process bears a closer look. Clearly, one way they can be created is by assigning a string literal (we'll get to literals in a moment) to a `String` object variable:

```
String myString = "Whose whiskers were so strong";
```

This is the easiest way to create a string, as we've been doing for some time. However, you'll notice that the `String` class gives us seven different constructors as well. The previous statement is functionally equivalent to the following:

```
String myString = new String ("Whose whiskers were so strong");
```

And, for that matter, these are both functionally equivalent to creating an array of characters that are then supplied to the constructor capable of converting arrays into `String` objects:

```
char myChars[] = {'W', 'h', 'o', 's', 'e', ' ', 'w', 'h', 'i',
's', 'k', 'e', 'r', 's', ' ', 'w', 'e', 'r', 'e', ' ', 's',
'o', ' ', 's', 't', 'r', 'o', 'n', 'g'};  // create array of
characters
String myString = new String(myChars);  /* use array to create
                                        new String object */
```

Of course, we can also create `String` objects from arrays of bytes, and even subsections of arrays. Using the same character array declared in the previous example, we can grab a portion of it for use as a string:

```
String myString = new String(myChars,6,8);
```

Here, we create a `String` object using a slice of the `myChars` array. By providing the index in the array at which to start, together with the number of elements to use, we can create a string from a subsection of that array. In the current example, the `String` object would now contain "whiskers."

Perhaps you noticed that the beginning index I provided for a slice of the array, 6, seems to indicate the `String` object should include a space and drop the last character(s) in the word "whiskers?"

Although this seems like a mistake, it's not. You might recall from Chapter 7 that array indexing begins at zero (0), and not at one (1), as you'd think. While C and C++ programmers are already familiar with such zero-based array indexing, we'll revisit the topic later, when we talk about arrays.

As it stands, this line of code creates a string using the characters "w h i s k e r s" not "h i s k e r". However, if you happen upon a mouse from Nantucket having strong hiskers, be sure to drop me a line; I'd be most curious to see such a creature.

Depending on your needs, there's likely to be a constructor to fit the bill. As you can see, arrays and strings work hand in hand; indeed, four of the seven constructors accept array parameters.

You'll also note that we can create an empty `String` object, which we can fill with characters later:

```
String myString = new String(); // create empty string object
myString = "Whose whiskers were so strong"; // fill with
characters
```

If you tried to print the empty `myString` before it was filled with characters, nothing would actually print. Keep in mind that `myString` isn't null, it's simply empty—sort of like a mug of coffee without any coffee in it. Sort of.

The `null` keyword has no meaningful value associated with it; it simply means an object is not referenced anywhere. To determine if an object has a reference, you can test it against `null`:

```
if (anyObject = = null){
   . . . // if true, object has no reference
}
```

This is particularly helpful when dealing with `String` objects, and in fact is how you determine if an applet's `PARAM` tag is provided. When an HTML document doesn't contain a particular `PARAM` tag, you'll know by testing for `null`. In this case, you can supply a default value:

```
soundFile = getParameter("sound"); // get sound PARAM
if (soundFile = = null){
   soundFile = "audio\welcome.au";  // set default if not
provided
}E
```

Once we have a `String` object, it's easy to make a copy of it using the appropriate constructor:

```
String anotherString = new String(myString); /* create copy of
                                          myString */
```

Of course, we can also assign one `String` object to another. The following assignment is the functional equivalent of the preceding constructor:

```
anotherString = myString; // copy myString into anotherString
```

Finally, we can create a `String` object from a `StringBuffer` object:

```
String myString = new String(anyStringBufferObject);
```

The contents of the `StringBuffer` object are copied into the new `String` object, effectively creating an immutable copy of a once-mutable string.

Accessor methods

Once you've created a `String` object, chances are you'll want to do something with it. This stands to reason; why would you bother creating an object if you didn't want to do something with it? As luck would have it, we can do a lot with `String` objects.

We've already sent `String` objects to the standard output stream, which typically writes the contents to the display (although they may be redirected, for example to a file):

```
System.out.print(myString);
System.out.println(myString);
```

We also use `String` objects in a variety of other methods, a few of which we're already familiar with:

```
drawString(myString, 100, 100); // draw the string on screen
getImage(getCodeBase(), myString); // get an image file
getAudioClip(getCodeBase(), myString); // get an audio file
setTitle(myString); // set window/frame title
new Menu(myString); // create new menu with this name
new Button(myString); // create button with this name
```

However, aside from being used as parameters in method calls, there are a number of methods that operate on `String` objects, as seen in Table 12-1.

We might, for example, want to change a few characters in an existing String object. This we can do easily by using the replace() method, specifying the characters to be replaced, and specifying the character to replace them with. However, since we can't alter a String as we can a StringBuffer, the result is returned as a new String:

```
String myString = "Hickory, Dickory, Dock";
String alterString = myString.replace('k', 'c'); /* creates a
brand new string, an exact copy of the original with one major
exception — this one has all occurrences of k replaced with c
*/
```

After executing, alterString would contain "Hiccory, Diccory, Docc," and myString would remain unchanged.

As you can see, the methods that would normally alter the contents of the string—such as replace()—don't. Instead, they return a new String object, since they can't physically alter the one they are given. While you may not make much use of such methods, depending on your needs, it's nice to know they exist, giving us a way to work around the restriction of Java strings being immutable.

One of the string methods you're likely to use on a regular basis, on the other hand, is length(). This method returns the number of characters in a String object, which you'll need if you do any type of work that requires a run through each of the characters.

For example, suppose you wanted to output a string in reverse. I'm not certain why you might want to do such a thing, but you can do it as long as you know the length of the string:

```
String myString = "Hickory, Dickory, Dock";
int len = myString.length(); // get number of chars in array
for (; len>0; len—) {
  System.out.print(myString.charAt(len-1)); // output a
    character
  }
System.out.println(); // flush output
```

Notice the parameter to charAt()? Again, since String objects are stored in the same fashion as arrays, you need to be aware that the first character begins at zero (0), and the last character is at the position "length of the array minus one." If the concept of beginning at zero throws you off, you might want to revisit Chapter 9 for a few moments.

A particularly handy method when gathering user input is `trim()`, which takes a string and returns a copy of it without any preceding or trailing white space. For example, if you prompt the user for input, he or she might enter spaces before and/or after the string.

Suppose, for instance, that you developed a spreadsheet applet that required valid numeric input. If, instead of entering only the numerals 23415, the user added a few spaces, the result would need to be trimmed:

```
String origString = "    23415    ";
String trimmedString = origString.trim();
```

When executed, the preceding code copies the characters "23415" into the `trimmedString` object. However, all the whitespace before and after the characters is left out. We now have a nice, freshly trimmed string. You'll notice, however, that it's still a `String` object, not a numeric value such as an `int` or `long`. If we attempted to use this string in a loop, for example, the compiler would laugh out loud (if it could):

```
for (int i=0; i<trimmedString; i++) {
  System.out.println("Iteration: " + i);
}
Survey says:
Incompatible type for <. Can't convert java.lang.String to int.
for (int i=0; i<trimmedString; i++) {
                ^
1 error
```

At first glance, the `valueOf()` constructors seem like they might do the trick; feed 'em a string and they'll return the value of it, right? Nope; they do just the opposite. If you supply `valueOf()` with a number, it returns a string containing the character equivalent of those numbers:

```
String numString = new String().valueOf("23415");
```

For example, if we supplied `valueOf()` with "23415," we'd get a string equal to that of `trimmedString`. In fact, we can test for equality just to prove it:

```
String numString = new String().valueOf(23415);
if (trimmedString.equals(numString)) // test for equality
  System.out.println(numString + " and " + trimmedString +
    " ARE EQUAL");
else
  System.out.println(numString + " and " + trimmedString +
    " ARE NOT EQUAL");
```

But can't we check for equality using the `==` operator? Sure, and in most cases you'll get the result you'd expect. However, you need to be extremely cautious. When you create a string using `valueOf()`, as shown earlier, it won't evaluate to `true` when compared with a `String` object created as usual. For example, although the preceding snippet of code will tell you the two `String` objects are equal, try this:

```
String numString = new String().valueOf("23415");
if (numString == trimmedString)
  System.out.println(numString + " and " + trimmedString +
    " ARE EQUAL");
else
  System.out.println(numString + " and " + trimmedString +
    " ARE NOT EQUAL");
```

In this case, you'd still expect the evaluation to produce "true." But it doesn't. As a matter of fact, if you want to test the concept of testing for equality, try this:

```
String numString1 = new String().valueOf(12345);
String numString2 = "12345";
if (numString1 == numString2)
  System.out.println(numString1 + " and " + numString2 +
    " ARE EQUAL");
else
  System.out.println(numString1 + " and " + numString2 +
    " ARE NOT EQUAL");
```

Even though they look equal, and are when using the `equals()` method, the internal representation of these two `String` objects is different. The result is an equality evaluation of "false," which can really throw you off the mark, since you'd expect them to evaluate to "true." The reason is that we've supplied an `int` to `valueOf()`, which is different from supplying characters:

```
String numString1 = new String().valueOf("12345");
String numString2 = "12345";
if (numString1 == numString2)
  System.out.println(numString1 + " and " + numString2 +
    " ARE EQUAL");
else
  System.out.println(numString1 + " and " + numString2 +
    " ARE NOT EQUAL");
```

Now, this would indeed evaluate to "true." We didn't supply `valueOf()` with an `int` this time around; we supplied a string literal. As a result, the `==` operator recognizes these as being the same. However, no matter which way you create a string using `valueOf()`, it won't be the same as one returned as the result of the `trim()` method, as far as the `==` operator is concerned. To be safe, it's best to use the `equals()` method whenever you're evaluating `String` objects for equality.

Tip

As you can see, I didn't supply curly braces ({ }) in the `if` statements here. Since only one line of code is to be executed in both cases (that is, only one line of code follows the `if` clause, and only one follows `else`), we aren't required to use them.

In such cases, where you only have one line of code to execute following an evaluation, you don't have to bother surrounding it with curly braces. For example,

```
if (boolean) {
   System.out.println ("Blah, Blah, Blah . . . ");
}
```

is functionally equivalent to:

```
if (boolean)
   System.out.println ("Blah, Blah, Blah . . . ");
```

This is all useful, but it doesn't solve our original problem of wanting to use a `String` object such as `trimmedString` as an actual number. Remember, the compiler won't let us use a string in our loops, even if that string is a set of digit characters. And since `valueOf()` converts values to `String` objects, not the other way around as we originally thought, it's of no help. So what do we do? Brace yourself; we wrap.

Type wrappers

I'd be willing to bet that most new programmers are drawn to their field because of the cool names used for everything. We have "protocols," "stacks," "bits," "bytes," "RAM," and "ROM." On a good day, we "push," "poke," "tunnel," "loop," and "bit-blit." On a bad day, we crawl through the "stack," "trap" errors, and hunt "bugs."

And now we "wrap to the beat of primitive data types." (This is, of course, a joke. Keep your flamemail out of my inbox. Hmmm . . . flamemail . . . there's another one.)

Aside from providing a nifty new term, type wrappers give us exactly what we're looking for: a way to extract numerical values from `String` objects.

And they do much more.

Since most Java methods expect objects as parameters, many don't know how to deal with true numeric data types such as `int`, `long`, `float`, `double`, and so on. You may recall that these are actually primitive data types that can't be reduced any further; in order to use them as objects, we must first wrap an object around them.

For example, if we have an `int` value of 235, that value isn't an object; it's a primitive data type. In order to treat it as an object, we must first wrap an `Integer` object around it. Now, don't confuse the `Integer` class (`java.lang.Integer`) with an `int` data type: they're two different beasts. The `Integer` class defines the methods we'll use to treat an `int` as an object. As such, it's known as a *type wrapper;* it allows us to wrap an object around numeric data types. To be even more specific, the `Integer` class can be called an *integral type wrapper.*

In order to use a type wrapper, you supply it with a value. What you receive in return is an object that may be treated like any other object. You can send it messages to invoke methods and pass it as a parameter to other methods:

```
Object myIntObject = new Integer(235); // create Integer object
```

Now we have an object that can be treated like any other object. However, this still doesn't help us use our original `trimmedString` variable as part of the `for` loop condition. It just allows us to create an `Integer` object from an `int` data type. We need to do the reverse; we need to create an `int` data type from a `String` object!

Wrapper classes allow us to do just that. First, we use the `Integer` constructor that takes as its parameter a string. Once we've created an object using this type wrapper, we can use the `intValue()` method to retrieve from it the `int` value we need:

```
    int  theInt = new Integer(trimmedString).intValue(); // get
that int!
    for (int i=0; i<theInt; i++) { // and use it . . .
       System.out.println("Iteration: " + i);
    }
```

We've finally solved our problem of treating a `String` object as a primitive data type: We don't actually treat it as a primitive. Instead, we wrap an `Integer` object around the `String` object, then use the `intValue()` method to extract the primitive.

At this point, you might ask, "Hey, why not just cast the `String` object into an `Integer` object instead of instantiating a brand new object?" That's a good question, since it would save three keystrokes by not requiring us to type new code:

```
    int theInt = ((Integer) trimmedString).intValue(); // ILLEGAL!
```

Unfortunately, this doesn't fly. The compiler beats it to the ground, as if to make up for all the time it spends sorting out your uninitialized variables (perhaps, if it didn't bother assigning default values to your uninitialized variables, the compiler would have the wherewithal to perform this cast). Instead, you must instantiate an `Integer` object, as we did earlier. Anyway, if you take into account the extra parentheses needed to perform the cast and make the statement readable, you would only save one keystroke.

Although we've been wrapped up in integral type wrappers, you'll be happy to know there are many other wrapper flavors—one to satisfy every primitive data type need. Since there are several primitive data types, there are several type wrapper classes. These are listed here, with the appropriate tables for their constructors, methods, and variables:

✦ Boolean (java.lang.Boolean) (see Tables 12-2, 12-3, and 12-4)

✦ Character (java.lang.Character) (see Tables 12-5, 12-6, and 12-7)

✦ Integer (java.lang.Integer) (see Tables 12-8, 12-9, and 12-10)

✦ Float (java.lang.Float) (see Tables 12-11, 12-12, and 12-13)

✦ Double (java.lang.Double) (see Tables 12-14-, 12-15, and 12-16)

✦ Long (java.lang.Long) (see Tables 12-17, 12-18, and 12-19)

Table 12-2
java.lang.Boolean Constructors

Signature	Description
Boolean(boolean)	Constructs a Boolean object initialized to the specified boolean value.
Boolean(String)	Constructs a Boolean object initialized to the value specified by the String parameter.

Table 12-3
java.lang.Boolean Methods

Method	Signature	Description
booleanValue	public boolean booleanValue()	Returns the value of this Boolean object as a boolean.
equals	public boolean equals (Object obj)	Compares this object against the specified object.
getBoolean	public static boolean getBoolean (String name)	Gets a boolean from the properties.
hashCode	public int hashCode()	Returns a hash code for this boolean.
toString	public String toString()	Returns a new String object representing this boolean's value.
valueOf	public static boolean valueOf (String s)	Returns the boolean value represented by the specified string.

Table 12-4
java.lang.Boolean Variables

Variable	Signature	Description
FALSE	public final static Boolean FALSE	Assigns this boolean to be false.
MAX_VALUE	public final static char MAX_VALUE	The maximum value a character can have.
MIN_VALUE	public final static char MIN_VALUE	The minimum value a character can have.
TRUE	public final static Boolean TRUE	Assigns this boolean to be true.

Table 12-5
java.lang.Character Constructors

Signature	Description
public Character(char value)	Constructs a Character object with the specified value.

Table 12-6
java.lang.Character Methods

Method	Signature	Description
charValue	public char charValue()	Returns the value of this Character object.
digit	public static int digit(char ch int radix)	Returns the numeric value of the character digit using the specified radix*.
equals	public boolean equals(Object obj)	Compares this object against the specified object.
forDigit	public static char forDigit (int digit, int radix)	Returns the character value for the specified digit in the specified radix*.
hashCode	public int hashCode()	Returns a hash code for this character.

Method	Signature	Description
isDigit	public static boolean is Digit(char ch)	Determines whether the specified character is an ISO-LATIN-1 digit.
isLowerCase	public static boolean isLowerCase(char ch)	Determines whether the specified character is ISO-LATIN-1 lowercase.
isSpace	public static boolean isSpace (char ch)	Determines whether the specified character is ISO-LATIN-1 whitespace, according to Java.
isUpperCase	public static boolean isUpperCase(char ch)	Determines whether the specified character is ISO-LATIN-1 uppercase.
toLowerCase	public static char toLowerCase (char ch)	Returns the lowercase character value of the ISO-LATIN-1 character. Characters that are not uppercase letters are returned unmodified.
toString	public String toString()	Returns a String object representing this character's value.
toUpperCase	public static char toUpperCase (char ch)	Returns the uppercase character value of the specified ISO-LATIN-1 character. Characters that are not lowercase letters are returned unmodified. Note that the German and Latin ÿ have no corresponding uppercase letters, even though they are lowercase. There is a capital ÿ, but not in ISO-LATIN-1.

Table 12-7
java.lang.Character Variables

Variables	Signature	Description
MAX_RADIX	public final static int MAX_RADIX	The maximum radix* available for conversion to and from strings.
MIN_RADIX	public final static int MIN_RADIX	The minimum radix* available for conversion to and from strings.

*A positive integer, where the weight of the digit place is multiplied to obtain the weight of the digit place with the next higher weight.

Note

Table 12-8
java.lang.Integer Constructors

Signature	Description
`Integer(int value)`	Constructs an `Integer` object initialized to the specified `int` value.
`public Integer(String s)`	Constructs an `Integer` object initialized to the value specified by the `String` parameter.

Table 12-9
java.lang.Integer Methods

Method	Signature	Description
`doubleValue`	`public double doubleValue()`	Returns the value of this integer as a `double`.
`equals`	`public boolean equals(Object obj)`	Compares this object to the specified object.
`floatValue`	`public float floatValue()`	Returns the value of this integer as a `float`.
`getInteger`	`public static Integer getInteger (String nm)`	Gets an `Integer` property.
`getInteger`	`public static Integer getInteger (String nm, int val)`	Gets an `Integer` property. If the property does not exist, it returns a `val`. Deals with hexadecimal and octal numbers.
`getInteger`	`getInteger (String nm, Integer val)`	Gets an `Integer` property. If the property does not exist, it returns a `val`. Deals with hexadecimal and octal numbers.
`hashCode`	`public int hashCode()`	Returns a hash code for this integer.
`intValue`	`public int intValue()`	Returns the value of this integer as an `int`.
`longValue`	`public long longValue()`	Returns the value of this integer as a `long`.

Method	Signature	Description
parseInt	public static int parseInt (String s)	Assuming the specified string represents an integer, returns that integer's value. Throws NumberFormatException if the string does not contain a parsable integer.
parseInt	public static parseInt(String s, int radix)	Assuming the specified string represents an integer, returns that integer's value. Throws NumberFormatException if the string does not contain a parsable integer.
toString	public String toString()	Returns a String object representing this integer's value.
toString	public static String toString (int i)	Returns a new String object representing the specified integer.
toString	public static toString(int i, int radix)	Returns a new String object representing the specified integer in the specified radix.
valueOf	public static Integer valueOf (String s, int radix)	Assuming the specified string represents an integer, returns a new Integer object initialized to that value. Throws NumberFormatException if the string cannot be parsed as an integer.
valueOf	public static Integer valueOf (String s)	Assuming the specified string represents an integer, returns a new Integer object initialized to that value. Throws NumberFormatException if the string cannot be parsed as an integer.

Table 12-10
java.lang.Integer Variables

Variable	Signature	Description
MAX_VALUE	MAX_VALUE	The maximum value an integer can have.
MIN_VALUE	MIN_VALUE	The minimum value an integer can have.

Table 12-11
java.lang.Float Constructor

Signature	Description
`public Float(double value)`	Constructs a `Float` wrapper for the specified `double` value.
`public Float(float value)`	Constructs a `Float` wrapper for the specified `float` value.
`public Float(String s)`	Constructs a `Float` object initialized to the value specified by the string parameter. Throws `NumberFormatException` if the string does not contain a parsable number.

Table 12-12
java.lang.Float Methods

Method	Signature	Description
`doubleValue`	`public double doubleValue()`	Returns the `double` value of this float.
`equals`	`public boolean object. equals (Object obj)`	Compares this object against some other object.
`floatToIntBits`	`public static int floatToIntBits (float value)`	Returns the bit representation of a single `float` value.
`floatValue`	`public float floatValue()`	Returns the `float` value of this `Float` object.
`hashCode`	`public int hashCode()`	Returns a hash code for this `float`.
`intBitsToFloat`	`public static intBitsToFloat (int bits)`	Returns the single `float` value corresponding to a given bit representation.
`intValue`	`public int intValue()`	Returns the integer value of this `float` (by casting to an `int`).

Method	Signature	Description
isInfinite	public boolean isInfinite()	Returns true if this float value is infinite in magnitude.
isInfinite	public static boolean isInfinite(float v)	Returns true if the specified number is infinite in magnitude.
isNaN	public boolean isNaN()	Returns true if this float value is Not-a-Number (NaN).
isNaN	public static boolean isNaN(float v)	Returns true if the specified number is the special Not-a-Number (NaN) value.
longValue	public long longValue()	Returns the long value of this float (by casting to a long).
toString	public String toString()	Returns a string representation of this Float object.
toString	public static String toString (float f)	Returns a string representation for the specified float value.
valueOf	public static Float valueOf (String s)	Returns the floating-point value represented by the specified string. Throws Number FormatException if the string does not contain a parsable float.

Table 12-13
java.lang.Float Variables

Variable	Signature	Description
MAX_VALUE	public final static float MAX_VALUE	The maximum value a float can have.
MIN_VALUE	public final static float MIN_VALUE	The minimum value a float can have.
NaN	public final static float NaN	Not-a-Number (NaN).
NEGATIVE_INFINITY	public final static float NEGATIVE_ INFINITY	Negative infinity.
POSITIVE_INFINITY	public final static float POSITIVE_ INFINITY	Positive infinity.

Table 12-14
java.lang.Double Constructor

Signature	Description
`public Double(double value)`	Constructs a `Double` wrapper for the specified `double` value.
`public Double(String s)`	Constructs a `Double` object initialized to the value specified by the string parameter.
	Throws `NumberFormat Exception` if the string does not contain a parsable number.

Table 12-15
java.lang.Double Methods

Method	Signature	Description
`doubleToLongBits`	`public static long doubleToLongBits (double value)`	Returns the bit representation of a `double` `float` value.
`doubleValue`	`public double doubleValue()`	Returns the `double` value of this `double`.
`equals`	`equals(Object obj)`	Compares this object against the specified object.
`floatValue`	`public float floatValue()`	Returns the `float` value of this `double`.
`hashCode`	`public int hashCode()`	Returns a hash code for this `double`.
`intValue`	`public int intValue()`	Returns the integer value of this `double` (by casting to an `int`).
`isInfinite`	`public boolean isInfinite()`	Returns `true` if this `double` value is infinite in magnitude.
`isInfinite`	`public boolean isInfinite(double v)`	Returns `true` if the specified number is infinite in magnitude.
`isNaN`	`public boolean isNaN()`	Returns `true` if this `double` value is the special Not-a-Number (`NaN`) value.

Method	Signature	Description
isNaN	public static boolean isNaN (double v)	Returns true if the specified number is the special Not-a-Number (NaN) value.
longBitsToDouble	public static double longBitsToDouble (long bits)	Returns the double float corresponding to a given bit representation.
longValue	public long longValue()	Returns the long value of this double (by casting to a long).
toString	public String toString()	Returns a string representation of this Double object.
toString	public static String toString (double d)	Returns a string representation for the specified double value.
valueOf	valueOf(String)	Returns a new double value initialized to the value represented by the specified string.

Table 12-16
java.lang.Double Variables

Variable	Signature	Description
MAX_VALUE	public final static double MAX_VALUE	The maximum value a double can have.
MIN_VALUE	public final static double MIN_VALUE	The minimum value a double can have.
NaN	public final static double MIN_VALUE	Not-a-Number (NaN).
NEGATIVE_INFINITY	public final static double NEGATIVE_ INFINITY	Negative infinity.
POSITIVE_INFINITY	public final static double POSITIVE_ INFINITY	Positive infinity.

Table 12-17
java.lang.Long Constructors

Signature	Description
`public Long(long value)`	Constructs a Long object initialized to the specified value.
`public long Long(String s)`	Constructs a Long object initialized to the value specified by the string parameter. Throws `NumberFormatException` if the string does not contain a parsable long.

Table 12-18
java.lang.Long Methods

Method	Signature	Description
doubleValue	`public double doubleValue()`	Returns the value of this long as a double.
equals	`public boolean equals(Object obj)`	Compares this object against the specified object.
floatValue	`public float floatValue()`	Returns the value of this long as a float.
getLong	`public static long getLong (String nm)`	Gets a long property. Returns zero (0) if it does not exist.
getLong	`public static long getLong (String nm, long val)`	Gets a long property. Returns val if it does not exist. Deals with hexadecimal and octal numbers.
hashCode	`public int hashCode()`	Computes a hash code for this long.
intValue	`public int intValue()`	Returns the value of this long as an int.
longValue	`public long longValue()`	Returns the value of this long as a long
parseLong	`public static long parseLong (String s)`	Assuming the specified string represents a long, return that long's value. Throws `NumberFormatException` if the string cannot be parsed as a long.

Method	Signature	Description
parseLong	public static long parseLong (String s, int radix)	Assuming the specified string represents a long, returns that long's value. Throws NumberFormatException if the string cannot be parsed as a long.
toString	public String toString()	Returns a String object representing this long's value.
toString	public static String toString (long i)	Returns a new String object representing the specified integer.
toString	public static String toString (long i,	Returns a new String object representing the specified long in the specified radix.
valueOf	public static Long valueOf (String s)	Assuming the specified string represents a long, returns a new Long object initialized to that value. Throws NumberFormat Exception if the string does not contain a parsable long.
valueOf	public static Long valueOf (String s, int radix)	Assuming the specified string represents a long, returns a new Long object initialized to that value. Throws NumberFormat Exception if the string cannot be parsed as a parsable long.

Table 12-19
java.lang.Long Variables

Variable	Signature	Description
MAX_VALUE	public final static long MAX_VALUE	The maximum value a long can have.
MIN_VALUE	public final static long MIN_VALUE	The minimum value a long can have.

As you can see, each of these primitive data types is part of the java.lang package. Since this package is automatically available to our programs, we don't need to bother importing it. You might also be interested to know that each one, with the exception of Boolean, descends from an abstract class called java.lang. Number (Boolean is a direct subclass of Object).

Aside from providing the wrapper functionality we've just discovered, these classes also allow us to extract values of different types from the wrapped value. For example, we could have retrieved the value from our Integer object in the form of a long, a float, or a double, in addition to the int we actually received:

```
long theLong = new Integer(trimmedString).longValue();
double theDouble = new Integer(trimmedString).doubleValue();
float theFloat = new Integer(trimmedString).floatValue();
```

String literals

String literals are characters surrounded by double quotation marks (" "). We've been using them all along, most obviously when we create a String object:

```
String myString = "You're looking at a string literal";
```

In fact, we use string literals in method calls all the time:

```
drawString("Hello World", 100, 100);
getImage(getCodeBase(), "images/world.gif");
getAudioClip(getCodeBase(), "audio/hello.au");
setTitle("Widget Window");
new Menu("Edit");
new Button("Click Me");
```

Anywhere a String object is used, we can substitute a string literal. This is because the compiler actually instantiates a String object from our literal. String literals can be any number of characters surrounded by double quotation marks, even no characters at all:

```
""
```

The example shows an empty string literal. It's just as valid a string as any others we've seen, even though it happens to be empty.

Concatenation and the + operator

Java supports the use of a *concatenation operator* that joins two or more strings together to form one string:

```
String myString1 = "Hickory";
String myString2 = "Dickory";
String myString3 = "Dock";
String allInOne = myString1 + myString2 + myString3;
```

We can also concatenate string literals:

```
String allInOne = "Hickory" + "Dickory" + "Dock";
```

The result is one string containing the contents of all three. In this case, we assign the result to a string variable. If we were to take a peek at the contents of allInOne, it would look like this:

```
HickoryDickoryDock
```

Since we didn't specify any spaces when concatenating these strings, they were placed one right after the other. If we wanted spaces, we could have provided them in the string literals, or when performing the concatenating operation:

```
String allInOne = "Hickory " + "Dickory " + "Dock";
```

Or:

```
String allInOne = "Hickory" + " " + "Dickory" + " " + "Dock";
```

When either of these two approaches is used, the result is a single string with spaces between each set of characters being joined:

```
Hickory Dickory Dock
```

As you now know, we can join both String objects and string literals. In both cases, you are free to break them up across several lines:

```
String brokenString = "The string literal you are now " +
    "reading has been broken up " +
    "intentionally. In total, it spans " +
    "four lines";
```

All four of the preceding string literals are joined as one using the string concatenation operator you'll read about in a moment. Using this operator, we can also break up strings inside constructors and method calls:

```
String brokenString = new String ("The string literal you are "
+
    " now reading has been broken up " +
    "intentionally. In total, it spans " +
    "four lines");
drawString("Hello " +
    "World", 100, 100);
```

And, although we've used string literals already, this applies to String objects as well. In fact, we can concatenate them both in any fashion we require:

```
String allInOne = myStringObject + "Here's a literal" +
    anotherStringObject + andAnotherStringObject +
    "Plus one more string literal";
```

Character constants

When specifying string literals, we can include escape sequences that represent characters such tabs, carriage returns, and form feeds:

```
String myString = "There is a tab between here and \t there.";
String myString = "There's a carriage return between here and \r
    there.";
String myString = "There's a new line between here and \n
    there.";
String myString = "The word \"mouse\" is in double quotes";
```

In addition, we can include Unicode escape sequences:

```
String myString = "There is a trademark symbol between here and
    \u2122 there.";
```

Tip

When adding Unicode escapes, however, keep in mind that just because you can do it doesn't mean users will see what you intend. If the system on which your program is executed doesn't support the full suite of Unicode characters, or the font used during output doesn't support that character, they'll never see what you specify. As a result, be frugal with Unicode and test your programs on as wide a range of systems as possible, if you do utilize it in this way.

StringBuffer (java.lang.StringBuffer)

By now, you're probably pretty comfortable with immutable `String` objects. When you want to change them, you can't. Instead, you create a completely new `String` object that receives the result of whatever you want to do to the original. In this way, the original string is preserved, pristine, untouched.

`StringBuffer` objects, however, allow you to create mutable strings (see Table 12-20). That is, we can rip 'em up without worrying about the compiler having a stroke. However, we don't have the plethora of methods to choose from with `StringBuffer` as we do with `String`, as you can see from Table 12-21.

Since `StringBuffer` objects are typically less efficient than `String` objects, they are usually used only in the ultimate creation of `String` objects. In fact, the Java compiler uses `StringBuffer` objects to implement the string concatenation operator we saw earlier:

```
"The string literal you are now " +
    "reading has been broken up " +
    "intentionally. In total, it spans " +
    "four lines";
```

The string concatenation compiles like this:

```
new StringBuffer().append("The string literal you are now ").
append("reading has been broken up").append("intentionally. In
total, it spans ").append("four lines").toString();
```

Although this might be a bit messy at first glance, begin reading carefully from left to right. You'll see that a new `StringBuffer` object is created, to which each string literal is appended using the `append()` method. Finally, the results contained in the `StringBuffer` object are converted into a `String` object by way of the `toString()` method.

Table 12-20
java.lang.StringBuffer Constructors

Constructor	Signature	Description
`StringBuffer`	`public StringBuffer()`	Constructs an empty string buffer.
`StringBuffer (int)`	`public StringBuffer (int length)`	Constructs an empty string buffer with the specified initial length.
`StringBuffer (String)`	`StringBuffer (String str)`	Constructs a string buffer with the specified initial value.

Table 12-21
java.lang.StringBuffer Methods

Method	Signature	Description
`append`	`public StringBuffer append(boolean b)`	Appends a `boolean` to the end of this buffer.
`Append`	`public synchronized StringBuffer append (char c)`	Appends a `char` to the end of this buffer.
`Append`	`public StringBuffer append(double d)`	Appends a `double` to the end of this buffer.
`Append`	`public StringBuffer append(float f)`	Appends a `float` to the end of this buffer.
`Append`	`public StringBuffer append(int i)`	Appends an `int` to the end of this buffer.
`Append`	`public StringBuffer append(long l)`	Appends a `long` to the end of this buffer.
`Append`	`public synchronized StringBuffer append (Object obj)`	Appends an object to the end of this buffer.

(continued)

Table 12-21 *(continued)*

Method	Signature	Description
Append	`public synchronized StringBuffer append (String str)`	Appends a string to the end of this buffer.
Append	`public synchronized StringBuffer append (char str[])`	Appends an array of character strings to the end of this buffer.
Append	`public synchronized StringBuffer append (char str[], int offset, int len)`	Appends part of an array of characters to the end of this buffer.
Capacity	`public int capacity()`	Returns the current capacity of the string buffer.
CharAt	`public synchronized char charAt(int index)`	Returns the character at the specified index.
Ensure Capacity	`public synchronized void ensureCapacity (int minimumCapacity)`	Ensures that the capacity of the buffer is at least equal to the specified minimum.
GetChars	`public synchronized void getChars(int srcBegin, int srcEnd, char dst[], int dstBegin)`	Copies the characters of the specified substring (determined by `srcBegin` and `srcEnd`) into the character array, starting at the array's `dstBegin` location.
Insert	`public StringBuffer insert(int offset, boolean b)`	Inserts a `boolean` into the string buffer.
Insert	`public synchronized StringBuffer insert (int offset, char c)`	Inserts a `char` into the string buffer.
Insert	`public synchronized StringBuffer insert (int offset, char[] str[])`	Inserts an array of characters into the string buffer.
Insert	`public StringBuffer insert(int offset, double d)`	Inserts a `double` into the string buffer.

Method	Signature	Description
Insert	`public StringBuffer insert(int offset, float f)`	Inserts a `float` into the string buffer.
Insert	`public StringBuffer insert(int offset, int i)`	Inserts an `int` into the string buffer.
Insert	`public StringBuffer insert(int offset, long l)`	Inserts a `long` into the string buffer.
Insert	`public synchronized StringBuffer insert (int offset, Object obj)`	Inserts an object into the string buffer.
Insert	`public synchronized StringBuffer insert (int offset, String str)`	Inserts a string into the string buffer.
Length	`public int length()`	Returns the length (character count) of the buffer.
SetCharAt	`public synchronized void setCharAt(int index, char ch)`	Changes the character at the specified index to be `ch`.
SetLength	`public synchronized void setLength(int newLength)`	Sets the length of the string.
ToString()	`public String toString()`	Converts to a string representing the data in the buffer.

As you can see, the bulk of `StringBuffer` methods are variations of `append()` and `insert()`. This is because `StringBuffer` is specifically built to grow as input is appended to it, and also to allow changes to the data, as seen with the `insert()` method.

Creating StringBuffer objects

You'll also notice three `StringBuffer` constructors, each of which creates a "buffer of strings." One constructor creates an empty string buffer, another creates an empty string buffer set to the initial length you specify, and the last creates a string buffer from the `String` object you provide:

```
StringBuffer myBuffer = new StringBuffer(); // empty
StringBuffer myBuff2 = new StringBuffer(50); /* empty, 50
    characters in length */
StringBuffer myBuff3 = new StringBuffer("Hello"); // using String
```

Although it may be tempting to create empty buffers of unspecified length, it's much more efficient to specify the length if possible. When you don't, or if you use a `String` object when creating a string buffer, memory must be allocated whenever something is appended to the buffer. When the size is known, as in the last two examples, the buffer allocates the memory in advance and doesn't need to allocate more, unless it grows beyond that size.

Thus, the following is discouraged:

```
StringBuffer myBuffer = new StringBuffer();
myBuffer.append("There once was a mouse from Nantucket");
```

In favor of this:

```
StringBuffer myBuffer =
    new StringBuffer("There once was a mouse from Nantucket");
```

Or this:

```
StringBuffer myBuffer = new StringBuffer(37); /* exactly what we
                                              need */
myBuffer.append("There once was a mouse from Nantucket");
```

Or even this:

```
StringBuffer myBuffer = new StringBuffer(50); /* a little more
                                              than we need */
myBuffer.append("There once was a mouse from Nantucket");
```

Modifying StringBuffer objects

Once we've created a `StringBuffer` object, whether of a specified length or empty, we can add data to it or change data already in it. To append data, we use one of the many `append()` methods. To change data, we use one of the various `insert()` methods.

Although you've already seen `append()` in action, there are a number of other data types you can append. In the preceding examples, we've appended strings. However, as you can see from Tables 12-2 through 12-19, we could add primitive data types (`boolean`, `char`, `int`, `long`, `float`, `double`) and other objects.

For example, assume in each of the following examples that the `StringBuffer` variable, `myBuff`, contains `"Hickory"` already.

We can append a `boolean` such as this:

```
myBuff.append(false); // results in "Hickoryfalse".
```

An `int` such as this:

```
myBuff.append(13565); // results in "Hickory13565"
```

What if we append a `long`?

```
myBuff.append(35356253565L); // results in "Hickory35356253565"
```

Perhaps a floating-point value?

```
myBuff.append(4564.62); // results in "Hickory4564.62"
```

Let's not forget the `double`:

```
myBuff.append(4.76645D); // results in "Hickory4.76645"
```

However, we might want to append an object, as opposed to these primitive data types:

```
Button myButton = new Button("Click Me");
myBuff.append(myButton); // append the button object
```

Before the appending takes place, the `Button` object is converted into a string. As a result, `myBuffer` would be:

```
"Hickoryjava.awt.Button[0,0,0x0,invalid,label=Click Me]"
```

Note

Since all objects know how to output themselves in string format, you can append them to or insert them into `StringBuffer` objects. You can also determine whether `String` objects are equal to other objects:

```
myString.equals(anyObject);
```

In addition to appending data to the end of a `StringBuffer`, you can insert data into a specific location. All you need to do is provide an offset into the buffer:

```
myBuff.insert(3,true); // results in "Hictruekory"
myBuff.insert(6,13565); // results in "Hickor13565y"
myBuff.insert(2,4564.62); // results in "Hi4564.62ckory"
```

However, `insert()` won't grow the buffer if you mistakenly provide an offset outside its bounds. For example, suppose we tried to add the last floating-point value with an offset of 8:

```
myBuff.insert(8,4564.62); // exceeds bounds!
```

Since the buffer isn't large enough to accommodate this insertion, the following exception is spit out at runtime:

```
java.lang.StringIndexOutOfBoundsException
        at java.lang.StringBuffer.insert(StringBuffer.java:333)
        at java.lang.StringBuffer.insert(StringBuffer.java:432)
        at StringTest.main(StringTest.java:97)
```

Although `StringBuffer` objects are most commonly used to create larger strings by appending and inserting, you can directly change the contents of any of the elements in buffer using `setCharAt()`.

Although this example, and our previous treatment of `String` objects, might lead to us believe that both the `String` and `StringBuffer` classes are really arrays, the truth is they are both descendants of `Object`. However, they do indeed seem to be arrays at times, especially when accessing or setting contents at a specific offset.

Yet, they are not arrays. `String` and `StringBuffer` are defined in their own distinct classes, and merely support the type of behavior we're accustomed to seeing with arrays. To understand the difference, let's take a look at arrays.

Arrays

In Java, arrays are truly first-class objects. Not only are they impossible to subclass, you won't even find a class definition for them. Instead, Java knows internally about arrays and how to treat them, just as it knows how to deal with primitive data types without offering a class for each (keep in mind that type wrappers for primitives are different from the primitives themselves; there are type wrapper classes, but no primitive classes).

Unlike `String` and `StringBuffer` objects, which can contain only character data, arrays are capable of holding any type of data we need, even other arrays. The only restriction is that each element in the array must be of the same type. You can't, for example, have an `int` in one element of an array, and a `char` in another. All of the elements in a given array must be of the same type.

As you might recall from Chapter 7, to declare an array we need specify only two things:

 ✦ A variable through which we'll access the array

 ✦ The data type of the elements the array will contain

To signal that this isn't a standard variable, we use a pair of braces ([ ]) to identify the object as an array:

```
int myIntegers[]; // declare an array of integers
char myCharacters[]; // declare an array of characters
float myFloats[]; // declare an array of floating point numbers
String myStrings[]; // declare an array of String objects
StringBuffer myStringBuffs[]; // declare array of StringBuffers
```

When you see the braces attached to a variable, you know immediately that it's actually an array of elements instead of a single element:

```
However, there is another way to declare arrays in Java:
int[] myIntegers; // declare an array of integers
char[] myCharacters; // declare an array of characters
float[] myFloats; // declare an array of floating point numbers
String[] myStrings; // declare an array of String objects
StringBuffer[] myStringBuffs;// declare array of StringBuffers
```

Here, we've declared exactly the same arrays, but used a slightly different notation to do so. Some programmers prefer this approach because they don't have to look at the variable name to see that they're dealing with an array. Instead, they can quickly scan the data type listing to see which elements are arrays and which are standard variables.

Although it may not seem like a big deal, consider the following:

```
int myInt, aInt, myInt, theInt, anotherInt, anyInt; // ints
float myFloat, aFloat, myFloater, theFloats[], floating,
    anyFloat; // floats
char myChar, aChar, myChar, theChar, character, anyChar; // chars
```

Granted, it takes only a moment to scan the list of variables to see that theFloats[] is an array. However, it's much more apparent in the following variable declaration:

```
int myInt, aInt, myInt, theInt, anotherInt, anyInt; // ints
float myFloat, aFloat, myFloater , floating, anyFloat; // floats
float[] theFloats; // floats
char myChar, aChar, myChar, theChar, character, anyChar; // chars
```

By scanning the data types, you can see immediately which are arrays, thanks to the pair of brackets immediately following the data type. Using this notation saves the time of scanning through each variable in search of brackets. Although insignificant when you're wide awake and dealing with a relatively small group of variables, it's quite significant at the end of a long day, with half a page of variables to wade through.

Instantiating arrays

Once you've declared an array, chances are you'll want to do something with it. In order to use it, you must first instantiate an Array object. Without an Array object, you have only an empty array variable.

In order to create an Array object, we typically use the new operator:

```
int myIntegers[]; // array declaration
  . . .
myIntegers = new int[25]; // instantiation
```

While this example illustrates the fact that array declaration and instantiation are two distinct steps, as with standard Java objects, they're often more closely associated in practice. Usually, the array declaration and instantiation happen at the same time:

```
int myIntegers[] = new int[25]; // declare and instantiate
```

When creating an Array object, we supply what is known as a *dimension* for that array. In the preceding examples, the dimension is 25. As a result, the array has 25 elements in it. If we supplied a dimension of 2483, the array would have 2483 elements.

Auto-initialization

So, when an `Array` object is instantiated as shown, it contains the number of elements you specify as the dimension. The array is effectively empty at this time, and each element is initialized to a default value.

With integral arrays, each element is initialized to zero (0). Each element in an array of `booleans`, on the other hand, is automatically initialized to `false`. In all other cases, such as with `String` objects and other compound data types (that is, any non-primitive), each element is initialized to `null`.

In-line initialization

In cases where you already know the elements you'd like to have in an array, you can save the time and effort of placing each into its position by providing them at the time of declaration:

```
int[] myIntegers2 = {123, 354, 235, 6255, 1, 35, 42563};
```

In this case, you don't have to explicitly dimension the array. We can have a good deal of work done for us by setting the array equal to the elements surrounded with curly braces, each separated by a comma.

In the last example, the compiler sees that we want to add seven elements, and therefore does the rest of the work automatically. The array is created and each element is added. We don't have to dimension the array and we don't have to fill it ourselves (more on filling arrays in a moment).

This applies to arrays of any type; as long as you know what elements you want, you can add them in-line at the time of declaration:

```
String[] myStrings = {"Hickory", "Dickory", "Dock"};
float[] myFloats = {253.35, 2.0, 644.13, 35612., 6.7};
char[] myCharacters = {'H', 'e', 'l', 'l', 'o'};
```

Of course, as with any array, the data in each element in a given array must be of the same type. For example, you can't add a `String` object to an array of floating-point numbers. If you try, the compiler will rap your knuckles.

Anonymous arrays

With JDK 1.0, you can only use the curly-braces syntax when you're defining an array. With JDK 1.1, however, the usage of the array initializer syntax has been extended. One of the most important benefits of this is that you can now create an anonymous array, and using the curly brace syntax, initialize the array when it is allocated. For example:

```
int[] a;
a = new int[] {1, 2, 3, 4, 5};
```

This creates an anonymous array a, which is created and initialized when new is called to allocate the array. When memory for a is allocated, enough space is allocated to hold the initialization items found in the curly braces—in this example, enough space for five integer array elements. While this new feature won't revolutionize your Java applications, it does make the process of creating dynamic arrays just a little bit easier.

Setting and retrieving array elements

In certain circumstances, we can fill an array in-line at the time it's declared. Where possible, this is helpful, since we don't have to do it ourselves. Unfortunately, it's not usually possible to do this. Often, we're not certain which elements are going to be in an array at the time it's created. In these cases, we must fill the array later.

To fill an array, or a portion of an array, we access a particular element in it with an index value and set it equal to whatever we want to be stored in it. Of course, the data we're trying to stuff into an array element must be the same type as the array is declared to hold:

```
int[] myIntegers = new int[25]; // create array with 25 elements
myIntegers[1] = 2353; // set element at index 1 to 2353
```

In this code, we're stuffing the int value of 2353 into index 1 of the array. Because this is an array of integers, the assignment is legal. To attempt a string assignment, on the other hand, would prevent your code from compiling.

Note

The term *index*, or *subscript*, is used to refer to a particular position in an array. If we supply the value of 5 as an index or subscript for an array, we're said to be accessing the array at index 5, yet retrieving the value stored at position 6.

This is because indexing begins at zero (0)! When you supply an index/subscript value of 5, you'll actually receive the sixth item in the array.

As you may recall from Chapter 7, array indexing begins at zero (0). C and C++ programmers are already familiar with this approach, although it can sometimes result in problems. If you're not careful, you might attempt to access an element beyond the legal range of index values.

In our example, the legal range of index values is 0 to 24. The first item in the array is set or retrieved using:

```
myIntegers[0]
```

while the last item is available with:

```
myIntegers[24]
```

If you attempt to access an element with an index of 25, you're in for trouble:

```
myIntegers[25]; // ILLEGAL - INDEX OUT OF RANGE!
```

Although the compiler will let this pass, the runtime system throws an `ArrayIndexOutOfBoundsException` exception. This is one of the particularly nice things about both arrays and strings in Java; the system catches oversights such as this and throws an exception. Rather than slipping through to the customer's hands, this bug is caught the first time the line of code is executed.

Tip

At times, you may want all items in an array to be set to the same value. In this case, it's much easier to use a loop than to set each manually:

```
int highScores[] = new int[25]; /* declare array of 25
                                    integers */
for (short i=0; i < 25; i++) {
  highScores[i] = 9999; /* initialize each array element
                            to 9999 */
}
```

This approach can be used even in cases where each element is different. As long as you can get the data you need for each element while inside the body of the loop, you can fill an array with this technique. For example, you might fill an array with characters typed by the user:

```
char keyStrokes[] = new char[500]; // declare array of 500
characters
char keyChar; // variable to hold keyboard input
for (short i=0; i < 500; i++) { // load up to 500 characters
  keyChar = System.in.read(); /* Get character from standard
                                  input stream */
  if (keyChar == -1) /* has user attempted to break out of
                        the process? */
    break; // break out of loop
  else
    keyStrokes[i] = keyChar; // stuff keyboard input into array
}
```

To retrieve an element in an array, you do the opposite of setting an element. Rather than stuffing an item into an element, you set a variable equal to that element:

```
myVariable = myIntegers[4]; // get 5th item in array
myString = myStrings[10]; // get 11th item in array
```

When retrieving elements in an array, it's often helpful to subtract 1 from the value representing the item you want. For example, if you want to retrieve the tenth item in an array, you can use either of the following approaches:

```
theNum = myIntegers[9]; // explicit
theNum = myIntegers[10-1]; // using "off by one" technique
```

Although the latter is less efficient, since the calculation must take place before the element is accessed, it's often easier to understand if you haven't dealt much with arrays. (For more details on this technique, see Chapter 7.)

Tip

To determine the number of elements in an array, use the length variable:

```
int len = myArray.length; // get the length and assign to
                             a variable */
```

Keep in mind that the *length* used here is a variable, not a method as seen with `String` and `StringBuffer` objects.

Array of Arrays

Although Java doesn't support multidimensional arrays, it offers essentially the same capability by allowing us to create an array of arrays:

```
int grid[][] = new int[10][10];
grid[0][0] = 1230;
grid[0][5] = 4;
grid[9][5] = 355;
System.out.println("Grid value at 0,0 is " + grid[0][0]);
System.out.println("Grid value at 0,5 is " + grid[0][5]);
System.out.println("Grid value at 9,5 is " + grid[9][5]);
```

In the preceding snippet of code, we created two arrays of integer values, both accessible through the grid variable. Although we created each array with ten elements, they didn't have to be of the same dimension:

```
int grid[][] = new int[15][10];
grid[14][9] = 2265;
System.out.println("Grid value at 14,9 is " + grid[14][9]);
```

We can create as many arrays as necessary, each accessible through the single variable:

```
int grid2[][][] = new int[15][10][5];
grid2[0][0][0] = 4630;
grid2[4][5][1] = 7345;
grid2[9][5][0] = 35;
grid2[14][9][0] = 6465;
grid2[14][9][4] = 16547;
System.out.println("Grid2 value at 0,0,0 is " +
    grid2[0][0][0]);
System.out.println("Grid2 value at 0,5,1 is " +
    grid2[4][5][1]);
System.out.println("Grid2 value at 9,5,0 is " +
    grid2[9][5][0]);
System.out.println("Grid2 value at 14,9,4 is " +
    grid2[14][9][4]);
```

And we can even use an array of arrays in another array of arrays, to give us as many dimensions as we'd like.

Exceptions

Thanks to arrays being objects, we're alerted any time something illegal is done with them. Rather than allowing such activity to slip through the cracks, Java let's us know right away when our program is doing something it shouldn't.

The two exceptions you're most likely to encounter when dealing with arrays are ArrayIndexOutOfBoundsException and ArrayStoreException.

Whenever an attempt is made to access an item with an index that is out of the legal range, whether that index is too low (negative) or too high, an ArrayIndexOutOfBoundsException is thrown. If, however, you attempt to store an element in an array that's of a type different than was declared for the array, you'll receive an ArrayStoreException.

Utility Classes (java.util Package)

In addition to the String, StringBuffer, and Array data storage and retrieval mechanisms provided by Java, we have a number of additional classes to choose from, thanks to the java.util package. These are shown in Table 12-22.

Table 12-22
Package java.util Interfaces, Classes, and Exceptions

Interfaces	
Enumeration	Observer

Classes	
BitSet	Calendar
Dictionary	Hashtable
ListResourceBundle	Observable
Properties	PropertyResourceBundle
Random	ResourceBundle
Stack	StringTokenizer
Date	Vector
TimeZone	

Exceptions	
EmptyStackException	NoSuchElementException

Note

In this package, you'll find classes for dealing with hash tables, stacks, vectors, and bit sets. While each of these has a specific function, you'll find they each provide a mechanism for storing and retrieving data.

Hashtable

A *hash table* maps keys to values, values which can be any Java object. Whatever object you use as a key, however, must implement the hashCode() and equals() methods.

In the following snippet of code, we create a hash table to track the amount of stock a store might have. We use the names of the items in stock as keys, and give each a value:

```
Hashtable stockLevels = new Hashtable();
stockLevels.put("Radios", new Integer(4343));
stockLevels.put("Bikes", new Integer(523));
stockLevels.put("Chairs", new Integer(3563));
stockLevels.put("Bananas", new Integer(646));
```

```
    // now retrieve the number of Bananas in stock:
Integer n = (Integer)stockLevels.get("Bananas");
if (n != null) {
    System.out.println("Yes, we have " + n + " bananas.");
}
```

The `Hashtable` class (see Tables 12-23 and 12-24) is a descendant of the abstract `Dictionary` class, which allows for the association of items using keys and values. A particularly powerful feature of hash tables is their ability to store more than one type of data. While `String` and `StringBuffer` objects can contain only characters, and arrays can have only elements of the same type, we can mix and match the data types stored in a hash table.

Even though we stored values of `Integer` objects in the preceding example, each could have been a different data type. If, for example, we wanted to store a string as the `Banana` value, we might have written the following:

```
stockLevels.put("Bananas", new String("lots o' naners"));
```

However, when retrieving this element, we'd have to get it as a `String` object. If we attempted to extract it as an `Integer` object, as we did earlier, a `ClassCastException` would be thrown (since a string can't be cast into an `int`). As a result, we would use something like the following to output the value of the `Bananas` key:

```
System.out.println(stockLevels.get("Bananas"));
```

Table 12-23
java.util.Hashtable Constructors

Signature	Description
`public Hashtable()`	Constructs a new, empty hash table.
`public Hashtable (int initialCapacity)`	Constructs a new, empty hash table with the specified initial capacity.
`Hashtable(int initialCapacity float loadFactor)`	Constructs a new, empty hash table with the specified initial capacity and the specified load factor. Throws `IllegalArgumentException` if the initial capacity or load factor is less than or equal to zero.

Table 12-24
java.util.Hashtable Methods

Method	Signature	Description
clear	clear()	Clears the hash table so that it has no more elements in it.
Clone	clone()	Creates a clone of the hash table.
Contains	public synchronized boolean contains (Object value)	Returns true if the specified object is an element of the hash table.
ContainsKey	public synchronized boolean containsKey (Object key)	Returns true if the collection contains an element for the key.
Elements	public synchronized Enumeration elements()	Returns an enumeration of the elements.
Get	public synchronized Object get(Object key)	Gets the object associated with the specified key in the hash table.
IsEmpty	public boolean isEmpty()	Returns true if the hash table contains no elements.
Keys	public synchronized Enumeration keys()	Returns an enumeration of the hash table's keys.
Put	public synchronized Object put(Object key, Object value)	Puts the specified element into the hash table, using the specified key.
Rehash	protected void rehash()	Rehashes the content of the table into a bigger table.
Remove	public synchronized Object remove(Object key)	Removes the element corresponding to the key.
Size	public int size()	Returns the number of elements contained in the hash table.
ToString	public synchronized String toString()	Converts to a rather lengthy string.

Vectors

Although arrays are nice and convenient to use, sometimes you need the ability to grow them. However, as you know, arrays must be dimensioned to a certain size before they are used. And once set, you can't change that dimension.

Vectors, on the other hand (see Tables 12-25, 12-26, and 12-27), are growable arrays. Rather than being constrained to a specific number of elements, you can expand them as needed. In the following example, we'll create an empty Vector and add two elements to it:

```
Vector myVector = new Vector(); // create a vector
String myString = "Obla-de, obla-da"; // any 'ol String
Button myButton = new Button("life goes on"); // a Button

/* Add objects to our vector: */
myVector.addElement(myString);
myVector.addElement(myButton);

/* Now retrieve the button (notice the cast): */
anotherButton = (Button) myVector.lastElement();
```

Notice how we managed to cram a Button object and a String object into the Vector object? Anything you put into a vector is first converted into a plain vanilla object, meaning you can put anything you'd like into it. But in order to get something out, you have to know what to cast it to! This is seen in the last line of the preceding code, where we retrieve the last item as a Button; because it was a Button object going in, we need to cast it to a Button object coming out.

Note

You can take a great deal of work off the runtime system by creating your vectors with an initial storage capacity; if you don't, each new element that is added forces the Vector to expand—a significant effort on Java's part and one to avoid if at all possible.

Table 12-25
java.util.Vector Constructors

Signature	Description
public Vector()	Constructs an empty vector.
public Vector(int initialCapacity)	Constructs an empty vector with the specified storage capacity.
public Vector(int initialCapacity, int capacity Increment)	Constructs an empty vector with the specified storage capacity and the specified capacity increment.

Table 12-26
java.util.Vector Methods

Method	Signature	Description
addElement	public final synchronized void addElement(Object obj)	Adds the specified object as the last element of the vector.
Capacity	public final int capacity()	Returns the current capacity of the vector.
Clone	public synchronized Object clone()	Clones this vector. Elements are not cloned.
Contains	public final boolean contains (Object elem)	Returns true if the specified object is a value of the collection.
CopyInto	public final synchronized void copyInto(Object AnArray[])	Copies the elements of this vector into the specified array.
ElementAt	public final synchronized Object elementAt(int index)	Returns the element at the specified index.
Elements	public final synchronized Enumeration elements()	Returns an enumeration of the elements.
Ensure Capacity	public final synchronized void ensureCapacity(int minCapacity)	Ensures that the vector has at least the specified capacity.
First Element	public final synchronized Object firstElement()	Returns the first element of the sequence.
IndexOf	public final int indexOf(Object elem)	Searches for the specified object, starting from the first position, and returns an index to it.
IndexOf	public final synchronized int indexOf(Object elem, int index)	Searches for the specified object, starting at the specified position, and returns an index to it.

Method	*Signature*	*Description*
Insert ElementAt	public final synchronized void insertElementAt (Object obj, int index)	Inserts the specified object as an element at the specified index.
IsEmpty	public final boolean isEmpty()	Returns true if the collection contains no values.
LastElement	public final synchronized Object lastElement()	Returns the last element of the sequence.
LastIndexOf	public final int lastIndexOf(Object elem)	Searches backwards for the specified object, starting from the last position, and returns an index to it.
LastIndexOf	public final synchronized int lastIndexOf(Object elem, int index)	Searches backwards for the specified object, starting from the specified position, and returns an index to it.
RemoveAll Elements	public final synchronized void removeAllElements()	Removes all elements of the vector.
Remove Element	public final synchronized boolean removeElement(Object)	Removes the element from the vector.
Remove ElementAt	public final synchronized void removeElementAt(int index)	Deletes the element at the specified index.
Set ElementAt	public final synchronized void setElementAt(Object obj, int index)	Sets the element at the specified index to be the specified object.
SetSize	public final synchronized void setSize(int newSize)	Sets the size of the vector.
Size	public final int size()	Returns the number of elements in the vector.
ToString	public final synchronized String toString()	Converts the vector to a string.
TrimToSize	public final synchronized void trimToSize()	Trims the vector's capacity to the appropriate size.

Table 12-27
java.util.Vector Variables

Variable	Signature	Description
capacityIncrement	protected int capacityIncrement	The size of the increment.
ElementCount	protected int elementCount	The number of elements in the buffer.
ElementData	protected Object elementData	The buffer where elements are stored.

Stacks

A common data storage mechanism used by many programmers is the stack (see Table 12-28), which allows you to push() objects onto it and pop() objects off when they need to be retrieved. Stacks follow a Last-In-First-Out (LIFO) ordering, meaning the last object you push() onto the stack will be the first one you receive when you call pop().

Table 12-28
java.util.Stack Constructor, Methods, and Variables

Constructor	Signature	Description
Stack	public Stack()	Creates a new Stack object.
Methods	**Signature**	**Description**
empty	public boolean empty()	Returns true if the stack is empty.
Peek	public Object peek()	Peeks at the top of the stack.
Pop	public Object pop()	Pops an item off the stack.
Push	public Object push (Object item)	Pushes an item onto the stack.
Search	public int search (Object item)	Sees if an object is on the stack.

The Stack class is a subclass of Vector, meaning you don't have to worry about how many items a Stack object will contain. You can simply create one and begin using it without worrying about how many items you'll eventually push() onto it.

StringTokenizer

At times, you'll need to retrieve the chunks of information stored in a `String` object. Such chunks, or *tokens*, must each be separated by a delimiter, such as a comma or a space. When you have such elements in a string, you can retrieve them using the `StringTokenizer` class.

For example, suppose you've stored a series of words into a string, as we've done in earlier examples:

```
String myString = "There once was a mouse from Nantucket";
```

Since each of the words is separated by a space, you could retrieve them as follows:

```
StringTokenizer tokens = new StringTokenizer(myString);
while (tokens.hasMoreTokens()) {
   System.out.println(tokens.nextToken());
}
```

When executed, the preceding code would output each word in the string on its own line:

```
There
once
was
a
mouse
from
Nantucket
```

Since the default delimiter for `StringTokenizer` is a space, we didn't have to do anything special to retrieve these words. If we were dealing with a delimiter other than a space, we could specify that delimiter when creating the `StringTokenizer` object, or when reading tokens.

Resource bundles

New to the `jav.util` package in JDK 1.1 is the concept of *resource bundles*. You use the `ResourceBundle` classes to define sets of localized resources that can be loaded dynamically based on the location the program is running. For example, text, images, and menus can be stored and retrieved from a resource bundle stream. While a `ResourceBundle` class is provided, it is not directly used. The `ListResourceBundle` and `PropertyResourceBundle` classes are used to access resource bundle streams. The `ListResourceBundle` class (see Table 12-29) is used to access resources as a list, while the `PropertyResourceBundle` class (see Table 12-30) is used to access resources through a property key. I discuss streams and storing objects on streams in more detail in Chapter 13.

Table 12-29
java.util.ListResourceBundle

Constructor	Signature	Description
ListResource Bundle	ListResourceBundle()	Creates a list resource bundle

Method	Signature	Description
getKeys	Enumeration getKeys()	Enumerates the keys available in the resource bundle
HandleGet Object	Object handleGet Object(String key)	Gets the object with the specified key from the resource bundle

Table 12-30
java.util.PropertyResourceBundle

Constructor	Signature	Description
Property Resource Bundle	PropertyResource Bundle(InputStream stream)	Creates a property resource bundle that reads from the specified stream

Method	Signature	Description
getKeys	Enumeration getKeys()	Enumerates the keys available in the resource bundle
HandleGet Object	Object handleGet Object(String key)	Gets the object with the specified key from the resource bundle

Miscellany

In addition to the various data storage and retrieval classes we've seen, the java.util package includes others that may be of use.

For example, you might consider the BitSet class if ever you require a growable storage mechanism for bits. If you're dealing with streams and need to include the functionality of a hash table, you'll want to take a look at the Properties() class, which allows you to create a hash table that can be saved and loaded from a stream.

Finally, this package features a few classes that don't have anything to do with saving and retrieving your own data: Calendar, Date, Random, and TimeZone. The Calendar and TimeZone classes are new to JDK 1.1. The constructors, methods, and variables for these classes are listed in Tables 12-31 through 12-38.

Table 12-31
java.util.Date Constructors

Signature	Description
publicDate()	Creates today's date/time.
public Date(long date)	Creates a date.
public Date(int year, int month, int date)	Creates a date.
public Date(int year, int month, int date, int hours, int minutes)	Creates a date.
public Date(int year, int month, int date, int hours, int minutes, int sec)	Creates a date.
public Date(String s)	Creates a date from a string, according to the syntax accepted by parse().

Table 12-32
java.util.Date Methods

Method	Signature	Description
UTC	public static longUTC (int year, int month, int date, int hrs, int min, int sec)	Calculates a UTC[1] value from YMDHMS[2].
After	public boolean after (Date when)	Checks whether this date comes after the specified date.
Before	public boolean before (Date when)	Checks whether this date comes before the specified date.
Equals	public boolean equals (Object obj)	Compares this object against the specified object.
GetDate	public int getDate()	Returns the day of the month.
GetDay	public int getDay()	Returns the day of the week.
GetHours	public int getHours()	Returns the hour.
GetMinutes	public int getMinutes()	Returns the minute.
GetMonth	public int getMonth()	Returns the month.
GetSeconds	public int getSeconds()	Returns the second.
GetTime	public long getTime()	Returns the time in milliseconds since the epoch.

(continued)

Table 12-32 *(continued)*

Method	Signature	Description
GetTimezone Offset	`public int getTime zoneOffset()`	Returns the time zone offset in minutes for the current locale that is appropriate for this time.
GetYear	`public int getYear()`	Returns the year after 1900.
HashCode	`public int hashCode()`	Computes a hash code.
Parse	`public static long parse(String s)`	Given a string representing a time, parses it and returns the time value.
SetDate	`public void setDate(int date)`	Sets the date.
SetHours	`public void setHours (int hours)`	Sets the hours.
SetMinutes	`public void setMinutes (int minutes)`	Sets the minutes.
SetMonth	`public void setMonth (int month)`	Sets the month.
SetSeconds	`public void setSeconds (int Seconds)`	Sets the seconds.
SetTime	`public void setTime (long time)`	Sets the time.
SetYear	`public void setYear(int year)`	Sets the year.
ToGMTString	`public String toGMT String()`	Converts a date to a string, using the Internet GMT[3] conventions.
ToLocale String	`public String toLocale String()`	Converts a date to a string, using the locale conventions.
ToString	`public String toString()`	Converts a date to a string, using the UNIX time conventions.

[1]UTC: Coordinated Universal Time

[2]YMDHMS: Year, Month, Day, Hour, Minute, Second

[3]GMT: Greenwich Mean Time

The Date class allows us to retrieve the current date and supports a number of methods for dealing with dates and times:

```
Date today = new Date();
System.out.println("The date today is: " + today);
```

Note

In the current release of Java, Date doesn't properly represent days prior to January 1, 1970. This is expected to be resolved in a future release of the language.

The Calendar class (see Tables 12-33, 12-34, and 12-35) is used to perform date and time arithmetic. It also includes methods used to convert dates and times between binary representations used by the Date class and standard units—such as minutes, hours, days, weeks, months, and years—that are more understandable to people.

Table 12-33
java.util.Calendar Constructors

Signature	Description
Calendar()	Creates an empty Calendar object using the default time zone and locale.
Calendar(TimeZone zone, Locale aLocale)	Creates a calendar for a specific time zone and locale.

Table 12-34
java.util.Calendar Constants

Constant	Signature	Description
ERA	final int ERA	Era field constant.
YEAR	final int YEAR	Year field constant.
MONTH	final int MONTH	Month field constant.
WEEK_OF_YEAR	final int WEEK_OF_YEAR	The week number of the date in the year field constant.
WEEK_OF_MONTH	final int WEEK_OF_MONTH	The week number of the date in the month field constant.
DATE	final int DATE	The date field constant.
DAY_OF_MONTH	final int DAY_OF_MONTH	The day of the month field constant.
DAY_OF_YEAR	final int DAY_OF_YEAR	The day of the year field constant.
DAY_OF_WEEK	final int DAY_OF_WEEK	The day of the week field constant.

(continued)

	Table 12-34 *(continued)*	
Constant	**Signature**	**Description**
DAY_OF_WEEK _IN_MONTH	final int DAY_OF_WEEK _IN_MONTH	The day of the week in the month field constant.
ZONE_OFFSET	final int ZONE_OFFSET	The time zone offset field constant.
DST_OFFSET	final int DST_OFFSET	The daylight savings time field constant.
AM_PM	final int AM_PM	The AM/PM field constant.
HOUR	final int HOUR	The hour field constant.
HOUR_OF_DAY	final int HOUR_OF_DAY	The hour of the day field constant.
MINUTE	final int MINUTE	The minute field constant.
SECOND	final int SECOND	The second field constant.
MILLISECOND	final int MILLSECOND	The millisecond field constant.
JANUARY	final int JANUARY	January month field constant.
FEBURARY	final int FEBRUARY	February month field constant.
MARCH	final int MARCH	March month field constant.
APRIL	final int APRIL	April month field constant.
MAY	final int MAY	May month field constant.
JUNE	final int JUNE	June month field constant.
JULY	final int JULY	July month field constant.
AUGUST	final int AUGUST	August month field constant.
SEPTEMBER	final int SEPTEMBER	September month field constant.
OCTOBER	final int OCTOBER	October month field constant.
NOVEMBER	final int NOVEMBER	November month field constant.
DECEMBER	final int DECEMBER	December month field constant.
SUNDAY	final int SUNDAY	Sunday day field constant.
MONDAY	final int MONDAY	Monday day field constant.
TUESDAY	final int TUESDAY	Tuesday day field constant.
WEDNESDAY	final int WEDNESDAY	Wednesday day field constant.
THURSDAY	final int THURSDAY	Thursday day field constant.
FRIDAY	final int FRIDAY	Friday day field constant.
SATURDAY	final int SATURDAY	Saturday day field constant.
AM	final int AM	AM field constant.
PM	final int PM	PM field constant.

Table 12-35
java.util.Calendar Methods

Methods	Signature	Description
getAvailable Locales	Local[] getAvailable Locales()	Gets the set of locales for which Calendars are installed.
GetInstance	Calendar getInstance ()	Gets a Calendar using the default time zone and locale.
GetInstance	Calendar getInstance (TimeZone zone)	Gets a Calendar using the time zone specified.
GetInstance	Calendar getInstance (Locale aLocale)	Gets a Calendar using the locale specified.
GetInstance	Calendar getInstance (TimeZone zone, Locale aLocale)	Gets a Calendar using the time zone and locale specified.
Add	void add(int field, int amount)	Adds the specified amount to the given time field.
After	boolean after(Object when)	Compares the time fields and returns true if the Calendar field is after the current Calendar field.
Before	boolean before (Object when)	Compares the time fields and returns true if the Calendar field is before the current Calendar field.
Clear	void clear()	Clears the values of all time and date fields.
Clear	void clear(int field)	Clears the value of the specified field.
Clone	Object clone()	Clones the Calendar object.
Equals	boolean equals (Object when)	Compares the time fields and returns true if the Calendar field is equal to the current Calendar field.
Get	int get(int field)	Gets the value of the specified field.

(continued)

Table 12-35 *(continued)*

Methods	Signature	Description
GetFirstDay OfWeek	`int getFirstDayOf Week()`	Gets the first day of the week for the specified local (for example, returns Sunday in the U.S. and Monday in France).
GetGreatest Minimum	`int getGreatest Minimum(int field)`	Gets the highest minimum value for the field specified.
GetLeastMaximum	`int getLeastMaximum (int field)`	Gets the lowest maximum value for the specified field.
GetMaximum	`int getMaximum(int field)`	Gets the maximum value of the field specified.
GetMinimalDays InFirstWeek	`int getMinimalDatsIn FirstWeek()`	Gets what the minimal days required in the first week of the year are.
GetMinimum	`int getMinimum(int field)`	Gets the minimum value of the field specified.
GetTime	`Date getTime()`	Gets the `Calendar`'s current time as a `Date` object.
GetTimeZone	`TimeZone getTime Zone()`	Gets the current time zone.
IsLenient	`boolean isLenient()`	Determines whether date/time interpretations are lenient.
IsSet	`boolean isSet(int field)`	Determines whether a field has been set.
Roll	`void roll(int field, boolean up)`	Adds or subtracts one unit to the specified field.
Set	`void set(int field, int value)`	Sets the field with the specified value.
Set	`void set(int year, int month, int date)`	Sets the specified year, month, and date fields.
Set	`void set(int year, int month, int date, int hour, int minute)`	Sets the specified year, month, date, hour, and minute fields.
Set	`void set(int year, int month, int date, int hour, int minute, int second)`	Sets the specified year, month, date, hour, minute, and second fields.

Methods	Signature	Description
SetFirstDayOf Week	void setFirstDayOf Week(int value)	Sets what the first day of the week is.
SetLenient	void setLenient (boolean lenient)	Specifies whether date/time interpretations will be lenient.
SetMinimalDays InFirstWeek	void setMinimalDays InFirstWeek(int value)	Sets the minimal days required in the first week of the year.
SetTime	void setTime(Date date)	Sets the Calendar's date and time with the value of the Date field.
SetTimeZone	void setTimeZone (TimeZone value)	Sets the current time zone.

The following example demonstrates how to create a Calendar object, specify a date and time, and perform some simple arithmetic:

```
Calendar Date1 = new Calendar();
Date1.set(1998,1,1,11,5);  /* Set the date to 1/1/1998
                              and time to 11:05 */
System.out.println("The current time is " +
                Date1.get(Date1.HOUR) + ":" +
                Date1.get(Date1.MINUTE));
Date1.add(3, Date1.HOUR);  // Add 3 hours to the time
System.out.println("The new time is " +
                Date1.get(Date1.HOUR) + ":" +
                Date1.get(Date1.MINUTE));
```

The TimeZone class (see Table 12-36) is used to represent geographical time zones.

Table 12-36
java.util.TimeZone Constructor and Methods

Methods	Signature	Description
TimeZone	TimeZone()	Creates a time zone object
getAvailableIDs IDs(int rawOffset)	String[] getAvailable	Gets the available time zone IDs for the given time zone offset
getAvailableIDs	String[] getAvailable IDs()	Gets all of the IDs supported

(continued)

Table 12-36 *(continued)*		
Methods	**Signature**	**Description**
getDefault	TimeZone getDefault()	Gets the current default time zone
getTimeZone	TimeZone getTimeZone (String ID)	Gets the TimeZone for the specified ID
setDefault	void setDefault(Time Zone zone)	Sets the default time zone
clone	Object clone()	Clones the current TimeZone object
getID	String getID()	Gets the ID of the current time zone
getOffset	int getOffset(int era, int year, int month, int day, int dayOfWeek, int milliseconds)	Gets the time zone offset, for current date, modified in case of daylight savings time
getRawOffset	int getRawOffset()	Gets the unmodified offset, *not* modified for daylight savings time
inDayLightTime	boolean inDaylight Time(Date date)	Determines if the date is using daylight savings time
setID	void setID(String ID)	Sets the current time zone ID
setRawOffset	void setRawOffset(int offsetMillis)	Sets the base time zone offset to GMT (Greenwich Mean Time)
useDaylightTime	boolean useDaylight Time()	Determines if the time zone uses daylight savings time

You can use the TimeZone class to determine the current time zone by calling the getDefault method, or to enumerate the available time zones. The Calendar class is the primary user of TimeZone objects.

The TimeZone class can be used to retrieve the current time zone and its attributes. The following example demonstrates how to retrieve the current time zone and determine if it uses daylight savings time:

```
TimeZone tz = new TimeZone();
if(tz.useDaylightTime()) {
  System.out.println("Daylight savings time is used");
} else {
  System.out.println("Daylight savings time is NOT" +
                     "used");
};
```

The Random class (see Tables 12-37 and 12-38) is used to create randomly generated numbers:

```
Random myRand = new Random();
int aRandomInt = myRand.nextInt();
long aRandomLong = myRand.nextLong();
float aRandomFloat = myRand.nextFloat();
double aRandomDouble = myRand.nextDouble();
double aRandomGaussian = myRand.nextGaussian();
```

In this example, we've created a Random object and extracted a variety of random values from it.

Table 12-37
java.util.Random Constructors

Signature	Description
public Random()	Creates a new random-number generator.
public Random(long seed)	Creates a new random-number generator using a single long seed.

Table 12-38
java.util.Random Methods

Methods	Signature	Description
nextDouble()	public doublenext Double()	Generates a pseudorandom, uniformly distributed double value between 0.0 and 1.0.
nextFloat()	public floatnext Float()	Generates a pseudorandom, uniformly distributed float value between 0.0 and 1.0.
nextGaussian()	public synchronized doublenext Gaussian()	Generates a pseudorandom, Gaussian-distributed double value with mean 0.0 and standard deviation 1.0.
nextInt()	public intnextInt()	Generates a pseudorandom, uniformly distributed int value.
nextLong()	public int next Long()	Generates a pseudorandom, uniformly distributed long value.
setSeed(long)	public int setSeed (long)	Sets the seed of the random number generator, using a single long seed.

The `nextGaussian()` method returns a Gaussian distributed `double` that is centered at 0.0 with a standard deviation of 1.0, which is also known as a *bell curve*.

The `java.lang.Math` class also defines a random-number generator that returns a double-precision floating-point value between 0.0 and 1.0:

```
double random();
```

In both cases, the values returned aren't considered truly random, since they tend to repeat themselves after a period of time.

With `java.util.Random`, you can change the generator's seed value as needed. By supplying the same seed, the sequence of generated numbers will be the same.

Summary

Now you understand how to add strings, arrays, and other fundamental programming structures to your Java applications. You're well on your way now to creating your own complex Java programs. Key concepts to remember from this chapter include these:

✦ Java strings aren't like the ones we're accustomed to in C and C++. In those languages, strings are simply an array of null-terminated characters. Java strings, however, are actually objects defined by the `String` class. As a result, they feature a number of methods that are used to access their contents. With Java, strings are first-class objects that support a well-defined set of methods.

✦ Java provides two distinct string classes: `String` and `StringBuffer`. The `String` class is used to create `String` objects which are immutable; their contents can't be altered once characters have been stored in them. `StringBuffer`, on the other hand, is specifically for strings that are mutable, or able to be changed even after characters have been stored in them.

✦ In Java, arrays are truly first-class objects. Not only are they impossible to subclass, you won't even find a class definition for them. Instead, Java knows internally about arrays and how to treat them, just as it knows how to deal with primitive data types without offering a class for each (keep in mind that type wrappers for primitives are different from the primitives themselves; there are type wrapper classes, but no primitive classes). Unlike `String` and `StringBuffer` objects, which can contain only character data, arrays are capable of holding any type of data we need, even other arrays. The only restriction is that each element in the array must be of the same type.

✦ The Hashtable class is a descendant of the abstract Dictionary class, which allows for the association of items using keys and values. A particularly powerful feature of hash tables is their ability to store more than one type of data. While String and StringBuffer objects can contain only characters, and arrays can have only elements of the same type, we can mix and match the data types stored in a hash table.

✦ Vectors are growable arrays. Rather than being constrained to a specific number of elements, you can expand them as needed.

✦ A common data storage mechanism used by many programmers is the stack, which allows you to push() objects onto it and pop() objects off when they need to be retrieved. Stacks follow a Last-In-First-Out (LIFO) ordering, meaning the last object you push() onto the stack will be the first one you receive when you call pop().

✦ At times, you'll need to retrieve the chunks of information stored in a String object. Such chunks, or *tokens*, must each be separated by a delimiter, such as a comma or a space. When you have such elements in a string, you can retrieve them using the StringTokenizer class.

✦ New to the jav.util package in JDK 1.1 is the concept of *resource bundles*. You use the ResourceBundle classes to define sets of localized resources that can be loaded dynamically based on the location the program is running. For example, text, images, and menus can be stored and retrieved from a resource bundle stream.

✦   ✦   ✦

Input/Output: Java Streams

Streams can be thought of as flowing buffers of data, providing our programs with a relatively easy mechanism for reading and writing data. You may already know of at least one way of sending data using streams; you've been using the system input stream all along. As you'll see throughout this chapter, `System.out` is only a very small way in which to use streams. In this chapter, you'll also learn how to create and use input and output (I/O) streams. You will also learn about `FilterInputStream` and `FilterOutputStream`, which provide an enhanced I/O mechanism for streams, and object serialization which allows any Java object to be written to an output stream, and then recreated later by reading the object back from the input stream.

About Streams

Streams are a conduit for sending and receiving information in Java programs. When sending a stream of data, it is said that we are *writing a stream*. When receiving a stream of data, we are said to be *reading a stream*.

Whenever a stream is being written or read, it blocks all other threads. This is not a major issue, however, if you use threads. As you'll see in Chapter 14, you can place input and output streams in a separate process to allow other program execution to continue while these processes are reading and writing. If an error occurs when reading or writing a stream, an `IOException` is thrown. As a result, you must surround your stream statements with a `try-catch` clause, in order to handle any of the potential exceptions (for details on exceptions, see Chapter 10).

Java has not only a standard system stream, but also a more complex and complete set of streams dedicated entirely to input/output: the `java.io` package. Before we get into this package, however, a look at standard system input/output will set the stage.

Standard System Streams (java.lang.System)

The `java.lang.System` class defines a standard input and a standard output stream. So far, we've been using output streams to output data to the display monitor in our applications.

There are three types of standard streams:

✦ The standard output stream (accessed through the `System.out` class variable); this is typically the display, or the monitor, of the machine on which your program is running, and is normally used to communicate textual information with the user.

✦ The standard input stream (accessed through the `System.in` class variable); this usually comes from the keyboard, and is often used for reading character data.

✦ The standard error stream (accessible through the `System.err` class variable).

Let's take a look at each.

Note

`System`'s class constructor is private, preventing the class from being instantiated. It also cannot be subclassed, since it has been declared as final (with all methods and variables specified as `static`). Since `System` methods and variables are static, you simply refer to them directly, as we've been doing throughout the book. For details on the `private`, final, and `static` modifiers, see Chapter 11.

Standard output (System.out)

So far, this book has used the standard output in all of its Java applications. You haven't, however, seen how to use standard output in applets, since we paint and draw information upon the applet canvas rather than sending output directly to `System.out`. Standard out, as you may recall, is often the display or the monitor, and is used in applications to output information directly to the screen. With applets, we already have a surface to draw on; with applications, however, we typically output information to the command line. This is done by sending either a `print()` or `println()` method to the `System.in` variable:

```
System.out.print ("Hello World"); // print
System.out.println("Hello World"); // print line
```

The `print()` method sends information into a buffer. This buffer is not flushed until an end-of-line character is sent via `print()`, or the `println()` method is called. As a result, all of the information is printed on one line until an end-of-line character is encountered or the `println()` method is invoked. By contrast, `println()` takes the information provided and prints it on a line followed by a carriage-return/line feed.

Standard input (System.in)

The second standard stream is `System.in`, which hasn't been used yet in this book; however, there's no time like the present.

Let's assume we wanted to read information from the keyboard. In an applet, we already know how to do this: We would test for `keyDown` events in either an `action()` or `handleEvent()` method. In an application, we don't usually have the luxury of dealing with those types of events (unless a GUI is created for the application; see Part IV for details) . What we do have, however, is access to the standard input stream by sending the `read()` method to the `System.in` variable:

```
int keyInput;
int i = 0;
while ((keyInput = System.in.read()) != -1) {
 i++;
 System.out.println(i + " = " + keyInput);
 } catch (IOException e) { ... }
```

As you can see, this fragment of code simply reads in character input from the keyboard, incrementing the counter each time through, outputting the character that is read to standard out, along with the character count, and then repeating the process. This loop can only be broken when the read returns –1. With `read()`, a –1 is returned only when an end-of-line character is received.

End-of-line characters are generated in different ways for UNIX and DOS/Windows-based machines. With UNIX, Ctrl+D (^D) must be used (holding down the Control and D keys at the same time). In DOS/Windows environments, Ctrl+Z (^Z) is used.

Standard error (System.err)

Although you'll use `System.out` most of the time, you may wish to use the standard error output stream, rather than sending output to `System.out`, as we've done above. This is because the system output may be redirected from the current device (typically the monitor) to another device (such as a file).

The difficulty in using this type of stream occurs when you have an error message to display to users; it may never get to them. After all, how would they be able to look at an error message if it's being output to a file instead of the screen? To ensure output goes to the display screen, you could simply send your data to the system-error variable like this:

```
System.err.println("Warning!");
```

Now the data doesn't run the risk of being "hidden" when output; it is always sent to the display.

java.io Streams

Although the system streams are very handy, they really aren't robust enough to be of much use when dealing with substantial I/O. For the full power of streams, we need to turn to the `java.io` package. As you can see from the diagram in Figure 13-1, this package supports two streams—one input and one output stream—from which all other streams are subclassed.

`java.io.InputStream` and `java.io.OutputStream` are actually abstract classes. They are implemented in the subclasses shown in Figure 13-1. However, they are the parent classes of all other streams, and as such, they have a common element that all streams share. To better understand the types of streams that are supported by the `java.io` package, we'll need to take a closer look at the `InputStream` and `OutputStream` classes.

InputStream

`InputStream` is an abstract class that defines how data is received. Where this data comes from really doesn't matter; what's important is that it is accessible. In fact, the data can come from just about anywhere. It may come from the keyboard, from a file on your local file system, or from across the Web—the program doesn't care. This is the strength of streams: It isn't necessary to know where the data is coming from or where it's going in order to use it.

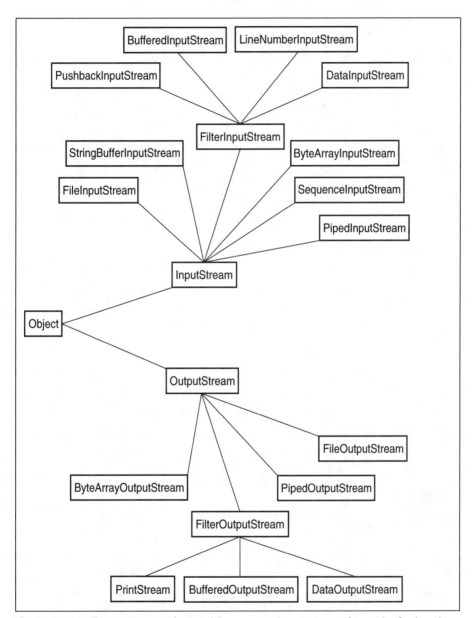

Figure 13-1: All Java streams descend from one of two parent classes in the java.io package: InputStream or OutputStream.

InputStream methods

The InputStream object provides a number of methods which allow you to create, read, and process input streams. Table 13-1 lists a few methods that operate on input streams, and how they might be used.

Table 13-1
Class java.io.InputStream

Method	Signature	Description
read	`public abstract int read() throws IOException`	Reads a byte of data. This method blocks if no input is available. Returns the byte read, or –1 if the end of the stream is reached. Throws `IOException` if an I/O error has occurred.
read	`public int read(byte b[]) throws IOException`	Reads into an array of bytes. This method blocks until some input is available. Returns the actual number of bytes read; is returned when the end of the stream is reached. Throws `IOException` if an I/O error has occurred. Parameter: b – buffer into which the data is read.
read	`public int read(byte b[], int off, int len) throws IOException`	Reads into an array of bytes. This method blocks until some input is available. Parameters: b – buffer into which the data is read off – start offset of the data len – maximum number of bytes read Returns the actual number of bytes read; –1 is returned when the end of the stream is reached. Throws `IOException` if an I/O error has occurred.
available	`public int available() throws IOException`	Returns the number of bytes that can be read without blocking. Returns the number of available bytes.

Method	Signature	Description
skip	`public long skip(long n) throws IOException`	Skips n bytes of input.
		Parameter: n – number of bytes to be skipped
		Returns the actual number of bytes skipped.
		Throws `IOException` if an I/O error has occurred.
mark	`public synchronized void mark(int readlimit)`	Marks the current position in the input stream. A subsequent call to `reset()` repositions the stream at the last marked position so that subsequent reads can re-read the same bytes. The stream promises to allow `readlimit` bytes to be read before the mark position is invalidated.
		Parameter: `readlimit` – maximum limit of bytes allowed to be read before the mark position becomes invalid.
reset	`public synchronized throws IOException void reset()`	Repositions the stream to the last marked position. Throws `IOException` if the stream has not been marked or if the mark has been invalidated (see note below).
markSupported	`public boolean markSupported()`	Returns a `boolean` indicating whether or not this stream type supports mark/reset. Returns `true` if this stream type supports mark/reset; `false` otherwise.
close	`public void close() throws IOException`	Closes the input stream. Must be called to release any resources associated with the stream.
		Throws `IOException` if an I/O error has occurred.

Note

Stream marks are intended to be used in situations where you need to read ahead a little to see what's in the stream. Often, this is most easily done by invoking some general parser. If the stream is of the type handled by the parser, it just chugs along happily. If the stream is not of that type, the parser should toss an exception when it fails—which, if it happens within `readlimit` bytes, allows the outer code to reset the stream and try another parser.

read()

We see three read() methods, each of which takes a different set of parameters; the most basic is the one we've been using with the system input stream. This read() method simply reads one byte from the input stream. The other two methods let you specify either an array of bytes or a portion of an array of bytes:

```
anyStream.read(); // reads one byte
byte byteArray = new byte[2048];
anyStream.read(byteArray[]); // reads into an array of bytes
anyStream.read(byteArray[], 25, 100); // reads into a portion of an
array
```

In the second example, read() tries to fill up the entire array we've passed to it. If it's not successful, meaning there were fewer characters in the stream than there were indexes in the array, -1 is returned.

However, –1 doesn't indicate an error; it simply lets us know that the process didn't run all the way through. If an actual error had occurred, an IOException would have been thrown.

In the third example, we specify the location in the array to begin writing the stream, along with how many positions in the array to actually fill. This is useful when we have an array that we want partially filled with data. We can begin reading data at any index and continue for the remainder of the array, or just a portion of it.

available()

The available() method enables you to find out how many bytes there are in a stream that can be read without blocking. Unfortunately, a number of the stream classes don't support available(). As a result, unless you're certain that the stream you're using supports available(), you can't guarantee this method will return a valid number. Sometimes, zero is returned; at other times, the actual number of bytes in the stream is returned. It's a good idea to avoid using available(), if possible, unless you're certain of exactly what you're doing.

skip()

At times, you'll want to skip over a number of bytes in a stream. This is easy enough; just invoke the skip() method. Supply it with a numeric parameter, telling it how many bytes to skip over, and the stream begins reading again at the position after that skip. This assumes, of course, that you are in the process of reading a stream:

```
anyStream.skip(200); // skip over next 200 bytes
```

Tip

Although you may be tempted to provide an actual `long` value to the `skip()` method, you should keep the range of your values to those of an `int`. This is because Java actually converts your `long` integer into an `int`. In future releases, `skip()` may indeed use a `long`, but for now, assume that it uses an `int`.

mark() and reset()

At times, you may want to revisit a particular position in a stream, and return to read there once again. This is possible by marking that position in the stream using the `mark()` method. When you want to return, simply call `reset()`:

```
anyStream.mark(256); // mark the 256th byte
... do something ...
anyStream.reset(); // return to the 256 byte, and begin from there
```

As you can see in the preceding example, we've marked byte 256 in the stream. When we call `reset()` on that stream, we begin reading at position 256. You should note, however, that if we read more than 256 characters between the time that we've set the `mark()` and called `reset()`, a problem occurs.

This is because the stream must keep track of the number of bytes you supply in `mark()`. If you read more than that number, it can't guarantee you can go back to the same position.

Suppose you read beyond the 256 characters; that is, you read 257 characters after setting the mark. The memory allocated for that mark may not be available, in which case, when you call `reset()`, an exception may be thrown.

Keep this in mind whenever you use `mark()` and `reset()`. Make certain that, once you mark a stream, you don't read more characters than you marked, minus one. For instance, if you set a mark at 1000, read only up to 999 more characters before calling `reset()`.

Not all stream types support `mark()`. In order to test whether it can, call the `markSupported()` method:

```
anyStream.markSupported(); /* returns true if mark() is
                              supported */
```

close()

Streams support the notion of being *closed*; that is, when you're done with them, you can close them down. This is easily done by sending the `close()` method to a stream:

```
anyStream.close (); // close this stream
```

Although the garbage collector in Java is supposed to take care of this for you, it's a good idea to do it yourself. Since you can't guarantee when the garbage collector will come around and close an unused stream for you, you might attempt to reopen it before the garbage collector has finished with it.

By closing the stream yourself, you guarantee it to be closed. The next time you try to open it, you won't run into this potential problem:

```
try {
    ... work with the stream ...
} catch (Exception e) {
    anyStream.close(); // close this stream
}
```

From the snippet just given, you can see that the best place to close a stream may be the finally clause in a try-catch clause. The finally clause is always a good way to close a stream, because it's the last thing called in a try-catch clause. And, as you know, since streams may generate or throw off exceptions, you need the try-catch clause anyway. So, why not simply close a stream in the finally clause when you're done using it? It's a good, safe way to ensure that your stream is closed before going on with the rest of your program.

In most of these examples, I haven't bothered to use the try-catch clause. Since working with streams can result in exceptions being thrown, you'll need to write your stream code using exception handlers.

InputStreamReader

JDK 1.1 has introduced a new set of classes—Reader and Writer—which handle text-based input/output more efficiently than the byte-stream counterparts. They are used in basically the same manner as their byte-stream counterparts. The Reader and Writer classes automatically provide the appropriate Unicode character conversions—making your applications and applets more portable between locales. The InputStreamReader (see Table 13-2) class reads bytes from a data source and converts them to their appropriate Unicode character counterparts.

Table 13-2
java.io.InputStreamReader

Constructor	Example	Description
InputStream Reader	public InputStreamReader (InputStream in)	Creates an input stream reader that uses the default character encoding.
InputStream Reader	public InputStreamReader (InputStream in, String enc)	Creates an input stream that uses the character encoding specified.

Methods	Example	Description
close	void close() throws IOException	Closes the input stream.
getEncoding	String getEncoding()	Returns the name of the encoding currently used.
read	int read() throws IOException	Reads a single character.
read	in read(char[] cbuf, int off, int len) throws IOException	Reads len number characters into buffer cbuf, starting at off.
ready	boolean ready() throws IOException()	Determines whether the input stream is ready to be read.

OutputStream

The OutputStream class is an abstract class that defines the way in which all streams are written.

OutputStream Methods

The OutputStream object provides methods to create, write, and process output streams. Every type of stream uses the methods shown in Table 13-3. Let's take a closer look at each.

	Table 13-3 java.io.OutputStream	
Methods	**Example**	**Description**
write	public abstract void write(int b) throws IOException	Writes a byte. This method blocks until the byte is actually written. Parameter: b – byte Throws IOException if an I/O error has occurred.

(continued)

	Table 13-3 *(continued)*	
Methods	**Example**	**Description**
write	`public void write(byte b[]) throws IOException`	Writes an array of bytes. This method blocks until the bytes are actually written. Parameter: `b`–data to be written. Throws `IOException` if an I/O error has occurred.
write	`public void write(byte b[], int off, int len) throws IOException`	Writes a subarray of bytes. Parameters: `b`–data to be written. `off`–start offset in the data. `len`–number of bytes written. Throws `IOException` if an I/O error has occurred.
flush	`public void flush() throws IOException`	Flushes the stream. This writes any buffered output bytes. Throws `IOException` if an I/O error has occurred.
close	`public void close() throws IOException`	Closes the stream. This method must be called to release any resources associated with the stream. Throws `IOException` if an I/O error has occurred.

write() and flush()

The three `write()` methods write bytes to a stream. Use the one that makes sense for your program (see the descriptions in Table 13-3):

- ✦ `write(int)` writes a single byte
- ✦ `write(byte[])` writes an array of bytes
- ✦ `write(byte[], int, int)` writes a particular section of an array of bytes

You'll note that these are similar, at least in their parameters, to the `read()` methods defined in `InputStream`. This is no surprise, since `OutputStream` can be considered the reverse of `InputStream`: While `InputStream` allows you to read bytes in from a stream, `OutputStream` sends bytes to a stream. Drawing from our previous `InputStream` examples, we might use the following to write a stream:

```
byte myByte = System.in.read(); // read a keyboard character
anOutputStream.write(myByte); // write it to a stream
anOutputStream.write(byteArray); // write array into a stream
anOutputStream.write(byteArray, 25, 100); /* write portion of
                                             an array */
flush()
```

The flush() method is used to write bytes that may be in memory to the stream. This may be necessary, for instance, when a stream is being built up in memory and needs to be flushed out to the disk.

This can also happen when the stream you are creating is being written to the network. In this case, while the stream may be written to memory, the flush() method will actually send it:

```
anOutputStream.flush(); // ensure all writing to stream is
flushed
```

close()

After you've opened an OutputStream, it's a good idea to close it. Just as with its InputStream counterpart, don't rely on the garbage collector to come around and close it for you. It's best to explicitly close any stream you're using when you're done:

```
try {
   ... work with the stream ...
} finally {
 anOutputStream.close(); // close this stream when done
}
```

OutputStreamWriter

The OutputStreamWriter (see Table 13-4) class writes characters to an output stream, translating the characters into bytes as specified by the character encoding scheme. This ensures characters are written in the appropriate format according to the translation scheme specified.

Table 13-4
java.io.OutputStreamWriter

Example	Description
Public OutputStreamWriter (OutputStream out)	Creates an output stream writer that uses the default character encoding.
Public OutputStreamWriter (OutputStream out, String enc)	Creates an output stream that used the character encoding specified.

(continued)

	Table 13-4 *(continued)*	
Methods	**Example**	**Description**
`close`	`void close() throws` `IOException`	Closes the output stream.
`flush`	`void flush() throws` `IOException`	Flushes the stream.
`write`	`void write(int b)` `throws IOException`	Writes a single character.

`write`	`in read(char[] cbuf,`
	`int off, int len)`
	`throws IOException`
		Reads `len` number characters into buffer `cbuf`, starting at `off`.

`write`	`boolean ready() throws` `IOException()`	Determines whether the input stream is ready to be read.

Special-purpose streams

As you know, the `InputStream` and `OutputStream` classes are the parents for all other streams in the `java.io` package. They define the basic behavior each stream supports. However, there are a number of special-purpose streams supported in `java.io` that allow you to do specific stream work. Since you already know how the `InputStream` and `OutputStream` methods are used, it's time to take a look at each of their special-purpose "children." (Take a look back at Figure 13-1, where the class hierarchy is laid out.)

File input

One of the most useful things you'll do with streams is read and write files with them. Two special classes, `FileInputStream` and `FileOutputStream`, make this process a breeze. As you can see in Table 13-5, there are several constructors—three constructors that allow you to create an input stream from a file.

Table 13-5	
java.io.FileInputStream Constructors	
Signature	**Description**

`public FileInputStream`
`(String name) throws`
`FileNotFoundException.`
	Creates input file with the specified `name` (`name` is system-dependent).

	Parameter: `name` – a system-dependent filename.
	Throws `IOException` if the file is not found.

Signature	Description
public FileInputStream (File fileObj) throws FileNotFoundException	Creates input file from the specified file object. Parameter: fileObj – file to be opened for reading. Throws IOException if the file is not found.
public FileInputStream (FileDescriptor fdescObj)	Creates input file from the specified file descriptor object. Parameter: fdescObj – valid file descriptor object.

The first constructor takes a string that is the actual path name of a file. The path name that you provide is system-dependent. You can use UNIX conventions for UNIX-based files, DOS conventions for DOS and Windows-based files, and Macintosh conventions for Macintosh-based files; and, as Java is ported to other platforms, these will each have their own conventions.

However, since Java automatically converts a path to accommodate whatever platform it is running on, you can use the one most convenient for you (I prefer the UNIX convention, since it requires less typing and is easy to read):

```
InputStream myUNIXFile =
newFileInputStream("/java/aewcode/HelloWorld.java");

InputStream myDOSFile =
newFileInputStream("\\java\\aewcode\\HelloWorld.java");
/* DOS slashes are escaped! (see Files and Directories sidebar) */

InputStream myMacFile =
newFileInputStream(":java:aewcode:HelloWorld.java");
```

In addition, you can create a FileInputStream using a FileDescriptor (defined in the java.io.FileDescriptor class). Once you've opened a file, it has what's known as a descriptor associated with it. You can get the FileDescriptor for a file you've just opened using the getFD() method. Once you have a FileDescriptor, you can hang onto it and use it to reference the file at a later time:

```
InputStream myFile =
newFileInputStream("/java/aewcode/HelloWorld.java");
FileDescriptor myDesc = myFile.getFD(); // get descriptor
...
InputStream myFile2 = newFileInputStream(myDesc); // new stream
```

This is particularly useful when you're creating applications that need to access information in a file, and you know which file you'll be using (such as a temporary data file that your program creates). However, there are times when you want to use files that come from a server.

This is common when using applets; in fact, this is the best way to handle files when dealing with applets. Since applets are prevented from accessing files on the local machine, unless specified to do so by the user, it's best to always load applet files from the server. This is done by creating a `FileInputStream` using a `File` object as a parameter. (A `File` object is created using the `File` class defined in `java.io.File`.)

Note   When using `FileInputStream`, the `available()` method works properly. This is because files are of a known size (that is, they're not infinite). As a result, `available()` can calculate how many characters or bytes are in a file. Keep in mind, however, that not all streams support the `available()` method!

File Output

In addition to reading streams that come from files, you may want to write a stream out to a file. Table 13-6 shows the various constructors the `FileOutput Stream` class supports. These are effectively the reverse of `FileInputStream`, creating an output stream instead of an input stream. The various output methods discussed earlier act as you would expect on the resulting stream.

<table>
<tr><th colspan="2">Table 13-6
java.io.FileOutputStream Constructors</th></tr>
<tr><td>*Signature*</td><td>*Description*</td></tr>
<tr><td>`public FileOutputStream (String name) throws IOException`</td><td>Creates an output file with the filename (filename is system-dependent).

Parameter: `name` – system-dependent filename.

Throws `IOException` if the file is not found.</td></tr>
<tr><td>`public FileOutputStream (File file) throws IOException`</td><td>Creates an output file using the `File` object passed to it.

Parameter: `file` – file to be opened for reading.

Throws `IOException` if the file is not found.</td></tr>
<tr><td>`public FileOutputStream (FileDescriptor fdescObj)`</td><td>Creates an output file from the specified `FileDescriptor` object.

Parameter: `fdescObj` – A valid file descriptor object.</td></tr>
</table>

Warning   A bug (or is it a feature?) in Java prevents us from being able to open a `FileOutputStream` to append information to a file. The moment you attempt to do so, the original contents of the file are blown away!

Listing 13-1 illustrates how to open a connection to the Web, using a URL, and retrieve the contents of whatever the URL points to. The object (page, graphic, sound file, and so on) is pulled off the Net and placed in a file inside the directory of your choice. Keep in mind that this is an application, not an applet, and so is invoked from the command line:

```
> java GetURL stuff http://www.pepsi.com
```

In this example, the home page at `http://www.pepsi.com` is retrieved and placed inside the `stuff` directory (located inside the same directory as the `GetURL` application). The program uses an input stream to download the data, and a `FileOutputStream` stream to spit the contents out to a local file.

Listing 13-1: GetURL.java—An Example of FileOutputStream in Action

```java
/*
 * GetURL takes a list of URLs and copies the contents to files
 * with the same name as in the URL (minus the path); these files
 * are put in the directory 'dir'.
 *
 * Useage: java GetURL dir URL [ URL ... ]
 *
 * @author: Ronald Tschaler
 */

import java.net.*;
import java.io.*;

class GetURL {
 static final int buf_size = 4000; // size of buffer for copying

  public static void main (String args[]) {

  int   dx, tail, numb, dir_idx = 0;
  boolean  noisy = false;
  byte     buffer[] = new byte[buf_size];
  String   outfile;
  URL      url;

  InputStream     in;
  FileOutputStream out;

  /*** Get command-line options ***/
```

(continued)

Listing 13-1 *(continued)*

```
while (dir_idx < args.length  && args[dir_idx].startsWith("-
")) {
  if (args[0].equals("-noisy")) {
    noisy = true;
  } else {
    System.err.println("Unknown option: "+args[0]);
    return;
  }
  dir_idx++;
}

/*** Check for correct number of command-line arguments ***/
 if (args.length < dir_idx+2) {
 System.err.println("Usage: java GetURL [-noisy] directory URL
   " + "[URL ...]");

 System.err.println("         copies the files specified by the "
    + "URL's into directory");

 return;
 }

/*** Get the files ***/
for (idx=dir_idx+1; idx<args.length; idx++) {

/*** Open URL ***/
 try {
   url = new URL(args[idx]);
 } catch (MalformedURLException e) {
   System.err.println("Error: malformed URL " + args[idx]);
   System.err.println(e.getMessage());
   continue;
 }

 try {
   in = url.openStream();
 } catch (IOException e) {
   System.err.println("Error: couldn't access " + args[idx]);
   System.err.println(e.getMessage());
   continue;
 }

 /*** Extract filename and open file ***/
 tail  = args[idx].lastIndexOf('\\');
 if (tail == -1) { tail = args[idx].lastIndexOf('/'); }

 outfile = args[idx].substring(tail + 1);
```

```
    try {
      out = new FileOutputStream(args[dir_idx] + '/' + outfile);
    } catch (IOException e) {
      System.err.println("Error: couldn't create " +
        args[dir_idx] +
          '/' + outfile);
      System.err.println(e.getMessage());
      continue;
    }

  /*** Get the file ***/
    if (noisy) {System.out.println("Copying "+outfile+"...");}

    try  {
      while ((numb = in.read(buffer)) != -1)
      out.write(buffer, 0, numb);
    } catch (IOException e) {
        System.err.println("Error: IOException during copy");
        System.err.println(e.getMessage());
        continue;
    }

  /*** Cleanup ***/
    try {in.close();}  catch (IOException e) { }
    try {out.close();} catch (IOException e) { }
    }
    if (noisy){System.out.println("Done");}
  }
}
```

The source code for GetURL is provided on the CD-ROM that comes with this book; save yourself the trouble of typing it in! See Appendix B for information on how to locate files on the CD-ROM.

Files and Directories

The java.io.File class supports objects that reference disk files. With this class, you can create files, rename them, and delete them. Typically, you would use it to create a file object, and then pass it to a FileInputStream or FileOutputStream constructor to create a stream linked to the file. Using the stream to perform I/O, you would use the File class methods to rename the file as needed, or delete it altogether when it is no longer required.

The File class offers three constructors, and a number of methods for dealing with files, as shown in Table 13-7.

Table 13-7
The File Class

Constructor	Description
File(String)	Creates a File object using the directory path passed to it.
File(String, String)	Creates a File object using the directory path and filename passed to it.
File(File, String)	Creates a File object using a directory File object (File) and filename.

Method	Description
canRead()	Returns boolean indicating whether or not a readable file exists.
canWrite()	Returns boolean indicating whether or not a writeable file exists.
delete()	Deletes specified file.
equals(Object)	Compares this object against the specified object.
exists()	Returns boolean indicating whether or not a file exists.
getAbsolutePath()	Gets absolute path of file.
getName()	Gets name of file.
getParent()	Gets name of parent directory.
getPath()	Gets path of file.
hashCode()	Computes hash code for file.
isAbsolute()	Returns boolean indicating whether filename is absolute.
isDirectory()	Returns boolean indicating whether a directory file exists.
isFile()	Returns boolean indicating whether a normal file exists.
lastModified()	Returns the last modification time.
length()	Returns the length of the file.
list()	Lists the files in a directory.
list(FilenameFilter)	Uses the specified filter to list files in a directory.
mkdir()	Creates a directory and returns a boolean indicating the success of the creation.
mkdirs()	Creates all directories in this path.
renameTo(File)	Attempts to rename the file and returns a boolean indicating if successful.
toString()	Returns a String object representing the file's path.

In Java, a directory is simply treated as a File object that has additional information—a list of names that may be examined with the list() method. The following code creates a file, in the java/aewcode directory, and then queries it using several of the File class methods:

```java
import java.io.File;
class FileQuery {
 public static void main(String args[]) {
   String dirname = "/java/aewcode"; // directory must exist!
   String filename = "readme.txt";
   File myFile = new File(dirname, filename);
   System.out.println("File Name:" + myFile.getName());
   System.out.println("Is it a directory? " +
      myFile.isDirectory());
   System.out.println("Is it a real file? " + myFile.isFile());
   System.out.println("File Path:" + myFile.getPath());
   System.out.println("Absolute Path:" +
      myFile.getAbsolutePath());
   System.out.println("Is file Readable? " + myFile.canRead());
   System.out.println("Is file Writeable? " + myFile.canWrite());
   System.out.println("Modified on: " + myFile.lastModified());
   System.out.println("Size (in bytes):" + myFile.length());
   System.out.println();
   System.out.println("--- Directory Listing ---");
   File dir = new File(dirname);
   if (dir.isDirectory() == false) {
     System.out.println(dirname + " is not a directory");
   }
   else {
     System.out.println("Directory of " + dirname);
     String d[] = dir.list();
     for (int i=0; i < d.length; i++) {
      System.out.println(d[i]);
     }
   }
 }
}
```

When it comes to path separators, you can use whatever is most convenient for you. Java converts between the Windows and UNIX path separators automatically, so you don't have to worry about how to enter them. Of course, if you choose to use the Windows (DOS) convention of backslashes, you'll have to enter them as escape codes, since the compiler can't handle them in strings directly. For this reason, the preceding code uses UNIX-style path separators (forward slashes) even though it was written on a Windows machine; using a backslash with escape codes ("\\") isn't quite as clean when it comes to reading the source. However, the following would have been fine:

```java
String dirname = "\\java\\aewcode";
```

Keep in mind that the directory must exist for this code to work properly. However, you can always augment the code to include the `File` class `mkdir()` or `mkdirs()` methods if you want the directory (or directories) to be created on the fly, if they don't already exist. Unfortunately, your program won't be able to remove any directories it creates, because the `File` class only allows you to create directories. Deletion isn't supported.

Note

A runtime `NullPointerException` is thrown if you call `list()` on an object that isn't actually a directory.

At times, you may want to exclude certain files from a directory listing. For instance, suppose you only wanted to view .TXT files. To do this, you'd implement the `FilenameFilter` interface found in `java.io`, which can be completed by creating an object that implements the interface and the abstract `accept()` method it defines. In this method you define what files will be accepted. By passing the resulting object to the `list()` method, only those items that match the criteria are returned.

For example, here's a class that allows you to filter files based on the extension of the filename:

```
public class ExtensionFilter implements FilenameFilter {
  private String extension;
  public ExtensionFilter (String e) {
    this.extension = "." + e; // tack on constructor param
  }
  public boolean accept(File dir, String fileName) {
    return fileName.endsWith(extension); /* accept only these
                                             files */
  }
}
```

To use this filter in our earlier example, we'd first create an object with it, passing in the extension we'd like all files to have in order to be listed. By passing the resulting object to `list()`, only files that are accepted by the filter (that is, files that cause the `accept` method to return a `boolean` value of `true`) are listed:

```
FilenameFilter textFiles = new ExtensionFilter("txt");
// create filter object
String d[ ] = dir.list(textFiles); // use it in list()
```

FileWriter and FileReader

JDK 1.1 has introduced a new classes, `FileReader` (see Table 13-8) and `FileWriter` (see Table 13-9), which process text files more efficiently than the `FileInputStream` and `FileOutputStream` classes. Both the `FileReader` and `FileWriter` classes operate in the same manner as their `FileInputStream` and `FileOutputStream` counterparts.

Table 13-8
java.io.FileReader Constructors

Signature	Description
public FileReader(String name) throws FileNotFoundException	Creates input file with the specified name (name is system-dependent). Parameter: name – a system-dependent filename. Throws IOException if the file is not found.
public FileReader(File fileObj) throws FileNotFoundException	Creates an input file from the specified file object. Parameter: fileObj – file to be opened for reading. Throws IOException if the file is not found.
public FileReader (File Descriptor fdescObj)	Creates input file from the specified file descriptor object. Parameter: fdescObj – valid file descriptor object.

Table 13-9
java.io.FileWriter Constructors

Signature	Description
public FileWriter(String name) throws IOException	Creates an output file with the filename (filename is system-dependent). Parameters: name – system-dependent filename. Throws IOException if the file is not found.
public FileWriter(String name, boolean append) throws IOException	Creates an output file with the filename (filename is system-dependent). Parameters: name – system-dependent filename. append – if true file is open for append. Throws IOException if the file is not found.

(continued)

Table 13-9 *(continued)*

Signature	Description
`public FileWriter(File file) throws IOException`	Creates an output file using the `File` object passed to it. Parameter: `file` – file to be opened for reading. Throws `IOException` if the file is not found.
`public FileWriter(File Descriptor fdescObj)`	Creates an output file from the specified `FileDescriptor` object. Parameter: `fdescObj` – A valid file descriptor object.

Strings

At times, you may wish to create a stream using strings. This is simple enough, using the `StringBufferInputStream` class. You provide a `String` object as the parameter, and as you might expect, you'll be given a stream containing its contents:

```
String myString = "If a chicken and a half lays an egg and a
half in a day in a half, how much time does it take a one-eyed
grasshopper to poke a hole through a donut?"
InputStream riddle = new StringBufferInputStream(myString);
```

Since all `String` objects have a length (they aren't infinite!), `available()` works perfectly on it. However, `reset()` sets the buffer back to the beginning, not to a previously set mark as you might expect. Win some, lose some.

Byte arrays

The `ByteArrayInputStream` class allows you to create input streams using arrays of bytes, as Table 13-10 shows.

Table 13-10
Class java.io.ByteArrayInputStream Constructors

Signature	Description
`public ByteArrayInputStream (byte buf[])`	Creates a byte array input stream from the array of bytes passed to it. Parameter: `buf` – input buffer.
`public ByteArrayInputStream (byte buf[], int offset, int length)`	Creates a byte array input stream from the array of bytes passed to it. Parameters: `buf` – input buffer. `offset` – offset into first byte to read. `length` – total number of bytes to read.

The ByteArrayOutputStream class, seen in Table 13-11, allows you to create output streams based on arrays.

| Table 13-11 | |
| **java.io.ByteArrayOutputStream** | |
Signature	**Description**
public ByteArrayOutputStream()	Creates byte-array output stream.
public ByteArrayOutput Stream(int size)	Creates array output stream of the specified size.
	Parameter: size – initial size.

Because arrays are of a known size, the available() method works as you would expect. However, the reset() method returns the stream to the beginning because marks are not available (see Listing 13-2). When you create a ByteArrayOutput Stream, the buffer continues to grow as data is written to it. Once a byte array buffer has been filled, that data can then be retrieved using the methods toByte Array() and toString(). This is useful when you want to extract the contents of a ByteArrayOutputStream and assign them to an array, or to a string.

The following program, Flip, creates a ByteArrayInputStream stream using an array of characters that together form the words "HELLO WORLD!" in uppercase letters. It then extracts each character in a loop for output; if the convert variable is true, the character is converted to lowercase before being printed. Since the reset() method returns the stream to the very beginning, Flip alternates between uppercase and lowercase output indefinitely (or until terminated by the user), as seen in Figure 13-2.

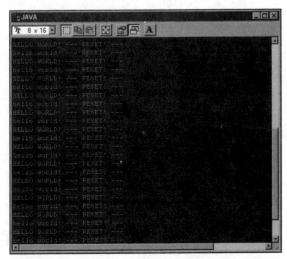

Figure 13-2: Flip takes advantage of ByteArrayInputStream's reset() method to toggle between uppercase and lowercase output.

Listing 13-2: Flip.java—An Example of ByteArrayInputStream in Action

```
/**
 * Flip.java
 *
 * "Flip" creates a ByteArrayInputStream stream, then extracts
 * each character in a loop. If "convert" boolean is true, the
 * character is converted to lowercase before being printed.
 *
 * Running in an infinite while loop, the stream is reset() each
 * time through to permit a fresh read of the data.
 *
 * @author Aaron E. Walsh
 * @version 1.0, 14 Feb 96
 */

import java.io.*;
import java.util.*;

class Flip {

public static void main(String args[]) throws Exception {

  byte myBytes[]={'H','E','L','L','O',' ', 'W','O','R','L','D',
'!'};
  ByteArrayInputStream myStream = new
    ByteArrayInputStream(myBytes);

  /* — PROCESS STREAM — */
  int c;
  boolean convert = false;

  while (true) { /* enter infinite loop! User can only terminate
                    with key combination (ctrl-c for Windows) */
    while ((c=myStream.read())!= -1) {
      if (convert)
        System.out.print(Character.toLowerCase((char)c));
      else
        System.out.print((char)c);
    }
    convert = !convert; // reverse value of convert
    System.out.println(" — RESET! — ");
    myStream.reset();
  }
 }
}
```

CharArrayReader and CharArrayWriter

JDK 1.1

JDK 1.1 has introduced the classes `CharArrayReader` (see Table 13-12) and `CharArrayWriter` (see Table 13-13), which return and use character arrays. Both the `CharArrayReader` and `CharArrayWriter` classes operate in the same manner as their `ByteArrayInputStream` and `ByteArrayOutputStream` counterparts.

Table 13-12
java.io.CharArrayInputStream Constructors

Signature	Description
`public CharArrayInput Stream(char buf[])`	Creates a character array input stream from the array of bytes passed to it.
	Parameter: `buf` – input buffer.
`public CharArrayInput Stream(char buf[], int offset, int length)`	Creates a character array input stream from the array of bytes passed to it.
	Parameters: `buf` – input buffer. `offset` – offset into first byte to read. `length` – total number of bytes to read.

Table 13-13
java.io.CharArrayOutputStream Constructors

Signature	Description
`public CharArrayOutput Stream()`	Creates a character array output stream.
`public CharArrayOutput Stream(int size)`	Creates a character array output stream of the specified size.
	Parameter: `size` – initial size.

Sequences

You are able to join streams using the `SequenceInputStream` class. Much like concatenating strings, `SequenceInputStream` allows you to specify two different streams that will be used to create a third—the result of the first two streams being joined. As you can see from Table 13-14, `SequenceInputStream` also has a constructor that supports enumeration. This is useful when you have more than two streams that you want to join.

Table 13-14 java.io.SequenceInputStream Constructors	
Signature	*Description*
public SequenceInputStream (Enumeration e)	Constructs sequence input stream using the specified list (enumeration).
	Parameter: e - list.
public SequenceInputStream (InputStream s1, InputStream s2)	Constructs sequence input stream set to the two input streams passed to it.
	Parameters: s1 - input stream. s2 - input stream.

Note

Enumeration is an interface defined in the java.util package. It specifies a number of methods that are used to enumerate or count through a number of values. For details on enumeration, see the java.util package section in Sun's application programming interface (API) documentation.

Pipes

The java.io package supports piped streams. PipedInputStream (shown in Table 13-15) and PipedOutputStream (shown in Table 13-16) work in tandem.

These piped streams are used specifically to pass streams back and forth between two different threads. You'll learn about threads in Chapter 14, but for now, it's worth understanding that the two piped streams work together; it's not useful to have one without the other. To use piped input and piped output, we simply create one of each kind of stream and reference them to each other, as follows:

```
PipedInputStream pipeIn = new PipedInputStream();
PipedOutputStream pipeOut = new PipedOutputStream(pipeIn);
```

Whenever a thread reads from the pipeIn, it is actually reading data that another thread is writing to pipeOut. Conversely, whenever a thread is writing to pipeOut, it is actually providing the input for another thread.

Table 13-15
java.io.PipedInputStream Constructors

Signature	Description
`public PipedInputStream (PipedOutputStream src) throws IOException`	Creates input file using the piped output stream passed to it. Parameter: `src` – the stream to connect to.
`public PipedInputStream()`	Creates input file that isn't initially connected to anything, and that must be connected to a piped output stream before being used.

Table 13-16
java.io.PipedOutputStream Constructors

Signature	Description
`public PipedOutputStream (PipedInputStream snk) throws IOException`	Creates output file connected to the piped input stream passed to it. Parameter: `snk` – the `InputStream` to connect to.
`public PipedOutputStream()`	Creates output file that isn't initially connected to anything, and that must be connected before being used.

JDK 1.1 has introduced the classes `PipedReader` (see Table 13-17) and `PipedWriter` (see Table 13-18), which return and use character arrays. Both the `PipedReader` and `PipedWriter` classes operate in the same manner as their `PipedInputStream` and `PipedOutputStream` counterparts.

Table 13-17
java.io.PipedReader Constructors

Signature	*Description*
`public PipedInputStream (PipedWriter src) throws IOException`	Creates input file using the piped output stream passed to it. Parameter: `src` – the stream to connect to.
`public PipedInputStream()`	Creates input file that isn't initially connected to anything, and that must be connected to a piped output stream before being used.

Table 13-18
java.io.PipedWriter Constructors

Signature	*Description*
`public PipedWriter(Piped Reader snk) throws IOException`	Creates output file connected to the piped input stream passed to it. Parameter: `snk` – the `InputStream` to connect to.
`public PipedWriter()`	Creates output file that isn't initially connected to anything, and that must be connected before being used.

Filtered Streams

The `java.io` package contains two abstract classes, `FilterInputStream` and `FilterOutputStream`, that provide an enhanced I/O mechanism for streams. These classes allow streams to be chained together, providing additional functionality to one another as they are processed. There are a number of subclasses from these abstract filter classes, each of which we'll take a look at.

Buffered I/O

Java supports buffered streams, which are kept in memory to allow much faster access than would otherwise be possible. These particular streams, `BufferedInputStream` and `BufferedOutputStream`, are actually the only ones that properly use the `mark()` and `reset()` methods.

However, since `BufferedInputStream` and `BufferedOutputStream` are subclasses of `FilterInputStream` and `FilterOutputStream`, respectively, we can pass on their buffered functionality to other streams using a simple stream filtering technique:

```
// create buffered String stream:
myString = "Obviously the question is false, since ice-cream has
    no bones."
OutputStream theStream = new BufferedOutputStream (new
    StringBufferInputStream(myString));

// create buffered File stream:
OutputStream myStream = new BufferedOutputStream
    (FileOutputStream("HelloWorld.java"));
```

As you can see, we've created two different buffered streams, even though the original stream types (`StringBufferInputStream` and `FileOutputStream`) don't support buffering. We've used the filter capability of `BufferedOutputStream` to create buffered versions of each.

As a result, these streams are not only faster, but use the `mark()` and `reset()` methods properly. It can be said that we've run our two streams through a `BufferedOutputStream` filter, which passes on functionality that they normally don't have.

Line numbers

Line-number input streams understand and use the concept of line numbering; they remember each line as a stream's data is input. This is a special-purpose class that is also a subclass of `FilterInputStream` is `LineNumberInputStream` (see Table 13-19).

Table 13-19
java.io.LineNumberInputStream Constructor

Signature	Description
`public LineNumberInputStream (InputStream in)`	Constructs line-number input stream initialized using the input stream passed to the constructor.
	Parameter: `in` – input stream.

To retrieve the line number of a particular portion of the stream, use the `getLineNumber()` method. To read lines from the stream, use the `readLine()` method, defined in `java.io.DataInputStream` (see the section on "Typed I/O" later in this chapter). An example follows in Listing 13-3.

Listing 13-3: **LineByLine.java—An Example of LineNumberInputStream in Action**

```java
/**
 * LineByLine.java
 *
 * "LineByLine" opens a file as a FileInputStream stream, then
 * passes it to LineNumberInputStream to gain line numbering
 * functionality.
 *
 * @author Aaron E. Walsh
 * @version 1.0, 14 Feb 96
 */

import java.io.*;

class LineByLine {

   public static void main (String args[]) throws
FileNotFoundException {

   String fileName = "letter.txt"; // name of file to open

   /* — OPEN THE STREAMS: — */
   FileInputStream f = new FileInputStream(fileName);
   LineNumberInputStream fileStream = new LineNumberInputStream (f);

   /* — PROCESS LINE-BY-LINE: — */
   try {
     int c; // variable to hold each character
     System.out.print("Line 1: "); // print 1st line # before loop

     while ((c=fileStream.read())!= -1) { /* loop until end of
                                              line */
       System.out.print((char)c); // output each character
       if (c=='\n') { // is this the last character in the line?
                      // if so, print the next line number:
         System.out.print("Line " + (fileStream.getLineNumber()+1)
             + ":");
       }
     }
   } catch (IOException e) {
     System.out.println("Can't open stream!");
   }
  }
 }
```

LineByLine **opens a text file using a** `FileInputStream` **stream. It passes this to the** `LineNumberInputStream` **constructor, which returns a stream capable of understanding line numbers. Each line in the text file is output on the command line, preceded by its line number (see Figure 13-3).**

Figure 13-3: FileInputStream understands line numbers, a particularly useful feature for text editing of any kind.

LineNumberReader

JDK 1.1 has introduced a `LineNumberReader` (see Table 13-20) which returns character arrays. The `LineNumberReader` works in the same way as its `LineNumberInputStream` counterparts.

Table 13-20
java.io.LineNumberReader Constructors

Signature	Description
`public LineNumberReader (InputStream in)`	Constructs line number input stream initialized using the input stream passed to it.
	Parameter: `in` – input stream.
`public LineNumberReader (InputStream in, int size)`	Constructs line number input stream initialized using the input stream passed to it.
	Parameters: `in` – input stream. `size` – initial size.

Pushing back

PushbackInputStream provides an interesting method called unread(), which allows us to place the last character back where it was read, as if we had never actually read it. This is useful in cases where you need to see what the next character in a buffer will be, but don't necessarily want to advance the stream. With PushbackInputStream, if the character is not what you want, you can put it back using the unread() method.

PushbackInputStream invalidates the mark() and reset() methods of the InputStream created with it.

JDK 1.1 also provides provides a PushbackReader class which processes character strings instead of byte arrays. PushbackReader functions in the same manner as the PushbackInputStream class.

Typed I/O

Up until now, we've been dealing with streams of bytes, which are a rather ineffective way to deal with data. While it's true that they provide an efficient mechanism for spitting data out and reading data in, we have no convenient way of using specific data types, such as booleans, shorts, integers, longs, floats, and doubles.

To help us deal with typed data streams, DataInputStream and DataOutputStream classes are available. They are described in Tables 13-21 and 13-22.

Table 13-21		
java.io.DataInputStream		
Constructor	**Signature**	**Description**
DataInputStream	public DataInputStream (InputStream in)	Creates data input stream using the input stream passed to it. Parameter: in – input stream.
Method	**Signature**	**Description**
read()	public read(byte[] b)	Reads data into an array of bytes.
read()	public read(byte[] b, int off, int len)	Reads data into an array of bytes from off until len.
readBoolean()	public readBoolean()	Reads a boolean.
readByte()	public readByte()	Reads an 8-bit byte.
readChar()	public readChar()	Reads a 16-bit char.

Method	Signature	Description
readDouble()	public readDouble()	Reads a 64-bit double.
readFloat()	public readFloat()	Reads a 32-bit float.
readFully()	public readFully (byte[])	Reads bytes, blocking until all are read.
readFully()	public readFully (byte[] b, int off, int len)	Reads bytes, blocking until the bytes from off to len are read.
readInt()	public readInt()	Reads a 32-bit int.
readLine()	public readLine()	Reads a line that is terminated with \n, \r, \r\n, or EOF.
readLong()	public readLong()	Reads a 64-bit long.
readShort()	public readShort()	Reads a 16-bit short.
readUTF()	public readUTF()	Reads a UTF format string.
readUTF()	public readUTF (DataInput)	Reads a UTF format string from the given input stream.
readUnsigned Byte()	public readUnsigned Byte()	Reads an unsigned 8-bit byte.
readUnsigned Short()	public readUnsigned Short()	Reads a 16-bit short.
skipBytes()	public skipBytes(int len)	Skips bytes, blocking until all are skipped.

Table 13-22
java.io.DataOutputStream

Constructor	Signature	Description
DataOutputStream	public DataOutput Stream(Output Stream out)	Creates data output stream using the output stream passed to it. Parameter: out - output stream.

Method	Signature	Description
flush()	flush()	Flushes the stream.
size()	size()	Returns total number of bytes written.
write()	write(int b)	Writes a byte.

(continued)

	Table 13-22 *(continued)*	
Method	*Signature*	*Description*
write()	write(byte[] b, int off, int len)	Writes a subarray of bytes.
writeBoolean()	writeBoolean (boolean b)	Writes a boolean.
writeByte()	writeByte(int b)	Writes an 8-bit byte.
writeBytes()	writeBytes(String s)	Writes String as a sequence of bytes.
writeChar()	writeChar(int b)	Writes a 16-bit char.
writeChars()	writeChars(String	Writes String as a sequence of chars.
writeDouble()	writeDouble(double b)	Writes a 64-bit double.
writeFloat()	writeFloat(float b)	Writes a 32-bit float.
writeInt()	writeInt(int b)	Writes a 32-bit int.
writeLong()	writeLong(long b)	Writes a 64-bit long.
writeShort()	writeShort(int b)	Writes a 16-bit short.
writeUTF()	writeUTF(String s)	Writes String in UTF format.

Now, rather than having to deal with streams in terms of bytes, we can use them as standard data types. If we want to write a byte, we can write a byte; if we want to write a boolean, we can write a boolean. As you can see from the last two tables, we can read and write the data types that we are most comfortable with. In this way, we're not restricted to dealing simply with bytes.

Listing 13-4, the GetFortuneString() method taken from the KzmFortune applet found on the CD-ROM that comes with this book, shows how DataInputStream is used to read lines of text. Specifically, this method opens an input stream using a URL that points to a text file residing either locally or on the Web. If a valid stream is opened, a line of text is read from it for display in a scrolling ticker tape. Pay particular attention to the try-catch clauses surrounding the stream code.

Listing 13-4: **How to Use the DataInputStream Object**

```
//  GetFortuneString, a method of KzmFortune
//  (by Alessandro Garbagnati)
//      input: filename, the number of line to show
//      output: message to show
//
```

```
public String GetFortuneString (String FileName, int TheNum) {
  String TheLine, TheUrl, result = "NO FORTUNE";
  int cnt = 1;

  TheUrl = DirectoryURL() + FileName;
  try {
   URL url = new URL(TheUrl);
    try {
      InputStream TheFile = url.openStream();
      try {
        DataInputStream MyData = new DataInputStream(TheFile);
        try {
            while ((TheLine = MyData.readLine()) != null) {
            if (TheNum == cnt) {result = TheLine;}
            cnt++;
            }
          }catch (Exception e) {
            System.out.println("Err ReadLine" + e.toString()); }
        }catch (Exception e) {
          System.out.println("Err DataInputStream " +
            e.toString()); }
      }catch (Exception f) {
        System.out.println("Err OpenStream" + f.toString()); }
    }catch (Exception g) {
      System.out.println("URL" + g.toString()); }
 return result; // return the "fortune" string
 }
```

On the CD-ROM

The entire source code for KzmFortune is provided on the CD-ROM that comes with this book. On this disc, you'll find a large number of applets that make use of streams, and you may wish to supplement this chapter by looking at them.

When you're dealing with data input streams, you must be aware that, when the end of the stream is reached, an EOFException is thrown. This is quite helpful, since it allows you to know exactly when the end of the stream has been reached. In order to trap and process this exception, you simply surround your stream code with a try-catch clause:

```
try {
   ... work with the stream ...
} catch (EOFException e) {
   // we now know the end of the stream has been reached
 } finally {
  anInputStream.close (); // close this stream
 }
```

If you're dealing with data output streams, however, you're likely to run into an IOException. If the DataOutputStream methods shown in Table 13-22 are ever unable to actually write the stream out, they throw an IOException. Of course, to handle this, simply surround your data output with the try-catch clause, just as we did with the data input streams:

```
try {
   ... work with the stream ...
} catch (IOException e) {
  // we know stream couldn't be written
 } finally {
  anOutputStream.close (); // close this stream
}
```

Tip

As you learned in the chapter covering exceptions (Chapter 10), you don't necessarily have to use the try-catch clause when dealing with these. You can, of course, explicitly say that the method in which the code appears throws the error itself.

Although this gets around having to capture and deal with the error yourself, and that isn't a very elegant way of coping with errors. As a general rule of thumb, you should capture all the exceptions that are thrown, rather then pretend to throw them yourself.

You'll also notice that the KzmFortune example shown didn't provide a specific exception name in the catch clause. The author of this applet chose to catch all possible exceptions at once, using catch (Exception e), instead of providing a catch clause for each possible type of exception.

PrintStream

You may or may not be aware that you've been using the PrintStream class in some fashion already. Whenever you send the print() or println() method to the System.out or System.err class variables, you are, in fact, sending PrintStream methods. System.out and System.err are actually PrintStream variables defined in the System class:

```
public static PrintStream out;
// System class standard out variable
public static PrintStream err;
// System class standard err variable
```

PrintStream is the most commonly used output stream, and that's not surprising. This class provides a plethora of methods (see Tables 13-23 and 13-24) for outputting text, and makes doing so a pleasure. Chances are good that you're already familiar with print() and println(), and their ability to handle a great number of parameters and different types; you might want to experiment with the other methods to gain full appreciation of the PrintStream class.

Table 13-23
java.io.PrintStream Constructors

Signature	Description
`public PrintStream(OutputStream out)`	Creates print stream using the output stream passed to it.
	Parameter: `out` – output stream.
`public PrintStream(OutputStream out, boolean autoflush)`	Creates print stream, with optional auto flushing.
	Parameters: `out` – output stream. `autoflush` – a `boolean`; `true` specifies the stream automatically flushes its output when a newline character is printed.

Table 13-24
java.io.PrintStream Methods

Method	Signature	Description
write	`public void write(int b)`	Writes the `byte`, blocking until it is written.
		Parameter: `b` – byte.
		Throws `IOException` if an I/O error has occurred. This method overrides `write` in `FilterOutputStream` class.
write	`public void write(byte b[], int off, int len)`	Writes the subarray of `byte`s.
		Parameters: `b` – data to write. `off` – offset into the data. `len` – number of bytes to write.
		Throws `IOException` if an I/O error has occurred. This method overrides `write` in `FilterOutputStream` class.
flush	`public void flush()`	Flushes the stream, writing all buffered output `byte`s. This method overrides `flush` in `FilterOutputStream` class.

(continued)

Table 13-24 *(continued)*

Method	Signature	Description
close	`public void close()`	Closes the stream. This method overrides `close` in `FilterOutputStream` class.
check Error	`public boolean checkError()`	Flushes the print stream, returning `true` if there was an error on the output stream, `false` otherwise. (Note: Errors are cumulative; if the print stream encounters an error, `checkError()` returns `true` on all successive calls. Thus, `true` is returned if the print stream has ever encountered an error on the output stream.)
print	`public void print(Object obj)`	Prints the object passed to it. Parameter: `obj` – object to print.
print	`public synchronized void print(String s)`	Prints the `String` passed to it. Parameter: `s` – `String` to print.
print	`public synchronized void print(char s[])`	Prints the array of characters passed to it. Parameter: `s` – array of `chars` to print.
print	`public void print(char c)`	Prints the character passed to it. Parameter: `c` – character to print.
print	`public void print(int i)`	Prints the integer passed to it. Parameter: `i` – integer to print.
print	`public void print(long l)`	Prints the `long` passed to it. Parameter: `l` – `long` to print.
print	`public void print(float f)`	Prints the `float` passed to it. Parameter: `f` – `float` to print.
print	`public void print(double d)`	Prints the `double` passed to it. Parameter: `d` – `double` to print.
print	`public void print (boolean b)`	Prints the `boolean` passed to it. Parameter: `b` – `boolean` to print.

Method	Signature	Description
println	public void println()	Prints a newline.
println	public synchronized void println(Object obj)	Prints the object passed to it, followed by a newline. Parameter: obj – object to print.
println	public synchronized void println(String s)	Prints the String passed to it, followed by a newline. Parameter: s – string to print.
println	public synchronized void println(char s[])	Prints the array of characters passed to it, followed by a newline. Parameter: s – array of characters to print.
println	public synchronized void println(char c)	Prints the character passed to it, followed by a newline. Parameter: c – character to print.
println	public synchronized void println(int i)	Prints the integer passed to it, followed by a newline. Parameter: i – integer to print.
println	public synchronized void println(long l)	Prints the long passed to it, followed by a newline. Parameter: l – long to print.
println	public synchronized void println(float f)	Prints the float passed to it, followed by a newline. Parameter: f – float to print.
println	public synchronized void println(double d)	Prints the double passed to it, followed by a newline. Parameter: d – double to print.
println	public synchronized void println(boolean b)	Prints the boolean passed to it, followed by a newline. Parameter: b – boolean to print.

Warning

Although these methods are extremely flexible, able to accept and output a wide variety of data types, they do not accept Unicode characters, only Latin-1 characters (ISO 8859-1). If you attempt to pass Unicode characters to PrintStream methods, be warned: The top 8 bits of these 16-bit characters are ignored!

PrintWriter

JDK 1.1 has also introduced a `PrintWriter` class, which operates in the same manner as the `PrintStream` class. Instead of creating a byte output stream, `PrintWriter` produces a character output stream. The `PrintStream` and `PrintWriter` classes use the same constructors and methods.

Object Serialization

A major new concept in the JDK 1.1 is the concept of object serialization. Object serialization allows any Java object to be written to an output stream, and then recreated later by reading the object back from the input stream. The cornerstone of object serialization is the `ObjectInput` (see Table 13-25) and `ObjectOutput` (see Table 13-26) classes. You can serialize objects by simply calling the `writeObject()` method, and recreate an object by calling the `readObject()` method.

Only objects that subclass the `Serializable` (or `Externalizable`) interface can be serialized. If a class field is declared as transient, it is not serialized.

Table 13-25 java.io.ObjectInput		
Constructor	**Signature**	**Description**
Object Input	public ObjectInput (InputStream in)	Creates an object input stream using the input stream passed to it. Parameter: in – input stream.
Method	**Signature**	**Description**
available	int available() throws IOException	Returns the number of bytes that can be read without blocking. Throws IOException if an I/O error has occurred.
close	void close() throws IOException	Closes the input stream. Throws IOException if an I/O error has occurred.
read	int read() throws IOException	Reads a byte of data. Throws IOException if an I/O error has occurred.

Method	Signature	Description
read	`int read(byte[] b) throws IOException`	Reads an array of bytes in array b. Throws `IOException` if an I/O error has occurred.
read	`int read(byte[]b, int off, int len) throws IOException`	Reads a `len` number bytes into array b, starting at offset `off`. Throws `IOException` if an I/O error has occurred.
readObject	`Object readObject() throws ClassNotFoundException`	Reads and returns an object. Throws `ClassNotFound Exception` if an I/O error has occurred.
skip	`long skip(long n) throws IOException`	Skips *n* bytes of input. Throws `IOException` if an I/O error has occurred.

Table 13-26
java.io.ObjectOutput

Signature	Description
`public ObjectInput (OutputStream out)`	Creates an object output stream using the input stream passed to it. Parameter: `in` – input stream

Method	Signature	Description
close	`int close() throws IOException`	Closes the output stream. Throws `IOException` if an I/O error has occurred.
flush	`void flush() throws IOException`	Flushes the output stream. Throws `IOException` if an I/O error has occurred.
write	`void write(int b) throws IOException`	Writes a byte of data. Throws `IOException` if an I/O error has occurred.

(continued)

Table 13-26 (continued)

Method	Signature	Description
write	void write(byte[] b) throws IOException	Writes an array of bytes. Throws IOException if an I/O error has occurred.
write	void write(byte[] b, int off, int len) throws IOException	Writes len number bytes from array b, starting at offset off. Throws IOException if an I/O error has occurred.
writeObject	void writeObject (Object obj) throws IOException	Writes object obj to the output stream. Throws IOException if an I/O error has occurred.

More I/O

In addition to the streams we've covered that are supported in the java.io package, other streams in the File and RandomAccessFile classes offer enhanced capabilities for working with data files. We'll return to a discussion of data files in later chapters.

For now, if you want to attain greater mastery of streams, you may want to do some research farther afield on the Web—for example, consider investigating the StreamTokenizer class, which allows you to break an input stream and put it into a stream of tokens. This class can be particularly helpful if you are parsing languages (either programming languages or those we use in everyday life), and clearly bear a close look if you require such functionality.

When dealing with streams, you must handle the potential exceptions that may be thrown in the process. The java.io package defines several exceptions, as shown in Table 13-27. To handle these exceptions, surround your stream-usage statements with a try-catch clause, or declare the methods that use them to throw the particular type of exception the statements are likely to generate.

Table 13-27
java.io Package Exceptions

Exception	Description
EOFException	Indicates that an unexpected End Of File (EOF) was reached during input.
FileNotFoundException	Indicates that a requested file couldn't be found.
IOException	Indicates that an error had occurred reading or writing a stream.
InterruptedIOException	Indicates that an interruption had occurred while reading or writing a stream.
UTFDataFormatException	Indicates that a malformed UTF-8 string was read in a data input stream.

Summary

In this chapter you learned all about Java streams as an essential aspect of input and output.

✦ Streams are a conduit for sending and receiving information in Java programs.

✦ Sending a stream of data is called *writing a stream*.

✦ Receiving a stream of data is called *reading a stream*.

✦ Streams are a versatile way to manage input, output, and object serialization.

✦   ✦   ✦

Threads

If you've spent any time looking at the source code of the applets included on the CD-ROM accompanying this book, you may have noticed that a number of them use *threads*. Threads are independent processes that can be run simultaneously.

In this chapter, you learn how threads operate and affect programs both indirectly and directly. You also see how threads can be used to speed up your programs and prevent bottlenecks when long processes in your code begin.

About Threads

In everyday life, we take the concept of threads for granted. For example, often the most critical task in my day is filled with threads: When I create a cup of coffee in the morning, I perform a number of smaller tasks in the process.

To begin, I place a pot of cold water on the stove and turn the burner on underneath it. While waiting for the water to heat up, I take the coffee beans and cream out of the refrigerator, then pour a little cream into the cup and add a teaspoon of sugar to it. Because I know exactly how much cream I like in my coffee, and all my coffee cups hold the same amount of liquid, I don't have to wait until the coffee is poured before I add these coffee condiments.

As the water gradually shows signs of letting off steam, I toss a fistful of beans into the grinder and give 'em a whirl. While dumping the pulverized beans into the coffee press with my right hand, the water usually comes to a rapid boil, so I take it off the heat with my left hand and place it onto a cold burner.

Tip

If coffee is as dear and life-saving a beverage to you as it is to me, I highly recommend investing in a French press. These elegant devices allow the grinds and water to stand together as long as you want, extracting caffeine and flavor, and caffeine, and more caffeine . . . and, well, you get the picture . . . with every passing second. With the use of a special press, you push the grinds to the bottom of the glass container. With the exception of a Neapolitan flip-drip pot, you can't make a better cup of coffee in your own home.

Because it's a bad idea to pour boiling water directly onto freshly ground beans, lest the poor babies are scalded and produce a bitter cup of Joe (and who wouldn't be bitter after having boiling water poured over his freshly pulverized body?), I spend the next minute or so slowly swirling the cream and sugar with a teaspoon to blend the two into a perfect, granular-free mixture. By the time the sugar has completely dissolved in the cream, I become impatient and figure the water temperature's had time to come down a few degrees.

I grab the pot of water and pour it into the press, all the while stirring the mix with the same teaspoon I used to prepare the cream and sugar. At this point, I may have cradled a portable phone between my cheek and neck to get a jump on the work day—and why not? They'll never know I'm still in my boxer shorts and furry slippers (I dread the arrival of video-phones). If I'm not on the phone by now, I'm probably knocking back a fine assortment of vitamins to counteract the damaging effects of my caffeine habit.

Regardless, within a few minutes I begin the pressing process, separating grounds from water. After pushing all the solid stuff to the bottom of the glass press, I pour the steaming liquid into my cup of waiting sugary sweet cream. Within moments, I lift the nectar to my lips, and, for the first time that day, a smile creeps across my face and my hands stop shaking.

Perhaps this process sounds vaguely familiar to you, perhaps not. The point is, by the time I take my first gulp of coffee, I've accomplished a number of tasks. Each of these has a distinct beginning, an end, and a sequence of steps that happen in between before the task is complete and I move on to the next one. In a number of cases, these tasks happen concurrently.

In essence, my morning coffee ritual has a number of threads of execution. As a result, the process of creating coffee can be considered multithreaded. In fact, just about everything we do in life can be broken down into threads. Can you chew gum and avoid the cracks in the sidewalk at the same time? Chalk up two threads; one for chewing, the other for avoidance behavior. Do you brush your teeth while looking in the mirror for signs of premature aging? Chalk up two more threads, plus one more to keep your ego in check.

As you can see, our lives can be broken down into threads. And, because they're going on in our lives all the time, we can be thought of as multithreaded beings.

In software, a thread is a single sequential flow of control. We're already familiar with sequential flow of control; it's what happens when we execute a program. The program begins, runs through a sequence of executions, and eventually ends. At any given time in the life of a program, there's only one point of execution; that is, the lines of code we write are executed sequentially, not at the same time.

Threads, also known as *execution contexts* or *lightweight processes*, are similar to the sequential programs we're accustomed to writing; they have a beginning, middle, and an end. During its life, a thread executes a sequence of commands and, at any given time, there's only one point of execution.

Does this sound like a program?

In fact, threads and programs are very similar concepts. Unlike programs, however, threads don't exist as discrete collections of executable commands. That is, the end user doesn't execute a thread directly. Instead, threads run *within* a program. It might help to think of them as mini programs that exist within the lifetime of an actual program (hence the name *lightweight process*).

There is nothing new about the concept of a single thread. The excitement in this industry is about multiple threads in a single program all running at the same time and performing different tasks. As you know, having more than one thread executing at a time is known as multithreading. It's this subject that has become a popular topic in computer science circles, especially when discussion turns to Java.

Threads are the reason browsers, such as HotJava and Netscape Navigator, can download a file to your hard drive, display a Web page in one window while opening another in a new window, output one or more Web pages to the printer, and perform a number of other processes concurrently. This is exactly the behavior multiple concurrent threads offer: many things can happen at once (or, more accurately, appear to happen at once). Instead of waiting for a connection to finish before going on to the next one, a number of threads can be created, or "spawned," each of which is responsible for handling its own connection. Because a different thread is taking care of each of these processes, the processes appear to happen in parallel.

Note

In truth, these multiple processes don't really happen at once. Unless threads are executing on a true multiprocessing computer system (a system with more than one processor, capable of executing commands in parallel), threads must take turns using a single CPU. However, because this happens so fast, we often are convinced that things are happening simultaneously.

Rather than going from start to finish in one large program, you can think of threads as divvying up your program into little chunks, or separate tiny programs that can run concurrently. The result is a dramatic improvement in the overall speed of your program. Without threads, the program would have to follow a predetermined set of instructions and wait for each one to be completed before going on to the next.

This approach might not sound all that bad. After all, it's what we're used to. However, what if one of the steps in a program takes a particularly long time to finish? Imagine if we had to wait every time an image or sound file was pulled off the network before we could go on to the next step. This would be a long process, and the larger the file, the longer the wait would be. Thankfully, Java automatically uses threads for just such things. As a result, the rest of our program is free to execute while the files come across the wire.

We can also add threads of our own to further increase the efficiency of our programs. Using them is extremely easy in Java. All we have to do is create a new Thread object and tell it to start executing. Take a look at how we can do this with our applets.

Using Threads in Applets

To use threads in applets, we need only implement the Runnable interface. The Runnable interface declares the methods that we'll need in order to implement threads in our program. The following code is the class signature for a program that uses the Runnable interface:

```
public class AnyClass extends java.applet.Applet implements
Runnable {
...
}
```

Once we've claimed that our applet will use the Runnable interface, there are only three easy things left to do:

✦ Declare a variable to hold a Thread object.

✦ Create a run() method, the nerve center of a thread.

✦ Transfer the contents of our start() method into run() and use start() to kick off the thread.

Because these basic steps take place in all applets that support threads, you can use Listing 14-1 as the basis for future threaded applets:

Listing 14-1: **A Basic Threaded Class Example**

```
public class AnyClass extends java.applet.Applet implements
Runnable {
    Thread myThread; // a variable to hold our thread
    public void start() {
        if (myThread == null) {
            myThread = new Thread(this); // create Thread
object
            myThread.start(); // start it
        }
    }
    public void run() {
        while (myThread != null) {
            .... // code that used to be in the original applet
start() method goes here...
        }
    }

    public void stop() {
        myThread.stop(); // stop it
        myThread = null; // prepare for garbage collection
    }
}
```

Note

Note that we didn't bother to import the `Thread` class (`java.lang.Thread`); the `java.lang` package is automatically available to all our programs, so we don't have to explicitly import it.

The `start()` method creates, or spawns, a new `Thread` object and starts it running. As you can see, this method doesn't do anything but begin the thread. It's the `run()` method that has the bulk of the responsibility.

The `run()` method contains the *thread body*, the sequence of code that the thread will execute. After a thread has been created and started, the runtime system calls its `run()` method. The code in this method is the entire reason the thread was created in the first place and is what the thread is responsible for executing.

As the thread's nerve center, `run()` is the method that defines the life of every thread. When `run()` is complete, the thread dies (more on `Thread` life and death later). Often, `run()` contains code that takes a long time to execute (such as downloading a large file off the network). As a result, this code executes in parallel with other threads, thereby eliminating a potential bottleneck.

Typically, the run() method makes use of a loop control structure, as in the animation applet seen in Listing 14-2. As you can see, we've created an instance variable of the Thread object called kicker. In the start() method, we determine whether or not kicker has already been instantiated and, if it hasn't, we create a new one:

```
kicker=new Thread(this);
```

Essentially, the line instantiates a new Thread object with our class as the parameter (this). This argument, our applet, becomes the thread's target. Because a thread executes the run() method of its target, our new thread knows to execute the run() method of this applet.

After the new Thread object is created, it is put into motion:

```
myThread.start(); // start it
```

When a thread is sent the start() method, as above, it begins to execute by invoking the run() method of its target. Until this point, the thread is simply instantiated and does us no good. Listing 14-2 demonstrates how to use the start() and run() methods:

Listing 14-2: **BlinkItem.java**

```
/**
 * BlinkItem.java
 * Display a Blinking Neon Light by alternating between two
 * images.
 * @author: Mattias Flodin
 */
import java.awt.Graphics;
import java.awt.Image;
import java.lang.Math;
public class BlinkItem extends java.applet.Applet implements
Runnable {
  Image imPic[]; // An array that holds the two images
  int iPicIndex=0; // Keeps track of which image is displayed
  Thread kicker;
  public void init() {
    resize(512,243);
  }
  public void paint(Graphics g) {
    update(g);
  }
  // Using the update method will get rid of some flickering
  public void update(Graphics g) {
```

```
    // Display an error message if something
    // unexpected has happened to the images
    if(imPic[iPicIndex]==null) {
      g.drawString("Error when loading picture", 0, 172);
    }
    // Draw the current image (method won't draw a null image)
    g.drawImage(imPic[iPicIndex],0,0, this);
  }
  public void start() {
    if(kicker == null) {     // If no thread is started yet
      kicker=new Thread(this);  // then create one
      kicker.start();           // and start it
    }
  }
  public void stop() {
   kicker.stop();
   kicker=null;
  }

  public void run() {
    imPic=new Image[2];     // Dimension the image array
    // Load the two images in our 'animation'
    imPic[0]=getImage(getCodeBase(), "images/Homepage1.gif");
    imPic[1]=getImage(getCodeBase(), "images/Homepage2.gif");
    for(;;) { // Loop forever
      repaint();        // Redraw the window
      iPicIndex=iPicIndex==0 ? 1 : 0;    // Switch image
      // The sleep method below might be interrupted and cause
an
      // InterruptedException, so we'll have to catch it.
      try {
        // Wait for a random amount of time
        Thread.sleep( (int) (Math.random()*500));
      } catch (InterruptedException e){}
    }
  }
}
```

Because the run() method contains the body of a thread, we move the contents of our previous start() method here and simply use the original start() method to create and get the thread running.

In this applet, which is a threaded and more elegant version of the BruteForce animation program discussed in Chapter 17, run() simply loads two different images into an array and then enters an infinite for loop. In this loop, the images are repainted one after another.

After an image is drawn, however, the thread is told to sleep a random amount of time:

```
Thread.sleep( (int) (Math.random()*500));
```

As seen in Tables 14-1, 14-2 and 14-3, a thread can be put to sleep, or suspended, for a specified amount of time.

Table 14-1
java.lang.Thread Constructors

Signature	Description
public Thread()	Constructs a new thread. Threads created this way must override their run() method to do anything. An example illustrating this method is shown in the sidebar "Using the Thread() Constructor."
public Thread (Runnable target)	Constructs a new thread, which applies the run() method of the specified target. Parameter: target–object whose run() method is called.
public Thread (ThreadGroup group, Runnable target)	Constructs a new thread in the specified thread group that applies the run() method of the specified target. Parameters: group–the thread group. target–object whose run() method is called.
public Thread (String name)	Constructs a new thread with the specified name. Parameter: name–name of the new thread.
public Thread (ThreadGroup group, String name)	Constructs a new thread in the specified thread group with the specified name. Parameters: group–thread group. name–name of the new thread.

Signature	Description
`public Thread (Runnable target,String name)`	Constructs a new thread with the specified `name` and applies the `run()` method of the specified `target`. Parameters: `target`–object whose `run()` method is called. `name`–name of the new thread.
`public Thread (ThreadGroup group, Runnable target, String name)`	Constructs a new thread in the specified thread group with the specified `name` and applies the `run()` method of the specified target. Parameters: `group`–thread group. `target`–object whose `run()` method is called. `name`–name of the new thread.

Table 14-2
java.lang.Thread Methods

Method	Signature	Description
`currentThread`	`public static Thread currentThread()`	Returns a reference to the currently executing `Thread` object.
`yield`	`public static void yield()`	Causes the currently executing `Thread` object to yield. If there are other runnable threads, they will be scheduled next.
`sleep`	`public static void sleep(long millis) throws Interrupted Exception`	Causes the currently executing thread to sleep for the specified number of milliseconds. Parameter: `millis`–length of time to sleep in milliseconds. Throws `InterruptedException` if another thread has interrupted this thread.

(continued)

	Table 14-2 *(continued)*	
Method	**Signature**	**Description**
sleep	public static void sleep(long millis, int nanos) throws InterruptedException	Sleep, in milliseconds and additional nanoseconds. Parameters: millis–length of time to sleep in milliseconds. nanos–0 – 999999 additional nanoseconds to sleep. Throws InterruptedException if another thread has interrupted this thread.
start	public synchronized void start()	Starts this thread. This causes the run() method to be called. This method returns immediately. Throws IllegalThreadState Exception if the thread was already started.
run	public void run()	The actual body of this thread. This method is called after the thread is started. You must either override this method by subclassing class Thread, or you must create the thread with a runnable target.
stop	public final void stop()	Stops a thread by tossing an object. By default, this routine tosses a new instance of ThreadDeath to the target thread. ThreadDeath is not actually a subclass of Exception, but is a subclass of Object. Users should not normally try to catch it unless they must perform an extraordinary cleanup operation. If ThreadDeath is caught, it's important to rethrow the object so the thread actually dies. The top-level error handler does not print a message if it falls through.

Method	Signature	Description
stop	`public final synchronized void stop(Throwable o)`	Stops a thread by tossing an object. Normally, users should call the `stop()` method without any argument. However, in some exceptional circumstances used by the `stop()` method to kill a thread, another object is tossed. `ThreadDeath` is not actually a subclass of `Exception`, but it is a subclass of `Throwable`. Parameter: o—object to be thrown.
interrupt	`public void interrupt()`	Sends an interrupt to a thread.
interrupted	`public static boolean interrupted()`	Asks whether you have been interrupted.
isInterrupted	`public boolean isInterrupted()`	Asks whether another thread has been interrupted.
destroy	`public void destroy()`	Destroys a thread without any cleanup In other words, this method just tosses its state; any monitors it has locked remain locked. A last resort.
isAlive	`public final boolean isAlive()`	Returns a `boolean` indicating whether the thread is active. Having an active thread means it has been started and has not been stopped.
suspend	`public final void suspend()`	Suspends this thread's execution.
resume	`public final void resume()`	Resumes this thread's execution. This method is only valid after `suspend()` has been invoked.
setPriority	`public final void setPriority(int newPriority)`	Sets the thread's priority. Throws `IllegalArgumentException` if the priority is not within the range `MIN_PRIORITY, MAX_PRIORITY`.

(continued)

Table 14-2 *(continued)*

Method	Signature	Description
getPriority	`public final int getPriority()`	Gets and returns the thread's priority.
setName	`public final void setName(String name)`	Sets the thread's name. Parameter: `name`–new name of the thread.
getName	`public final String getName()`	Gets and returns this thread's name.
getThreadGroup	`public final Thread Group getThreadGroup()`	Gets and returns this thread group.
activeCount	`public static int activeCount()`	Returns the current number of active threads in this thread group.
enumerate	`public static int enumerate(Thread tarray[])`	Copies, into the specified array, references to every active thread in this thread's group. Returns the number of threads put into the array.
countStack Frames	`public int count StackFrames()`	Returns the number of stack frames in this thread. The thread must be suspended when this method is called. **Throws** `IllegalThreadState Exception` if the thread is not suspended.
join	`public final synchronized void join(long millis) throws Interrupted Exception`	Waits for this thread to die. A time-out in milliseconds can be specified. A time-out of 0 (zero) milliseconds means to wait forever. Parameter: `millis`–time to wait in milliseconds. **Throws** `InterruptedException` if another thread has interrupted this one.
join	`public final synchronized void join(long millis, int nanos) throws InterruptedException`	Waits for the thread to die, with more precise time. **Throws** `InterruptedException` if another thread has interrupted this thread.

Method	Signature	Description
join	public final void join() throws InterruptedException	Waits forever for this thread to die. Throws InterruptedException if another thread has interrupted this thread.
dumpStack	public static void dumpStack()	A debugging procedure to print a stack trace for the current thread.
setDaemon	public final void setDaemon(boolean on)	Marks this thread as a daemon thread or a user thread. When there are only daemon threads left running in the system, Java exits. Parameter: on—determines whether the thread will be a daemon thread. Throws IllegalThreadState Exception if the thread is active.
isDaemon	public final boolean isDaemon()	Returns the daemon flag of the thread.
checkAccess	public void check Access()	Checks whether the current thread is allowed to modify this thread. Throws SecurityException if the current thread is not allowed to access this thread group.
toString	public String toString()	Returns a string representation of the thread, including the thread's name, priority, and thread group. Overrides toString in class Object.

Table 14-3
java.lang.Thread Variables

Variable	Signature	Description
MIN_PRIORITY	public final static int MIN_PRIORITY	The minimum priority that a thread can have. The lowest priority is equal to 1.
NORM_PRIORITY	public final static int NORM_PRIORITY	The default priority that is assigned to a thread. The default priority is 5.
MAX_PRIORITY	public final static int MAX_PRIORITY	The maximum priority that a thread can have. The highest priority is 10.

While a thread is sleeping, it is said to enter a *Not Runnable* state. All the other threads are free to continue, but a sleeping thread is inactive until the amount of time specified has passed. Although this applet specifies a random amount of time, we can also specify exactly how long a thread should sleep:

```
Thread.sleep(2000); // sleep 2,000 milliseconds (2 seconds)
```

Because threads execute extremely fast, the sleep parameter is expressed in milliseconds. To help make sense of this parameter, just remember that 1,000 milliseconds equal one second.

You might have noticed that we didn't send the `Kicker` object the `sleep()` method. Instead, we called the `Thread` class method directly. The current thread is known, because we're in its `run()` method, so we don't have to send it the `sleep()` method directly. The preceding line of code applies the `sleep()` method to the current thread, which happens to be `kicker`. In a more complicated program, we'd prefer to invoke the `sleep()` method of the thread we want to take a nap to avoid confusion, instead of taking direct advantage of the `Thread` classes' `sleep()` method, as seen here. However, in this simple example, the result is the same and fairly clear regardless of how we forced the thread to sleep. We could just as easily have called `kicker.sleep( (int) (Math.random()*500));`.

Because invoking `sleep()` may result in an exception being thrown, as most methods that operate on threads have the potential of doing, we must wrap a `try-catch` clause around this statement. You'll see, however, that nothing is done if an error is thrown.

What can we do? Nothing really, except perhaps break out of the loop and terminate the life of the thread:

```
try {
   Thread.sleep( (int) (Math.random()*500));
} catch (InterruptedException e){break;}
```

However, we just let the loop continue. If an error occurs while sleeping, we really don't want to terminate the entire animation. So, perhaps it will repaint the next image a little faster than expected. But it's not worth terminating the entire thread simply because our `sleep()` request wasn't fulfilled.

In this case, the result of a random sleep parameter is quite effective. The images used in the animation (see Figure 14-1) seem to blink on and off, with a little stutter between each blink, just like a neon sign.

When the browser in which this applet is viewed loads another page, the applet's `stop()` method is called. It's here that we bring the life of our thread to an abrupt end:

```
kicker.stop(); // kill thread
kicker=null; // mark for garbage collection
```

Homepage 1.gif

Homepage 2.gif

Figure 14-1: Using threads, the BlinkItem applet alternates between these two images to give the appearance of a neon sign.

The stop() method "kills" a thread and sends it into a "dead" state. When it's dead, we mark the thread as null, allowing the garbage collector to reclaim the memory allocated for it.

Don't Kill That Thread by Mistake!

arning

As you can see from Table 14-2, you can get the currently executing process using the following statement:

```
Thread.currentThread();
```

You might be tempted to send stop() to the currently executing thread, assuming it's yours. Don't do it! If you blindly assume the current thread is yours, you might kill the main thread your applet is running under, or perhaps even the garbage collector thread. If you want to be able to distinguish your thread from others, use the constructor that allows you to supply a name for your thread:

```
kicker = new Thread(this, "BlinkThread");
```

You can then use the getName() method to ensure that the thread you're dealing with is, in fact, yours.

When the page is revisited, the applet's own start() method kicks off another thread, and the entire process is repeated. Alternatively, we could have suspended the thread when the applet's stop() method was called, and resumed it when the page was revisited (see the suspend() and resume() methods in Table 14-2).

However, in this case there is no good reason to keep the thread alive when the page itself is left. We can't guarantee that the webber will return, and it's just as easy to start a new one every time the page is visited. Threads are easy and efficient to create, so we don't have to be stingy with them. We can create and kill them, acting as Lord of the Threads, if you will.

Using the Thread() Constructor

The following code illustrates how to create a threaded class by implementing the Runnable interface. Notice that the run() method is overridden, a must for all threads created in this way:

```
class myThread implements Runnable {
  String name;
    myThread() { // standard constructor
    name = null;
  }
  myThread(String str) { // constructor with name
    name = str;
  }
  public void run() {
    if (name == null)
      System.out.println("A new thread was created");
    else
      System.out.println("A new thread named " +
        name + " was created");
  }
}
class testThread {
    public static void main (String args[]) {
      myThread t = new myThread();
      if(t != null) {
        System.out.println("new myThread() succeed");
      }else {
        System.out.println("new myThread() failed");
      }
    }
}
```

Creating Threaded Objects

In addition to implementing the Runnable interface, we can use threads by extending the Thread class. In this way, we can create our own objects that use threads:

```
class AnyClass extends Thread {
   ...
}
```

As you can see, all we have to do is extend the Thread class. Because the java.lang package is automatically available to all of our programs, we don't have to import it explicitly. Take a look at a class that extends Thread:

```
class EZThread extends Thread {
    public EZThread(String str) {
        super(str);  // pass up to Thread constructor
    }
    public void run() {
        for (int i = 0; i < 5; i++) {
            System.out.println(i + " " + getName());
            try {
                sleep((int)(Math.random() * 500));
            } catch (InterruptedException e) {}
        }
        System.out.println(getName() + " HAS EXPIRED!");
    }
}
```

The first thing this class does is implement a constructor that takes a string parameter and passes it along to the constructor of its superclass. The Thread class constructor that takes a string is invoked, returning a Thread object with this name. By naming threads, we can keep track of which are currently running.

Aside from this, we've implemented a run() method. Whenever an EZThread object is created, its start() method must be invoked before it can execute. Because we don't bother to define a start() method in this class, the superclass start() method is actually used (that is, the Thread class start() method is invoked). This method, in turn, invokes the EZThread run() method.

This run() method is quite simple: It executes a loop five times, outputting the loop iteration (i) on the same line as the name of the thread. In order to test this class, we can use the following:

```
class EZTest {
  public static void main (String args[]) {
    new EZThread("Hickory").start();
    new EZThread("Dickory").start();
    new EZThread("Dock").start();
    }
}
```

As you can see, this test is quite simple. We merely instantiate three new threads and start each of them. We don't even need to hold onto the `Thread` objects that are created. We create the threads, start them, and sit back as they execute. The output is shown in Figure 14-2. You may note that it's not sequential; it doesn't follow any exact order. The threads are running independently of one another—each one executes whenever it has the chance. The order is determined on the Java thread scheduler and the underlying system architecture. However, you'll see in "Bringing It All Together," later in this chapter, how you can synchronize threads to execute in a nice, orderly fashion.

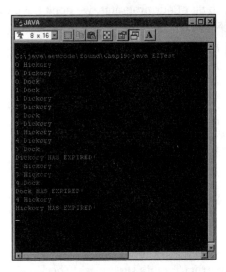

Figure 14-2: Because threads don't run in a predetermined order, the three in this program don't generate output sequentially.

Clearly, creating and using threads is easy in Java. In fact, it's recommended you use threads whenever you have a specific sequence of events that can be executed independently of others. In this way, you can divvy up your program into a number of threads, each executing independently, and potential bottlenecks can be significantly reduced or eliminated entirely.

Keep in mind that each time you create a Java thread, an underlying system thread is actually created. That is, the operating system of your computer—together with the Java runtime system—is responsible for handling the flow of execution of each thread you create. The more threads you create, the more the system is taxed. If you go mad, creating threads for everything you can think of, eventually you'll bring the system to its knees. It's best to think about the sequence of events you want to wrap inside a thread, rather than assume that everything needs to be threaded.

In fact, the Java runtime system already has threads running with which yours must share a slice of the CPU pie. For example, there's the Java garbage collector thread. If the garbage collection mechanism weren't running in a thread, it would have to interrupt your program each time it tried to reclaim objects no longer in use. However, because this system is operating in a thread, it goes about its business without greatly affecting the performance of your program.

In addition, there's a thread always running that is responsible for gathering user input from the keyboard and the mouse. So there are already two threads running before you add your own to the mix.

We're not telling you to be stingy with threads; they are fast and easy to create, and when used properly can greatly enhance the performance of your programs. However, you must consider what operations lend themselves to threads. We recommend that whenever you have a sequence of steps that can operate independently from the rest of your program (such as the animation of a graphic), you place it into a thread.

Tip

When creating threads, you may wonder, *Should I implement the* Runnable *interface or extend the* Thread *class?* The answer, of course, depends on what the class you're creating requires. If it must extend another class, you have no choice but to implement the Runnable interface, because your classes can only inherit from one superclass. We recommend that you use the Runnable interface whenever you need to override only run() and no other thread methods. Classes shouldn't be subclassed unless you are modifying or enhancing their fundamental behavior, so there's no reason to subclass Thread if you need only to implement the run() method.

Under the Covers

As you know, Java threads are implemented by the Thread class, which is part of the java.lang package. Because java.lang is automatically included in your programs, you don't need to import this class to add thread support to your own programs.

This class provides you with a system-independent mechanism for dealing with threads. But under the covers, the actual implementation of threads is dependent on whatever operating system architecture Java is running on. As a result, your threaded programs are really taking advantage of the thread support of the OS on which they are executed. Luckily, you're isolated from the intricacies of individual platforms, thanks to the Thread class.

When creating a thread, you can give it a priority. The higher its priority, the more clout it carries with the runtime system. The Java runtime system uses a scheduler that is responsible for running all existing threads within all executing Java programs. This scheduler uses a fixed-priority scheduling algorithm that, in essence, ensures that the highest-priority threads in each program get the processor—the highest-priority thread is allowed to execute before any others.

(continued)

(continued)

In a case where a single program has more than one thread of the same priority waiting to execute, the scheduler chooses them in a round-robin fashion, choosing a thread not previously executed when the next choice must be made. All threads of the same priority receive equal treatment. Threads of lesser priority are given a chance to execute after those of higher priority have been killed or have entered a nonrunnable state (see "Not Runnable" in the next section).

Thread Attributes

To use threads efficiently and without incident, you must understand the various aspects of threads and the Java runtime system. Specifically, you need to know about:

✦ Thread body: how to provide a body for a thread

✦ Thread state: the life-cycle of a thread

✦ Thread priority: how the runtime system schedules threads

✦ Daemon threads: what they are and how to write them

✦ Thread groups: all Java threads must be part of a thread group

Thread body

As you now know, thread activity takes place in the body of a thread. Specifically, the thread's body is implemented in its run() method. You can provide a thread body by creating a subclass of the Thread class and then overriding its run() method, as we did with EZThread. Or, you can create a class that implements the Runnable interface. In that case, you must instantiate a Thread object and supply it with a Runnable object as the target:

```
kicker=new Thread(this);
```

Accordingly, we have two options when it comes to using threads. However, when writing applets, we have no such choice, because we can only extend one class. Applets must inherit from the java.awt.Applet class, so we must implement the Runnable interface.

If we don't need to extend another class, we can choose to extend the `Thread` class. However, as a general rule, unless we need to override more than the `run()` method, there's no reason to use this approach rather than implement the `Runnable` interface.

Thread state

During the lifetime of a thread, there are many states it can enter. Off the top of your head, you can probably think of at least one of these states: the Runnable state. A thread enters this state whenever it receives the `start()` method.

There are three other states a thread can enter, as shown in Figure 14-3. In all, the four states are:

✦ New Thread

✦ Runnable

✦ Not Runnable

✦ Dead

Take a look at each of them in turn.

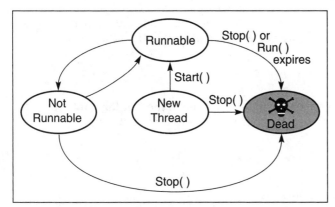

Figure 14-3: Threads may be in one of four states at any given time.

New Thread

Whenever you instantiate a `Thread` object, that thread enters a New Thread state:

```
Thread myThread = new Thread(this);
```

At this point, no system resources have been allocated for the thread; it is only an empty object. As a result, the only thing you can do with it is start or stop it:

```
myThread.start();
myThread.stop();
```

If you attempt to invoke any other method at this point, an IllegalThreadStateException is thrown. This happens because a thread in this state has no way of dealing with methods.

Runnable

Once a Thread object receives the start() method, it enters what is known as the Runnable state. You may think it should be called the "Running" state because, at first thought, you might assume it is executing.

However, this is not necessarily true. Even though threads seem to operate and execute at the same time, it's the underlying system architecture that determines this capability. Specifically, in order to execute at the same time, or in parallel, more than one CPU must be available. Because true multiprocessing computers are rare, your threads are more likely to wait around while each takes a crack at a single CPU.

Simply having multiple CPUs installed in a single computer does not result in a true multiprocessing system. The system architecture (the system hardware and software) must support the capability to execute commands in parallel. True multiprocessing machines are currently a high-end option; they're just beginning to be marketed for everyday desktop use.

Not Runnable

If a thread isn't in the Runnable state, it may be in the Not Runnable state. Not Runnable is entered when a thread is in one of four conditions:

✦ Suspended

✦ Sleeping

✦ Waiting on a condition variable

✦ Blocked by another thread

Three of these are each the result of a specific method:

✦ suspend()

✦ sleep()

✦ join()

The remaining condition is a result of a thread being blocked by an input/output operation (see Chapter 13).

Because each of these is a Not Runnable condition, sending messages to a thread in one of them results in an exception being thrown. For each possible way a thread may become Not Runnable, there is a single and distinct way that it may re-enter the Runnable state. Take a close look at each of these conditions and how each can be reversed.

Suspended

Whenever a thread's suspend() method is invoked, that thread effectively goes into limbo. When suspended, the thread is not in a position to be executed; it must be awakened first by the resume() method. This is helpful when you want to suspend a thread's execution but don't want to kill it.

Sleeping

As you saw earlier, we can put threads to sleep for a period of time (measured in milliseconds). Once a thread is put to sleep, it cannot run. Even if it has a crack at a processor, a sleeping thread won't take it. Until the "sleep time" has expired, the thread simply won't execute. When its time has passed, it re-enters the Runnable state.

What if you called resume() on a sleeping thread? A nice idea, but it would do absolutely no good. When a thread is sleeping, the resume() method is ignored altogether. It's only useful for taking suspended threads out of limbo.

Waiting for a condition variable

A thread can be told to wait on a conditional variable, forcing it to hang out until that condition is satisfied. After sending a thread the join() method, you must wait indefinitely until that thread's run() method has finished. Sending the join() method to a thread may be dangerous, however, if you have important things to do and are forced to wait around for a long period of time. If you refer back to Table 14-2, you'll notice a time-out period may be supplied with two of the join() methods, in which case the thread continues after the specified time passes, regardless of the outcome of the condition.

Whatever object is in control of the condition we're waiting on must alert waiting threads using either the notify() or notifyAll() methods. If a thread is waiting on something to happen, it can proceed only once notify() or notifyAll() has been issued, or if the (optional) time-out period has passed.

Blocked

If a thread is blocked by an input/output operation, it has no choice but to wait around until the input/output command is finished. In this case, the thread is considered Not Runnable, even though it may be fully qualified to run otherwise.

Dead

Just like us, threads have a life cycle. Once a thread's run() method is complete, its life is up: Sorry, buddy, it's time to die!

For example, if the loop in the run() method for our BlinkItem example was to iterate only a thousand times, the life cycle of that thread would be one thousand iterations of that loop. However, because the loop is intentionally infinite, the life cycle of that thread is also infinite, as long as you don't exit the page in which it's embedded.

As soon as the page is exited, the applet's stop() method is called, which in turn calls the thread's stop() method. In this case, the thread does not die from "natural causes," as our EZThread threads do: it's murdered.

The thread is killed by the stop() message being sent to it. When a thread receives this, it commits digital hara-kiri and terminates itself.

As a general rule of thumb, you should send stop() to all threads whenever your applet's own stop() method is invoked. Unless you have a very good reason, whenever someone moves out of the page in which your applet is running, you should kill all threads (or, at the very least, suspend them). It is extremely bad style to allow threads to run in the background when your applet is not actually executing.

Note

Actually, the stop() method sends the thread what is known as a ThreadDeath object (an actual subclass of Object, not an exception). When a thread receives a ThreadDeath object, it realizes that it's time to die and kills itself. You shouldn't try to catch the ThreadDeath object, unless you have an extraordinary cleanup operation to perform before your thread dies. If this object is caught, it's a better idea to rethrow it, allowing the thread to die with some dignity.

The Thread class provides a method called isAlive(), enabling our program to determine whether a thread has been started and not stopped. isAlive() returns true if a thread has been created and started but hasn't been stopped. It returns false if the thread is dead, or if it has been created but not started.

As a result, when isAlive() returns true, you know that a thread is either in the Runnable or Not Runnable state. Unfortunately, there is no way to know which of these two states the thread is in. Conversely, you know that when isAlive() returns false, the thread is either dead or has not yet been started.

Thread Exceptions

The Java runtime system throws IllegalThreadStateException whenever you attempt to invoke a method that the thread cannot handle in its current state. For example, a sleeping thread can't deal with the resume() method. The thread is busy sleeping; it doesn't know how to react to it.

The same holds true when you try to invoke suspend() in a thread that isn't in its Runnable state. If it's already suspended, sleeping, waiting on a condition variable, or blocked by I/O, a thread won't understand how to deal with suspend().

Whenever you call a thread method that may potentially throw an exception, you have to supply an exception handler to catch whatever exceptions may be generated.

As you can see in the following snippet of code, you can determine whether a thread was killed cleanly, or whether an exception occurred:

```
try {
... // deal with threads here...
} catch (ThreadDeath death){
    // was killed... be sure to re-throw:
    throw death;
} catch (IllegalThreadStateException e){
    // thread was sent a method it couldn't handle in its state
} catch (InterruptedException e){
  // the thread was interrupted
}
```

If the thread surrounded by the try-catch clause was killed, the first exception handler captures it. In this case, we need to rethrow the ThreadDeath object to ensure the thread is killed cleanly. However, if the thread was sent a method it couldn't handle in its current state, the second catch clause catches it.

Finally, if the thread is unexpectedly interrupted, the InterruptedException exception is thrown. In this case, our last handler catches it.

Thread priority

In Java, each thread has a priority that affects the order in which it is run. Threads of high priority run before threads of low priority. This is essential, because there are times when threads must be separated in this way. For example, the thread responsible for handling user input is of a higher priority than one that crunches a data file in the background.

Note

A thread inherits its priority from the thread that created it. Unless a new priority is assigned to a thread, the thread keeps this priority until it dies.

You can set the priority of a thread using the setPriority() method, assigning it a value between the Thread class constants MIN_PRIORITY and MAX_PRIORITY (refer to Table 14-1). For example, we could make our BlinkItem thread the highest priority with the following line:

```
kicker.setPriority(MAX_PRIORITY); //
```

Because kicker is the only thread in this applet, changing its priority doesn't make much sense. In programs with multiple threads, however, the ability to assign priority is quite important. Certain parts of our programs vary in how critical they are, and by setting their threads accordingly, we can ensure they are given the attention (or lack of attention) they deserve.

Java threads are scheduled using fixed-priority scheduling. This algorithm essentially executes threads based on their priority relative to one another, and can be summed up in a simple rule: *At any given time, the "Runnable" thread with the highest priority will be running.*

Relinquishing Control with Yield( )

Although threads of the same priority are given equal treatment by the Java thread scheduler, it's possible for a thread to hog the CPU. Consider the following code, and assume it is part of a thread body:

```
int i = 0;
while (i++ < 500000) {
    System.out.println("Iteration: " + i);
}
```

You'll see that, once the loop is entered, there's no way other threads have a chance to run and the current thread cannot move into the Not Runnable state. So this thread monopolizes the CPU entirely and all 500,000 iterations happen without so much as a second of time going to other threads of equal priority. Unless a thread of a higher priority comes along and preempts this one, the loop completes naturally. If this is the case, you should use the yield() method to force the thread to relinquish control of the CPU:

```
int i = 0;
while (i++ < 500000) {
    System.out.println("Iteration: " + i);
    yield(); // relinquish control
}
```

Here, we still execute the loop, but we also give threads of the same priority a chance to execute. Keep in mind that threads of a lower priority must still wait until all these threads enter a Not Runnable state or die.

Whenever multiple threads are ready for execution, the Java runtime system chooses whichever has the highest priority and executes it. When that thread stops running yields (see the "Relinquishing Control with Yield( )" sidebar), or becomes Not Runnable, the lower priority threads have an opportunity to run. If there are two threads with the same priority waiting to be executed, the scheduler executes them in a round-robin fashion, as described earlier.

Tip

The Java runtime system's scheduler is preemptive. If the scheduler is running one thread, and another thread of a higher priority comes along, the thread that is currently executed is put on the back burner and the one with the higher priority is placed in execution. In this sense, the highest priority thread is said to preempt the currently running thread.

The Java scheduler doesn't preempt the currently running thread for another of the same priority, however. And although the scheduler itself isn't time-sliced (that is, it doesn't give threads of the same priority a slice of time in which to execute), the system implementation of threads underlying the `Thread` class may support time-slicing.

Because you can't be certain what systems your applets will be executed on, never write your program to rely on time-slicing. That is, you should use `yield()` to allow threads of the same priority an opportunity to execute rather than expecting each to get a slice of the CPU pie automatically.

Daemon threads

Java supports what are known as *daemon threads*. A daemon thread can be considered a head honcho, or taskmaster thread that supports other threads. The body of a daemon thread, the `run()` method, often uses an infinite loop that waits for a request from an object or other threads. When such a request is made, the daemon thread carries it out, dispatching the appropriate methods. For example, the HotJava browser has a daemon thread named Background Image Reader. This thread is responsible for downloading images from the network and handing them off to objects and other threads that need them.

To set a daemon thread, invoke the `setDaemon()` method with a `true` parameter:

```
myThread.setDaemon(true); // myThread is now a daemon
```

You can find out if a thread is a daemon by using `isDaemon()`:

```
myThread.isDaemon();
```

The `isDaemon()` method returns `true` if the thread is a daemon; otherwise, it returns `false`.

Thread groups

All Java threads are part of a thread group (see Tables 14-4 and 14-5), whether or not you explicitly specify one when creating them. However, there are three constructors in the Thread class that enable you to specify which group a thread should be part of, if you want to specify one other than the default group:

✦ Thread(ThreadGroup, Runnable);

✦ Thread(ThreadGroup, String);

✦ Thread(ThreadGroup, Runnable, String);

Table 14-4
Class java.lang.ThreadGroup Constructors

Signature	Description
public ThreadGroup (String name)	Creates a new thread group. Its parent is the thread group of the current thread.
	Parameter: name–name of the new thread group created.
public ThreadGroup (ThreadGroup parent, String name)	Creates a new thread group with a specified name in the specified thread group.
	Parameters: parent–specified parent thread group. name–name of the new thread group being created.
	Throws NullPointerException if the given thread group is equal to null.

Table 14-5
Class java.lang.ThreadGroup Methods

Method	Signature	Description
activeCount	public synchronized int activeCount()	Returns an estimate of the number of active threads in the thread group.
activeGroupCount	public synchronized int activeGroup Count()	Returns an estimate of the number of active groups in the thread group.

Method	Signature	Description
checkAccess	public final void checkAccess()	Checks to see if the current thread is allowed to modify this group.
		Throws SecurityException if the current thread is not allowed to access this thread group.
destroy	public final synchronized void destroy()	Destroys a thread group. This does *not* stop the threads in the thread group.
		Throws IllegalThreadState Exception if the thread group is not empty, or if it was already destroyed.
enumerate	public int enumerate (Thread list[])	Copies, into the specified array, references to every active thread in this thread group. You can use the activeCount() method to get an estimate of how big the array should be.
		Parameter: list–an array of threads. Returns the number of threads put into the array.
enumerate	public int enumerate (Thread list[], boolean recurse)	Copies, into the specified array, references to every active thread in this thread group. You can use the activeCount() method to get an estimate of how big the array should be.
		Parameters: list–an array list of threads. recurse–a boolean indicating whether a thread has reappeared. Returns the number of threads placed into the array.

(continued)

Table 14-5 *(continued)*		
Method	**Signature**	**Description**
enumerate	public int enumerate (ThreadGroup list[])	Copies, into the specified array, references to every active thread in this thread group. You can use the activeGroupCount() method to get an estimate of how big the array should be.
		Parameter: list–an array of thread groups. Returns the number of thread groups placed into the array.
enumerate	public int enumerate (ThreadGroup list[], boolean recurse)	Copies, into the specified array, references to every active thread in this thread group. You can use the activeGroupCount() method to get an estimate of how big the array should be.
		Parameters: list–an array list of thread groups.
		recurse–a boolean indicating whether a thread group has reappeared.
		Returns the number of thread groups placed into the array.
getMaxPriority	public final int getMaxPriority()	Gets the maximum priority of the group. Threads that are part of this group cannot have a higher priority than the maximum priority.
getName	public final String getName()	Gets the name of this thread group.
getParent	public final Thread Group getParent()	Gets the parent of this thread group.
isDaemon	public final boolean isDaemon()	Returns the daemon flag of the thread group. A daemon thread group is automatically destroyed when it is found empty after a thread group or thread is removed from it.

Method	Signature	Description
list	`public synchronized void list()`	Lists this thread group. Useful for debugging only.
parentOf	`public final boolean parentOf(ThreadGroup g)`	Checks to see whether this thread group is a parent of, or is equal to, another thread group. Parameter: g–thread group to be checked. Returns `true` if this thread group is equal to, or is the parent of, another thread group; `false` otherwise.
resume	`public final synchronized void resume()`	Resumes all the threads in this thread group and all of its subgroups.
setDaemon	`public final void setDaemon(boolean daemon)`	Changes the daemon status of this group. Parameter: daemon–daemon `boolean` that is to be set.
setMaxPriority	`public final synchronized void setMaxPriority(int pri)`	Sets the maximum priority of the group. Threads that are already in the group can have a higher priority than the set maximum. Parameter: `pri`–priority of the thread group.
stop	`public final synchronized void stop()`	Stops all the threads in this thread group and all of its subgroups.
suspend	`public final synchronized void suspend()`	Suspends all the threads in this thread group and all of its subgroups.
toString	`public String toString()`	Returns a string representation of the thread group. Overrides `toString` in class `Object`.
uncaught Exception	`public void uncaught Exception(Thread t, Throwable e)`	Called when a thread in this group exists because of an uncaught exception. Parameters: t–the thread. e–a `Throwable` object.

Thread groups are particularly useful, because you can start or suspend all threads within them, meaning you don't have to deal with each thread individually. Thread groups provide a general way of dealing with a number of threads at once, saving you a great deal of time and effort tracking them down individually.

The following snippet creates a thread group called `genericGroup`. Once we've created the group, we then create a few threads that are part of it:

```
ThreadGroup genericGroup = new ThreadGroup("My Generic
Threads");
Thread aThread = new Thread(genericGroup, this);
Thread aThread2 = new Thread(genericGroup, this);
Thread aThread3 = new Thread(genericGroup, this);
```

You don't necessarily have to create the group of which your threads are a part. You can use one created by the Java runtime system, or one created by the application in which your applet is running. If you don't specify a particular thread group when creating a new thread, as we have in the preceding examples, the thread becomes part of Java's main thread group. This is sometimes referred to as the *current thread group*.

With applets, the default group may not be the main group. It's up to the browser to give the thread a name. To find out what the name is, use the `getName()` method (refer to Table 14-2).

To find out what group a thread is in, use the `getThreadGroup()` method defined in the `Thread` class. This method returns a thread group to which you can send a variety of methods that act on each member of the group. As you may recall, Table 14-2 shows the various methods that operate on groups.

Thread groups support the notion of access privileges. If you don't specify an access privilege for a group, the threads in that group are allowed to query and find out information about threads in other groups.

By default, the threads you create don't have a specific security level assigned to them. As a result, any thread in any group is free to inspect or modify threads in other groups. You can, however, use the abstract `SecurityManager` class (`java.lang.SecurityManager`) to specify access restrictions for thread groups.

To specify access restrictions, you would create a subclass of the `SecurityManager` class and override those methods that are utilized in thread security. Keep in mind, however, that most browsers (such as Netscape) won't allow you to change or alter security managers, so this procedure only applies to applications.

Multithreaded Programs

Whenever you have multiple threads running simultaneously (or almost at the same time, as is the case with single-CPU systems), they may need to access the same piece of data at the same time. In fact, unless your program is running on a true multiprocessor system that supports parallel processing, your threads will never access a specific piece of data at exactly the same time. They will, however, be able to access the same piece of data at roughly the same time, with perhaps only milliseconds or less between each access.

The problem is that when threads share data, none of them can be certain that the data hasn't been changed by another thread before they got to it.

Think in terms of a basket full of eggs. If you're the only person at your Easter egg decorating party, you can be pretty sure that, when you reach into the basket, you'll get an egg (at least until there are no more eggs, or the cops break up your little party).

However, suppose you invite the local chapter of the Hell's Angels over to decorate eggs with you. Whenever you reach into the basket, you now run the risk of brushing up against a hairy forearm or two. Worse still, you might be expecting an egg, only to find that Alphonse got the last one. In this case, Alphonse is busy throwing his egg at Sebastian while you get hot under the pinstriped collar. And who's going to yell at a Hell's Angel? Not me, that's for sure.

Aside from the likelihood of encountering hirsute appendages, the same thing can happen when a number of threads operate on the same data. Unless their access to the data is synchronized, there's no way of guaranteeing that the data hasn't been changed by another thread.

Synchronization

Up until this point, we've only looked at threads that operated where all the data and methods required for execution were inside the body of the thread. We have not considered threads that access data outside themselves.

A sticky situation can occur when multiple threads need to access the same piece of information. For example, suppose you wrote a simple `Counter` class that provided methods for incrementing and returning the counter variable. Using the class within a single thread is just fine, but what happens when multiple threads attempt to use this class?

Because each thread has the potential for accessing these methods at exactly (or nearly) the same time, the counter may become inconsistent. Suppose, for example, that one thread was incrementing the value of the counter at the same time another was retrieving it. Should the returned value reflect the incremented value? Suppose a dozen threads all tried to update the value at the same time, and only one attempted to retrieve it. What value should be returned in that case?

In effect, the data becomes unreliable, yet it's almost impossible to track down precisely what's going on, because everything seems to be jogging along smoothly. Then, every once in a while, seemingly inexplicably, the data gets clobbered. You might expect to retrieve a number such as 12, but find that only 2 is returned because of a synchronization error.

The way to avoid this distress is to use the `synchronized` keyword, as shown in the following snippet of code. In this way, you can guarantee that only one thread is accessing a method at a time. Every other thread has to wait its turn until the object is free:

```
synchronized void myMethod( ) {
    // all code in here is now synchronized!
    }
```

Tip   The `synchronized` keyword can be applied to any block of code, not just methods:

```
synchronized (anyObject) {
    // the object and this block of code are synchronized
    }
```

Although this may be tempting, locking objects—as the preceding code snippet does—can lead to trouble, because the rest of the code around it isn't synchronized. As a result, you'll have more difficulty keeping track of what is and what isn't synchronized. For this reason, it's best to synchronize the entire method, rather than a smaller block of code inside it.

The `synchronized` keyword makes use of *monitors*. A monitor acts like a bouncer at the door of an exclusive nightclub, allowing only one person in and out at any given time (not a very fun club, from the sound of it, but a club nonetheless). Whenever an object enters a synchronized method, the bouncer, or monitor, marks it as locked and prevents any other threads from accessing it until the current thread is finished. Using the proper terminology, any time you apply the `synchronized` keyword to a method or to a block of code, you are marking a critical section.

Using `synchronized` to mark critical sections of code enables you to share data among threads without worrying that it will be clobbered. The `hit( )` method in class `PingPong`, shown in Listing 14-2 in the "Bringing It All Together" section later in this chapter, is an example of a synchronized method.

Whenever a thread enters `hit()`, all others are locked out until it has finished. The others wait, blocked, until `hit()` becomes unlocked. In this way, we never have to worry about synchronization errors again.

Tip

Java has a reserved keyword, called `volatile`, that enables you to specify variables as being, you guessed it, volatile. A variable that is volatile is read from memory every time it's used and then stored after each use. This means that each time you access a variable, it's guaranteed not to have come from a register and not to have been stored in a previous memory location.

Deadlock

An interesting condition occurs when two or more threads are waiting for each other to unlock a synchronized block of code, where each thread relies on another to do the unlocking. This *deadlock* situation can occur if you're not careful in writing your synchronized methods. If the method being called attempts to access the synchronized method that invoked it, and must wait for that method to become free before it can become free itself, the two methods will end up waiting on each other for eternity!

There are a few things you can do to ensure that your synchronized programs don't end up in deadlock. For one, try to execute locked code in as short an amount of time as possible. The longer you hold the lock, the more likely it is that another thread will come along and require that object.

Also, be careful when you're actually invoking synchronized methods from within another synchronized method. Whenever a synchronized method invokes another synchronized method, there is a potential for deadlock. The best way to avoid deadlock is to define the task each thread has clearly, and consider what data is to be used and when. Although you may not anticipate all potential scenarios, you'll be in better shape than if you simply attempt to wrap a thread around everything. By ensuring that every thread in your program has a specific purpose, you eliminate the threads that aren't required and reduce the chance of deadlock.

Bringing It All Together

The following code listings bring many of the aspects you've just read about to life. Together, Listings 14-2, 14-3, and 14-4 illustrate a very simple example of a synchronized, threaded program that implements `wait()` and `notify()`. The program, `Ping Pong`, has a very simple algorithm:

```
If it is my turn,
    note whose turn it is next,
    then PING,
    and then notify anyone waiting.
otherwise,
    wait to be notified.
```

The first class is named PingPong and consists of a single synchronized method named hit(), whose only parameter is the name of the "player" who goes next. Any thread with a reference to an instance of class PingPong can synchronize itself with other threads holding that same reference. To illustrate this concept, the Player class (Listing 14-3) was written to instantiate a PingPong thread, and the Game class (Listing 14-4) was written to create several players and run them all at once.

Because each of these is a public class, they can't be stored in the same .java file (remember, only one public class to a file!). As a result, each resides in its own file. When compiled and executed, the output looks something like the following:

```
PING! (alice)
PING! (bob)
PING! (alice)
PING! (bob)
PING! (alice)
PING! (bob)
PING! (alice)
PING! (bob)
PING! (alice)
PING! (bob)
PING! (alice)
PING! (bob)
PING! (alice)
PING! (bob)
PING! (alice)
PING! (bob)
PING! (alice)
PING! (bob)
PING! (alice)
PING! (bob)
PING! (alice)
PING! (bob)
PING! (alice)
PING! (bob)
PING! (alice)
PING! (bob)
```

Because these threads are synchronized with each other, they run nice and orderly, each in turn and quite unlike our EZThread example earlier where it was every thread for itself. Thanks to PingPong's use of synchronization, only one thread at a time can enter hit(), so each waits for the other to finish before taking its turn. Contrast this with unsynchronized methods, where multiple threads can access the code at the same time.

The Ping Pong program is part of the JavaWorld "Synchronizing Threads in Java" article available at http://www.JavaWorld.com. Refer to this article (or one of the other two articles on threads) for a step-by-step breakdown of this program and detailed information regarding Java threads.

Listing 14-2: **PingPong.java by Chuck McManis**

```java
// The "Player" class
public class PingPong {

// state variable identifying whose turn it is.
  private String whoseTurn = null;

  public synchronized boolean hit(String opponent) {

  String x = Thread.currentThread().getName();

  if (whoseTurn == null) {
    whoseTurn = x;
    return true;
  }

  if (whoseTurn.compareTo("DONE") == 0)
   return false;

  if (opponent.compareTo("DONE") == 0) {
    whoseTurn = opponent;
    notifyAll();
    return false;
  }

  if (x.compareTo(whoseTurn) == 0) {
    System.out.println("PING! ("+x+")");
    whoseTurn = opponent;
    notifyAll();
  } else {
   try {
     long t1 = System.currentTimeMillis();
     wait(2500);
     if ((System.currentTimeMillis() - t1) > 2500) {
       System.out.println("****** TIMEOUT! "+x+
       " is waiting for "+whoseTurn+" to play.");
     }
   } catch (InterruptedException e) { }
  }
 return true; // keep playing.
}
}
```

Listing 14-3: Player.java by Chuck McManis

```
// The "Player" class
public class Player implements Runnable {
 PingPong myTable;        // Table where they play
 String myOpponent;

 public Player(String opponent, PingPong table) {
   myTable  = table;
   myOpponent = opponent;
 }

 public void run() {
  while (myTable.hit(myOpponent))
   ;
  }
}
```

Listing 14-4: Game.java by Chuck McManis

```
// The "Game" class
public class Game {
  public static void main(String args[]) {
    PingPong table = new PingPong();
    Thread alice = new Thread(new Player("bob", table));
    Thread bob   = new Thread(new Player("alice", table));

    alice.setName("alice");
    bob.setName("bob");
    alice.start();    // alice starts playing
    bob.start();      // bob starts playing
    try {
      // Wait 5 seconds
     Thread.currentThread().sleep(5000);
    } catch (InterruptedException e) { }

    table.hit("DONE"); // cause the players to quit their
threads.
    try {
      Thread.currentThread().sleep(100);
    } catch (InterruptedException e) { }
  }
}
```

Threads and Future Versions of the Java SDK

Future revisions of the Java SDK promise threading performance enhancements. These future performance enhancements will be realized in three ways. First, Java will provide Solaris native thread support. Native thread support will provide enhanced performance on multiprocessor-based systems. Second, faster memory allocation and garbage collection will be provided. The local heap for threaded processes will be cached — resulting in shorter garbage-collection times. Finally, the thread local monitor will also be cached, enabling synchronization methods to be nearly as fast as normal methods.

Summary

A thread, also known as an execution context or lightweight process, is a single sequential flow of control. Think of it as a way to divide your programs into chunks, each capable of executing independent of others. When used properly, threads help eliminate bottlenecks and improve overall programming performance. Threads are quick and easy to add to your programs, but with such power comes the responsibility of clearly defining which tasks deserve their own threads.

✦ You can use threads by implementing the `Runnable` interface, or by extending the `Thread` class.

✦ Threads have three key aspects: body, state, and priority.

✦ A thread can be specified as a daemon thread, which serves other threads, and may also be assigned to a thread group when you need to manage more than one at a time.

✦ The body of a thread is its `run()` method, which is where all the action takes place and can be thought of as the heart of a thread.

✦ Be careful to include in the body of a thread (its `run()` method) only those tasks that may operate independently from the rest of your program.

✦ Be aware that multithreaded programs can deadlock your program when they use synchronized methods; be careful when you use monitors in your methods.

✦   ✦   ✦

Weaving Applets into Web Pages

In this chapter, you learn the ins and outs of weaving Java applets into World Wide Web documents or HTML documents. Although we also explain aspects of this process in previous chapters (specifically Chapter 7), we explore each of the pieces of the puzzle in more detail.

In particular, we explore the ⟨APPLET⟩ tag, which is used to embed a Java applet into a Web page. This tag is created specifically for Java-savvy browsers. If a browser doesn't understand the applet tag, it simply ignores it. As you'll see, there are a few ways to let non-Java browsers know about your applet, or at least allow them to tell the user there's an applet on your page.

Applet Tag Syntax

The following is the syntax of the ⟨APPLET⟩ tag, which is currently supported only by Java-savvy browsers such as Netscape Navigator 2.0 (and later), Internet Explorer 3.0 (and later), and HotJava. While these aren't the only Java-savvy browsers on the market, they're the most popular. Regardless, any Java-savvy browser supports the ⟨APPLET⟩ tag, as you'll see in the following definition (items in square brackets ([ ]) are optional):

```
<APPLET
  [CODEBASE = base_URL]                  — applet code base —
  CODE = classname.class                 — applet code file —
  [ALT = alternate_Text]                 — alternate text —
  [NAME = applet_Name]                   — applet name —
  WIDTH = width_Value                    — applet width (pixels) —
  HEIGHT = height_Value                  — applet height (pixels)—
  [ALIGN = (left|right|top|texttop|middle|
            absmiddle|baseline|bottom|absbottom) baseline]
  [VSPACE = vert_Value]                  — vertical space (pixels)—
  [HSPACE = horiz_Value]                 — horizontal space (pixels)—
  [ARCHIVE = archive_list]               — comma separated list of
  JAR files —
  [OBJECT = serialized_app]              — serialized applet file —
>
[PARAM NAME=param1_Name VALUE = "param1_Value"]
[PARAM NAME=param2_Name VALUE = "param2_Value"]
[PARAM NAME=param3_Name VALUE = "param3_Value"]
  [alternate_HTML_CODE]
</APPLET>
```

As you can see from the preceding definition, there are only three portions, or
attributes, that this tag requires: CODE, HEIGHT, and WIDTH, as shown in Table 15-1.
Optional attributes are shown in Table 15-2.

Note

Applet attributes provide information that either the browser, the Java runtime
system, or your applet itself uses to execute properly. The CODE, HEIGHT, and
WIDTH items specified in all the HTML documents we've created so far are actually
applet attributes.

Table 15-1
Required Applet Attributes

Attribute	Description
CODE	Specifies the name of the file containing the bytecode for your applet.
HEIGHT	Specifies the initial height of your applet in pixels.
WIDTH	Specifies the initial width of your applet in pixels.

Table 15-2
Optional Applet Attributes

Attribute	Description
ALIGN	Specifies where your applet is placed on the page in respect to the text around it. It can have one of the following nine alignments: left, right, top, texttop, middle, absmiddle, baseline, bottom, and absbottom.
ALT	Specifies alternate text to be displayed by text-only browsers.
ARCHIVE	Specifies one or more archives (for example, JAR files) that will be preloaded. Classes are loaded using an instance of the AppletClassLoader with the CODEBASE specified.
CODEBASE	Specifies the base URL for your applet. The applet itself must be located relative to this URL. If CODEBASE isn't specified, the URL of the HTML document in which the applet is embedded is used.
HSPACE	Specifies the horizontal space surrounding your applet. The value you specify for HSPACE is used only when the ALIGN attribute is set to left or right.
NAME	Specifies the symbolic name of your applet, allowing other applets embedded in the same page to locate your applet by name.
OBJECT	Specifies the name of a class that contains a serialized version of an Applet. When a serialized applet is loaded its init() method is not invoked, but its start() method will. An applet must have either the OBJECT or CODE attribute specified.
VSPACE	Specifies the vertical space surrounding your applet. The value you specify for VSPACE is used only when the ALIGN attribute is set to top or bottom.

CODEBASE attribute

Aside from CODE or OBJECT, HEIGHT, and WIDTH, no other attributes are required for the <APPLET> tag. As you know, providing only these three parameters specifies that the applet (the class file) will be located in the same directory as the HTML file in which it is embedded. However, you can use the CODEBASE attribute to specify a location other than this default.

With `CODEBASE`, we can supply either an *absolute URL* (one that specifies a complete address) or a *relative URL*, which specifies an address relative to the current document's location. For example, if we wanted an applet embedded in a page to be loaded from a directory named `stuff` residing in the directory of the page itself, we would provide the following relative URL to `CODEBASE`:

```
<APPLET CODEBASE = "stuff"
CODE = "MyApplet.class"
WIDTH = 200
HEIGHT = 200>
</APPLET>
```

Or we can go down a few levels:

```
<APPLET CODEBASE = "stuff/games/strategy"
CODE = "MyApplet.class"
WIDTH = 200
HEIGHT = 200>
</APPLET>
```

Tip

Although you aren't required to enter attribute names (`CODEBASE`, `CODE`, `WIDTH`, `HEIGHT`, and the others) as all uppercase letters, it's a good idea. Supplying attribute names as all uppercase makes your HTML code easier to read.

We could also supply an absolute URL and have our applet loaded from anywhere on the Web:

```
<APPLET CODEBASE =
"http://www.mantiscorp.com/jstuff/games/strategy"
CODE = "MyApplet.class"
WIDTH = 200
HEIGHT = 200>
</APPLET>
```

Keep in mind, however, that an applet can only access files from the same Web server on which it's located. As a result, if you provide an absolute URL for `CODEBASE`, that applet will only be able to access files off the server on which it resides. For example, in the preceding applet tag, once the applet is loaded, it can only grab files off the server the `www.mantiscorp.com` host resides on.

This is due to one of the security measures protecting applets: They are not allowed to reach out and grab code and resources from just anywhere. JDK 1.2 includes security checks, using a permission/policy-based mechanism, that allow applets to load files from anywhere on the Web.

JDK 1.2 Security

In JDK 1.2, when code is loaded, it is assigned "permissions" based on the security policy currently in effect. Each permission specifies a permitted access to a particular resource (such as "read" and "write" access to a specified file or directory, "connect" access to a given host and port, and so on). The policy, specifying which permissions are available for code from various signers/locations, can be initialized from an external configurable policy file. Unless a permission is explicitly granted to code, it cannot access the resource that is guarded by that permission. These new security features enable fine-grain, highly configurable, flexible, and extensible access control. Such access control now can not only be specified for applets but also for all Java code, including applications, beans, and servlets. For more detailed information on the new JDK 1.2 security model, consult Sun's Java Web site at `http://java.sun.com/products/jdk/1.2/docs/guide/security/spec/security-specTOC.doc.html`.

Typically, your applet will require the use of support files (such as sound or image files). Your applet can be written in one of the following three ways to affect how these support files load:

✦ It can access files using a URL, allowing the file to be located anywhere on the server (as long as it's on the same server as the applet).

✦ It can access files stored relative to the applet itself.

✦ It can access files stored relative to the HTML document in which it is embedded.

The most convenient techniques are the last two—loading files relative to the applet or the Web page in which it is embedded. However, in order to load a file relative to the applet or Web page, you must first find out the URL of the applet or page. Luckily, the `java.applet.Applet` class provides two methods for doing this.

Note

For details on loading files using a URL, see Chapter 7. In that chapter we create the `FlexibleMediaHello` applet, which loads a sound file and an image file using URLs supplied in applet parameters.

To find out the base URL of your applet, use the `getCodeBase()` method:

```
URL myImageURL = getCodeBase(); // get the URL of applet
Image img = getImage(myImageURL, "images/world.gif"); // load
image file
```

This example shows how you can use the `getCodeBase()` method to load an image relative to the applet itself. The applet's own URL is retrieved and used in a call to `getImage(·)`, which accepts a URL as its first parameter. When executed, `getImage()`looks for the `world.gif` file in the `images` directory, located in the same directory as the applet itself.

We can also find the URL for the Web page (HTML document) the applet is embedded in:

```
URL myImageURL = getDocumentBase();
Image img = getImage(myImageURL, "images/world.gif");
```

In this example we load an image relative to the document, not the applet. As you can guess, this method is necessary when you need to retrieve files that are relative to the Web page and not the applet.

Often, applets and the Web pages they are referenced in reside in the same directory. In this case, it doesn't matter which method you use: the URLs are the same! However, if the applet and Web page are in different directories, you have to use the appropriate method to locate your support files.

Tip

You don't have to store the URL in a variable before passing it as a parameter to one of these methods, as we do here. Instead, you can combine both lines of code as follows:

```
getImage(getCodeBase (),"images/world.gif");
```

or

```
getImage(getDocumentBase(),"images/world.gif");
```

In fact, unless you have a reason to hang onto the URL, this is the preferred way of doing it!

NAME attribute

Names are used to uniquely identify more than one applet on a page. This is particularly helpful when you want your applets to communicate with one another. Using the `NAME` attribute, you can give your applet a unique name:

```
<APPLET CODEBASE = "stuff/games/strategy"
CODE = "MyApplet.class"
NAME = "A Very Special Applet"
WIDTH = 200
HEIGHT = 200>
</APPLET>
```

Suppose, for example, that you had two applets on a page, and assigned the names TaskMaster and Grunt to them. In the TaskMaster applet, you can have a bit of code that "talks" to Grunt:

```
// get a reference to Grunt:
Applet theGrunt = getAppletContext().getApplet("Grunt");
// invoke Grunt's method
( (gruntClassName) theGrunt).aMethod(param1, param2, ...);
```

In the preceding two lines of code, we do something quite powerful. First, we use the getApplet() method to retrieve a reference to the Grunt applet. We do this by way of the getAppletContext() method, which returns a "context" to the applet's environment context.

Since an applet's context is the browser, we effectively say, "Look in the browser for an applet named Grunt, and give me a reference to it." Once we have a reference to Grunt (poor little devil), we can invoke any of the methods in it, as if it were just another object in the TaskMaster program. All we do is cast out the Grunt reference into its appropriate class, and we are golden.

The *JavaWorld* magazine articles provided on the CD-ROM with this book show several ways you can use interapplet communications to get your applets talking to one another. For details, refer to the *JavaWorld* article entitled "Tin Cans and String: Four Methods of Inter-Applet Communication."

WIDTH and HEIGHT attributes

You know, of course, about the HEIGHT and WIDTH attributes; we deal with them from the beginning, with our fi st applet, and all along the way—they're required attributes no applet can live without. They specify the width and the height of the applet when first executed. However, the applet itself can, and often does, resize itself using the resize() method.

Unfortunately, you can never be sure whether resize() will work properly. It's completely up to the browser to respond to (or ignore) calls to resize(). In fact, the first Java-savvy version of Netscape Navigator (version 2.0) ignored all such calls, meaning your applets couldn't resize themselves once loaded in this browser, while Applet Viewer responds to this method as you'd expect. As a result, you shouldn't rely on this method always working. Instead, insist that the user set the appropriate values in the HEIGHT and WIDTH attributes.

Alignment

Since applets are integral portions of Web pages, the ALIGN <APPLET> tag definition allows us to align our applets in nine different ways:

```
ALIGN=left
ALIGN=right
ALIGN=top
ALIGN=texttop
ALIGN=middle
ALIGN=absmiddle
ALIGN=baseline
ALIGN=bottom
ALIGN=absbottom
```

When aligning applets to the left or right, the text following the applet is arranged accordingly. When the applet is on the left, the text appears to the right. Conversely, if your applet is aligned to the right, the text appears to the left, as shown in Figure 15-1.

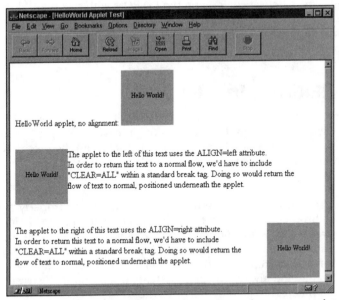

Figure 15-1: The ALIGN attribute determines where your applet will be placed in the browser window, and affects the flow of text following the <APPLET> tag.

You should note that all subsequent text continues to flow in this manner, so you must supply a break at the point you want the text to start flowing normally again. The break tag `<BR>` accepts a `CLEAR` attribute, which allows you to specify how the remaining text will flow. `CLEAR` can be `left`, `right`, or `all`. To set the text back to a normal flow, set `CLEAR` to `all`:

```
<BR CLEAR=ALL>
```

The remaining align values specify how the applet is aligned in relation to the text. Examples of each are shown in Figure 15-2.

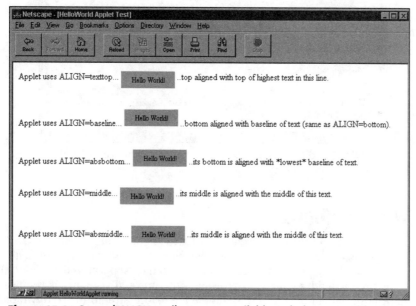

Figure 15-2: Several ALIGN attributes are available to help you position an applet in relation to a line of text.

Vertical and horizontal space

You can gain even more control over your applet's position relative to the text around it by using the `VSPACE` and `HSPACE` attributes. `VSPACE` specifies how much space will appear in a vertical relation—that is, above or below—to your applet. `HSPACE` specifies the amount of horizontal space (from left to right) that will appear. Figure 15-3 shows how vertical and horizontal spacing affects the visual impact of your applet in relation to the text.

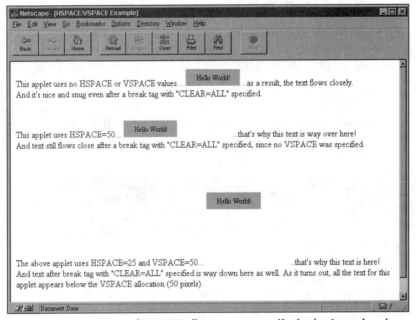

Figure 15-3: HSPACE and VSPACE allow you to specify the horizontal and vertical space around your applet.

ARCHIVE attribute

In Chapter 11 we discuss how to create JAR (Java Archive) files. You can use JAR files to compress and store a number of class files so they are downloaded all at once. The `ARCHIVE` tag can be used to specify a comma-separated list of JAR files that will be pre-loaded by your Web browser. Any time a file or class is required, the Web browser will first search the archive file before attempting to download it over the network. The `ARCHIVE` tag is used as follows:

```
<APPLET CODE="AnyClass.class"
ARCHIVE="AnyJar1.jar,AnyJar2.jar">
</APPLET>
```

Whenever any file or class is required by the `AnyClass` applet, the `AnyJar1.jar` and `AnyJar2.jar` files are searched first. Creating and managing JAR files is explained in detail in Chapter 11.

Communicating with Non-Java Browsers

In cases where a non-Java browser loads a Web page that contains an applet, we have an opportunity to display a message indicating that this particular page contains an applet. To do this, we provide standard HTML between the beginning and closing applet tags:

```
<APPLET CODE="AnyClass.class" WIDTH=90 HEIGHT=50 ALIGN=top>
This page requires a Java-savvy browser!
</APPLET>
```

As you can see, we supply a text message that says "This page requires a Java-savvy browser!" Whenever a non-Java browser comes to this page, it won't be able to launch the applet, but it will be able to display this text message to the user. In this way, users are made aware that they can come back later with a Java browser and have some particular effect take place.

Any standard HTML can be used in this area. You are not limited to text alone; in fact, you can supply graphics tags, as well. You can also supply hyperlinks for graphics and pieces of text, so that when a user visits the page with a non-Java browser, it may look like a fully functional Web page and, in fact, act like one:

```
<APPLET CODE="AnyClass.class" WIDTH=90 HEIGHT=50 ALIGN=top>
This page requires a Java-savvy browser!
<A HREF="http://www.javasoft.com">GET ONE!</A>
</APPLET>
```

However, when someone visits with a Java-powered browser, the applet portion kicks in, and they'll be off and running under Java steam. In this case, the "alternate HTML," as it's called, is ignored, meaning only users of non-Java browsers will see it.

It's always good style to attempt to provide both sides of the coin; that is, if it's possible that your applet can be rendered using standard HTML code (as in the case of graphics and text), you should do it. In this way, both non-Java and Java-powered browsers benefit from your site.

Applet Parameters

As you know, we can supply our applet with parameters from within the applet tag. This is simple enough, using the PARAM attribute. Each PARAM attribute has a name and a value associated with it:

```
<PARAM NAME=hello VALUE="How are you?">
```

The name tells us which parameter we're talking about, `hello` in this case, while the value specifies the value for that parameter ("How are you?"). Whenever we retrieve a parameter from within our applet, it's received in the form of a string. To retrieve a parameter, we simply use the `getParameter()` method:

```
String helloString = getParameter ("hello");
```

If we attempt to retrieve a parameter that is not included in an HTML file, this method returns `null`. As a result, we need to test to ensure that we are receiving valid parameters. When we receive an invalid parameter, we can use a default:

```
if (helloString == null) {
  helloString = "Hello World";
}
```

There are a number of things for which you can use the parameter tag. You may want to specify the color for which graphics or text are drawn. Or you may want to specify an image or sound file associated with the applet. It's up to you how to use parameters. They're provided so you can gain greater flexibility without having to hard-code such things into your applets.

Be careful, however, when specifying parameter tags in your HTML code. If you don't enclose the `VALUE` you supply in quotes, or type an extra quote by mistake (such as `VALUE = "Hello""`), the browser will likely pass garbage instead of what you want! In fact, some browsers may even crash, since they expect a single value to appear between a set of quotes (`VALUE = "Hello"`, for example). For more information on applet parameters, see Chapter 7.

Typically, parameters are retrieved in your applet's `init()` method. You're free to get them when you like, of course, although the conventional way of retrieving parameters is similar to how you initialize variables: right off the bat!

You may have noticed that a number of the applets on the CD-ROM provided with this book allow you to specify a list or array of parameters associated with a single `PARAM` name. This is particularly useful when you don't want to take up a lot of space and assign each of these potential variables to a specific `PARAM` name. The easiest way of doing this is to separate each element on the name line with the traditional pipe separator:

```
<PARAM NAME=sounds
VALUE="1.au|2.au|3.au|4.au|5.au|6.au|7.au|8.au|9.au|0.au">
```

The preceding example, taken from the `Animator` applet supplied on the CD-ROM, shows one long string associated with a single-parameter name (`sounds`). However, this string contains many different parameters, each separated by the pipe character (|). To extract and process these parameters, Listing 15-1 is used. The parseSounds method takes a parameter string containing a list of sound files, and stores them in a hash table for easy retrieval.

Listing 15-1: **parseSounds Stores a Parameter String in a Hash Table**

```
Hashtable parseSounds(String attr, Vector images)
   throws MalformedURLException {
   Hashtable result = new Hashtable();

   int imageNum = 0; // the counter index
   int numImages = images.size(); // max sounds to get
   for (int i = 0; i < attr.length(); ) { // begin loop
       if (imageNum >= numImages) break; // too many!?

       int next = attr.indexOf('|', i); // pipe?
       if (next == -1) next = attr.length(); // done?

       String sound = attr.substring(i, next);
       if (sound.length() != 0) {
           result.put(new Integer(imageNum),
                   new URL(soundSource, sound));
       }
       i = next + 1;
       imageNum++;
   }
   return result;
   }
```

This method, `parseSounds()`, breaks apart the sound string, passed into it by the `attr` parameter, placing each sound file in a `HashTable` object. Since each sound is played in sync with the individual frames of an animation sequence, an additional `Vector` object parameter is used to establish the maximum number of sounds to read in. While this may be a bit complex, depending on your needs, an alternative approach might have been to use a `StringTokenizer` object.

For more details on the `HashTable`, `Vector`, and `StringTokenizer` classes, see Chapter 12.

Going Gold

Whenever you decide to actually embed an applet inside an HTML file, you're working under the assumption that the applet is ready to be used. If it's not, you can do a number of things to ensure it's prepared for prime time.

Of course, you need to test your applets internally before releasing them to the general public, since you can't always guarantee they'll work the way you want in widespread distribution. However, even before entering the test phase, you can do the following things to prepare your applets for mass consumption:

✦ You can remove debugging output.

✦ You can stop the applet from running any of its threads when it's no longer onscreen.

In Proper Context

The `getAppletContext()` method, defined in `java.applet.Applet`, allows us to obtain a reference to the environment our applets are running in, which is usually the browser or Applet Viewer. Once you have an applet's context, there are a handful of methods declared in the `java.applet.AppletContext` interface (Table 15-3) that you can use with it.

Two of the methods you may find particularly interesting are `showStatus()` and `showDocument()`. The former allows us to send messages to the browser's status area, while the latter makes is possible to open URLs, as if the applet itself were at the controls:

```
getAppletContext().showStatus("I'm working...please wait!");
```

You can keep the Web user informed of what's going on in your applet by sending messages to the browser's status area:

```
getAppletContext().showDocument("http://www.anywhere.org");
```

By sending the message `showDocument()`, along with a valid URL, the browser can make a connection to that address, as if the user of the browser had entered it manually. This example opens the page in the existing frame, although another `showDocument()` method is available which allows you to control which frame the page is displayed in. While applets are restricted from accessing files from anywhere on the Web but the server they come from, this does not apply to `showDocument()`! Feel free to pass any URL you'd like to this method; it can handle any URL you can enter manually into the browser, regardless of where it may point.

Table 15-3
java.applet.AppletContext Interface

Method	Signature	Description
getApplet	public abstract Applet getApplet (String name)	Gets an applet by name. Returns null if the applet doesn't exist.
GetApplets	public abstract Enumeration getApplets()	Enumerates the applets in this context. Only applets that are accessible are returned. This list always includes the applet itself.
GetAudioClip	public abstract Audio Clip get AudioClip (URL url)	Gets an audio clip. This usually involves downloading it over the Internet. However, the environment may decide to cache sounds. This method takes an array of URLs, each of which is tried until the sound is found.
GetImage	public abstract get Image(URL url) Image	Gets an image. This usually involves downloading it over the Internet. However, the environment may decide to cache images. This method takes an array of URLs, each of which is tried until the image is found.
ShowDocument	public abstract void showDocument (URL url)	Shows a new document. This may be ignored by the applet context.
ShowDocument	public abstract void showDocument(URL url, String target)	Show a new document in a target window or frame. This may be ignored by the applet context. This method accepts the following target strings: self—show in current frame. parent—show in parent frame. top—show in topmost frame. blank—show in new unnamed top-level window. "other"—show in new top-level window named "other".
showStatus	public abstract void show Status(String status)	Shows a status string, usually located at the bottom of the browser window.

In addition, you may wish to supply the Web user with information from inside your applet. You can do this in one of two ways. You can either throw information directly onto the applet itself, such as `initializing, please wait`, or you can use the status portion of the browser to send a message:

```
getAppletContext().showStatus("initializing, please wait");
```

Although you can't guarantee that the status method will be implemented in every browser, it's an elegant way of communicating with the user.

Either of these two ways of communication work, and are useful for supplying a variety of information. You may wish to inform the user of each step when something is happening in your applet, such as when you're loading a large file or preparing to do a time-consuming process. Or you may wish to alert users that something has gone wrong, as in the case of an exception that is too serious to ignore.

Since you can't guarantee that users will see or understand what you throw into a text string, it may be possible to pop up a dialog box or window that forces them to respond. This, however, assumes that whatever has occurred in your program requires dramatic and drastic user interaction. If you can get away with it, don't display a dialog box or a window at all; simply provide a way for the user to know what's going on (such as placing text on the applet itself) and you'll be all set. Only in the most extreme cases do you really want to force the user to interact with your program in such a manner.

The `<APPLET>` tag can be surrounded by other HTML tags, such as "center". These are treated just like any other standard HTML tags, allowing you to use the applet tag as you would any other HTML tag.

Dual-Purpose Applets

As you may have realized, it's possible to include applet and application functionality in one body of code. This is easy enough; simply include both a `main()` method and an `init()` method in the same program. The trick is in the `main()` method. First you'll need to create a frame in the `main()` method, for which all subsequent AWT graphics methods called from the application will be used, and then an instance of the class itself. Using this instance, you can invoke its `init()` and `start()` methods, kicking off the applet as you normally would.

Of course, applications don't accept parameters through an HTML file as an applet does. And so, you'd have to pass all parameters in on the command line, just as you would standard command-line arguments, then process them as you would in the applet. For example, suppose you wanted to create a dual-purpose class called `DuneBuggy`. You'd write the applet as normal, and then add the following `main()` method:

```java
public static void main (String args[]) {

    // process params passed on command line  before doing
    // anything else (see Chapter 10 for details)

    // then, create the frame:
    Frame theFrame = new Frame ("Running as an application!");
    theFrame.resize(500,500); // and resize as needed

    // next, create an instance of DuneBuggy class:
    DuneBuggy theApplet = new DuneBuggy();

    // now, add the applet to the frame and show it.
    // Use add() method defined in java.awt.Container,
    // which adds a component to a container:
    theFrame.add("Center", theApplet); // add it
    theFrame.show(); // and show it

    // finally, kick start the applet instance!
    theApplet.init(); // invoke init()
    theApplet.start(); // invoke start()
}
```

That's all there is to it. Just include a souped-up `main()` method along with the standard applet methods, and you have a dual-purpose piece of code. This is helpful when you have a program that you want to function as both an applet and an application and don't want to write or create separate versions of each. It creates a dual-purpose program for you.

Warning

There is one fatal flaw to dual-purpose programs: applications aren't executed inside a browser, so all calls to `getAppletContext()` return `null`. The result is a crash whenever you try to invoke a method that deals with the applet context, such as the following:

```java
getAppletContext().showStatus("Hello!"); // will crash!
getAppletContext().showDocument("http://www.anywhere.org");
    // will crash!
```

Preparing for the Future

Before placing your applet on the Web, it's a good idea to override the `getAppletInfo()` and `getParameterInfo()` methods. While `getAppletInfo()` is used to provide your applet with a version and author string, `getParameterInfo()` ensures parameters used are well documented.

Taking advantage of `getAppletInfo()` is simple. You need only override the method and return a string. Although this method is intended to provide your applet with a way to identify itself, its author, and the copyright, you're free to supply whatever you'd like:

```
public String getAppletInfo() {
        return "MyCoolApplet version 1.1, by J. Schmo. " +
                "Copyright 1998, all rights reserved!";
    }
```

While you may be tempted to go nuts here, it's a good idea to at least include your name and the name and version of your applet. If you don't care about the copyright to your work, you don't have to bother including a copyright notice as shown above. While this method doesn't serve any practical purpose at the moment, it will likely be put to use by browsers and Web page development software in the future. By including your applet's vital statistics today, you'll be well prepared for tomorrow.

The other "planning for the future" method you'll want to override is `getParameterInfo()`. This method provides a mechanism for your applet to formally document what parameters it can accept, and what is likely to be used in search engines and graphical applet configuration tools of the future (see Chapter 8, "Surfing The Web for Java Source Code" for details). However, unlike `getAppletInfo()`, this method is a bit more complex:

```
public String[][] getParameterInfo() { }
```

The `getParameterInfo()` method returns an array of strings describing the parameters that are understood by your applet. The array consists of groups of three strings, which must fall in specific order: the parameter name, the parameter's type, and a description of the parameter. Take, for example, the following snippet of code:

```
public String[][] getParameterInfo() {
  String[][] info = {
      {"imagesource", "URL", "a directory"},
      {"startup", "URL", "displayed at startup"},
      {"background", "URL", "displayed as background"},
      {"startimage", "int", "start index"},
      {"endimage", "int", "end index"},
      {"namepattern", "URL", "used to generate indexed names"},
      {"pause", "int", "milliseconds"},
      {"pauses", "ints", "milliseconds"},
      {"repeat", "boolean", "repeat or not"},
      {"positions", "coordinates", "path"},
      {"soundsource", "URL", "audio directory"},
      {"soundtrack", "URL", "background music"},
      {"sounds", "URLs", "audio samples"},
  };
  return info;
}
```

This example, taken from Sun's own `Animator` applet, lists each of the parameters the applet accepts, using the format "name, type, description." Of course, just as with `getAppletInfo()`, you're free to supply any information you'd like. However, in the interest of future compatibility with browsers and special tools that might make use of this information, it's best to use these methods as they were intended.

Summary

With this chapter you have added the ability to include applets into your Web pages using the `<APPLET>` tag. You should remember the following key attributes of the `<APPLET>` tag:

✦ With `CODEBASE`, you can supply either an absolute URL (one that specifies a complete address) or a relative URL, which specifies an address relative to the current document's location.

✦ Names are used to uniquely identify more than one applet on a page. This is particularly helpful when you want your applets to communicate with one another. Using the `NAME` attribute, you can give your applet a unique name.

✦ The `WIDTH` and `HEIGHT` attributes specify the width and the height of the applet when first executed. However, the applet itself can, and often does, resize itself using the `resize()` method.

✦ Since applets are integral portions of Web pages, the `ALIGN <APPLET>` tag definition allows us to align our applets in nine different ways: `left`, `right`, `top`, `texttop`, `middle`, `absmiddle`, `baseline`, `bottom`, and `absbottom`.

✦ You can gain even more control over your applet's position relative to the text around it by using the `VSPACE` and `HSPACE` attributes. `VSPACE` specifies how much space will appear in a vertical relation — that is, above or below — to your applet. `HSPACE` specifies the amount of horizontal space (from left to right) that will appear.

✦ The `ARCHIVE` tag can be used to specify a comma-separated list of JAR files that will be pre-loaded by your Web browser. Any time a file or class is required, the Web browser will first search the archive file before attempting to download it over the network.

✦ As you may have realized, it's possible to include applet and application functionality in one body of code. This is easy enough; simply include both a `main()` method and an `init()` method in the same program. The trick is in the `main()` method. First you'll need to create a frame in the `main()` method, for which all subsequent AWT graphics methods called from the application will be used, and then an instance of the class itself. Using this instance, you can invoke its `init()` and `start()` methods, kicking off the applet as you normally would.

✦   ✦   ✦

Abstract Windowing Toolkit

You're probably itching to learn how to develop even more complex Java applications. If you are, then the Abstract Windowing Toolkit is still your key to developing full-featured user interfaces for your Java applications. Although the AWT is being replaced by the Java Foundation Classes (JFC) in Java 1.2, understanding the AWT will help you support older Java applications and give you a solid foundation for understanding the JFC.

This part shows you how to add graphics, fonts, windows, and user interface controls—such as buttons, list boxes, combo boxes, menus, and sliders—to your own Java applications. Each AWT object described also includes a complete reference for you to use when you develop your own applications.

The best way to learn how to use the Java user interface classes is to use them to develop an actual application. This part wraps up with the step-by-step development of the JavaDraw application—a basic graphic-drawing application. You'll learn how to use the AWT classes to design and implement your application.

Finally, to get you ready to move to the latest and greatest Java Development Kit—version 1.2—this part introduces the powerful newcomers to JDK 1.2: the Java Foundation Classes (JFC), and the new user interface classes JFC includes—nicknamed Swing. A detailed review of each interface component in the Swing classes demonstrates why these classes are poised to replace the Abstract Windowing Toolkit for Java-based user interface development.

Abstract Windowing Toolkit Overview

Until now, the programs I've created have lacked a true graphical user interface (GUI). However, to create really compelling and useful software programs with Java, you're likely to need to implement one. After all, what good is a program without buttons, scroll bars, text fields, menus, check boxes, windows, and other GUI goodies?

To be fair, you can do quite a bit without a GUI (as DOS and UNIX programmers are quick to point out). However, whether you're creating Web applets or standalone applications, chances are good that you'll need a GUI component at some point, even if it's only a simple button.

This chapter introduces you to Java's GUI classes, known formally as the *Abstract Windowing Toolkit (AWT)*. The AWT is quite large and complex, as you soon see. As a result, I've broken the discussion of it into several chapters. In this chapter you learn about the AWT in a general sense: how it's organized, what it can do, and the basic concepts you need to understand to use it. In the chapters that follow, we put the pedal to the metal and make good use of the things you learn here.

Abstract Windowing Toolkit

The Java AWT is actually a generic user interface (UI) toolkit, a collection of classes that lets you create platform-independent user interfaces. Just as Java programs are platform independent, capable of running on any computer that has the Java runtime system installed, so too are the user interfaces created with the AWT.

You'll note that I didn't use the term *graphical user interface* to describe the AWT. This is because most people associate only a specific set of elements with a GUI, namely those things that a program uses to present windows and their contents (such as scroll bars, menus, and buttons).

Although the term *Windowing Toolkit* might lead you to believe that's all the AWT does, it really goes above and beyond the typical GUI to encompass all aspects of a user interface—not just GUI elements. An image that you draw on the screen, for example, is considered part of the UI. Whatever users see and, many believe, whatever they hear is part and parcel of a user interface.

The AWT actually includes methods that enable your applets to access and play audio clips. Because I've used these in earlier chapters, I'll stay focused on the portions of the `java.awt` package that provide a visual user interface.

A UI that you create using the AWT looks and acts appropriately for any platform on which it runs. With Java, you don't have to worry about writing code for a specific platform. And thanks to the AWT, you don't have to bother learning specific UI routines, either.

The AWT doesn't attempt to support every UI feature of every platform. Its aim is more modest: to provide the minimum necessary to develop a complete interface that is functional and consistent across all platforms. Even so, the AWT encompasses dozens of classes. Windows, dialog boxes, menus, buttons, scroll bars, text fields, check boxes, and drawing and painting canvases are but a few of the UI components the AWT offers. In addition, it provides an event mechanism that allows your UI to respond to user input, such as mouse clicks and key presses.

The AWT is designed to be extensible, allowing developers to subclass existing AWT classes and create their own, special-purpose GUI elements (animated 3D scroll bars, anyone?). Thanks to platform independence, the result is a brand-spanking new GUI widget that looks smashing on every user's computer.

This assumes, of course, that whatever special-purpose GUI element you create is, in fact, smashing. If it is dull and lifeless, it will look dull and lifeless on all platforms. But with Java, at least you have to write dull, lifeless GUI widgets only once, rather than having to write a special version for each platform on which your dull, lifeless program runs.

Fundamental organization

The AWT is quite complex and so large that it is organized into a main package (`java.awt`) and four supporting packages (`java.awt.event`, `java.awt.image`, `java.awt.datatransfer`, and `java.awt.peer`). Although you'll probably never use classes in the `java.awt.peer` package, the other packages contain a host of classes you'll want to dig right into. These classes are described in the following sections.

Note

Typically, peer objects are used only by those porting Java to a new platform, because they act as the glue between the AWT classes you use and the underlying operating system. Thanks to peers, AWT elements (windows, dialog boxes, buttons, menus, scroll bars, and so on) look and act as the underlying operating system dictates; actually, the underlying system creates and handles the AWT elements. Although you won't use them directly, peers ensure that your GUI appears exactly as the user would expect, regardless of what platform your program is executed on. Your applications will look slightly different on varying platforms because they will take on the look and feel of the platform on which they are running.

java.awt

The main `java.awt` package contains most of the classes and interfaces for creating graphical user interfaces. In this package, all the classes for creating windows, menus, buttons, check boxes, and other essential GUI elements are found. See Tables 16-1 and 16-2 for a listing of the interfaces and classes defined in `java.awt`.

Table 16-1
Package java.awt Interfaces

Interfaces	Description
Adjustable	Interface for objects that have an adjustable numeric value.
ItemSelectable	Interface for objects that contain selectable items
LayoutManager	Interface for objects that know how to lay out containers.
LayoutManager2	Interface for constraint-based layout managers.
MenuContainer	The superclass of all menu-related containers.
PrintGraphics	Ancestor of classes that define a graphics context for a printed page.
Shape	Interface for objects that represent geometric shapes.

Table 16-2
Package java.awt Classes

Classes	Description
AWTEvent	Granddaddy of all AWT event classes.
AWTEvent Multicaster	Defines a multicasting event dispatcher.
BorderLayout	An NSEW-style (North, South, East, West, and Center) border bag layout.

(continued)

Table 16-2 *(continued)*

Classes	Description
Button	A class that produces a labeled button component.
Canvas	A canvas component. This is a generic component that needs to be subclassed to produce some functionality.
CardLayout	A layout manager that contains several "cards." Only one card is visible at a time, allowing you to flip through them.
Checkbox	A Checkbox object is a graphical user interface element that has a boolean state.
CheckboxGroup	This class is used to create a multiple-exclusion scope for a set of check box buttons.
CheckboxMenu Item	This class produces a check box that represents a choice in a menu.
Choice	The Choice class is a pop-up menu of choices. The current choice is displayed as the title of the menu.
Color	A class to encapsulate RGB and HSB (hue saturation) colors.
Component	A generic Abstract Windowing Toolkit component.
Container	A generic Abstract Windowing Toolkit container-object component that can contain other components.
Cursor	Encapsulates a bitmap that represents a mouse cursor.
Dialog	A class that produces a dialog box (a window that takes input from the user).
Dimension	A class to encapsulate a width and height dimension.
Event	A platform-independent class that encapsulates events from the graphical user interface.
EventQueue	A platform-independent class that queues events from the underlying system and from trusted applications.
FileDialog	Displays a file selection dialog.
FlowLayout	This is used to lay out buttons in a panel.
Font	A class that produces font objects.
FontMetrics	A fontmetrics object.
Frame	A frame is a top-level window with a title.
Graphics	Graphics is the abstract base class for all graphic contexts for various devices.
GridBag Constraints	GridBagConstraints is used to specify constraints for components laid out using the GridBagLayout class.
GridBagLayout	A flexible layout manager for positioning components.

Classes	Description
GridLayout	A layout manager for a container that lays out grids.
Image	The Image class is an abstract class. The image must be obtained in a platform-specific way.
Insets	The insets of a container. This class is used to lay out containers.
Label	A component that displays a single line of read-only text.
List	A scrolling list of text items.
MediaTracker	A utility class to track the status of a number of media objects.
Menu	A menu that is a component of a menu bar.
MenuBar	A class that encapsulates a platform's concept of a *menu bar* bound to a frame.
MenuComponent	The superclass of all menu-related components.
MenuItem	A string item that represents a choice in a menu.
MenuShortcut	Defines the class of keyboard accelerators for menu items.
Panel	A panel Container class. This produces a generic container.
Point	An *x,y* coordinate.
Polygon	A polygon consists of a list of *x* and *y* coordinates.
PopupMenu	A menu that can dynamically pop up at a specified location in a component.
PrintJob	Provides printing support for applications.
Rectangle	A rectangle defined by *x, y,* width, and height.
Scrollbar	A scroll bar component.
ScrollPane	A container that provides scrolling support for its client.
TextArea	A multiline area that displays text.
SystemColor	Provides symbolic names for the colors of UI features, such as buttons, captions, control highlights and shadows, and so on.
TextComponent	A component that allows the editing of some text.
TextField	A component that allows the editing of a single line of text.
Toolkit	An AWT toolkit. It is used to bind the AWT classes to a particular native toolkit implementation.
Window	A window is a top-level window with no borders and no menu bar. It can be used to implement a popup menu.

The basic java.awt class hierarchy is shown in Figure 16-1.

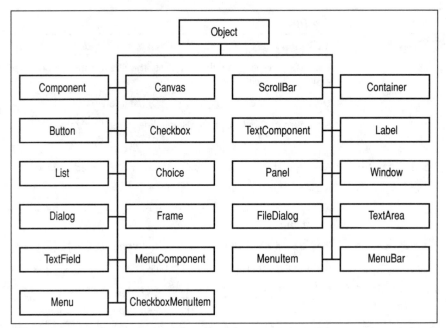

Figure 16-1: The java.awt class hierarchy is comprised of a large number of classes that together form the AWT.

As you can see, the `java.awt` package contains a number of classes that together form the AWT. There are three aspects to the class hierarchy:

✦ Primitive graphics

✦ Fonts

✦ Standard GUI elements

Let's take a closer look at each aspect.

Note

The word *windowing* in *Abstract Windowing Toolkit* might lead you to believe that the AWT is only used to create and manage window objects. In truth, it's used to create window and dialog objects, along with anything you might associate with them (buttons, menus, scroll bars, and the like), and whatever you see going on inside windows and dialog boxes (text output, text output in a specific font, drawing of vector graphics, painting of bitmap graphics, animation of both vector and bitmap graphics, and anything else the user sees).

Primitive graphics

The main `java.awt` package includes `Graphics`, a class that defines a primitive set of drawing methods that enable you to draw and fill lines, rectangles, ovals, polygons, and arcs. These can be drawn and filled by using a preset range of colors or by using ones you define yourself (see Figure 16-2). In addition, the `java.awt` package provides methods for clearing, clipping, and copying the drawing area, giving you the ability to manipulate images and graphics after they are placed on the screen.

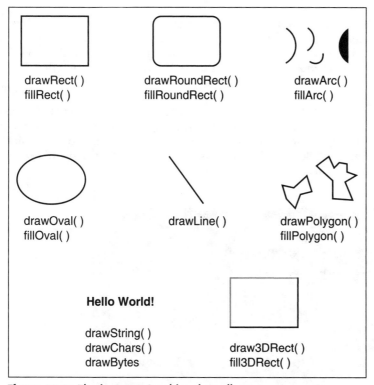

Figure 16-2: The java.awt.Graphics class allows you to create and draw primitive graphics.

The AWT contains an abstract class called Image and a subpackage of classes (java.awt.image), both for dealing with bitmap images. Initially, you won't work with these classes directly, because the Graphics class implements all the methods you'll need to use bitmap images.

In addition to using the image methods provided in the Graphics class, you can always create a subclass of Image for your own purposes. The Image class contains abstract methods that you must implement for a specific platform. For example, you might create a subclass of Image in order to create a class that allows you to use .BMP (BitMaP) format images.

Tip

At times, the only way to tell if I'm talking about the Image class (java.awt.Image) or the image package (java.awt.image) is by the capitalization of the word *Image* for a class. Class names begin, by convention, with a capital letter. Packages, however, are typically all lowercase.

Currently, the AWT supports .GIF and .JPEG image formats. You can easily retrieve and draw graphics of both formats, either directly from the local hard drive or over the network, just as you did with the MediaHelloWorld applet.

Fonts

Many graphics systems treat fonts as actual graphics, and the AWT is no different. After all, fonts are the graphical representation of characters. If characters, strings, numbers, and letters were never displayed on the screen, there would be no need for fonts. However, as soon as you output these things to the screen, they become graphics.

With the `Font` class (`java.awt.Font`), you can output text using any typeface you want; for example, Times Roman, Courier, Helvetica, and Zapf Dingbats. You can also choose from styles such as regular, bold, italic, and underlined, and point sizes such as 8pt, 12pt, 36pt, and 72pt. Figure 16-3 shows an example of text output in a number of faces, styles, and point sizes.

Figure 16-3: The java.awt.Font class enables you to draw text on the screen in a variety of faces (fonts), sizes, and styles.

Warning

Although you can tell Java to use any font you like, be warned that not all users have the same fonts on their computer as you do. Although you may be able to see a specific font when the applet is running on your computer, others may see a substitute that doesn't look anything like what you want! Play it safe, and be conservative in your font choices (see the next section, "Standard GUI elements").

Standard GUI elements

When most people think of the AWT, they think of it in terms of a graphical user interface toolkit. Indeed, the AWT is often considered a GUI toolkit simply because of the name. After all, what do you think of when you hear the word *windowing*? You think of all the widgets that usually come along for the ride: menus, scroll bars, buttons, text fields, check boxes, and Bill Gates.

Note   Be honest—you can't possibly hear the word *windowing* without thinking of Bill Gates. I won't venture to guess exactly what runs through your mind at that moment, and I'm not about to share the contents of mine (at least not here . . . drop me a line), but don't lie to yourself. I'll be spending the next quarter-century shaking the residue of Bill's $200,000,000 Windows 95 promotional campaign out of my subconscious. Heck, I'll be lucky if, by the year's end, I can get myself to stop breaking into a spontaneous Rolling Stones "Start Me Up" lip-synch and shimmy every time I hear *windows*. And by that time, I'll almost certainly be facing a Windows 98 campaign!

All such widgets, including windows and dialog boxes themselves, descend from the Component class (see Figure 16-4). To keep our terminology clear and simple, I refer to anything that falls under the Container class (panels, applets, windows, dialog boxes, file dialogs, and frames) as containers. You can put other components and containers in them.

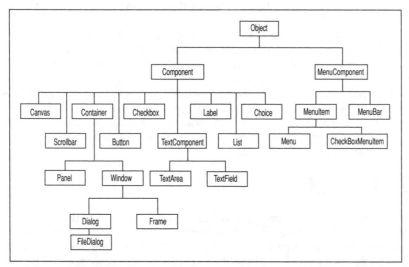

Figure 16-4: The majority of AWT classes you'll use are direct descendants of the java.awt.Component class.

As for the buttons, scroll bars, text fields, and other user interface elements, I'll refer to them all as *widgets*. If the term *widgets* gets under your skin, feel free to substitute your favorite term every time I say it (might I suggest *doohickey*, *dealybobber*, or perhaps *thingamajig?*).

It's not that I mean to belittle these essential creatures, but I think *element* is a bit too stuffy and serious to use when referring to buttons, scroll bars, and their ilk. And I don't want to refer to them as components because I use that term when talking about anything that falls under the `Component` class.

Some folks might like the term *control*, which most of these things are, but I prefer to group them all under a more general term, since some of them (labels and canvases, specifically) don't actually control anything. More importantly, I just can't let go of the word *widget* when it comes to classifying these things. Whenever I see one, the words *widget . . . Widget . . . WIDGET!!* insidiously enter my mind, refusing to go away. Sadly, I'm compelled to pass this compulsion on to you.

When referring to both containers and widgets, I'll use the term *component*. With this, we have a simple and effective jargon for AWT elements:

✦ **Containers:** Panels, applets, windows, dialogs, file dialogs, and frames.

✦ **Widgets:** Buttons, scroll bars, text fields, and other user interface elements; need I say more?

✦ **Components:** Encompassing every descendant of the `Component` class.

As you'll soon see, using the AWT to build a UI is quite easy. You just create a container, if you even need one (more on that later), and slap on widgets to your heart's desire. Of course, they'll do you no good whatsoever, but they sure look cool.

What's this? Worthless widgets? Delinquent doohickeys? Trivial thingamajigs? Yes, indeed. They may look pretty, but don't be deceived: It's all fluff. Clicking them will get you nowhere—until, of course, you respond to the events they generate.

Notice how I refer to interacting with the user, not webber (even though webber is nearly as gratifying to say as widget)? This is because you can use the AWT to develop both applications and applets. Although the bulk of this chapter and the next are geared towards developing applets, you can apply what you read to developing Java applications as well.

Handling Events

Events are what enable your program to interact with a user. (See the "About Events" sidebar.) Whenever a user interacts with an element of your program's user interface through the keyboard, the mouse, a button, or a menu item, the element generates an event. To react to an event, it's necessary to create some code that executes whenever the event occurs—this is called *trapping* the event. By trapping events, your program can respond to the user's input in a meaningful way.

About Events

An *event* refers to any unpredictable change of state in a program's environment. Two kinds of events occur in a typical environment: physical events and simulated events. A *physical* event corresponds to a change of state in the system's physical environment, such as a user's mouse movement. A *simulated* event corresponds to a change of state in a simulated environment, such as a graphical user interface. For example, window systems, such as Windows 95 and Motif, generate a simulated event whenever a user interacts with a visual control, such as a push button or a menu item.

Semantic events are an important subclass of simulated events. A *semantic* event conveys a specific meaning to the application program and is often defined independently of a particular type of widget. For example, in the Java environment, several different types of widgets, including buttons, menu items, and check boxes, can generate a type of semantic event known as an action event. An *action* event means "Perform the action associated with this component."

Every system provides a standard mechanism for detecting, queuing, and responding to events. This mechanism, known as an *event model,* typically divides event-handling duties between the operating system and the application. The operating system handles event detection and queuing, because these tasks are generic. The application program handles the task of responding to events in specific ways, as dictated by the application.

Java provides two system-independent mechanisms, or models for handling events, known as the *hierarchical model* and the *delegation model.* The hierarchical model, so-called because it assigns event-handling duties to a program's widget-container hierarchy, came first and is considered obsolete. However, at this point only standalone Java interpreters support its replacement, the delegation model, which lets a program delegate event-handling chores to any properly qualified object. If you want to create an applet, you must use the hierarchical model, at least until browsers that support the delegation model become available. Because you may have occasion to use either model, you will learn how to use both in this chapter.

From a practical perspective, the main difference between the two models lies in how a program traps events. In the hierarchical model, a program traps events by overriding certain default methods defined by the AWT's `Component` class. For example, if you want to trap a button click, you override the button's `action()` method or the `action()` method of its container. With the delegation model, on the other hand, you trap events by registering event handlers, called *listeners*, with the components in which the events occur. For example, if you want to trap a button click, you register an action listener with the button. In either case, you need to have a basic understanding of how the model operates in order to use the model successfully. So let's explore each model in turn.

The hierarchical model

The hierarchical model is an object-oriented model: It treats events as objects and as if they occur in objects, specifically UI components, such as button or panels. From your perspective as a Java developer, the most important feature of the hierarchical model is that it provides a means for you to trap and respond to events as they occur in your program's UI. The way you do this is by overriding default AWT event-handling methods, replacing them with your own. Which methods you override depends on the type of events you want to trap and where they occur in your program's UI. To know which methods to override, you need to know the basics of the hierarchical model event-handling mechanism.

The mechanism works as follows. Whenever an event occurs, the Java interpreter calls the handleEvent() method of the UI component in which the event occurs, passing it an instance of the java.awt.Event class. The method processes the event, using information about the event provided by the fields of the Event object, which includes the event's type (ID), the object in which it occurred (target), the time it occurred, and other data specific to that type of event, such as the position of the mouse in the case of mouse events (see Table 16-3).

Table 16-3
java.awt.Event Instance Variables

Variable	Description
int ID	The ID of the event (refer to Table 16-2).
Object target	The "target" of an event (CheckBox, Button, ScrollBar, Textfield objects, and so on). Use the instanceof keyword to find the target.
long when	Time-stamp (when the event was generated).
int x, int y	The coordinates (x,y) where the event occurred.
int key	Key that was pressed (keyboard events).
Object arg	Arbitrary argument associated with an event (such as the name of the button selected).
int modifiers	State of the modifier keys when an event was generated.

The Event class simplifies the job of handleEvent() by defining constants for every type of event recognized by the hierarchical model (see Table16-4).

Table 16-4
Component-Generated Events

Component	Event ID	Description
Button	ACTION_EVENT	The user clicked the button.
Check Box	ACTION_EVENT	The user clicked the check box.
Choice	ACTION_EVENT	The user selected an item.
Component	GOT_FOCUS	The user got input focus.
Component	KEY_ACTION	The user pressed a function key.
Component	KEY_ACTION_RELEASE	The user released a function key.
Component	KEY_PRESS	The user pressed a key.
Component	KEY_RELEASE	The user released a key.
Component	LOST_FOCUS	The user lost input focus.
Component	MOUSE_ENTER	The mouse entered the component.
Component	MOUSE_EXIT	The mouse exited the component.
Component	MOUSE_DOWN	The user pressed a mouse button.
Component	MOUSE_UP	The user released a mouse button.
Component	MOUSE_MOVE	The user moved the mouse.
Component	MOUSE_DRAG	The user dragged the mouse.
List	ACTION_EVENT	The user double-clicked a list item.
List	LIST_SELECT	The user selected a list item.
List	LIST_DESELECT	The user deselected a list item.
MenuItem	ACTION_EVENT	The user selected a menu item.
ScrollBar	SCROLL_LINE_UP	The user requested scroll line up.
ScrollBar	SCROLL_LINE_DOWN	The user requested scroll line down.
ScrollBar	SCROLL_PAGE_UP	The user requested scroll page up.
ScrollBar	SCROLL_PAGE_DOWN	The user requested scroll page down.
ScrollBar	SCROLL_ABSOLUTE	The user requested an absolute change.
TextField	ACTION_EVENT	The user pressed Enter.
Window	WINDOW_DESTROY	The window was destroyed.
Window	WINDOW_ICONIFY	The window was iconified.
Window	WINDOW_DEICONIFY	The window was deiconified.
Window	WINDOW_MOVED	The window was moved.

The AWT supports the hierarchical model by defining a default `handleEvent()` method in the `Component` class, the ancestral class for all AWT UI components. Every AWT widget either inherits or overrides this default method. Aha! Finally, we've discovered the secret to handling events in the hierarchical method. Just override the `handleEvent()` method of components in which events of interest occur. Actually, the situation is a bit more complicated than that.

For one thing, the AWT's default `handleEvent()` method acts as an event-handling switch, diverting certain common types of events, specifically keyboard, mouse, and action events, to more specific event-handling methods. For these types of events, it makes more sense to override the more specific default methods (see Table 16-5). Moreover, if the event is not an action or mouse event, or the more specific method does not handle the event, the default `handleEvent()` method kicks the event upstairs to the `handleEvent()` method of its containing object, where the whole process is repeated on a higher level in your UI's hierarchy (hence the name hierarchical model). What this means is that it is possible for you to handle all events at a high level in the hierarchy. In fact, in the case of applets, you can handle all events at the highest level, namely the applet itself. That's because unless your applet spawns secondary windows—it is the top-level container in its UI hierarchy.

Table 16-5
Default Event-Handling Methods

Event ID	Method	Description
ACTION_EVENT	`action(Event, Object)`	User selected a menu item, a button or check box, or the contents of a choice, text, or list control.
KEY_PRESS	`keyDown(Event, int)`	Key-press keyboard event.
KEY_RELEASE	`keyUp(Event, int)`	Key-release keyboard event.
KEY_ACTION	`keyDown(Event, int)`	Key action (press + release) keyboard event, generated when Function keys are pressed.
KEY_ACTION_ RELEASE	`keyUp(Event, int)`	Key action (press + release) keyboard event.
MOUSE_DOWN	`mouseDown(Event, int, int)`	Mouse-down event.
MOUSE_UP	`mouseUp(Event, int, int)`	Mouse-up event.
MOUSE_MOVE	`mouseMove(Event, int, int)`	Mouse-move event.
MOUSE_ENTER	`mouseEnter(Event, int, int)`	Mouse-enter event.
MOUSE_EXIT	`mouseExit(Event, int, int)`	Mouse-exit event.
MOUSE_DRAG	`mouseDrag(Event, int, int)`	Mouse-drag event.

When developers use the hierarchical model, they generally elect to handle events at the highest possible level in the UI hierarchy, specifically at the applet level in the case of applets. Here's the reason why. To trap events at a lower level in the hierarchy, you must override the default event-handling methods of the lower-level components. This, in turn, entails creating a new class derived from the appropriate AWT component class, for example, the `Button` class. If you elect to handle events at a low level, you end up having to create a bunch of new classes, often for no reason other than to customize event handling. In contrast, if you handle events at a higher level, you cut down significantly on the number of new classes you need to create. In the case of applets, you need to create only one new class, namely a derivative of the AWT's `Applet` class. This is hardly a burden, because as you've seen, developing an applet entails subclassing `Applet` anyway.

Now let's take a look at handling a common type of event.

Handling action events

The AWT provides a set of widgets that lets a user control various aspects of a Java program. This set includes the widgets defined by the AWT's `Button`, `CheckBox`, `Choice`, `List`, `MenuItem`, and `TextField` classes. The following chapters explore these widgets in detail. For the moment, it's enough for you to know that when a user interacts with any of them—for example, when a user clicks a button or double-clicks a list item—the widget posts an `ACTION_EVENT` event. You can trap and handle the event by overriding the `action()` method of the target widget or its container.

As Table 16-5 reveals, when an action event occurs, the `handleEvent()` method of the relevant component passes two parameters to the `action()` method: an Event instance and an Object parameter:

```
public boolean action(Event evt, Object what) {
  ...
}
```

The Event instance provides all the information you really need to identify an event. However, as a convenience, `handleEvent()` passes additional information in the Object parameter that simplifies identifying the event's target, such as the target's label in the case of buttons and menu items. The Object parameter is particularly useful when you assign action-handling chores to an `Applet action()` method. In this case, the `action()` method typically must identify the target of an action event to respond appropriately. The Object parameter makes this easy in the case of buttons and menu items. Simply query the Object parameter to find out the button or menu item's label:

```
public boolean action(Event evt, Object what) {
  if (evt.target instanceof Button) {// is this a Button event?
    String buttonName = (String)what; // retrieve name of
button
    ... // process based on which button it is
```

```
      return true; // terminate event; keep from going up
  hierarchy
    }
    if (evt.target instanceof Choice) {// is this a Choice menu
        event?
        // next, get rid of the selected Choice menu item:
      int item = Integer.getInteger((String)what)).intValue();
      ... // process based on which item it is
      return true;
    }
    return false;
  }
```

Notice that the preceding example returns true when it handles an event.
Returning true prevents handleEvent() from passing the event on up the UI
hierarchy.

Handling non-action events

AWT widgets produce other types of events besides action events. If the events are
any of the types specified in Table 16-5, you can process them by overriding the
corresponding default handler. If you want to trap events for which there is no
specific handler—for example, scroll bar or window events—you'll have to
override the target widget's (or its container's) handleEvent() method.

As you have already seen, whenever an event occurs, the Java runtime
environment invokes the handleEvent() method of the component in which it
occurs, passing it an Event instance. Because the default handleEvent() method
automatically passes the event up the widget hierarchy, you can override this
method at any convenient point in the hierarchy. The first thing your customized
method should do is test the ID field of the Event instance to determine the type of
event being processed. If the event is of interest, go ahead and process it.
Otherwise, invoke the AWT's default handleEvent() method:

```
  public boolean handleEvent(Event e) {
    if (e.id == Event.WINDOW_DESTROY) {
    // Do window exit cleanup.
    return true; // indicate event was handled
    }
    return super.handleEvent(e);
  }
```

Note that a common mistake is to forget to invoke the default AWT
handleEvent() method for events not handled by a custom handleEvent()
method. This can short-circuit the handling of other events. For example, suppose
that your program includes a custom action() method as well as a custom
handleEvent() method. If the custom handleEvent() method does not invoke
the default handleEvent() method, your custom action() method is not invoked
either. As a result, your program ignores all action events, which is probably not
what you want to happen.

The delegation model

Like the hierarchical model, the delegation model is object-oriented: events are objects and occur in objects (widgets, for example). Some significant differences show up, however. For one, unlike the hierarchical model, which defines only one event class, the delegation model defines an entire hierarchy of events (see Table 16-6) derived from a common ancestor, the AWTEvent class. AWTEvent class defines the general characteristics of events. The specific classes extend this common definition to include the characteristics of specific types of events, such as mouse events, action events, and so on. Representing events by a class hierarchy instead of a single class is not only more object-oriented, it also makes it possible for developers to extend the event hierarchy (by defining new subclasses of AWTEvent).

The delegation model differs from the hierarchical model in another important way. The hierarchical model predetermines which object handles events. By contrast, the delegation model lets a program delegate event handling to any object it chooses as long as that object implements an interface of type EventListener. An object that implements the EventListener interface, which is defined in the java.util package, is called a *listener*. The jave.awt.event package defines specific listener interfaces for all the event classes defined by the AWT (see Table 16-5). Each listener interface declares methods for handling a particular class of events. Any object that implements a listener interface can be a listener for the corresponding class of events.

A program delegates event handling to a listener by registering the listener at run-time with a component. A program can register as many listeners with a component as it likes, including multiple listeners for a particular class of events. A program can also remove listeners at any time. Each AWT component provides methods for registering listeners for each of the classes of events that can occur in it. By convention, these methods are named addEVENTListener(), where EVENT is the name of the class of event handled by the listener; for example, addActionListener(). Each component also provides methods for removing listeners. By convention, these methods are named removeEVENTListener(), where EVENT is the corresponding event class; for example, removeActionListener().

Whenever an event occurs in a component, the component dispatches the event to all the listeners registered for that class of event. If more than one listener is registered for a particular class of events, the component calls the listeners, although not necessarily in the order in which the program registered them. The program dispatches an event by calling a method specifically defined for that event in the corresponding interface. For example, the MouseListener interface defines mouseClicked(), mouseEntered(), mouseExited(), mousePressed(), and mouseReleased() methods for mouse clicked, entered, exited, pressed, and released events, respectively. Whenever one of the events occurs in a component, the component calls the corresponding method of any previously registered mouse listeners. For example, if the event is a mouse click, the component calls the mouseClicked() method.

Note that the delegation model does not guarantee that a component will dispatch events to listeners in a particular order. Moreover, when passing an event to multiple listeners, a component makes a fresh copy of the event for each listener. Thus, one listener cannot communicate with another by altering an event's instance variables. The moral is, if you want to set up a chain of event listeners, register only the root of the chain with the component, and make each handler responsible for invoking the next handler in the chain.

Table 16-6
Delegation Model Event Hierarchy

Class	Listener	Description
ActionEvent	ActionListener	Generated when a user selects a menu item, button, or check box; selects a choice or list element; or presses Enter in a text field.
AdjustmentEvent	AdjustmentListener	Generated when the size of an adjustable object, such as a scroll bar, changes.
ComponentEvent	ComponentListener	Generated when the layout of a component changes (for internal use only).
ContainerEvent	ContainerListener	Generated when a container object changes.
FocusEvent	FocusListener	Generated when a widget gains or loses keyboard input focus.
InputEvent	n/a	For internal use.
ItemEvent	ItemListener	Produced when the user selects a check box, or a list or choice item.
KeyEvent	KeyListener	Produced by a key down or up event.
MouseEvent	MouseListener, MouseMotionListener	Produced by a mouse event.
PaintEvent	n/a	For internal use.
TextEvent	TextListener	Generated when the contents of a text widget changes.
WindowEvent	WindowListener	Generated when a window opens or closes or changes its state in some other way.

Creating listeners

Because event handling depends on the application, the delegation model does not define event listeners for you. This is a task you have to perform yourself. The way you define a listener for a specific class of events is by creating a class that implements the corresponding interface. For example, to handle a button click, create a class that implements the methods declared by the ActionListener interface, and then register it with the button:

```
public class MyApplet extends Applet

  // Define "Do" button handler.
  class DoButtonListener implements ActionListener {
    public void actionPerformed(Event e) {
      // Perform "Do" button action.
    }
  }
class MyApplet extends Applet {
  // Construct applet.
  public MyApplet {
    // Create "Do" button and register listener.
    Button doButton = new Button("Do");
    // Register button listener.
    doButton.addActionListener(new DoButtonListener());
    // Add button to layout.
    add("Center", doButton);
  }
}
```

Dedicated versus non-dedicated listeners

The delegation model gives you a great deal of flexibility in implementing listener interfaces. At one extreme, you can define non-dedicated event listeners for each event type and each event source in your program (as in the preceding example). At the other extreme, you can define dedicated event listeners that handle multiple event types for multiple source objects as well as performing other functions. For example, in the preceding example I could have defined MyApplet as a listener for all action events that occur within it, effectively mimicking the hierarchical event model.

Although you are free to design listeners in any way you want, the dedicated listener approach makes sense in most applications. For one thing, dedicated listeners isolate event handling to small, easily identifiable chunks of code, making it easier to understand and modify your program. Also, dedicated listeners eliminate the need to identify the source of an event, greatly simplifying your code. But, you protest, using dedicated event handlers will mean a proliferation of classes—at least one class for every action widget in my applet or application— and this will make my program tedious to create and to read. In fact, it seems at first sight rather silly to clutter up a program with a lot of one-shot classes, each of which will never spawn more than one instance. The latest version of Java, however, introduces two facilities that greatly mitigate this objection: *event adapters* and *anonymous classes*.

Event adapters

The `java.awt.event` package defines a set of adapter classes specifically intended to simplify creation of dedicated listeners. Each mouse adapter class implements an interface for a corresponding listener interface. For example, the `MouseAdapter` class implements each of the methods declared by the `MouseListener` interface. Close inspection reveals that event adapter methods do nothing, so what's the big deal? The point is that when you derive a dedicated listener from an adapter class, you only have to implement the methods for the specific events that you want to handle. In contrast, if you derive your listener class from a listener interface, you have to implement all the methods declared by the interface, regardless of whether you are interested in all the events they handle.

Event adapters can greatly simplify listener creation. For example, suppose you want to create a listener to handle mouse down and mouse up events on a Canvas instance. Deriving your listener from the `MouseAdapter` class requires you to define only two methods, versus five methods if you derive your listener from the `MouseListener` interface.

Anonymous classes

An *anonymous class* is a class that has no name and only one instance. Version 1.1 of the Java Developers Kit extends the syntax of the `new` expression to let you define and instantiate an anonymous class in the same expression. The syntax consists of the `new` keyword, followed by the constructor of the parent class, followed by the class body of the anonymous class:

```
Object obj = new Object() {
  public String toString() {
    return "I am an instance of a class with no name";
  }
}
```

Anonymous classes are instances of *inner classes*, a new type of class defined by JDK 1.1. Unlike outer classes, which can appear only at the package level, inner classes can appear anywhere an expression can appear—even in the argument list of a function call. Anonymous inner classes allow you to code very tersely. In particular, they let you define, instantiate, and pass an object to a function in a single statement. This greatly facilitates creating dedicated event handlers, as the following example demonstrates:

```
public class MyApplet extends Applet
  // Construct applet.
  public MyApplet {
    // Create "Do" button and register listener.
    Button doButton = new Button("Do");
    // Define, instantiate and register button listener.
    doButton.addActionListener(new ActionListener() {
      public void actionPerformed(Event e) {
        // Perform "Do" button action.
```

```
        }
    });
    // Add button to layout.
    add("Center", doButton);
  }
}
```

Note that in this example, the anonymous listener appears to derive from an interface (`ActionListener`). In fact, Java derives the anonymous class from the `Object` class with the specified listener interface. The anonymous class body implements the specified listener interface.

Coordinate System

In all graphics systems, including Java, a coordinate system allows programmers to explicitly place items on the screen for users to see.

The *x,y* coordinates

As with most graphics systems, Java's coordinate system begins in the upper-left corner, at the *x,y* coordinate of 0,0. The *x* axis runs from left to right, and the *y* axis runs from top to bottom. This coordinate system is shown in Figure 16-5.

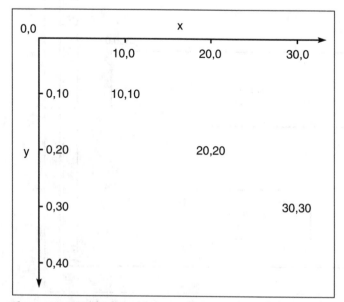

Figure 16-5: Java's graphics coordinate system, showing the horizontal *x* axis and the vertical *y* axis.

When you are drawing and painting in an applet, however, the coordinate system isn't what you might expect. The browser window has its own coordinate system, which your applet can't draw to. Your applet's coordinate system begins wherever the applet is placed on the screen, and you're allowed to draw only inside it (or create a window and draw inside that; more on windows in the next chapter). When you draw or paint in an applet, you're doing so in the coordinate system relative to that applet, not in the one relative to the browser (see Figure 16-6).

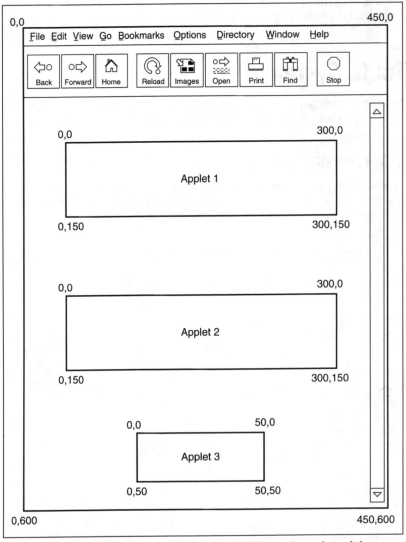

Figure 16-6: Your applet coordinate system is different from that of the browser in which it is executed.

Integer values

Keeping the Java coordinate system in mind, you can precisely place graphic elements directly on your applet using either two or four integer values:

✦ X: The *x* coordinate

✦ Y: The *y* coordinate

✦ width: Width of the item (optional in many methods)

✦ height: Width of the item (optional in many methods)

For example, when you painted a .GIF image on the screen (in Chapter 16), you supplied only the *x* and *y* coordinates to specify where on the applet to place the upper-left corner of that image. The width and height parameters for the image were automatically calculated for you.

Suppose, for example, that you wanted to draw an image on the screen with *x* and *y* coordinates of 25 and 16, respectively:

```
drawImage (myImage, 25, 18, this); // drawImage at 25, 18
```

When the image was drawn to the screen, you'd see the upper-left corner of the image appear at exactly 25, 18. The rest of the image would be drawn to the right and down, taking up as many pixels on the screen as the image measured in width and height. In this example, assume that the image is 45 pixels wide and 20 pixels high. When drawn on the screen, you'd see something similar to Figure 16-7.

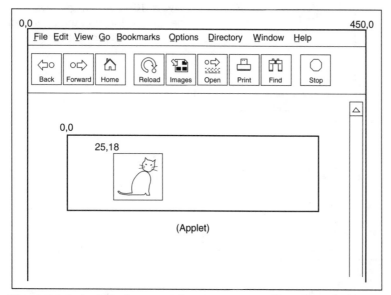

Figure 16-7: Images drawn on the screen are positioned precisely at the *x* and *y* coordinates supplied.

Tip

Another `drawImage()` method exists that takes both *x* and *y* and width and height parameters. (This method is described in the next chapter.) If the image isn't exactly the same width and height as the specifications you supply, it is scaled to fit. Using this method, you can stretch or shrink images at will.

Many other methods also take width and height parameters. Such is the case with `drawOval()`, which draws an oval of the size you choose:

```
drawOval(5, 5, 100, 150);// draw at 5,5 (100 pixels wide, 150 high)
```

Bounding box

Text, images, and graphics are contained in what is known as a *bounding box*. The upper-left corner of the bounding box is placed at the exact *x,y* coordinates you provide. This is important to realize, because you may rip your hair out trying to figure out why the image you positioned on the screen is appearing several pixels off the mark.

Images don't have to begin at the upper-left corner of their bounding box. For example, when you use graphics software to create .GIF and .JPEG images, you can control the size of the bounding box (often called a *canvas* in graphics programs, but not to be confused with the canvas component in Java). You might assume that the image begins at the upper-left corner, but it may not, as shown in Figure 16-8. If it doesn't, you may have a problem positioning it precisely where you want.

Figure 16-8: An image doesn't necessarily begin in the upper-left corner of its bounding box.

To see just how big the bounding box for an image is, open the image in a graphics package. If there is excessive space around the image, just crop it.

Dimension class

Because we use width and height parameters so often, the AWT provides a Dimension class that we can use to hold such values:

```
Dimension mySize = new anyAWTObject.size(); // place object's
size in mySize variable
int width = mySize.width; // width instance variable in
Dimension object
int height = mySize.height; // height instance variable in
Dimension object
```

This can be particularly helpful if you need to know the size of your applet. Simply call size() or this.size() in the init() method of your applet, and place the results in a Dimension object method. You can then retrieve the size of your applet through the Dimension object's width and height instance variables as needed later on.

Putting It All Together

As you may have noticed in Figure 16-4, an applet is actually a subclass of Panel, which is itself a subclass of Container. And Container, of course, is a descendant of Component. As a result of this inheritance tree, every applet already knows a great deal about handling user interaction, and also supports drawing and painting directly on it.

In fact, you've been taking advantage of this all along. You didn't have to create a container in which to draw your images, because applets inherit indirectly from the Container class. You just began slapping your text and image right on the applet, without bothering with such details.

However, as you get deeper into the AWT in the next chapter, you need to know how everything fits together. In particular, you need to see how the graphics coordinate system and the event-handling mechanism are affected as you create a real UI for your programs.

Without much effort, you can begin adding widgets to your applets. With a little more effort, you can handle the events that the applets generate when the user interacts with them. Again, because your applets are already containers, you can start slapping on the various UI elements you want without concerning yourself with the details.

Eventually, however, this may become impractical. In many cases, you'll want to create a nice, clean way to group the various widgets your program supports. You may also want a user to be able to resize the applet without screwing up the placement of your various graphics and widgets.

Note   Containers are things that we can draw to, paint on, and add widgets to. Windows, dialog boxes, and even your applets are descendants of the `Container` class.

Containers

To deal with both the grouping and resizing issue, you can create a container for each distinct group of UI elements. Suppose, for example, that you are developing a painting applet that supports a number of brushes and palettes. You might create two new windows and make them much like floating palettes in today's most popular graphics programs (see Figure 16-9).

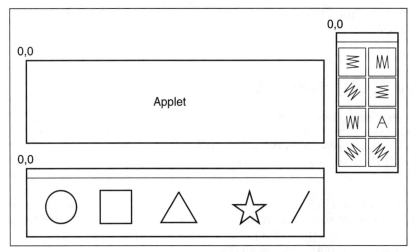

Figure 16-9: You can create a window container to group controls. Each container (such as these windows) has its own coordinate system.

You may also choose to instantiate a `Panel` object (which you learn about in more detail in Chapter 19) for each container and add them both to the applet. If you did this, you would be nesting containers. In either case, each container has its own coordinate system. As a result, you need to be aware of the containers your program uses, and take care to draw and paint according to their respective coordinate systems.

For example, an *x,y* coordinate of 250,300 might be valid for your applet, but completely out of the range of the other containers. However, because you can declare a `paint()` method for each container you create, you don't have to worry about managing the drawing and painting for every container through a single method.

Layout managers

Whenever you add a widget to a container, it gets placed on the screen according to placement rules imposed by whatever layout manager is associated with that container. As you learn in the next chapter, you don't place widgets on the screen using explicit *x,y* coordinates. Instead, you simply create them and add them using an add() method. Where they actually appear is based entirely on the layout manager being used by that container.

At first this may seem strange, but in reality it's quite necessary. Because all Java programs are supposed to be platform independent, allowing widgets to be placed at explicit screen locations would create a real problem. The coordinate system for your computer and for the computers of other potential users around the world aren't going to be the same. What looks just beautiful on your screen might be a jumbled mess on another.

And what if the user resizes the container? If you want your program to respond to resize directives, as real applications do, you'd have to rearrange your widgets accordingly. Because you would need to know details about the system on which the container has been resized to do a decent job, the whole idea becomes an utter nightmare to implement.

Rather than making you deal with such details, Java provides a layout mechanism that you can rely on instead. Your widgets are drawn in the order that you add them, according to the layout manager associated with the container to which they are added. When the container is resized, the layout manager rearranges and redraws each widget you've added to it, so you don't have to. As you learn in the next chapter, you can choose from a number of different layout managers, each of which lays out widgets differently.

Summary

The Java AWT is actually a generic user interface (UI) toolkit, a collection of classes that lets you create platform-independent user interfaces. Just as Java programs are platform independent, capable of running on any computer that has the Java runtime system installed, so too are the user interfaces created with the AWT.

✦ Whenever a user interacts with an element of your program's user interface, such as the keyboard, mouse, a button, or a menu item, the element generates an event. To react to an event, you must create some code that executes whenever the event occurs—this is called *trapping the event.*

✦ Even though I've discussed a good deal of the AWT, I really didn't do much in the way of actually programming. This should tip you off to how large the AWT is, since I've covered a considerable amount of material without getting into the nuts and bolts of it.

✦ As with most graphics systems, Java's coordinate system begins in the upper-left corner, at the x,y coordinate of 0,0. The x axis runs from left to right, and the y axis runs from top to bottom.

✦ You have learned about the fundamental organization of the AWT and how it encompasses graphics, text, fonts, color, bitmap images, and GUI components. This gives you a better understanding of how each part of the AWT works and how you can make use of it in your own programs.

✦   ✦   ✦

Graphics, Fonts, Color, and Images

In the previous chapter, we learned the fundamentals of the Abstract Windowing Toolkit (AWT). Now that we have an understanding of how it's organized and what it provides, it's time to put that knowledge to good use.

In this chapter we'll learn how to use the AWT to add graphics primitives, fonts, colors, and bitmap images to our programs. Along the way, we'll update our `FlexibleHelloWorld` applet to take advantage of color, and use a few new methods to position the image so that the cursor no longer obscures a portion of it when drawn.

We'll also take a look at graphics and animation techniques. We'll cover what I call "brute force" animation, and discuss a few of the ways to build a more elegant solution.

Finally, we'll show you how to print what you see on the screen. After all, what's the point of a snazzy-looking interface if you can't have the satisfaction of viewing it on good old-fashioned paper?

Graphics (java.awt.Graphics)

Java provides a set of graphics primitives that allow you to draw lines, rectangles, ovals, polygons, arcs, and even text directly on the screen. You can draw these primitives either outline (that is, without a fill) or with a fill, and in any color you desire.

As you may recall, drawing on the screen requires that you first have a Graphics object. We saw this in our previous HelloWorld applets. In these applets we used the paint() method to draw strings and images on the screen. The paint() method is provided, as its sole parameter, such a Graphics object. Using that object, we invoked graphics-based methods that did the work of placing text and bitmap images on the screen:

```
public void paint(Graphics g) {
    g.drawString("Hello World!",50,100); // text
    g.drawImage(myImage, horizontal, vertical, this); // image
    super.paint(g); // pass Graphics object up to the
                    // superclass paint() method
    }
```

Graphics operations, such as the drawString() and drawImage() methods shown previously, are always performed on a Graphics object. However, as you know, we don't have to actually create a new Graphics object just to draw on our applet. We simply override the paint() method, as we've been doing all along, and use the Graphics object that comes with it.

Note   In many of the code snippets sprinkled throughout this chapter, I don't bother to wrap a paint() method around graphics methods. This is to save you from seeing paint() over and over again, because I reckon you're pretty comfortable with it by now. However, I will always use a Graphics object:

```
g.drawString("Hello", 10, 10);
// invoke g's drawString method
```

If you assume that the g variable is a valid Graphics object, we'll get along just fine.

Of course, before you can send methods to a Graphics object, you have to import the Graphics class:

```
import java.awt.Graphics;
```

Note   In truth, you don't have to explicitly import a class (or package) before you can use it. You can always include the fully qualified name of the class directly in the body of your code. For details, see Chapter 11.

Once imported, the Graphics class is available for use, and can provide our programs with the capabilities we'll talk about in this chapter (see Table 17-1).

Table 17-1
java.awt.Graphics Constructor and Methods

Constructor	Signature	Description
Graphics	protected Graphics()	Constructs a new Graphics object.

Method	Signature	Description
clearRect	public abstract void clearRect(int x, int y, int width, int height)	Clears the specified rectangle by filling it with the current background color of the current drawing surface.
ClipRect	public abstract void clipRect(int x, int y, int width, int height)	Clips to a rectangle.
CopyArea	public abstract void copyArea(int x, int y, int width, int height, int dx, int dy)	Copies an area of the screen.
Create	public abstract Graphics create()	Creates a new Graphics object that is a copy of the original Graphics object.
Create	public Graphics create(int x, int y, int width, int height)	Creates a new Graphics object with the specified parameters, based on the original Graphics object.
Dispose	public abstract void dispose()	Disposes of this graphics context.
draw3DRect	public void draw3Drect(int x, int y, int width, int height, boolean raised)	Draws a highlighted 3D rectangle.

(continued)

	Table 17-1 *(continued)*	
Method	**Signature**	**Description**
DrawArc	public abstract void drawArc(int x, int y, int width, int height, int startAngle, int arcAngle)	Draws an arc bounded by the specified rectangle from startAngle to endAngle.
DrawBytes	public void drawBytes(byte drawData [], int offset, int length, int x, int y)	Draws the specified bytes using the current font and color.
DrawChars	public void drawChars(char data[], int offset, int length, int x, int y)	Draws the specified characters using the current font and color.
DrawImage	public abstract boolean drawImage(Image img, int x, int y, Image Observer observer)	Draws the specified image at the specified coordinate (*x,y*).
drawImage	public abstract boolean drawImage(Image img, int x,int y, int width, int height, Image Observer observer)	Draws the specified image inside the specified rectangle.
DrawImage	public abstract boolean drawImage(Image img, int x, int y, Color bgcolor, ImageObserver observer)	Draws the specified image at the specified coordinate (*x,y*), with the given solid background color.
DrawImage	public abstract boolean drawImage(Image img, int x, int y, int width, int height, Color bgcolor, ImageObserver observer)	Draws the specified image inside the specified rectangle, with the given solid background color.

Method	Signature	Description
DrawLine	public abstract void drawLine(int x1, int y1, int x2, int y2)	Draws a line between the coordinates (*x1,y1*) and (*x2,y2*).
DrawOval	public abstract void drawOval(int x, int y, int width, int height)	Draws an oval inside the specified rectangle using the current color.
DrawPolygon	public abstract void drawPolygon(int xPoints [],int yPoints[], int nPoints)	Draws a polygon defined by an array of *x* points and *y* points.
DrawPolygon	public void drawPolygon(Polygon p)	Draws a polygon defined by the specified polygon.
DrawRect	public void drawRect(int x, int y, int width, int height)	Draws the outline of the specified rectangle using the current color.
DrawRoundRect	public abstract void drawRoundRect(int x, int y, int width, int height, int arcWidth, int arcHeight)	Draws an outlined rounded corner rectangle using the current color.
DrawString	public abstract void draw String(String str, int x, int y)	Draws the specified string using the current font and color
fill3Drect	public void fill3Drect(int x, int y, int width, int height, boolean raised)	Paints a highlighted 3D rectangle using the current color.
FillArc	public abstract void fillArc(int x, int y, int width, int height, int startAngle, int arcAngle)	Fills an arc using the current color.

(continued)

Table 17-1 *(continued)*

Method	Signature	Description
FillOval	public abstract void fillOval (int x, int y, int width, int height)	Fills an oval inside the specified rectangle using the current color.
FillPolygon	public abstract void fillPolygon(int xPoints [], int yPoints[], int nPoints)	Fills a polygon with the current color.
FillPolygon	public void fillPolygon(Polygon p)	Fills the specified polygon with the current color.
FillRect	public abstract void fillRect(int x, int y, int width, int height)	Fills the specified rectangle with the current color.
FillRoundRect	public abstract void fillRoundRect(int x, int y, int width, int height, int arcWidth, int arcHeight)	Draws a rounded rectangle filled in with the current color.
Finalize	public void finalize()	Disposes of this graphics context once it is no longer referenced.
GetClip	public abstract Shape getClip()	Returns the current clipping area as a Shape object.
GetClipBounds	public abstract Rectangle getClip Bounds()	Returns the bounding rectangle of the current clipping area.
getClipRect	public abstract Rectangle getClipRect()	Deprecated—use getClipBounds instead.

Method	Signature	Description
GetColor	Public abstract Color getColor()	Gets the current color.
GetFont	public abstract Font getFont()	Gets the current font.
GetFontMetrics	public FontMetrics getFontMetrics()	Get the font metrics for the current font.
GetFontMetrics	public abstract FontMetrics getFontMetrics(Font f)	Get the font metrics for the specified font.
SetClip	public abstract void setClip(int x, int y, int width, int height)	Sets a rectangular clip area.
SetClip	public abstract void setClip(Shape clip)	Sets an arbitrarily shaped clip area.
SetColor	public abstract void setColor(Color c)	Sets the current color to the specified color.
SetFont	public abstract void setFont(Font font)	Sets the font for all subsequent text-drawing operations.
SetPaintMode	public abstract void setPaintMode()	Sets the paint mode to overwrite the destination with the current color.
SetXORMode	public abstract void setXORMode(Color c1)	Sets the paint mode to alternate between the current color and the new specified color.
ToString	public String toString()	Returns a String object representing this graphic's value.
Translate	public abstract void translate(int x, int y)	Translates the specified parameters into the origin of the graphics context.

For detailed descriptions of parameters and return types for each method, see Sun's API documentation, available at http://java.sun.com/.

Lines

Perhaps the simplest method in the `Graphics` class is the one that creates a straight line, so let's begin our exploration by using one. The `drawLine()` method takes four parameters, which specify the top, left, right, and bottom values that make up the coordinates for that line, thereby setting its position, width, and length:

```
g.drawLine(20,20,150,150); // a line at an angle
g.drawLine(200,10,200,300); // a vertical line
g.drawLine(0,200,120,200); // a horizontal line
```

If this example were executed, the lines in Figure 17-1 would be produced.

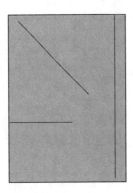

Figure 17-1: Examples of lines using the drawLine() method.

Rectangles

Java provides three different types of rectangles, each of which may be filled or left empty when drawn on the screen. To draw any one of these we must supply, at a minimum, four arguments: the two coordinates of the upper-left corner, and the rectangle's width and height. For the most basic of rectangles, that's all we need:

```
g.drawRect(15,20,150,150); // draw a plain rectangle
g.fillRect(15,185,150,150); // fill a plain rectangle
```

The first line of code draws a plain rectangle, beginning at the *x,y* position of 15,20. As it turns out, this rectangle is actually a perfect square, since it's as wide (150) as it is high (150).

The second line of code fills a plain rectangle of the same size as the first, but appears below the first one, since the vertical value of 185 is supplied. As you can see from Figure 17-2, there's nothing particularly special about these rectangles; they look exactly as you'd expect them to look.

Figure 17-2: A plain and a filled rectangle, created with drawRect() and fillRect().

Java also provides for rectangles with rounded corners, rather than the sharp, crisp corners of the rectangles we have just created. The methods that make this possible, drawRoundRect() and fillRoundRect(), accept two additional parameters that basic rectangles do not:

✦ arcWidth—horizontal diameter of the arc at the four corners (integer value)

✦ arcHeight—vertical diameter of the arc at the four corners (integer value)

These parameters determine just how sharp or rounded the corners of rounded rectangles are. The first determines how sharp the angle is on the horizontal, and the second determines how sharp the angle is on the vertical. Following is an example of drawing a rounded rectangle, as well as an example of how to fill one. The last two parameters in each method call control the arc width and height:

```
g.drawRoundRect(20,20,130,150,50,10);
g.fillRoundRect(20,185,150,150,30,30);
```

The larger the last two parameters become, the more rounded the rectangle. Increasingly large numbers begin to make a rectangle look more like a circle, until eventually it looks *exactly* like one.

Tip It is preferable to draw a circle using the oval methods, described in the next section. However, to draw a circle using the rounded rectangle methods, simply provide the height and the width of the rectangle for these two additional parameters:

```
g.drawRoundRect(20,185,150,150,150,150); // draws a circle
```

3D (beveled) rectangles

In addition to the plain and rounded rectangles we've just seen, the Graphics class provides methods for creating three-dimensional rectangles. No, these aren't three-dimensional in the sense that you may be thinking; they're simply beveled rectangles that look raised or pressed in, depending on one of the parameters you supply.

To create a 3D rectangle (or beveled rectangle, to be more precise) you merely supply the method draw3DRect() with the same parameters you would a standard rectangle, with one additional boolean value:

```
g.draw3DRect(10,10,100,100, false); // draw 3D rect, not raised
g.draw3DRect(150,10,100,100, true); // draw 3D rect, raised
```

If you provide a boolean value of true, the rectangle is raised, and it looks beveled. If you provide false, the rectangle is depressed (sigh) and looks as if it's been pressed in. You can draw and fill 3D rectangles in the same way as for the other two types of rectangles provided by Java:

```
g.fill3DRect(10,150,100,100, true); // fill 3D rect, raised

g.fill3DRect(150,150,100,100, false); // fill 3D rect, not raised
```

Figure 17-3 shows several 3D rectangles, both plain and filled.

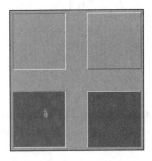

Figure 17-3: Java supports 3D rectangles, both plain and filled.

Ovals

Ovals are just as easy to use as the plain rectangle we learned about. In fact, when you draw an oval, you actually define a rectangle in which the oval will appear. You can draw in outline or filled ovals:

```
g.drawOval(10,10,50,100); // draw an oval
g.fillOval(150,10,130,20); // fill an oval
g.drawOval(150,50,40,20); // draw an oval
g.drawOval(100,50,40,10); // draw an oval
```

```
g.drawOval(200,50,40,90); // draw an oval
g.drawOval(10,150,100,100); // draw circle (same height width)
g.fillOval(150,150,30,30); // fill circle (same height width)
```

Figure 17-4 shows several ovals, the result of running the preceding code. As you can see, ovals can be a variety of shapes. They can look long and elliptical, or as round as a circle. In fact, in order to create a circle you should use the oval methods, by creating an oval that is exactly as wide as it is high. You can see this in the last two lines of code.

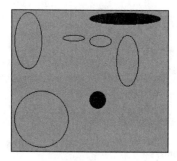

Figure 17-4: An example of ovals, which you can use to create circles.

Polygons

In addition to basic lines, rectangles, and ovals, you can also create polygons. These are much more complex than the simple graphics we have been discussing thus far. Polygons (affectionately known as "polys" to many programmers) can have any number of sides, each of which is specified as a pair of *x,y* coordinates. In fact, you can think of a polygon as a digital game of connect-the-dots.

Simply supply all the dots as *x,y* coordinates. When drawn, a line travels from dot-to-dot, connecting them in the order they were provided. You can optionally fill a polygon, as you can other graphics primitives. Figure 17-5 shows a plain and a filled polygon.

Figure 17-5: Polygons can have any number of sides, and are created by "connecting the dots." You specify these as a series of *x,y* points.

To create a polygon we use either the `drawPolygon()` or `fillPolygon()` method. When invoking these methods, we can either provide an array of *x* and *y* coordinates to specify the dots to be connected, or we can supply a `Polygon` object. Let's first take a look at how to create a polygon and then we will fill it and draw with it.

To create a polygon we simply instantiate a `Polygon` object:

```
Polygon myPoly = new Polygon(); // create new, empty poly
```

This creates an empty polygon, which we can then fill with *x,y* coordinates (dots, or points) using the `addPoint()` method:

```
myPoly.addPoint(40,40);
myPoly.addPoint(55,38);
myPoly.addPoint(65,55);
myPoly.addPoint(80,30);
myPoly.addPoint(80,75);
myPoly.addPoint(40,40);
```

Here we've added a number of points to our `Polygon` object. When we're done, we can give this polygon to the `drawPolygon()` or `fillPolygon()` methods:

```
g.drawPolygon(myPoly); // draw it
g.drawPolygon(myPoly); // fill it
```

Although this may be the easiest way to deal with polygons, it's not the only way. We could instantiate a `Polygon` object and supply an array of *x* coordinates, an array of *y* coordinates, and an integer number that specifies the total number of coordinates we'll be using. Instead of creating a `Polygon` object and then adding a point at a time, this allows us to create a polygon with all its points right off the bat:

```
int xCoords[] = {40,55,65,80,80,40}; // create x values
int yCoords[] = {40,38,55,30,75,40}; // create y values
Polygon myPoly =
    new Polygon(xCoords,yCoords,xCoords.getLength());
    // create poly from arrays
```

We can now pass this new polygon to the `fillPolygon()` or `drawPolygon()` method.

However, we don't necessarily have to create a `Polygon` object first. By supplying an array of *x* and *y* coordinates, in addition to the total number of points to connect, we can draw or fill the polygon directly:

```
g.drawPolygon(xCoords,yCoords,xCoords.getLength());
    // draw polygon
g.fillPolygon(xCoords,yCoords,xCoords.getLength());

    // fill polygon
```

Rather than instantiate a `Polygon` object, we can directly provide all the essential information to these `drawPolygon()` and `fillPolygon()` methods. This is useful if we want to draw or fill a polygon on the fly, but have no need to hang onto the object for later reference.

Tip

You can supply any number of points for your polygon. They can be incredibly complex or simple, depending on how you like them.

You can also have polygons that are "open," meaning the last point does not connect to the first point. Since we've specified the last *x,y* coordinate in these examples to be the same as the first *x,y* coordinate, the result is a "closed" polygon. However, if the first and last set of *x,y* coordinates are not the same, an "open" polygon is created.

Arcs

Finally, we come to the primitive graphic that may, at first, seem the most difficult to understand: the arc.

The first four coordinates of the arc are nothing new. They define the rectangle we used for the oval graphics described moments ago. Again, we provide an upper-left coordinate, and the height and width. The last two coordinates, however, can be quite confusing if you've never dealt with arcs before:

✦ x—the standard *x* coordinate

✦ y—the standard *y* coordinate

✦ width—the width of the arc's bounding box (rectangle)

✦ height—the height of the arc's bounding box (rectangle)

✦ startAngle—the angle to begin drawing the arc

✦ arcAngle—the angle of the arc (relative to startAngle)

The first of these two new parameters, startAngle, is the beginning angle of the arc. This value can run from 0 to 360. Contrary to intuition, these angles increase counterclockwise. Zero is at three o'clock, while 90 degrees is at twelve, 180 is at nine o'clock, and 270 is at six o'clock. It may help to draw this clock on a piece of paper. The value that you choose for the start angle determines, of course, where that arc's going to start. To get a better feel for the degrees you can choose for your start angle, see Figure 17-6.

It's the last parameter, arcAngle, however, that determines where the arc ends, by indicating how far the arc is going to travel.

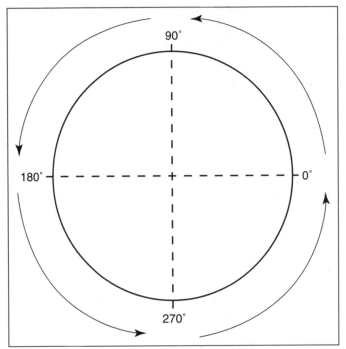

Figure 17-6: The arc startAngle parameter specifies an angle between 0 and 360 degrees. Such values begin at three o'clock (0), and run counterclockwise for the full 360 degrees.

Don't be confused by this ending argument. The `arcAngle` argument is not actually a specific angle, in the way that `startAngle` is. It's a magnitude—simply a value that tells you how far, in degrees, the arc is going to continue in your rectangle (here, a perfect square). For instance, if you wanted an arc that begins at twelve o'clock (90) and runs to three o'clock (–90), you would specify the following:

```
g.drawArc(10,10,100,100,90,-90); // run clockwise
```

Since positive `arcAngle` values result in an arc sweeping counter-clockwise, we used a negative value (-90) to effectively say "run clockwise for 90 degrees."

However, if we wanted an arc that began at twelve o'clock and ran to nine o'clock, we would use the following:

```
g.drawArc(10,150,100,100,90,90); // run counter-clockwise
```

As you can see, values that are positive take an arc counter-clockwise and values that are negative take them clockwise. The following snippet of code produces the arcs in Figure 17-7. Arcs, just like their rectangular, polygonal, and oval brethren, can be filled or left empty:

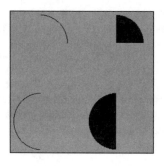

Figure 17-7: You can think of arcs as lines drawn around an invisible circle inscribed in an invisible rectangle.

```
g.drawArc(10,10,100,100,90,-90);
g.fillArc(150,10,100,100,90,-90);
g.drawArc(10,150,100,100,90,180);
g.fillArc(150,150,100,100,90,180);
```

Fonts (java.awt.Fonts)

In addition to the graphics primitives we've just explored, the Graphics class allows us to place text on the screen. We saw this earlier using the drawString() method. In this section, we learn how to specify and draw text in a variety of font faces, styles, and sizes. We also use the drawChars() method to place individual characters on the screen, in a way that's similar to drawing strings.

Creating and using fonts

In order to use fonts, we must first create a Font object. This is simple enough. All we have to do is provide a font name (string), a font style (int), and a font point size (int):

```
Font myFont = new Font("Serif", Font.BOLD, 72);
```

Here we've created a Font object using a serif font face, bold style (via Font.BOLD, which accesses the BOLD static integer variable of the Font class) and 72 point size. I chose "Serif" since every system is likely to have at least one serif font. If you specify "Serif," Java will substitute the system's default serif face, usually Times Roman. If you choose a specific font face that isn't installed on a particular machine, Java will substitute a default font (Courier, for example).

Note

Serif fonts have feet at the base line. The font in this book is a serif font. Typically, most people find serif fonts easier to read—that's why you see them in most books. Sans serif fonts eliminate the feet (*sans* is a French word that means *without*). The Arial and Helvetica typefaces are prime examples of sans serif fonts. With monospace fonts, every character is the same width. The Courier typeface is a good example of a monospace font.

Generic Typefaces in JDK 1.0.2

JDK 1.0.2 does not support the notion of a generic typeface. However, you can use the names *Times Roman, Courier,* and *Helvetica* to produce the same effect. For example, if you specify *Times Roman* as the typeface name, a JDK 1.0.2 interpreter supplies a Times Roman font if it's available on the current system; otherwise, it supplies the closest matching serif face. Similarly, if a Courier or Helvetica font is not available, the interpreter provides the closest matching monospaced and sans serif font, respectively.

Even though you can choose any font face you want, I recommend that you use only a narrow set—those likely to be available on the systems on which your applets will be running. If you stick to the following, you'll be in good shape:

 ✦ `Serif`—default serif font, typically Times Roman

 ✦ `Monospaced`—default monospaced font, typically Courier

 ✦ `SansSerif`—default sans serif font, typically Helvetica

Tip

You can use the `getFontList()` method defined in `java.awt.Toolkit` to find out which fonts are installed on your machine at the time of execution. This method is used in `FontTest`, shown in the next chapter.

As you can see from the preceding example, you create fonts using three arguments, a string, and two integers. The `Font()` constructor, methods, and variables are listed in Table 17-2.

Table 17-2
Class java.awt.Font

Constructor	Signature	Description
Font	`Font(String name, int style, int size)`	Creates a new font with the specified name, style, and point size.

Method	Signature	Description
decode	`public static Font decode(String str)`	Gets the specified font using the name passed in.
getFamily	`public string getFamily()`	Gets the platform-specific family name of the font. Use `getName` to get the logical name of the font.
getName	`public string getName()`	Gets the logical name of the font.

Method	Signature	Description

getStyle	`public int`
	
	`getStyle()`
		Gets the style of the font.

getSize	`public int`
	
	`getSize()`
		Gets the point size of the font.

IsPlain	`public boolean`
	
	`isPlain()`
		Returns `true` if the font is plain.

IsBold	`public boolean`
	
	`isBold()`
		Returns `true` if the font is bold.

isItalic	`public boolean`
	
	`isItalic()`
		Returns `true` if the font is italic.

getFont	`public static`
	
	`Font getFont(String nm)`
		Gets a font from the system properties list.
		
		Parameter: `nm`—the property name.

getFont	`public static`
	
	`Font getFont(String nm, Font, font)`
		Gets the specified font from the system properties list.
		
		Parameters:
		`nm` — the property name.
		`font`—a default font to return if property `nm` is not defined.

hashCode	`public int`
	
	`hashCode()`
		Returns a hash code for this font.
		
		Overrides `hashCode()` in class `Object`.

equals	`public boolean`
	
	`equals(Object obj)`
		Compares this object to the specified object.
		
		Parameter: `obj`—the object with which to compare.
		
		Returns `true` if the objects are the same; `false` otherwise. Overrides `equals()` in class `Object`.

(continued)

Table 17-2 *(continued)*

Method	Signature	Description
toString	`public string toString()`	Converts this object to a string representation. Overrides `toString()` in class `Object`.

Variables	Signature	Description

PLAIN	`public final static`
	
	`int PLAIN`
		The plain style constant. This can be combined with the other style constants for mixed styles.

BOLD	`public final static`
	
	`int BOLD`
		The bold style constant. This can be combined with the other style constants for mixed styles.

ITALIC	`public final static`
	
	`int ITALIC`
		The italicized style constant. This can be combined with the other style constants for mixed styles.

Name	`protected String name`	The logical name of this font.
Style	`protected int style`	The style of the font. This is the sum of the constants PLAIN, BOLD, or ITALIC.
Size	`protected int size`	The point size of this font.

When creating a `Font` object, the string parameter specifies a specific or generic family name, such as `Serif`, `SansSerif`, or `Monospaced`. This is also known as the *font face*; it's the visual appearance of the font, which is consistent and recognizable regardless of what style or point size is used.

Both the style and point size are specified as `int` values. You can determine the style of a font by using variables that the `Font` class provides, such as `BOLD`, `ITALIC`, and `PLAIN`. In fact, you can combine these styles as follows:

```
Font myFont = Font("SansSerif", Font.BOLD+Font.ITALIC, 32);
    // bold and italic
```

The point size, however, is simply a plain `int` that you provide as an integer literal. The point size can be so small that you might not see the font when it is drawn on a screen, or it may be so large that it won't fit on the screen at all.

Once you've created a `Font` object, you have to tell the `Graphics` object to use it for all subsequent text drawing:

```
g.setFont(myFont); // set the Font
```

Now, any calls to drawString() or drawChars() will be done using the face, style, and point size specified in myFont. The following snippet of code uses several different font styles, sizes, and font families to produce what you see in Figure 17-8. Note that we can either create a Font object, and then set it, or simply provide these parameters directly in setFont():

Figure 17-8: Fonts allow you to draw text in a variety of faces, styles, and sizes.

```
Font f = new Font("Serif", Font.PLAIN, 72); // create a Font
g.setFont(f); // set the Font
g.drawString("Serif Plain, 72pt.", 5,60); // draw string using
Font
   // create and set all in one step:
g.setFont(new Font("Serif", Font.BOLD, 72));
g.drawString("Serif Bold, 72pt.", 5,120);
g.setFont(new Font("Serif", Font.ITALIC, 72));
g.drawString("Serif Italic, 72pt.", 5,180);
g.setFont(new Font("Serif", Font.BOLD+Font.ITALIC, 72));
g.drawString("Serif Bold Italic, 72pt.", 5,240);
g.setFont(new Font("Serif", Font.PLAIN, 18));
g.drawString("Serif Plain, 18pt.", 5,270);
g.setFont(new Font("Monospaced", Font.PLAIN,18));
g.drawString("Monospaced Plain, 18pt.", 5,300);
g.setFont(new Font("Monospaced", Font.BOLD,18));
g.drawString("Monospaced Bold, 18pt.", 300, 300);
g.setFont(new Font("Monospaced", Font.ITALIC,18));
g.drawString("Monospaced Italic, 18pt.", 5,325);
g.setFont(new Font("Monospaced", Font.BOLD+Font.ITALIC,18));
```

```
g.drawString("Monospaced Bold Italic, 18pt.", 300, 325);
g.setFont(new Font("SansSerif", Font.PLAIN,32));
g.drawString("SansSerif Plain, 32pt.", 5,400);
g.setFont(new Font("SanSerif", Font.BOLD,32));
g.drawString("SansSerif Bold, 32pt.", 340, 400);
g.setFont(new Font("SansSerif", Font.ITALIC,32));
g.drawString("SansSerif Italic, 32pt.", 5,440);
g.setFont(new Font("SansSerif", Font.BOLD+Font.ITALIC,32));
g.drawString("SansSerif Bold Italic, 32pt.", 340, 440);
```

Here, just as with the previous example, we've used drawString() to place text on the screen. However, there is another method which may be of use, depending on your particular implementation:

```
public void drawChars(char data[], int offset, int length,
    int x, int y);
```

The drawChars() method can be extremely helpful when you need to draw characters stored in an array. You can see this in Listing 17-1, which draws each character in the array one at a time, each in a different color (more on color later). In fact, this program is an example of text animation, and of using threads as well (hence the "inherits Runnable" portion of the class declaration).

We'll discuss each of these in time, but for now, take a look at the paint() method. It sets a random color, then chooses a random *x,y* value (within a range) for the subsequent call to drawChars().

Listing 17-1: **WildWords.java — Animating Text with drawChars()**

```
/**
*  WildWords.java
*  @author: Scott Clark
*/

import java.awt.Graphics;
import java.awt.Font;
import java.awt.FontMetrics;
import java.awt.Event;
import java.awt.Color;

public class WildWords extends java.applet.Applet implements
Runnable {

  // parameters
  String text = "Java"; // string to be displayed
  int delay = 100; // # of milliseconds between updates
  int delta = 5; // "wildness" factor: max pixel offset
  boolean clear = false; // background cleared on update?
  String fontName = "Serif";
```

```
int fontSize = 36;
boolean fontBold = true;
boolean fontItalic = false;

// implementation
char chars[]; // individual chars in 'text'
int positions[]; // base horizontal position
FontMetrics fm;
Thread thread = null;
int newWidth, newHeight;

public void init() {
  String param;
  param = getParameter("text");
  if (param != null) { text = param; }

  param = getParameter("delay");
  if (param != null) { delay = Integer.parseInt(param); }
  param = getParameter("delta");
  if (param != null) { delta = Integer.parseInt(param); }
  param = getParameter("clear");
  if (param != null) { clear = param.equals("true"); }
  param = getParameter("fontName");
  if (param != null) { fontName = param; }
  param = getParameter("fontSize");
  if (param != null) { fontSize = Integer.parseInt(param); }
  param = getParameter("fontBold");
  if (param != null) { fontBold = param.equals("true"); }
  param = getParameter("fontItalic");
  if (param != null) { fontItalic = param.equals("true"); }
  int fontStyle = (fontBold ? Font.BOLD : 0)+(fontItalic ?
                   Font.ITALIC : 0);
  setFont(new Font(fontName, fontStyle, fontSize));
  fm = getFontMetrics(getFont());
  chars = new char[text.length()];
  text.getChars(0, text.length(), chars, 0);
  positions = new int[text.length()];
  for (int i = 0; i < text.length(); i++) {
   positions[i] = fm.charsWidth(chars, 0, i);
  }

 newWidth = delta * 2 + fm.stringWidth(text);
 newHeight = delta * 2 + getFont().getSize();

// Note: resize() works in AppletViewer, but has no effect in
Netscape 4.0 */
 resize(newWidth, newHeight){
 }

 public void start() {
   if (thread == null) {
    thread = new Thread(this);
```

(continued)

Listing 17-1 *(continued)*

```
      thread.start();
    }
  }

  public void stop() {
    thread = null;
  }

  public void run() {
    while (thread != null) {
      try {Thread.sleep(delay);} catch (InterruptedException e) {}
      repaint();
    }
  }

  public void paint(Graphics g) {
    // set random color:
    g.setColor(new Color((float)Math.random(),
      (float)Math.random(), (float)Math.random()));

    for (int i = 0; i < text.length(); i++) {
      int x = (int)(Math.random() * delta*2) + positions[i];
      int y = (int)(Math.random() * delta*2) + fm.getAscent()-1;
      g.drawChars(chars, i, 1, x, y); // draw a char in array
    }
  }

  public void update(Graphics g) {
    if (clear) {
      super.update(g);
    } else {
      paint(g);
    }
  }

}
```

choose a ranc
color

choose a ranc
x, y, value

draw each
character

As you now know, drawChars() takes as arguments an array of characters:

✦ An offset, or index, into that array (specifying which element int to begin the array)

✦ A length parameter (specifying how many array elements, or characters, should be drawn)

✦ The *x* and *y* for the coordinates with drawString()

In the example shown in Listing 17-1, only one array element, or character, is drawn at a time. This is because the length parameter supplied here, 1, only allows for a single element to be accessed. Figure 17-9 shows the results of this program.

Figure 17-9: The drawChars() method allows you to draw characters stored in an array.

FontMetrics

As you can see in Table 17-2, Java provides a number of methods that allow you to find out about the current font. At times, however, you may find you need more specific typographical information, such as the exact height and width of each character, how much leading there is between lines, font ascent and descent, and other information not available using the methods in the Font class.

If this is the case, you can use methods in the FontMetrics class. To use these, simply provide a Font object to the FontMetrics() constructor. This results in a FontMetrics object, to which you can send any of the methods shown in Table 17-3.

Table 17-3
Class java.awt.FontMetrics

Constructor	Signature	Description
FontMetrics	protected FontMetrics (Font font)	Creates a new FontMetrics object with the specified font.

Method	Signature	Description
getFont	public Font getFont()	Gets the font.
GetLeading	public int getLeading()	Gets the standard leading, or line spacing, for the font. This is the logical amount of space to be reserved between the descent of one line of text and the ascent of the next line. The height metric is calculated to include this extra space.
GetAscent	public int getAscent()	Gets the font ascent. The font ascent is the distance from the baseline to the top of the characters.

(continued)

Table 17-3 *(continued)*

Method	Signature	Description
GetDescent	public int getDescent()	Gets the font descent. The font descent is the distance from the baseline to the bottom of the characters.
GetHeight	public int getHeight()	Gets the total height of this font. This is the distance between the baseline of adjacent lines of text. It is the sum of: leading + ascent + descent.
GetMax Ascent	public int getMaxAscent()	Gets the maximum ascent of all characters in this font. No character will extend further above the baseline than this metric.
GetMax Descent	public int getMaxDescent()	Gets the maximum descent of all characters. No character will descend further below the baseline than this metric.
GetMax Decent	public int getMaxDecent()	For backward compatibility only.
GetMax Advance	public int getMaxAdvance()	Gets the maximum advance width of any character in this font. Returns -1 if the maximum advance is not known.
CharWidth	public int charWidth(int ch)	Returns the width of the specified character in this font. Parameter: ch—specified font.
charWidth	public int charWidth(char ch)	Returns the width of the specified character in this font. Parameter: ch—specified font.
stringWidth	public int stringWidth (String str)	Returns the width of the specified string in this font. Parameter: str—string to be checked.

Method	Signature	Description
charsWidth	`public int charsWidth(char data[], int off, int len)`	Returns the width of the specified character array in this font. Parameters: `data`—data to be checked. `off`—start offset of data. `len`—maximum number of bytes checked.
bytesWidth	`public int bytesWidth(byte data[], int off, int len)`	Returns the width of the specified array of bytes in this font. Parameters: `data`—data to be checked. `off`—start offset of data. `len`—maximum number of bytes checked.
getWidths	`public int[] getWidths()`	Gets the widths of the first 256 characters in the font.
ToString	`public String toString()`	Returns the string representation of this `FontMetric`'s values. Overrides `toString()` in class `Object`.

Variable	Signature	Description
font	`protected Font font`	The actual font.

We can also reference these methods directly, without having to create a
`FontMetrics` object. In the following snippet, we get the width of "Hello," as it
would be drawn in the current font:

```
int len = g.getFontMetrics().stringWidth("Hello");
```

Color (java.awt.Color)

When you took a look at Listing 17-1, you may have noticed an interesting line of
code in the `paint()` method:

```
g.setColor(new Color((float)Math.random(), (float)Math.random(),
    (float)Math.random()));
```

This line creates a new random `Color` object and passes it to the `Graphics` object using `setColor()`. This method sets the current `Graphics` object to whatever color is specified through the three `Color` parameters it accepts; it happens to be randomly generated in this example. All subsequent drawing is done in this color, meaning that primitive graphics and text will appear in it.

The Java color model is a 24-bit *RGB* (red, green, blue) model, so its `Color` objects can contain 24 bits' worth of color information (that weighs in at approximately 16 million different colors) specified as red, green, and blue components.

To use a color, we simply create a new `Color` object and supply values of red, green, and blue. Together, these values determine the final color:

```
Color myColor = new Color (255,0,0);      // create red color
Color myColor = new Color (0,255,0);      // create green color
Color myColor = new Color (0,0,255);      // create blue color
Color myColor = new Color (255,255,255);  // create black color
Color myColor = new Color (0,0,0);        // create white color
Color myColor = new Color (100,100,100);  // create gray color
```

From these examples, you can see that the range of integer values is from 0 to 255. We can use any combination of these values to create a color.

As Table 17-4 illustrates, Java provides a number of preset colors that we can use, without having to specify their values. As a matter of fact, we don't even have to create a new `Color` object if we use one of these; we simply write the following:

```
g.setColor(Color.red); // set color to red
g.setColor(Color.green); // set color to green
g.setColor(Color.blue); // set color to blue
```

The example in Listing 17-1, however, specifies random red, green, and blue values. And it uses floating-point values rather than the integers we've been using so far. This particular `Color()` constructor accepts float values, while another `Color()` constructor allows all red, green, and blue values to be specified in a single `int`. We can use any of the three to create colors.

Regardless of how a color is mixed, we use the same methods on the resulting `Color` object. We can query the object to find out its red component, its green component, and its blue component. We can also use a number of methods to derive variations of a color. The methods `brighter()` and `darker()`, for example, return brighter and darker versions of the current color.

Table 17-4
Class java.awt.Color

Constructor	Signature	Description
Color	public Color(int r, int g, int b)	Creates a color with the specified red, green, and blue values in the range 0 to 255. The actual color used in rendering depends on finding the best match, given the color space available for a given output device. Parameters: r—red component. g—green component. b—blue component.
Color	public Color(int rgb)	Creates a color with the specified combined RGB value, consisting of the red component in bits 16–23, the green component in bits 8–15, and the blue component in bits 0–7. The actual color used in rendering depends on finding the best match, given the color space available for a given output device. Parameter: rgb—combined RGB components.
Color	public Color(float r, float g, float b)	Creates a color with the specified red, green, and blue values in the range 0.0–1.0. The actual color used in rendering depends on finding the best match, given the color space available for a given output device. Parameter: r—red component. g—green component. b—blue component.

Method	Signature	Description
getRed	public int getRed()	Gets the red component.
GetGreen	public int getGreen()	Gets the green component.
GetBlue	public int getBlue()	Gets the blue component.

(continued)

Table 17-4 *(continued)*

Method	Signature	Description

GetRGB	`public int`
	
	`getRGB()`
		Gets the RGB value representing the color in the default RGB ColorModel. (Bits 24–31 are 0xff, 16–23 are red, 8–15 are green, and 0–7 are blue.)

Brighter	`public`
	
	`Color brighter()`
		Returns a brighter version of this color.

Darker	`public`
	
	`Color darker()`
		Returns a darker version of this color.

HashCode	`public int`
	
	`hashCode()`
		Computes the hash code. Overrides `hashCode()` in class `Object`.

Equals	`public boolean`
	
	`equals(Object obj)`
		Compares this object against the specified object.
		
		Parameter:
		`obj`—the object with which to compare. Returns `true` if the objects are the same; `false` otherwise.
		Overrides `equals()` in class `Object`.

ToString	`public String`
	
	`toString()`
		Returns the string representation of this color's values. Overrides `toString()` in class `Object`.

Decode	`public static Color`
	`decode(String nm)`
	`throws NumberFormat`
	`Exception`
		Returns the specified color.
		
		Parameter:
		`nm`—representation of the color as a 24-bit integer.

getColor	`public static`
	
	`Color getColor`
	`(String nm)`
		Gets the specified color property.
		
		Parameter:
		`nm`—name of the color property.

getColor	`public static`
	
	`Color getColor`
	`(String nm, Color`
	`v)`
		Gets the specified color property of the specified color.
		
		Parameters:
		`nm`—name of the color property.
		`v`—specified color.
		Returns the new color.

Method	Signature	Description

GetColor	`public static`
	
	`Color getColor`
	`(String nm, int v)`
		Gets the specified color property of the color value.
		
		Parameters:
		`nm`—name of the color property.
		`v`—the color value.
		Returns the new color.

HSBtoRGB	`public static int`
	
	`HSBtoRGB (float hue,`
	`float saturation,`
	`float brightness)`
		Returns the RGB value, defined by the default RGB ColorModel, of the color corresponding to the given HSB (hue, saturation, brightness) color components.
		
		Parameters:
		`hue`—hue component
		`saturation`—saturation of the color
		`brightness`—brightness of the color

RGBtoHSB	`public static float`
	`[]RGBtoHSB(int r,`
	`int g, int b, float`
	`hsbvals[])`
		Returns the HSB values corresponding to the color defined by the red, green, and blue components.
		
		Parameters:
		`r`—red component
		`g`—green component
		`b`—blue component
		
		`hsbvals`—array used to return the three HSB values, or null (returns the array used to store the results [`hue, saturation, brightness`]).

getHSBColor	`public static`
	
	`Color getHSBColor`
	`(float h, float s,`
	`float b)`
		A static color factory for generating a `Color` object from HSB values.
		
		Parameters:
		`h`—hue component.
		`s`—saturation of the color.
		`b`—brightness of the color.
		
		Returns the `Color` object for the corresponding RGB color.

(continued)

	Table 17-4 *(continued)*	
Variable	*Final Static Color*	*Description*
white	`public final static` `color white`	The color white.
LightGray	`public final static` `color lightGray`	The color light gray.
Gray	`public final static` `color gray`	The color gray.
DarkGray	`public final static` `color darkGray`	The color dark gray.
Black	`public final static` `color black`	The color black.
Red	`public final static` `color red`	The color red.
Pink	`public final static` `color pink`	The color pink.
Orange	`public final static` `color orange`	The color orange.
Yellow	`public final static` `color yellow`	The color yellow.
Green	`public final static` `color green`	The color green.
Magenta	`public final static` `color magenta`	The color magenta.
Cyan	`public final static` `color cyan`	The color cyan.
Blue	`public final static` `color blue`	The color blue.

Tip Although it's possible to create millions of colors, most webbers don't have that many at their disposal. If you use colors in your Web page that are out of the range of many users' display capabilities, they will be mapped or dithered to the closest possible match. In some cases, the results will be quite ugly.

To ensure the best possible results over a wide range of displays, it's recommended that you work with 256 colors or less. And, whenever possible, use the standard colors specified by the `Color` class variables, rather than defining your own. The `Color` class provides a number of static variables which define typical colors. The static data elements use common color names such as `Color.red`, `Color.green`, `Color.blue`, and so on.

Foreground and background colors

In addition to setting the drawing color for both text and graphics, you can set foreground and background colors in Java. To do this, two methods are defined in `java.awt.Component`:

```
setForeground(Color c); // set foreground color
setBackground(Color c); // set background color
```

While these might seem straightforward enough, it's worth taking a closer look at each.

setBackground()

Normally, the background color of your applet is the same as the browser window in which it's running (usually gray). However, with `setBackground()`, you can specify any color you like. This method takes as its sole argument a `Color` object.

Whenever your applet calls `repaint()`, the background color comes into play. The `repaint()` method actually calls an `update()` method that clears the screen. This "clearing" is performed by a call to `clearRect()` which, in essence, fills a rectangle with the current background color.

Whenever you change the background color, all subsequent calls to `clearRect()` result in your color being used. As a result, whenever your applet is updated, or whenever you call `repaint()`, the background color you set is used instead of the default.

setForeground()

This method also takes one parameter, a `Color` object. It changes the foreground color so that everything on the screen is immediately redrawn in it. This can be particularly helpful when you have a number of items on the screen that you wish to be redrawn in a new color. Rather than redrawing each item individually, you can reset the foreground color and let it do the work for you.

Tip Before you change the color in which you are drawing, or change the foreground or background color, you may wish to get the current color first and stash it away in a Color object for later use. To do this, use the getForeground() and getBackground() methods. Both return a Color object, which you can later feed to setForeground() or setBackground() if you want to return these colors to their original state.

Images (java.awt.image and java.awt.Image)

By now, you're aware that we can use bitmap images to draw on the screen. Unlike the graphics primitives that we draw from hand, as shown previously, bitmap images come prerendered and ready to slap on the screen. We did this, in fact, with our MediaHelloWorld application. After loading a GIF image into an Image variable, we were able to draw it on the screen using the drawImage() method. At this point, however, it's worth getting a little more sophisticated in our image use.

Tip Those users who run Java on systems that can't distinguish between uppercase and lowercase letters may run into difficulty installing Java documentation, because java.awt.Image and java.awt.image are seen as the same file. In this situation, documentation (HTML) files having these names wouldn't be able to reside in the same directory: One or the other would have to be renamed.

If you do run into problems, keep in mind that classes, by convention, begin with an uppercase letter while packages are generally all lowercase. Thus, you would know just by the name that java.awt.image is a package while java.awt.Image is a class, even if your computer system can't tell the difference.

Here, we learn how to use the getHeight() and getWidth() methods defined in java.awt.Image. These methods allow us to find out the dimensions of a bitmap graphic. This is particularly useful when we want to resize images or if we want to know how large they are for proper display on the screen.

For example, in our FlexibleMediaHello applet, we can use getHeight() and getWidth() to calculate the size of the image. Without this information, we can't properly place the image on the screen with regard to the mouse cursor. Until now, we've simply drawn it at the coordinates of the mouse. As a result, the mouse cursor (an arrow) appears directly on top of our image, obscuring a portion of it.

Using getHeight() and getWidth(), however, we can draw the image to the upper left-hand side of the cursor. In this way, the cursor is always at the lower right-hand corner of our image. If done properly, the cursor will never obscure our image again (see Figure 17-10).

Figure 17-10: Thanks to getHeight() and getWidth(), this image is no longer obscured by the cursor.

Listing 17-2 contains a slightly refined version of our FlexibleMediaHello applet. Rather than drawing the image directly on top of the cursor, which causes unnecessary flickering and the image to be partially obscured, this version of the applet uses getHeight() and getWidth() to calculate the size of the image and position it on the upper left-hand side of the cursor when drawn. In addition, the text is displayed in a randomly selected color each time the paint() method is invoked.

Listing 17-2: **FlexibleHelloWorld.java — a Slightly Refined Version**

```
/**
 * FlexibleMediaHello.java
 *
 * Now draws "Hello World!" in a random color, and adjusts
                                              drawing
 * of the image to accommodate the cursor.
 *
 * @author Aaron E. Walsh
 * @version 1.2, 29 May 97
 */
import java.applet.*;
import java.awt.*;
import java.awt.event;
import java.net.URL;
import java.net.MalformedURLException;
public class FlexibleMediaHello extends HelloWorldApplet   {
  String     helloString;
  Image      myImage;
  AudioClip  myAudio;
  int        horizontal, vertical;
  int        imageW, imageH; // image's width and height
  boolean    SoundOn = true;
  public void init() {
    /* GET THE APPLET PARAMETERS: */
    helloString = getParameter ("hello");
    String  imageString = getParameter ("image");
    String  audioString = getParameter ("sound");
    /* GET FILES USING PARAMETERS: */
    if (imageString==null) {
      myImage=getImage(getCodeBase(), "images/world.gif");
```

(continued)

Listing 17-2 *(continued)*

```
  }
  else {
    URL      imageURL=null;
    try {
      imageURL = new URL(imageString);
    }catch (MalformedURLException e) { ; }
  myImage=getImage(imageURL);
  }
  if (audioString==null) {
    myAudio=getAudioClip(getCodeBase(), "audio/hello.au");
  }
  else {
    URL      audioURL=null;
    try {
      audioURL= new URL(audioString);
    }catch (MalformedURLException e) {   }
  myAudio=getAudioClip(audioURL);
  }
  /* REGISTER MOUSE LISTENERS   */
  addMouseListener(new MouseAdapter() {
    public void mousePressed(MouseEvent event) {
      if (SoundOn) {
        myAudio.loop();
        SoundOn = false;
      }
      else {
        myAudio.stop();
        SoundOn = true;
      }
    }
  });
  addMouseMotionListener(new MouseMotionAdapter() {
    public void mouseMoved(MouseEvent event) {
      horizontal=event.getX();
      vertical=event.getY();
      repaint();
    }
  });
}
public void paint(Graphics g) {
  imageW = myImage.getWidth(this); // get image width
  imageH = myImage.getHeight(this); // get image height
  /* draw the image to the upper left of cursor: */
  if (myImage != null) {
    g.drawImage(myImage, horizontal-imageW, vertical-imageH,this);
  }
  //...now, onto the text...how about a nice, random color?
  g.setColor(new Color((float)Math.random(),
  (float)Math.random(), (float)Math.random()));
```

get the image width and he

draw images using height width values

get a random color to draw

```
   if (helloString==null) {
      super.paint(g);
    }
   else {
      g.drawString(helloString,50,100);
    }
 }
 public void start() {
   myAudio.loop();
 }
 public void stop() {
   myAudio.stop();
 }


 }
```

Looking at our refined FlexibleMediaHello code, the paint() method in particular, you can see that getHeight() and getWidth() both receive the this object. Actually, these methods require an ImageObserver object:

```
int getHeight(ImageObserver observer);
int getWidth(ImageObserver observer);
```

An image observer is an object that watches, or observes, an image. It's the ImageObserver that knows when an image has been completely downloaded from the network. In our case, it tells us how high and wide our image is.

We don't have to instantiate an ImageObserver object, however, since the applet understands how to perform ImageObserver tasks. We simply pass the reference to our applet—this—to getHeight() and getWidth(), and let it take care of giving us the information.

If the image has been fully loaded, these methods return valid information. However, if the image is still downloading off the network, or is not currently available, these methods return a negative 1 (-1). If this is the case, we'll have to wait around a little longer until the image is loaded. Waiting around proves not to be a problem, however, since we're constantly looping through the paint() method. Eventually, these methods will return the true dimensions of our image.

Tip   The FlexibleMediaHello implementation shown in Listing 17-2 uses the delegation event model and thus runs only on JDK 1.1/1.2-compatible browsers. See the electronic version of *Java Bible* on the CD-ROM (Chap 17 folder) for a JDK 1.0.2-compatible version of the FlexibleMediaHello applet.

Animation

One of the most interesting things we can do with images and graphics is to animate them. The easiest way is to draw a series of images in the same place, with each one slightly different from the previous. This is much like a cartoon flip-book. We start with a series of images, or frames, and draw each in the same place. When we run through them, displaying each in turn, the result appears to be an animation.

In Java, there are two methods for doing this:

✦ When animating bitmap images, we use two, three, or more slightly different images, drawn to the screen in sequence.

✦ When animating graphics primitives, we slightly change the values used to create the image (for example, the height and width parameters) for each sequential image, working them into a loop, and then draw the results on the screen.

In both cases, we must clear the screen after each frame is drawn, and then redraw the next one in its place. You can accomplish the "clearing" process by calling repaint(), or by using the clearRect() method:

```
clearRect(int, int, int, int);
```

This method, described earlier, "clears" the specified rectangle by filling it with the current background color. However, when you call the repaint() method, clearRect() is automatically called immediately before paint() is executed. In this case, you don't have to call clearRect() directly; repaint() does it for you.

There are three techniques for dealing with bitmap images used in an animation:

✦ You can load each into a variable and manually specify the drawing order.

✦ You can load them into an array of Image objects and then run through the array, drawing each in turn.

✦ You can use the MediaTracker class, discussed in detail in Chapter 29 (and also in JavaWorld's "Javamation" article, which provides more control over how you can access the individual elements in your animation).

This snippet of code shows the manual approach to loading images:

```
public void init() {
  Image myImage1, myImage2, myImage3; // image variables
  myImage1 = getImage(getDocumentBase(), "images/anImage.gif");
  myImage2 = getImage(getDocumentBase(),
                    "images/anotherImage.gif");
  myImage3 = getImage(getDocumentBase(),
"images/xyzImage.gif");
}
```

This is rather inflexible, however, since you have to refer to each image variable by name in order to draw it. Also, you have to keep track of which one you are in to properly advance to the next one. Finally, you have to check whether the image you've just drawn is the last in the sequence, and then "wrap around" to the first one and begin again. As a result, loading and animating images manually isn't the most elegant approach.

Listing 17-3 illustrates the array-based animation technique. Here, we load two images into an array and then draw each on the screen. By calling repaint(), the paint() method is continually invoked. Without having to do anything more, our drawing surface is wiped clean (by an intermediate call repaint() makes to clearRect()), before paint() is actually called.

Listing 17-3: **BruteForce.java — It's Not Pretty, but It Gets the Job Done**

```
/**
 * BruteForce.java
 *
 * A fast, "brutish" approach to animating bitmap images.
 * A BAD example of animation, since threads aren't supported and
 * nothing is done to reduce the flicker caused by repaint().
 * Additionally, we have paint() essentially calling itself; it's
 * an attention hog, not giving time to any other tasks.
 *
 * This serves only as an example of how to load images into an
 * array and run through them. It's definitely not the recommended
 * way to animate images. For details on how to refine this code,
 * see Chapter 14, "Threads," Chapter 29, "Multimedia," and the
 * "Javamation: Creating animation in Java applets" JavaWorld
 * article (provided on CD-ROM).
 *
 * @author Aaron E. Walsh
 * @version 1.1, 14 Feb 96
 */
import java.awt.*;
public class BruteForce extends java.applet.Applet {
   Image myImages[] = new Image[2]; // array for holding 2 images
   int index=0; // Keep track of which image is displayed

   public void init() {
    resize(500,300);
    // Load the two images into array:
     myImages[0]=getImage(getCodeBase(), "images/image1.gif");
     myImages[1]=getImage(getCodeBase(), "images/image2.gif");
   }
   public void paint(Graphics g) {
```

(continued)

Listing 17-3 *(continued)*

```
    g.drawImage(myImages[index], 0, 0, this);
    index=index==0 ? 1 : 0; // Switch image index
    repaint(); // force paint() again; works, but VERY BAD STYLE!
  }
}
```

This is what I call a brute-force animation; it's terribly primitive (if it were a person, you'd see lots of hair on its back and knuckles dragging on the ground). In fact, you never really want to animate using this technique, since it monopolizes the system by calling repaint() every time through the paint() method. As a result, nothing else gets a chance to execute.

Although it's not a good idea to use this approach when animating graphics, it's a clear illustration of the technique of using an array to hold your images. We simply load two images into the array and draw one after the other on the screen. Since the drawing surface is being cleared each time throughout the process, the animation flickers a lot. In addition, there's no way to pause between the frames; we barrel ahead without giving the eyes a moment to focus.

There are a number of techniques we can use to remedy these problems. First, we can pause for a moment or two between each frame, allowing the user's eyes to get adjusted to the current frame before going on to the next. In this way, our animation appears smoother than with the brute force approach.

In order to pause between each frame, you need to use threads. These are discussed in Chapter 14. They not only provide a way to add pauses to your animations, but they don't monopolize the processor (as this program clearly does!).

However, without reading either of these chapters or referring to the CD-ROM, you can create simple animations by following the principles described here.

Although BruteForce loads only two images, you could load as many as you like. A clean and easy way of doing that is to have a directory of images to load, each having the same name, but with a number that indicates their position in the array.

Figure 17-11 shows the images used in the NotSoBrutish animation program provided on CD-ROM (see Appendix B). We load them up and draw one after the other at the same position on the screen. Take a look at NotSoBrutish: you'll see how we can add thread support and override the paint() method to make a more elegant animation.

Figure 17-11: Images that are slightly different result in an animation when played rapidly in sequence.

For example, if I had a directory with ten images, I'd name them something like: `myImage0.gif, myImage1.gif, myImage2.gif, myImage3.gif, myImage4.gif`, and so on. Since array indexing begins at 0, the last image would be named `myImage9.gif`. When such a naming convention is used, we can use an efficient loop to load each into an array, rather than having to refer to them by name:

```
int count = 10; // number of images to load (10, in this example)
String dir = "images/"; // the name of the directory to load from
String name = "myImage"; // first part of name
String extension = ".gif"; // extension of every image to load
    // Load images into an array:
Image imgs[] = new Image[count]; // create the array
for (int i = 0; i < count; i++) {
  imgs[i] = getImage(getDocumentBase(), dir + name + i +
                     extension);
}
```

Since the reference to each image is automatically taken care of in the previous example, we sit back and let the loop do the work for us. This is particularly helpful when these variables are supplied as <APPLET> parameters, because it gives the people adding your applet to their pages a great deal of flexibility in specifying the number, names, and format of the images to animate.

Now, when you want to animate the images, you simply run through a loop and increment the index in each iteration:

```
if (i==count) {i=0;}
    // "wrap around" to first element when at end
g.drawImage(imgs[i++], 0, 0, this); // draw image in i position
```

Although we've been discussing animations of images and graphics that are drawn to the same location on the screen, we can also move items across the screen. To do this, simply change the *x* and *y* coordinates when drawing each image in the sequence. Adding a value to *x* moves the image to the right, while subtracting a value moves it to the left. Likewise, adding a positive value to *y* moves it down, while subtracting a value moves it up:

```
g.drawImage(imgs[i++], x, y, this); // draw image at x,y
x = x + 5; // next time, draw 5 pixels over
y = y + 2; // and 2 pixels down
```

The values you add or subtract from the *x* and *y* coordinates will vary from animation to animation. You'll have to monkey around with these until you get the desired effect.

Scaling images

In addition to the drawImage() method we've been using so far, there are a few others to choose from:

```
drawImage(Image, int, int, int, int, ImageObserver);
drawImage(Image, int, int, Color, ImageObserver);
drawImage(Image, int, int, int, int, Color, ImageObserver);
```

The first drawImage() method shown earlier takes both a height and a width argument:

```
drawImage(Image img, int x, int y, int width, int height,
ImageObserver observer);
```

If the image size is not that of the height and the width passed to drawImage(), it is scaled accordingly. Using this method, we can stretch the images out or compress them into ever smaller spaces, making for interesting visual effects (see Figure 17-12).

Figure 17-12: Would you like to stretch or compress images?

Two new methods have been added to the AWT `Graphics` class to provide a complete scaling, flipping, cropping image-rendering facility. The new methods are:

```
drawImage(Image img,
          int dx1, int dy1, int dx2, int dy2,
          int sx1, int sy1, int sx2, int sy2,
          ImageObserver observer)
drawImage(Image img,
          int dx1, int dy1, int dx2, int dy2,
          int sx1, int sy1, int sx2, int sy2,
          Color bgcolor, ImageObserver observer)
```

The original `drawImage()` methods may create a totally new representation of the image for the screen by rereading the raw image data. In contrast, these new methods always use the pixels from the unscaled version of the image to draw to the screen. Also, the coordinate specification has been changed in these new methods. Two coordinates are used to define the bounding rectangle. Because negative widths and heights carry existing meanings in the rest of the Java APIs, the new methods use the new coordinate-pair specification to allow explicit control over which dimensions get flipped.

This sample code shows the use of the new API to perform image cropping:

```
// Draw a background image
g.drawImage(bgimg, 0, 0, this);
// Draw the upper left 200x200 portion of another image
// at 20,20
g.drawImage(img,
            20, 20, 220, 220,
            0, 0, 200, 200, this);
```

Following is sample code showing the use of the new API to perform image flipping:

```
// Draw the center 200x200 portion of a 400x400 image
// at location 20, 20, flipped horizontally.
g.drawImage(img,
            20, 20, 220, 220,
            200, 100, 100, 200, this);
```

Printing (java.awt.PrintJob)

So far we've concerned ourselves with displaying graphics and images on a computer screen. Though the Web promises to do away with the need for paper (or so we're told), many unenlightened users continue to demand a printed hard copy of what they see on the screen. Unfortunately, the good folks at JavaSoft have decreed that applets shall not print, at least not until they figure out some way of keeping a devilish applet from sneaking into your office network through the Web and spewing out pages from networked printers 'til they drop. On the other hand, if you're creating a Java application, you can easily add a printing capability using the AWT's `PrintJob` class (see Table 17-5).

<table>
<tr><td colspan="3" align="center">Table 17-5
Class java.awt.PrintJob</td></tr>
<tr><td>*Constructor*</td><td>*Signature*</td><td>*Description*</td></tr>
<tr><td>PrintJob</td><td>public PrintJob()</td><td>Default constructor. Note that the Toolkit for a particular platform creates print jobs at the behest of application programs.</td></tr>
<tr><td>*Method*</td><td>*Signature*</td><td>*Description*</td></tr>
<tr><td>get Graphics</td><td>public abstract Graphics getGraphics()</td><td>Gets a Graphics object that draws to the next page. The page is sent to the printer when the graphics object is disposed. This graphics object implements the Print Graphics interface.</td></tr>
<tr><td>GetPage Dimension</td><td>public abstract Dimension getPageDimension()</td><td>Returns the dimensions of the page in pixels.

Note: This method returns an incorrect value on Windows 95 and perhaps on other platforms, as well.</td></tr>
<tr><td>GetPage Resolution</td><td>public abstract int getPageResolution()</td><td>Returns the resolution of the page in pixels per inch. This doesn't have to correspond to the physical resolution of the printer.

Note: This method returns the actual physical resolution (dots per inch) of the printer on Windows 95 and perhaps on other platforms, as well.</td></tr>
</table>

Method	Signature	Description
LastPage First	`public abstract boolean lastPageFirst()`	Returns `true` if the last page will be printed first.
End	`public abstract void end()`	Ends the print job and does any necessary cleanup.
Finalize	`public void finalize()`	Ends this print job once it is no longer referenced.

There are two important things to keep in mind about `PrintJob`. First, you cannot create an instance of `PrintJob` because it is an abstract class. Instead, when you need to print, you actually request what's known as a *print job* from the Toolkit for the platform on which your application is running, using the Toolkit's `getPrintJob()` method. This method constructs and returns a platform-specific `PrintJob` class that you can then use to print your data. This seemingly roundabout way of doing things shields you from having to deal with the peculiarities of printing on a particular platform.

Note

The `java.awt.Toolkit` class is used to bind the platform-independent `java.awt` classes with their `java.awt.Peer` class counterparts. Many of the methods in the `java.awt.Toolkit` classes should not be called directly because they interact directly with the platform operating system.

The other important point to keep in mind is that the aim of `PrintJob` is to make printing a hard copy as easy as drawing on the screen. Indeed, `PrintJob` assumes that you want to print exactly what is on the screen. If that is the case, `PrintJob` makes the job easy because it lets you use the same Java code that you use to display output on the screen for the printer, effectively redirecting output from the screen device to a printer (nifty, huh?). On the other hand, if you want to print a document that doesn't fit entirely inside a window on the computer screen (a long document, such as word processor file, a large drawing, or some other large and complex body of material that doesn't fit into the dimensions of a computer screen), you have to work a bit harder to get the job done with `PrintJob`.

Keeping this in mind, let's drill down into the specifics of printing with `PrintJob`. The first step is to get a `PrintJob` instance for the platform on which your application is running, which you do by invoking the `getPrintJob()` method of the Toolkit for the current platform. The `getPrintJob()` method is defined as follows:

```
PrintJob getPrintJob(Frame frame,
                     String jobtitle,
                     Properties props)
```

The `getPrintJob()` method returns a `PrintJob` object that is the result of initiating a print operation on the toolkit platform. It returns null if the user canceled the print job.

You can accomplish this by either invoking the `getDefaultToolkit()` static method of the `Toolkit` class or by calling the `getToolkit()` method of your application's frame window, as shown here:

```
Toolkit tk = frame.getDefaultToolkit();
PrintJob pj = tk.getPrintJob(frame, "My Print Job", null);
```

You pass your application's frame and a print job title to the `getPrintJob()` method. The method then displays a dialog box that allows a user to select a printer and various print job options (see Figure 17-13). If the user selects the OK button in the dialog, the `getPrintJob()` method returns a `PrintJob` instance. Otherwise, the method returns `null`.

Tip   As of this writing, the `getPrintJob` method accepts, but ignores, a `java.util.Properties` object as a third argument, which is why `null` is passed in this example. In the future, perhaps by the time you read this, the `java.util.Properties` argument will let you get and set print job options programmatically. Who knows? By then, `PrintJob` may have even more remarkable powers as well. Remember `PrintJob` is a work in progress.

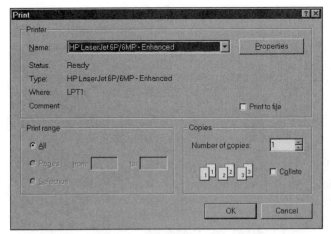

Caption 17-13: PrintJob allows Java applications to print just as native programs do.

Once you have obtained a `PrintJob` instance, as we've done before, the next step is to call the `PrintJob` instance's `getGraphics()` method:

```
public abstract Graphics getGraphics()
```

This method returns a `Graphics` object that represents the page currently in the printer's feed station. This `Graphics` object is essentially identical to a display `Graphics` object. It has the same drawing methods and uses the same coordinate system. In fact, a printer `Graphics` instance views the printed page as just another widget. For example, a printer `Graphics` object measures distances in terms of screen pixels and locates the origin at the upper-left corner of the drawing area (the page). Sound familiar? It should, and for good reason: This is exactly the same way a display `Graphics` object deals with measurements and coordinates!

Such similarities make using printer `Graphics` objects relatively painless once you've got the hang of display graphics in general. However, an important difference exists between a printer `Graphics` object and a display `Graphics` object: whatever you draw to a display `Graphics` object appears on the screen immediately, while drawing to a print `Graphics` object doesn't immediately result in output appearing on a printed page. Instead, Java saves the drawing in memory until either you or Java's garbage collector calls the `Graphics` object's `dispose()` method, at which point, Java sends your drawing to the printer as a series of printer commands.

While this may seem odd at first, it makes sense if you think about it for a while. After all, there's no sense in physically running a page through the printer until the output that should appear on that page has been completely received. And, as long as you're working with a printer `Graphics` object, it won't be disposed of by the automatic garbage collector (nor would you want to dispose of it yourself at this point). However, once you're done working with the object, Java realizes that it's available for garbage collection, and sweeps it away. But not, of course, before it has sent the output information it contains to the printer!

Because printer and display `Graphics` objects are essentially interchangeable, you can pass an instance of either to your application's `paint()` methods. The `paint()` methods draw equally well with either. The only difference is that the results of painting with a `Graphics` object appear on the printer (when you or Java's garbage collector calls the `dispose()` method of the `Graphics` object) rather than on the screen.

To help put this all in perspective, let's take a look at a bit of printing code. The `PrintJava` application in Listing 17-4 illustrates just how easy it is, thanks to `PrintJob`, to reproduce on paper what you see on the screen. This application displays and prints the word *Java* in blue letters, and it centers the word in a two-inch yellow square. The code for this program uses the `PrintCanvas`'s `paint()` method for both displaying and printing the vibrant "Java" square, illustrating how you can use one body of code to send output to both screen and printer devices.

Listing 17-4: **PrintJava.java**

```java
/**
 * PrintJava.java
 * Displays and prints a yellow square containing
 * the word "Java" in blue letters.
 * @author: Paul Kinnucan
 * @version: 1.0
 */
import java.awt.*;
import java.awt.event.*;
import java.util.*;
import jshapes.*;

public class PrintJava extends Frame {
  PrintCanvas canvas;
  public PrintJava() {
    super("PrintJava");
    // Exit when user clicks the frame's close button.
    this.addWindowListener(new WindowAdapter() {
      public void windowClosing(WindowEvent e) {
        System.exit(0);
      }
    });
    canvas = new PrintCanvas();
    add("Center", canvas);
    pack();
  }

  public void run() {
    // Display the print dialog.
    PrintJob pj =
      getToolkit().getPrintJob(this, "Print Java", null);
    // Null indicates user canceled print job.
    if (pj != null) {
      // Get the graphics context for the current
      // page and "paint" the page.
      Graphics gc = pj.getGraphics();
      canvas.paint(gc);
      // Deleting the graphics context causes the
      // page to be printed.
      gc.dispose();
      pj.end();
    }
  }
```

```
  public static void main(String argv[]) {
    PrintJava app = new PrintJava();
    app.show();
    app.run();
  }
}

class PrintCanvas extends Canvas {
  // Set size of canvas to 2x2 inches.
  public Dimension getPreferredSize() {
    int res = getScreenResolution();
    return new Dimension(2*res, 2*res);
  }

  public int getScreenResolution() {
    Frame parent = (Frame) getParent();
    return parent.getToolkit().getScreenResolution();
  }

  public void paint(Graphics g) {
    // Draw a yellow rectangle the size of
    // the canvas.
    Rectangle r = getBounds();
    g.setColor(Color.yellow);
    g.fillRect(0, 0, r.width, r.height);

    // Draw "Java" in blue letters centered on
    // the canvas.
    g.setColor(Color.blue);
    Font f = new Font("Serif", Font.PLAIN, 72);
    g.setFont(f);
    FontMetrics fm = g.getFontMetrics();
    String str = "Java";
    int fw = fm.stringWidth(str);
    int fh = (f.getSize()*getScreenResolution())/72;
    int x = (r.width - fw)/2;
    int y = r.height - fh;
    g.drawString(str, x, y);
  }
}
```

Need to handle longer more complex print jobs? See the next section, "Printing pages."

Printing Components

The AWT provides some specialized printing methods that simplify making hard copies of your application's screens. For example, to print a hard copy of a simple component, such as a button, simply invoke the component's `print()` method, passing it the printer `Graphics` object obtained from `PrintJob`:

```
public void print(Graphics g)
```

The `print()` method passes the `Graphics` object to the component's `paint()` method, thereby reproducing the component's screen appearance on the printer. A corresponding function, `printAll()`, lets you reproduce dialog boxes and other complex objects that have subcomponents:

```
public void printAll(Graphics g)
```

The `printAll()` function invokes the `paint()` methods of the component and all its subcomponents, adjusting the coordinate system of the `Graphics` object as necessary to assure that the subcomponents appear on the printed page in the same position relative to each other that they appear on the screen.

Printing pages

What happens if you want to print a long text file, a large drawing, or another object that does not fit on a single printed page? You can do this with `PrintJob` by dividing up your text or graphics into page-size chunks, printing each sequentially by repeatedly creating (via calls to a `PrintJob` instance's `getGraphics()` method as shown earlier) and disposing of printer `Graphics` objects, one for each page.

The tricky part of this task is assuring that the height and width of each printer `Graphics` object is set to the height and width of the *printable area* of a physical page measured in *screen pixels,* while taking into account the fact that most printers cannot print close to the edges of a piece of paper. Most printers are incapable of placing ink or toner any closer than .25 inches from each edge. Thus, the printable area is usually smaller than the nominal page size by a small factor, typically .25 inches.

Warning

It's important to remember that `PrintJob` deals with coordinates and measurements in terms of screen pixels, since the printed page is treated as nothing more than a screen component by Java. As a result, you must be careful to calculate the size of printable areas using screen pixels. If you don't, your output will almost certainly take on an abstract quality—output won't appear where you expect it!

To compute the printable area in pixels, first get the current display's resolution in pixels-per-inch (ppi) by calling the getScreenResolution() method of the platform's Toolkit object. You can obtain the Toolkit object by calling the static getDefaultToolkit() method of the AWT's Toolkit class or by calling the getToolkit() method of your application's Frame object as you did earlier when working with PrintJob:

```
Toolkit tk = frame.getToolkit();
int res = tk.getScreenResolution();
```

Once you have obtained the screen resolution, as we've already done, multiply the printable area's dimension (measured in inches) by the resolution to obtain the area's dimensions (measured in pixels). Finally, each time you obtain a Graphics object for printing the next chunk of data (remember, you have to chop up large amounts of output into page-sized chunks of data), set the page Graphics object's clip area to the dimensions of the printer's printable area before drawing to it:

```
int w = res * 8; // assume a .25 inch border
int h = res * 10.5;
g.setClip(0, 0, w, h); // g = page Graphics object
```

You may have noticed that the first two lines of code in this example accommodate the fact that most printers can't print on the far edges of a page. As a result the printable area is the nominal area minus a border of .25 inches. The clipping methods are discussed in Chapter 16.

While this is all well and good for the printer in my office, the harsh reality is that printable areas differ among different types of printers. What's .25 inches on my printer may be .125 inches on yours, or .5 inches on a printer down the hall! As a result, what we really need is a way to determine the printable area at run time (or, at least, it would be useful to know the type of the printer selected by the user, which would allow us to build a little data file in advance that contains the precise printable areas for the most popular printers out there). Unfortunately, Java does not yet provide a way of determining the characteristics or even the identity of the printer selected by the user. The bottom line? If you need to print accurately on a variety of printers, you must either wait until JavaSoft gets around to implementing the printer property querying feature of the PrintJob class or else implement such a facility yourself through native methods. Personally, I plan to wait patiently.

Summary

In this chapter we learned how to display and print graphics, images, and text, using the AWT.

✦ With the Graphics class Java provides a set of graphics primitives that allow you to draw lines, rectangles, ovals, polygons, arcs, and even text directly on the screen. You can draw these primitives either outline (that is, without a fill) or with a fill, and in any color you desire.

✦ The Graphics class allows us to place text on the screen.

✦ In order to use fonts, we must first create a Font object. Java provides a number of methods that allow you to find out about the current font.

✦ Java can display GIF and JPEG type images using the Image class.

✦ You can use the java.awt.PrintJob class to put information from your Java applications onto paper.

✦   ✦   ✦

Widgets

◆ ◆ ◆ ◆

In This Chapter

Adding graphical
user interface (GUI)
Components to your
Java applications

Using buttons, check
boxes, choice menus,
and scrolling list
objects in your Java
applications

◆ ◆ ◆ ◆

In the last chapter you explored the graphical side of the
Abstract Windowing Toolkit (AWT): graphics primitives,
fonts, colors, and images. Although you can create impressive
looking applets and jazz up your applications, you still haven't
created a true graphical user interface (GUI). The next five
chapters cover the Components that make up Java's GUI
classes.

In these chapters you learn how to use the AWT to create a
GUI for your own programs. You'll explore containers (panels,
applets, windows, and other objects capable of containing
Components and other containers), widgets (a term I've
adopted to cover buttons, pop-up menus, scroll bars, labels,
choice menus, and all their widgety friends), and the layout
managers responsible for how our widgets are arranged in a
Container class.

In this chapter you begin with a look at the Component class,
the parent of all other GUI classes. Then you go on to learn
about buttons, check boxes, choice menus, and scrolling lists.

GUI Components (java.awt.Component)

As you learned in the previous chapter, the Java graphics
environment is based on the Component class. Any time you
put something on the screen, you're dealing (either directly
or indirectly) with a Component. Applets, as you know, are
actually descendants of the Component class, which is why
you're able to draw directly on an applet without having to do
anything special.

Note

AWT Components communicate with the underlying operating system's windowing environment using *peers*, which actually implement the platform-specific behavior of Components. Although peers are a vital part of Java, allowing the AWT to present an interface consistent with the platform on which it is executing, you won't deal with them directly, unless you're porting Java to a new platform.

The Component class contains a large number of methods, as you can see in Table 18-1.

Table 18-1
java.awt.Component Methods

Method	Signature	Description
getName	public String getName()	Gets the name of the Component.
SetName	public void setName (String name)	Sets the name of the Component to the specified string. Parameter: name – the name of the Component.
getParent	public Container getParent()	Gets parent of Component.
GetPeer	public ComponentPeer getPeer()	Gets peer of Component. Note: getPeer() is deprecated. As of JDK version 1.1, programs should not directly manipulate peers.
GeTreeLock	public final Object geTreeLock()	Gets the locking object for AWT Component—tree and layout operations.
GeToolkit	public Toolkit geToolkit()	Gets the Toolkit of the Component. The Toolkit creates the peer for this Component. Note: The Frame that contains a Component controls which Toolkit is used. If the Component has not yet been added to a Frame (or is later moved to a different Frame), the Toolkit it uses may change.
isValid	public boolean isValid()	Checks whether Component is valid. Components are invalidated when first shown on-screen.

Method	Signature	Description
isVisible	public boolean isVisible()	Checks whether Component is visible. Components are initially visible (with the exception of top-level Components such as Frame).
isShowing	public boolean isShowing()	Checks whether Component is visible and showing onscreen. The Component must be visible and in a container that is both visible and showing.
isEnabled	public boolean isEnabled()	Checks whether Component is enabled. Components are initially enabled.
setEnabled	public void setEnabled(boolean b)	Enables a Component.
enable	public synchronized void enable()	Enables a Component. Note: enable() is deprecated. Replaced by setEnabled(boolean) in JDK version 1.1.
enable	public void enable (boolean cond)	Conditionally enables Component. Parameter: cond–enables Component when true; disables otherwise.
disable	public synchronized void disable()	Disables Component. Note: disable() is deprecated. Replaced by setEnabled(boolean) in JDK version 1.1.
setVisible	public void set Visible(boolean b)	Shows or hides the Component depending on the boolean flag b. Parameter: b–if true, shows the Component; otherwise, hides the Component.
show	public synchronized void show()	Shows Component. Note: show() is deprecated. Replaced by setVisible(boolean) in JDK version 1.1.

(continued)

Table 18-1 *(continued)*

Method	Signature	Description
show	`public void show (boolean cond)`	Conditionally shows the `Component`. Parameter: cond–if `true`, shows `Component`; otherwise hides it. Note: `show()` is deprecated. Replaced by `setVisible(boolean)` in JDK version 1.1.
hide	`public synchronized void hide()`	Hides `Component`. Note: `hide()` is deprecated. Replaced by `setVisible(boolean)` in JDK version 1.1.
getForeground	`public Color getForeground()`	Gets foreground color (or that of its parent if the `Component` has no foreground color).
setForeground	`public synchronized void setForeground (Color c)`	Sets foreground color. Parameter: c–color.
getBackground	`public Color getBackground()`	Gets background color (or that of its parent if the `Component` has no background color).
setBackground	`public synchronized void setBackground (Color c)`	Sets background color. Parameter: c–color.
getFont	`public Font getFont()`	Gets font of the `Component` (or that of its parent if the `Component` has no font).
setFont	`public synchronized void setFont(Font f)`	Sets font of `Component`. Parameter: f–font.
getLocale	`public Locale getLocale()`	Gets the locale of the `Component` (or that of its parent if the `Component` has no locale). Throws `Illegal ComponentStateException` if the `Component` does not have its own locale and has not yet been added to a containment hierarchy such that the locale can be determined from the containing parent.

Method	Signature	Description
setLocale	public void setLocale(Locale l)	Sets the locale of the Component. Parameter: l–the locale.
getColorModel	public synchronized ColorModel getColor Model()	Gets color model used to display Component on the output device.
getLocation	public Point getLocation()	Returns the current location of this Component. The location is in the parent's coordinate space.
getLocationOn Screen	public Point getLocationOn Screen()	Returns the current location of this Component in the screen's coordinate space.
location	public Point location()	Returns the Component's location. Note: location() is deprecated. Replaced by getLocation() in JDK version 1.1.
setLocation	public void setLocation(int x, int y)	Moves the Component to a new location. The x and y coordinates are in the parent's coordinate space. Parameters: x–the x coordinate. y–the y coordinate.
move	public void move (int x, int y)	Moves the Component to a new location. Note: move() is deprecated. Replaced by setLocation(int, int) in JDK version 1.1.
setLocation	public void set Location(Point p)	Moves the Component to a new location. The point p is given in the parent's coordinate space. Parameter: p–the new location for the coordinate.
getSize	public Dimension getSize()	Returns the current size of this Component.

(continued)

Table 18-1 *(continued)*

Method	Signature	Description
size	`public Dimension size()`	Returns the size of the Component. Note: `size()` is deprecated. Replaced by `getSize()` in JDK version 1.1.
setSize	`public void setSize (int width, int height)`	Resizes the Component to the specified width and height. Parameters: `width`–the width of the Component. `height`–the height of the Component.
resize	`public void resize (int width, int height)`	Resizes the Component. Note: `resize()` is deprecated. Replaced by `setSize(int, int)` in JDK version 1.1.
setSize	`public void setSize (Dimension d)`	Resizes the Component to the specified dimension. Parameter: `d`–the Component dimension.
resize	`public void resize (Dimension d)`	Resizes the Component. Note: `resize()` is deprecated. Replaced by `setSize(Dimension)` in JDK version 1.1.
getBounds	`public Rectangle getBounds()`	Returns the current bounds of this Component.
Bounds	`public Rectangle bounds()`	Returns the bounds of the Component. Note: `bounds()` is deprecated. Replaced by `getBounds()` in JDK version 1.1.

Method	Signature	Description
setBounds	public void set Bounds(int x, int y, int width, int height)	Reshapes Component to specified bounding box. Parameters: x–the *x* coordinate. y–the *y* coordinate. width–width of Component. height–height of Component.
reshape	public synchronized void reshape(int x, int y, int width, int height)	Reshapes Component. Note: reshape() is deprecated. As of JDK version 1.1, replaced by set Bounds(int, int, int, int).
setBounds	public void set Bounds(Rectangle r)	Reshapes the Component to the specified bounding box. Parameter: r–the new bounding rectangle for the Component.
getPreferred Size	public Dimension getPreferredSize()	Returns the preferred size of this Component.
preferredSize	public Dimension preferredSize()	Note: preferredSize() is deprecated. Replaced by getPreferredSize() in JDK version 1.1.
getMinimum Size	public Dimension getMinimumSize()	Returns the minimum size of this Component.
minimumSize	public Dimension minimumSize()	Returns the minimum size of this Component. Note: minimumSize() is deprecated. Replaced by getMinimumSize() in JDK version 1.1.
getMaximum Size	public Dimension getMaximumSize()	Returns the maximum size of this Component.
getAlignmentX	public float getAlignmentX()	Returns the alignment along the *x* axis. Specifies how the Component would like to be aligned relative to other Components. The value should be a number between 0 and 1, where 0 represents alignment along the origin, 1 is aligned farthest away from the origin, 0.5 is centered, and so on.

(continued)

Table 18-1 *(continued)*

Method	Signature	Description
getAlignmentY	public float getAlignmentY()	Returns the alignment along the y axis. Specifies how the Component would like to be aligned relative to other Components. The value should be a number between 0 and 1, where 0 represents alignment along the origin, 1 is aligned farthest away from the origin, 0.5 is centered, and so on.
doLayout	public void doLayout()	Lays out the Component. Usually called when the Component (specifically, its container) is validated.
layout	public void layout()	Lays out the Component. Note: layout() is deprecated. Replaced by doLayout() in JDK version 1.1.
validate	public void validate()	Ensures that a Component has a valid layout. Intended to operate primarily on Container instances.
invalidate	public void invalidate()	Invalidates the Component. The Component and all parents above it are marked as needing to be laid out. Can be called often, so it needs to execute quickly.
getGraphics	public Graphics getGraphics()	Gets graphics context for Component. Returns null if Component is currently not on the screen.
getFont Metrics	public FontMetrics getFontMetrics(Font font)	Gets font metrics for Component. Parameter: font–font.
setCursor	public synchronized void setCursor (Cursor cursor)	Sets the cursor image to that of a predefined cursor. Parameter: cursorType–one of the cursor constants defined in the next entry.
getCursor	public Cursor getCursor()	Gets the cursor set on this Component.

Method	Signature	Description
paint	public void paint (Graphics g)	Paints the Component; the clip rectangle in the Graphics parameter is set to the area to be painted. Called when the Component's contents should be painted, as when the Component is first shown or needs repair.
		Parameter: g–the specified graphics context (window).
update	public void update (Graphics g)	Updates Component. The update() method is called in response to repaint(). You can assume that the background is not cleared.
		Parameter: g–the specified graphics context (window).
paintAll	public void paint All(Graphics g)	Paints Component and its subcomponents.
		Parameter: g–the specified graphics context (window).
repaint	public void repaint()	Repaints Component (results in a call to update() as soon as possible).
repaint	public void repaint (long t)	Repaints Component, resulting in a call to update within t milliseconds.
		Parameter: t–maximum time in milliseconds before update.
repaint	public void repaint (int x, int y, int width, int height)	Repaints part of the Component, resulting in a call to update() as soon as possible.
		Parameters: x–the *x* coordinate. y–the *y* coordinate. width–the width. height–the height.

(continued)

Table 18-1 *(continued)*

Method	*Signature*	*Description*
repaint	public void repaint (long t, int x, int y, int width, int height)	Repaints part of the Component. This results in a call to update within t milliseconds. Parameters: t–maximum time in milliseconds before update. x–the *x* coordinate. y–the *y* coordinate. width–the width. height–the height.
print	public void print (Graphics g)	Prints the Component. The default implementation of this method calls paint. Parameter: g–the specified graphics context (window).
printAll	public void print All(Graphics g)	Prints Component and its subcomponents. Parameter: g: The specified graphics context (window).
imageUpdate	public boolean imageUpdate(Image img, int flags, int x, int y, int w, int h)	Repaints Component when image has changed. Returns true if the image has changed; false if it has not.
createImage	public Image create Image(ImageProducer producer)	Creates image from the specified image producer. Parameter: producer–image producer.
createImage	public Image create Image(int width, int height)	Creates off-screen drawable image for double buffering. Parameters: width–the width. height–the height.

Method	Signature	Description
prepareImage	public boolean prepareImage(Image image, ImageObserver observer)	Prepares image for rendering on this Component (downloads image data asynchronously, in separate thread; generates appropriate screen representation of the image). Parameters: image—the image to prepare screen representation for. observer—the ImageObserver object to be notified as image is being prepared (returns true if image is already fully prepared; false if it is not).
prepareImage	public boolean prepareImage(Image image, int width, int height, Image Observer observer)	Prepares an image to render on this Component at specified width and height. Downloads image data asynchronously, in a separate thread, and generates an appropriately scaled screen representation of the image. Parameters: image—the image to prepare screen representation for. width—the width of desired screen representation. height—the height of desired screen representation. observer—the ImageObserver object to be notified as image is being prepared (returns true if the image is already fully prepared; false if it is not).
checkImage	public int check Image(Image image, ImageObserver observer)	Returns status of construction for the screen representation of the specified image. Does not force the image to begin loading; use prepareImage() method to force loading. Parameters: image—the image to check. observer—the ImageObserver object to be notified as image is being prepared (returns the boolean OR of ImageObserver flags for currently available data).

(continued)

Table 18-1 *(continued)*

Method	Signature	Description
`checkImage`	`public int check Image (Image image, int width, int height, Image Observer observer)`	Returns status of construction of a scaled screen representation of a specified image. Does not force the image to begin loading; use `prepare Image()` method to force loading.
		Parameters: `image`–the image to check. `width`–the width of the scaled version to check. `height`–the height of the scaled version to check. `observer`–the ImageObserver object to be notified as image is being prepared (returns the boolean `OR` if the `ImageObserver` flags for currently available data).
`contains`	`public boolean contains(int x, int y)`	Checks whether an *x,y* location is "inside" Component. By default, *x* and *y* are "inside" if they fall within the bounding box of the Component.
		Parameters: `x`–the *x* coordinate. `y`–the *y* coordinate.
`inside`	`public boolean inside(int x, int y)`	By default, *x* and *y* are "inside" if they fall within the bounding box of the Component.
		Note: `inside()` is deprecated. Replaced by `contains(int, int)` in JDK version 1.1.
`contains`	`public boolean contains(Point p)`	Checks whether this Component "contains" a specified point. *x* and *y* in the specified point are defined relative to the coordinate system of this Component.
		Parameter: `p`–the point.
`getComponentAt`	`public Component getComponentAt(int x, int y)`	Returns Component or subcomponent containing the *x,y* location.
		Parameters: `x`–the *x* coordinate. `y`–the *y* coordinate.

Method	Signature	Description
locate	public Component locate(int x, int y)	Returns Component or subcomponent containing location.
		Note: locate() is deprecated. Replaced by getComponentAt(int, int) in JDK version 1.1.
getComponentAt	public Component getComponentAt(Point p)	Returns the Component or subcomponent that contains the specified point.
		Parameter: p–the point.
deliverEvent	public void deliverEvent(Event e)	Dispatches an event.
		Note: deliverEvent() is deprecated. Replaced by dispatchEvent in JDK version 1.1; use dispatchEvent instead.
dispatchEvent	public final void dispatchEvent(AWT Event e)	Dispatches an event to this Component or one of its subcomponents.
		Parameter: e–the event.
postEvent	public boolean postEvent(Event e)	Note: postEvent() is deprecated. As of JDK version 1.1, replaced by dispatchEvent(AWTEvent).
addComponentListener	public synchronized void addComponentListener(ComponentListener l)	Adds the specified Component Listener to receive Component events from this Component.
		Parameter: l–the Component listener.
removeComponentListener	public synchronized void removeComponentListener(ComponentListener l)	Removes the specified listener so it no longer receives Component events from this Component.
		Parameter: l–the Component Listener.

(continued)

Table 18-1 *(continued)*

Method	Signature	Description
addFocus Listener	public synchronized void addFocus Listener(Focus Listener l)	Adds the specified FocusListener to receive focus events from this Component. Parameter: l: The FocusListener.
removeFocus Listener	public synchronized void removeFocus Listener(Focus Listener l)	Removes the specified FocusListener so it no longer receives focus events from this Component. Parameter: l: The FocusListener.
addKeyListener	public synchronized void addKeyListener (KeyListener l)	Adds the specified key listener to receive key events from this Component. Parameter: l: The KeyListener.
removeKey Listener	public synchronized void removeKey Listener(KeyListener l)	Removes the specified key listener so it no longer receives key events from this Component. Parameter: l: The KeyListener.
addMouse Listener	public synchronized void addMouse Listener(Mouse Listener l)	Removes the specified Mouse Listener so it no longer receives mouse events from this Component. Parameter: l: The MouseListener.
removeMouse Listener	public synchronized void removeMouse Listener(Mouse Listener l)	Adds the specified MouseMotion Listener to receive mouse motion events from this Component. Parameter: l: The MouseMotionListener.
addMouseMotion Listener	public synchronized void addMouseMotion Listener(MouseMotion Listener l)	Adds the specified MouseMotion Listener to receive mouse motion events from this Component. Parameter: l: The MouseMotionListener.

Method	Signature	Description
removeMouse MotionListener	`public synchronized void removeMouse MotionListener(Mouse MotionListener l)`	Removes the specified `MouseMotion Listener` so it no longer receives mouse motion events from this `Component`.
		Parameter: l: The `MouseMotion Listener`.
enableEvents	`protected final void enableEvents(long eventsToEnable)`	Enables the events defined by the specified event mask parameter to be delivered to this `Component`. Event types are automatically enabled when a listener for that type is added to the `Component`. This method need be invoked only by those subclasses of a `Component` that need specified event types delivered to `processEvent` regardless of whether a listener is registered.
		Parameter: `eventsToEnable`: The event mask defining the event types.
disableEvents	`protected final void disableEvents(long eventsToDisable)`	Disables the events defined by the specified event mask parameter from being delivered to this `Component`.
		Parameter: `eventsToDisable`: The event mask defining the event types.
processEvent	`protected void processEvent(AWT Event e)`	Processes events occurring on this `Component`. By default, calls the appropriate `processXXXEvent` method for the class of event. Not called unless an event type is enabled for this `Component`, which happens when (a) a listener object is registered for that event type, or (b) the event type is enabled via `enableEvents()`.
		Note: Classes that override this method should call `super.processEvent()` to ensure that default event processing continues normally.
		Parameter: e: The event.

(continued)

Table 18-1 *(continued)*

Method	Signature	Description
Component Eventprocess	`protected void processComponent Event(ComponentEvent e)`	Processes `Component` events occurring on this `Component` by dispatching them to any registered `ComponentListener` objects. Not called unless `Component` events are enabled for this `Component`, which happens when (a) a `Component Listener` object is registered via `addComponentListner()` or (b) `Component` events are enabled via `enableEvents()`. Note: Classes that override this method should call `super.process ComponentEvent()` to ensure that default event processing continues normally. Parameter: e: The `Component` event.
Eventprocess Focus	`protected void processFocusEvent (FocusEvent e)`	Processes `FocusEvents` occurring on this `Component` by dispatching them to any registered `FocusListener` objects. Not called unless focus events are enabled for this `Component`, which happens when (a) a `FocusListener` object is registered via `addFocusListener()` or (b) `FocusEvents` are enabled via `enableEvents()`. Note: Classes that override this method should call `super.processFocusEvent()` to ensure that default event processing continues normally. Parameter: e: The `FocusEvent`.

Method	Signature	Description
processKey Event	protected void processKeyEvent(Key Event e)	Processes key events occurring on this Component by dispatching them to any registered KeyListener objects. Not called unless key events are enabled for this Component, which happens when (a) a KeyListener object is registered via addKeyListener() or (b) Key events are enabled via enableEvents(). Note: Classes that override this method should call super.processKey Event() to ensure that default event processing continues normally. Parameter: e: The key event.
processMouse Event	protected void processMouseEvent (MouseEvent e)	Processes mouse events occurring on this Component by dispatching them to any registered MouseListener objects. Not called unless mouse events are enabled for this Component, which happens when (a) a Mouse Listener object is registered via addMouseListener() or (b) Mouse events are enabled via enable Events(). Note: Classes that override this method should call super.processMouse Event() to ensure that default event processing continues normally. Parameter: e: The mouse event.

(continued)

	Table 18-1 *(continued)*	
Method	*Signature*	*Description*
processMouse MotionEvent *(continued)*	protected void processMouseMotion Event(MouseEvent e)	Processes MouseMotionEvents occurring on this Component by dispatching them to any registered MouseMotionListener objects. Not called unless mouse motion events are enabled for this Component, which happens when (a) a MouseMotion Listener object is registered via addMouseMotionListener() or (b) Mouse Motion events are enabled via enableEvents(). Note: Classes that override this method should call super.processMouse MotionEvent() to ensure that default event processing continues normally. Parameter: e–the MouseMotion Event.
handleEvent	public boolean handleEvent(Event evt)	Note: handleEvent() is deprecated. Replaced by (AWTEvent) in JDK version 1.1.
mouseDown	public boolean mouse Down(Event evt, int x, int y)	Note: mouseDown() is deprecated. Replaced by processMouseEvent (MouseEvent) in JDK version 1.1.
mouseDrag	public boolean mouse Drag(Event evt, int x, int y)	Note: mouseDrag() is deprecated. Replaced by processMouseMotion Event(MouseEvent) in JDK version 1.1.
mouseUp	public boolean mouse Up(Event evt, int x, int y)	Note: mouseUp() is deprecated. Replaced by processMouseEvent(Mouse Event) in JDK version 1.1.
mouseMove	public boolean mouse Move(Event evt, int x, int y)	Note: mouseMove() is deprecated. Replaced by processMouseMotion Event(MouseEvent) in JDK version 1.1.

Method	Signature	Description
mouseEnter	public boolean mouse Enter(Event evt, int x, int y)	Note: mouseEnter() is deprecated. Replaced by processMouseEvent (MouseEvent) in JDK version 1.1.
mouseExit	public boolean mouse Exit(Event evt, int x, int y)	Note: mouseExit() is deprecated. Replaced by processMouseEvent(Mouse Event) in JDK version 1.1.
keyDown	public boolean key Down(Event evt, int key)	Note: keyDown() is deprecated. Replaced by processKeyEvent (KeyEvent) in JDK version 1.1.
keyUp	public boolean key Up(Event evt, int key)	Note: keyUp() is deprecated. Replaced by processKeyEvent (KeyEvent) in JDK version 1.1.
action	public boolean action(Event evt, Object what)	Note: action() is deprecated. Replaced by registering this Component as ActionListener on the Component that fires action events in JDK version 1.1.
addNotify	public void addNotify()	Notifies a Component that it has been added to a container, and that if a peer is required, it should be created. This method should be called by Container.add() and not by user code directly.
removeNotify	public synchronized void removeNotify()	Notifies Component to destroy peer.
gotFocus	public boolean got Focus(Event evt, Object what)	Note: gotFocus() is deprecated. Replaced by processFocusEvent (FocusEvent) in JDK version 1.1.
lostFocus	public boolean lost Focus(Event evt, Object what)	Note: lostFocus() is deprecated. Replaced by processFocusEvent (FocusEvent) in JDK version 1.1.

(continued)

Table 18-1 *(continued)*

Method	Signature	Description
isFocus Traversable	public boolean isFocusTraversable()	Returns a determination of whether this Component can be traversed by using Tab or Shift-Tab keyboard focus traversal. If this method returns false, this Component may still use requestFocus() to request the keyboard focus, but will not be assigned a focus automatically during Tab traversal.
requestFocus	public void request Focus()	Requests the input focus. A Focus Gained event will be delivered if this request succeeds. The Component must be visible on the screen for this request to be granted.
transferFocus	public void transferFocus()	Transfers the focus to the next Component.
nextFocus	public void nextFocus()	Note: nextFocus() is deprecated. Replaced by transferFocus() in JDK version 1.1.
add	public synchronized void add(PopupMenu popup)	Adds the specified pop-up menu to the Component. Parameter: popup–the popup menu to be added to the Component.
remove	public synchronized void remove(Menu Component popup)	Removes the specified pop-up menu from the Component. Parameter: popup–the pop-up menu to be removed.
paramString	protected String paramString()	Returns parameter string of Component.
toString	public String toString()	Returns a string that represents the Component's values. Overrides toString in the Object class.
list	public void list()	Prints listing to a print stream.

Method	Signature	Description
list	public void list (PrintStream out)	Prints listing to the specified print stream. Parameter: out–stream name.
list	public void list (PrintStream out, int indent)	Prints out list, beginning at specified indention, to specified print stream. Parameters: out–stream name. indent–start of list.
list	public void list (PrintWriter out)	Prints a listing to the specified print writer.
list	public void list (PrintWriter out, int indent)	Prints out a list, starting at the specified indention, to the specified print writer.

Note

You may have noticed that a number of the methods in the Component class are specified as being *synchronized*. Synchronized methods may only be accessed by one thread at a time, preventing others from potentially changing the state or behavior of the method out from under the current thread. For details on synchronized methods and threads, see Chapter 14.

To draw an image, write some text, or place a UI element on the screen, you must use a container (java.awt.Container). Containers are those things that can "contain" Components. Components, you'll recall, are those things that fall under the Component class: buttons, check boxes, scroll bars, labels, choice menus, and so forth. Even containers can fall under this class, implying that they may be nested or placed inside one another. And, in fact, this is often the case.

Because Applet is a subclass of Panel, which is a subclass of Container, which is itself a subclass of Component, all applets inherently (no pun intended) know how to add and display Components. You simply create the Component and add it to your applet. Nothing special; simply create and add.

In the next two chapters you take a look at how to create your own panels and windows, but right now I discuss what I've been calling widgets. You'll see how to add *widgets* (buttons, check boxes, scroll bars, labels, choice menus, text areas, and text fields) to your applets. I begin with buttons.

Buttons

Chances are, I don't have to explain buttons to you (or most other widgets, for that matter). Buttons are simple widgets that initiate actions when you click them. You see buttons in use all the time. In fact, all modern personal computer operating systems use them.

The button widget, along with all its companions, is seen in Figure 18-1. To create a button, you simply instantiate a `Button` object, give it a name, and add it:

```
Button myButton = new Button("Click Me");
add(myButton);
```

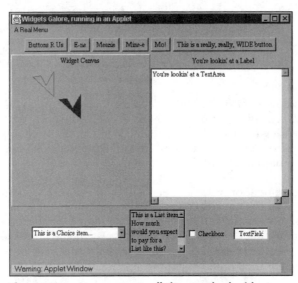

Figure 18-1: Java supports all the standard widgets (GUI Components) found on modern computer operating systems.

In fact, you don't even need to assign the button to a variable:

```
buttonPanel.add(new Button("Click Me"));
```

You'll note that I didn't supply *x,y* coordinates for the button, as I've been doing all along with images and graphics primitives. This is because widgets, as with all Components, are placed on the screen according to a layout manager; explicit coordinates are not used. You learn about layout managers later on (in Chapter 23, to be precise). For now, all you need to know is that you instantiate a `Button` object and add it to the screen. Tables 18-2 and 18-3 show the various constructors and methods associated with buttons.

Java Layout Managers

Java supports five layout managers:

- ✦ FlowLayout
- ✦ GridLayout
- ✦ GridBagLayout
- ✦ BorderLayout
- ✦ CardLayout

`FlowLayout` supports three types of alignments: left, right, or center. `FlowLayout` doesn't provide much control over where Components are placed on the screen. You simply add them, and they are placed on the panel from left to right in the order added. When a Component reaches the right side of the screen, it is wrapped around to the next row, where the process continues.

There are many instances in which you need more control over where the Components are placed. In these situations, you might use `GridLayout`. The order in which you lay down Components with `GridLayout` is very important. The first Component is placed in the first element of the grid, going from left to right. Each element you add to a grid layout takes up one position of the grid, much like adding only one number per cell in a spreadsheet. `GridLayout` is constraining in that you can place only one Component inside each cell in the grid.

If you want a Component to occupy one or more cells, you should use `GridBagLayout`. Although considerably more complicated to use than other layout managers, `GridBagLayout` has definite advantages when it comes to controlling your Components' placement on the screen. `GridBagConstraints` specifies how the Component is positioned over one or more cells, known as the *display area*. To use the `GridBagLayout`, you must customize one or more of a Component's `GridBagConstraints`. You do this by setting the instance variables of a `GridBagConstraints` object.

`BorderLayout` arranges Components along the border of the container, as opposed to placing Components on the inside, as `FlowLayout`, `GridLayout`, and `GridBagLayout` do.

Finally, unlike the other layout managers, `CardLayout` allows only one Component to be viewed at a time. You can specify which Component to display, so you have control over how and when Components are visible.

Table 18-2
java.awt.Button Constructors

Signature	Description/Parameter(s)
public Button()	Constructs button with no label.
public Button (String label)	Constructs button with a given string label. Parameter: label: The button label.

Table 18-3
java.awt.Button Methods

Method	Signature	Description
addNotify	public synchronized void	Creates peer of the button. Note: AddNotify() overrides addNotify in class Component.
getLabel	public String getLabel()	Gets the label of a button.
SetLabel	public void setLabel (String label)	Sets the button's label. Parameter: label—the label.
setAction Command	public void setActionCommand (String command)	Sets the command name of the action event fired by this button. By default this will be set to the label of the button.
GetAction Command	public String getActionCommand()	Returns the command name of the action event fired by this button.
AddAction Listener	public void addActionListener (ActionListener l)	Adds the specified ActionListener to receive action events from this button. Parameter: l—the action listener.
removeAction Listener	public void removeAction Listener(ActionListener l)	Removes the specified ActionListener so it no longer receives action events from this button. Parameter: l—the action listener.

Method	Signature	Description
processEvent	protected void process Event(AWTEvent e)	Processes events on this button. If the event is an ActionEvent, it invokes the processActionEvent method; otherwise, it invokes its superclass's processEvent. Parameter: e–the event.
processAction Event	protected void process ActionEvent(ActionEvent e)	Processes action events occurring on this button by dispatching them to any registered ActionListener objects. Not called unless action events are enabled for this Component, which happens when (a) an ActionListener object is registered via addActionListener() or (b) Action events are enabled via enableEvents(). Parameter: e–the action event.
paramString	protected String paramString()	Returns button's parameter string. Overrides paramString in class Component.

Check Boxes

Java supports two types of check boxes, exclusive and non-exclusive:

✦ In **exclusive** check boxes, only one item can be selected at a time. If you choose another item, the current check box is deselected and your new selection is highlighted.

✦ In **non-exclusive** check boxes, any number of items in the group can be selected.

The following pieces of code give examples of both types of check boxes. The first is non-exclusive and is derived from the Checkbox class (see Tables 18-4 and 18-5). The second is an exclusive check box, instantiated from the CheckboxGroup class (see Table 18-6):

```
/* -- Create a single check box: -- */
add(new Checkbox("This is a check box"));
/* -- Create a CheckboxGroup: -- */
Checkbox hickory;
Checkbox dickory;
Checkbox dock;
String hickoryLabel = "Hickory";
String dickoryLabel = "Dickory";
String dockLabel = "Dock";
 // create the group
CheckboxGroup myGroup = new CheckboxGroup();
 // add each to the current panel
add(hickory=new Checkbox(hickoryLabel,myGroup,true)); // "on"
 // the following two will be "off"
add(dickory=new Checkbox(dickoryLabel,myGroup,false));
add(dock=new Checkbox(dockLabel,myGroup,false));
```

Don't let the word *box* in CheckboxGroup deceive you! Depending on the underlying system on which your program is executed (Sun Solaris, MS Windows, Apple Macintosh, and so on) the check boxes will actually appear as circles or diamonds. In non-Java lingo, they're often called *radio buttons*.

Table 18-4
java.awt.Checkbox Constructors

Signature	Description
public Checkbox()	Constructs check box with no label or check box group, and is initialized to false.
public Checkbox (String label)	Constructs check box with a label but no check box group, and is initialized to false.
	Parameter: label–the label.
public Checkbox (String label, boolean state)	Constructs check box with a label. The check box starts in the specified state and is not part of any check box group.
	Parameters: label–the label. State–the initial state of this check box.

Signature	Description
`public Checkbox (String label, CheckboxGroup group, boolean state)`	Constructs a check box with a label, check box group, and specified initial value. If `CheckboxGroup` is not null, check box becomes a check box button (meaning only one check box in the group may be set at a time). Parameters: `label`–the label. `Group`–the check box group this check box is part of. `State`–the initial state of check box.

Table 18-5
java.awt.Checkbox Methods

Method	Signature	Description
`addNotify`	`public synchronized void addNotify()`	Creates peer of the check box. Overrides `addNotify` in class `Component`.
`getLabel`	`public String getLabel()`	Gets button label.
`setLabel`	`public void setLabel (String label)`	Sets the button with specified label. Parameter: `label`–the label.
`getState`	`public boolean getState()`	Returns check box state.
`setState`	`public void setState (boolean state)`	Sets check box to the specified state. Parameter: `state`: The boolean state.
`getSelected Objects`	`public Object[] getSelectedObjects()`	Returns an array (length 1) containing the check box label or null if the check box is not selected.
`getCheckbox Group`	`public CheckboxGroup getCheckboxGroup()`	Returns check box group.

(continued)

Table 18-5 *(continued)*

Method	Signature	Description
setCheckbox Group	public void setCheckboxGroup (CheckboxGroup g)	Sets check box group to the specified group. Parameter: g–the check box group.
addItem Listener	public void addItem Listener(ItemListener l)	Adds the specified item listener to receive item events from this check box. Parameter: l_the item listener.
removeItem Listener	public void remove ItemListener(Item Listener l)	Removes the specified item listener so that it no longer receives item events from this check box. Parameter: l–the item listener.
processEvent	protected void processEvent(AWT Event e)	Processes events on this check box. If the event is an ItemEvent, it invokes the processItemEvent method; otherwise, it calls its superclass's processEvent. Parameter: e–the event.
processItem Event	protected void processItemEvent (ItemEvent e)	Processes item events occurring on this check box by dispatching them to any registered ItemListener objects. Not called unless item events are enabled for this Component, as when (a) an ItemListener object is registered via addItemListener() or (b) Item events are enabled via enableEvents(). Parameter: e–the item event.
paramString	protected String paramString()	Returns parameter string of check box. Overrides paramString in class Component.

Table 18-6
java.awt.CheckboxGroup Constructor and Methods

Constructor	Signature	Description
CheckboxGroup	public CheckboxGroup()	Creates check box group.

Method	Signature	Description
getSelected Checkbox	public Checkbox getSelectedCheckbox()	Gets the current choice.
GetCurrent	public Checkbox deprecated. getCurrent()	Note: getCurrent() is Replaced by getSelectedCheckbox () in JDK version 1.1.
SetSelected Checkbox	public synchronized void setSelectedCheck box(Checkbox box)	Sets the current choice to the specified check box. If the check box belongs to a different group, returns no result. Parameter: box–the current check box choice.
setCurrent	public synchronized void setCurrent (Checkbox box)	Note: setCurrent() is deprecated. Replaced by setSelectedCheckbox (Checkbox) in JDK version 1.1.
ToString	public String toString()	Returns this check box group's values. Overrides toString in class Object.

As you can see in Figure 18-2, check boxes provide an on/off state that is well suited to toggling program options off and on.

Figure 18-2: The check box widget has two states: true (checked) and false (not-checked).

Choice Menus

Choice menus (see Table 18-7) are really pop-up menus; they enable you to build a list of choices that pop up on the screen as a menu.

Table 18-7
java.awt.Choice Constructor and Methods

Constructor	Signature	Description
Choice	public Choice()	Constructs new choice.

Method	Signature	Description
addNotify	public synchronized void addNotify()	Creates choice's peer. Overrides addNotify in class Component.
GetItem Count	public int getItem Count()	Returns the number of items in this choice.
CountItems	public int countItems()	Note: countItems() is deprecated. Replaced by getItemCount() in JDK version 1.1.
GetItem	public String getItem(int index)	Returns String at specified index in choice. Parameter: index–the index.
add	public synchronized void add(String item)	Adds an item to this choice. Parameter: item–the item to be added.
addItem	public synchronized void addItem(String item)	Identical to the add method; adds an item to choice list. Throws NullPointerException if item's value is null. Parameter: item–the item to add.
Insert	public synchronized void insert(String item, int index)	Inserts the item into this choice at the specified position. Parameters: item–the item to be inserted. index–the position at which the item should be inserted.

Method	*Signature*	*Description*
remove	public synchronized void remove(String item)	Removes the first occurrence of item from the choice menu. Parameter: item–the item to remove from the choice menu.
remove	public synchronized void remove(int position)	Removes an item from the choice menu.
RemoveAll	public synchronized void removeAll()	Removes all items from the choice menu.
GetSelected Item	public String getSelectedItem()	Returns a string representing the current selection.
GetSelected Objects	public synchronized Object[] getSelectedObjects()	Returns an array (length 1) containing the currently selected item. If this choice has no items, returns null.
GetSelected Index	public int getSelectedIndex()	Returns index of currently selected item.
Select	public synchronized void select(int pos)	Selects item having the specified position. Throws IllegalArgumentException if choice item position is invalid. Parameter: pos–the item position.
Select	public void select (String str)	Selects item with specified String. Parameter: str–the specified String.
addItem Listener	public void addItemListener (ItemListener l)	Adds the specified ItemListener to receive item events from this check box. Parameter: l–the item listener.

(continued)

Table 18-7 *(continued)*

Method	Signature	Description
removeItem Listener	public void removeItemListener (ItemListener l)	Removes the specified item listener so that it no longer receives item events from this check box. Parameter: l_the item listener.
processEvent	protected void processEvent (AWTEvent e)	Processes events on this check box. If the event is an ItemEvent, it invokes the processItemEvent method; otherwise, it calls its superclass's processEvent. Parameter: e–the event.
processItem Event	protected void processItemEvent (ItemEvent e)	Processes item events occurring on this check box by dispatching them to any registered ItemListener objects. Note: Not called unless item events are enabled for this Component, as when (a) an ItemListener object is registered via addItemListener() or (b) item events are enabled via enableEvents(). Parameter: e–the item event.
paramString	protected String paramString()	Returns the parameter string of this choice. Overrides paramString in class Component.

Unlike the menus that are used in windows, choice menus can appear anywhere on your screen, as shown in Figure 18-3. The following code is for creating choice menus:

```
Choice theChoice = new Choice(); // create it
  // add a few items:
theChoice.addItem("This is a Choice item...");
theChoice.addItem("This is another Choice item!");
theChoice.addItem("Yet another Choice item");
theChoice.addItem("And, yes, a fourth Choice item");
add(theChoice); // finally, add the choice menu
```

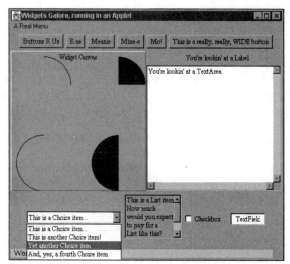

Figure 18-3: You can place choice menus, typically called pop-up menus, anywhere in your applet.

As you can see, you first create a `Choice` object and then add the various items you want to appear in that menu list. When you're finished adding items, add the choice menu itself.

With choice menus, you're allowed to select only one item; multiple selections aren't permitted. Sometimes, however, you may want the functionality of a choice menu yet require multiple selections. In such a case, you would use a scrolling list.

You don't necessarily have to add all the items to a choice menu before you add it to the container. You can create the menu, add it to the container, and then add individual items later, as you wish.

You may also decide to change items in the choice menu after you've created it. Do this when you're not certain what the contents of your choice menu will be, or whether they will change over time.

Note

Choice menus under JDK 1.1 are a little different from their JDK 1.0.2 friends—in 1.0.2, choice menu items cannot be removed! Indeed, if you want to remove an item from a choice menu in JDK 1.0.2, you actually have to create a brand new menu, and then copy the items you want from the old menu into the new one. Clearly this is a royal pain, so JDK 1.1 makes removing choice items as easy as adding them.

Scrolling Lists

Scrolling lists are particularly helpful when you need the basic functionality of a choice menu but must also select more than one item. Not surprisingly, scrolling lists have scroll bars, which let you create long lists of items without consuming the amount of screen real estate that you might with a scroll pane. (Scroll panes are discussed in the next chapter.)

To create a scrolling list, you simply create a `List` object and then add items to it. When you're done, you add the list:

```
// create list with 5 rows and multiple selections:
List theList = new List(5, true);
theList.addItem("This is a list item...");
theList.addItem("How much");
theList.addItem("would you expect");
theList.addItem("to pay for a");
theList.addItem("list like this?");
theList.addItem("$150?");
theList.addItem("$100?");
add(theList);
```

As you can see in Table 18-8, two constructors are available for scrolling lists. The first simply creates the `List` object; the second requires both an integer and a boolean parameter. In the second constructor, which I used earlier, the `int` parameter defines how many visible lines will be in the list; the boolean parameter specifies if multiple selections are supported. If the boolean argument is true, the list can accept multiple selections. If it is false, the list will act like a choice menu, allowing only one selection at a time. Table 18-9 shows the List methods.

Table 18-8 java.awt.List Constructors	
Signature	**Description**
`public List()`	Creates scrolling list with no visible lines or multiple selections.
`public List(int rows, boolean MultipleSelections)`	Creates scrolling list with the specified number of visible lines (boolean parameter specifies whether multiple selections are permitted).
	Parameters: `rows`–number of items to show. `MultipleSelections`–multiple selections are allowed when `true`, but prohibited otherwise.

Table 18-9
java.awt.List Methods

Method	Signature	Description
addNotify	public synchronized void addNotify()	Creates peer for the list. Overrides addNotify in class Component.
RemoveNotify	public synchronized void removeNotify()	Removes peer for list. Overrides removeNotify in class Component.
GetItemCount	public int getItemCount()	Returns the number of items in the list.
countItems	public int countItems()	Note: countItems() is deprecated. Replaced by getItemCount() in JDK version 1.1.
getItem	public String getItem(int index)	Gets item at specified index. Parameter: index–position of item.
getItems	public synchronized String[] getItems()	Returns the items in the list.
add	public void add(String item)	Adds the specified item to the end of scrolling list. Parameter: item–the item to be added.
addItem	public synchronized void addItem(String item)	Adds item to the end of the list. Parameter: item–the item to be added.
replaceItem	public synchronized void replaceItem (String newValue, int index)	Replaces item at the index with the value you pass in. Parameters: newValue–the new value. index–position of item to replace.
removeAll	public synchronized void removeAll()	Removes all items from the list.
clear	public synchronized void clear()	Note: clear() is deprecated. As of JDK version 1.1, replaced by removeAll().

(continued)

Table 18-9 *(continued)*

Method	Signature	Description
remove	public synchronized void remove(String item)	Removes the first occurrence of item from the list. Throws Illegal ArgumentException if the item doesn't exist in the list. Parameter: item–the item to remove from the list.
remove	public synchronized void remove(int position)	Removes item from the list.
delItem	public synchronized void delItem(int position)	Deletes item from the list.
delItems	public synchronized void delItems(int start, int end)	Note: delItems() is deprecated. As of JDK version 1.1, not for future public use. This method is expected to be retained only as a package private method.
getSelected Index	public synchronized int getSelected Index()	Retrieves the currently selected item on the list (returns −1 if no item is selected).
getSelected Indexes	public synchronized int[]getSelected Indexes()	Returns indexes of currently selected items on the list.
getSelected Item	public synchronized String getSelected Item()	Returns currently selected item on the list (returns null if no item is selected).
getSelected Items	public synchronized String[] getSelectedItems()	Returns selected items on list.
getSelected Objects	public Object[] getSelectedObjects()	Returns the selected items on the list in an array of objects.

Method	Signature	Description
select	public synchronized void select(int index)	Selects item at specified index. Parameter: index–position of item to select.
deselect	public synchronized void deselect(int index)	Deselects item at specified index. Parameter: index–position of item to deselect.
isIndex Selected	public boolean isIndexSelected(int index)	Returns true if the item at the specified index has been selected; false otherwise. Parameter: index–the position of item to be checked.
isSelected	public synchronized boolean isSelected (int index)	Note: isSelected() is deprecated. As of JDK version 1.1, replaced by isIndexSelected(int).
getRows	public int getRows()	Returns number of visible lines in list.
isMultiple Mode	public boolean isMultipleMode()	Returns true if this list allows multiple selections.
allows Multiple Selections	public boolean allowsMultiple Selections()	Note: allowsMultiple Selections() is deprecated. As of JDK version 1.1, replaced by isMultipleMode().
setMultiple Mode	public synchronized void setMultipleMode (boolean b)	Sets whether this list should allow multiple selections or not. Parameter: b–the boolean to allow multiple selections.
setMultiple Selections	public void set MultipleSelections (boolean v)	Note: setMultipleSelections() is deprecated. Replaced by setMultiple Mode(boolean) in JDK version 1.1.
getVisible Index	public int get VisibleIndex()	Gets index of item last made visible by the makeVisible() method.
makeVisible	public void make Visible(int index)	Forces item at specified index to become visible. Parameter: index–position of item.

(continued)

Table 18-9 *(continued)*		
Method	**Signature**	**Description**
getPreferred Size	public Dimension getPreferredSize (int rows)	Returns the preferred dimensions needed for the list with the specified amount of rows.
preferredSize	public Dimension preferredSize(int rows)	Note: preferredSize() is deprecated. Replaced by getPreferredSize(int) in JDK version 1.1.
getPreferred Size	public Dimension getPreferredSize()	Returns the preferred dimensions needed for the list.
preferredSize	public Dimension preferredSize()	Note: preferredSize() is deprecated. As of JDK version 1.1, replaced by getPreferredSize().
getMinimum Size	public Dimension getMinimumSize(int rows)	Returns the minimum dimensions needed for the amount of rows in the list. Parameter: rows–minimum quantity of rows in the list.
minimumSize	public Dimension minimumSize(int rows)	Note: minimumSize() is deprecated. Replaced by getMinimumSize(int) in JDK version 1.1.
getMinimum Size	public Dimension getMinimumSize()	Returns the preferred size with the specified number of rows if the row size is greater than zero.
minimumSize	public Dimension minimumSize()	Note: minimumSize() is deprecated. Replaced by getMinimumSize() in JDK version 1.1.
addItem Listener	public void addItem Listener(Item Listener l)	Adds the specified item listener to receive item events from this list box. Parameter: l–the ItemListener.
removeItem Listener	public void remove ItemListener(Item Listener l)	Removes the specified ItemListener so that it no longer receives item events from this check box. Parameter: l–the item listener.
addAction Listener	public void add ActionListener (ActionListener l)	Adds the specified ActionListener to receive action events from this button. Parameter: l–the ActionListener.

Method	Signature	Description
removeAction Listener	public void remove ActionListener (ActionListener l)	Removes the specified Action Listener so it no longer receives ActionEvents from this button.
		Parameter: l–the ActionListener.
processEvent	protected void processEvent(AWT Event e)	Processes events on this check box. If the event is an ItemEvent, it invokes the processItemEvent method. If the event is an ActionEvent, it invokes the processActionEvent method; otherwise, it invokes the superclass's processEvent.
		Parameter: e–the event.
processItem Event	protected void processItemEvent (ItemEvent e)	Processes item events occurring on this check box by dispatching them to any registered ItemListener objects. Note: Not called unless item events are enabled for this Component, as when (a) an ItemListener object is registered via addItemListener() or (b) Item events are enabled via enableEvents().
		Parameter: e–the item event.
process ActionEvent	protected void processActionEvent ActionListener (ActionEvent e)	Processes action events occurring on this button by dispatching them to any registered objects. Note: Not called unless action events are enabled for this Component, as when (a) an ActionListener object is registered via addAction Listener() or (b) Action events are enabled via enableEvents().
		Parameter: e–the action event.
paramString	protected String paramString()	Returns list's parameter string. Overrides paramString in class Component.

One of the nicest attributes of scrolling lists is that you don't have to deal with the interaction of the scroll bar. When users click your scroll bar, the scroll list acts appropriately, scrolling the text up and down as the users expect it to.

Summary

Although I covered quite a bit in this chapter, there's still a considerable amount lurking under the AWT covers. In the next chapter I turn to scroll bars, labels, text, canvases, containers, and panels—all things you're likely to use in your applets and applications. I strongly recommend that you explore these classes at your own leisure and walk through the source code samples provided on the CD-ROM accompanying this book.

The AWT can be overwhelming at first, but stick with it. If you approach it a little at a time and come back as needed, then before long you're hooking up full-blown user interfaces for your own Java programs. After you get over the initial learning curve of dealing with Components, it all makes infinite sense. You may find yourself whipping up powerful and attractive programs on the weekends, since so much of the UI is taken care of for you when you use the AWT.

✦ The Java graphics environment is based on the `Component` class. Any time you put something on the screen, you're dealing (either directly or indirectly) with a Component.

✦ The AWT supports using buttons, check boxes, choice menus, and scrolling list objects in your Java applications.

✦　✦　✦

More Widgets and Containers

In this chapter, you continue to look at the components that make up Java's graphical user interface (GUI). I'll run through scroll bars, labels, text, canvases, containers, and panels—all things you're likely to use in your applets and applications.

JDK 1.2 Although many older Java applications completely rely on the AWT for user interface components, JDK 1.2 is geared to using the JFC/Swing classes, which are discussed in more detail in Chapters 23, 24, and 25.

Scroll Bars

Scroll bars by themselves are particularly helpful as generic controls, and they come in handy when you need to provide the user with a *sliding* widget that has some control over an aspect of your program:

```
add(new Scrollbar(Scrollbar.HORIZONTAL, 25, 3,
1, 100));
```

As you can tell from Tables 19-1 through 19-3, the previous line of code creates and adds a scroll bar in the horizontal orientation. I've set the initial value (see later in this section) to 25 and specified a visible area of 3. The minimum value is set to 1, and the maximum value is 100.

Table 19-1
java.awt.Scrollbar Constructors

Signature	Description
`public Scrollbar()`	Constructs a new vertical scroll bar.
`public Scrollbar(int orientation)`	Constructs a new scroll bar with the specified orientation. Throws `IllegalArgumentException` when an illegal scroll bar orientation is given. Parameters: `orientation`–either `Scrollbar.HORIZONTAL` or `Scrollbar.VERTICAL`.
`public Scrollbar(int orientation, int value, int visible, int minimum, int maximum)`	Constructs a new scroll bar with the specified orientation, value, page size, minimum value, and maximum value. Parameters: `orientation`–either `Scrollbar.HORIZONTAL` or `Scrollbar.VERTICAL`. `value`–the scroll bar's value. `visible`–the size of the visible portion of the scrollable area; the scroll bar uses this value when paging up or down a page at a time. `minimum`–the minimum value of the scroll bar. `maximum`–the maximum value of the scroll bar.

Table 19-2
java.awt.Scrollbar Methods

Method	Signature	Description
`addNotify`	`public synchronized void addNotify()`	Creates the scroll bar's peer. The peer allows you to modify the appearance of the scroll bar without changing any of its functionality. Overrides `addNotify` in class `Component`.
`GetOrientation`	`public int getOrientation()`	Returns the orientation for this scroll bar.

Method	Signature	Description
setOrientation	`public synchronized void setOrientation (int orientation)`	Sets the orientation for this scroll bar. Parameter: `orientation`–either `Scrollbar.HORIZONTAL` or `Scrollbar.VERTICAL` to set the orientation (HORIZONTAL or VERTICAL) of this scroll bar.
getValue	`public int getValue()`	Returns the current value of this scroll bar.
SetValue	`public void setValue(int value)`	Sets the value of this scroll bar to the specified value. Parameter: `value`–the new value of this scroll bar. If this value is below the current minimum or above the current maximum, it becomes the new value.
GetMinimum	`public int getMinimum()`	Returns the minimum value of this scroll bar.
setMinimum	`public synchronized void setMinimum(int newMinimum)`	Sets the minimum value for this scroll bar. Parameter: `minimum`–the minimum value of the scroll bar.
getMaximum	`public int getMaximum()`	Returns the maximum value of this scroll bar.
setMaximum	`public synchronized void setMaximum(int newMaximum)`	Sets the maximum value for this scroll bar. Parameter: `maximum`–the maximum value of the scroll bar
getVisible Amount	`public int getVisibleAmount()`	Returns the visible amount of this scroll bar.
GetVisible	`public int getVisible()`	Note: `getVisible()` is deprecated. As of JDK version 1.1, replaced by `getVisibleAmount()`.

(continued)

	Table 19-2 *(continued)*	
Method	**Signature**	**Description**
SetVisible Amount	`public synchronized void setVisible Amount(int newAmount)`	Sets the visible amount of this scroll bar, which is the range of values represented by the width of the scroll bar's bubble. Parameter: `Visible`—the amount visible per page.
setUnit Increment	`public synchronized void setUnit Increment(int v)`	Sets the unit increment for this scroll bar. This is the value that will be added (subtracted) when the user hits the unit down (up) gadgets.
SetLine Increment	`public void setLine Increment(int l)`	Note: `setLineIncrement()` is deprecated. As of JDK version 1.1, replaced by `setUnitIncrement (int)`.
getUnit Increment	`public int getUnitIncrement()`	Gets the unit increment for this scroll bar.
GetLine Increment	`public int getLine Increment()`	Note: `getLineIncrement()` is deprecated. As of JDK version 1.1, replaced by `getUnitIncrement()`.
SetBlock Increment	`public synchronized void setBlock Increment(int v)`	Sets the block increment for this scroll bar. This is the value that will be added (subtracted) when the user hits the block down (up) gadgets.
SetPage Increment	`public void setPage Increment(int l)`	Note: `setPageIncrement()` is deprecated. As of JDK version 1.1, replaced by `setBlockIncrement()`.
GetBlock Increment	`public int getBlock Increment()`	Gets the block increment for this scroll bar.
GetPage Increment	`public int getPage Increment()`	Note: `getPageIncrement()` is deprecated. As of JDK version 1.1, replaced by `getBlockIncrement ()`.

Method	Signature	Description
SetValues	public void set Values(int value, int visible, int minimum, int maximum)	Sets the values for this scroll bar and enforces the following constraints: ✦ The maximum must be greater than the minimum. ✦ The value must be greater than or equal to the minimum and less than or equal to the maximum minus the visible amount. ✦ The visible amount must be greater than 1 and less than or equal to the difference between the maximum and minimum values. (Values that do not meet these criteria are quietly coerced to the appropriate boundary value.) Parameters: value – position in the current window visible – amount visible per page minimum – minimum value of the scroll bar maximum – maximum value of the scroll bar.
removeAdjustment Listener	public synchronized void remove Adjustment Listener (AdjustmentListener l)	Removes the specified adjustment listener so that it no longer receives adjustment events from this scroll bar.
processEvent	protected void processEvent(AWT Event e)	Processes events on this scroll bar. If the event is an Adjustment Event, it invokes the process AdjustmentEvent method, else it invokes its superclass's processEvent. Parameter: e – the event.

(continued)

Table 19-2 *(continued)*

Method	Signature	Description
process AdjustmentEvent	protected void processAdjustment Event(Adjustment Event e)	Note: This method will not be called unless adjustment events are enabled for this component, which happens when one of the following occurs: (a) An `AdjustmentListener` object is registered via `addAdjustmentListener()`. (b) Adjustment events are enabled via `enableEvents()`.
ParamString	protected String paramString()	Returns the string parameters for this scroll bar. Overrides `paramString` in class `Component`.

Table 19-3
java.awt.Scrollbar Variables

Variable	Signature	Description
HORIZONTAL	public final static int HORIZONTAL	The horizontal scroll bar variable.
VERTICAL	public final static int VERTICAL	The vertical scroll bar variable.

Actually, the component methods shown in Tables 19-1 through 19-3 are applicable to any container, including windows and dialog boxes, as you'll see in the next two chapters.

Scroll bars enable you to select a value between a maximum and a minimum, both of which you can define. After you've created a scroll bar with a minimum/maximum, you can change what is known as the value of the scroll bar in three ways:

   ✦ Using the up arrow (or the left arrow, if the scroll bar is horizontally positioned)

   ✦ Using the down arrow (or the right arrow, if the scroll bar is horizontally positioned)

   ✦ Using the thumb (or areas on either side of the thumb)

You can see these three alternatives in Figure 19-1.

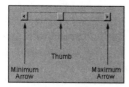

Figure 19-1: You can change the value of a scroll bar by clicking the up (maximum) and down (minimum) arrows, the thumb, or the areas on either side of the thumb.

The thumb is a visual indication of the current value of the scroll bar. If it is at the maximum position, the scroll bar's value is the maximum allowed. If it is at the minimum position, the value of the scroll bar is at the minimum. By looking at the thumb, you can tell approximately what value is associated with the scroll bar.

You can grab the thumb with your mouse and move it in either direction. You can even click directly inside the contents of the scroll bar and jump the thumb in that direction by several values (the default values for clicking here are ten).

When you need to get the value of a scroll bar, use the getValue() method. Also, you can set the value needed by using the setValue() method.

Unlike the widgets discussed in Chapter 18, scroll bars do not generate an *action* event. If you want to intercept a scroll bar event, you must register an Adjustment Listener, using the scroll bar's addAdjustmetListener () method (or override the handleEvent() method, if you are programming for JDK 1.0.2 browsers). For details on Abstract Windowing Toolkit (AWT) events, see Chapter 16.

Labels

Labels are the most simple of widgets. They don't generate an action and they don't have what you might consider a true user interface (UI). You use labels to place specific pieces of text on the screen, similar to how you draw a string. As you learn later, however, the advantage of labels over drawString() or drawChars() is that they can automatically reposition themselves on the screen according to a layout manager, whenever the container they are in is resized.

You can read more about layouts in Chapter 21. For now, think of labels as being a nice, easy way to identify areas on the screen and other widgets in your programs. To better position them, you can choose between one of three possible alignments (Label class variables): LEFT, CENTER, or RIGHT.

```
add(new Label("You're lookin' at a Label", Label.LEFT));
add(new Label("You're lookin' at a Label", Label.CENTER));
add(new Label("You're lookin' at a Label", Label.RIGHT));
```

The tables that follow provide details of class `java.awt.Label`. Table 19-4 shows the various signatures of the `Label` constructor; Tables 19-5 and 19-6 show (respectively) the methods and variables associated with labels.

Table 19-4
Class java.awt.Label Constructors

Signature	Description
`public Label()`	Constructs an empty label.
`public Label (String label)`	Constructs a new label with the specified string of text.
	Parameter: `label` – the text that makes up the label.
`public Label(String label, int alignment)`	Constructs a new label with the specified string of text and the specified alignment.
	Parameters: `label` – the string that makes up the label. `alignment` – the alignment value.

Table 19-5
java.awt.Label Methods

Method	Signature	Description
addNotify	`public synchronized void addNotify()`	Creates the peer for this label. The peer allows us to modify the appearance of the label without changing its functionality. Overrides `addNotify` in class `Component`.
GetAlignment	`public int getAlignment()`	Gets the current alignment of this label.
SetAlignment	`public void setAlignment(int alignment)`	Sets the label's alignment to that specified. Parameter: `alignment` – the alignment value. Throws `IllegalArgumentException` if an improper alignment is given.

Method	Signature	Description
GetText	public String getText()	Gets the text of this label.
SetText	public void setText (String label)	Sets the label's text to that specified.
		Parameter: label – the text that makes up the label.
paramString	protected String paramString()	Returns the parameter string of this label. Overrides paramString in class Component.

Table 19-6
Class java.awt.Label Variables

Variable	Signature	Description
LEFT	public final static int LEFT	The left alignment.
CENTER	public final static int CENTER	The center alignment.
RIGHT	public final static int RIGHT	The right alignment.

Text Components

The AWT implements a TextComponent class (see Tables 19-7) from which two subclasses are derived: TextField (see Tables 19-8 and 19-9) and TextArea (see Tables 19-10 and 19-11). Let's take a look at each of these classes.

Table 19-7
java.awt.TextComponent

Constructor	Signature	Description
TextComponent	public class TextComponent extends Component	A text component allows the editing of some text. This class can't be instantiated by itself (hence, no constructors are listed here), yet it provides methods common to this type of component.

(continued)

Table 19-7 *(continued)*

Method	Signature	Description
removeNotify	`public void remove Notify()`	Removes the text component's peer. The peer allows us to modify the appearance of the text component without changing its functionality. Overrides `remove Notify` in class `Component`.
SetText	`public synchronized void setText(String t)`	Sets the text of this text component to the specified text. Parameter: `t` – the new text to be set.
getText	`public synchronized String getText()`	Returns the text contained in this text component.
GetSelectedText	`public synchronized String getSelected Text()`	Returns the selected text contained in this text component.
IsEditable	`public boolean isEditable()`	Returns the `boolean` indicating whether this text component is editable.
SetEditable	`public synchronized void setEditable (boolean t)`	Sets the specified boolean to indicate whether this text component should be editable. Parameter: `t` – the `boolean` to be set.
getSelectionStart	`public synchronized int getSelection Start()`	Returns the selected text's start position.
SetSelectionStart	`public synchronized void setSelection Start(int selection Start)`	Sets the selection start to the specified position. The new starting point is constrained to be before or at the current selection end. Parameter: `selectionStart` – the start position of the text.
getSelectionEnd	`public synchronized int getSelectionEnd ()`	Returns the selected text's end position.

Method	Signature	Description
SetSelectionEnd	public synchronized void setSelectionEnd (int selectionEnd)	Sets the selection end to the specified position. The new end point is constrained to be at or after the current selection start. Parameter: selectionEnd–the end position of the text.
select	public synchronized void select(int sel Start, int selEnd)	Selects the text found between the specified start and end locations. Parameters: selStart–the start position of the text. SelEnd–the end position of the text.
selectAll	public synchronized void selectAll()	Selects all the text in the text component.
SetCaretPosition	public void setCaret Position(int position)	Sets the position of the text insertion caret for the TextComponent. Parameters: position–the position. Throws IllegalArgument Exception if position is less than 0.
GetCaretPosition	public int getCaret Position()	Returns the position of the text insertion caret for the Text Component.
AddTextListener	public synchronized void addTextListener (TextListener l)	Adds the specified text event listener to receive text events from this text component. Parameters: l–the TextEvent listener.
removeTextListener	public void remove TextListener(Text Listener l)	Removes the specified text event listener so that it no longer receives text events from this text component. Parameter: l–the TextEvent listener.

(continued)

Table 19-7 *(continued)*

Method	Signature	Description
processEvent	protected void processEvent(AWT Event e)	Processes events on this text component. If the event is a TextEvent, it invokes the processTextEvent method; otherwise, it invokes its superclass's processEvent. Parameter: e – the event.
processTextEvent	protected void processTextEvent (TextEvent e)	Processes text events occurring on this text component by dispatching them to any registered Text Listener objects. Note: This method will not be called unless text events are enabled for this component; as when one of the following occurs: (a) A TextListener object is registered via addText Listener() or (b) Text events are enabled via enableEvents(). Parameter: e – the text event.
paramString	protected String paramString()	Returns the string of parameters for this text component. Overrides paramString in class Component.

Table 19-8
java.awt.TextField Constructors

Signature	Description
public TextField()	Constructs a new text field.
public TextField(int cols)	Constructs a new text field initialized with the specified columns. Parameter: cols – the number of columns.
public TextField(String text)	Constructs a new text field initialized with the specified text. Parameter: text – the text to be displayed.

Signature	Description
`public TextField(String text, int cols)`	Constructs a new text field initialized with the specified text and columns. Parameters: `text`–the text to be displayed. `cols`–the number of columns.

Table 19-9
java.awt.TextField Methods

Method	Signature	Description
addNotify	`public void addNotify()`	Creates the text field's peer. The peer allows you to modify the appearance of the text field without changing its functionality. Overrides `addNotify` in class `Component`.
GetEchoChar	`public char getEcho Char()`	Returns the character to be used for echoing.
SetEchoChar	`public void setEcho Char(char c)`	Sets the echo character for this text field. This is useful for fields in which the user input shouldn't be echoed to the screen, as in the case of a text field that represents a password. Parameter: `c`–the echo character for this text field.
setEcho Character	`public void setEcho Character(char c)`	Note: `setEchoCharacter()` is deprecated. As of JDK version 1.1, replaced by `setEchoChar(char)`.
EchoCharIsSet	`public boolean echoCharIsSet()`	Returns `true` if this text field has a character set for echoing.
GetColumns	`public int getColumns()`	Returns the number of columns in this text field.
SetColumns	`public void set Columns(int columns)`	Sets the number of columns in this text field. Parameter: `columns`–the number of columns. Throws `IllegalArgument Exception` if `columns` is less than 0.

(continued)

Table 19-9 *(continued)*

Method	Signature	Description
GetPreferred Size	public Dimension getPreferredSize (int cols)	Returns the preferred size dimensions needed for this text field with the specified amount of columns. Parameter: cols – the number of columns in this text field.
preferredSize	public Dimension preferredSize(int cols)	Note: preferredSize() is deprecated. As of JDK version 1.1, replaced by getPreferredSize (int).
getPreferred Size	public Dimension getPreferredSize()	Returns the preferred size dimensions needed for this text field. Overrides getPreferredSize in class Component.
PreferredSize	public Dimension preferredSize()	Note: preferredSize() is deprecated. As of JDK version 1.1, replaced by getPreferredSize ().
GetMinimum Size	public Dimension getMinimumSize(int cols)	Returns the minimum size dimensions needed for this text field with the specified amount of columns. Parameter: cols – the number of columns in this text field.
minimumSize	public Dimension minimumSize(int cols)	Note: minimumSize() is deprecated. As of JDK version 1.1, replaced by getMinimumSize (int).
getMinimum Size	public Dimension getMinimumSize()	Returns the minimum size dimensions needed for this text field. Overrides getMinimumSize in class Component.
MinimumSize	public Dimension minimumSize()	Note: minimumSize() is deprecated. As of JDK version 1.1, replaced by getMinimumSize().
AddAction Listener	public synchronized void addAction Listener(Action Listener l)	Adds the specified action listener to receive action events from this text field. Parameter: l – the action listener.

Method	Signature	Description
removeAction Listener	public void removeActionListener (ActionListener l)	Removes the specified action listener so that it no longer receives action events from this button. Parameters: l –the action listener.
processEvent	protected void processEvent(AWTEvent e)	Processes events on this text field. If the event is an ActionEvent, it invokes the processActionEvent method; otherwise, it invokes its superclass's processEvent. Parameter: e –the event.
processAction Event	protected void processActionEvent (ActionEvent e)	Processes action events occurring on this text field by dispatching them to any registered ActionListener objects. Note: This method will not be called unless action events are enabled for this component; as when one of the following occurs: (a) An ActionListener object is registered via addAction Listener() or (b) Action events are enabled via enableEvents(). Parameter: e –the action event.
paramString	protected String paramString()	Returns the string of parameters for this text field.

Table 19-10
java.awt.TextArea Constructors

Signature	Description
public TextArea()	Constructs a new text area.
public TextArea (String text)	Constructs a new text area with the specified text displayed. Parameter: text –text to be displayed.

(continued)

Table 19-10 *(continued)*

Signature	Description
`public TextArea(int rows, int cols)`	Constructs a new text area with the specified number of rows and columns. Parameters: `rows` – number of rows. `cols` – number of columns.
`public TextArea (String text, int rows, int cols)`	Constructs a new text area with the specified text and number of rows and columns. Parameters: `text` – text to be displayed. `rows` – number of rows. `cols` – number of columns.
`public TextArea(String text, int rows, int columns, int scrollbars)`	Constructs a new text area with the specified text and number of rows, columns, and scroll bar visibility. Parameters: `text` – the text to be displayed. `rows` – the number of rows. `columns` – the number of columns.

Table 19-11
java.awt.TextArea Methods

Methods	Signature	Description
`addNotify`	`public synchronized void addNotify()`	Creates the text area's peer. The peer allows us to modify the appearance of the text area without changing any of its functionality. Overrides `addNotify` in class `Component`.
`Insert`	`public synchronized void insert(String str, int pos)`	Inserts the specified text at the specified position. Parameters: `str` – the text to insert. `pos` – the position at which to insert.

Methods	Signature	Description
insertText	public void insertText (String str, int pos)	Note: insertText() is deprecated. As of JDK version 1.1, replaced by insert(String, int).
append	public synchronized void append(String str)	Appends the given text to the end. Parameter: str—the text to insert.
appendText	public void appendText (String str)	Note: appendText() is deprecated. As of JDK version 1.1, replaced by append(String).
Replace Range	public synchronized void replaceRange(String str, int start, int end)	Replaces text from the indicated start to end position with the new text specified. Parameters: str—the text to use as the replacement. start—the start position. end—the end position.
replace Text	public void replaceText (String str, int start, int end)	Note: replaceText() is deprecated. As of JDK version 1.1, replaced by replaceRange (String, int, int).
getRows	public int getRows()	Returns the number of rows in the text area.
SetRows	public void setRows(int rows)	Sets the number of rows for this text area. Parameter: rows—the number of rows. Throws IllegalArgument Exception if rows is less than 0.
GetColumns	public int getColumns()	Returns the number of columns in the text area.
SetColumns	public void setColumns (int columns)	Sets the number of columns for this text area. Parameter: columns—the number of columns. Throws IllegalArgument Exception n if columns is less than 0.

(continued)

Table 19-11 *(continued)*

Methods	Signature	Description
Get Scrollbar Visibility	`public int getScrollbar Visibility()`	Returns the enumerated value describing which scroll bars the text area has.
Get Preferred Size	`public Dimension get PreferredSize(int rows, int columns)`	Returns the specified row and column dimensions of the text area. Parameters: `rows` – the preferred rows amount. `columns` – the preferred columns amount.
preferred Size	`public Dimension preferredSize(int rows, int cols)`	Note: `preferredSize()` is deprecated. As of JDK version 1.1, replaced by `getPreferredSize (int, int)`.
get Preferred Size	`public Dimension getPreferredSize()`	Returns the preferred size dimensions of the text area.
Preferred Size	`public Dimension preferredSize()`	Note: `preferredSize()` is deprecated. As of JDK version 1.1, replaced by `getPreferredSize ()`.
GetMinimum Size	`public Dimension getMinimumSize(int rows, nt columns)`	Returns the specified minimum size dimensions of the text area. Parameters: `rows` – the minimum row size. `columns` – the minimum column size.
minimum Size	`public Dimension minimum Size(int rows, int cols)`	Note: `minimumSize()` is deprecated. As of JDK version 1.1, replaced by `getMinimumSize (int, int)`.
getMinimum Size	`public Dimension getMinimumSize()`	Returns the minimum size dimensions of the text area.
MinimumSize	`public Dimension minimumSize()`	Note: `minimumSize()` is deprecated. As of JDK version 1.1, replaced by `getMinimumSize()`.

Methods	Signature	Description
Param String	`protected String paramString()`	Returns the string of parameters for this text area. Overrides `paramString` in class `TextComponent`.

TextField

At times, you'll need to create an area in which the user can enter a relatively small piece of information, such as a social security number, a name, or an address. When you need a single line of text entry, you use the `TextField()` method:

```
TextField ssnField = new TextField("Enter SSN", 11);
add(ssnField);
```

In this example, I've created a `TextField` object 11 characters wide. The words *Enter SSN* actually appear inside the text field. If I didn't want this text to appear inside, I could always use a label (see "Labels" earlier in this chapter).

Text fields support the notion of echo characters, which echo a specific character to the screen during input, instead of the ones that are actually typed. This is particularly helpful for allowing the user to enter sensitive information, such as passwords, without worrying whether someone is looking over his or her shoulder:

```
ssnField.setEchoCharacter('x');
```

Tip

I wouldn't recommend using echo characters when processing credit card numbers. These numbers are so long that users will invariably mistype them if they aren't able to see what they're entering. Echo characters are best used for small pieces of text that the user isn't either likely to forget or have difficulty entering without the benefit of seeing each character appear after it is typed.

TextArea

Text fields are strictly limited. They allow you to create only small pieces of text, are restricted to one line, and don't support scroll bars.

Clearly, you may well need to go beyond these basic capabilities. You may need to display or allow the user to edit large portions of text, such as a mailing address, a resume, or even a novel. In these cases, a much larger area is required. You may even need scroll bars to allow the user to scroll up, down, left, or right.

Text areas enable you to do these things. They create large portions of text on the screen, which the user may or may not be able to edit. In fact, if you apply the isEditable() method, both TextField and TextArea allow you to specify whether the user should be able to change what is inside of them. Because TextField and TextArea inherit from the TextComponent class, the methods listed in Table 19-3 apply to both:

```
TextField myTextField = new TextField("You're lookin' at a
    TextField", 5, 20); // 5 columns by 20 rows
add(myTextField);
```

You can, of course, supply an actual String object when creating a text field. This enables you to keep your program neat, clean, and more readable:

```
String theString = "You can use any length string you want...";
TextField myTextArea = new TextField(theString, 5, 20);
add(myTextArea);
```

Canvases

Although each of the widgets I've discussed so far are obviously UI elements (perhaps with the exception of labels, which don't support user interaction), Java supplies an additional type of UI item, known as a *canvas*. The Canvas constructor and methods are shown in Table 19-12.

Table 19-12 **java.awt.Canvas**		
Constructor	**Signature**	**Description**
Canvas	public Canvas()	Creates a custom canvas.
Method	**Signature**	**Description**
addNotify	public synchronized void addNotify()	Creates the peer of the canvas. This peer enables you to change the UI of the canvas without changing its functionality. Overrides addNotify in class Component.
Paint	public void paint (Graphics g)	Paints the canvas in the default background color. Overrides paint in class Component. Parameter: g—the specified graphics context. Overrides paint in class Component.

Think of canvases as drawing or painting surfaces. They don't have special user-interaction traits, as do the widgets you've taken a look at so far. Nor do they provide a GUI-like purpose, as you might expect. You don't click them to initiate an action, scroll from left to right to view their contents, or choose items from a list.

So far, you haven't had to use a canvas because the applet itself has provided this functionality for you. In most cases, you simply draw on the applet what you want.

However, you eventually may want to reserve a certain area for such things. To do so, you can create a custom canvas by overriding or subclassing the Canvas class. This is particularly useful when you have a paint program or a game, or simply wish to have a specific type of canvas on which to paint and draw, as in Listing 19-1.

Listing 19-1: **Creating a Pie-Chart Canvas**

```
/**
 *
 * PieChartCanvas Class - Draws a 3D pie chart
 *
 * @version   1.03    27-Jun-1995
 * @author    Ciaran Treanor
 *
 */
class PieChartCanvas extends Canvas {
   final double aspectFudge = 2.5;
   int    radius,
    depth,
    called = 1,
    numSlices = 0;
   float    total = 0, value[] = new float[10];
   Color    color[] = new Color[10];
   Graphics    offGraphics;
   Image gfxBuff;
   public PieChartCanvas(int radius, int depth) {
     this.value = value;
     this.color = color;
     this.radius = radius;
     this.depth = depth;
   }
   public void paint(Graphics g) {
      int startAngle;
      float angle;
      Dimension d = size();
      if(gfxBuff == null) {
         gfxBuff = createImage(d.width, d.height);
         offGraphics = gfxBuff.getGraphics();
         offGraphics.setColor(getBackground());
         offGraphics.fillRect(0, 0, d.width, d.height);
      }
// This is less than optimal, but we don't have a floodfill.
// Draw depth-1 ovals in a darker color
```

(continued)

Listing 19-1 *(continued)*

```
        for(int x = depth; x >= 1; x-) {
            startAngle = -45;
            for(int i = 0; i < numSlices; i++) {
          offGraphics.setColor(color[i].darker());
          angle = Math.round(360 * (value[i] / total));

            offGraphics.fillArc(0, x, radius,
            (int)(radius / aspectFudge),
          startAngle, (int)angle);
            startAngle += angle;
          }
      }
  // Now draw the final (top) oval in the undarkened color
   startAngle = -45;
   for(int i = 0; i < numSlices; i++) {
     offGraphics.setColor(color[i]);
     angle = Math.round(360 * (value[i] / total));
     offGraphics.fillArc(0, 0, radius, (int)(radius /
   aspectFudge), startAngle, (int)angle);
     startAngle += angle;
   }
   g.drawImage(gfxBuff, 0, 0, null);
      }
    public void addSlice(float value, Color color) {
        this.value[numSlices] = value;
        this.color[numSlices++] = color;
        total += value;
    }
    public Dimension getPreferredSize() {
      return getMinimumSize();
    }
    public Dimension getMinimumSize() {
      return new Dimension(radius, (int)((radius / aspectFudge)
          +depth));
    }
  }
```

The code in Listing 19-1, taken from the PieChart applet example on the CD-ROM provided with this book, creates a PieChartCanvas class by extending the standard Canvas class. The result is a drawing surface that has all the properties the author wanted. Rather than simply creating the pie chart directly on the applet screen, the programmer decided to create a special canvas in which to display all pie charts. You can do the same yourself, especially in cases where you need better control over a drawing surface.

To create a canvas, simply instantiate a new Canvas object and add it as you would any other UI item:

```
PieChartCanvas c = new PieChartCanvas(radius, depth);
```

Containers (java.awt.Container)

As you learned in our discussion in Chapter 16, containers (see Table 19-13) enable you to place components inside them. They are, in fact, a direct subclass of the `Component` class. There are two main types of containers that you'll be dealing with: `Panel`, of which `Applet` is a subclass, and `Window`, of which `Dialog` and `Frame` are subclasses.

Table 19-13 java.awt		
Class	**Signature**	**Description**
`Container`	`public class Container`	Extends the `Component` class. A generic Abstract Windowing Toolkit (AWT) container object is a component that can contain other AWT components.
Method	**Signature**	**Description**
`getComponentCount`	`public int getComponentCount()`	Returns the number of components in this panel.
`CountComponents`	`public int countComponents()`	Note: `countComponents()` is deprecated. As of JDK version 1.1, replaced by `getComponentCount()`.
`GetComponent`	`public synchronized getComponent(int n)`	Gets the *n*th component in this container. Parameter: n – number of the component to get. Throws `ArrayIndexOutOfBoundsException` if the nth value does not exist.
`GetComponents`	`public synchronized Component[] getComponents()`	Gets all the components in this container.
`GetInsets`	`public Insets getInsets()`	Returns the insets of the container. The insets indicate the size of the border of the container. A frame, for example, will have a top inset that corresponds to the height of the frame's title bar.

(continued)

Table 19-13 *(continued)*

Method	Signature	Description
Insets	`public Insets insets()`	Note: `insets()` is deprecated. As of JDK version 1.1, replaced by `getInsets()`.
Add	`public Component add(Component comp)`	Adds the specified component to this container. Parameter: `comp` – component to be added.
add	`public synchronized Component add(String name, Component comp)`	Adds the specified component to this container. The component is also added to the layout manager of this container, using the name specified. Parameters: `name` – component name. `comp` – component to be added.
add	`public synchronized Component add (Component comp, int pos)`	Adds the specified component to this container at the given position. Parameters: `comp` – component to be added. `pos` – position at which to insert the component (–1 means insert at the end).
add	`public void add (Component comp, Object constraints)`	Adds the specified component to this container at the specified index. Also notifies the layout manager to add the component to the container's layout using the specified `constraints` object. Parameters: `comp` – the component to be added. `constraints` – an object expressing layout constraints for this component.

Method	Signature	Description
add	`public void add (Component comp, Object constraints, int index)`	Adds the specified component to this container with the specified constraints at the specified index. Also notifies the layout manager to add the component to this container's layout using the specified `constraints` object. Parameters: `comp`: The component to be added. `constraints`: An object expressing layout constraints for this. `index`: The position in the container's list at which to insert the component. A value of −1 means insert at the end.
raddImpl	`protected void add Impl(Component comp, Object constraints, int index)`	Adds the specified component to this container at the specified index. Also notifies the layout manager to add the component to this container's layout using the specified `constraints` object. This is the method to override if you want to track every add request to a container. An over-riding method should usually include a call to `super.addImpl (comp, constraints, index)`. Parameters: `comp`–the component to be added. `constraints`–an object expressing layout constraints for this component. `index`–the position in the container's list at which to insert the component. A value of −1 means insert at the end.
Remove	`public void remove (int index)`	Removes the component at the specified index from this container. Parameters: `index`–the index of the component to be removed.

(continued)

Table 19-13 (continued)

Method	Signature	Description
remove	public synchronized void remove (Component comp)	Removes the specified component from this container. Parameter: comp – component to be removed.
removeAll	public synchronized void removeAll()	Removes all the components from this container.
GetLayout	public LayoutManager getLayout()	Gets the layout manager for this container.
SetLayout	public void setLayout(Layout Manager mgr)	Sets the layout manager for this container. Parameter: mgr – specified layout manager. Overrides doLayout in class Component. Note: Most programs should not call this method directly, but should invoke validate instead.
Layout	public synchronized void layout()	Note: layout() is deprecated. As of JDK version 1.1, replaced by doLayout(). Overrides layout() in class Component.
Invalidate	public void invalidate()	Invalidates the container. The container and all parents above it are marked as needing to be laid out. This method can be called often, so it needs to execute quickly. Overrides invalidate() in class Component.
validate	public synchronized void validate()	Validates this container and all the components contained within it. Overrides validate() in class Component.

Method	Signature	Description
ValidateTree	protected void validateTree()	Recursively descends the container tree and recomputes the layout for any subtrees marked as needing it (those marked as invalid).
		Synchronization should be provided by the method that calls validate.
getPreferredSize	public Dimension getPreferredSize()	Returns the preferred size of this container.
		Overrides getPreferredSize() in class Component.
preferredSize	public synchronized Dimension preferred Size()	Note: preferredSize() is deprecated. As of JDK version 1.1, replaced by getPreferredSize().
		Overrides preferredSize() in class Component.
GetMinimumSize	public Dimension getMinimumSize()	Returns the minimum size of this container.
		Overrides getMinimumSize() in class Component.
minimumSize	public synchronized Dimension minimum Size()	Note: minimumSize() is deprecated. As of JDK version 1.1, replaced by getMinimumSize().
		Overrides minimumSize() in class Component.
GetMaximumSize	public Dimension getMaximumSize()	Returns the maximum size of this container.
		Overrides getMaximumSize() in class Component.
getAlignmentX	public float getAlignmentX()	Returns the alignment along the *x* axis. This specifies how the component would like to be aligned relative to other components.
		The value should be a number between 0 and 1, where 0 represents alignment along the origin, 1 is aligned the farthest away from the origin, 0.5 is centered, and so on.
		Overrides getAlignmentX() in class Component.

(continued)

Table 19-13 (continued)

Method	Signature	Description
getAlignmentY	public float getAlignmentY()	Returns the alignment along the y axis. This specifies how the component would like to be aligned relative to other components. The value should be a number between 0 and 1, where 0 represents alignment along the origin, 1 is aligned the furthest away from the origin, 0.5 is centered, and so on. Overrides getAlignmentY() in class Component.
paint	public void paint (Graphics g)	Paints the container. This forwards the paint call to any lightweight components that are children of this container. If this method is reimplemented, super.paint(g) should be called so that lightweight components are properly rendered. If a child component is entirely clipped by the current clipping setting in g, paint() will not be forwarded to that child. Overrides paint() in class Component. Parameter: g – the specified graphics window. Overrides paint() in class Component.

Method	Signature	Description
print	public void print (Graphics g)	Prints the container. This forwards the print to any lightweight components that are children of this container. If this method is reimplemented, super.print(g) should be called so that lightweight components are properly rendered. If a child component is entirely clipped by the current clipping setting in g, print() will not be forwarded to that child. Overrides print() in class Component. Parameter: g – the specified graphics window. Overrides print() in class Component.
paintComponents	public void paint Components(Graphics g)	Paints the components in this container. Parameter: g – the specified graphics window.
printComponents	public void print Components(Graphics g)	Prints the components in this container. Parameter: g – the specified graphics window.
addContainer Listener	public synchronized void addContainer Listener(Container Listener l)	Adds the specified container listener to receive container events from this container. Parameter: l – the container listener.
removeContainer Listener	public void remove ContainerListener (ContainerListener l)	Removes the specified container listener so that it no longer receives container events from this container. Parameter: l – the container listener.

(continued)

Table 19-13 (continued)

Method	Signature	Description
processEvent	protected void processEvent(AWT Event e)	Processes events on this container. If the event is a Container Event, it invokes the process ContainerEvent() method; otherwise, it invokes its superclass's processEvent(). Overrides processEvent() in class Component. Parameter: e –the event.
processContainer Event	protected void processContainer Event(ContainerEvent e)	Processes container events occurring on this container by dispatching them to any registered ContainerListener objects. Note: This method will not be called unless container events are enabled for this component; this happens when one of the following occurs: (a) A ContainerListener object is registered via addContainerListener() (b) Container events are enabled via enableEvents() Parameter: e –the container event.
deliverEvent	public void deliver Event(Event e)	Note: deliverEvent() is deprecated. As of JDK version 1.1, replaced by dispatchEvent(AWTEvent e). Overrides deliverEvent() in class Component.

Method	Signature	Description
GetComponentAt	`public Component getComponentAt(int x, int y)`	Locates the component that contains the *x,y* position. The top-most child component is returned in the case where there is overlap in the components. This is determined by finding the component closest to the index 0 that claims to contain the given point via `Component.contains()`.
		Returns null if the component does not contain the position. If there is no child component at the requested point, and the point is within the bounds of the container, the container itself is returned; otherwise, the top-most child is returned.
		Overrides `getComponentAt()` in class `Component`.
		Parameters: x – the *x* coordinate. y – the *y* coordinate.
locate	`public Component locate(int x, int y)`	Note: `locate()` is deprecated. As of JDK version 1.1, replaced by `getComponentAt(int, int)`.
		Overrides `locate()` in class `Component`.
GetComponentAt	`public Component getComponentAt (Point p)`	Locates the component that contains the specified point.
		Returns null if the component does not contain the point; returns the component otherwise.
		Overrides `getComponentAt()` in class `Component`.
		Parameter: p – the point.

(continued)

	Table 19-13 *(continued)*	
Method	*Signature*	*Description*
addNotify	public void addNotify()	Notifies the container to create a peer. It will also notify the components contained in this container. This method should be called by `Container.add()` and not by user code directly.
		Overrides `addNotify()` in class `Component`.
RemoveNotify	public void removeNotify()	Notifies the container to remove its peer. It will also notify the components contained in this container. This method should be called by `Container.remove` and not by user code directly.
		Overrides `removeNotify()` in class `Component`.
IsAncestorOf	public boolean isAncestorOf (Component c)	Checks whether the component is contained in the component hierarchy of this container.
		Parameter: `c` – the component.
paramString	protected String paramString()	Returns the parameter string of this container.
		Overrides `paramString()` in class `Component`.
List	public void list (PrintStream out, int indent)	Prints a list of container objects, starting at the specified indention, to the specified out-stream. Overrides `list()` in class `Component`.
		Parameters: `out` – stream name. `indent` – start of the list.
list	public void list (PrintWriter out, int indent)	Prints a list, starting at the specified indention, to the specified print writer.
		Overrides `list()` in class `Component`.

Layout Managers Are Relevant Here

By default, containers have what's known as a *layout manager* associated with them. Layout managers allow your applications and applets to lay out components on the screen in a way that is appropriate for each platform on which they are running. I discuss layout managers in Chapter 21; they are relevant here because you're likely to encounter them as parameters.

Panels

Panel (see Table 19-14) is a subclass of the Container class. And, as you know, Applet is a subclass of Panel. As a result, your applets are, technically speaking, special-purpose panels.

Table 19-14
java.awt.Panel

Constructor	Example	Description
Panel	public Panel()	Creates a new panel. The default layout for all panels is FlowLayout.
Panel	public Panel(Layout Manager layout)	Creates a new panel with the specified layout manager.
		Parameter: layout – the layout manager for this panel.

Method	Signature	Description
addNotify	public synchronized void addNotify()	Creates the panel's peer. The peer allows you to modify the appearance of the panel without changing its functionality.
		Overrides addNotify() in class Container.

Whatever you want to do with panels and containers, you can do directly inside your applet. This is the reason you're able to draw directly on your applets. You don't have to worry about creating a special canvas or container. To create a panel, you simply instantiate a Panel object and add it, just as you do with individual components:

```
Panel anyPanel = new Panel();
add.anyPanel; // add it to the current container (such as an applet)
```

There is, however, a difference in this procedure: Instead of creating a specific interface widget, you are creating and adding an area that can contain within itself a number of user-interface components. You could create a panel, for example, on the upper left-hand side of your applet that had a specific grouping of buttons, scroll bars, and other widgets. Then you could create an additional panel, place it in the lower left-hand corner, and have whatever widgets you like associated there.

In addition, you can nest panels inside each other. In fact, when you create a panel inside an applet, this is exactly what you're doing, as seen in the previous code example: You created a new panel and added it to the applet, which is, of course, a panel itself.

Grouping components

Panels are used to group components; most often, they are used to group widgets. As you may be able to tell from Figure 19-2, this program uses three panels:

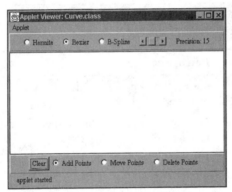

Figure 19-2: Panels are useful for grouping components.

✦ The top panel contains controls that let you decide the type of curve you want to create. In addition to check boxes, there's a scroll bar to customize how fine or how rough the curve will be.

✦ Directly beneath the top panel is a drawing area in which the curve will be drawn. This is itself contained in a panel.

✦ Immediately below the drawing area is yet another panel, which contains a Clear button (to clear out the residue of the previous drawing) and a group of check boxes that enable you to choose whether you're adding new points to the curve, removing points you've placed up there already, or simply moving points around.

Using panels allowed the developer to neatly separate and group the various components that this particular applet uses.

Coordinates

Each panel has its own coordinate system. As you now know, the basic coordinate system starts with the upper left-hand corner being 0,0 and extends to the right (*x* axis) and to the bottom (*y* axis) in positive values. When you create a new panel, it has an identical coordinate system: The upper left-hand coordinates are 0,0, and they extend along *x* and *y* axes (width and height).

As a result, coordinate systems become nested. For example, while the applet may have a coordinate system of (0,0,200,400), the top panel in this example has its own coordinate system, perhaps of (0,0,200,100). The bottom panel might be (0,0,200,100) as well, because both are the same size. And the middle panel might be something like (0,0,200,200).

Note

When you position text and graphics inside a panel, use *x* and *y* coordinates relative to the coordinate system of that panel. The scroll bar in Figure 19-2 is not positioned according to the coordinate system of the applet (0,0,200,400), but it is positioned in accordance with the coordinate system of the panel it is in (0,0,200,100).

Listing 19-2 contains code used to create panels. As you can see by referring back to Table 19-8, only one method and a constructor are defined in `java.awt.Panel`. However, because `Panel` is a subclass of `Container`, it inherits all the methods seen in Table 19-7. And because `Container` is a subclass of `Component`, the methods in Table 21-1 are also available to Panel objects.

Listing 19-2: **The Code That Creates Panels**

```
/*
 * WidgetsInWindow.java
 *
 * A sample applet/application combo to show how to create
 * a frame and add widgets to it.
 * The frame supports menus, the last three of which are
 * functional and create dialogs.
 *
 * @author Aaron E. Walsh
 * @version 1.1, 8 Jul 97
 */
import java.awt.*;
import java.awt.event.*;
public class WidgetsInWindow extends java.applet.Applet {
  public void init() {
    resize(250,250);
    WidgetsFrame window = new WidgetsFrame();
    window.applet=true; /* set flag to tell we're running as
                           an applet, not an application */
```

(continued)

Listing 19-2 *(continued)*

```
    window.setTitle(""Widgets Galore, running in an Applet"");
    window.pack();
    window.show();
  }

  public static void main(String[] args) {
    WidgetsFrame window = new WidgetsFrame();
    window.applet=false; /* set flag to tell we're running as
                                              an application */
    window.setTitle(""Widgets Galore"");
    window.pack();
    window.show();
  }

  public void paint(Graphics g) {
    g.drawString(""Here come the widgets..."",50,100);
  }
}
class WidgetsFrame extends Frame {
  boolean applet= true;
  final String GET_FILE = ""Get a file..."";
  final String SAVE_FILE = ""Save a file..."";
  final String BASIC_WINDOW = ""Create a basic window..."";
  public static void main(String args[]) {
   WidgetsFrame window = new WidgetsFrame();
   window.applet= false; /* set a flag to tell we're
                            running as an application,
                            not as an applet */
   window.setTitle(""Widgets galore, running as an application"");
   window.pack();
   window.show();
  }
  public WidgetsFrame() {
   Panel centerPanel = new Panel(); // main panel
   Panel buttonPanel = new Panel(); // panel for buttons
   Panel widgetPanel = new Panel(); // for other widgets
   /* --- Begin by creating a menubar and menu for this
                           frame --- */
   MenuBar theMenuBar = new MenuBar(); /* create a new menubar
                                            object */
   Menu theMenu = new Menu(""A Real Menu""); /* and create a menu
                                                to put it in */
   theMenu.add(new MenuItem(""This is a menu item..."")); /*add a
                                                few items... */
   theMenu.add(new CheckboxMenuItem(""This is another menu
                                        item!""));
   theMenu.add(new CheckboxMenuItem(""Yet another menu item""));
   theMenu.add(new MenuItem(""And, yes, a fourth menu item""));
   theMenu.add(new MenuItem(""-"")); // create a menu separator
```

```
MenuItem mi = new MenuItem(GET_FILE);
  /* Add action handler for this menu item. */
mi.addActionListener(new ActionListener() {
  public void actionPerformed(ActionEvent e) {
    FileDialog dlog  = new FileDialog(WidgetsFrame.this,
      ""Get A File..."",FileDialog.LOAD);
    dlog.show();
  }
});
theMenu.add(mi);
mi = new MenuItem(SAVE_FILE);
theMenu.add(mi);
mi.addActionListener(new ActionListener() {
  public void actionPerformed(ActionEvent e) {
    FileDialog dlog = new FileDialog(WidgetsFrame.this,
      ""Save A File..."",  FileDialog.SAVE);
    dlog.show();
  }
});
mi = new MenuItem(BASIC_WINDOW);
mi.addActionListener(new ActionListener() {
  public void actionPerformed(ActionEvent e) {
    Window myWindow = new Window(new Frame());   /* myWindow is
      initially invisible */
    myWindow.setSize(200, 350); // make window 200 by 350
    myWindow.setLocation(50,50);  /* then move it to desired
                                     location */
    myWindow.show(); // and finally show it
  }
});
theMenu.add(mi);
theMenuBar.add(theMenu);
setMenuBar(theMenuBar);    /* and finally add the menubar to
                             the menu */
Menu subMenu = new Menu(""Here's a submenu""); /* create
                                                 another menu */
subMenu.add(new MenuItem(""Hello!"")); // add an item...
theMenu.add(subMenu); // and add the submenu to the menu
/* --- Add buttons to the buttonPanel -- */
buttonPanel.add(new Button(""Buttons R Us""));
buttonPanel.add(new Button(""Eeny""));
buttonPanel.add(new Button(""Meeny""));
buttonPanel.add(new Button(""Miney""));
buttonPanel.add(new Button(""Mo!""));
buttonPanel.add(new Button(""This is a really, really, WIDE
  button""));
/* --- Add widgets to the widgetPanel --- */
// first add a choice menu:
Choice theChoice = new Choice(); // create it
```

(continued)

Listing 19-2 *(continued)*

```
theChoice.addItem(""This is a Choice item..."");  /* add an item
                                                    or six */
theChoice.addItem(""This is another choice item!"");
theChoice.addItem(""Yet another choice item"");
theChoice.addItem(""And, yes, a fourth choice item"");
theChoice.addItem(""-"");  //can't create a menu separator!
theChoice.addItem(""The above isn't a separator!"");
widgetPanel.add(theChoice); // and add it to the widgetPanel.

// then Create a new list and add it:
List theList = new List(5, true);  /* five rows, multiple
                                      selections allowed */
theList.addItem(""This is a list item..."");
theList.addItem(""How much"");
theList.addItem(""would you expect"");
theList.addItem(""to pay for a"");
theList.addItem(""list like this?"");
theList.addItem(""$150?"");
theList.addItem(""$100?"");  /* notice that seven items (two
                               more than specified) are added,
                               forcing scroll bars to appear
                               when drawn */
widgetPanel.add(""West"", theList);
 // next, add a check box and text field...
widgetPanel.add(new Checkbox(""Check box""));
widgetPanel.add(new TextField(""TextField""));

/* --- Add Canvas, Label and TextArea to centerPanel --- */
centerPanel.setLayout(new GridLayout(1,2));  /* GridLayout
                                                (2 rows, 2
                                                columns) */
   //Put a canvas in the left column.
centerPanel.add(new WidgetCanvas()); // see WidgetCanvas class
Panel p = new Panel();     /* this panel is nested inside
                              centerPanel */
p.setLayout(new BorderLayout());
p.add(""North"", new Label(""You're lookin' at a Label"",
      Label.CENTER));
p.add(""Center"", new TextArea(""You're lookin' at a
   TextArea"", 5,  20));
centerPanel.add(p);
/* -- Now set the layout manager for this frame -- */
 setLayout(new BorderLayout()); /* change the layout to
                                   BorderLayout */
add(""North"", buttonPanel); // place buttonPanel at top
add(""South"", widgetPanel); // place widgetPanel at bottom
add(""Center"", centerPanel); // and the centerPanel in the
                                                    center
```

```
    addWindowListener(new WindowAdapter() {
      public void Iconified(WindowEvent e) {// should we just hide?
         setVisible(false);
      }
      public void windowDeiconified(WindowEvent e) {
         setVisible(true);
      }
      public void windowClosing(WindowEvent e) {// or die?
        System.exit(0);
        if (applet)
          dispose();
        else
          System.exit(0);
      }
    });
  }
}
class WidgetCanvas extends Canvas {
 public void paint(Graphics g) {
  int canW = getSize().width; // get width of canvas
  int canH = getSize().height; // get height of canvas
  g.setColor(Color.lightGray); // set the color to lightGray
  g.draw3DRect(0, 0, canW -1, canH-1, true); /* frame canvas with
                                                 rectangle */
  g.setColor(Color.black); // set the color to black
   /* draw string centered in canvas width: */
  g.drawString(""Widget Canvas"", (canW -
    g.getFontMetrics().stringWidth(""Widget Canvas""))/2, 15);
// POLYGONS:
  g.setColor(Color.red); // set the color to red
  int xCoords[] = {40, 55, 65, 80, 80, 40}; // create x values
  int yCoords[] = {40, 38, 55, 30, 75, 40}; // create y values
   // create the polygon:
  Polygon thePoly = new Polygon(xCoords,yCoords,xCoords.length);
  g.drawPolygon(thePoly); // then draw it
       /* however, we can always feed the arrays directly to
          drawPolygon() without creating a polygon object using
          g.drawPolygon(xCoords,yCoords,xCoords.length); */
// This polygon will be blue, offset, and filled:
  g.setColor(Color.blue); // set the color to blue
  int xOffset = 50; // the x offset
  int yOffset  = 40; // the y offset
  int xlen = xCoords.length;
  for (int i=0;i<xlen;i++) { // offset the contents of each array
    xCoords[i] += xOffset; // offset
    yCoords[i] += yOffset; // offset
  }
  g.fillPolygon(xCoords,yCoords,xCoords.length); // now, fill
```

(continued)

Listing 19-2 *(continued)*

```
  }
  public Dimension getMinimumSize() {
   return new Dimension(250,250);
  }
  public Dimension getPreferredSize() {
   return getMinimumSize();
  }
 }
```

Creating Panels with JDK 1.0.2

Creating panels with JDK 1.0.2 is almost exactly the same as creating them with JDK 1.1/1.2. The only difference lies in how you handle events. In JDK 1.1, the *delegation event model* governs handling of events that occur inside panels. In JDK 1.0.2, Java's original *hierarchical event model* rules. The difference between the two event models is significant, and is one of the most major differences between JDK 1.0 and JDK 1.1/1.2. Specifically, when an event occurs when running in a JDK 1.0.*x* applet or application, the hierarchical event model is used: If the event takes place within a component inside a panel, that component has first crack at handling the event. If the component chooses not to handle the event, it passes it to its containing panel. The panel can process the event or pass it to its container, which might be another panel, and so on, until the event reaches the application or applet's top-level container. In the case of an applet, of course, the applet itself is the top-level container, so the applet itself is the event handler of last resort.

With this hierarchical model, you are free to choose at what point in your UI hierarchy to handle events, including those that occur inside panels. For example, you can let your panel handle events that occur inside it, or you can handle them at the applet level. All you need to do is override the appropriate event-handling methods of the container that you want to handle the events, as discussed in Chapter 16.

For example, Listing 19-3 contains a JDK 1.0.2-compatible version of the `WidgetsIn Window` code (shown in Listing 19-2), that is functionally the same as its JDK 1.1/1.2 counterpart: It creates panels. In this version, however, you're dealing with the hierarchial event model instead of the delegation event model. As such, I have chosen to let this applet/application combination program handle menu events that occur inside the applet/application's frame window.

Listing 19-3: **JDK 1.0.2-Compatible Code for Creating Panels**

```
WidgetsInWindow-1.02.java
/*
 * WidgetsInWindow-1.02.java
 *
 * A sample applet/application combo to show how to create
 * a frame and add widgets to it.
 * The frame supports menus, the last three of which are
 * functional and create dialogs.
 *
 * @author Aaron E. Walsh
 * @version 1.0, 14 Jan 98
 */
import java.awt.*;
public class WidgetsInWindow extends java.applet.Applet {
  public void init() {
  resize(250,250);
  WidgetsFrame window = new WidgetsFrame();
  window.applet=true; /* set flag to tell we're running as
                         an applet, not an application */
  window.setTitle("Widgets Galore, running in an Applet");
  window.pack();
  window.show();
  }
  public static void main(String[] args) {
    WidgetsFrame window = new WidgetsFrame();
    window.applet=false; /* set flag to tell we're running as
                            an application */
    window.setTitle("Widgets Galore");
    window.pack();
    window.show();
  }
  public void paint(Graphics g) {
    g.drawString("Here come the widgets... ",50,100);
  }
}
class WidgetsFrame extends Frame {
 boolean applet= true;
 final String GET_FILE = ""Get a file...."";
 final String SAVE_FILE = "Save a file...";
 final String BASIC_WINDOW = "Create a basic window...";
 public static void main(String args[]) {
  WidgetsFrame window = new WidgetsFrame();
  window.applet= false; /* set a flag to tell we're
                           running as an application,
                           not as an applet */
  window.setTitle("Widgets galore, running as an application");
  window.pack();
  window.show();
 }
```

(continued)

Listing 19-3 *(continued)*

```java
public WidgetsFrame() {
 Panel centerPanel = new Panel(); // main panel
 Panel buttonPanel = new Panel(); // panel for buttons
 Panel widgetPanel = new Panel(); // for other widgets
 /* --- Begin by creating a menubar and menu for this
    frame --- */
 MenuBar theMenuBar = new MenuBar(); // create a new menubar
object
 Menu theMenu = new Menu("A Real Menu"); /* and create a menu to
                                    put it in */
theMenu.add(new MenuItem("This is a menu item..."));/* add a few
                                            items */
theMenu.add(new CheckboxMenuItem
        ("This is another menu item!"));
theMenu.add(new CheckboxMenuItem("Yet another menu item"));
theMenu.add(new MenuItem("And, yes, a fourth menu item"));
theMenu.add(new MenuItem("-")); // create a menu separator
theMenu.add(new MenuItem(GET_FILE));
theMenu.add(new MenuItem(SAVE_FILE));
theMenu.add(new MenuItem(BASIC_WINDOW));
theMenuBar.add(theMenu);
setMenuBar(theMenuBar);
   // and finally add the menubar to the menu
Menu subMenu = new Menu("Here's a submenu"); /* create another
                       menu */
subMenu.add(new MenuItem("Hello!")); // add an item...
theMenu.add(subMenu); // and add the submenu to the menu
/* --- Add buttons to the buttonPanel --- */
buttonPanel.add(new Button("Buttons R Us"));
buttonPanel.add(new Button("Eeny"));
buttonPanel.add(new Button("Meeny"));
buttonPanel.add(new Button("Miney"));
buttonPanel.add(new Button("Mo!"));
buttonPanel.add(new Button("This is a really, really, WIDE
            button"));
/* --- Add widgets to the widgetPanel --- */
// first add a choice menu:
Choice theChoice = new Choice(); // create it
theChoice.addItem("This is a Choice item..."); /* add an item
                                        or six */
theChoice.addItem("This is another choice item!");
theChoice.addItem("Yet another choice item");
theChoice.addItem("And, yes, a fourth choice item");
theChoice.addItem("-"); //can't create a menu separator!
theChoice.addItem("The above isn't a separator!");
widgetPanel.add(theChoice); // and add it to the widgetPanel.

// then Create a new list and add it:
List theList = new List(5, true); /* five rows, multiple
                              selections allowed */
```

```
theList.addItem("This is a list item...");
theList.addItem("How much");
theList.addItem("would you expect");
theList.addItem("to pay for a");
theList.addItem("list like this?");
theList.addItem("$150?");
theList.addItem("$100?"); /* notice that seven items (two
                             more than specified) are added,
                             forcing scroll bars to appear
                             when drawn */
widgetPanel.add("West", theList);
  // next, add a check box and text field...
widgetPanel.add(new Checkbox("Check box"));
widgetPanel.add(new TextField("TextField"));

/* --- Add Canvas, Label and TextArea to centerPanel --- */
centerPanel.setLayout(new GridLayout(1,2));
/* GridLayout (2 rows, 2 columns) */
  //Put a canvas in the left column.
centerPanel.add(new WidgetCanvas()); // see WidgetCanvas class
Panel p = new Panel();
  // this panel is nested inside centerPanel
p.setLayout(new BorderLayout());
p.add("North", new Label("You're lookin' at a Label",
  Label.CENTER));
p.add("Center", new TextArea("You're lookin' at a TextArea",
  5, 20));
centerPanel.add(p);
/* -- Now set the layout manager for this frame --- */
setLayout(new BorderLayout()); /* change the layout to
                                  BorderLayout */
add("North", buttonPanel); // place buttonPanel at top
add("South", widgetPanel); // place widgetPanel at bottom
add("Center", centerPanel); // and the centerPanel in the center
}
public boolean handleEvent(Event e) {
if ((e.id == Event.ACTION_EVENT) && (e.target instanceof
  MenuItem)) {
  String label = (String)e.arg;
  if (label.equals(GET_FILE)) {
  FileDialog dlog = new FileDialog(this, "Get A File...",
    FileDialog.LOAD);
  dlog.show();
  } else if (label.equals(SAVE_FILE)) {
    FileDialog dlog = new FileDialog(this, "Save A File...",
      FileDialog.SAVE);
    dlog.show();
    } else if (label.equals(BASIC_WINDOW)) {
    Window myWindow = new Window(new Frame());/* myWindow is
                                      initially invisible */
    myWindow.resize(200, 350); // make window 200 by 350
```

(continued)

Listing 19-3 *(continued)*

```
      myWindow.move(50,50); // then move it to desired location
      myWindow.show(); // and finally show it
      }
    return true;
  }

  if (e.id == Event.WINDOW_ICONIFY) { // should we just hide?
    hide();
    return true;
  }
  if (e.id == Event.WINDOW_DESTROY) { // or is it time to die?
    if (applet) {
      dispose();
      return true;
    } else {
      System.exit(0);
    }
  }
  return super.handleEvent(e);
  }
}
class WidgetCanvas extends Canvas {
  public void paint(Graphics g) {
  int canW = size().width; // get width of canvas
  int canH = size().height; // get height of canvas
  g.setColor(Color.lightGray); // set the color to lightGray
  g.draw3DRect(0, 0, canW -1, canH-1, true); /* frame canvas with
                                                rectangle */
  g.setColor(Color.black); // set the color to black
   /* draw string centered in canvas width: */
  g.drawString("Widget Canvas", (canW -
    g.getFontMetrics().stringWidth("Widget Canvas"))/2, 15);
// POLYGONS:
  g.setColor(Color.red); // set the color to red
  int xCoords[] = {40, 55, 65, 80, 80, 40}; // create x values
  int yCoords[] = {40, 38, 55, 30, 75, 40}; // create y values
   // create the polygon:
  Polygon thePoly = new Polygon(xCoords,yCoords,xCoords.length);
  g.drawPolygon(thePoly); // then draw it
     /* however, we can always feed the arrays directly to
        drawPolygon() without creating a polygon object
        using g.drawPolygon(xCoords,yCoords,xCoords.length); */
// This polygon will be blue, offset, and filled:
  g.setColor(Color.blue); // set the color to blue
  int xOffset = 50; // the x offset
  int yOffset = 40; // the y offset
  int xlen = xCoords.length;
  for (int i=0;i<xlen;i++) { // offset the contents of each array
    xCoords[i] += xOffset; // offset
    yCoords[i] += yOffset; // offset
  }
```

```
g.fillPolygon(xCoords,yCoords,xCoords.length); // now, fill
}
public Dimension minimumSize() {
return new Dimension(250,250);
}
public Dimension preferredSize() {
return minimumSize();
}
}
```

For example, to change the size of a panel (or to set the size initially), you use the resize() method. If you want to place the panel at a specific place on the screen, you move it to the desired location using the move() method. Because all the UI elements I'm discussing are descendants of Component, they all understand and respond to these methods.

Summary

This chapter examined the components that make up Java's graphical user interface because these features are commonly found in Java applets and applications. How you use these components depends on which version of the JDK you use.

✦ Java enables you to use scroll bars, labels, text components, canvases, containers, and panels as features of your application's user interface.

✦ Older Java applications may rely on the AWT for user interface components; JDK 1.2 uses the JFC and Swing classes instead.

✦ Labels have a small but appropriate role in a Java user interface.

✦ AWT components enable you to listen for events.

✦ JDK versions 1.0.2, 1.1, and 1.2 have significantly different approaches to event handling.

✦   ✦   ✦

Windows

T his chapter continues the discussion of the graphical user interface (GUI) components available in Java's Abstract Windowing Toolkit (AWT). Having come this far in the book, you've dealt with most of the widgets you're likely to encounter or need; therefore this chapter is devoted to explaining how to work with windows.

Windows

All windows are `Window` objects. The `Window` class is a subclass of `Container`, and is in the same position in the class hierarchy as `Panel`. However, this class has a very specific purpose: to create those `Window` objects. For applets, this has a special connotation, since windows exist "outside" them altogether.

Until now, everything we've been doing with respect to applets has been happening inside the applet. Even the panels we discussed in the last chapter are created inside the applet context (browser). At times, however, we need to create a full-blown window or dialog box; perhaps in order to create the equivalent of a floating palette, with widgets on a window instead of inside the applet.

Or maybe we'd like to give users access to files on the local machine, as seen in Figure 20-1. In this case, we'd use the `FileDialog` class to present this special-purpose window.

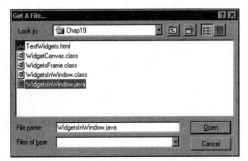

Figure 20-1: The FileDialog class allows us to easily create file-access dialog boxes.

Table 20-1 lists the constructors and methods that apply to windows. Note that they also apply to dialogs (see Table 20-6 later in this chapter).

	Table 20-1	
	java.awt.Window Constructor and Methods	
Constructor	**Signature**	**Description**
Window	public Window (Frame parent)	Constructs a new window initialized to an invisible state. It behaves as a modal dialog box in that it will block input to other windows when shown. Parameter: parent – the owner of the dialog box
Method	**Signature**	**Description**
addNotify	public synchronized void addNotify()	Creates the window's peer. The peer allows us to modify the appearance of the window without changing its functionality. Overrides addNotify() in class Container.
pack	public synchronized void pack()	Packs the components of the window.
show	public synchronized void show()	Shows the window. This will bring the window to the front if it is already visible. Overrides show() in class Component.
dispose	public synchronized void dispose()	Disposes of the window. This method must be called to release the resources used for the window.
toFront	public void toFront()	Places this window at the top of the stacking order and shows it in front of any other windows.

Method	Signature	Description
toBack	`public void toBack()`	Places this window at the bottom of the stacking order and makes the corresponding adjustment to other visible windows.
getToolkit	`public Toolkit getToolkit()`	Returns the toolkit of this frame. Overrides `getToolkit()` in class `Component`.
getWarning String	`public final String getWarningString()`	Gets the warning string for this window. This string will be displayed somewhere in the visible area of windows that are not secure.
getLocale	`public Locale getLocale()`	Gets the locale for the window, if it has been set. If no locale has been set, then the default locale is returned. Overrides `getLocale()` in class `Component`.
addWindow Listener	`public synchronized void addWindow Listener(Window Listener l)`	Adds the specified window listener to receive window events from this window. Parameter: l – the window listener.
removeWindow Listener	`public synchronized void removeWindow Listener(Window Listener l)`	Removes the specified window listener so that it no longer receives window events from this window. Parameter: l – the window listener
processEvent	`protected void processEvent(AWT Event e)`	Processes events on this window. If the event is a `WindowEvent`, it invokes the `processWindowEvent()` method, else it invokes its superclass's `process Event()`. Overrides `processEvent()` in class `Container`. Parameter: e – the event.

(continued)

	Table 20-1 *(continued)*	
Method	**Signature**	**Description**
process WindowEvent	protected void processWindowEvent (WindowEvent e)	Processes window events occurring on this window by dispatching them to any registered WindowListener objects. Note: This method will not be called unless window events are enabled for this component; this happens when one of the following occurs: a) A Window Listener object is registered via add WindowListener() b) Window events are enabled via enableEvents(). Parameter: e – the window event.
getFocus Owner	public Component getFocusOwner()	Returns the child component of this window that has focus if and only if this window is active. Returns the component with focus, or null if no children have focus assigned to them.
postEvent	public boolean postEvent(Event e)	Note: postEvent() is deprecated. As of JDK version 1.1, replaced by dispatchEvent(AWTEvent). Overrides postEvent() in class Component.
isShowing	public boolean isShowing()	Checks whether this window is showing on-screen. Overrides isShowing() in class Component.

Just as with panels, you can use any of the container methods with windows. For example, once you create a window or dialog box, you can move it anywhere on the screen using setLocation(), or change its dimensions using setSize().

Because windows initially are created invisibly, you can't see them until the show() method is invoked. In the next fragment of code, we create a new window, supplying to the constructor a newly created Frame object. The frame, discussed in detail below, is a required parameter for the Window() constructor. However, we can create one on the fly without bothering to keep a reference to it:

```
Window myWindow = new Window(new Frame()); // myWindow is
invisible
```

```
myWindow.show(); // but now it's visible
```

When you first create a window, you'll need to make it visible (as shown in this sample code), before the user can interact with it. However, it's a good idea to resize the window to whatever dimensions you want, and to move it to the position you want on the screen first. If you do these things after making the window (or any other container, for that matter) visible, it can result in an unattractive flashing:

```
Window myWindow = new Window(new Frame()); // myWindow is
invisible
myWindow.setSize(200, 350); // make window 200 by 350
myWindow.setLocation(50,50);
myWindow.show();
```

In addition, once the window is visible, you can make it invisible as necessary. To do this, simply send it the `setVisible(false)` method. This is helpful when you need to get a window off the screen, but want it to reappear later in the same position.

Tip

You may have realized that `setSize()` and `setLocation()` are defined in `java.awt.Component`, but not in the `Window` or `Container` classes. Because you can move and resize all components and their subclasses in the same way, there is no need for a special method for each. You'll see that quite a few methods defined in `Component` are useful for windows as well (see Table 20-1 earlier in this chapter).

Frames

The basic window is created without a menu bar, and doesn't even support menus. As a result, it's most useful for popping up a set of controls that can't fit inside your applet — a floating control panel, for example. You can draw and paint in a window, just as you would in an applet, so you may choose to use one as a surface for just such things. You won't be able to use menus with standard windows (although choice menus are fine; they don't require a menu bar).

Frames, on the other hand, allow you to implement a menu bar with menus, resulting in windows that look and act as you would expect (see Table 20-2).

Table 20-2
java.awt.Frame Constructor, Methods, and Variables

Constructor	Signature	Description
Frame	public Frame()	Constructs a new frame that is initially invisible.
Frame	public Frame (String title)	Constructs a new, initially invisible, frame with the title specified. Parameter: title – title specified.

Method	Signature	Description
addNotify	public synchronized void addNotify()	Creates the frame's peer. The peer allows us to change the look of the frame without changing its functionality. Overrides addNotify() in class Window.
getTitle	public String getTitle()	Gets the title of the frame.
setTitle	public void setTitle (String title)	Sets the title for this frame to the specified title. Parameter: title – specified title.
getIconImage	public Image getIconImage()	Returns the icon image for this frame.
setIconImage	public void setIcon Image(Image image)	Sets the image to display when this frame is iconized. Note that not all platforms support the concept of iconizing a window. Parameter: image – icon image to be displayed.
getMenuBar	public MenuBar getMenuBar()	Gets the menu bar for this frame.
setMenuBar	public synchronized void setMenuBar (MenuBar mb)	Sets the menu bar for this frame to the specified menu bar. Parameter: mb – menu bar being set
isResizable	public boolean isResizable()	Returns true if the user can resize the frame.
setResizable	public synchronized void setResizable (boolean resizable)	Sets the resizable flag. Parameter: resizable – true if resizable; false otherwise.

Method	Signature	Description
remove	public synchronized void remove(Menu Component m)	Removes the specified menu bar from this frame.
dispose	public synchronized void dispose()	Disposes of the frame. This method must be called to release the resources that are used for the frame. Overrides dispose in class Window.
isResizable	public boolean isResizable()	Returns true if the user can resize the frame.
setResizable	public void setResizable (boolean resizable)	Sets the resizable flag. Parameter: resizable – true if resizable; false otherwise.
setCursor	public void setCursor(int cursorType)	Sets the cursor image to a predefined cursor. Parameter: cursorType - one of the cursor constants defined below.
getCursorType	public int getCursorType()	Note: getCursorType() is deprecated. As of JDK version 1.1, replaced by Component.getCursor().
paramString	protected String paramString()	Returns the parameter string of this frame. Overrides paramString() in class Container.

Variable	Signature
DEFAULT_CURSOR	public final static int DEFAULT_CURSOR
CROSSHAIR_CURSOR	public final static int CROSSHAIR_CURSOR
TEXT_CURSOR	public final static int TEXT_CURSOR
WAIT_CURSOR	public final static int WAIT_CURSOR
SW_RESIZE_CURSOR	public final static int SW_RESIZE_CURSOR
SE_RESIZE_CURSOR	public final static int SE_RESIZE_CURSOR
NW_RESIZE_CURSOR	public final static int NW_RESIZE_CURSOR
NE_RESIZE_CURSOR	public final static int NE_RESIZE_CURSOR
N_RESIZE_CURSOR	public final static int N_RESIZE_CURSOR

(continued)

Table 20-2 *(continued)*	
Variable	**Signature**
S_RESIZE_CURSOR	public final static int S_RESIZE_CURSOR
W_RESIZE_CURSOR	public final static int W_RESIZE_CURSOR
E_RESIZE_CURSOR	public final static int E_RESIZE_CURSOR
HAND_CURSOR	public final static int HAND_CURSOR
MOVE_CURSOR	public final static int MOVE_CURSOR

When you create frames from within an applet, however, the words *Warning: Applet Window* are always displayed at the bottom to alert the webber that an applet created this window.

This is something you can neither change nor avoid, since it's a security measure designed to prevent applets from impersonating applications that are run locally.

As you can see by looking at the constructors in Table 20-2, you can supply a name for a frame. A string you supply to the Frame() constructor is taken to be the title of the window that will be constructed from it. In this way, our Java windows can have names that appear in the title area just as their fully functional native brethren do.

To create a frame, we first extend the Frame class:

```
class WidgetsFrame extends Frame {
    ...
}
```

In this new class, we provide a constructor to create and add the various components (widgets, panels, and so on) that the objects instantiated from this frame will have. We also handle the events that this frame needs to deal with by registering the appropriate listeners with it. Once that's done, you can instantiate a new object based on it:

```
WidgetsFrame window = new WidgetsFrame();
```

Of course, we don't have to create a new Frame subclass just to see a window with a menu bar. We could just as easily instantiate a Frame object:

```
Frame window = new Frame();
```

However, the real power of using both frames and windows comes when we define our own subclasses that encapsulate the state and behavior we require. If we do that, then whenever we need to use those frames or windows later, we simply instantiate new ones.

The Window() constructor accepts, as its sole parameter, a frame. To create a window, simply create a new frame — with or without a title — and feed that object to the Window() constructor. You don't have to go through the process of creating a Frame subclass just to use a standard window:

```
Window myWindow = new Window(new Frame());// myWindow is
invisible
```

Table 20-1 earlier in this chapter shows a number of methods and variables associated with windows, frames, and dialogs. You can, for instance, retrieve the title of a window, frame, or dialog box using the getTitle() method. You can also retrieve or change the current menu bar. Additionally, you can set the cursor to one of the cursor types shown. This is useful, for instance, when you need to change the appearance of the cursor when it moves into a particular area on the screen (such as over text or in a drawing area).

Frame menu bars and menus

Chances are, if you create a frame, you'll also want to create a menu bar (see Table 20-3) that has menus in it (see Table 20-4).

<table>
<tr><td colspan="3">Table 20-3
java.awt.MenuBar Constructor and Methods</td></tr>
<tr><td>**Constructor**</td><td>**Signature**</td><td>**Description**</td></tr>
<tr><td>MenuBar</td><td>public MenuBar()</td><td>Creates a new menu bar.</td></tr>
<tr><td>**Method**</td><td>**Signature**</td><td>**Description**</td></tr>
<tr><td>addNotify</td><td>public synchronized void addNotify()</td><td>Creates the menu bar's peer. The peer allows us to change the appearance of the menu bar without changing any of its functionality.</td></tr>
<tr><td>removeNotify</td><td>public void remove Notify()</td><td>Removes the menu bar's peer. Overrides removeNotify() in class MenuComponent.</td></tr>
<tr><td>getHelpMenu</td><td>public Menu get HelpMenu()</td><td>Gets the Help menu on the menu bar.</td></tr>
</table>

(continued)

Table 20-3 *(continued)*

Method	Signature	Description
setHelpMenu	public synchronized void setHelpMenu (Menu m)	Sets the Help menu to the specified menu on the menu bar. Parameter: m – menu to be set.
add	public synchronized Menu add(Menu m)	Adds the specified menu to the menu bar. Parameter: m – menu to be added to the menu bar.
remove	public synchronized void remove(int index)	Removes the menu located at the specified index from the menu bar. Parameter: index – position of the menu to be removed.
remove	public synchronized void remove (Menu Component m)	Removes the specified menu from the menu bar. Parameter: m – menu to be removed.
getMenuCount	public int getMenu Count()	Counts the number of menus on the menu bar.
countMenus	public int count Menus()	Note: countMenus() is deprecated. As of JDK version 1.1, replaced by getMenuCount().
getMenu	public Menu getMenu (int i)	Gets the specified menu. Parameter: i – menu to be returned.
shortcuts	public synchronized Enumeration shortcuts()	Gets an enumeration of all menu shortcuts this menu bar manages.
getShortcut	public MenuItem get ShortcutMenuItem (MenuShortcut s)	Returns the menu item associated with a menu shortcut, or null if none has been specified. Parameter: s – menu shortcut to search for.
delete Shortcut	public void delete Shortcut(MenuShort cut s)	Deletes the specified menu shortcut. Parameter: s – menu shortcut to delete.

Table 20-4
java.awt.Menu Constructor and Methods

Constructor	Signature	Description
Menu	public Menu()	Constructs a new menu with an empty label. This menu can not be torn off.
Menu	public Menu(String label)	Constructs a new menu with the specified label. This menu can't be torn off; it will still appear on-screen after the mouse button has been released. Parameter: label – label to be added to this menu.
Menu	public Menu(String label, boolean tearOff)	Constructs a new menu with the specified label. If tearOff is true, the menu can be torn off; it will still appear on-screen after the mouse button has been released. Note: Tear-off functionality may not be supported by all AWT implementations. If a particular implementation doesn't support tear-offs, this value will be silently ignored. Parameters: label – label to be added to this menu. tearOff – boolean indicating whether or not the menu can be torn off.

Method	Signature	Description
addNotify	public synchronized void addNotify()	Creates the menu's peer. The peer allows us to modify the appearance of the menu without changing its functionality. Overrides addNotify() in class MenuItem.
removeNotify	public synchronized void removeNotify()	Removes the menu's peer. Overrides removeNotify() in class MenuComponent.
isTearOff	public boolean isTearOff()	Returns true if this is a tear-off menu.
getItemCount	public int getItemCount()	Returns the number of elements in this menu.
countItems	public int countItems()	Note: countItems() is deprecated. As of JDK version 1.1, replaced by getItemCount().

(continued)

	Table 20-4 *(continued)*	
Method	**Signature**	**Description**
getItem	public MenuItem getItem(int index)	Returns the item located at the specified index of this menu.
		Parameter: index – position of the item to be returned.
add	public synchronized MenuItem add(Menu Item mi)	Adds the specified item to this menu.
		Parameter: mi – item to be added.
add	public void add (String label)	Adds an item with the specified label to this menu.
		Parameter: label – text on the item.
insert	public synchronized void insert(MenuItem menuitem, int index)	Inserts the menu item to this menu at the specified position.
		Parameters: menuitem – menu item to be inserted index – the position at which the menu item should be inserted.
		Throws IllegalArgument Exception if index is less than 0.
insert	public void insert (String label, int index)	Inserts an item with the specified label to this menu at the specified position.
		Parameters: label – text on the item. index – position at which the menu item should be inserted.
addSeparator	public void addSeparator()	Adds a separator line, or a hyphen, to the menu at the current position.
Insert Separator	public void insert Separator(int index)	Inserts a separator at the specified position.
		Parameter: index position at which the menu separator should be inserted.
		Throws IllegalArgument Exception if index is less than 0.

Method	Signature	Description
remove	`public synchronized void remove(int index)`	Deletes the item from this menu at the specified index.
		Parameter: `index` – position of the item to be removed.
remove	`public synchronized void remove(Menu Component item)`	Deletes the specified item from this menu.
		Parameter: `item` – item to be removed from the menu.
removeAll	`public synchronized void removeAll()`	Deletes all items from this menu.
paramString	`public String paramString()`	Returns the `String` parameter of the menu. Overrides `paramString()` in class `MenuItem`.

Creating a menu bar that has menus in it is easy enough:

```
MenuBar theMenuBar = new MenuBar();
   // create a new MenuBar object
Menu theMenu = new Menu("A Real Menu"); // create a menu
// add items...
theMenu.add(new MenuItem("Menu item one"));
theMenu.add(new CheckboxMenuItem("Menu item two"));
theMenu.add(new MenuItem("-")); // create a menu separator
theMenu.add(new MenuItem("Yet another menu item"));
theMenu.add(new MenuItem("And, yes, another"));
theMenuBar.add(theMenu); // add menu to the menu bar
setMenuBar(theMenuBar);
   // and finally add the menu bar to the frame
```

Here we've created a new menu bar and added several items to it. Once complete, we added the menu bar to the current frame. If we wanted to add it to a specific frame, we would have supplied it as the target of `setMenuBar()`:

```
anyFrame.setMenuBar(theMenuBar); // add to specific frame
```

Keep in mind that this is not the type of menu we discussed earlier. This is a window-style menu, while the choice menu is a pop-up menu. Although they are altogether different types of menus, the process of creating and adding them to a frame is very similar. We simply create a new `Menu` object and add whatever items we'd like to it. When we're done, the menu bar that the menu is attached to is set for the window. Of course, we can add more than one menu to a menu bar.

Since `Menu` is actually a subclass of the `MenuItem` class (see Table 20-5), you can retrieve the name of a particular menu item with `getLabel()`, and change it with `setLabel()`.

Table 20-5
java.awt.MenuItem Constructor and Methods

Constructor	Signature	Description
MenuItem	`public MenuItem()`	Constructs a new menu item with an empty label and no keyboard shortcut.
MenuItem	`public MenuItem(String label)`	Constructs a new menu item with the specified label and no keyboard shortcut.
		Parameter: `label` – label for this menu item.
		Note: The hyphen (-) is reserved to mean a separator between menu items.
MenuItem	`public MenuItem(String label, MenuShortcut s)`	Creates a menu item with an associated keyboard shortcut.
		Parameter: `label` – label for this menu item. Note: The hyphen (-) is reserved to mean a separator between menu items. `s` – menu shortcut associated with this menu item.

Method	Signature	Description
addNotify	`public synchronized void addNotify()`	Creates the menu item's peer. The peer allows us to modify the appearance of the menu item without changing its functionality.
getLabel	`public String getLabel()`	Gets the label for this menu item.
setLabel	`public void setLabel(String label)`	Sets the label to be the one specified.
		Parameter: `label` – label for this menu item.
isEnabled	`public boolean isEnabled()`	Checks whether the menu item is enabled.
Set Enabled	`public synchronized void setEnabled(boolean b)`	Sets whether or not this menu item can be chosen.
		Parameter: `b` – if `true`, enables this menu item; otherwise, disables it.

Method	*Signature*	*Description*
enable	public void enable()	Note: enable() is deprecated. As of JDK version 1.1, replaced by setEnabled(boolean).
enable	public void enable (boolean cond)	Note: enable(boolean) is deprecated. As of JDK version 1.1, replaced by setEnabled(boolean).
disable	public void disable()	Note: disable() is deprecated. As of JDK version 1.1, replaced by setEnabled(boolean).
Get Shortcut	public MenuShortcut getShortcut()	Returns the menu shortcut associated with this menu item, or null if none has been specified.
set Shortcut	public void setShort cut(MenuShortcut s)	Sest this menu item's menu shortcut. If a menu shortcut is already associated with this menu item, it will be replaced. Parameter: s – menu shortcut to associate with this menu item
delete Shortcut	public void delete Shortcut()	Deletes any menu shortcut associated with this menu item.
enable Events	protected final void enableEvents(long eventsToEnable)	Enables the events defined by the specified event mask parameter to be delivered to this menu item. Event types are automatically enabled when a listener for that type is added to the menu item; therefore, this method only needs to be invoked by subclasses of a menu item that want to have the specified event types delivered to processEvent() regardless of whether a listener is registered. Parameter: eventsToEnable – event mask defining the event types.
disable Events	protected final void disableEvents(long eventsToDisable)	Disables the events defined by the specified event mask parameter from being delivered to this menu item. Parameter: eventsToDisable – event mask defining the event types.
setAction Command	public void setAction Command(String command)	Sets the command name of the action event fired by this menu item. By default, this will be set to the label of the menu item.

(continued)

Table 20-5 *(continued)*

Method	Signature	Description
getAction Command	public String get ActionCommand()	Returns the command name of the action event fired by this menu item.
addAction Listener	public synchronized void addActionListener (ActionListener l)	Adds the specified action listener to receive action events from this menu item. Parameter: l – the action listener.
remove Action Listener	public synchronized void removeAction Listener(ActionListener l)	Removes the specified action listener so it no longer receives action events from this menu item. Parameter: l – the action listener.
process Event	protected void process Event(AWTEvent e)	Processes events on this menu item. If the event is an ActionEvent, it invokes the handleActionEvent() method. Overrides – processEvent in class MenuComponent. Note: Menu items currently support only action events. Parameter: e – the event.
process Action Event	protected void process ActionEvent(Action Event e)	Processes action events occurring on this menu item by dispatching them to any registered ActionListener objects. Note: This method will not be called unless action events are enabled for this component; this happens when one of the following occurs: a) An ActionListener object is registered via addActionListener() b) Action events are enabled via enableEvents(). Parameter: e – the action event.
param String	public String param String()	Returns the string parameter of the menu item. Overrides paramString() in class MenuComponent.

You can also disable menu items so the user cannot select them, using disable(). Table 20-6 describes the methods provided by the CheckboxMenuItem.

Table 20-6
java.awt.CheckboxMenuItem Constructor and Methods

Constructor	Signature	Description
Checkbox MenuItem	public Checkbox MenuItem()	Creates a check box menu item with an empty label, initially set to off (false state).
Checkbox MenuItem	public Checkbox MenuItem(String label)	Creates the check box item with the specified label. Parameter: label – the button label.
Checkbox MenuItem	public Checkbox MenuItem(String label, boolean state)	Creates a check box menu item with the specified label and state. Parameters: label – the button label. state – the initial state of the menu item; true indicates on, and false indicates off.

Method	Signature	Description
addNotify	public synchronized void addNotify()	Creates the peer of the check box item. This peer allows us to change the look of the check box item without changing its functionality. Overrides addNotify () in class MenuItem.
getState	public boolean getState()	Returns the state of this menu item. This method is only valid for a check box.
setState	public void setState (boolean t)	Sets the state of this menu item if it is a check box. Parameter: t – the specified state of the check box.
getSelected Objects	public synchronized Object[] getSelected Objects()	Returns an array (length 1) containing the check box menu item label or null if the check box is not selected.
addItem Listener	public synchronized void addItemListener (ItemListener l)	Adds the specified item listener to receive item events from this check box menu item. Parameter: l – the item listener.

(continued)

Table 20-6 *(continued)*

Method	Signature	Description
removeItem Listener	`public synchronized void removeItem Listener(ItemListener l)`	Removes the specified item listener so it no longer receives item events from this check box menu item. Parameter: `l` – the item listener.
processEvent	`protected void processEvent(AWTEvent e)`	Processes events on this check box menu item. If the event is an `ItemEvent`, it invokes the `handleItemEvent()` method. Overrides `processEvent` in class `MenuItem`. Note: Check box menu items currently only support action and item events. Parameter: `e` – the event.
processItem Event	`protected void processItemEvent (ItemEvent e)`	Processes item events occurring on this check box menu item by dispatching them to any registered `Item Listener` objects. Note: This method will not be called unless item events are enabled for this check box menu item; this happens when one of the following occurs: a) An `ItemListener` object is registered via `addItemListener()` b) Item events are enabled via `enableEvents()`. Parameter: `e` – the item event.
paramString	`public String param String()`	Returns the parameter string of this button. Overrides `paramString()` in class `MenuItem`.

At times, you might need to add submenus to an existing menu. Simply create a new menu, which will be the submenu, and add it to whichever menu you wish:

```
Menu subMenu = new Menu("Here's a submenu"); // create another menu
subMenu.add(new MenuItem("Hello!")); // add an item...
anyMenu.add(subMenu); // add to a menu, creating a submenu
```

This snippet of code creates a new menu and adds it as a submenu to the `anyMenu` menu. Of course, `anyMenu` is just a variable name for a nonexistent menu; you'd use a real menu variable instead.

Note

A special type of menu item, CheckboxMenuItem, allows you to toggle items on a menu. When a CheckboxMenuItem is selected, it displays a check mark next to it to indicate it is on. In fact, the second menu item we created in the above example code is a CheckboxMenuItem.

As with traditional menus, you may want to add a separator to your Java menus from time to time. A separator is a thin, horizontal line that breaks up and groups items on a menu. To add a separator, you can use the addSeparator() method, creating a new menu item with an "-" argument:

```
add(new MenuItem("-")); // add a separator
```

Menu shortcuts

If you want to make your application really slick, assign a shortcut key to each of your menu items. That way, your users can select a menu item simply by pressing the Ctrl key and the corresponding shortcut key. To assign a shortcut key to a menu item, create an appropriate instance of MenuShortcut and register it with the menu item in question:

```
Menu m = new Menu("File"); // Create File menu
MenuItem mi = new MenuItem("New",
                            new MenuShortcut('n'));
m.add(mi);  // add File -> New item to File menu
```

The AWT adds the shortcut for each menu item to the item's label so that a user can easily determine the shortcut for any item. Table 20-7 describes the methods provided by the MenuShortcut object, which allows you to define keyboard shortcuts to access menu items.

Table 20-7
java.awt.MenuShortcut Constructor and Methods

Constructor	Signature	Description
MenuShort cut	public MenuShortcut (int key)	Constructs a new menu shortcut for the specified key. Parameter: key—the raw keycode for this menu shortcut, as would be returned in the keyCode field of a KeyEvent if this key were pressed.

(continued)

Table 20-7 (continued)

Constructor	Signature	Description
MenuShort cut	public MenuShortcut (int key, boolean useShiftModifier)	Constructs a new menu shortcut for the specified key. Parameters: key – the raw keycode for this menu shortcut, as would be returned in the keyCode field of a KeyEvent if this key were pressed. useShiftModifier – indicates whether this menu shortcut is invoked with the Shift key down.

Method	Signature	Description
getKey	public int getKey()	Returns the raw keycode of this menu shortcut.
usesShift Modifier	public boolean uses ShiftModifier()	Returns whether this menu shortcut must be invoked using the Shift key.
equals	public boolean equals (MenuShortcut s)	Returns whether this menu shortcut is the same as another: Equality is defined to mean that both menu shortcuts use the same key and both either use or don't use the Shift key. Parameter: s – menu shortcut to compare with this one.
toString	public String toString()	Returns an internationalized description of the menu shortcut. Overrides toString in class Object.
paramString	protected String paramString()	Returns an internationalized description of the menu item parameter string.

Menu events

A menu is simply window dressing unless your application responds when a user selects an item. The way to make your application responsive is to register appropriate action listeners with the menu items. That way, the AWT will know how to invoke the appropriate code when a user selects a particular item:

```
Menu m = new Menu("File"); // Create File menu
MenuItem mi = new MenuItem("New"); // Create File -> New menu
item.
mi.addActionListener(new ActionListener() { // register listener
   public void actionPerformed(ActionEvent e) {
       // Add code to create document here.
       // The AWT will invoke this code when the user
       // selects the File -> New menu item.
   }
});
m.add(mi); // add File -> New item to File menu
```

Menu Events in JDK 1.0.2

Menus in JDK 1.0.2, as with other interface widgets created with this version of Java, invoke the `action()` method when selected. Each menu item creates its own specific event, meaning you can find out exactly which item in which menu was selected by simply overriding the `action()` method in your program. Inside the overridden `action()` method, you can then test the target of the event to find out if it's an instance of `MenuItem`, and, if it is, use the Object argument (`arg`) to find out the name of the selected menu item:

```
if (e.target instanceof MenuItem) {
   String label = (String)arg; // get menu's label/name
   if (label.equals("XYZ")) { // is it equal to "XYZ"?
     // process appropriately
   }
}
```

You can also override the `handleEvent()` method, test to see if the event that comes through that mechanism is, in fact, a menu item, and then act accordingly:

```
public boolean handleEvent(Event e) {
   if ((e.id == Event.ACTION_EVENT) && (e.target instanceof
     MenuItem)) {
     String label = (String)e.arg;
     if (label.equals("XYZ")) { // is it equal to "XYZ"?
       // process appropriately
     }
   }
   return true;
}
```

Dialogs

In addition to the windows and frames we've just discussed, a special subclass of `Window` known as the *dialog* exists; many users know these special windows as *dialog boxes*. Dialogs allow you to present users with a window that they *must* respond to. For instance, suppose you want to require a password at some point in your applet or application; you could pop up a dialog box and insist the user either supplies the information or cancels the operation. To do this, you don't need a menu bar with menus or even a window title; you just have to toss up a dialog box and request the information.

Table 20-8 lists the constructors and methods that apply to dialogs.

	Table 20-8	
	java.awt.Dialog Constructor and Methods	
Constructor	**Signature**	**Description**
Dialog	`public Dialog(Frame parent)`	Constructs an initially invisible dialog box with an empty title.
		Parameter: `parent` – owner of the dialog box.
Dialog	`public Dialog(Frame parent, boolean modal)`	Constructs an initially invisible dialog. A modal dialog grabs all the input from the user.
		Parameters: `parent` – owner of the dialog `modal` – if `true`, the dialog blocks input to other windows when shown.
Dialog	`public Dialog(Frame parent, String title)`	Constructs an initially invisible dialog with a title.
		Parameters: `parent` – owner of the dialog. `title` – title of the dialog.
Dialog	`public Dialog(Frame parent, String title, boolean modal)`	Constructs an initially invisible dialog with a title. A modal dialog grabs all the input from the user.
		Parameters: `parent` – owner of the dialog. `title` – title of the dialog. `modal` – if `true`, the dialog blocks input to other windows when shown.

Method	Signature	Description
addNotify	`public synchronized void addNotify()`	Creates the dialog's peer. The peer allows us to change the appearance of the dialog box without changing its functionality. Overrides `addNotify()` in class `Window`.
isModal	`public boolean isModal()`	Returns true if the dialog is modal. A modal dialog grabs all the input from the user.
setModal	`public void set Modal(boolean b)`	Specifies whether this dialog is modal. A modal dialog grabs all the input to the parent frame from the user.
getTitle	`public String getTitle()`	Gets the title of the dialog.
setTitle	`public synchronized void setTitle (String title)`	Sets the title of the dialog box. Parameter: `title` – new title being given to the dialog box.
show	`public void show()`	Shows the dialog box. This will bring the dialog box to the front if the dialog is already visible. If the dialog is modal, this call will block input to the parent window until the dialog box is taken down by calling hide or dispose. It is permissible to show modal dialogs from the event dispatching thread because the toolkit will ensure that another dispatching thread will run while the one that invoked show is blocked. Overrides `show()` in class `Window`.
isResizable	`public boolean isResizable()`	Returns true if the user can resize the dialog box.
setResizable	`public synchronized void setResizable (boolean resizable)`	Sets the `resizable` flag. Parameter: `resizable` – true if resizable; `false` otherwise.
paramString	`protected String paramString()`	Returns the parameter string of this dialog. Overrides `paramString()` in class `Container`.

In addition to the generic dialog box that is created with the dialog method, there is a special-purpose `FileDialog` class—a descendant of `Dialog`—that allows you to create dialogs to open or save files. Such dialogs supply the basic type of file interaction users expect on their platforms. Keep in mind, however, that applets must be configured for local file access to use file dialogs:

```
FileDialog loaddlg = new FileDialog(this, "Get A File...",
                                    FileDialog.LOAD);
loaddlg.show();
  /* Create a SAVE file dialog */
FileDialog savedlg = new FileDialog(this, "Save A File...",
FileDialog.SAVE);
savedlg.show();
```

Window Events

Windows, frames, and dialogs support a small fleet of window events. These events let you know when something significant is happening to the window as a whole, for example, that it is being iconified or destroyed. You can intercept these events by registering a `WindowListener` with the window.

```
Frame f = new MyAppFrame("My App");
f.addWindowListener(new WindowAdapter() {
  public void windowClosing(WindowEvent e) {
     System.exit(0);
}});
```

Note that in this example, we created an anonymous descendant of the `WindowAdapter` class to avoid having to implement all the methods defined by the `WindowListener` interface (see Table 20-9).

Table 20-9
java.awt.event.WindowListener Methods

Method	Signature	Description
WindowOpened	`public abstract void windowOpened(Window Event e)`	Invoked when a window has been opened.
windowClosing	`public abstract void windowClosing(Window Event e)`	Invoked when a window is in the process of being closed. The close operation can be overridden at this point.
windowClosed	`public abstract void windowClosed(Window Event e)`	Invoked when a window has been closed.

Method	Signature	Description
windowIconified	public abstract void windowIconified(Window Event e)	Invoked when a window is iconified.
windowDei conified	public abstract void windowDeiconified (WindowEvent e)	Invoked when a window is deiconified.
window Activated	public abstract void windowActivated (WindowEvent e)	Invoked when a window is activated.
window Deactivated	public abstract void windowDeactivated (WindowEvent e)	Invoked when a window is deactivated.

Window Events in JDK 1.0.2

You can handle window events in JDK 1.0.2 by overriding a window's handleEvent() method:

```
public boolean handleEvent(Event e) {
  if (e.id == Event.WINDOW_DESTROY) {
    System.exit(0);
    }
  }
```

The AWT Event class defines the types of window-related events that can occur in JDK 1.0.2 windows (see Table 20-10).

Table 20-10
Variables as JDK 1.0.2 Window Event Types

Variable	Signature	Description
WINDOW_DESTROY	public final static int	The "destroy window" event.
WINDOW_EXPOSE	public final static int	The "expose window" event.
WINDOW_ICONIFY	public final static int	The "iconify window" event.
WINDOW_DEICONIFY	public final static int	The "deiconify window" event.
WINDOW_MOVED	public final static int	The "move window" event.

Summary

All windows are Window objects. The Window class is a subclass of Container, and is in the same position in the class hierarchy as Panel. However, this class has a very specific purpose: to create Window objects.

✦ The basic window is created without a menu bar, and doesn't even support menus. As a result, it's most useful for popping up a set of controls that can't fit inside your applet — a floating control panel, for example. You can draw and paint in a window, just as you would in an applet, so you may choose to use one as a surface for just such things. However, you won't be able to use menus with standard windows (although choice menus are fine, since they don't require a menu bar).

✦ A menu is simply window dressing unless your application responds when a user selects an item. The way to make your application responsive is to register appropriate action listeners with the menu items. That way, the AWT will know how to invoke the appropriate code when a user selects a particular item.

✦ In addition to windows and frames, a special subclass of window known as the *dialog* exists. Dialogs allow you to present users with a window that they *must* respond to.

✦   ✦   ✦

Laying Out Components

◆   ◆   ◆   ◆

In This Chapter

Using layouts to
position applications
controls

A review of the
layout managers
supported by Java

Drawing and
updating components

◆   ◆   ◆   ◆

In this chapter, we look at how to lay out all the wonderful widgets and components we've been considering in the last three chapters. These include buttons, check boxes, choice menus, scrolling lists, scroll bars, labels, text, canvases, containers, panels, windows, frames, menu bars, and dialogs. Even if you haven't used it much, you'll soon see just how powerful and flexible Java's Abstract Windowing Toolkit (AWT) really is when it comes to cross-platform interface development.

Types of Layouts

As you learned in Chapter 19, the way in which you position components on the screen depends upon the layout manager the panel has installed. For example, the default layout manager for your applet is `FlowLayout` (`java.awt.Flow-Layout`). In fact, this is the default layout for the `Panel` class, which applet inherits from.

Default: FlowLayout

With `FlowLayout`, you add components one after another, row by row. There are several alignments that you can use with `FlowLayout`. You can specify that components begin to the left of the layout, or have them begin at the center, which is the default. As you begin to lay them down using `FlowLayout`, they appear in order one after another with a default gap of five pixels between them. If a component reaches the far right side of the panel, it will wrap around and begin on the next line.

You can control the layout mechanism by providing it with an actual argument that specifies the alignment. Each time the window is resized, all the components reorder themselves appropriately.

For example, if we resize the window that contains our curve applet (see Figure 21-1), all the components reposition themselves according to the layout manager used in each panel. The applet itself has a default panel layout, and each of the specific panels we created have their own layouts. When the applet is resized, the layout manager ensures that its basic look doesn't change.

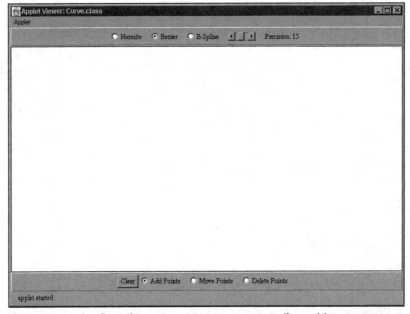

Figure 21-1: Thanks to layout managers, you can easily position components on the screen. Even when we resize a container (such as this applet), the components inside automatically reposition themselves.

Layout Managers

Java supports five layout managers:

- ✦ FlowLayout
- ✦ GridLayout
- ✦ GridBagLayout
- ✦ BorderLayout
- ✦ CardLayout

As Tables 21-1 through 21-5 illustrate, each layout manager positions components in a specific way and accepts a different number of parameters in the constructor.

Table 21-1
Java Layout Managers: FlowLayout Constructors

Signature	Description
`public FlowLayout()`	Constructs a new flow layout with centered alignment and a default 5-unit horizontal and vertical gap.
`public FlowLayout(int align)`	Constructs a new flow layout with the specified alignment and a default 5-unit horizontal and vertical gap. Parameter: `align` – alignment value.
`public FlowLayout(int align, int hgap, int vgap)`	Constructs a new flow layout with the specified alignment and gap values. Parameters: `align` – alignment value. `hgap` – horizontal gap. `vgap` – vertical gap.

Table 21-2
Java Layout Managers: GridLayout Constructors

Signature	Description
`public GridLayout()`	Creates a grid layout with a default of one column per component, in a single row.
`public GridLayout(int rows, int cols)`	Creates a grid layout with the specified rows and columns. Parameters: `rows` – rows. `cols` – columns.
`public GridLayout(int rows, int cols,int hgap, int vgap)`	Creates a grid layout with the specified rows, columns, horizontal gap, and vertical gap. Parameters: `rows` – rows; zero means "any number." `cols` – columns; zero means "any number." (Note: Only `rows` or `cols` can be zero, not both.) `Hgap` – horizontal gap. `vgap` – vertical gap. Throws `IllegalArgumentException` if the rows and columns are invalid.

Table 21-3
Java Layout Managers: GridBagLayout Constructor

Signature	Description
`public GridBagLayout()`	Creates a gridbag layout.

Table 21-4
Java Layout Managers: BorderLayout Constructors

Signature	Description
`public BorderLayout()`	Constructs a new border layout with no gaps between components.
`public BorderLayout(int hgap, int vgap)`	Constructs a border layout with the specified gaps. Parameters: `hgap`–horizontal gap. `vgap`–vertical gap.

Table 21-5
Java Layout Managers: CardLayout Constructors

Signature	Description
`public CardLayout()`	Creates a new card layout with gaps of size zero.
`public CardLayout(int hgap, int vgap)`	Creates a card layout with the specified gaps. Parameters: `hgap`–horizontal gap. `vgap`–vertical gap.

To change the layout for a panel, simply create a new layout object of the desired type and use the `setLayout` method:

```
setLayout(new GridLayout(2,2));
    // GridLayout with 2 rows, 2 columns
```

Let's take a detailed look at each of the layout managers.

FlowLayout

FlowLayout (see Table 21-6) supports three types of alignments: left, right, or center. The default alignment is center, as the buttons in Figure 21-2 illustrate.

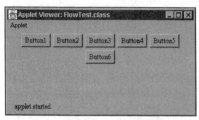

Figure 21-6: FlowLayout has center alignment as its default panel layout.

Table 21-6
java.awt.FlowLayout Methods and Variables

Method	Signature	Description
getAlignment	public int getAlignment()	Returns the alignment value for this layout, LEFT, CENTER, or RIGHT.
setAlignment	public void setAlignment(int align)	Sets the alignment value for this layout. Parameter: align–the alignment value, one of LEFT, CENTER, or RIGHT.
getHgap	public int getHgap()	Returns the horizontal gap between components.
setHgap	public void setHgap(int hgap)	Sets the horizontal gap between components. Parameter: hgap–horizontal gap.
getVgap	public int getVgap()	Returns the vertical gap between components.

(continued)

Table 21-6 (continued)

Method	Signature	Description
setVgap	public void setVgap(int vgap)	Sets the vertical gap between components.
		Parameter: vgap—vertical gap.
addLayout Component	public void addLayoutComponent (String name, Component comp)	Adds the specified component to the layout. Not used by this class.
		Parameters: name—name of the component. comp—component to be added.
removeLayout Component	public void removeLayout Component(Component comp)	Removes the specified component from the layout. Not used by this class.
		Parameter: comp—component to remove.
preferred LayoutSize	public Dimension preferredLayoutSize (Container target)	Returns the preferred dimensions for this layout, given the components in the specified target container.
		Parameter: target—container that needs to be laid out.
minimum LayoutSize	public Dimension minimumLayoutSize (Container target)	Returns the minimum dimensions needed to lay out the components contained in the specified target container.
		Parameter: target—component that needs to be laid out.

Method	Signature	Description
layout Container	public void layoutContainer (Container target)	Lays out the container. This method actually reshapes the components in the target to satisfy the constraints of the FlowLayout object. Parameter: target—specified component being laid out
toString	public String toString()	Returns the string representation of this flow layout's values. Overrides toString() in class Object.

Variable	Signature	Description
LEFT	public final static int LEFT	The left-alignment variable.
CENTER	public final static int CENTER	The center-alignment variable.
RIGHT	public final static int RIGHT	The right-alignment variable.

As you remember from Table 21-1, FlowLayout has three constructors:

✦ The constructor with no parameters creates a flow layout with a centered alignment.

✦ The constructor having one integer as a parameter creates a flow layout of whatever alignment is specified.

✦ The constructor with three parameters creates a flow layout with the specified alignment, in addition to a gap value supplied by the remaining two parameters.

The gap value is the horizontal and vertical space between the components in a panel. The default is five pixels. If you want a larger amount of space between components, you can simply change the gap values.

GridLayout

FlowLayout doesn't provide much control over where components are placed on the screen. You simply add them, and they are placed on the panel from left to right in the order added. When a component reaches the right side of the screen, it is wrapped around to the next row, where the process continues.

However, there are many cases where you need more control over where the components are placed. In this case, you might use `GridLayout` (see Table 21-7).

<table>
<tr><td colspan="3" align="center">

Table 21-7
java.awt.GridLayout Methods
</td></tr>
<tr><td>*Method*</td><td>*Signature*</td><td>*Description*</td></tr>
<tr><td>getRows</td><td>public int getRows()</td><td>Returns the number of rows in this layout.</td></tr>
<tr><td>setRows</td><td>public void setRows (int rows)</td><td>Sets the number of rows in this layout.

Parameter:
rows—number of rows in this layout.</td></tr>
<tr><td>getColumns</td><td>public int getColumns()</td><td>Returns the number of columns in this layout.</td></tr>
<tr><td>setColumns</td><td>public void setColumns(int cols)</td><td>Sets the number of columns in this layout.

Parameter:
cols—number of columns in this layout.</td></tr>
<tr><td>getHgap</td><td>public int getHgap()</td><td>Returns the horizontal gap between components.</td></tr>
<tr><td>setHgap</td><td>public void setHgap (int hgap)</td><td>Sets the horizontal gap between components.

Parameter:
hgap—horizontal gap.</td></tr>
<tr><td>getVgap</td><td>public int getVgap()</td><td>Returns the vertical gap between components.</td></tr>
<tr><td>setVgap</td><td>public void setVgap (int vgap)</td><td>Sets the vertical gap between components.

Parameter:
vgap—vertical gap.</td></tr>
<tr><td>addLayout Component</td><td>public void add LayoutComponent (String name, Component comp)</td><td>Adds the specified component with the specified name to the layout.

Parameters:
name—name of the component.
comp—component to be laid out.</td></tr>
</table>

Method	Signature	Description
removeLayout Component	public void remove LayoutComponent (Component comp)	Removes the specified component from the layout. Parameter: comp – component to be removed.
preferred LayoutSize	public Dimension preferredLayoutSize (Container parent)	Returns the preferred dimensions for this layout, given the components in the specified panel. Parameter: parent – component that needs to be laid out.
minimum LayoutSize	public Dimension minimumLayoutSize (Container parent)	Returns the minimum dimensions needed to lay out the components contained in the specified panel. Parameter: parent – component that needs to be laid out.
layout Container	public void layout Container(Container parent)	Lays out the container in the specified panel. Parameter: parent – specified component being laid out.
toString	public String toString()	Returns the string representation of this grid layout's values. Overrides toString() in class Object.

GridLayout organizes the panel in a way that is very similar to a spreadsheet – by rows and columns.

The second GridLayout constructor (see Table 21-2) requires two integers (the first constructor doesn't take any arguments). It specifies the number of rows and the number of columns for your layout. If you want to specify a different horizontal and vertical gap, you can supply those in the third type of constructor.

The order in which you lay down components with GridLayout is very important. The first component is placed in the first element of the grid, going from left to right. Each element you add to a grid layout takes up one position of the grid, very much like adding only one number per cell in a spreadsheet. This is shown in Figure 21-3.

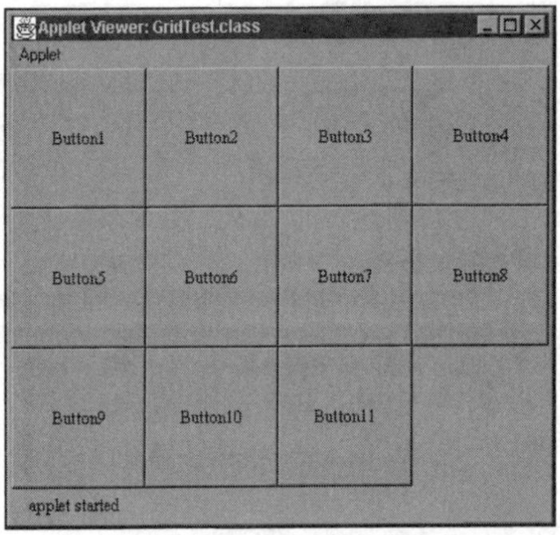

Figure 21-3: GridLayout is arranged in rows and columns, much like a spreadsheet.

When you've reached the right-hand side of the panel, the next grid item wraps underneath the first one, much like FlowLayout would with a left alignment. However, GridLayout lets you specify exactly how many rows and columns to use, so it is much more precise.

Listing 21-1 illustrates the basic use of GridLayout. Here, in the init() method, a GridLayout object is created and set for our applet. Once this new layout is set, a number of buttons are created and added to the applet. Since the applet's layout is now GridLayout, instead of the default FlowLayout, the buttons are positioned according to a grid-like system in the order they are added (see Figure 21-3).

Listing 21-1: **Using GridLayout to Create an Object**

```
GridTest.java
/**
 * GridTest.java
 *
 * GridLayout is a layout manager that aligns components
 * vertically and horizontally as a rectangular grid of cells.
 * Each component is placed into its own cell.
 *
 * @author Aaron E. Walsh
 * @version 1.1, Jan 97
 */
import java.awt.*;
import java.applet.Applet;
public class GridTest extends Applet {
  protected void addGridButton (String buttonName) {
    Button button = new Button(buttonName); // create new
button
```

```
      add(button); // add it
    }
  public void init() {
    resize(400, 300); // resize applet
    /* --- Set GridLayout and add buttons: ---- */
    GridLayout grid = new GridLayout(3,4); // create GridLayout
    setLayout(grid); // set the layout to GridLayout

    addGridButton("Button1");
    addGridButton("Button2");
    addGridButton("Button3");
    addGridButton("Button4");
    addGridButton("Button5");
    addGridButton("Button6");
    addGridButton("Button7");
    addGridButton("Button8");
    addGridButton("Button9");
    addGridButton("Button10");
    addGridButton("Button11");
  }
}
```

GridBagLayout

GridLayout is constraining in that you can only place one component inside each cell in the grid. There are instances when you may want a component to occupy one or more cells. In these situations, you should use GridBagLayout (see Table 21-8). While considerably more complicated to use than other layout managers, GridBagLayout has definite advantages when it comes to controlling your components' placement on the screen.

Table 21-8
java.awt.GridBagLayout Methods and Variables

Method	Signature	Description
setConstraints	public void setConstraints (Component comp, GridBagConstraints constraints)	Sets the constraints for the specified component. Parameters: comp – component to be modified constraints – constraints to be applied.

(continued)

Table 21-8 *(continued)*

Method	Signature	Description
getConstraints	public GridBag Constraints getConstraints (Component comp)	Retrieves the constraints for the specified component. A copy of the constraints is returned. Parameter: comp – the component to be queried.
lookup Constraints-	protected GridBagConstraints lookupConstraints (Component comp)	Retrieves the constraints for the specified component. The return value is not a copy, but is the actual Constraints class used by the layout mechanism. Parameter: comp – component to be queried.
getLayout Origin	public Point getLayoutOrigin()	Returns the origin of the layout grid.
getLayout Dimensions	public int[][] getLayoutDimensions()	Returns column widths and row heights for the layout grid.
getLayoutpublic Weights	double[][] getLayoutWeights()	Returns the weights of the layout grid's columns and rows.
location	public Point location(int x, int y)	Returns the cell in the layout grid that contains the point specified by the location *x, y*.
addLayout Component	public void addLayout Component(String name, Component comp)	Adds the specified component with the specified name to the layout. Parameters: name – name of the component. comp – component to be added.

Method	Signature	Description
addLayout Component	public void addLayout Component(Component comp, Object constraints)	Adds the specified component to the layout, using the specified constraint object. Parameters: comp–the component to be added. constraints–where/how the component is added to the layout.
removeLayout Component	public void removeLayoutComponent (Component comp)	Removes the specified component from the layout. Parameter: comp–component to be removed.
preferred LayoutSize	public Dimension preferredLayoutSize (Container parent)	Returns the preferred dimensions for this layout, given the components in the specified panel. Parameter: parent–component that needs to be laid out.
minimumLayout Size	public Dimension minimumLayoutSize (Container parent)	Returns the minimum dimensions needed to lay out the components contained in the specified panel. Parameter: parent–component that needs to be laid out.
getLayout AlignmentX	public float getLayoutAlignmentX (Container parent)	Returns the alignment along the x axis. This specifies how the component would like to be aligned relative to other components. The value should be a number between 0 and 1, where 0 represents alignment along the origin, 1 is aligned the furthest away from the origin, 0.5 is centered, and so on.

(continued)

Table 21-8 *(continued)*

Method	Signature	Description
getLayout AlignmentY	public float getLayoutAlignmentY (Container parent)	Returns the alignment along the y axis. This specifies how the component would like to be aligned relative to other components. The value should be a number between 0 and 1, where 0 represents alignment along the origin, 1 is aligned the furthest away from the origin, 0.5 is centered, and so on.
invalidate Layout	public void invalidateLayout (Container target)	Invalidates the layout, indicating that if the layout manager has cached information, it should be discarded.
layoutContainer	public void layoutContainer (Container parent)	Lays out the container in the specified panel. Parameter: parent – specified component being laid out.
toString	public String toString()	Returns the string representation of this grid layout's values.
DumpLayoutInfo	protected void DumpLayoutInfo (GridBagLayoutInfo s)	Prints the layout information. Useful for debugging.
GetLayoutInfo	protected GridBag LayoutInfo GetLayout Info(Container parent, I nt sizeflag)	Returns the layout constraints.
AdjustFor Gravity	protected void AdjustForGravity (GridBagConstraints constraints, Rectangle r)	Adjusts the grid layout on the basis of the cell weights.
GetMinSize	protected Dimension GetMinSize (Container parent, GridBagLayout Info info)	Returns the minimum size required by the layout
ArrangeGrid	protected void ArrangeGrid(Container parent)	Rearranges the grid.

Variable	Signature
MAXGRIDSIZE	protected final static int MAXGRIDSIZE
MINSIZE	protected final static int MINSIZE
PREFERREDSIZE	protected final static int PREFERREDSIZE
comptable	protected Hashtable comptable
defaultConstraints	protected GridBagConstraints defaultConstraints
layoutInfo	protected GridBagLayoutInfo layoutInfo
columnWidths	public int columnWidths[]
rowHeights	public int rowHeights[]
columnWeights	public double columnWeights[]
rowWeights	public double rowWeights[]

GridBagLayout is more flexible than GridLayout, although it shares the concept of positioning items according to a grid. Furthermore, unlike GridLayout, GridBagLayout has a GridBagConstraints object associated with it.

GridBagConstraints specifies how the component is positioned over one or more cells, known as the *display area*. To use the GridBagLayout, you must customize one or more of the components' GridBagConstraints. You do this by setting the instance variables of a GridBagConstraints object.

The source code in Listing 21-2 creates the GridBagLayout shown in Figure 21-4.

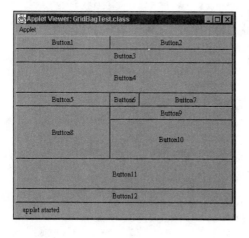

Figure 21-4: GridBagLayout is similar to GridLayout, although it allows components (such as these buttons) to take up more than one cell in the spreadsheet-like grid.

Listing 21-3: **Creating an Example of GridBagLayout**

```
/**
 * GridBagTest .java
 *
 * GridBagLayout is a layout manager that aligns components
 * vertically and horizontally as a rectangular grid of cells.
 * By specifying the GridBagConstraints of a component, a
 * component can occupy more than one cell. The cells a component
 * occupies are called the "display area" for that component.
 *
 * @author Aaron E. Walsh
 * @version 1.1, Jan 97
 */
import java.awt.*;
import java.applet.Applet;
public class GridBagTest extends Applet {
  protected void addGridBagButton (String buttonName,
  GridBagLayout gb, GridBagConstraints gbc) {
    Button button = new Button(buttonName); // create new
    button
    gb.setConstraints(button, gbc); // set the constraints for
    it
    add(button); // add it
  }
  public void init() {
    resize(400, 300); // resize applet
    /* -- Create GridBagLayout and add 12 buttons: -- */
    GridBagLayout gridbag = new GridBagLayout();
 // and create new Constraints object for GridBagLayout:
    GridBagConstraints c = new GridBagConstraints();

    setLayout(gridbag); // set the layout
      // Next,  specify components to resize themselves both
      // horizontally and vertically as needed to fit:
    c.fill = GridBagConstraints.BOTH;
      // Set a "weight" for columns (weighty) and rows
        (weightx),
      // determining how to distribute space between
        components.
      // The default weight is 0, which clumps all components
      // together in the center of the container — we don't
      // want that!
    c.weightx = 1.0;
      // add first button, using current constraints:
    addGridBagButton("Button1", gridbag, c);
      // specify a "last in row" constraint (determines how
        many
      // cells are in a row):
    c.gridwidth = GridBagConstraints.REMAINDER;
      // the next button will be last in its row...
    addGridBagButton("Button2", gridbag, c);
      // and so will this button...
```

```
    addGridBagButton("Button3", gridbag, c);
      // set vertical (column) weight:
    c.weighty = 1.0;
      // and add another button...
    addGridBagButton("Button4", gridbag, c);
      // reset width of grid of default (number of  cells in
        row):
    c.gridwidth = 1;
      // reset vertical (column) weight to default:
    c.weighty = 0.0;
      // this one begins on a new row:
    addGridBagButton("Button5", gridbag, c);
      // reset row weight to the default, so the next button is
      // "squeezed" between those either side of it:
    c.weightx = 0.0;
      // this one will be next to last on the current row:
    addGridBagButton("Button6", gridbag, c);
      // specify a "last in row" constraint:
    c.gridwidth = GridBagConstraints.REMAINDER;
      // and this one will be the last in this row:
    addGridBagButton("Button7", gridbag, c);
      // reset width to default (number of cells in a row):
    c.gridwidth = 1;
      // specify component to take up 2 cells in a column:
    c.gridheight = 2;
      // specifying 1.5 weight distribution on y axis:
    c.weighty = 1.5;
      // next button will take up two columns:
    addGridBagButton("Button8", gridbag, c);
    c.weighty = 0.0; //reset to the default
      // specify a "last in row" constraint:
    c.gridwidth = GridBagConstraints.REMAINDER;
      // specify component to take up 1 cell in a column:
    c.gridheight = 1;
      /* this one will be the last in its row, and take
        up one cell: */
    addGridBagButton("Button9", gridbag, c);
      // also last in its row, takes up one cell. However, this
      // cell extends to bottom of component 8 (button 8), to
      // balance out:
    addGridBagButton("Button10", gridbag, c);

    c.weighty = 1.0; // specifying 1.0 distribution of space
      // also last in row (gridwidth hasn't changed):
    addGridBagButton("Button11", gridbag, c);

    c.weighty = 0.0; //reset to the default
    addGridBagButton("Button12", gridbag, c);
  }
}
```

BorderLayout

BorderLayout (see Table 21-9) arranges components along the border of the container, as opposed to placing components on the inside, as FlowLayout, GridLayout, and GridBagLayout do.

<table>
<tr><td colspan="3" align="center">Table 21-9
Class java.awt.BorderLayout</td></tr>
<tr><td>Method</td><td>Signature</td><td>Description</td></tr>
<tr><td>getHgap</td><td>public int getHgap()</td><td>Returns the horizontal gap between components.</td></tr>
<tr><td>setHgap</td><td>public void setHgap (int hgap)</td><td>Sets the horizontal gap between components.

Parameter:
hgap–the horizontal gap between components.</td></tr>
<tr><td>getVgap</td><td>public int getVgap()</td><td>Returns the vertical gap between components.</td></tr>
<tr><td>setVgap</td><td>public void setVgap (int vgap)</td><td>Sets the vertical gap between components.

Parameter:
vgap–the vertical gap between components.</td></tr>
<tr><td>addLayoutComponent</td><td>public void addLayoutComponent (Component comp, Object constraints)</td><td>Adds the specified component to the layout, using the specified constraint object.

Parameters:
comp–the component to be added.

constraints–where/how the component is added to the layout.</td></tr>
</table>

Method	Signature	Description
addLayoutComponent	public void addLayoutComponent (String name, Component comp)	Note: addLayout Component() is deprecated. Replaced by addLayoutComponent (Component, Object).
removeLayout Component	public void remove LayoutComponent (Component comp)	Removes the specified component from the layout. Parameter: comp – component to be removed.
preferred LayoutSize	public Dimension preferredLayoutSize (Container parent)	Returns the preferred dimensions for this layout, given the components in the specified panel. Parameter: parent – component that needs to be laid out.
minimumLayoutSize	public Dimension minimumLayoutSize (Container parent)	Returns the minimum dimensions needed to lay out the components contained in the specified panel. Parameter: parent – component that needs to be laid out.
getLayoutAlignmentX	public float getLayoutAlignmentX (Container parent)	Returns the alignment along the *x* axis. This specifies how the component would like to be aligned relative to other components. The value should be a number between 0 and 1, where 0 represents alignment along the origin, 1 is aligned the furthest away from the origin, 0.5 is centered, and so on.

(continued)

	Table 21-9 *(continued)*	
Method	**Signature**	**Description**
getLayoutAlignmentY	public float getLayoutAlignmentY (Container parent)	Returns the alignment along the *y* axis. This specifies how the component would like to be aligned relative to other components. The value should be a number between 0 and 1, where 0 represents alignment along the origin, 1 is aligned the furthest away from the origin, 0.5 is centered, and so on.
invalidateLayout	public void invalidateLayout (Container target)	Invalidates the layout, indicating that if the layout manager has cached information, it should be discarded.
layoutContainer	public void layout Container(Container parent)	Lays out the container in the specified panel. Parameter: parent- specified component being laid out.
toString	public String toString()	Returns the string representation of this grid layout's values.

With BorderLayout, you specify a placement of North, South, East, West, or Center. When a BorderLayout panel is resized, the components reposition themselves along the borders according to their placement. If there is a component in the center, it happens to occupy whatever space remains. There may not be any space left over, however, if the panel has shrunk too much. In this case, the component on the inside becomes clipped, or partially obscured, if it can be seen at all.

This code creates the basic border layout shown in Figure 21-5.

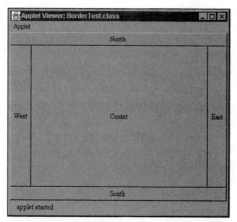

Figure 21-5: BorderLayout arranges components on the North, South, East, and West borders of a container. A Center position is also available.

```java
/**
* BorderTest.java
*
* BorderLayout is a layout manager that aligns components to the
* borders of the container:
* "North", "South", "East", "West", and "Center".
*
* All but the "Center" component get laid out according to
* their preferred sizes and the constraints of the container's
* size, while the "Center" component is placed in the remaining
* space (if any).
*
* @author Aaron E. Walsh
* @version 1.1, Jan 97
*/
import java.awt.*;
import java.applet.Applet;
public class BorderTest extends Applet {
  public void init() {
    resize(400, 300);  // resize applet
    /* -- Create BorderLayout and add buttons: -- */
    setLayout(new BorderLayout());  // set the layout

    add("North", new Button("North"));
    add("South", new Button("South"));
    add("East", new Button("East"));
    add("West", new Button("West"));
    add("Center", new Button("Center"));
  }
}
```

In this example, we didn't bother to create a `BorderLayout` object and then feed it to `setLayout()`. Unless you need to hold onto the `BorderLayout` object, you can save a line of code, as we've done here, simply by creating the object inside of the `setLayout()` method. The same is true for all layouts—if you don't need to hold onto the layout object, you can create it and pass it to `setLayout()` in one step as I've done here.

CardLayout

Unlike the previous layout managers, `CardLayout` (see Table 21-10) only allows one component to be viewed at a time. You can specify which component to display, so you have control over how and when components are visible.

<table>
<tr><td colspan="3" align="center">Table 21-10
Class java.awt.CardLayout</td></tr>
<tr><td>*Methods*</td><td>*Signature*</td><td>*Description*</td></tr>
<tr><td>getHgap</td><td>public int getHgap()</td><td>Returns the horizontal gap between components.</td></tr>
<tr><td rowspan="2">setHgap</td><td rowspan="2">public void setHgap (int hgap)</td><td>Sets the horizontal gap between components.</td></tr>
<tr><td>Parameter:
hgap—horizontal gap.</td></tr>
<tr><td>getVgap</td><td>public int getVgap()</td><td>Returns the vertical gap between components.</td></tr>
<tr><td rowspan="2">setVgap</td><td rowspan="2">public void setVgap (int vgap)</td><td>Sets the vertical gap between components.</td></tr>
<tr><td>Parameter:
vgap—vertical gap.</td></tr>
<tr><td rowspan="2">addLayoutComponent</td><td rowspan="2">public void addLayoutComponent (Component comp, Object constraints)</td><td>Adds the specified component to the layout, using the specified constraint object.</td></tr>
<tr><td>Parameters:
comp—the component to be added.
constraints—where/how the component is added to the layout.</td></tr>
</table>

Methods	Signature	Description
addLayoutComponent	public void addLayoutComponent (String name, Component comp)	Note: addLayout Component() is deprecated. Replaced by addLayoutComponent (Component, Object).
removeLayout Component	public void remove LayoutComponent (Component comp)	Removes the specified component from the layout. Parameter: comp – component to be removed.
preferred LayoutSize	public Dimension preferredLayoutSize (Container parent)	Calculates the preferred size for the specified panel. Parameter: parent – name of the parent container. Returns the dimensions of this panel.
minimumLayoutSize	public Dimension minimumLayoutSize (Container parent)	Calculates the minimum size for the specified panel. Parameter: parent – name of the parent container. Returns the dimensions of this panel.
getLayout AlignmentX	public float getLayoutAlignmentX (Container parent)	Returns the alignment along the *x* axis. This specifies how the component would like to be aligned relative to other components. The value should be a number between 0 and 1, where 0 represents alignment along the origin, 1 is aligned the furthest away from the origin, 0.5 is centered, and so on.

(continued)

Table 21-10 *(continued)*

Methods	Signature	Description
getLayoutAlignmentY	public float getLayoutAlignmentY (Container parent)	Returns the alignment along the *y* axis. This specifies how the component would like to be aligned relative to other components. The value should be a number between 0 and 1, where 0 represents alignment along the origin, 1 is aligned the furthest away from the origin, 0.5 is centered, and so on.
invalidateLayout	public void invalidateLayout (Container target)	Invalidates the layout, indicating that if the layout manager has cached information, it should be discarded.
layoutContainer	public void layoutContainer (Container parent)	Performs a layout in the specified panel. Parameter: parent – name of the parent container.
first	public void first (Container parent)	Flips to the first card. Parameter: parent – name of the parent container.
next	public void next (Container parent)	Flips to the next card of the specified container. Parameter: parent – name of the parent container.
previous	public void previous (Container parent)	Flips to the previous card of the specified container. Parameter: parent – name of the parent container.
last	public void last (Container parent)	Flips to the last card of the specified container. Parameter: parent – name of the parent container.

Methods	Signature	Description
show	public void show (Container parent, String name)	Flips to the specified component name in the specified container. Parameters: parent–name of the parent container. ame–component name.
toString	public String toString()	Returns the string representation of this card layout's values. Overrides toString in class Object

With CardLayout, you generally add panels or containers inside each card. You can specify a layout for each card independently.

CardLayout lets you flip from card to card, displaying the component in each. When a component is showing, all others are invisible. Figure 21-6 shows the card layout created with the code shown in Listing 21-3:

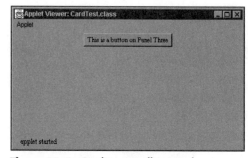

Figure 21-6: CardLayout allows only one component to be visible at a time.

In the example shown in Figure 21-6, four panels actually exist but only the third is visible. Listing 21-3 provides the code required to create this card layout.

Listing 21-3: **Card Test Example (JDK 1.1, 1.2, and Later)**

```java
/**
 * CardTest.java
 *
 * CardLayout is a layout manager which allows only one component
 * to be visible at once; all others are invisible. Components in
 * a card layout are often panels, each capable of having a
 * different layout. In this way, you can "flip" the screen to
 * display a new layout (card).
 *
 * This test simply creates four different cards, each having a
 * button in them. All have the default "FlowLayout", although
 * we can specify a different layout for each.
 * When the mouse is clicked, the next card is made visible.
 *
 * @author Aaron E. Walsh
 * @version 2.0, 20 Jul 97
 */
import java.awt.*;
import java.applet.Applet;
import java.awt.event.*;

public class CardTest extends Applet {
  CardLayout card = new CardLayout(); // create new CardLayout

  public void init() {
    resize(400, 300); // resize applet
/* -- set CardLayout and add  buttons: -- */
    setLayout(card); // set the layout to CardLayout

    Panel p1 = new Panel(); // create new panel
    p1.add(new Button("This is a button on Panel One"));
    add(p1, "");
    addMouseListener(p1);
    Panel p2 = new Panel(); // create new panel
    p2.add(new Button("This is a button on Panel Two"));
    add(p2,"");
    addMouseListener(p2);
    Panel p3 = new Panel(); // create new panel
    p3.add(new Button("This is a button on Panel Three"));
    add(p3,"");
    addMouseListener(p3);
    Panel p4 = new Panel(); // create new panel
    p4.add(new Button("This is a button on Panel Four"));
    add(p4,"");
    addMouseListener(p4);
    card.first(this); // begin by displaying the first card
  }

  void addMouseListener(Panel p) {
    p.addMouseListener(new MouseAdapter() {
      public void mousePressed(MouseEvent e) {
```

```
                    card.next(CardTest.this); // "flip" to next card
            }
        });
    }
}
```

The code in Listing 21-3 runs only under JDK 1.1 environments, or later. See
Listing 21-4 for the original version of this code, written in JDK 1.0.2, which runs
under earlier versions of the Java environments.

Versions 1.1 and 1.2 of the JDK both use the new event model to capture mouse
events.

Listing 21-4: **Card Test Example (1.0.2 Version)**

```
/**
 * CardTest.java
 *
 * CardLayout is a layout manager which allows only one component
 * to be visible at once; all others are invisible. Components in
 * a card layout are often panels, each capable of having a
 * different layout. In this way, you can "flip" the screen to
 * display a new layout (card).
 *
 * This test simply creates four different cards, each having a
 * button in them. All have the default "FlowLayout", although
 * we can specify a different layout for each.
 * When the mouse is clicked, the next card is made visible.
 *
 * @author Aaron E. Walsh
 * @version 1.0, 14 Feb 96
 */
import java.awt.*;
import java.applet.Applet;
public class CardTest extends Applet {
  CardLayout card = new CardLayout(); // create new CardLayout

  public void init() {
    resize(400, 300); // resize applet
/* -- set CardLayout and add  buttons: -- */
    setLayout(card); // set the layout to CardLayout

    Panel p1 = new Panel(); // create new panel
    p1.add(new Button("This is a button on Panel One"));
    add(p1);
    Panel p2 = new Panel(); // create new panel
    p2.add(new Button("This is a button on Panel Two"));
```

(continued)

Listing 21-4 *(continued)*

```
    add(p2);
    Panel p3 = new Panel(); // create new panel
    p3.add(new Button("This is a button on Panel Three"));
    add(p3);
    Panel p4 = new Panel(); // create new panel
    p4.add(new Button("This is a button on Panel Four"));
    add(p4);
    card.first(this); // begin by displaying the first card
  }
  public boolean mouseDown(Event e, int x, int y) {
    card.next(this); // "flip" to next card
    return true;
  }
}
```

Insets

As you know, components in a panel have a gap, either horizontal or vertical, that separates them from each other. You've seen this in all the layouts described earlier in this chapter. In addition, every container has an inset. An inset surrounds a panel. You can specify whatever size you'd like it to be. For instance, if you wanted your grid layout to appear 25 pixels in from each border, you would specify insets of 25 for the top, bottom, left, and right, as follows:

```
public Insets insets() {
  return new Insets(25,25,25,25);
}
```

Figure 21-7 shows the example just given and how it would affect the border layout. As you can see, this isn't a method that you can apply to a panel; it's a method that you should override for each panel you create. For example, if you had several different panels defined in your program, you might override an insets() method.

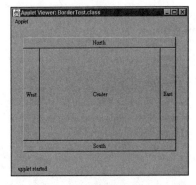

Figure 21-7: Insets determine how much space appears around a panel.

Drawing and Updating Components

By now you've probably realized that there is no way to explicitly place a component at a specific *x,y* location when using layouts. This is no mistake! The reason is that if you were to place a component in an exact location on the screen, it wouldn't appear consistently across a wide range of systems.

Pixel-perfect alignment of components on a Macintosh, for instance, wouldn't necessarily appear so on any other system because the Mac's interface components are uniquely designed (in both size and appearance) for that platform alone. And, since the AWT is designed to use the native components for each platform it runs on, actual size and appearance varies from platform to platform. While this is wonderful when it comes to developing software interfaces that look and feel exactly as the user of each platform expects, it also prevents us from using pixel-perfect placement of components.

Instead, we allow the layout manager to determine where each component is positioned on the screen. Although it may seem rather constraining, you can use various combinations of layout managers to accurately position a component on the screen without resorting to explicit *x,y* coordinates.

Furthermore, since the AWT takes on the responsibility of drawing and updating components, we don't have to keep track of which ones had been obscured and then revealed. We simply sit back and let the AWT do the work for us.

As we discussed earlier, you know that panels are drawn according to the order in which you add them. The applet is drawn first (if you're creating an applet), then the first panel that was created and added to the applet is drawn, then the second, and so on.

If you'd like to draw specific information on an individual panel, simply override the `paint()` method for that panel. In order to redraw graphics on the screen, it's necessary to invoke the `paint()` method. We've done this all along using the `repaint()` method. Unfortunately, when you call `repaint()`, it doesn't call `paint()` directly. Instead, it calls an intermediary method, `update()`. This then fills the entire screen with the background color.

As a result, you may see a great deal of flickering in your panels when they are updated. In many cases, you can greatly reduce this flicker in your animation by overriding the `update()` method. When you do this, you can eliminate the process of filling the screen with the background color by calling your `paint()` method directly:

```
public void update(Graphics g) {
  paint(g); // call your paint method with the Graphics object
}
```

Depending on what type of drawing your `paint()` method does, the flicker may or may not be reduced with this technique. Luckily, there are a number of tricks we can try. For details on reducing flicker in your applets, see Chapter 31 and read the JavaWorld "Javamation" article provided on the enclosed CD-ROM.

Overriding the `update()` method, as shown in the previous code snippet, is particularly effective when you're animating an image "in place" (it doesn't move on either the *x* or *y* axis). Since each image, or frame, in such animations is drawn over the previous one, there's no need to refresh the screen at all.

Summary

The way in which you position components on the screen depends upon the layout manager the panel has installed.

✦ `FlowLayout` supports three types of alignments: left, right, or center. The default alignment is center.

✦ `FlowLayout` doesn't provide much control over where components are placed on the screen. You simply add them, and they are placed on the panel from left to right in the order added. When a component reaches the right side of the screen, it is wrapped around to the next row, where the process continues.

✦ There are many cases where you need more control over where the components are placed. In this case, you might use `GridLayout`.

✦ `GridLayout` is constraining in that you can only place one component inside each cell in the grid. There are instances when you may want a component to occupy one or more cells. In these situations, you should use `GridBagLayout`.

✦ `BorderLayout` arranges components along the border of the container, as opposed to placing components on the inside, as `FlowLayout`, `GridLayout`, and `GridBagLayout` do.

✦ Unlike the other layout managers, `CardLayout` only allows one component to be viewed at a time. You can specify which component to display, so you have control over how and when components are visible.

✦   ✦   ✦

Bringing It All Together with JDK 1.1

◆ ◆ ◆ ◆

In This Chapter

Designing and
implementing
JavaDraw

Using an interface-
driven approach
to application
development

Designing your Java
applications carefully
before you rush to
implementation

Digging into the
implementation
phase and becoming
a code warrior

◆ ◆ ◆ ◆

The past six chapters have helped you learn the various parts of the Abstract Windowing Toolkit and understand how to call each part into action using Java source code, but the real meat and potatoes lie in bringing it all together in a real-world program. Without a real example to work through, everything else is simply academic; you might know the concepts, but nothing hits home like actually doing it.

In this chapter we develop a simple drawing program called JavaDraw, and then implement it as a dual-purpose application/applet. We put the past 21 chapters to work, starting with basic design specification and working all the way through the code implementation details.

Designing the JavaDraw Application/Applet

Before jumping keys-first into code, we need to consider exactly what it is that we're programming, and sketch out the user interface using paper and pen, just as we discussed in Chapter 3. Taking this approach frees us to think in detail about the project, refining our goals and plan of attack as we go along, without committing to a single line of code before we're actually ready.

To begin, we need to know what it is that we're working on. In this case, the answer is simple: JavaDraw, a simple drawing program that can be run as both an applet or application. Creating this dual-purpose program will give us experience using nearly all the material presented so far in this book without being too complicated to cover in a single chapter.

And so, there you have it. Your mission, should you choose to accept it, is to develop a simple drawing program that can be executed as an applet in a Web page or as a standalone application. Although this specification is rather loose, there are a few requirements we'll have to work into the program. Specifically, JavaDraw should allow users to do several things:

✦ Choose a variety of drawing shapes (line, oval, rectangle, and so on)

✦ Choose plain, filled, or 3D drawing modes, and mix and match them at will

✦ Select ink colors for drawing (red, green, blue, black, yellow, and so on)

✦ Draw using an image, such as a GIF or JPEG, as a paintbrush

✦ Clear the drawing surface to erase everything and start drawing from scratch

✦ Find out details about the program, such as the product name, version number, author, and so on

Now that you know these requirements, you might be tempted to dive in and start programming. Instead, restrain yourself for a few moments as we approach the task from an entirely different angle—the user's perspective.

Interface-Driven Development

Too often, software developers approach programming from an engineering perspective. Although this isn't a bad idea, it tends to result in a more complicated product for the end user. Instead of focusing on what the user should see and do, developers often concentrate their efforts on the underlying code. As a result, the interface becomes almost an afterthought, shoe-horned into the constraints imposed by the implementation.

In Chapter 3, we suggested that you first design the interface before writing a single line of code. Doing so actually reverses the typical software development process; it becomes *interface-driven*, not code-driven. At best, the result is a product that is as easy to use as it is powerful. At worst, you've saved yourself buckets of recoding, because you developed a clear mission plan long before launching into implementation.

Using this interface-driven approach to software development, let's press ahead with JavaDraw. At the moment, we know what the product must do, but we don't know how it should appear to the user. Now it's time to attack the interface!

A call to arms: pencil and paper first

Before going further, grab a pad of paper and a freshly sharpened pencil. (Okay, a mechanical pencil is fine if there's one handy, but beware of ink pens — they're permanent, don't ya know?!) Now, think for a moment about the nicest, cleanest interface you can conjure up for JavaDraw. Don't be shy; let yourself go and dream it up.

We like the idea of a single toolbar area, where all the drawing tools are in one place, and an open area for actually drawing. So far, so good, but where should the toolbar appear? We're not overly fond of toolbars at the bottom of windows. We prefer them at the top, where they are in the majority of today's drawing and painting programs, so for us the ideal position is clear: toolbar at top, drawing canvas beneath.

This interface is easy enough to dream up, and easy enough to sketch, as you can see in Figure 22-1. Nope, it's not the fanciest interface in the word, but it's a start, and that's the important part. The interface is coming first, long before the code. So what next? Well, how about fleshing out that toolbar?

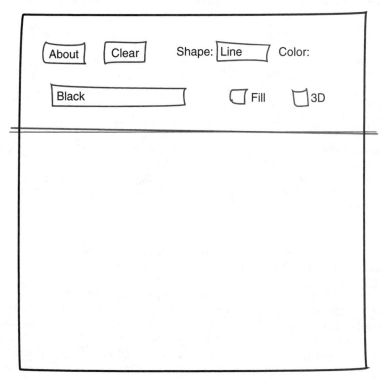

Figure 22-1: A rough sketch of the JavaDraw application user interface

Fleshing out bare bones

With the rough sketch of our ideal interface in place, it's now time to flesh it out. At this point we reconsider the requirements of the program and try out a few ideas for presenting features to the user.

Should the user select drawing shapes by clicking a button and then choosing items in a dialog box? How about the colors? Should I use the same dialog box, just as a word processor includes text and style options in the same dialog box to conserve space? And what about getting information about the program—should that be a menu item or a button? Hmmm . . .

Since it's impossible to make a decision without choices, you might as well sketch out a few different approaches. You are only using paper and pencil, after all; the worst that can happen is you'll chuck a few of the bad ideas into the waste basket or fireplace. No harm there.

After a few trips to the idea buffet, you'll likely come upon a solid interface for your toolbar. Of course, if you're new to interface development, it'll take more time and practice, but don't fret—as long as you put in the effort using pencil and paper first, you're certain to hit upon a more effective interface than if you simply begin coding right off the bat.

For us, the interface took hold after a few revisions. We decided against using dialog boxes altogether because they're really not necessary in this case. Opening a dialog box to change shapes and colors just doesn't make sense when a nice, fast, and clean pop-up menu does the trick even better. Of course, labeling these puppies makes it even easier for the user to identify which to use and when, so we decided to label the two menus Shape and Color.

After much consideration, we decided to place the "draw with an image" option inside the Shape pop-up menu. Since this is, in effect, a specialized drawing shape, it makes sense to group it with the other possible shapes. After all, when drawing with an image, you can't draw with any other shape. Image thus becomes the last item on the Shape menu.

I decided to use buttons for the "clear canvas" and "get program information" features, shortening the name of each as much as possible without reducing them so much that they make no sense. And so the Clear! and About buttons took shape.

Since each shape can potentially be drawn plain, filled, and/or in 3D mode, we decided that the default mode would be plain. Placing check boxes directly on the toolbar instead of making them multiple-choice selection menus allows users to quickly toggle between Fill and 3D options. In addition, the check boxes allow users to see exactly which options are selected without forcing them to first choose a menu—another argument for placing them directly on the toolbar and in plain view.

Finally, we decided that just seeing a text description of the color wasn't enough. In most drawing and painting programs, you choose a color by clicking on a palette. For our purposes, implementing a color palette wasn't practical; it's simply too complicated to do within the amount of space we have to present the code here, and so we had to come up with something else. The pop-up is a good idea, but seeing the name of a color just doesn't cut it—you have to see the color, too.

And so, with a little more thought, we decided to take advantage of the natural interface issues that we were already grappling with. Specifically, we had to create a toolbar that was obviously a toolbar, and not part of the drawing canvas. To do this, we chose to the make the toolbar gray and the canvas area white, so that the visual contrast between the two is obvious.

Now we can show the current color on the screen in a place where the user will see it but not be distracted by it. We had already decided to draw a thin line between the bottom of the toolbar and the top of the canvas area to further distinguish the two, so after a bit more consideration, we decided to draw the line in the current color instead of black. That's a perfect way to let users know what the current color is without being intrusive.

Voilà! We've designed the JavaDraw interface, and it took little more than a pencil, paper, and a few cups of coffee. We made the transformations entirely on paper and in our minds; this saved hours of recoding that would have been required had we jumped directly into code. But don't jump in quite yet; we still need to model the objects our program will use.

Objects, Shmobjects!

We know you're just itching to get to the code. But trust us, the next step is just as important as sketching the user interface, perhaps more so. You certainly could begin coding right here and now, but you're almost as certain to waste your time if you don't first consider what objects you'll need to create. Yep, more up-front work with a pencil and paper, but it's well worth it. We promise.

Tip

You don't have to go nuts with applying complicated object-oriented analysis and design here; at least get a lay of the land before you blaze new trails. Consider your interface and how it dictates the objects you'll end up coding.

If you take a look at our final interface design (shown in Figure 22-2), you'd be right to assume that at least two objects are necessary: a toolbar object and a canvas object. So, why not sketch these out as the amorphous blobs that they are? Actually, strictly speaking, we do not need the canvas object. We can draw directly on the area of the applet below the toolbar. In effect, we can let the applet be our canvas. This is the strategy that we will adopt (see Figure 22-2).

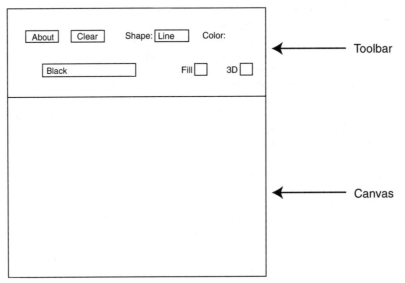

Figure 22-2: Final user interface for the JavaDraw application

What other objects will JavaDraw need? Well, we need a frame in which to display our applet when it is running as an application. (Remember, our specification calls for an applet that can run standalone as an application.) Thus, all in all, we need at least the following objects:

✦ An applet that we can run in a browser

✦ A toolbar to let a user select drawing features

✦ A frame in which to display our applet when running it as an application

Now that we know what we must do, let's get to work.

Code Warrior — Digging into the Implementation Phase

Of course, the question arises: Where to begin? Let's begin with the toolbar. Listing 22-1 shows our implementation of the toolbar, which we call `WidgetPanel`, because it's a panel containing a bunch of widgets.

Listing 22-1: **WidgetPanel.java**

```java
import java.awt.*;
import java.awt.event.*;
import java.awt.Image;
import java.applet.*;
import java.net.*;
import Shape;

/*
 *
 * WidgetPanel
 *
 */
class WidgetPanel extends Panel {

  private final String AboutButtonName = "About...",
    ClearButtonName = "CLEAR!";

  protected boolean About_Mode = false;

  protected  Choice shapeChoice = null,
    colorChoice = null;


  private Checkbox fillCheckbox = null,
  threeDCheckbox = null;


  private final static int _WIDTH = 400, // default width
                           _HEIGHT = 60; // default height


  private int width=0, height=0;   // used to size this panel

  // CONSTRUCTOR: WidgetPanel()
  public WidgetPanel() {
    this(0,0);
  }

  // CONSTRUCTOR: WidgetPanel(int, int)
  public WidgetPanel(int width, int height) {
    // Begin by setting dimensions of this panel:
   setSize(width, height);

    // Now, let's actually create the panel:
    new Panel();

    setBackground(Color.lightGray);
```

(continued)

Listing 22-1 *(continued)*

```
/* --- Add buttons --- */

// Add About JavaDraw button
Button b = new Button(AboutButtonName);
b.addActionListener(new ActionHandler() {
  public void actionPerformed(ActionEvent e) {
    super.actionPerformed(e);
    WidgetPanel.this.about();
  }
});
add(b);

// Clear canvas button
b = new Button(ClearButtonName);
b.addActionListener(new ActionHandler() {
  public void actionPerformed(ActionEvent e) {
    super.actionPerformed(e);
    WidgetPanel.this.clearDrawCanvas();
  }
});
add(b);

/* --- Add Choice menus --- */
// let's start with the "Shape" choice item:
add (new Label("Shape:"));   // label first...
shapeChoice = new Choice();  // choice next...
shapeChoice.addItem("Line");
shapeChoice.addItem("Rectangle");
shapeChoice.addItem("Oval");
shapeChoice.addItem("Polygon");
shapeChoice.addItem("Arc");
shapeChoice.addItem("Text");
shapeChoice.addItem("Image");
add(shapeChoice);

// now do the same for the "Color" choice:
add (new Label("Color:"));   // label first...
colorChoice = new Choice();  // choice next...
colorChoice.addItem("Black");
colorChoice.addItem("Blue");
colorChoice.addItem("Cyan");
colorChoice.addItem("DarkGray");
colorChoice.addItem("Gray");
colorChoice.addItem("Green");
colorChoice.addItem("LightGray");
colorChoice.addItem("Magenta");
colorChoice.addItem("Orange");
colorChoice.addItem("Pink");
```

```
  colorChoice.addItem("Red");
  colorChoice.addItem("White");
  colorChoice.addItem("Yellow");

  colorChoice.addItemListener(new ItemListener() {
    public void itemStateChanged(ItemEvent e) {
      String colorStr =
        WidgetPanel.this.colorChoice.getSelectedItem();
        WidgetPanel.this.getParent().
          setForeground(UltraColor.stringColor(colorStr));
        WidgetPanel.this.repaint();
    }
  });

  add(colorChoice);

  /* --- Add Checkboxes --- */
  fillCheckbox = new Checkbox("Fill");
  add(fillCheckbox);

  threeDCheckbox = new Checkbox("3D");
  add(threeDCheckbox);
}


// getPreferredSize()
// Set the preferred size (width, height) of this panel.
public Dimension getPreferredSize() {
  return new Dimension (width, height);
}

// setSize()
// Set the "height" and "width" variables of the panel,
// the values passed into this method if valid, or
// defaults (_WIDTH and _HEIGHT) if not.
public void setSize(int width, int height) {
  if (width > 0)
    this.width = width;
  else
    this.width = _WIDTH;

  if (height > 0)
    this.height     = height;
  else
    this.height = _HEIGHT;
}

// clearDrawCanvas()
// Clear the drawing surface.
//   NOTE: This method ASSUMES that the parent
// component is the surface to clear!
```

(continued)

Listing 22-1 *(continued)*

```java
public void clearDrawCanvas () {
  Graphics g = getParent().getGraphics();
  int w = getParent().getSize().width,
      h = getParent().getSize().height;
  g.clearRect(0,0,w,h);
}

// Display program "about" info in drawing area...
public void about() {
  About_Mode = true;
  clearDrawCanvas();
  // Save foreground color
  Color fg = getParent().getForeground();
  // set to black for about text
  getParent().setForeground(Color.black);
  // get AFTER setting foreground; work around bug in JDK...
  Graphics g = getParent().getGraphics();

  g.drawString("JavaDraw!", 10, 70);
  g.drawString("by Aaron E. Walsh", 10, 80);
  g.drawString("version 1.0", 10, 90);
  g.drawString("revised 7.26.97", 10, 100);
  // restore original foreground color
  getParent().setForeground(fg);
}

// Define an actionlistener superclass to handle
// processing common to all actions.
class ActionHandler implements ActionListener {
  public void actionPerformed(ActionEvent e) {
    // Handle about mode
    if (About_Mode) {
      // if about message is on screen, clear screen
      // then return to normal mode by setting
      // About_Mode flag to false...
      WidgetPanel.this.clearDrawCanvas();
      WidgetPanel.this.About_Mode = false;
    }
  }
}

// paint()
// Handle painting of this panel...
public void paint(Graphics g) {

  // draw "divider line" between widget panel and canvas:
```

```
      for (int yOffset = 0; yOffset < 3; yOffset++) {
        g.drawLine (0,
           getSize().height - yOffset,
           getSize().width,
           getSize().height - yOffset);
      }
    }


    /* ------------- ACCESSOR METHODS: ------------- */
    public int getShape() {
      return shapeChoice.getSelectedIndex();
    }


    public boolean isFilled() {
      return fillCheckbox.getState();
    }


    public boolean isThreeD() {
      return threeDCheckbox.getState();
    }


  }
```

The heart of `WidgetPanel` is its main constructor, `WidgetPanel(int width, int height)`. This constructor creates a panel of a specified width and height and populates it with the widgets dictated by our design: buttons for displaying information about JavaDraw and for clearing the drawing area, choice menus for selecting colors and shapes to draw, and check boxes for specifying filled and 3D shapes. The constructor also sets the size of the toolbar and its background color (light gray). Note that our constructor does not specify a layout manager. As a result, the toolbar will have a default flow layout that arranges widgets from left to right across the panel in the order in which we add them to the toolbar panel. This is just fine for our purposes.

Besides creating the toolbar widgets, `WidgetPanel`'s main constructor also registers event handlers for some of them, specifically the About and Clear! buttons and the `colorChoice` widget. The handler for the About button displays information about the JavaDraw applet. The Clear! button handler clears the drawing area. Note that both event handlers derive from an `ActionHandler` class defined within the `WidgetPanel` class. The `ActionHandler` class defines action processing common to the About and Clear! buttons. In particular, it clears any previous About message from the drawing area.

The handler for the `colorChoice` widget sets the applet's current foreground drawing color to the color selected by the user. By so doing, it absolves our drawing code (see the `JavaDraw` class below) from having to set the foreground color itself. Note that the `WidgetPanel` constructor does not register a listener for the `shapeChoice` widget. How, then, does JavaDraw know when a user selects a new shape to draw? In a word, it doesn't. Instead, we rely on the drawing portion of our code to get the current shape selection from the `shapeChoice` widget. Of course, we could have added a listener to detect when a user selects a new shape and set a state variable in our applet accordingly. However, this would have entailed adding a state variable to our applet. We found it simpler to let the `shapeChoice` widget itself serve as our shape state variable.

Now that we have implemented a toolbar for the JavaDraw applet, let's proceed to defining a frame in which to display the applet. Listing 22-2 shows the code for the frame.

Listing 22-2: **JavaDrawFrame.java**

```
//**********************************************************
// JavaDrawFrame.java:
//
//**********************************************************
import java.awt.*;
import java.awt.event.*;

//=========================================================
// This frame class acts as a top-level window in which the
// applet appears when it's run as a standalone application.
//=========================================================
class JavaDrawFrame extends Frame {

  // JavaDrawFrame constructor
  //-------------------------------------------------------
  public JavaDrawFrame(String str) {
    super (str);
    addWindowListener(new WindowAdapter() {
      public void windowClosing(WindowEvent e) {
        dispose();
        System.exit(0);
      }
    });
  }
}
```

The JavaDraw frame is really not much, just a constructor that registers a window listener with the frame. The job of the window listener is to detect when a user selects the Close button or Close menu item on the frame, signaling a wish to end JavaDraw immediately. The window listener obliges by disposing of any resources associated with it and then invoking the System.exit() function.

At last we are ready to code the JavaDraw applet itself. Listing 22-3 shows the code for the applet.

Listing 22-3: **JavaDraw.java**

```
//***************************************************************
// JavaDraw.java: Applet
//
//***************************************************************
import java.applet.*;
import java.awt.*;
import java.awt.event.*;
import JavaDrawFrame;
import WidgetPanel;
import Shape;

//===============================================================
// Main Class for applet JavaDraw
//
//===============================================================
public class JavaDraw extends Applet {

  // STANDALONE APPLICATION SUPPORT:
  // m_fStandAlone will be set to true if applet is run
  // standalone
  //-----------------------------------------------------------
  boolean m_fStandAlone = false;

  // OTHER CLASS VARIABLES:
  //-----------------------------------------------------------
  private WidgetPanel guiPanel = null;

  private int oldX=0,  // last mouse x value
              oldY=0; // last mouse y value

  // image to draw when in "image" mode
  private Image theImage = null;
  private String imagePath = "images/logo.gif"; // path to image

  // PARAMETER SUPPORT:
  // Parameters allow an HTML author to pass information to the
  // applet; the HTML author specifies them using the <PARAM> tag
```

(continued)

Listing 22-3 *(continued)*

```java
// within the <APPLET> tag.  The following variables are used
// to store the values of the parameters.
//----------------------------------------------------------
// Members for applet parameters
// <type>         <MemberVar>    = <Default Value>
//----------------------------------------------------------
private String m_foregroundColor = null;
private String m_backgroundColor = null;

// Parameter names.  To change a name of a parameter, you need
// only make a single change.  Simply modify the value of the
// parameter string below.
//----------------------------------------------------------
private final String PARAM_foreColor = "foreColor";
private final String PARAM_backColor = "backColor";

// STANDALONE APPLICATION SUPPORT
// The GetParameter() method is a replacement for the
// getParameter() method defined by Applet. This method returns
// the value of the specified parameter; unlike the original
// getParameter() method, this method works when the applet
// is run as a standalone application, as well as when run
// within an HTML page. This method is called by
// GetParameters().
//----------------------------------------------------------
String GetParameter(String strName, String args[]) {

  if (args == null) {
    // Running within an HTML page, so call original
    // getParameter().
    //----------------------------------------------------------
    return getParameter(strName);
  }

  // Running as standalone application, so parameter values are
  // obtained from the command line. The user specifies them as
  // follows:
  //
  // JView JavaDraw param1=<val> param2=<"val with spaces"> ...
  //----------------------------------------------------------
  int    i;
  String strArg = strName + "=";
  String strValue = null;

  for (i = 0; i < args.length; i++) {
    if (strArg.equalsIgnoreCase(args[i].substring(0,
        strArg.length())))  {
```

```
        // Found matching parameter on command line, so extract
                                                            its
        // value. // If in double quotes, remove the quotes.
      //----------------------------------------------------------
        strValue= args[i].substring(strArg.length());
        if (strValue.startsWith("\"")) {
          strValue = strValue.substring(1);
          if (strValue.endsWith("\""))
            strValue = strValue.substring(0, strValue.length()
              - 1);
        }
      }
    }

  return strValue;
}

// STANDALONE APPLICATION SUPPORT
// The GetParameters() method retrieves the values of each of
// the applet's parameters and stores them in variables. This
// method works both when the applet is run as a standalone
// application and when it's run within an HTML page. When the
// applet is run as a standalone application, this method is
// called by the main() method, which passes it the command-
// line arguments. When the applet is run within an HTML page,
// this method is called by the init() method with args ==
// null.
//----------------------------------------------------------
void GetParameters(String args[]) {

  // Query values of all Parameters
    //----------------------------------------------------------
  String param;

  // foreColor: Specifies default foreground color of this
  // program (must be a Color class variable)
    //----------------------------------------------------------
  param = GetParameter(PARAM_foreColor, args);
  if (param != null)
    m_foregroundColor = param;

  // backColor: Specifies default background color of this
  // program (must be a Color class variable)
    //----------------------------------------------------------
  param = GetParameter(PARAM_backColor, args);
  if (param != null)
    m_backgroundColor = param;

}

// STANDALONE APPLICATION SUPPORT
// The main() method acts as the applet's entry point when it
```

(continued)

Listing 22-3 *(continued)*

```
// is run as a standalone application. It is ignored if the
// applet is run from within an HTML page.
//------------------------------------------------------------
public static void main(String args[]) {

  // Create Toplevel Window to contain applet JavaDraw
  //----------------------------------------------------------
  JavaDrawFrame frame = new JavaDrawFrame("JavaDraw!");

  // Must show Frame before we size it so getInsets() will
  // return valid values
  //----------------------------------------------------------
  frame.show();
  frame.setVisible(false);
  frame.setSize(frame.getInsets().left +
     frame.getInsets().right + 400, frame.getInsets().top +
     frame.getInsets().bottom + 350);

  // The following code initializes the applet within the frame
  // window. It also calls GetParameters() to retrieve
  // parameter values from the command line, and sets
  // m_fStandAlone to true to prevent init() from trying to get
  // them from the HTML page.
  //----------------------------------------------------------
  JavaDraw applet_JavaDraw = new JavaDraw();

  frame.add("Center", applet_JavaDraw);
  applet_JavaDraw.m_fStandAlone = true;
  applet_JavaDraw.GetParameters(args);
  applet_JavaDraw.init();
  frame.show();
}

// JavaDraw Class Constructor
//------------------------------------------------------------
public JavaDraw() {
}

// APPLET INFO SUPPORT:
// The getAppletInfo() method returns a string describing the
// applet's author, copyright date, or miscellaneous
// information.
//------------------------------------------------------------

public String getAppletInfo() {
  return "Name: JavaDraw\r\n" +
    "Author: Aaron E. Walsh\r\n";
}
```

```
// PARAMETER SUPPORT
// The getParameterInfo() method returns an array of strings
// describing the parameters understood by this applet.
//
// JavaDraw Parameter Information:
//   { "Name", "Type", "Description" },
//-----------------------------------------------------------
public String[][] getParameterInfo() {
  String[][] info =
  {
    { PARAM_foreColor, "String", "Specifies default foreground
      color of this program (must be a Color class variable)" },
    { PARAM_backColor, "String", "Specifies default background
      color of this program (must be a Color class variable)" },
  };
  return info;
}


// The init() method is called by the AWT when an applet is
// first loaded or reloaded.
//-----------------------------------------------------------
public void init() {

  if (!m_fStandAlone)
    GetParameters(null);

  resize(400, 350);
  this.setLayout(new BorderLayout());
  setBackground(Color.white);
  guiPanel = new WidgetPanel();
  add("North", guiPanel);
  addMouseListener(getMouseListener());
  addMouseMotionListener(getMouseMotionListener());
}

MouseListener getMouseListener() {
  return new MouseAdapter() {

    // The mousePressed() method is called if the mouse button
    // is pressed while the mouse cursor is over the applet's
    // portion of the screen.
    //
    // We simply update the variables that hold the x and y
    // position (oldX, oldY)
    //-------------------------------------------------------
    public void mousePressed(MouseEvent e) {
      oldX = e.getX();
      oldY = e.getY();
    }

    // The mouseReleased() method is called if the mouse button
    // is released while the mouse cursor is over the applet's
```

(continued)

Listing 22-3 *(continued)*

```
    // portion of the screen.
    //-----------------------------------------------------------
    public void mouseReleased(MouseEvent e) {
      // force redraw of the "dividing line" between panel
      // and canvas in case it was drawn over by user...
      update(getGraphics());
    }
  };
}

MouseMotionListener getMouseMotionListener() {
  return new MouseMotionAdapter() {

    public void mouseDragged(MouseEvent e) {
      // MOUSE SUPPORT:
      // The mouseDragged() method is called if the mouse cursor
      // moves over the applet's portion of the screen while the
      // mouse button is being held down.
      // This is where the real drawing takes place.
      JavaDraw.this.draw(e.getX(), e.getY());
    }
  };
}

void draw(int x, int y) {
  // We start by getting a
  // reference to the graphics drawing area, then check to see
  // what kind of drawing should take place (line, circle, etc.).
  // In cases where "filled" and/or 3D drawing can take
  // place, it's allowed (assuming these options
  // have been selected by the user).
  //
  // Note: Although we get a graphics context each time
  // this method is called, performance isn't a problem.
  // However, you can always make the "g" variable a global and
  // test for null to determine if a new graphics context
  // should be loaded. This technique is illustrated with
  // "theImage" seen below in the "Shape.IMAGE" case.
    //-----------------------------------------------------------

  // get graphics context in which to  draw
  Graphics g=getGraphics();

  boolean fill = guiPanel.isFilled(), // filled mode?
    threeD = guiPanel.isThreeD();     // 3D mode?

  switch (guiPanel.getShape()) { // what shape should be drawn?

  case Shape.LINE:
    g.drawLine(oldX, oldY, x, y);
    break;
```

```
case Shape.RECT:
  if (fill) {
    if (threeD)
      g.fill3DRect(oldX, oldY,x, y, true); // fill 3D rect
    else
      g.fillRect(oldX, oldY, x, y);   // fill regular rect
  } else {
    if (threeD)
      g.draw3DRect(oldX+1, oldY+1, x+1, y+1, true); //3D rect
    else
      g.drawRect(oldX, oldY, x, y); // draw regular rect
  }
  break;


case Shape.OVAL:
  if (fill) {
    g.fillOval(oldX, oldY, x, y);
  } else {
    g.drawOval(oldX, oldY, x, y); // just draw it
  }
  break;

case Shape.ARC:
  if (fill) {
    g.fillArc(oldX, oldY, 100, 100, x, y); // fill it
  } else {
    g.drawArc(oldX, oldY, 100, 100, x, y); // just draw it
  }
  break;

case Shape.POLY:
  // create x values
  int xCoords[] = {x+oldX, x+55, x+65, x+80, x+80, x+oldX};
  // create y values
  int yCoords[] = {y+oldY, y+38, y+55, y+30, y+75, y+oldY};
  // create polygon
  Polygon thePoly = new
    Polygon(xCoords,yCoords,xCoords.length);

  if (fill) {
    g.fillPolygon(thePoly);  // fill it
  } else {
    g.drawPolygon(thePoly);  // just draw it
  }
  break;


case Shape.TEXT:
```

(continued)

Listing 22-3 *(continued)*

```java
        g.setFont( new Font ("Courier", Font.BOLD, y/6) );
        g.drawString("JavaDraw!", x, y);
        break;


    case Shape.IMAGE:

      if (theImage==null)
        if (m_fStandAlone) {
          theImage =
             Toolkit.getDefaultToolkit().getImage(imagePath);
        } else {
            theImage = getImage(getCodeBase(),imagePath);
        }

      int h = theImage.getHeight(this);
      int w = theImage.getWidth(this);

      if (fill) {
        // draw image and fill transparent parts
        // with foreground color:
        g.drawImage(theImage, x - (w/2), y - (h/2),
                    getForeground(), this);
      } else {
        // just draw it:
        g.drawImage(theImage, x - (w/2), y - (h/2), this);
      }
      break;

    default: break;
    }

    // dispose graphics context
    g.dispose();

    // update oldX,oldY to keep track of last mouse position:
    oldX=x;
    oldY=y;


  }
}
```

At first glance, the JavaDraw class looks pretty complicated. However, the essence of this class resides in only two methods: init() and draw(). The init() method creates an instance of WidgetPanel, JavaDraw's toolbar, and inserts it at the top (North) position of the applet window, using a Border layout. The init() method also registers a mouse button event listener and a mouse motion listener with the applet. These listeners enable a user to draw on the applet window by dragging the mouse over it. Specifically, when the user presses the mouse button, the mouse button listener records the location. Then, as the user drags the mouse over the applet window, the mouse motion listener draws a shape by invoking the applet's draw() method.

The draw() method itself is nothing but a big switch statement that draws the shape selected by the current setting of the toolbar's shapeChoice menu. Note that for readability, the draw() method uses symbolic constants, TEXT, POLY, LINE, and so on, to refer to types of shapes. The class Shape defines the values of these constants (see Listing 22-4). The draw() method also uses a class named UltraColor to convert color names to color objects (see Listing 22-5).

Listing 22-4: **Shape.java**

```
//*************************************************************
// Shape.java:
//
//*************************************************************
public final class Shape {

    public final static int LINE  = 0,
                            RECT  = 1,
                            OVAL  = 2,
                            POLY  = 3,
                            ARC   = 4,
                            TEXT  = 5,
                            IMAGE = 6;

    // CONSTRUCTOR: Shape()
    // PRIVATE — Don't let anyone instantiate this class!
        private Shape() {
        }
}
```

Listing 22-5: **UltraColor.java**

```
import java.awt.*;
/*
 *
 * UltraColor
 *
 */
```

(continued)

Listing 22-5 *(continued)*

```java
public class UltraColor
{
  // CONSTRUCTOR: UltraColor()
  // PRIVATE — Don't let anyone instantiate this class!
    private UltraColor() {
    }

  public static Color stringColor (String colorStr) {
    Color theColor = null;
    if (colorStr.equalsIgnoreCase("black")) {
      theColor = Color.black;
    } else if (colorStr.equalsIgnoreCase("blue")) {
      theColor = Color.blue;
    } else if (colorStr.equalsIgnoreCase("cyan")) {
      theColor = Color.cyan;
    } else if (colorStr.equalsIgnoreCase("darkGray")) {
      theColor = Color.darkGray;
    } else if (colorStr.equalsIgnoreCase("gray")) {
      theColor = Color.gray;
    } else if (colorStr.equalsIgnoreCase("green")) {
      theColor = Color.green;
    } else if (colorStr.equalsIgnoreCase("lightGray")) {
      theColor = Color.lightGray;
    } else if (colorStr.equalsIgnoreCase("magenta")) {
      theColor = Color.magenta;
    } else if (colorStr.equalsIgnoreCase("orange")) {
      theColor = Color.orange;
    } else if (colorStr.equalsIgnoreCase("pink")) {
      theColor = Color.pink;
    } else if (colorStr.equalsIgnoreCase("red")) {
      theColor = Color.red;
    } else if (colorStr.equalsIgnoreCase("white")) {
      theColor = Color.white;
    } else if (colorStr.equalsIgnoreCase("yellow")) {
      theColor = Color.yellow;
    } else {
      System.out.println("NO COLOR MATCH!");
    }
    return theColor;
    }

}
```

Most of the other methods in the `JavaDraw` class provide support for running JavaDraw either as an application or as an applet. For example, every Java application must have a static `main()` method to serve as an entry point. The `JavaDraw` class provides such a method. The `main()` method creates an instance of the JavaDraw applet inside the `JavaDrawFrame` class, extracts any command-line arguments, and initializes the applet. The `JavaDraw` class also provides a `GetParameter()` method analogous to the applet `getParameter()` method. The `applet` method extracts parameters from an HTML page that can be used to customize the applet, the background and initial foreground drawing colors in JavaDraw's case. The `JavaDraw` class's `main()` method uses the `GetParameter()` method to extract the same parameters from the command line. In this way, JavaDraw lets a user specify these parameters whether it is running as an application or as an applet.

Finally, Figure 22-3 illustrates the JavaDraw application in action. Now that you've seen how to approach the design and implementation of the JavaDraw applet/application, you're ready to begin putting all of your newly found Java knowledge to work.

Tip

Remember to take things a step at a time—begin with your application design and work your way to the code. Good luck!

Figure 22-3: The JavaDraw application in action

Summary

In this chapter you've learned about the basics of application development. You wouldn't try to build a house without a blueprint—so don't start developing your applications without a plan, either. Keep some ground rules in mind as you develop your own applications:

✦ Before jumping keys-first into code, consider exactly what you're programming; sketch out the user interface using paper and pen, as discussed in Chapter 3. Taking this approach frees you to think in detail about the project, refining your goals and plan of attack along the way, without committing to a single line of code before you're actually ready.

✦ Too often, software developers approach programming from an engineering perspective. Although this isn't a bad idea, it tends to result in a more complicated product for the end user. Instead of focusing on what the user should actually see and do, developers often concentrate their efforts on the underlying code. As a result, the interface becomes almost an afterthought, shoehorned into the constraints imposed by the implementation.

✦ We don't have to go nuts about applying complicated object-oriented analysis and design, but it's important to at least get a lay of the land before blazing new trails. At least consider your interface and how it dictates the objects you'll end up coding.

✦ Take a step-by-step approach to your application development. Start by building the basics of your user interface and flesh out your application from there.

✦ Finally, don't forget to take the necessary time to test and debug your application *before* you turn it loose on the unsuspecting public!

✦   ✦   ✦

Introducing Java Foundation Classes

Just what you need—another set of classes to learn before
you get to create a user interface for your programs. The
Java Foundation Classes (JFC) can give you more than just
another set of user-interface classes—JFC helps you add a
more professional look and feel to your Java applications than
you can with the Abstract Windowing Toolkit (AWT). The JFC
adds more than just a bit of polish to your user interface. It
provides the following features:

- ✦ Works with the Java Beans model
- ✦ Supports drag-and-drop
- ✦ Generates greater support for forms-based applications
- ✦ Uses a set of interface widgets
- ✦ Provides a pluggable look and feel
- ✦ Gives a framework for displaying your user interface

JFC's Components

So many components must come together to build the user
interface for your applications that it's important to take a
moment to sort them out.

The JFC isn't just a single component; it's actually made up of the following five different APIs:

✦ **AWT**—The original Java GUI component set. The AWT serves as the foundation for many of the Swing classes, described in the next section.

✦ **Java 2D**—A set of classes for 2D graphics and imaging. Primarily used to draw line-based graphics and images.

✦ **Accessibility**—Designed to provide user interface assistance for people with disabilities. Includes screen magnifiers and audible text readers.

✦ **Drag-and-Drop**—Enables data transfer between Java applications and between Java and native applications.

✦ **Swing**—The Swing classes include a new set of interface widgets, including existing AWT components and more interactive widgets. The Swing classes are loosely based on Netscape's Internet Foundation Classes.

So why did they call it *Swing*, anyway? While at the 1997 JavaOne show in San Francisco, JavaSoft engineers were showing off a new GUI component set in a musically-based demo. JavaSoft engineer George Saab joked that music critics were calling swing music the *in* sound. Since the classes didn't have a name yet, Swing seemed like a good choice—after all, Java already has its own Duke (that funky-looking dancing guy).

Examining Swing Classes

Yes, Swing brings along yet another revision to the Abstract Windowing Toolkit. A number of new classes are richer and more complicated than their AWT counterparts, but they're fairly lightweight and should be easy to use. The Swing classes are designed to be backward-compatible with older code. Figure 23-1 illustrates the widgets provided by Swing that replace the older AWT versions.

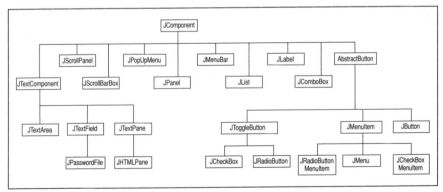

Figure 23-1: The class hierarchy of Swing classes that have AWT counterparts

Note

It's easy to remember the names of the new Swing classes that have AWT counterparts, Just put a *J* in front of the old AWT class name. For example, `Label` now becomes `JLabel`.

However, Swing actually includes twice the number of components than there were in the AWT. Figure 23-2 illustrates the hierarchy of these components.

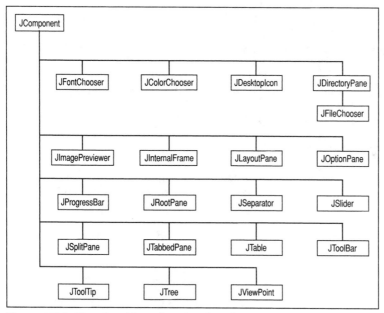

Figure 23-2: The class hierarchy of Swing classes

Most of the new widgets in Swing provide the basics of user interface design. There are classes for labels, buttons, check boxes, lists, combo boxes, text fields, and menus. But Swing also includes more sophisticated components, as well, such as sliders, progress bars, tree controls, tool tips, and tables. Swing also makes putting graphics into menus easier; Swing widgets offer other improvements as well:

✦ They redraw themselves more efficiently.

✦ They can be layered.

✦ They can be drawn transparently over one another.

In the earlier AWT models, user interface widgets were native classes. This meant that each component was mapped to its native operating system equivalent. While this worked well, the problem with this approach was that these classes had to be rewritten for each platform Java supported. This caused variations in the way a user interface of a Java application looked on different platforms. Swing brings the promise that the look and feel of controls across user interfaces will be much more consistent, because the interface elements were no longer implemented using the native operating system. All Swing interface elements are implemented using only Java. The new AWT event model is still present in the Swing classes. (The AWT 1.0 event model can't be used with the Swing widgets, though.)

Model-View-Controller (MVC) architecture

The look and feel of Java Swing components are implemented in pluggable modules, meaning it's possible to create custom look-and-feel modules to change the way Swing components work. You can even change the look and feel of your application components while your application is running. Another way Swing supports the separation of widgets from native code is through the use of the Model-View-Controller (MVC) architecture. The MVC architecture separates each widget component into three parts: a model, a view, and a controller. The model component contains the widget's data. The view component handles screen display. And the controller component contains the code that is used to manipulate the components. Swing components are also JavaBeans (see Chapter 26) and participate in the JavaBeans event model.

MVC is a methodology that is often used when building user interfaces. In an MVC-based user interface, there are three communicating objects: the *model, view,* and *controller.* The model is the underlying logical representation, the view is the visual representation, and the controller specifies how to handle user input. When a model changes, it notifies all views that depend on it. This provides two important, powerful features:

- ✦ You can base multiple views of the same object on the same model.
- ✦ Because models specify nothing in the way the user interface element looks, you can modify or create views without affecting the underlying model.

A view uses a controller to specify the way it responds. For example, the controller component determines what to do when receiving mouse or keyboard input.

While the primary purpose of the MVC model is for building user interfaces, it can be also used to establish a notification protocol between nonvisual objects. A model object can send change notifications to another set of objects without knowing details about those objects.

Note

This same behavior has been provided in Java since version 1.0 through the `Observer/Observable` objects in `java.util` package.

Swing represents components where the view and controller components are combined into an object called a *delegate.* Delegates represent the model, just like the view component in the MVC model, and translate user input into the model, just like the controller component in the MVC model. While the communication that occurs between the view and controller components is quite complex, it helps to simplify the component design process.

Swing widgets are subclasses of `JComponent`, such as `JButton`. A `JComponent` object has a single model and a single delegate associated with it. Models for a particular `JComponent` are classes that implement a model interface specific to that `JComponent`. For example, for a class to act as a `JButton`'s model, it must implement the `ButtonModel` interface. Delegates are also implementations of a delegate interface that is specific to the `JComponent`. The delegate/model hierarchy used by the `JButton` Swing component is illustrated in Figure 23-3.

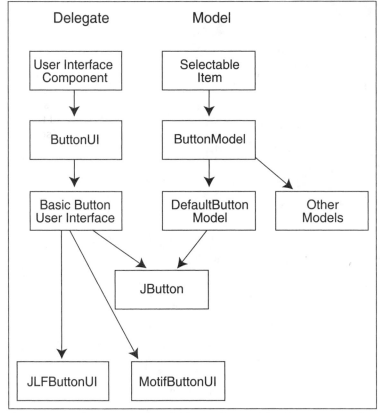

Figure 23-3: The delegate/model hierarchy used by the JButton Swing component

Inheritance differences between Swing and AWT

Figure 23-1 illustrates how a number of the Swing user interface classes are descended from the `JComponent` class. For those who have used the AWT in the past, after a quick look it could appear that all of the Swing classes are inherited from the `JComponent` class in the same way all classes are inherited from the `Component` class in the AWT. However, if you take a closer look at the figure, you'll notice some subtle and interesting differences between the way Swing classes are inherited from the JComponent class and the way AWT classes were inherited from the Component class. A closer look at the button and menu widget objects can help to illustrate the differences more clearly. (Chapter 24 examines all the Swing widgets in more detail.)

Button widget changes

There are a number of major differences between Swing and AWT button widget classes. The AWT provides only two button classes—Button and CheckBox, as shown in Figure 23-4.

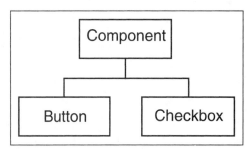

Figure 23-4: Button and Checkbox class inheritance with AWT

In Swing, two new kinds of buttons have been added, and the button-component hierarchy tree has been rearranged, as shown in Figure 23-5.

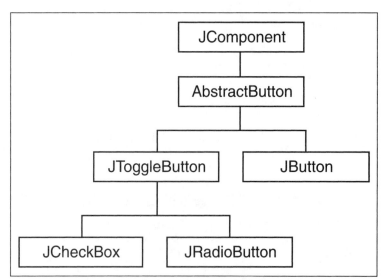

Figure 23-5: JCheckBox, JRadioButton, and JButton class inheritance with Swing

Swing has both a radio-button class and a check-box class. In the older AWT, there wasn't a radio-button class; the `CheckBox` functioned as both a check-box class and a radio-button class.

In Swing, the `JRadioButton` and `JCheckBox` descend from another new button class named `JToggleButton`. All of the Swing button classes (`JButton`, `JToggleButton`, `JRadioButton`, and `JCheckBox`) are inherited from an abstract class named `AbstractButton`, which neatly encapsulates all their common features and capabilities. The `AbstractButton` class is directly inherited from the `JComponent` class.

Menu widget changes

You may know that in the older AWT model, the menu classes descended from the `java.lang.Object` class (as shown in Figure 23-6), instead of from the `Component` class.

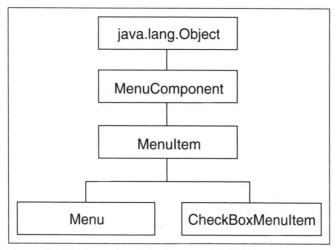

Figure 23-6: Menu class inheritance with AWT

In Swing, all menu classes are descended from the `JComponent` class, as shown in Figure 23-7. As you can see, the newer Swing model results in a more complex object hierarchy—the `JButton` and `JMenu` classes are closely linked together—this arrangement makes it easier to implement button and menu events.

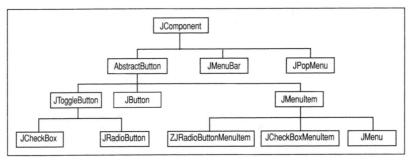

Figure 23-7: JMenu, JRadioButtonMenuItem, JCheckBoxMenuItem class inheritance with Swing

Swing also provides a new interface, the `Action` interface, which listens for both menu and button events simultaneously. This capability now makes it easier to coordinate button and menu events then was ever possible before.

Packages

Thirteen packages comprise the Swing classes. Each class has its own purpose:

✦ `com.sun.java.swing`—This high-level Swing package primarily contains components, adapters, default component models, and interfaces for all the delegates and models.

✦ `com.sun.java.swing.basic`—This `basic` Swing package contains the User Interface (UI) classes, which implement the default look and feel for Swing components.

✦ `com.sun.java.swing.beaninfo`—The `beaninfo` package contains `BeanInfo` support classes for when the Swing components are used within a Bean-connecting tool (see Chapter 26 for more information on the JavaBeans programming model).

✦ `com.sun.java.swing.border`—The `border` package declares the `Border` interface and classes, which define specific border rendering styles.

✦ `com.sun.java.swing.event`—The `event` package is for the Swing-specific event types and listeners. Swing components can generate their own event types, in addition to the `java.awt.event` types.

✦ `com.sun.java.swing.multi`—The `multi` package contains the multiplexing user interface classes, which permit the creation of components from different user interface factories.

✦ `com.sun.java.swing.plaf`—The `plaf` package contains the Pluggable Look-and-Feel API, used to define custom interfaces.

✦ `com.sun.java.swing.table`—The `table` package contains the interfaces and classes that support the Swing `JTable` component.

✦ `com.sun.java.swing.target`—The `target` package contains the support classes for action target management.

✦ `com.sun.java.swing.text`—The `text` package contains the support classes for the Swing document framework.

✦ `com.sun.java.swing.text.html`—The `text.html` package contains the support classes for basic HTML rendering.

✦ `com.sun.java.swing.undo`—The `undo` package provides the support classes for implementing undo/redo capabilities in a GUI.

Summarizing the Swing Classes

Table 23-1 summarizes the classes provided in the Swing component package. Each Swing user-interface class component is reviewed in detail in Chapter 24.

Table 23-1
Classes Provided in the Swing Component Package

Component	Description
`Japplet`	Implements a Java applet.
`JAppletBeanInfo`	Provides information about `JApplet` to bean-based tools.
`JButton`	Implements a button component.
`JButtonBeanInfo`	Provides information about `JButton` for bean-based tools.
`JCheckBox`	Implements a check-box component.
`JCheckBoxBeanInfo`	Provides information about `JCheckBox` for bean-based tools.
`JCheckBoxMenuItem`	Implements a check-box menu item.
`JCheckBoxMenuItem BeanInfo`	Provides information about `JCheckBoxMenuItem` for bean-based tools.
`JColorChooser`	Displays and manages a color-chooser dialog.
`JColorChooserBean Info`	Provides information about `JColorChooser` for bean-based tools.
`JComboBox`	Implements a combo-box component.
`JComboBoxBeanInfo`	Provides information about `JComboBox` for bean-based tools.
`JComponent`	The mother of all Swing components.

(continued)

Table 23-1 *(continued)*

Component	Description
JComponentBeanInfo	Provides information about JComponent for bean-based tools.
JDesktopIcon	Displays an iconified version of a JInternalFrame.
JDesktopIconBeanInfo	Provides information about JDesktopIcon for bean-based tools.
JDesktopPane	Provides a pluggable DesktopManager object for JInternalFrame objects.
JDesktopPaneBean	Provides information about JDesktopPane for bean-based Info tools.
JDialog	Adds enhancements to java.awt.Dialog.
JDialogBeanInfo	Provides information about JDialog for bean-based tools.
JFileChooser	Implements a file-chooser dialog box.
JFileChooserBeanInfo	Provides information about JFileChooser for bean-based tools.
JFrame	Adds enhancements to java.awt.Frame.
JFrameBeanInfo	Provides information about JFrame for bean-based tools.
JInternalFrame	Implements a frame object that can be placed inside a JDesktopPane object to emulate a native frame window.
JInternalFrameBean Info	Provides information about JInternalFrame for bean-based tools.
JLabel	Creates a display area for displaying read-only text, an image, or both.
JLabelBeanInfo	Provides information about JLabel for bean-based tools.
JLayeredPane	Can display multiple layered panes (JInternalFrame objects) inside a frame.
JLayeredPaneBeanInfo	Provides information about JLayeredPane for bean-based tools.
JList	Allows the user to select one or more objects from a list. A separate model, ListModel, represents the contents of the list.
JListBeanInfo	Provides information about JList for bean-based tools.
JMenu	Implements a menu component.
JMenuBeanInfo	Provides information about JMenu for bean-based tools.

Component	Description
JMenuBar	Implements a menu bar component.
JMenuBarBeanInfo	Provides information about JMenuBar for bean-based tools.
JMenuItem	Implements a menu item component.
JMenuItemBeanInfo	Provides information about JMenuItem for bean-based tools.
JOptionPane	Displays a dialog box that prompts the user for a choice and then passes that choice on to the executing program.
JOptionPaneBeanInfo	Provides information about JOptionPane for bean-based tools.
JPanel	Provides a generic container for organizing other components.
JPanelBeanInfo	Provides information about JPanel for bean-based tools.
JPasswordField	Displays a field in which the user can type a password. The text of the password does not appear in the field as it is being typed.
JPasswordFieldBean Info	Provides information about JPasswordField for bean-based tools.
JPopupMenu	Implements a pop-up menu.
JPopupMenuBeanInfo	Provides information about JPopupMenu for bean-based tools.
JProgressBar	Implements a progress-bar component.
JProgressBarBeanInfo	Provides information about JProgressBar for bean-based tools.
JRadioButton	Implements a radio-button control.
JRadioButtonBeanInfo	Provides information about JRadioButton for bean-based tools.
JRadioButtonMenuItem	Implements a radio-button menu item.
JradioButtonMenuItem BeanInfo	Provides information about JRadioButtonMenuItem for bean-based tools.
JRootPane	Instantiates in a single step an object made up of a glass pane, a layered pane, an optional menu bar, and a content pane.
JRootPaneBeanInfo	Provides information about JRootPane for bean-based tools.
JScrollBar	Implements a scroll-bar object.

(continued)

Table 23-1 *(continued)*

Component	Description
JScrollBarBeanInfo	Provides information about JScrollBar for bean-based tools.
JScrollPane	Implements a scroll-pane object.
JScrollPaneBeanInfo	Provides information about JScrollPane for bean-based tools.
JSeparator	Implements a menu separator object.
JSeparatorBeanInfo	Provides information about JSeparator for bean-based tools.
JSlider	Implements a slider-bar object.
JSliderBeanInfo	Provides information about JSlider for bean-based tools.
JSplitPane	Implements a split-pane component.
JSplitPaneBeanInfo	Provides information about JSplitPane for bean-based tools.
JTabbedPane	Implements a tabbed-pane ("property-page") component.
JTabbedPaneBeanInfo	Provides information about JTabbedPane for bean-based tools.
JTable	Implements a table component.
JTableBeanInfo	Provides information about JTable for bean-based tools.
JTextArea	Implements a multiline area that can display editable or read-only text.
JTextAreaBeanInfo	Provides information about JTextArea for bean-based tools.
JTextPane	Implements a text component that can be marked up with attributes to be represented graphically.
JTextPane-BeanInfo	Provides information about JTextPane for bean-based tools.
JToggleButton	Implements a two-stage button component.
JToggleButtonBeanInfo	Provides information about JToggleButton for bean-based tools.
JToolBar	Implements a dockable, floatable tool bar.
JToolBarBeanInfo	Provides information about JToolBar for bean-based tools.

Component	Description
JToolTip	Implements a tool-tip component (a component that can display a short string, such as the name of components or a user tip).
JToolTipBeanInfo	Provides information about JToolTip for bean-based tools.
JTree	A component that can display a set of hierarchical data in a graphical outline format.
JTreeBeanInfo	Provides information about JTree for bean-based tools.
JViewport	Provides a clipped view of an arbitrarily large component. Used by JScrollPane.
JViewportBeanInfo	Provides information about JViewport for bean-based tools.
JWindow	Adds enhancements to java.awt.Window.
JWindowBeanInfo	Provides information about JWindow for bean-based tools.

Other Foundation Classes

It's important to keep in mind that other competing interface classes are also being developed by Netscape and Microsoft. The Netscape Internet Foundation Classes (IFC) share a common foundation with the Swing classes. Like everything Microsoft, the Application Foundation Classes (AFC) are wholly Microsoft and take on their own approach to user interface design. Neither of the aforementioned foundation classes have made a major stake in the Java application development world. It's important to know, though, that there are other Java user-interface classes available. Hopefully a single user-interface class will dominate in the future. Our bet is it will be Swing.

Internet Foundation Classes

The design of the Swing class library borrowed heavily from Netscape's Internet Foundation Class library. The Swing class developers worked closely with Netscape to integrate the best features of both the old AWT and IFC into a new and better user-interface class library. Although both the IFC and Swing classes share the same background, the Swing classes as they exist today are quite different. If you're interested in finding out more about the Netscape Internet Foundation classes, visit the Internet Foundation Class library Web site at http://www.netscape.com/.

Application Foundation Classes

The Application Foundation Classes, or AFC, is Microsoft's answer to the AWT. The AFC builds on the AWT foundation to provide more user-friendly controls for your applications. The Application Foundation Classes are provided in the following three packages:

- ✦ `com.ms.ui`—This User Interface package, which provides the primary framework for applets, applications, and user interface controls. The User Interface package is what most people will be referring to when they speak of the AFC. The User Interface package includes menus, buttons, canvases, edit controls, frames, lists, marquees, panels, radio buttons, scrollers, and tree view controls.

- ✦ `com.ms.fx`—This FX package provides advanced graphic controls in your applications, including control over colors, fonts, curves, text, and textures. The FX package provides more flexibility than AWT because it is not limited to only system-defined standards. Especially when developing intranet applications, you can use the FX classes to use all of your system's available fonts and colors.

- ✦ `com.ms.resource`—This Resource package provides access to Win-32 resources, including dialog boxes and string tables, from your Java applications.

The User Interface package is the heart of the AFC. The AFC is built on the foundation laid by the AWT. If you're already familiar with using the AWT, much of what you already know will remain familiar. Figure 23-8 illustrates the AFC hierarchy. The class names preceded by an asterisk (*) are AWT classes. As you can see, all of the Application Foundation Classes extend from these base AWT classes. Figure 23-9 illustrates the class hierarchy of the user interface elements provided by the AFC. Many of these elements will be familiar to those familiar with AWT (for example, buttons, check boxes, and radio buttons) while others were not previously available (for example, tree control, marquee, and so on).

Before you think *There goes Microsoft, trying to usurp yet another piece of the Java world,* let's take a closer look. The AFC is built upon and extends the AWT, making it possible to mix both user interface models in your applications, which helps to preserve your user interface investment in your current applications and ease the transition over to a new programming model. Other user interface class models usually force a developer to choose between the AWT and another library.

Unlike the AWT and Swing, the AFC isn't entirely written in Java, and in some cases is based on DirectX components; thus, AFC only runs on Win32 platforms. The Application Foundation Classes provide new and better scroll bars and sliders, a tree control, a tab display, the ability to move through the user interface using just the keyboard, and a file-system explorer. The Application Foundation Classes permit the development of applications with user interfaces that are familiar to users of traditional Windows-based applications.

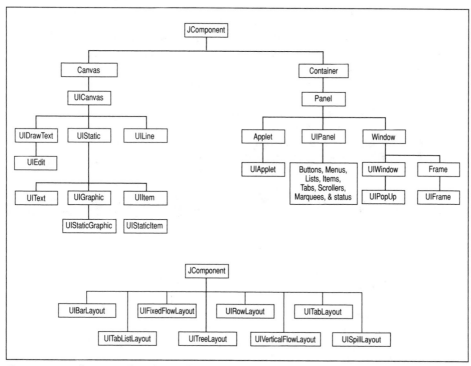

Figure 23-8: The MFC class hierarchy

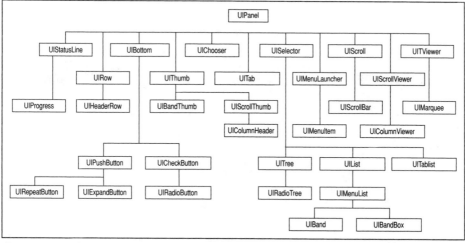

Figure 23-9: The MFC User Interface class hierarchy

Building Java applications with the Application Foundation Classes is no different from building your applications using the AWT. Instead of using the `Applet` and `Frame` classes, the `UIApplet` and `UIFrame` classes are substituted instead. Since the `UIApplet` and `UIFrame` classes are extended from the AWT `Applet` and `Frame` classes it is possible to mix both AWT and AFC components. Listing 23-1 demonstrates how to create a shell AFC applet. Listing 23-2 demonstrates how to create the HTML necessary to call the shell applet. The AFC can also be used to create standalone applications. Listing 23-3 demonstrates how to create a standalone shell application using the AFC. In its current release, the Application Foundation Classes support both the traditional event-handling model as used in these examples, and the event delegation model supported by JDK 1.1.

Listing 23-1: **How to Create a Shell AFC Applet**

```
// A shell AFC applet. Use this as a template
// for building your own AFC applets.

import java.applet.*;
import java.awt.*;
import com.ms.ui.*;
import com.ms.fx.*;

public class AFCAppletShell extends UIApplet {
   public init() {
      setBackground(FXColor.gray);
      // Add other user interface components here
   }
}
```

Listing 23-2: **HTML Required to Embed the AFC Applet**

```
<HTML>
<TITLE>A Shell AFC Applet</TITLE>
<CENTER>An Example AFC Applet</CENTER>
<APPLET CODE=AFCAppletShell.class
        ID=AFCAppletShell
        WIDTH=200
        HEIGHT=200>
</APPLET>
</HTML>
```

Listing 23-3: **How to Create a Shell AFC Applet**

```
// Listing 3: A shell AFC application. Use this
// as a template for building your own AFC
// applications.

import java.applet.*;
import java.awt.*;
import com.ms.ui.*;
import com.ms.fx.*;

public class AFCAppShell extends UIApplet {
  public static void main(String args[]) {
    AFCShellFrame frame = new
      new AFCShellFrame("AFC Application Shell");
    frame.show();
    frame.resize(200,200);

    AFCAppShell applet = new AFCAppShell();

    // Add the applet to the frame
    frame.add(applet);

    applet.init();
  }

  public init() {
    setBackground(FXColor.gray);
    // Add other user interface components here
  }
}

class AFCShellFrame extends UIFrame {
  // Frame constructor
  public AFCShellFrame(String str) {
    super(str);
  }

  // Frame event handler
  public boolean handleEvent(Event evnt) {
    switch(evnt.id) {
      // Close the application
      case Event.WINDOW_DESTROY:
        System.exit(0);
        return(true);
      // Pass all other events to the UIFrame
      // event handler
      default:
        super.handleEvent(evnt);
    }
  }
}
```

Summary

The Java Foundation Classes are more than just another set of user interface classes—they help you add a more professional look and feel to your Java applications than you can achieve with the AWT.

✦ The JFC isn't just a single component, it's actually a set of five different APIs: AWT, Java 2D, Accessibility, Drag-and-Drop, and Swing.

✦ Most of the new widgets in Swing provide the basics of user interface design. There are classes for labels, buttons, check boxes, lists, combo boxes, text fields, and menus. But Swing also includes more sophisticated components as well, such as sliders, progress bars, tree controls, tool tips, and tables.

✦ Swing supports the separation of widgets from native code through the use of the Model-View-Controller (MVC) architecture. The MVC architecture separates each widget component into three parts: a model, a view, and a controller. The model component contains the widget's data. The view component handles screen display. And the controller component contains the code which is used to manipulate the components.

✦ The JFC isn't the only game in town—competing interface classes are also being developed by Netscape and Microsoft. The Netscape Internet Foundation Classes (IFC) share a common foundation with the Swing classes. Like everything Microsoft, the Application Foundation Classes (AFC) are wholly Microsoft and take their own approach to user-interface design.

✦　　✦　　✦

Getting in the Swing of Things

Do you have your feet squared in the batter's box, all ready to take a swing? If so, then you're ready to take a look at Swing's user-interface classes—the major new component of the Java Foundation Classes. They are the new path to user interface design with JDK 1.2 and beyond. This chapter reviews the packages that comprise the Swing user-interface classes and reviews Swing's major interface components. A discussion of the Swing classes and user interface components could easily produce an entire book on its own. This chapter presents a simpler, down-and-dirty review of the Swing user-interface components, followed by a method reference. (If you're interested in a more in-depth treatment of the JFC, read *JFC: Java Foundation Classes* by Daniel I. Joshi and Pavel A. Vorobiev, IDG Books Worldwide.) There's no time to waste—it's time to get into the game and hit a home run.

Introduction to the Swing Packages

Swing user-interface classes come in thirteen different packages, as listed in Table 24-1.

Table 24-1
Swing Packages

Swing Package	Definition
com.sun.java.swing	This high-level Swing package primarily contains components, adapters, default component models, and interfaces for all the delegates and models.
com.sun.java.swing.basic	This basic Swing package contains the User Interface (UI) classes that implement the default look and feel for Swing components.
com.sun.java.swing.beaninfo	The beaninfo package contains BeanInfo support classes for when the Swing components are used within a Bean-connecting tool (see Chapter 26 for more information on the JavaBeans programming model).
com.sun.java.swing.border	The border package declares the Border interface and classes, which define specific border rendering styles.
com.sun.java.swing.event	The event package is for the Swing-specific event types and listeners. Swing components can generate their own event types, in addition to the java.awt.event types.
com.sun.java.swing.multi	The multi package contains the multiplexing user interface classes that permit the creation of components from different user interface factories.
com.sun.java.swing.plaf	The plaf package contains the Pluggable Look-and-Feel API used to define custom interfaces.
com.sun.java.swing.table	The table package contains the interfaces and classes that support the Swing table component.
com.sun.java.swing.target	The target package contains the support classes for action target management.
com.sun.java.swing.text	The text package contains the support classes for the Swing document framework.
com.sun.java.swing.text.html	The text.html package contains the support classes for basic HTML rendering.
com.sun.java.swing.undo	The undo package provides the support classes for implementing undo/redo capabilities in a GUI environment.

Swing Objects

A number of objects comprise the Swing user interface classes, as shown in Figure 24-1, which illustrates the Swing object hierarchy. As you'll notice, Swing has twice the number of components than there were in the AWT. Most of the new widgets in Swing provide the basics of user interface design. You'll find classes for labels, buttons, check boxes, lists, combo boxes, text fields, and menus. But Swing also includes more sophisticated components as well, such as sliders, progress bars, tree controls, tool tips, and tables. Let's look at the basic Swing objects in detail.

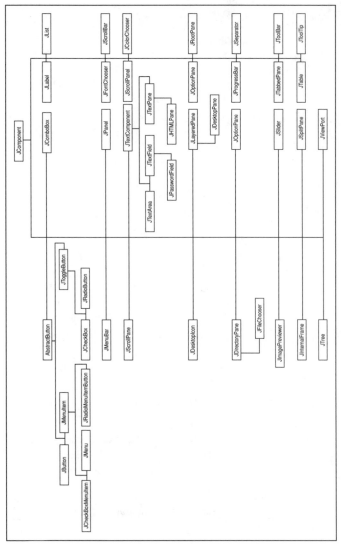

Figure 24-1: The Swing user-interface class hierarchy

AbstractButton

The AbstractButton class defines the inherent behavior of all Swing buttons. The AbstractButton class isn't a class you would use directly—though several of the more commonly used JComponent classes inherit a lot of their behavior from this object. For example, the icon usage methods getIcon() and setIcon() are inherited from the AbstractButton class. Table 24-2 lists and describes the methods provided by the AbstractButton class.

Table 24-2 AbstractButton Methods	
Method	*Description*
addAccessibleSelection(int)	Calls setSelected(true).
addActionListener (ActionListener)	Adds an ActionListener to the button.
addChangeListener (ChangeListener)	Adds a ChangeListener to the button.
addItemListener (ItemListener)	Adds an ItemListener to the checkbox.
checkHorizontalKey (int, String)	Ensures that the key is valid.
checkVerticalKey (int, String)	Ensures that the key is valid.
clearAccessibleSelection()	Calls setSelected(false).
createChangeListener()	Subclasses that want to handle ChangeEvents differently can override this to return another ChangeListener implementation.
doAccessibleAction(int)	Performs the specified Action on the object.
doClick()	Programatically performs a "click."
doClick(int)	Programatically performs a "click."
getAccessibleActionCount()	Returns the number of Actions available in this object.
getAccessibleAction Description(int)	Returns a description of the specified action of the object.
getAccessibleName()	Gets the accessible name of this object.
getAccessibleSelection(int)	Returns Accessible—representing the specified selected item in the object.

Method	Description
getAccessibleSelection Count()	Returns the number of items currently selected.
getAccessibleStateSet()	Gets the state set of this object.
getAccessibleValue()	Gets the value of this object as a `Number`.
getActionCommand()	Returns the action command for this button.
getDisabledIcon()	Returns the icon used by the button when it's disabled.
getDisabledSelectedIcon()	Returns the icon used by the button when it's disabled and selected.
getHorizontalAlignment()	Returns the horizontal alignment of the icon and text.
getHorizontalTextPosition()	Sets the horizontal position of the text relative to the icon.
getIcon()	Returns the default icon.
getKeyAccelerator()	Returns the keyboard accelerator from the current model.
getLabel()	This method is deprecated—it's no longer used.
getMargin()	Returns the margin between the button's border and the label.
getMaximumAccessibleValue()	Gets the maximum value of this object as a `Number`.
getMinimumAccessibleValue()	Gets the minimum value of this object as a `Number`.
getModel()	Gets the model that this button represents.
getPressedIcon()	Returns the pressed icon for the button.
getRolloverIcon()	Returns the rollover icon for the button.
getRolloverSelectedIcon()	Returns the rollover selection icon for the button.
getSelectedIcon()	Returns the selected icon for the button.
getText()	Returns the button's text.
getUI()	Returns the button's current UI.
getVerticalAlignment()	Returns the vertical alignment of the text and icon.
getVerticalTextPosition()	Returns the vertical position of the text relative to the icon valid keys: `CENTER` (the default), `TOP`, `BOTTOM`.

(continued)

Table 24-2 *(continued)*

Method	Description
isBorderPainted()	Returns whether the border should be painted.
isFocusPainted()	Returns whether focus should be painted.
isRolloverEnabled()	Checks whether rollover effects are enabled.
isSelected()	Returns the state of the button.
paintBorder(Graphics)	Paints the button's border if BorderPainted property is true.
removeAccessibleSelection (int)	Calls setSelected(false).
removeActionListener (ActionListener)	Removes an ActionListener from the button.
removeChangeListener (ChangeListener)	Removes a ChangeListener from the button.
removeItemListener (ItemListener)	Removes an ItemListener from the button.
selectAllAccessible Selection()	Calls setSelected(true).
setAccessibleValue(Number)	Sets the value of this object as a Number.
setActionCommand(String)	Sets the action command for this button.
setBorderPainted(boolean)	Sets whether the border should be painted.
setDisabledIcon(Icon)	Sets the disabled icon for the button.
setDisabledSelectedIcon (Icon)	Sets the disabled selection icon for the button.
setEnabled(boolean)	Enables (or disables) the button.
setFocusPainted(boolean)	Sets whether focus should be painted.
setHorizontalAlignment(int)	Sets the horizontal alignment of the icon and text.
setHorizontalTextPosition (int)	Sets the horizontal position of the text relative to the icon.
setIcon(Icon)	Sets the button's default icon.
setKeyAccelerator(int)	Sets the keyboard accelerator for the current model.

Method	Description
setLabel(String)	This method has been deprecated—it's no longer used.
setMargin(Insets)	Sets space for the margin between the button's border and the label.
setModel(ButtonModel)	Sets the model that this button represents.
setOpaque(boolean)	Fills the button's background with background color if true.
setPressedIcon(Icon)	Sets the pressed icon for the button.
setRolloverEnabled(boolean)	Enable or disable rollover effects.
setRolloverIcon(Icon)	Sets the rollover icon for the button.
setRolloverSelectedIcon (Icon)	Sets the rollover selected icon for the button.
setSelected(boolean)	Sets the state of the button.
setSelectedIcon(Icon)	Sets the selected icon for the button.
setText(String)	Sets the button's text.
setUI(ButtonUI)	Sets the button's UI.
setVerticalAlignment(int)	Sets the vertical alignment of the icon and text.
setVerticalTextPosition (int)	Sets the vertical position of the text relative to the icon.
updateUI()	Gets a new UI object from the default User Interface factory.

Other common behaviors inherited from the AbstractButton class include:

✦ The setDisabledIcon, setDisabledSelectedIcon, setPressedIcon, setRolloverIcon, setRolloverSelectedIcon, and setSelectedIcon methods are used to change the displayed icon, based on the button state.

✦ The doClick method is used to select the button.

✦ The setKeyAccelerator method is used to add a keyboard accelerator character to a text label.

✦ The setVerticalTextPosition and setHorizontalTextPosition methods are used to position text in different areas around an icon.

✦ The setVerticalAlignment and setHorizontalAlignment methods are used to anchor an icon or text in different areas of a button.

JButton

A Swing JButton object can be used just like the older AWT button (java.awt. Button)—to create a user interface push button. It also responds in the same manner as an AWT button by sending a message to an ActionListener whenever the button is clicked. By default the background color of a JButton is the same as the background color of the container control, so you need to set the background color to SystemColor.control whenever you create a JButton. Listing 24-1 demonstrates how to create a JButton.

Listing 24-1: **How to Create a Simple JButton Object**

```
public class ButtonPanel extends JPanel {
  public ButtonPanel () {
    JButton myButton = new JButton("My JButton");
    myButton.setBackground (SystemColor.control);
    add(myButton);
  }
}
```

You can also include an icon on a JButton, as demonstrated in Listing 24-2. Table 24-3 lists and describes the methods provided by the JButton class—remember that much of the JButton behavior is inherited from the AbstractButton class.

Listing 24-2: **How to Create a JButton Object That Also Displays an Icon**

```
public class ButtonPanel extends JPanel {
  public ButtonPanel() {
    Icon myIcon = new ImageIcon("MyButtonIcon.gif");
    JButton myButton = new JButton("My JButton", myIcon);
    myButton.setBackground (SystemColor.control);
    add(myButton);
  }
}
```

Table 24-3
JButton Methods

Method	Description
void updateUI()	Notification from the User Interface factory that the look and feel have changed.
public String getUIClassID()	Returns a string that specifies the name of the look-and-feel class that renders this component.
public AccessibleRole getAccessibleRole()	Gets the role of this object.

JCheckBox

A JCheckBox is similar to an AWT Checkbox that isn't part of a CheckboxGroup. You can specify your own icon to be used to illustrate the unchecked and checked state of the check box. Listing 24-3 demonstrates how to create a JCheckBox object. Table 24-4 lists and describes the methods provided by the JCheckBox class—once again, remember that much of the JCheckBox behavior is inherited from the AbstractButton class.

Listing 24-3: **How to Create a Simple JCheckBox Object**

```
public class ButtonPanel extends JPanel {
    public ButtonPanel () {
        // Create checkbox with its state initialized to true
        JCheckBox box1 = new JCheckBox("Check Box 1", true);
        box1.setIcon(unchecked);
        box1.setSelectedIcon(checked);
        // Create checkbox with its state initialized
        // to false
        JCheckBox box2 = new JCheckBox("Check Box 2", false);
        box2.setIcon(unchecked);
        box2.setSelectedIcon(checked);
        add(box1);
        add(box2);
    };
};
```

<table>
<tr><td colspan="2" align="center">Table 24-4
JCheckBox Methods</td></tr>
<tr><td>*Method*</td><td>*Description*</td></tr>
<tr><td>getAccessible
ActionDescription(int)</td><td>Returns a description of the specified action of the object.</td></tr>
<tr><td>getAccessibleRole()</td><td>Gets the role of this object.</td></tr>
<tr><td>updateUI()</td><td>Notification from the User Interface factory that the look and feel have changed.</td></tr>
</table>

JComboBox

The JComboBox works just like AWT's Choice component — providing a drop-down list of choices in an edit box — although some of the methods have been renamed. As with the Choice component, the JComboBox object also provides an editable option. You can create a JComboBox with a list of default choices, but still allow the entry of another value through the use of the editable option, as shown in Listing 24-4. Whenever the user presses a key that matches the first letter of a default choice, it is automatically displayed. Table 24-5 lists and describes the methods provided by the JComboBox class.

Listing 24-4: How to Create a Simple JComboBox Object

```
public class ComboPanel extends JPanel {
  String choices[] = {"Choice1", "Choice2","Choice3"};
  public ComboPanel() {
    JComboBox combo1 = new JComboBox();
    for (int i=0;i<choices.length;i++) {
      combo1.addItem (choices[i]);
    }
    // Allow the Combo Box to be editable
    combo1.setEditable(true);
    // Set the maximum number of rows to display
    combo1.setMaximumRowCount(4);
    add(combo1);
  }
}
```

Table 24-5
JComboBox Methods

Method	Description
actionPerformed (ActionEvent)	This method is public as an implementation side-effect.
addActionListener (ActionListener)	Adds an ActionListener.
addItem(Object)	Adds an item in the item list.
addItemListener (ItemListener)	Adds an ItemListener.
contentsChanged (ListDataEvent)	This method is public as an implementation side-effect.
getActionCommand()	Returns the action command that is included in the event sent to action listeners.
getItemCount()	Accesses the model.
getSelectedObjects()	Returns an array containing the selected item.
hidePopup()	Causes the combo box to hide its popup.
insertItemAt(Object, int)	Inserts an item in the item list at a given index.
isFocusTraversable()	Identifies whether or not this component can receive the focus.
isOpaque()	Returns true if this component is completely opaque.
processKeyEvent(KeyEvent)	Overrides processKeyEvent to process events.
removeActionListener (ActionListener)	Removes an ActionListener.
removeAllItems()	Convenience to remove all items. This method works only if the receiving JComboBox uses the default JComboBox data model.
removeItem(Object)	Removes an item from the item list.
removeItemAt(int)	Removes the item at anIndex.
removeItemListener (ItemListener)	Removes an ItemListener.
selectedItemChanged()	This method is called when the selected item changes.

(continued)

Table 24-5 *(continued)*	
Method	**Description**
setActionCommand(String)	Sets the action command that should be included in the event sent to action listeners.
setSelectedItem(Object)	Sets the receiving JComboBox selected item.
showPopup()	Causes the combo box to show its popup.
updateUI()	Overriden from JComponent to change the UI according to the default factory.

JFrame

The Window class hierarchy is different from the AWT. All the Swing Window classes are subclassed from the Window object, not JComponent, like many of the other Swing components. The JFrame class replaces the AWT's Frame class, providing a frame for your windows where you can add menus and toolbars. You have two ways to add a menu to your JFrame: you can add older java.awt.MenuBar objects using the setMenuBar method, or you can add a JMenuBar to a JFrame using the setJMenuBar method.

The other major difference between the JFrame class and the AWT Frame class is that you can no longer directly add components or use setLayout() to change the Frame LayoutManager. Now, you need to get a content pane, and then you can add components to that or change its layout. Listing 24-5 demonstrates how to create a JFrame object. Table 24-6 lists and describes the methods provided by the JFrame object.

Listing 24-5: **How to Create a Simple JFrame Object**

```
public class TestFrame {
  public static void main (String args[]) {
    JFrame f = new JFrame ("My JFrame Example");
    Container c = f.getContentPane();
    c.setLayout (new FlowLayout());
    for (int i = 0; i < 5; i++) {
      c.add (new JButton ("My Button")).setBackground
        (SystemColor.control);
    }
    c.add (new JLabel ("Swing Test Frame"));
    f.setSize (300, 200);
    f.show();
  }
}
```

Table 24-6
JFrame Methods

Method	Description
addAccessibleSelection(int)	Adds the *n*th selected item in the object to the object's selection.
clearAccessibleSelection()	Clears the selection in the object, so nothing in the object is selected.
createRootPane()	Creates the default rootPane when called by the constructor methods.
doAccessibleAction(int)	Performs the *n*th Action on the object
frameInit()	Acts to initialize the JFrame properly when called by the constructors.
getAccessibleActionCount()	Returns the number of Actions available in this object. If more than one exist, the first one is the "default" action (if any action is considered "default").
getAccessibleAction Description(int)	Returns a description of the *n*th Action of the object.
getAccessibleAt(Point)	Returns the accessible child contained at the local coordinate Point, if one exists.
getAccessibleChild(int)	Returns the *n*th accessible child of the object.
getAccessibleChildrenCount()	Returns the number of accessible children in the object.
getAccessibleDescription()	Gets the accessible description of this object.
getAccessibleName()	Gets the accessible name of this object.
getAccessibleParent()	Gets the accessible parent of this object.
getAccessibleRole()	Gets the role of this object.
getAccessibleSelection(int)	Returns an Accessible representing the *n*th selected item in the object.
getAccessibleSelection Count()	Returns the number of items currently selected.
getAccessibleStateSet()	Gets the state of this object.
getAccessibleText()	Gets the AccessibleText interface for the component.

(continued)

Table 24-6 *(continued)*	
Method	**Description**
getAccessibleValue()	Gets the value of this object as a `Number`.
getDefaultCloseOperation()	Returns the default operation, which occurs when the user initiates a "close" on this window.
getMaximumAccessibleValue()	Gets the maximum value of this object as a `Number`.
getMinimumAccessibleValue()	Gets the minimum value of this object as a `Number`.
getNextAccessibleSibling()	Gets the next sibling of this `Accessible`, if a preferred one exists.
getPreviousAccessible Sibling()	Gets the previous sibling of this `Accessible`, if a preferred one exists.
removeAccessible Selection(int)	Removes the *n*th selected item in the object from the object's selection.
selectAllAccessible Selection()	Causes every selected item in the object to be selected, if the object supports multiple selections (if `getAccessibleStateSet()` returns a state that is `MULTISELECTABLE`).
setAccessibleDescription (String)	Sets the accessible description of this object.
setAccessibleName(String)	Sets the localized accessible name of this object.
SetAccessibleValue(Number)	Gets the value of this object as a `Number`.
setDefaultClose Operation(int)	Sets the operation that will happen by default when the user initiates a "close" on this window.

JLabel

A Swing `JLabel` object provides a single-line label just like the `java.awt.Label` object. The `JLabel` object has additional functionality, including these options:

✦ The capability to set the relative position of the contents within the label

✦ The capability to add an icon

✦ The capability to set the vertical and horizontal position of the text (relative to the icon)

Listing 24-6 demonstrates how to create a simple `JLabel` object. Table 24-7 lists and describes the methods provided by the `JLabel` object.

Listing 24-6: **How to Create Simple JLabel Objects**

```
public class LabelPanel extends JPanel {
  public LabelPanel() {
    // Create and add a JLabel
    JLabel simpleLabel = new JLabel("A Simple Label");
    add(simpleLabel);
    // Create a label with an Icon
    JLabel iconLabel = new JLabel("A Label with an Icon");
    // Create an Icon
    Icon myIcon = new ImageIcon("MyIcon.gif");
    // Place the Icon in the label
    iconLabel.setIcon(myIcon);
    // Add to panel
    add(iconLabel);
  }
}
```

Table 24-7
JLabel Methods

Method	Description
getAccessibleName()	Gets the accessible name of this object.
getAccessibleRole()	Gets the role of this object.
getDisabledIcon()	Returns the value of the disabledIcon property if it's been set. If it hasn't been set, and the value of the icon property is an ImageIcon, we compute a "grayed out" version of the icon and update the disabledIcon property with that.
getDisplayedKeyAccelerator()	Returns the char that indicates a shortcut key.
getHorizontalAlignment()	Returns the alignment of the label's contents along the *x* axis.
getHorizontalTextPosition()	Returns the horizontal position of the label's text, relative to its image.
getIcon()	Returns the graphic image (glyph, icon) that the label displays.
getIconTextGap()	Returns the amount of space between the text and the icon displayed in this label.
getLabelFor()	Returns the component associated with this label.

(continued)

Table 24-7 *(continued)*	
Method	**Description**
getText()	Returns the text string that the label displays.
getUI()	Returns the current look and feel for this component.
getUIClassID()	Returns a string that specifies the name of the look-and-feel class that renders this component.
getVerticalAlignment()	Returns the alignment of the label's contents along the *y* axis.
getVerticalTextPosition()	Returns the vertical position of the label's text, relative to its image.
isOpaque()	Identifies whether the label's background is opaque or transparent.
setDisabledIcon(Icon)	Sets the icon to be displayed if this JLabel is "disabled" (for example).
setDisplayedKeyAccelerator (char)	Specifies a character that indicates a shortcut key.
setFont(Font)	Sets the font used to display the label's text.
setHorizontalAlignment(int)	Sets the alignment of the label's contents along the *x* axis.
setHorizontalText Position(int)	Sets the horizontal position of the label's text, relative to its image.
setIcon(Icon)	Defines the icon this component will display.
setIconTextGap(int)	If both the icon and text properties are set, this property defines the space between them.
setLabelFor(Component)	Sets the component this label is associated with.
setOpaque(boolean)	If true the label's background will be filled with the background color.
setText(String)	Defines the single line of text this component will display.
setUI(LabelUI)	Sets the look and feel for the component.
setVerticalAlignment(int)	Sets the alignment of the label's contents along the *y* axis.
setVerticalTextPosition(int)	Sets the vertical position of the label's text, relative to its image.
updateUI()	Notification from the User Interface factory that the look and feel have changed.

JList

The Swing JList object is much like its AWT List counterpart—providing a list of choices—in fact it's now even easier to add a list of elements to a list: You can add a String array of list elements by simply calling the setListData() method. You'll also find one important difference between the older AWT List and the Swing JList objects. The JList doesn't support scrolling directly. You need to place the JList within a ScrollPane (or JScrollPane) object, which will handle the scrolling (ScrollPane is discussed in more detail in Chapter 25). Listing 24-7 demonstrates how to create a simple JList object. Table 24-8 lists and describes the methods provided by the JList object.

Listing 24-7: **How to Create a Simple JList Object**

```
public class ListPanel extends JPanel {
   String labels [] = {"Choice1", "Choice2",
                       "Choice3","Choice4"};
   public ListPanel() {
     setLayout (new BorderLayout());
     JList mylist = new JList(labels);
     ScrollPane pane = new ScrollPane();
     pane.add (mylist);
     add(pane, BorderLayout.CENTER);
   }
}
```

Table 24-8
JList Methods

Method	Description
addListSelectionListener (ListSelectionListener)	Adds a listener to the list that's notified each time a change to the selection occurs.
addSelectionInterval (int, int)	Sets the selection to be the union of the specified interval with current selection.
clearSelection()	Clears the selection—after calling this method, isSelectionEmpty() will return true.
createSelectionModel()	Returns an instance of DefaultListSelectionModel.
ensureIndexIsVisible(int)	If this JList is being displayed within a JViewport and the specified cell isn't completely visible, scroll the viewport.

(continued)

Table 24-8 *(continued)*

Method	Description
fireSelectionValueChanged (int, int, boolean)	This method notifies JList ListSelectionListeners that the selection model has changed.
getAccessibleAt(Point)	Returns the accessible child contained at the local coordinate Point, if one exists.
getAccessibleChild(int)	Returns the *n*th accessible child of the object.
getAccessibleChildrenCount()	Returns the number of accessible children in the object.
getAccessibleRole()	Gets the role of this object.
getAccessibleStateSet()	Gets the state set of this object.
getAnchorSelectionIndex()	Returns the first index argument from the most recent addSelectionInterval() or setSelectionInterval() call.
getCellBounds(int, int)	Returns the bounds of the specified item in JList coordinates; null if index isn't valid.
getFirstVisibleIndex()	Returns the index of the cell in the upper-left corner of the JList or −1 if nothing is visible or the list is empty.
getLastVisibleIndex()	Returns the index of the cell in the lower-right corner of the JList or −1 if nothing is visible or the list is empty.
getLeadSelectionIndex()	Returns the second index argument from the most recent addSelectionInterval() or setSelectionInterval() call.
getMaxSelectionIndex()	Returns the largest selected cell index.
getMinSelectionIndex()	Returns the smallest selected cell index.
getPreferredScrollable ViewportSize()	Computes the size of the viewport needed to display visibleRowCount rows.
getScrollableTracks ViewportHeight()	Returns true if the list box tracks the height of the viewport; false otherwise.
getScrollableTracks ViewportWidth()	Returns true if the list box tracks the width of the viewport; false otherwise.
getScrollableUnitIncrement (Rectangle, int, int)	Returns the scrolling increment—if scrolling downward (direction is greater than 0), and the first row is completely visible with respect to visibleRect, then this method returns its height.

Method	Description
getSelectedIndex()	Returns the first selected index.
getSelectedIndices()	Returns an array of all of the selected indices in increasing order.
getSelectedValue()	Returns the first selected value, or null if the selection is empty.
getSelectedValues()	Returns an array of the values for the selected cells.
getUIClassID()	Returns the name of the User Interface factory class that generates the look and feel for this component.
getVisibleRowCount()	Returns the value of the visibleRowCount property.
indexToLocation(int)	Returns the origin of the specified item in JList coordinates; null if index isn't valid.
isOpaque()	JList components are always opaque.
isSelectedIndex(int)	Returns true if the specified index is selected.
isSelectionEmpty()	Returns true if nothing is selected; this is a convenience method that just delegates to the selectionModel.
locationToIndex(Point)	Converts a point in JList coordinates to the index of the cell at that location.
removeListSelectionListener (ListSelectionListener)	Removes a listener from the list that's notified each time a change to the selection occurs.
removeSelectionInterval (int, int)	Sets the selection to be the set difference of the specified interval and the current selection.
setCellRenderer (ListCellRenderer)	Sets the delegate that's used to paint each cell in the list.
setFixedCellHeight(int)	Defines the height of every cell in the list if this value is greater than zero.
setFixedCellWidth(int)	Defines the width of every cell in the list if this value is greater than zero.
setListData(Object[])	Creates a ListModel from the object array and then applies setModel() to it.

(continued)

<table>
<tr><td colspan="2" align="center">Table 24-8 (continued)</td></tr>
<tr><td>**Method**</td><td>**Description**</td></tr>
<tr><td>setListData(Vector)</td><td>Creates a ListModel from the Vector and then applies setModel() to it.</td></tr>
<tr><td>setModel(ListModel)</td><td>Sets the model that represents the contents or "value" of the list and clears the list's selection after notifying PropertyChangeListeners.</td></tr>
<tr><td>setPrototypeCellValue (Object)</td><td>Computes fixedCellWidth and fixedCellHeight by configuring the cellRenderer at index-equals-zero for the specified value and then computing the renderer component's preferred size if this value is non-null.</td></tr>
<tr><td>setSelectedIndex(int)</td><td>Selects a single cell.</td></tr>
<tr><td>setSelectedIndices(int[])</td><td>Selects a set of cells.</td></tr>
<tr><td>setSelectionInterval (int, int)</td><td>Selects the specified interval.</td></tr>
<tr><td>setSelectionModel (ListSelectionModel)</td><td>Sets the selectionModel for the list to a non-null ListSelectionModel implementation.</td></tr>
<tr><td>setUI(ListUI)</td><td>Sets the ListUI look-and-feel implementation delegate.</td></tr>
<tr><td>setVisibleRowCount(int)</td><td>Sets the preferred number of rows in the list that are visible within the nearest JViewport ancestor, if any.</td></tr>
<tr><td>updateUI()</td><td>Sets the UI property with the ListUI from the current default User Interface factory.</td></tr>
</table>

JMenu

Creating menus with Swing is the same as creating menus in the older AWT model. You'll find three important exceptions when using the Swing menu items, however:

✦ The menu classes are all descended from the JComponent class. Consequently, you can now place a JMenuBar within any Container, including Applet.

✦ A new menu class, JRadioButtonMenuItem (reviewed later in this chapter), provides a set of mutually exclusive check boxes on a menu.

✦ You can also now display an icon on any menu item.

Listing 24-8 demonstrates how to create a simple Swing menu. Table 24-9 lists and describes the methods provided by the JMenu class.

Listing 24-8: **How to Create a Simple Swing Menu**

```java
public class MenuTest extends JFrame
    implements ActionListener {

  public void actionPerformed (ActionEvent e) {
    System.out.println (e.getActionCommand());
  }

  public MenuTest() {
    super ("My Example Menu");

    JMenuBar jmb = new JMenuBar();
    JMenu file = new JMenu ("File");
    JMenuItem item;
    file.add (item = new JMenuItem ("New"));
    item.addActionListener (this);
    file.add (item = new JMenuItem ("Open"));
    item.addActionListener (this);
    file.addSeparator();
    file.add (item = new JMenuItem ("Close"));
    item.addActionListener (this);
    jmb.add (file);

    jmb.add (choice);

    setJMenuBar (jmb);
  }
}
```

Table 24-9
JMenu Methods

Method	Description
getAccessibleChild(int)	Returns the *n*th accessible child of the object.
getAccessibleChildrenCount()	Returns the number of accessible children in the object.
getAccessibleRole()	Gets the role of this object.
getDelay()	Returns the suggested delay before the menu's PopupMenu is popped up or down.
insertSeparator(int)	Inserts a separator at the specified position.

(continued)

Table 24-9 *(continued)*

Method	Description
isMenuComponent (Component)	Returns true if the component c exists in the submenu hierarchy.
isSelected()	Returns the state of the button.
paramString()	Gets the parameter string representing the state of this menu.
remove(int)	Removes the menu item at the specified index from this menu.
remove(JMenuItem)	Removes the specified menu item from this menu.
setDelay(int)	Sets the suggested delay before the menu's PopupMenu is popped up or down.
setModel(ButtonModel)	Sets the model that this button represents.
setSelected(boolean)	Sets the state of the button.
setUI(MenuUI)	Sets the menu's UI.
updateUI()	Gets a new UI object from the default User Interface factory.

JPanel

The Swing JPanel object is a lightweight Panel object that offers built-in support for double buffering. When buffering is enabled, either through the constructor or by calling the setBuffered() method, all the drawing operations of components within the panel will be drawn to an off-screen drawing buffer before they are drawn on the screen. The JPanel class is used in most of the examples in this section. Listing 24-9 demonstrates how to create a simple JPanel object. Table 24-10 lists and describes the methods provided by the JPanel object.

Listing 24-9: **How to Create a Simple JPanel Object**

```
public class MyPanel extends JPanel {
  public MyPanel() {
    // Add your panel objects here...
  }
}
```

Table 24-10
JPanel Methods

Method	Description
getAccessibleRole()	Gets the role of this object.
isOpaque()	Returns whether the receiving panel is opaque. This method is overridden from JComponent.
paintComponent(Graphics)	Paints the background if the component is opaque. This method is overridden from JComponent.
setBuffered(boolean)	Changes the buffering properties of the panel.
setOpaque(boolean)	Sets whether the receiving panel is opaque. If the JPanel is opaque, it will paint its background.

JPopupMenu

The JPopupMenu object lets you associate context-sensitive menus with any JComponent—similar to the AWT PopupMenu class. You can use the addSeparator() method to add a separator bar. Listing 24-10 demonstrates how to create a popup menu and listen for an event. Table 24-11 lists and describes the methods provided by the JPopupMenu item.

Listing 24-10: How to Create a Simple JPopupMenu Object

```
public class PopupPanel extends JPanel {
  JPopupMenu mypopup = new JPopupMenu ();
  public PopupPanel() {
    JMenuItem item;
    mypopup.add (item = new JMenuItem ("Cut"));
    mypopup.add (item = new JMenuItem ("Copy"));.
    mypopup.add (item = new JMenuItem ("Paste"));
    mypopup.addSeparator();
    mypopup.add (item = new JMenuItem ("Select All"));
    enableEvents (AWTEvent.MOUSE_EVENT_MASK);
  }
  protected void processMouseEvent (MouseEvent e) {
    if (e.isPopupTrigger())
      popup.show (e.getComponent(), e.getX(), e.getY());
    super.processMouseEvent (e);
  }
}
```

Table 24-11
JPopupMenu Methods

Method	Description
getAccessibleRole()	Gets the role of this object.
getMargin()	Returns the margin between the popup menu's border and its containees.
getUI()	Returns the popup menu's current UI.
isBorderPainted()	Checks whether the border should be painted.
isOpaque()	Checks whether the background should be painted.
paintBorder(Graphics)	Paints the popup menu's border if the BorderPainted property is true.
setBorderPainted(boolean)	Sets whether the border should be painted.
setOpaque(boolean)	Sets whether the background should be painted.
setUI(PopupMenuUI)	Sets the popup menu's UI.
updateUI()	Gets a new UI object from the default User Interface factory.

JProgressBar

The JProgressBar component lets you display a progress bar that reflects the status of an operation. Typically you will have an operation that executes in a thread and has the operation monitored by a progress bar. Listing 24-11 demonstrates how to create and use a JProgressBar object. Table 24-12 lists and describes the methods provided by the JProgressBar class.

Listing 24-11: How to Create and Use a Simple JProgressBar Object

```
public class ProgressBarPanel extends JPanel {
   Thread loadThread;
   Object lock = new Object();
   boolean Stop=false;
   JTextField progressText;
   JProgressBar progressBar;
   public ProgressBarPanel() {
     setLayout(new BorderLayout());

     progressText = new JTextField();
     add(progressText, BorderLayout.NORTH);

     JPanel bottomPanel = new JPanel();
```

```
      progressBar = new JProgressBar();
      bottomPanel.setLayout(new GridLayout(0,1));
      bottomPanel.add(progressBar);
      bottomPanel.add(new JLabel("Status"));
      JPanel buttonPanel = new JPanel();
      JButton startButton = new JButton("Start");
      startButton.setBackground (SystemColor.control);
      buttonPanel.add(startButton);
      startButton.addActionListener(new ActionListener() {
        public void actionPerformed(ActionEvent e) {
          startLoading();
        }
      });
      JButton stopButton = new JButton("Stop");
      stopButton.setBackground (SystemColor.control);
      buttonPanel.add(stopButton);
      stopButton.addActionListener(new ActionListener() {
        public void actionPerformed(ActionEvent e) {
          stopLoading();
        }
      });
      bottomPanel.add(buttonPanel);
      add(bottomPanel, BorderLayout.SOUTH);
  }
  public void startLoading() {
    if(loadThread == null) {
      loadThread = new LoadThread();
      Stop = false;
      loadThread.start();
    }
  }
  public void stopLoading() {
    synchronized(lock) {
      Stop = true;
      lock.notify();
    }
  }
  class LoadThread extends Thread {
    public void run () {
      int min = 0;
      int max = 100;
      progressBar.setValue(min);
      progressBar.setMinimum(min);
      progressBar.setMaximum(max);
      for (int i=min;i<=max;i++) {
        progressBar.setValue(i);
        progressText.setText (""+i);
        synchronized(lock) {
          if(Stop)
            break;
          try {
            lock.wait(100);
```

(continued)

Listing 24-11 *(continued)*

```
        } catch (java.lang.InterruptedException e) {
          // Ignore Exceptions
        }
      }
    }
    loadThread = null;
  }
}
}
```

Table 24-12
JProgressBar Methods

Method	Description
addChangeListener (ChangeListener)	Adds a ChangeListener to the button.
getAccessibleRole()	Gets the role of this object.
getAccessibleStateSet()	Gets the state set of this object.
getAccessibleValue()	Gets the accessible value of this object.
getMaximumAccessibleValue()	Gets the maximum accessible value of this object.
getMinimumAccessibleValue()	Gets the minimum accessible value of this object.
getOrientation()	Returns JProgressBar.VERTICAL or JProgressBar.HORIZONTAL depending on the orientation of the progress bar.
getValue()	Returns the value.
isBorderPainted()	Returns true if the progress bar has a border or false if it does not.
isOpaque()	Returns true if the progress bar is painting its background or false if it does not.
paintBorder(Graphics)	Paints the progress bar's border if the BorderPainted property is true.
removeChangeListener (ChangeListener)	Removes a ChangeListener from the button.
setAccessibleValue(Number)	Sets the value of this object as a Number.

Method	Description
setBorderPainted(boolean)	Sets whether the progress bar should have a border.setMaximum(int) Sets the maximum to int.
setMinimum(int)	Sets the model's minimum to int.
setOpaque(boolean)	Sets whether the progress bar should paint its background.
setOrientation(int)	Sets the progress bar's orientation to newOrientation, which must be JProgressBar.VERTICAL or JProgressBar.HORIZONTAL.
setValue(int)	Sets the value to int.
update(Graphics)	Overridden to call paint without filling the background.
updateUI()	Called to replace the UI with the latest version from the default User Interface factory.

JRadioButton

In AWT, radio buttons are check boxes that belong to the same CheckboxGroup, which ensures that only one check box is selected at a time. Swing has a separate widget called a JRadioButton. Each JRadioButton is added to a ButtonGroup so the group behaves as a set of radio buttons. Like CheckboxGroup, ButtonGroup is a functional object that has no visual representation.

Listing 24-12 demonstrates how to create and use a JRadioButton object. Table 24-13 lists and describes the methods provided by the JRadioButton class.

Listing 24-12: How to Create and Use a Simple JRadioButon Object

```
public class RadioButtonPanel extends JPanel {

    public RadioButtonPanel() {
        // Set the layout to a GridLayout
        setLayout(new GridLayout(2,1));

        // Declare a radio button
        JRadioButton radioButton;

        // Instantiate a ButtonGroup for functional
```

(continued)

Listing 24-12 *(continued)*

```
        // association among radio buttons
        ButtonGroup rbg = new ButtonGroup();

        // Add a new radio button
        radioButton = new JRadioButton("Radio-1");
        add(radioButton);
        // Add the button to the ButtonGroup
        rbg.add(radioButton);

        // Set this radio button to be the default
        radioButton.setSelected(true);

        // Set up another radio buttons
        radioButton = new JRadioButton("Radio-2");
        add(radioButton);
        rbg.add(radioButton);
    }
}
```

Table 24-13
JRadioButton Methods

Method	Description
getAccessibleAction Description(int)	Returns a description of the specified action of the object.
getAccessibleRole()	Gets the role of this object.
getUIClassID()	Returns a string that specifies the name of the look-and-feel class that renders this component.
updateUI()	Notification from the User Interface factory that the look and feel have changed.

JScrollBar

The Swing JScrollBar object is a lightweight version of the older AWT java.awt. Scrollbar component. Listing 24-13 demonstrates how to use a JScrollBar object. Table 24-14 lists and describes the methods provided by the JScrollBar object.

Listing 24-13: **How to Create a Simple JScrollBar Object**

```
public class ScrollbarPanel extends JPanel {

  public ScrollbarPanel() {
    setLayout(new BorderLayout());
    // Create a vertical scroll bar
    JScrollBar scroll1 =
      new JScrollBar (JScrollBar.VERTICAL,
                      0, 10, 0, 200);
    add(scroll1, BorderLayout.EAST);
    // Create a horizontal scroll bar
    JScrollBar scroll2 =
      new JScrollBar (JScrollBar.HORIZONTAL,
                      0, 10, 0, 100);
    add(scroll2, BorderLayout.SOUTH);
  }
```

Table 24-14
JScrollBar Methods

Method	Description
getAccessibleRole()	Gets the role of this object.
getAccessibleStateSet()	Gets the state set of this object.
getAccessibleValue()	Gets the accessible value of this object.
getMaximumAccessibleValue()	Gets the maximum accessible value of this object.
getMaximumSize()	The scroll bar is flexible along its scrolling axis and rigid along the other axis.
getMinimumAccessibleValue()	Gets the minimum accessible value of this object.
getMinimumSize()	The scroll bar is flexible along its scrolling axis and rigid along the other axis.

Method	Description
isOpaque()	Returns true if this component is completely opaque.
setAccessibleValue(Number)	Sets the value of this object as a Number.
setValues(int, int, int, int)	Ensures that the model is always in a consistent state by enforcing the constraints specified.
stateChanged(ChangeEvent)	Implemented for the ChangeListener interface support.
updateUI()	Notification from the User Interface factory that the look and feel have changed.

JSlider

The JSlider object is just like the JScrollBar object, except the JSlider object can

✦ Display a border around the slider.

✦ Display large and small tick marks as a scale.

Listing 24-14 demonstrates how to create a JSlider object. Table 24-15 lists and describes the methods provided by the JSlider object.

Listing 24-14: **How to Create a Simple JSlider Object**

```
public class SliderPanel extends JPanel {
  public SliderPanel() {
    setBackground (Color.lightGray);
    setLayout(new BorderLayout());
    setBackground (Color.lightGray);
    // Create a slider with tick small tick marks
    // and large tick marks
    JSlider slider1 =
      new JSlider (JSlider.VERTICAL, 0, 100, 50);
    slider1.setPaintTicks(true);
    slider1.setMajorTickSpacing(10);
    slider1.setMinorTickSpacing(2);
    add(slider1, BorderLayout.EAST);
  }
}
```

Table 24-15
JSlider Methods

Method	Description
addChangeListener (ChangeListener)	Adds a ChangeListener to the button.
GetAccessibleRole()	Gets the role of this object.
GetAccessibleStateSet()	Gets the state set of this object.
GetAccessibleValue()	Gets the accessible value of this object.
GetMaximumAccessibleValue()	Gets the maximum accessible value of this object.
GetMinimumAccessibleValue()	Gets the minimum accessible value of this object.
isOpaque()	Returns true if this component is completely opaque.
removeChangeListener (ChangeListener)	Removes a ChangeListener from the button.
setAccessibleValue(Number)	Sets the value of this object as a Number.
updateUI()	Called to replace the UI with the latest version from the default User Interface factory.

JSplitPane

The JSplitPane control can be used to create resizable controls inside a container. You can split a pane horizontally or vertically, and you can also embed split panes within each other to control the resizing of more than two components. Use the setContinuousLayout() method to have each pane update automatically as a user resizes the pane. Listing 24-15 demonstrates how to create a simple JSplitPane object. Table 24-16 lists and describes the methods provided by the JSplitPane object.

Listing 24-15: How to Create and Use a JSplitPane Object

```
public class JSplitPanel extends JPanel {

    public JSplitPanel() {
        // Set the layout to hold only one component
        setLayout(new BorderLayout(10, 10));

        JButton button1 = new JButton ("Button-1");
        button1.setBackground (SystemColor.control);
        add(new JSplitPane(JSplitPane.HORIZONTAL_SPLIT,
                           button1));
```

(continued)

Listing 24-15 *(continued)*

```
JButton button2 = new JButton ("Button-1");
button2.setBackground (SystemColor.control);
add(new JSplitPane(JSplitPane.VERTICAL_SPLIT,
                   button2));
  }
}
```

Table 24-16
JSplitPane Methods

Method	Description
addImpl(Component, Object, int)	If a constraint identifies the left/top or right/bottom child component, and a component with that identifier was previously added, it will be removed and then Component will be added in its place.
getAccessibleRole()	Gets the role of this object.
getAccessibleStateSet()	Gets the state set of this object.
getAccessibleValue()	Gets the accessible value of this object.
getBottomComponent()	Returns the component below or to the right of the divider.
getDividerLocation()	Returns the location of the divider from the look-and-feel implementation.
getDividerSize()	Returns the size of the divider.
getLastDividerLocation()	Returns the last location where the divider was.
getLeftComponent()	Returns the component to the left of or above the divider.
getMaximumAccessibleValue()	Gets the maximum accessible value of this object.
getMaximumDividerLocation()	Returns the maximum location of the divider from the look-and-feel implementation.
getMinimumAccessibleValue()	Gets the minimum accessible value of this object.
getMinimumDividerLocation()	Returns the minimum location of the divider from the look-and-feel implementation.
getOrientation()	Returns the orientation.
getRightComponent()	Returns the component to the right of or below the divider.

Method	Description
`getTopComponent()`	Returns the component above or to the left of the divider.
`getUI()`	Returns the `TreeUI` that is providing the current look and feel.
`isContinuousLayout()`	Returns `true` if the child components are continuously redisplayed and laid out during user intervention.
`isOneTouchExpandable()`	Returns `true` if the receiver provides a UI widget to collapse/expand the divider.
`paintChildren(Graphics)`	Subclassed to message the UI with `finishedPaintingChildren` after super has been messaged, as well as painting the border.
`remove(Component)`	Removes the child component from the receiver.
`remove(int)`	Removes the component at the passed-in index `int`.
`removeAll()`	Removes all the child components from the receiver.
`resetToPreferredSizes()`	Messaged to redo the layout of the `JSplitPane` based on preferred size of child components.
`setAccessibleValue(Number)`	Sets the value of this object as a `Number`.
`setBottomComponent(Component)`	Sets the component below or to the right of the divider.
`setContinuousLayout(boolean)`	Sets whether or not the child components are continuously redisplayed and laid out during user intervention.
`setDividerLocation(int)`	Sets the location of the divider.
`setDividerSize(int)`	Sets the size of the divider to `newSize`.
`setLastDividerLocation(int)`	Sets the last location where the divider was to `newLastLocation`.
`setLeftComponent(Component)`	Sets the component to the left of or above the divider.
`setOneTouchExpandable(boolean)`	If `newValue` is `true`, the receiver will provide UI widgets on the divider to quickly expand/collapse the divider.

(continued)

	Table 24-16 *(continued)*	
Method	**Description**
setOrientation(int)	Sets the orientation, or how the splitter is divided.
SetRightComponent(Component)	Sets the component to the right of or below the divider.
setTopComponent(Component)	Sets the component above or to the left of the divider.
setUI(SplitPaneUI)	Sets the TreeUI that will provide the current look and feel.
updateUI()	Called to replace the UI with the latest version from the default User Interface factory.

JTabbedPane

The JTabbedPane control is much like the older AWT CardLayout object. The JTabbedPane control adds the capability to switch between panes. Once you create a pane, you can add additional cards by calling the addTab() method—any JComponent object can be added to a tab. Listing 24-16 demonstrates how to create a JTabbedPane object. Table 24-17 lists and describes the methods provided by the JTabbedPane object.

Listing 24-16: How to Create and Use a JTabbedPane Object

```
public class TabbedPanel extends JPanel {
  String tabs[] = {"One", "Two", "Three"};
  public JTabbedPane tabbedPane = new JTabbedPane();
  public TabbedPanel() {
    setLayout (new BorderLayout());
    // Create three tabs
    for (int i=0;i<tabs.length;i++)
         // Create a pane to add to a tab
      tabbedPane.addTab (tabs[i], null,
                           createPane (tabs[i]));
    tabbedPane.setSelectedIndex(0);
    add (tabbedPane, BorderLayout.CENTER);
  }
  JPanel createPane(String s) {
    JPanel p = new JPanel();
    p.setBackground (SystemColor.control);
    p.add(new JLabel(s));
    return p;
  }
}
```

Table 24-17
JTabbedPane Methods

Method	Description
`addAccessibleSelection(int)`	Selects the given tab.
`addChangeListener (ChangeListener)`	Adds a `ChangeListener` to the button.
`addTab(String, Component)`	Adds a component represented by a title and no icon.
`addTab(String, Icon, Component)`	Adds a component represented by a title and/or icon, either of which can be null.
`addTab(String, Icon, Component, String)`	Adds a component and tip represented by a title and/or icon, either of which can be null.
`createChangeListener()`	Subclasses that want to handle `ChangeEvents` differently can override this to return a subclass of `ModelListener` or another `ChangeListener` implementation.
`getAccessibleAt(Point)`	Returns the accessible child contained at the local coordinate `Point`, if one exists.
`getAccessibleChild(int)`	Returns the *n*th accessible child of the object.
`getAccessibleChildren Count()`	Returns the number of accessible children in the object.
`getAccessibleRole()`	Gets the role of this object.
`getAccessibleSelection(int)`	Returns an `Accessible` representing the *n*th selected item in the object.
`getAccessibleSelection Count()`	Returns the number of items currently selected.
`getComponentAt(int)`	Returns the component at index `int`.
`getIconAt(int)`	Returns the icon at index `int`.
`getModel()`	Returns the model associated with the `TabbedPane`.
`getSelectedIndex()`	All of the `Model` methods are implemented by delegation.
`getTabCount()`	Returns the number of tabs.

(continued)

Table 24-17 *(continued)*

Method	Description
getTitleAt(int)	Returns the title at index.
getToolTipText(MouseEvent)	Returns the string to be used as the tool tip for the event.
getUI()	Returns the TabbedPane's UI controller.
indexOfComponent(Component)	Returns the index of the tab for the specified component.
indexOfTab(String)	Acts as a convenience method for locating the first tab with a given title, testing for equality with String.equals.
insertTab(String, Icon, Component, String, int)	Inserts a component at index int, represented by a title and/or icon, either of which may be null.
removeChangeListener (ChangeListener)	Removes a ChangeListener from the button.
removeTabAt(int)	Removes the tab at index.
setComponentAt(int, Component)	Sets the component at index int to Component.
setIconAt(int, Icon)	Sets the icon at index int to Icon, which can be null.
setModel(Single SelectionModel)	Sets the model to be used with the TabbedPane.
setTitleAt(int, String)	Sets the title at index int to title String, which can be null.
setUI(TabbedPaneUI)	Sets the TabbedPane's UI controller.
updateUI()	Acts as a notification from the User Interface factory that the look and feel have changed.

JTextArea and JTextField

The Swing JTextArea and JTextField components are very similar to their older AWT counterparts java.awt.TextArea and java.awt.TextField—they create single- and multiple-line edit boxes. Listing 24-17 demonstrates how to create and use these simple controls. Table 24-18 lists and describes the methods provided by the JTextArea object. Similiary, Table 24-19 lists and describes the methods provided by the JTextField object.

Listing 24-17: **How to Use the JTextArea and JTextField Objects**

```
// Instantiate a new TextField
JTextField textfld = new JTextField();
// Instantiate a new TextArea
JTextArea textarea = new JTextArea();
// Initialize the text of each
textfld.setText("TextField");
textarea.setText("JTextArea Supports\nMultiple Lines");
add(textfld);
add(textarea);
```

Table 24-18
JTextArea Methods

Method	Description
append(String)	Appends the given text to the end of the document.
createDefaultModel()	Creates the default implementation of the model to be used at construction if one isn't explicitly given.
getColumns()	Returns the number of columns in the text area.
getColumnWidth()	Gets the column width.
getMinimumSize()	Returns the minimum size dimensions of the TextArea.
getPreferred ScrollableViewportSize()	Returns the preferred size of the viewport if this component is embedded in a JScrollPane.
getRowHeight()	Defines the meaning of the height of a row.
getRows()	Returns the number of rows in the TextArea.
getScrollableUnit Increment(Rectangle, int, int)	Components that display logical rows or columns should compute the scroll increment that will completely expose one new row or column, depending on the value of orientation.
getTabSize()	Gets the number of characters used to expand tabs.
getUIClassID()	Returns the class ID for the UI.
insert(String, int)	Inserts the specified text at the specified position.
isManagingFocus()	Turns off tab traversal once the focus is gained.

(continued)

Table 24-18 *(continued)*

Method	Description
paramString()	Returns the String of parameters for this TextArea.
replaceRange(String, int, int)	Replaces text from the indicated start to end position with the new text specified.
setColumns(int)	Sets the number of columns for this TextArea.
setFont(Font)	Sets the current font.
setRows(int)	Sets the number of rows for this TextArea.
setTabSize(int)	Sets the number of characters that are replaced with tabs.

Table 24-19
JTextField Methods

Method	Description
addActionListener(Action Listener)	Adds the specified action listener to receive action events from this text field.
addMouseListener(Mouse Listener)	Adds a MouseListener.
addMouseMotionListener (MouseMotionListener)	Adds a MouseMotionListener.
createDefaultModel()	Creates the default implementation of the model to be used at construction if one isn't explicitly given.
createMouseListener()	Creates a MouseListener that listens to mouse events, shifting the event's x, y positions to the scrolled view translation, and refires them to any registered mouse listeners.
createMouseMotionListener()	Creates a MouseMotionListener that listens to mouse events, shifting the event's x, y positions to the scrolled view translation, and refires them to any registered mouse listeners.
fireActionPerformed()	Notifies all listeners that have registered interest for notification on this event type.
getActions()	Fetches the command list for the editor.
getColumns()	Returns the number of columns in this text field.

Method	Description
getColumnWidth()	Gets the column width.
getMinimumSize()	Returns the minimum size dimensions needed for this text field.
getPreferredSize()	Returns the preferred size dimensions needed for this text field.
getScrollOffset()	Gets the scroll offset.
getUIClassID()	Gets the class ID for a UI.
paint(Graphics)	Paints the component, translating the graphics by the scrolled amount.
paramString()	Returns the String of parameters for this text field.
postActionEvent()	Processes action events occurring on this text field by dispatching them to any registered ActionListener objects.
removeActionListener (ActionListener)	Removes the specified ActionListener so it no longer receives action events from this text field.
removeMouseListener (MouseListener)	Removes a MouseListener.
removeMouseMotion Listener(MouseMotion Listener)	Removes a MouseMotionListener.
repaint(long, int, int, int, int)	Repaints the component, shifting by the scrolled amount.
scrollRectToVisible (Rectangle)	Scrolls the field left or right.
setColumns(int)	Sets the number of columns in this text field.
setFont(Font)	Sets the current font.
setScrollOffset(int)	Sets the scroll offset.

JToggleButton

The JToggleButton class is the parent of both the JCheckBox and JRadioButton (it doesn't have an equivalent AWT object). The JToggleButton works just like a Button that stays depressed when clicked. When toggled off, you cannot tell a JToggleButton apart from a regular Button or JButton object. Listing 24-18 shows how to use the JToggleButton object, while Table 24-20 lists the JToggleButton's methods—remember that much of the JToggleButton behavior is inherited from the AbstractButton class.

Listing 24-18: **How to Use the JToggleButton Object**

```
public class ToggleButtonPanel extends JPanel {
  public ToggleButtonPanel() {
    // Set the layout to a GridLayout
    setLayout(new GridLayout(2, 1, 10, 10));
    add (new JToggleButton ("Button-1"));
    add (new JToggleButton ("Button-2"));
  }
}
```

Table 24-20
JToggleButton Methods

Method	Description
getAccessibleRole()	Gets the role of this object.
getUIClassID()	Returns a string that specifies the name of the look-and-feel class that renders this component.
updateUI()	Notification from the User Interface factory that the look and feel have changed.

Summary

The packages that comprise the Swing user interface classes, as well as the major interface components that comprise Swing, were reviewed in detail. The next chapter discusses how to install the Swing classes, implement Swing layouts, and listen for Swing events.

✦ Considered together, the Swing user interface classes represent a major new component of the Java Foundation Classes.

✦ Swing includes new design classes, objects, and user interface widgets.

✦ Swing has twice as many components as the Abstract Windowing Toolkit.

✦ Although Swing has important differences from the AWT, it retains some similar techniques.

✦ Swing is the new path to user interface design with JDK 1.2 and beyond.

✦   ✦   ✦

Bringing It All Together with JDK 1.2

✦   ✦   ✦   ✦

In This Chapter

Getting your applications off the ground with JDK 1.2 and Swing

Building the user interface of your Java applications using Swing components

Using Swing layouts

Listening for events in your Swing-based applications

✦   ✦   ✦   ✦

You're poised at the brink now—ready to jump into the fray with the Java JDK 1.2 by your side. This chapter will bring together much of the Java Foundation Class components discussed in the previous chapters and show you how to get started.

The Java JDK 1.2, as an evolutionary step in the development of Java, has made some changes in the language that could affect your existing programs; this chapter discusses them in detail.

Get Going with JDK 1.2

The Java JDK 1.2 includes all the components that comprise the Java Foundation Classes (JFC). To begin using the Swing and other JFC classes in your applications, you will need to make sure you have the JDK 1.2 installed on your system.

The JDK 1.2 revision is available on the CD-ROM included with your book, and also at the Sun Java Web site, `http://java.sun.com`.

Note

It is possible to download just the JFC classes from the Sun Web site, but to utilize the JFC and Swing classes to their maximum benefit you should first install the JDK 1.2.

JDK 1.2 incompatibilities

Although the JDK 1.2 is backward-compatible with JDK 1.0 and 1.1, it incorporates some changes that could affect your applications. Some potential and actual incompatibilities—binary, language, runtime, API, and tools—are known to exist. Many of these problems were by-products of an effort to close possible security holes or to fix implementation or design bugs.

Most of the compatibility problems in JDK 1.2 are minor and won't affect your Java applications greatly, but you need to be aware of them.

Changes in binary compatibility

Backward binary compatibility is supported, but it isn't guaranteed. Class files built with a 1.2 compiler, but relying only on APIs defined in JDK 1.0 or 1.1, will generally run on 1.0 and 1.1 versions of the Java Virtual Machine, but this "backward" compatibility has not been extensively tested and cannot be guaranteed. Of course, if the class files depend on any new 1.2 APIs, those files will not work on earlier platforms.

Changes in language compatibility

The JDK 1.0 and 1.1 compilers would compile some types of illegal Java code without producing warnings or error messages. Bug fixes in JDK 1.2 have made the compiler more stringent in ensuring that code conforms to the Java Language Specification. The following is a brief summary of code that did compile under previous versions but no longer compiles under JDK 1.2:

✦ Some initializations of `int` types to `long` types were passed by previous compilers but are flagged as errors in JDK 1.2. For example, consider this code:

```
public class foo {
    int i = 3000000000;
    int j = 6000000000;
}
```

Here the initializations of both `i` and `j` are in error. In JDKs earlier than 1.2, only the incorrect initialization of `i` would have been reported. The initialization of `j` would have overflowed without giving notice.

✦ In previous JDKs, implicit assignment conversion from `char` to `byte` and `short` would be allowed in the case of character literals that fit into 8 bits. Such implicit assignment conversion is not allowed by the JDK 1.2 compiler. (For example, `byte b = 'b';` is no longer allowed.) An explicit cast is required to perform this type of conversion.

✦ `0xL` is not a legal hex literal and the JDK 1.2 compiler does not accept it.

✦ `'''` and `\u000D` are not legal `char` literals and the JDK 1.2 compiler does not accept them. The literals `'\''` and `'\r'` must be used instead.

✦ The type `void[]` is not legal and the JDK 1.2 compiler does not accept it.

✦ You can no longer combine the `abstract` method modifier with `private`, `final`, `native`, or `synchronized` modifiers.

✦ In JDK 1.2, an assignment expression is not accepted as the third subexpression of a conditional statement. For example, the statement

```
myVal = condition ? x = 7 : x = 3;
```

would cause a parsing error in JDK 1.2. You would have to fix this problem by using parentheses:

```
myVal = condition ? x = 7 : (x = 3);
```

Changes in runtime compatibility

Two important differences in runtime compatibility set JDK 1.2 apart from previous versions:

✦ The `String` hash function implemented in JDK 1.1 releases did not match the function specified in the first edition of the Java Language Specification. To fix the performance problems, both the specification and implementation have been changed. The new `String` hash function as of JDK 1.2 is:

```
s[0] * 31^(n-1) + s[1] * 31^(n-2) + ... + s[n-1]
```

where `s[n]` is the nth character of string `s`.

✦ In JDK 1.2, an unimplemented abstract method or interface method will now cause an `AbstractMethodError` to occur at runtime when the method is invoked.

Changes in API compatibility

A few minor API changes will affect older code when it is run under the JDK 1.2 Virtual Machine and classes:

✦ In version 1.2 of the Java platform, the class `ActiveEvent` is in the package `java.awt`. In version 1.1, `ActiveEvent` was in the package `java.awt.peer`.

✦ The `stringFlavor` and `plainTextFlavor` fields of class `java.awt.datatransfer.DataFlavor` have been made final in version 1.2.

✦ Interface `java.util.List` has been added to version 1.2 of the Java platform. In JDK 1.2, using only the 'wildcard' import statements

```
import java.awt.*;
import java.util.*;
```

would cause a compiler error for code that contains the unqualified name `List`—a problem caused by the conflict between `java.awt.List` and `java.util.List`. You would have to use an additional import statement, either `import java.awt.List;` or `import java.util.List;` to resolve the conflict.

Changes in tools compatibility

Finally, a few changes have been introduced into the Java tools with JDK 1.2:

✦ In JDK 1.2, the `-0` option for `javac` has a different meaning, and may have different performance effects on generated code, than earlier compilers. The `-0` flag no longer implicitly turns on `-depend`, so you need to add `-depend` to the command line where desired.

✦ In JDK 1.2, the `javakey` tool has been replaced with the `keytool`, `PolicyTool`, and `jarsigner` tools.

✦ Due to bugs in JDK 1.1.x, code that is signed using the JDK 1.1.x `javakey` tool will be recognized as unsigned on JDK 1.2. Code signed using JDK 1.2 will be recognized as unsigned on JDK 1.1.x.

Advanced Swing Objects

Chapter 24 gives you a taste of how the new Swing user-interface classes are poised to replace the existing AWT (Abstract Windowing Toolkit) classes and become the way to write your future Java applications. Now it's time to take a closer look at more advanced Swing objects, including tooltips, toolbars, trees, and the text framework.

Tooltips and toolbars

Tooltips are context-sensitive text strings that are displayed in a popup window when the mouse is moved over a particular object on the screen. The Swing classes provide these tips to the the `JToolTip` class. `JToolTip` is rarely used directly, because you can call the `setToolTipText()` method of the `JComponent` object. Listing 25-1 demonstrates how to add a tooltip text string for a button. Table 25-1 lists and describes the methods provided by the `JToolTip` class.

Listing 25-1: **How to Add a Tooltip to a JComponent Object**

```
public class TooltipPanel extends JPanel {
  public TooltipPanel() {
    JButton myButton = new JButton("Button");
    myButton.setBackground (SystemColor.control);
    myButton.setToolTipText ("Button Tip");
    add(myButton);
  }
}
```

Table 25-1
JTooltip Methods

Method	Description
getAccessible Context()	Gets the AccessibleContext associated with this JComponent.
getTipText()	Retrieves the tool tip text.
setTipText(String)	Sets the tool tip text.
updateUI()	Called to replace the UI with the latest version from the default UIFactory.

The JToolBar control provides a container that can display components in a toolbar, across or down, in one row or column, depending where it's placed on the screen. Floatable toolbars are also even permitted. To disable toolbar floating, you can turn it off with setFloatable() method. When a toolbar is floating you can drag it to another area of the screen, or place it in a window external from the original container. Listing 25-2 demonstrates how to create a JToolBar object — any components can be included on a toolbar. Table 25-2 lists and describes the methods provided by the JToolBar class.

Listing 25-2: **Adding a Toolbar**

```
public class ToolbarPanel extends JPanel {
  ToolbarPanel() {
    setLayout (new BorderLayout());
    JToolBar toolbar = new JToolBar();
    JButton myButton = new JButton("Button 1");
    toolbar.add(myButton);
    Icon myIcon = new ImageIcon("MyImage.gif");
    myButton = new JButton(myIcon);
    toolbar.add(myButton);
    add (toolbar, BorderLayout.SOUTH);
  }
}
```

Table 25-2
JToolbar Methods

Method	Description
addSeparator()	Adds a separator to the ToolBar.
getAccessible Context()	Gets the AccessibleContext associated with this JComponent.
getMargin()	Returns the margin between the toolbar's border and its buttons.
getUI()	Returns the toolbar's current UI.
isBorderPainted()	Checks whether the border should be painted.
paintBorder (Graphics)	Paints the toolbar's border if BorderPainted property is true.
setBorderPainted (boolean)	Sets whether the border should be painted.
setMargin(Insets)	Sets the margin between the toolbar's border and its buttons.
setOpaque(boolean)	If true the buttons' background will be filled with the background color.
setUI(ToolBarUI)	Sets the toolbar's UI.
updateUI()	Gets a new UI object from the default UIFactory.

JTree

The JTree class can be used to display tree-based hierarchical information. JTree objects are comprised of TreeNode objects, which hold tree node information. The TreeModel interface describes a JTree's underlying data. A JTree object has a model that can be accessed using the getModel and setModel methods. The model is used to determine which TreeModel a JTree uses. The TreeModel interface specifies how a tree is mapped over a data structure. The DefaultTreeModel is a simple implementation of TreeModel that explicitly uses TreeNode and MutableTreeNode objects. The TreeSelectionModel is an interface that specifies how the user may select a path of arbitrary objects. JTree uses it to set up selection rules. DefaultTreeSelectionModel is a simple implementation of TreeSelectionModel. It allows for the usual selection model experienced when selecting files in a standard file dialog box.

The TreeCellRenderer interface is used by JTree to specify components that will visually represent tree nodes. For example, the default tree node renderer is the BasicTreeCellRenderer class, which uses folders as root and internal nodes and filled circles as leaf nodes. You can create custom-looking trees by defining classes that implement this interface that contain the getTreeCellRendererComponent method. The default model and view of a JTree can be used to create a file/directory-style tree. Listing 25-3 demonstrates how to create a simple tree object. Table 25-3 lists and describes the methods provided by the JTree class.

Listing 25-3: How to Create a Swing Tree

```
public class JTreePanel extends JPanel {

    JTreePanel() {
        // Set the layout to hold only one component
        setLayout(new BorderLayout());

        // Create root node of tree
        DefaultMutableTreeNode root =
            new DefaultMutableTreeNode("Tree-1");

        // Create a child
        DefaultMutableTreeNode level1 = new
            DefaultMutableTreeNode("Child");
        root.add(level1);

        // Create and add some 2nd level leaf nodes
        level1.add(new DefaultMutableTreeNode(
            "Leaf-1"));
        level1.add(new DefaultMutableTreeNode(
            "Leaf-2"));
        level1.add(new DefaultMutableTreeNode(
            "Leaf-3"));

        // Create a tree from the root
        JTree tree = new JTree(root);

        // Place tree in JScrollPane
        JScrollPane pane = new JScrollPane();
        pane.getViewport().add (tree);

        add(pane, BorderLayout.CENTER);
    }
}
```

<table>
<tr><td colspan="2" align="center">Table 25-3
JTree Methods</td></tr>
</table>

Method	Description
addSelectionInterval(int index0, int index1)	Adds the paths between index0 and index1 to the selection.
addSelectionPath(TreePath path)	Adds the path identified by path to the current selection.
addSelectionPaths(TreePath[] paths)	Adds each path in paths to the current selection.
addSelectionRow(int rows)	Adds the paths at each of the rows in rows to the current selection.
addSelectionRows(int[] rows)	Adds the paths at each of the rows in rows to the current selection.
addTreeExpansionListener(Tree ExpansionListener tel)	Adds tel as interested in receiving TreeExpansion events.
addTreeSelectionListener(Tree SelectionListener tsl)	Adds tsl as interested in receiving TreeSelection events.
clearSelection()	Clears the selection.
collapsePath(TreePath path)	Insures that the last item identified in path is collapsed and visible.
collapseRow(int row)	Insures that the item identified by row is collapsed.
convertValueToText(Object value, boolean selected, boolean expanded, boolean leaf, int row, boolean hasFocus)	This is called by the tree renderer to convert the passed-in value into text.
createTreeModel(Object value)	Returns a TreeModel wrapping the passed-in Object value.
expandPath(TreePath path)	Insures that the last item identified in path is expanded and visible.
expandRow(int row)	Insures that the item identified by row is expanded.
getAccessibleContext()	Gets the AccessibleContext associated with this Jcomponent.
getCellEditor()	Returns the editor used to edit entries in the tree.
getCellRenderer()	Returns the current TreeCellRenderer that is rendering each cell.

Method	Description
getClosestPathForLocation (int x, int y)	Returns the path to the node that is closest to x,y.
getClosestRowForLocation(int x, int y)	Returns the row to the node that is closest to x,y.
getDefaultTreeModel()	Creates and returns a sample TreeModel.
getEditingPath()	Returns the path to the element that is being edited.
getInvokesStopCellEditing()	Returns true if, when editing is to be stopped by changing the selection, changing data in tree, or by other means, then stop CellEditing will be invoked; if false, then cancelCellEditing will be invoked.
getEditingPath()	Returns the path to the element that is being edited.
getInvokesStopCellEditing()	Returns true if, when editing is to be stopped by changing the selection, changing data in the tree, or by other means, then stopCellEditing will be invoked; if false, then cancelCellEditing will be invoked.
getLastSelectedPathComponent()	Returns the last path component in the selection.
getLeadSelectionPath()	Returns the last path that was added.
getLeadSelectionRow()	Returns the lead selection index.
getMaxSelectionRow()	Gets the last selected row.
getMinSelectionRow()	Gets the first selected row.
getModel()	Returns the TreeModel that is providing the data.
getPathBetweenRows(int index0, int index1)	Returns JTreePath instances representing the path between index0 and index1 (including index1).
getPathBounds(TreePath path)	Returns the Rectangle that the last item in path will be drawn into.
getPathForLocation(int x, int y)	Returns the path for the given location.
getPathForRow(int row)	Returns the path for the passed-in row.

(continued)

Method	Description
getPreferredScrollableViewport Size()	Returns the preferred viewable size of a JTree.
getRowBounds(int row)	Returns the Rectangle that the item identified by row will be drawn into.
getRowCount()	Returns the number of rows that are currently being displayed.
getRowForLocation(int x, int y)	Returns the row for the passed-in location.
getRowForPath(TreePath path)	Returns the row that the last item identified in path is visible at.
getRowHeight()	Returns the height of each row.
getScrollableBlockIncrement (Rectangle visibleRect, int orientation, int direction)	Returns the amount for a block increment, which is the height or width of visibleRect, based on orientation.
getScrollableTracksViewport Height()	Returns false.
getScrollableTracksViewport Width()	Returns false.
getScrollableUnitIncrement (Rectangle visibleRect, int orientation, int direction)	Returns the amount to increment when scrolling.
getSelectionCount()	Returns the number of nodes selected.
getSelectionModel()	Returns the model for selections.
getSelectionPath()	Returns the path to the first selected value, or null if nothing is currently selected.
getSelectionPaths()	Returns the path of the selected values, or null if nothing is current selected.
getSelectionRows()	Returns all the currently selected rows.
getShowsRootHandles()	Returns true if handles for the root nodes are displayed.
getToolTipText(MouseEvent event)	Overriding to allow renderer's tips to be used if it has text set.
getUI()	Returns the TreeUI that is providing the current look and feel.
getVisibleRowCount()	Returns the number of rows that are to be made visible.

Table 25-3 *(continued)*

Method	Description
isCollapsed(int row)	Returns true if the value identified by row is currently collapsed.
isCollapsed(TreePath path)	Returns true if the value identified by path is currently collapsed; this will return false if any of the values in path are currently not being displayed.
isEditable()	Returns true if the tree is editable.
isEditing()	Returns true if the tree is being edited.
isExpanded(int row)	Returns true if the value identified by row is currently expanded.
isExpanded(TreePath path)	Returns true if the value identified by path is currently expanded; this will return false if any of the values in path are currently not being displayed.
isFixedRowHeight()	Returns true if the height of each row is a fixed size.
isLargeModel()	Returns true if the receiver is configured for a large model.
isOpaque()	Returns true if this component is completely opaque.
isPathEditable(TreePath path)	Returns true if the tree is editable.
isPathSelected(TreePath path)	Returns true if item identified by path is currently selected.
isRootVisible()	Returns true if the root node from the TreeModel is currently visible.
isRowSelected(int row)	Returns true if the row identified by row is selected.
isSelectionEmpty()	Returns true if the selection is currently empty.
isVisible(TreePath path)	Returns true if the value identified by path is currently visible; false otherwise.
makeVisible(TreePath path)	Insures that the value identified by path is currently visible.
removeSelectionInterval(int index0, int index1)	Removes the paths between index0 and index1 from the selection.

(continued)

Table 25-3 *(continued)*

Method	Description
removeSelectionPath(TreePath path)	Removes the path identified by path from the current selection.
removeSelectionPaths(TreePath[] paths)	Removes the paths identified by paths from the current selection.
removeSelectionRow(int row)	Removes the path at the index row from the current selection.
removeSelectionRows(int[] rows)	Removes the paths that are selected at each of the indices in rows.
removeTreeExpansionListener (TreeExpansionListener tel)	Removes tel as being interested in receiving TreeExpansion events.
removeTreeSelectionListener (TreeSelectionListener tsl)	Removes tsl as being interested in receiving TreeSelection events.
scrollPathToVisible (TreePath path)	Makes sure all the path components in path are expanded (except for the last path component) and tries to scroll the resulting path to be visible.
scrollRowToVisible(int row)	Scrolls the item identified by row to be visible.
setCellEditor(TreeCellEditor cellEditor)	Sets the cell editor to cellEditor.
setCellRenderer(TreeCell Renderer tcr)	Sets the TreeCellRenderer that will be used to draw each cell.
setEditable(boolean flag)	Sets the tree to being editable based on the boolean flag.
setInvokesStopCellEditing (boolean newValue)	If newValue is true, when editing is to be stopped by changing the selection, changing data in the tree, or by other means, then stop CellEditing will be invoked; if false, then cancelCellEditing will be invoked.
setLargeModel(boolean newValue)	Sets the receiver to being a large model based on newValue.
setModel(TreeModel model)	Sets the TreeModel that will provide the data.
setRootVisible(boolean rootVisible)	Sets, based on rootVisible, whether or not the root node from the TreeModel is visible.

Method	Description
setRowHeight(int rowHeight)	Sets the height of each row to be rowHeight.
setSelectionInterval(int index0, int index1)	Sets the selection to the paths of the nodes between index0 and index1.
setSelectionModel(TreeSelection Model selectionModel)	Sets the selection model to selectionModel.
setSelectionPath(TreePath path)	Sets the selection to the value identified by path.
setSelectionPaths(TreePath[] paths)	Sets the selection to paths.
setSelectionRow(int index)	Sets the selection to the path at index row.
setSelectionRows(int[] rows)	The selection is set to the paths for the items at each of the rows in rows.
setShowsRootHandles(boolean display)	Sets whether or not the root handles are to be displayed.
setUI(TreeUI ui)	Sets the TreeUI that will provide the current look and feel.
setVisibleRowCount(int count)	Sets the number of rows that are to be visible.
startEditingAtPath(TreePath path)	Selects the last item in path and tries to edit it.
stopEditing()	Stops the current editing session.
treeDidChange()	Sent when the tree has changed enough that we need to resize the bounds, but not enough that we need to remove the expanded node set (for example, nodes were expanded or collapsed, or nodes were inserted into the tree).
updateUI()	Called to replace the UI with the latest version from the default UIFactory.

Text framework/Document interface

The Document interface is used as an independent structure for holding text. It supports markup of styles, notification of changes, and tracking of changes to undo changes. Text is marked up with structures called *elements*. Elements describe the state of a document with an arbitrary set of attributes. A document can be viewed from its elements. Documents also contain methods to describe the number of lines and paragraphs of text. In many cases, a single document structure can describe a text component's model. The Document interface, however, permits multiple views of the text data. Several Document views are a part of the Swing classes. The simplest is AbstractDocument, which is intended primarily as a superclass to extend and form models that are more complete. The primary feature of the AbstractDocument class is its locking mechanism. It implements the readers/writers model to allow either one writer or multiple readers access to the content. Writers must wait for notification of all observers of a previous change before they can begin another mutation cycle. AbstractDocument is the abstract superclass of two full-featured document models, PlainDocument and DefaultStyledDocument. The purpose of PlainDocument is for short and simple text. It can manage text content as a string, and doesn't support history or undo operations. The DefaultStyledDocument also supports a document format similar to the Rich Text Format (RTF). It relies on structure elements to mark up the text into styles.

JTable

The Swing classes support tables through the com.sun.java.swing.table package. The package contains classes and interfaces that handle the creation and display of column-based data. The JTable class supports features such as editing, colorizing, simultaneous row-column selection, and getting information about the selected entries. Listing 25-4 demonstrates how to create a JTable object. Table 25-4 lists and describes the methods provided by the JTable object.

Listing 25-4: **Creating a Simple Table with the JTable Object**

```
public class TablePanel extends JPanel {
  TablePanel() {
    setLayout (new BorderLayout());

    // Create data model
    MyDataModel MyModel =
      new MyDataModel();

    // Create and setup the table
    JTable table = new JTable (MyModel);

    // Resize columns
    table.sizeColumnsToFit (false);

    // Place table in JScrollPane
    JScrollPane scrollPane =
      JTable.createScrollPaneForTable(table);

    // Add to Screen
    add(scrollPane, BorderLayout.CENTER);

  }
}
```

```java
class MyDataModel extends AbstractTableModel {

  // AbstractTableModel takes care of
  // TableModelListener list management

  String columns[] = {"Column-1", "Column-2",
                      "Column-3"};
  String rows[][] = {
    {"1", "7", "100"},
    {"2", "6", "99"},
    {"3", "5", "98"},
    {"4", "4", "97"},
    {"5", "3", "96"},
    {"6", "2", "95"},
    {"7", "1", "94"},
  };

  private int numColumns = columns.length;
  private int numRows = rows.length;

  public int getColumnCount() {
    return numColumns;
  }

  public int getRowCount() {
    return numRows;
  }

  public Object getValueAt (int row, int column) {
    return rows[row][column];
  }

  public void setValueAt (Object aValue,
      int row, int column) {
    String cellValue;
    if (aValue instanceof String)
      cellValue = (String)aValue;
    else
      cellValue = aValue.toString();
    rows[row][column] = cellValue;
    fireTableChanged (new TableModelEvent (this, row));
  }

  public String getColumnName (int columnIndex) {
    return columns[columnIndex];
  }
}
```

Table 25-4
JTable Methods

Method	Description
addColumn(TableColumn Column)	Appends a Column to the end of the array of columns held by the JTable's column model.
addColumnSelectionInterval(int index0, int index1)	Adds the columns from index0 to index1 inclusive to the current selection.
addRowSelectionInterval(int index0, int index1)	Adds the rows from index0 to index1 inclusive to the current selection.
clearSelection()	Deselects all selected columns and rows.
columnAtPoint(Point point)	Returns the index of the column that point lies in, or -1 if it lies outside the receiver's bounds.
convertColumnIndexToModel (int index)	Returns the index of the column in the model whose data is being displayed in the column viewColumnIndex in the display.
convertColumnIndexToView (int index)	Returns the index of the column in the view that is displaying the data from the column modelColumnIndex in the model.
createDefaultColumnModel()	Returns the default column model object that is a DefaultTableColumnModel.
createDefaultColumnsFromModel()	This method will create default columns for the table from the data model using the getColumnCount() and getColumnType() methods defined in the TableModel interface.
createDefaultDataModel()	Returns the default table model object, that is a DefaultTableModel.
createDefaultSelectionModel()	Returns the default selection model object, that is a DefaultListSelectionModel.
createDefaultTableHeader()	Returns the default table header object, that is a JTableHeader.
createScrollPaneForTable (Jtable table)	This static method is provided to simplify the task of wrapping a JTable in a scroll pane.
editCellAt(int x, int y)	Programmatically starts editing the cell at row x and column y, if the cell is editable.
editCellAt(int x, int y, EventObject event)	Programmatically starts editing the cell at row x and column y, if the cell is editable.

Method	Description
editingColumn()	If sent while isEditing() is true, this returns the index of the editing column; otherwise returns -1.
editingRow()	If sent while isEditing() is true, this returns the index of the editing row; otherwise returns -1.
getAccessibleContext()	Get the AccessibleContext associated with this Jcomponent.
getAutoCreateColumnsFromModel()	Returns whether the table will create default columns from the model.
getAutoResizeMode()	Returns auto resize mode of the table.
getCellEditor()	Sets the cellEditor variable.
getCellRect(int x, int y, boolean flag)	Returns a rectangle locating the cell that lies at the intersection of row and column.
getColumn(Object obj)	Returns the TableColumn object for the column in the table whose identifier is equal to obj, when compared using equals().
getColumnClass(int column)	Returns the type of the column at position column in the view.
getColumnCount()	Returns the number of columns in the column model; note that this may be different from the number of columns in the table model.
getColumnModel()	Returns the TableColumnModel that contains all column information of this table.
getColumnName(int column)	Returns the name of the column at position column in the view.
getDefaultEditor(Class editclass)	Returns the editor to be used when no editor has been set in a TableColumn.
getDefaultRenderer(Class rendclass)	Returns the renderer to be used when no renderer has been set in a TableColumn.
getEditorComponent()	If the receiver is currently editing, this will return the component that was returned from the CellEditor.
getGridColor()	Returns the color used to draw grid lines.
getIntercellSpacing()	Returns the horizontal and vertical spacing between cells.

(continued)

<table>
<tr><th colspan="2">Table 25-4 (continued)</th></tr>
<tr><th>Method</th><th>Description</th></tr>
<tr><td><code>getModel()</code></td><td>Returns the <code>TableModel</code> that provides the data displayed by the receiver.</td></tr>
<tr><td><code>getRowCount()</code></td><td>Returns the number of rows in the table.</td></tr>
<tr><td><code>getRowHeight()</code></td><td>Returns the height of a table row in the receiver.</td></tr>
<tr><td><code>getSelectionModel()</code></td><td>Returns the <code>ListSelectionModel</code> that is used to maintain row selection state.</td></tr>
<tr><td><code>getShowGrid()</code></td><td>Returns <code>true</code> if the receiver draws grid lines around cells, <code>false</code> if it doesn't.</td></tr>
<tr><td><code>getTableHeader()</code></td><td>Returns the <code>tableHeader</code> working with this <code>JTable</code>.</td></tr>
<tr><td><code>getToolTipText(MouseEvent event)</code></td><td>Overriding to allow renderer's tips to be used if it has text set.</td></tr>
<tr><td><code>getValueAt(int row, int column)</code></td><td>Returns the cell value at <code>row</code> and <code>column</code>.</td></tr>
<tr><td><code>isCellEditable(int row, int column)</code></td><td>Returns <code>true</code> if the cell at <code>row</code> and <code>column</code> is editable.</td></tr>
<tr><td><code>isOpaque()</code></td><td>Returns <code>true</code> if this component is completely opaque.</td></tr>
<tr><td><code>moveColumn(int column, int targetColumn)</code></td><td>Moves <code>column</code> to the position currently occupied by <code>targetColumn</code>.</td></tr>
<tr><td><code>removeColumn(TableColumn column)</code></td><td>Removes a <code>column</code> from the <code>JTable</code>'s array of columns.</td></tr>
<tr><td><code>removeColumnSelectionInterval (int index0, int index1)</code></td><td>Deselects the columns from <code>index0</code> to <code>index1</code> inclusive.</td></tr>
<tr><td><code>removeRowSelectionInterval(int index0, int index1)</code></td><td>Deselects the rows from <code>index0</code> to <code>index1</code> inclusive.</td></tr>
<tr><td><code>resizeAndRepaint()</code></td><td>Properly sizes the receiver and its header view, and marks it as needing display.</td></tr>
<tr><td><code>rowAtPoint(Point point)</code></td><td>Returns the index of the row that <code>point</code> lies in, or -1 if is not in the range [<code>0</code>, <code>getRowCount()-1</code>].</td></tr>
<tr><td><code>selectAll()</code></td><td>If a column is selected, then this selects all columns.</td></tr>
<tr><td><code>setAutoCreateColumnsFromModel (boolean flag)</code></td><td>Sets the table's <code>autoCreateColumns FromModel</code> flag.</td></tr>
<tr><td><code>setAutoResizeMode(int mode)</code></td><td>Sets the table's auto-resize mode when the table is resized.</td></tr>
</table>

Method	Description
setCellEditor(TableCellEditor cellEditor)	Sets the cellEditor variable.
setCellSelectionEnabled(boolean enable)	Sets whether this table allows both a column selection and a row selection to exist at the same time.
setColumnModel(TableColumnModel newModel)	Sets the column model for this table to newModel and registers with for listener notifications from the new column model.
setColumnSelectionAllowed (boolean flag)	Sets whether the columns in this model can be selected.
setColumnSelectionInterval(int index0, int index1)	Selects the columns from index0 to index1 inclusive, if column selection is allowed.
setDefaultEditor(Class class, TableCellEditor editor)	Sets a default editor to be used if no editor has been set in a TableColumn.
setDefaultRenderer(Class class, TableCellRenderer render)	Sets a default renderer to be used if no renderer has been set in a TableColumn.
setEditingColumn(int newValue)	Sets the editingColumn variable.
setEditingRow(int row)	Sets the editingRow variable.
setGridColor(Color color)	Sets the color used to draw grid lines to color and redisplays the receiver.
setIntercellSpacing(Dimension newSpacing)	Sets the width and height between cells to newSpacing and redisplays the receiver.
setModel(TableModel newModel)	Sets the data model for this table to newModel and registers with for listener notifications from the new data model.
setRowHeight(int newRowHeight)	Sets the height for rows to newRowHeight and invokes tile.
setRowSelectionAllowed(boolean flag)	Sets whether the rows in this model can be selected.
setRowSelectionInterval(int index0, int index1)	Selects the rows from index0 to index1 inclusive, if row selection is allowed.
setSelectionModel(List SelectionModel newModel)	Sets the row selection model for this table to newModel and registers with for listener notifications from the new selection model.
setShowGrid(boolean flag)	Sets whether the receiver draws grid lines around cells.

(continued)

Table 25-4 *(continued)*

Method	Description
setTableHeader(JtableHeader newHeader)	Sets the tableHeader working with this JTable to newHeader.
setValueAt(Object, int, int)	Sets the value for the cell at row and column.
sizeColumnsToFit(boolean flag)	Resizes one or more columns of the table so that the sum width of all columns will equal to the width of the table.
tableChanged(TableModelEvent newModel)	The TableModelEvent should be constructed in the coordinate system of the model, the appropriate mapping to the view coordinate system is performed by the JTable when it receives the event.
updateUI()	Called to replace the UI with the latest version from the default UIFactory.

Layouts

Swing has five primary layout managers:

✦ ScrollPaneLayout

✦ ViewportLayout

✦ BoxLayout

✦ OverlayLayout

✦ SpringLayout

The BoxLayout, OverlayLayout, and SprintLayout function like their counterparts in the older AWT user-interface model. The BoxLayout also happens to be built into the Box component.

BoxLayout

The BoxLayout layout manager allows you to arrange components along either an *x* axis or *y* axis. In a *y*-axis BoxLayout, for instance, components are arranged from top to bottom in the order they are added. Unlike GridLayout, BoxLayout allows components to occupy different amounts of space along the primary axis. Table 25-5 lists and describes the methods provided by the JBoxLayout object.

Table 25-5
JBoxLayout Methods

Method	Description
getLayoutAlignmentX(Container)	Returns the alignment along the x axis for the container.
getLayoutAlignmentY(Container)	Returns the alignment along the y axis for the container.
invalidateLayout(Container)	Indicates that a child has changed its layout-related information, and thus any cached calculations should be flushed.
layoutContainer(Container)	Called by the AWT when the specified container needs to be laid out.
maximumLayoutSize(Container)	Returns the maximum dimensions needed to lay out the components contained in the specified target container.
minimumLayoutSize(Container)	Returns the minimum dimensions needed to lay out the components contained in the specified target container.
preferredLayoutSize(Container)	Returns the preferred dimensions for this layout, given the components in the specified target container.

ScrollPaneLayout

The ScrollPaneLayout is the layout manager used by a JScrollPane. The layout defines nine different areas for the JScrollPane:

- ✦ JViewport—in the center for the content
- ✦ JScrollBar objects—one each for horizontal and vertical scrolling
- ✦ JViewport objects—one for column headers, the other row
- ✦ Component objects—one for each of the corners. The JScrollPane constants to specify the corners are: LOWER_LEFT_CORNER, LOWER_RIGHT_CORNER, UPPER_LEFT_CORNER, UPPER_RIGHT_CORNER

The center viewport portion of this layout is of primary interest for simple layouts. A JViewport is itself a container object that can hold components.

ViewportLayout

ViewportLayout is the layout manager used by a JViewport. You should never need to use the layout directly, as it is automatically associated with a JViewport object, and positions the internal component for you based upon the JViewport properties.

Event Listeners

Like the AWT, Swing has its own event package for Swing-specific events. There are events and event listeners within this package, while the event sources exist outside the package. Table 25-6 lists and describes the objects Swing uses to listen for events.

Table 25-6	
Event-Listener Objects	
Object	**Description**
AncestorEvent	An ancestor added, moved, removed.
ChangeEvent	An object's state change.
DocumentEvent	Document state change.
DragEvent	Drag support.
ListDataEvent	A list's contents were changed; an interval added or removed.
ListSelectionEvent	A list's selection status change.
MenuEvent	A menu was selected/posted, deselected, cancelled.
TableColumnModelEvent	A table column was changed.
TableModelEvent	A table model was changed.
TreeExpansionEvent	A tree was expanded or collapsed.
TreeModelEvent	A tree model was changed.
TreeSelectionEvent	A tree selection status changed.

Each listener interface is coupled with a single event type and contains a method for each type of event the event class embodies. For example, the ListDataListener contains three methods, one for each type of event that the ListDataEvent has: contentsChanged(), intervalAdded(), and intervalRemoved().

Wrapping Up JFC and Swing (for Now)

The last three chapters have covered a lot of ground in discussion of Java Foundation Classes and Swing user-interface classes. Even so, that discussion is only the beginning. There's always more to know about Swing and JFC; in effect, you've seen the future of Java user interface programming. If you'd like to stay on top of the latest Swing and JFC developments, check out the following Web sites:

✦ Using the JFC/Swing Packages:

`http://java.sun.com/docs/books/tutorial/ui/swing/index.html`

✦ The Swing Connection:

`http://java.sun.com/products/jfc/swingdoc-current/index.html`

✦ Creating a User Interface:

`http://java.sun.com/docs/books/tutorial/ui/index.html`

Swing 1.0 Release Notes

By the time you read this, Swing 1.0 should be shipping. The main Swing classes and APIs will be locked in when Swing 1.0 is released, although the APIs that implement Swing's pluggable look-and-feel designs will not be frozen. These are the main Swing API packages that will be frozen when Swing 1.0 is released:

✦ `com.sun.java.swing`

✦ `com.sun.java.swing.border`

✦ `com.sun.java.swing.event`

✦ `com.sun.java.swing.multi`

✦ `com.sun.java.swing.plaf`

✦ `com.sun.java.swing.table`

✦ `com.sun.java.swing.text`

✦ `com.sun.java.swing.tree`

✦ `com.sun.java.swing.undo`

✦ `com.sun.java.accessibility`

The APIs that implement Swing's pluggable look-and-feel designs will not be frozen—they will continue to evolve until they appear in the final version of JDK 1.2. These are the packages that will *not* be frozen when Swing 1.0 is officially released:

✦ `com.sun.java.swing.basic`

✦ `com.sun.java.swing.windows`

✦ `com.sun.java.swing.motif`

✦ `com.sun.java.swing.organic`

✦ `com.sun.java.swing.preview`

(continued)

(continued)

Also, when Swing 1.0 is released, the `JColorChooser` and `JFileChooser` components will be moved to a new `swing.preview` package. This is because the color-chooser and file-chooser APIs will still be changing for a few months after the official release. The look-and-feel implementation that has been known up to now as the *Java look and feel* (JLF) will be called the *Organic look and feel* (this means that the `swing.jlf` package will be renamed `swing.organic`). Also, a new package that implements the Macintosh look and feel will be named `swing.macintosh`.

Summary

This chapter reviewed how to make the most of Swing and Java Foundation Classes with the Java Development Kit 1.2. This chapter reviewed:

✦ Incompatibilities between JDK 1.2 and previous versions of Java include binary, language, runtime, API, and tools. Most of these problems are minor and won't affect your Java applications greatly—but you need to be aware of them.

✦ With its Swing and Java Foundation Classes, JDK 1.2 enables you to integrate Swing objects, layouts, and event listeners into your applications.

✦ Advanced Swing objects such as toolbars, tooltips, trees, and a text framework can lend sophistication to your user interfaces.

✦ More than just a current hot topic, the Swing and Java Foundation Classes are likely to dominate the future of user-interface programming in Java.

✦   ✦   ✦

Advanced Java

Although you have learned much about the basics of the Java programming language by this point in the book, this section introduces you to some advanced topics that outline exciting Java capabilities and directions. Due to the object-oriented nature and the class-based strategy of the Java programming language, it's easy to extend and its uses are diverse. In this part you'll learn how to implement and use JavaBeans—standalone components that can be used by other applications—including the Java applications you create.

Java also provides complete support for networking and database connectivity. The chapters in this part explore how to add network connectivity to your own Java applications, and how to add database support with the Java Database Classes (JDBC). The JDBC provides an open architecture, providing access to a number of native database platforms. This part also includes a review of Java multimedia support, and shows you how to enliven your applications with animation and sound.

With these capabilities in place and more to come, Java continues to change and evolve—so this part wraps up with a look at what to expect in the short- and long-term future of Java.

JavaBeans

JavaBeans Basics

In the preceding chapters, you learned how to create Java applets and applications using the Java programming language and the various tools that come with the Java Development Toolkit (JDK). Depending on your background in software development, writing Java applets and applications may not be radically different from what you already know.

JavaBeans, however, is likely to feel altogether new, even if Java came naturally to you. The reason for this is simple: JavaBeans builds on Java, so you have to know Java before you can work with JavaBeans. Assuming that you've worked through the chapters leading up to this one, or at least a good deal of them, you're ready for JavaBeans.

JavaBeans is a *software component model* for Java. It describes how to create and use reusable software components, known as *beans*, that you can manipulate visually using special-purpose *builder tools* (also known as *application builders*).

Assuming we have a few beans (whether we create them from scratch or use preexisting beans), we can use a builder tool such as the BeanBox utility that comes with the Beans Development Kit (BDK) to visually configure them to fit our needs. (See the "BeanBox Builder Tool Basics" section later in this chapter.)

Right out of the gate we're dealing with four new terms:

+ *JavaBeans*—a software component model specifically for Java.

+ *Software component model*—describes how to create and use reusable software components to build an application. The model tells you how to connect components so they can continue to function as intended and simultaneously cooperate with the other components in your application.

✦ *Bean*—a reusable Java program based on the JavaBeans component model.

✦ *Builder tool*—an application development tool, such as Borland's JBuilder or Symantec's Visual Café. This type of tool lets you both create new beans and use existing beans to create an application. You should treat these functions as two distinct operations. The BeanBox program that comes with the BDK performs the second function; it lets you visually manipulate existing beans to create an application.

Tip

Many developers mistakenly use the singular *JavaBean* interchangeably with the term *bean*, and you'll often hear the plural *JavaBeans* used to refer to more than one bean. For example, you might hear a developer claim to have created several really cool JavaBeans. In this context, the developer is clearly talking about beans, or reusable software programs, not the JavaBeans component model from which such beans are derived. You need to interpret the meaning of these terms differently depending on how they are used.

Software components and software component models

While the terms *software components* (or simply *components*) and *software component model* (or *component model*) may seem new, they have been around for many years. Software components and software component models go hand-in-hand; you can't have one without the other.

A software component is a self-contained program that behaves in a well-known, predictable manner, courtesy of a software component model. The component model functions as the "master plan" from which the component draws life. Component models are really just a means to an end—it's the components that we really want.

Software components—the next "big thing"?

Object-oriented languages such as Java represent a quantum leap forward in the field of software development. Objects help us rapidly build software programs and, if used properly, are reusable to an extent that the software industry hasn't seen before. And so, in a sense, objects are really the "next big thing," even though they've been around for a while.

Before objects, software programs were generally "hand crafted"—you had to reinvent the wheel each time you created a new program. But thanks to objects, we can create repositories of code (known as *packages* in Java) that can be used over and over again, greatly enhancing our productivity as software developers while also increasing the overall quality of the final program.

You can think of *objects* as the reusable building blocks (frames, doors, windows, steps, and so forth) that you use to build a larger structure. To be sure, building a house would be a daunting task if we had to build every little piece of it from scratch. However, if we only have to slap together a set of different prebuilt pieces, the job of building a house becomes a lot less challenging. By the same token, creating a software program is quite tedious if you have to create it from scratch, as you would if you used a procedural language such as Pascal or C. However, if you use objects (akin to building blocks) instead, the process goes much more quickly.

You can think of *software components* as fully prefabricated buildings. If you start with a completed building instead of a set of building blocks, the lion's share of work is already done; all you have to do is paint the house, put up some wallpaper, and plant a little grass out front. You just customize it a bit and you're ready to move in. To extend this idea to software development, a project that would require a reasonable amount of effort if you used objects requires practically no effort at all if you use components.

Of course, such an analogy oversimplifies the relationship between objects and components, but it captures the essence of the most significant difference: Objects are reusable *building blocks*, and components are reusable *programs* that you can customize using a builder tool such as BeanBox.

You usually build software components using objects. Objects and software components are complimentary, and they are useful and appropriate at different points in the software-development process.

Note

If you're familiar with visual software-development tools such as Visual Basic, Visual Age, and Delphi, then you've already been exposed to software components. All of these products let you create software components, and they've been around for some time. The biggest difference between the software components that you create with these tools and those you develop with JavaBeans is the language; beans are software components created with Java. Regardless of the language, the concept is the same: A component is a reusable program that greatly reduces the effort required to get a specific job done.

Software component models—"master plans" or "means to an end"?

To create and use software components, you have to use a software component model that describes *how* to develop and use components and supplies the *mechanism* for doing so. A software component model generally consists of two major elements:

✦ A detailed specification that describes how to create and use components

✦ A software implementation (in other words, an Application Programming Interface, or API) of the specification that supplies a concrete mechanism for building and using components

Naturally, how you create and use components depends on the specific component model. If you're working with the JavaBeans component model, you'll use the Java language, along with the JavaBeans specification—an official document that formally defines how to create and use beans—and the JavaBeans API.

Note

The JavaBeans specification is available on JavaSoft's Web site at `http://java.sun.com/beans/spec.html`, and is definitely worth getting your hands on if you're serious about JavaBeans. Heck, even if you're not serious about JavaBeans, it's worth checking out.

Some programmers regard software component models as the final word on developing and using components. They view the model as the "master plan" from which everything related to software components emanates. However, others don't pay much attention to the model itself because they're interested in using existing components and don't want to be bothered with the finer points of creating them from scratch.

In truth, you don't have to actively involve yourself with a software component model in order to create or use software components. However, even if you try to ignore the model, you can't escape it. Because the model describes *how* components are built and used and also provides the mechanism for creating and using them, you're always involved with it at some level. You just might not know or care. But that's okay.

You can run, but you can't hide . . .

Even if you don't care about the software component model, if you're using components, you'll find yourself dealing with the five standard *services* that component models (including JavaBeans) generally supply to their components:

- ✦ Property manipulation

- ✦ Customization (also known as *interface publishing*)

- ✦ Introspection (also known as *interface discovery*)

- ✦ Event support (also known as *event handling*)

- ✦ Persistence (the capability to *maintain state*)

Property manipulation

Just like objects, beans (and all other components) have certain properties. The background color of a button is a property. The time elapsed since its initial invocation can also be a property. Component models encourage developers to use a standard manner by which properties can be manipulated or changed— usually an explicitly defined method. In the case of beans, accessor methods are used. The JavaBeans specification calls for each property to have two associated accessor methods: a "get" method that reads the value of a property, and a "set" method that sets the value of a property.

Customization

Customization, or *interface publishing*, is a key feature of JavaBeans. One of the hallmarks of a properly designed bean is that you can visually customize it using a builder tool.

Builder tools, such as the BeanBox, are essential when working with software components such as beans—they let you visually customize the appearance and behavior of components. You can build sophisticated applications by simply stringing together beans that you've customized to fit your needs.

To do their magic, builder tools must be able to figure out exactly what capabilities a component supports and how these capabilities can be customized. If the builder tool has this information, it can let the user (typically a developer such as you or me) tweak its various properties using little more than the mouse and perhaps a few taps of the keys. Using builder tools and beans greatly reduces the coding effort traditionally required to create an application. However, you have to document your code very carefully. You have to know the capabilities and customizable parts of a bean before you can modify it, and you usually get this information by looking at the documentation accompanying the bean.

Note

Although beans are most useful when visually manipulated using builder tools, we can also tap into them through plain old-fashioned code. In fact, the JavaBeans specification (`http://java.sun.com/beans/spec.html`) shows how programmers can manually assemble and customize beans using nothing more than Java code. This is possible because beans are created using traditional Java APIs, meaning that they're built using standard Java classes and coding techniques.

Introspection

Introspection, or *interface discovery*, enables builder tools to understand how beans work by analyzing their internal structure. Builder tools use introspection to figure out which properties, events, and methods a bean supports. Using this intimate information, builder tools can control the appearance and behavior of a bean, which in turn enables us to visually manipulate and customize beans.

JavaBeans supports two distinct forms of introspection: implicit introspection and explicit introspection. *Implicit introspection* is a fundamental form of introspection supported by all beans. It's built into every bean and requires no extra effort by the bean creator to implement. *Explicit introspection* is a more sophisticated form of introspection that requires additional work on behalf of a bean's creator during the bean development process. Implicit introspection is information inherent to the bean and readily available, while *explicit introspection* depends on the willingness of the bean to provide additional information (in the form of extra code written for the bean).

Implicit introspection relies on Java's own reflection package, java.lang.reflect. This suite of APIs, new to JDK 1.1, allows a program to examine the internal structure of itself or any other Java class. By default, all beans support *reflection-based introspection*, which is used to deduce what properties, events, and public methods a bean supports. *Explicit introspection*, on the other hand, enables you to provide custom BeanInfo classes that are used in place of reflection to describe the internals of the bean. Thus, explicit introspection, by way of the BeanInfo class, gives you ultimate control over how your bean can be manipulated and customized, but it requires extra effort on your part.

Table 26-1 shows the SimpleBeanInfo class, which is a utility class used to construct BeanInfo classes.

Table 26-1
Class java.beans.SimpleBeanInfo

Constructor	Signature	Description
SimpleBeanInfo()	public SimpleBean Info()	This is a utility class. It simplifies creation of BeanInfo classes, should you choose to provide it. In the absence of BeanInfo classes, introspection is used to gather information about a bean.

Method	Signature	Description
getBean Descriptor	public BeanDescriptor getBeanDescriptor()	Override this if you want to provide explicit information about the class and the customizer of the bean.
getProperty Descriptors	public Property Descriptor[] get PropertyDescriptors ()	Override this if you want to provide explicit information about a property.
getDefault Property Index	public int getDefault PropertyIndex()	Override this if you want to define a default property for the bean supporting indexed properties.
getEventSet Descriptors	public EventSet Descriptor[] getEvent SetDescriptors()	Override this if you want to provide explicit information about an event set.
getDefault EventIndex	public int getDefault EventIndex()	Override this if you want to define a default event set.

Method	Signature	Description
getMethod Descriptors	`public Method Descriptor[] get MethodDescriptors()`	Override this if you want to provide explicit information about a method.
getAdditional BeanInfo	`public BeanInfo[] get AdditionalBeanInfo()`	Override this if you want to provide additional information on a bean.
getIcon	`public Image getIcon (int iconKind)`	Override this if you want to provide icons for your bean.
loadImage	`public Image loadImage (String resourceName)`	This utility method helps load icon images. It takes the name of a resource file associated with the current object's class file and loads an image object from that file. Typically images will be GIFs.
		Parameter: `resourceName`—a pathname relative to the directory holding the class file of the current class
		Returns an image object. May be null if the load failed.

We also have the `Introspector` class shown in Table 26-2. Along with the `SimpleBeanInfo` class, these two classes can provide us with a great deal of information about beans.

Table 26-2
Class java.beans.Introspector

Method	Signature	Description
getBeanInfo	`public static BeanInfo getBeanInfo(Class beanClass)`	Introspect on a Java bean and learn about all its properties, exposed methods, and events. When an error occurs an `Introspection Exception` object is thrown.

(continued)

Table 26-2 *(continued)*

Method	Signature	Description
decapitalize	public static String decapitalize(String name)	Utility method to take a string and convert it to normal Java variable name capitalization. This is done by converting the first character from uppercase to lowercase. If more than one character exists and both the first and second characters are uppercase, we leave it alone. For example, FooBah becomes fooBah and X becomes x, but URL stays as URL.
getBeanInfo SearchPath	public static String[] getBeanInfoSearchPath ()	Returns an array of package names that will be searched to find BeanInfo classes.
setBeanInfo SearchPath	public static void set BeanInfoSearchPath (String path[])	Sets the array of package names that will be used for finding BeanInfo classes.

Event support

Event support, or *event handling*, refers to a bean's capability to understand and deal with events. Events, as you may recall from previous chapters in this book, especially those chapters that discuss Java's Abstract Windowing Toolkit (AWT), are the programmatic mechanism used to exchange change-of-state notifications among objects. In simpler terms, events are used to tell objects that *something* (such as a mouse click or a key press) has happened, which in turn enables the object to react accordingly.

JavaBeans supports the same event model used by the AWT, and in doing so supports the notion of *source* beans and *listener* beans: Beans that produce an event are considered the *source* of the event, while those beans that are registered to receive the event are considered *listeners* of the event. JavaBeans uses an event as a simple communication device that enables us to connect beans, just as the AWT uses an event to connect objects. (For more details on events, refer to Part IV of this book, which covers the Abstract Windowing Toolkit.) While most AWT events result from user interaction and have a visual implication, bean events can (and in many cases do) have nonvisual contexts. When a number in a bean reaches a certain threshold, that could trigger an event that causes another bean to change its behavior. All of this could happen without the user ever "seeing" anything.

The "Cooking Up Your First Bean" section later in this chapter outlines the basic event model in JavaBeans. The event scheme can easily become complex, and careful design is a must for successful applications. For example, cases occur in which the source must send out a number of events simultaneously. Such a broadcast is encapsulated in the EventSetDecriptor class (see Table 26-3). Methods are provided to group such related events together and act on each one of them accordingly. For example, the getListenerMethods() method returns an array of method objects that are called when certain events occur.

	Table 26-3 Class java.beans.EventSetDescriptor	
Constructor	**Signature**	**Description**
EventSet Descriptor	public EventSetDescriptor (Class sourceClass, String eventSetName, Class listenerType, String listenerMethodName)	Sometimes an event source needs to fire more than a single event simultaneously. You do this by using an EventSetDescriptor where a group of events are delivered at once.
	public EventSetDescriptor (Class sourceClass, String eventSetName, Class listenerType, String listenerMethodNames[], String addListenerMethod Name, String remove ListenerMethodName)	Different constructors are used depending on how you want to create the EventSetDescriptor. Your choices are simple design patterns, introspection, and from scratch.
	public EventSetDescriptor (String eventSetName, Class listenerType, Method listenerMethods[], Method addListenerMethod, Method removeListenerMethod)	
	public EventSetDescriptor (String eventSetName, Class listenerType, Method Descriptor listenerMethod Descriptors[], Method add ListenerMethod, Method removeListenerMethod)	

(continued)

Table 26-3 *(continued)*

Method	Signature	Description
getListenerType	public Class get ListenerType()	Returns the Class object for the event handler that will be invoked when the event is fired.
getListenerMethods	public Method[] get ListenerMethods()	Returns an array of Method objects for the target methods within the target listener interface that will get called when events are fired.
getListenerMethod Descriptors	public Method Descriptor[] get ListenerMethod Descriptors()	Returns an array of MethodDescriptor objects for the target methods within the target listener interface that will get called when events are fired.
getAddListener Method	public Method get AddListenerMethod ()	Returns the method used to register a listener at the event source.
getRemoveListener Method	public Method get RemoveListener Method()	Returns the method used to register a listener at the event source.
setUnicast	public void set Unicast(boolean unicast)	Used to designate an event as unicast. Parameter: unicast—true if the event set is unicast
isUnicast	public boolean is Unicast()	Returns true if the event set is unicast.
setInDefault EventSet	public void setIn DefaultEventSet (boolean inDefault EventSet)	Marks an event set as being in the default set. By default this is true.
isInDefault EventSet	public boolean is InDefaultEventSet ()	Reports whether an event set is in the default set. Returns true if the event set is in the default set.

Persistence

Persistence is the capability of a bean to *save and restore* its state. In essence, this means that you can permanently save a bean to disk along with all of the runtime attributes that it possesses, and later "resurrect" it from disk with all its attributes intact. The capability to save and restore state is an important feature of beans. Without it, we'd have to reconfigure them from scratch each time we quit and then reran our builder tool.

Thanks to persistence, we can use builder tools to manipulate and configure beans to our heart's content without worrying that our work will be lost when we exit from the tool. Similar in nature to how a word processor enables us to save the state of each document we write, persistence gives builder tools the capability to save the changes we make to our beans.

JavaBeans supports two forms of persistence: automatic persistence and external persistence. *Automatic persistence* is near effortless, because it relies on Java's built-in serialization mechanism to save and restore the state of a bean. *External persistence*, on the other hand, gives you the option of supplying your own custom classes to control precisely how a bean's state is stored and retrieved. For example, your application may require you to save the state of a bean in a relational database. Externalization lets you do just that.

In most cases, you'll find that automatic serialization is the way to go. Because adding support for automatic persistence is a trivial effort when creating beans, there's no good reason to bother writing external persistence classes unless the automatic route fails to do the trick. While you may need to use external persistence if you're developing complicated beans that have special persistence requirements, in this chapter I focus on automatic persistence because it's probably all you'll need when you first start developing your own beans.

JavaBeans supports automatic persistence through Java's own Object Serialization mechanism, which is part of the `java.io` package in JDK 1.1. (JDK 1.0 does not inherently support serialization; you must manually craft your own solution if you want to save and restore object state.) Specifically, `java.io.Serializable` is an interface that a class can implement to indicate that it can be serialized. The `java.io.Serializable` interface is extended by the `java.ioExternalizable` interface. The `java.io.Externalizable` interface defines two methods, `readExternal()` and `writeExternal()`, which together enable a class to have complete control over the writing of its state. For more details on the `java.io` package and persistence, see Chapter 13.

BeanBox Builder Tool Basics

If you want to really understand the power of beans and fully appreciate the services each bean receives courtesy of the JavaBeans component model, you actually need to *work* with beans instead of merely *reading* about them. And to do that, you need to get your hands on a pile of premade beans and a bean-savvy builder tool that you can use to visually manipulate them. As luck would have it, the Beans Development Kit gives you both. Better still, the BDK is free.

The BDK is available on the CD-ROM that comes with this book and at Sun's Java Web site, http://java.sun.com/beans/. For more details, see Appendix B.

Introducing the Beans Development Kit

The Beans Development Kit (BDK) is created by JavaSoft, the same folks who created the Java Development Toolkit, and made freely available to developers such as yourself. It's important to note, however, that the BDK is not intended to be a full-blown beans development environment. Instead, its purpose in life is to support early-stage application development using beans while also acting as a "reference base" for both bean developers and tool vendors. In short, don't expect all the bells and whistles from the BDK that you would from a commercial bean development tool such as the BeanMachine created by Lotus Development Corporation.

The BDK is a bare-bones environment that offers just enough to get you started with beans, but not too much more than that. Just as you'll outgrow the JDK in time, you're certain to outgrow the BDK if you spend more than a little time working with beans. In the meantime, it's the perfect introduction to beans development, so we start here.

The BDK comes with a builder tool called the BeanBox, along with the JavaBeans API (the java.beans package) and a variety of bean source code examples. Although we explore the JavaBeans API and some of the source code examples provided with the BDK later, at the moment we focus on the BeanBox builder tool, because using it is perhaps the best way to really understand how beans work.

Many professional Java development tools also support JavaBean development. You can find the latest and greatest JavaBean tools online at http://java.sun. com/beans/tools.html. This site is devoted entirely to JavaBean development tools. If you're unsure of where to begin when it comes to finding the perfect JavaBeans development tool for your needs, be sure to consult this online site made available through Sun's JavaSoft division. Note that although many of today's tools support both bean development and application development based on beans, the two are different beasts. *Bean development* requires a tool that enables you to create beans with the intention that such beans will be used by others to create applications. Sun's Java Workshop is an example of such a tool. *Application development based on beans* means you already have access to a number of beans, and your job is to put them together to create an application. Java Studio is an example of this second type of tool.

The BeanBox

The BeanBox builder tool provided with the BDK is a pure Java application that runs under JDK 1.1. Because it's built entirely with Java, the BeanBox is platform-independent.

To run the BeanBox, simply move to the `beanbox` directory located inside the main BDK directory that is created on your hard drive when you run the BDK installer. (This assumes, of course, that you've installed the BDK. If you haven't, you'll have to do so now if you want to work through the examples in this chapter.) Windows 95 users can invoke the **run.bat** batch file by double-clicking it with the mouse in the Windows Explorer or by typing **run** at the command prompt in a DOS window. Solaris and other UNIX-flavor users can use the **run.sh** shell script.

When you run the BeanBox, three windows appear, as shown in Figure 26-1.

These windows perform the following functions:

✦ **ToolBox**—Lists the sample beans provided with the BDK. You can add your own beans to this list. You'll find out how later in this chapter.

✦ **BeanBox**—This window is a simple container in which you can manipulate and configure beans.

✦ **Properties**—Lists the properties of the bean currently selected in the BeanBox window.

Before you begin to explore the BeanBox in more detail, note that the BeanBox is a very simplistic example of a builder tool. Builder tools come in many flavors, so you're sure to find one that suits your personal tastes. They come in the form of Web site and Web page builders, visual application development tools, GUI layout builders, and just about any other type of software-development oriented tool you can think of. In fact, a plain-vanilla word processor that simply lets you drop beans into your documents is also considered a "builder tool."

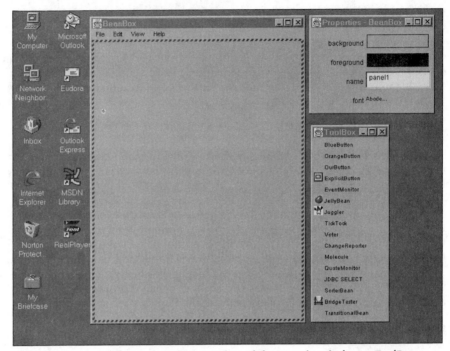

Figure 26-1: The BeanBox interface consists of three main windows: ToolBox, BeanBox, and Properties.

Tapping into existing beans

Now let's perform some very simple tasks to get you familiar with the BeanBox and its elements. In the ToolBox, click the OurButton bean, and then click in the BeanBox area. You have just instantiated your first JavaBean! The OurButton component (bean) has been placed inside the BeanBox container, as shown in Figure 26-2.

You can use the property sheet on the right side of the screen to customize the bean you have just created. Go ahead and change some of its properties, such as background color and label.

An important feature of beans is the event model, which lets two beans communicate with each other. To see this communication visually, we need another bean in addition to the OurButton bean. Let's use the Juggler bean, which shows the famous Duke juggling three beans in a continuous animation. We can use the OurButton bean to stop the animation with a click of the button.

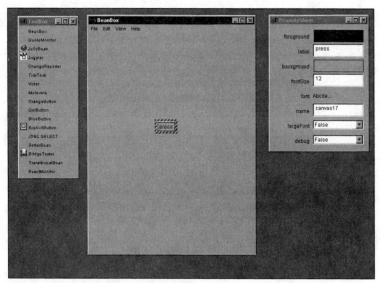

Figure 26-2: The OurButton bean

Place an instance of the `Juggler` bean inside the BeanBox, and then follow these steps:

1. Change the label property of `OurButton` to STOP.

2. Make sure that the `OurButton` bean is selected, and then choose Edit, Events; Select `action`, and then click `actionPerformed`.

3. Now you can see a red line starting from the STOP button. Connect the line to the `Juggler` and click the mouse button.

4. An `EventTargetDialog` box pops up. In this box, select `stopJuggling` and then click OK. The `stopJuggling` event is something that is supported by the `Juggler` bean. You are instructing the bean to do whatever it has to do to stop the Duke from juggling when it receives a "signal" from the `OurButton` bean.

5. Now click the STOP button and see what happens. The juggler stops juggling.

The event generated by clicking the `OurButton` bean caused another event (`stopJuggling`) to occur in the `Juggler` bean. This seemingly simple mechanism is the foundation of interaction among beans. Such interaction can quickly become complex as the number of beans grows.

Continue playing with the BeanBox until you are comfortable with the environment. Take a look at all the beans and their properties. Try connecting more beans together. For example, you can create a START button for the `Juggler`.

Under the File menu, you will find the Serialize command. You issue this command to make your beans persistent. For example, you can customize a button bean with the right background and foreground colors and the right label. You can then "serialize" the bean, give it a new name, and thus make it available for subsequent usage. You no longer have to start with the basic button and customize it every time.

You can't really see introspection with the BeanBox. The property sheet window, however, is mostly the result of introspection. The items in the property sheet change as you change beans. For each bean, its customizable properties are identified at runtime and are placed on the Property Sheet. Depending on the type of the property (color, text, and so on) an appropriate "customizer" is also provided. That's why you get a menu of colors for the Foreground property, but a text field for the Label property.

Cooking Up Your First Bean

A bean is not required to inherit from any particular base class or interface. Visible beans must inherit from java.awt.Component so that they can be added to visual containers, but invisible beans aren't required to do this.

Properties, events, and methods

As a software component, each bean has its own properties. Consider a simple push-button bean. It has a color property, a size property, and a label property. The label itself has other properties, such as font, size, and color. Properties that are meant to be accessible to other beans are called *public properties*. Those that are internal to the bean itself are classified as *private properties*.

Typically, in Java you can access a property belonging to a class directly and get or set its value. Properties are often stored as a simple variable. The JavaBeans specification changes this. JavaBeans requires that accessor methods be provided for all public (readable) properties. This means that, for a given property, a method must be provided to gets its value, and another method must be provided to set its value. This is a fundamental part of beans and one thing that distinguishes a bean from an ordinary class definition.

Aside from single-value properties, beans can have indexed, bound, and constrained properties. *Indexed* properties are similar to arrays. A *bound* property is linked to an event. When that property is changed, an event is fired to notify another bean of the change. Consider a radio button. When its property is changed from ON to OFF, you may need to gray out some other radio buttons or menu selections. This is where a bound property is useful. To facilitate dealing with bound properties, the utility class PropertyChangeSupport is often used. This class is shown in Table 26-4. You can add and remove listeners that must be notified when the value of a bound property is changed.

Table 26-4
Class java.beans.PropertyChangeSupport

Constructor	Signature	Description
PropertyChange Support	public PropertyChange Support(Object source)	This is a utility class. It handles the common things that a bean supporting bound properties must perform.

Method	Signature	Description
addProperty ChangeListener	public synchronized void addProperty ChangeListener (PropertyChange Listener listener)	Adds a PropertyChangeListener from the listener list. Parameter: listener—the PropertyChangeListener to be added.
removeProperty ChangeListener	public synchronized void removeProperty ChangeListener (PropertyChange Listener listener)	Removes a PropertyChange Listener from the listener list. Parameter: listener—the PropertyChangeListener to be removed.
fireProperty Change	public void fire PropertyChange (String property Name, Object old Value, Object new Value)	When a bound property changes, you can notify all registered listeners by invoking this method. Parameters: propertyName—the programmatic name of the property that was changed. oldValue—the old value of the property. newValue—the new value of the property.

You can use the PropertyDescriptor class to systematically specify the description of properties. Using the methods outlined in Table 26-5, you can, for example, find out the accessor methods for a property or determine whether it is bound or constrained.

Table 26-5
Class java.beans.PropertyDescriptor

Constructor	Signature	Description
Property Descriptor	public Property Descriptor()	This class describes a bean property. The property is supported via accessor methods per the JavaBeans specification.
		The class can be constructed in three ways. The first method is to use simple design patterns identified by get and set methods. The second approach is to specify the name of the property and the name of the methods used for reading and writing that property. The last option is to specify the name of the property and the objects used to read and write the property.

Method	Signature	Description
getProperty Type	public Class get PropertyType()	Returns the Java type info for the property.
getRead Method	public Method getReadMethod()	Returns the method that should be used to read the property value.
getWrite Method	public Method getWriteMethod()	Returns the method that should be used to write the property value.
isBound	public boolean isBound()	Returns true if the property is a bound property.
setBound	public void setBound (boolean bound)	Parameter: bound—true if the property is a bound property.
is Constrained	public boolean isConstrained()	Returns true if the property is a constrained property.
set Constrained	public void setConstrained (boolean constrained)	Parameter: constrained—Returns true if the property is a constrained property.
setProperty EditorClass	public void setPropertyEditor Class(Class property EditorClass)	Lets you associate a particular PropertyEditor with a property. Parameter: propertyEditorClass— the class for the desired Property Editor.
getProperty EditorClass	public Class getPropertyEditor Class()	Returns any explicit PropertyEditor class that has been registered for this property.

A *constrained* property is similar to a bound property with one difference. The bean being notified of a change must actually validate that change. For example, suppose you have a bean inside another bean. When the inner bean is resized, you can have the parent bean notified via a constrained property. The parent bean must then verify that the size change is valid and only after that verification does the resize actually occur. To facilitate this "veto" power of constrained properties, you can use the `VetoableChangeSupport` class (see Table 26-6). This is a utility class that lets you add listeners that allow or disallow a change in the value of a constrained property.

Table 26-6
Class java.beans.VetoableChangeSupport

Constructor	Signature	Description
VetoableChange Support	public VetoableChange Support(Object source)	This is a utility class. It handles the common things that a bean supporting constrained properties must perform.

Method	Signature	Description
addVetoable ChangeListener	public synchronized void addVetoableChange Listener(Vetoable ChangeListener listener)	Adds a VetoableChange Listener from the listener list. Parameter: listener—the VetoableChangeListener to be added.
removeVetoable ChangeListener	public synchronized void removeVetoable ChangeListener (VetoableChange Listener listener)	Removes a VetoableChange Listener from the listener list. Parameter: listener—the VetoableChangeListener to be removed.
fireVetoable Change	public void fireVetoable Change(String property Name, Object oldValue, Object newValue)	When a constrained property changes, you can notify all registered listeners by invoking this method. Parameters: propertyName—the programmatic name of the property that was changed. oldValue—the old value of the property. newValue—the new value of the property.

Properties basically define a component, and for the component to be reusable, it must allow customization and modification of its properties. But properties are only half of the story. A component must have a behavior and must be able to communicate with other components. The event model in JavaBeans addresses this need.

As mentioned before, events are what connect beans together. Beans use an event model that consists of two parts: a source object and a listener object. The source object is responsible for firing an event. This is like a broadcast message indicating that something has happened (a resize event, for example). The listener object is responsible for listening for events that it is interested in and performing certain actions when it receives notification that a relevant event has occurred.

Typically a bean registers itself with another bean to indicate its interest in some event. It is then notified when such an event has occurred. You can also use an adapter to filter events before they arrive at the listener. This gives you some control over propagation of events. Sometimes, the bean is only interested in a certain combination of events. In these cases, you can use an adapter to determine whether the special combination exists, and only pass the events on to their respective listeners if the combination does indeed exist.

Descriptors

Beans are only as useful as what we know about them. While simple introspection provides a mechanism to "inspect" a bean and learn about its properties, it often proves to be inadequate. Just as good documentation can be the key to successfully using an application and taking advantage of its features, a good description of a bean can do wonders for its successful deployment. Because beans can be used in a variety of builder tools, a great deal of effort has been made to create a systematic umbrella around the "descriptive" aspects of beans. As a result, we have classes that encompass descriptions of methods, properties, and parameters. Table 26-7 lists the FeatureDescriptor class, which is the base class for other "descriptor" classes. You can set/get a short textual description of a feature, set/get its attributes, determine whether the particular feature is hidden or not, and even determine whether the feature is intended for "expert" users or not.

Table 26-7
Class java.beans.FeatureDescriptor

Constructor	Signature	Description
Feature Descriptor	public Feature Descriptor()	The FeatureDescriptor class is the common base class for the "descriptor" classes such as PropertyDescriptor, EventSet Descriptor, and MethodDescriptor. It supports some common information that can be set and retrieved for any of the introspection descriptors. It also provides a generic mechanism for adding arbitrary attribute/value pairs.

Method	Signature	Description
getName	public String getName()	Returns the name of the property/method/event.
setName	public void setName (String name)	Parameter: name—the name of the property/method/event.
getDisplay Name	public String get DisplayName()	Returns the localized name for the property/method/event. The default is the same as its name from getName.
setDisplay Name	public void set DisplayName(String displayName)	Parameter: displayName—the localized name for the property/method/event.
isExpert	public boolean isExpert()	The expert flag lets you designate a feature intended for "expert" users. This provides a degree of feature customizability. Returns true if this feature is intended for use by experts only.
setExpert	public void set Expert(boolean expert)	The expert flag lets you designate a feature intended for "expert" users. This provides a degree of customizability to the feature. Parameter: expert—returns true if this feature is intended for use by experts only.
isHidden	public boolean isHidden()	The hidden flag is used to identify features that are intended only for the tool's internal use and should not be exposed to the user. Returns true if this feature should be hidden from users.

(continued)

Table 26-7 *(continued)*

Method	Signature	Description
setHidden	public void setHidden (boolean hidden)	The hidden flag is used to identify features that are intended only for the tool's internal use and should not be exposed to the user. Parameter: hidden—true if this feature should be hidden from users.
getShort Description	public String get ShortDescription()	Returns a localized description associated with this property/method/event. This defaults to be the name.
setShort Description	public void setShort Description(String text)	Associates a description with a feature. Parameter: text—a (localized) short description to be associated with this property/method/event.
setValue	public void setValue (String attributeName, Object value)	Associates a named attribute with this feature. Parameters: attributeName—the locale-independent name of the attribute value—the value.
getValue	public Object getValue (String attributeName)	Retrieves a named attribute with this feature. Parameter: attributeName—the locale-independent name of the attribute. Returns the value of the attribute. May be null if the attribute is unknown.
attribute Names	public Enumeration attributeNames()	Returns an enumeration of the locale-independent names of all attributes that have been registered with setValue.

A MethodDescriptor class also exists, based on the FeatureDescriptor class. This class provides a more detailed look at methods. In particular, it is important to have a good description of a method's parameters. Tables 26-8 and 26-9 show the MethodDescriptor, and Table 26-10 shows the ParameterDescriptor classes.

Table 26-8
Class java.beans.MethodDescriptor Constructors

Signature	Description
`public MethodDescriptor (Method method)`	A `MethodDescriptor` describes attributes of a method supported by the bean. Parameter: `method`—the low-level method information.
`public MethodDescriptor (Method method, ParameterDescriptor parameterDescriptors[])`	Parameters: `method`—the low-level method information. `parameterDescriptors`—descriptive information for each of the method's parameters.

Table 26-9
Class java.beans.MethodDescriptor Methods

Method	Signature	Description
`getMethod`	`public Method getMethod()`	Returns a description of the method.
`GetParameter Descriptors`	`public ParameterDescriptor[] getParameterDescriptors()`	Returns the locale-independent names of the parameters.

Table 26-10
Class java.beans.ParameterDescriptor

Constructor	Signature	Description
`Parameter Descriptor`	`public Parameter Descriptor()`	The `ParameterDescriptor` class is used to provide additional information on each of the parameters, beyond the low-level type information provided by the `java.lang.reflect.Method` class.

Two-bean example

Let's take a look at the code for a couple of beans. These beans are connected via the event model. The following example implements an increment function as two separate beans. The first bean contains a button. The second bean is a simple label. When you click the button, an event is generated notifying all registered listeners (in this case the label bean). The label bean then simply increments the value of the label. We have intentionally kept this example very simple so you can see the various aspects of beans you have learned so far, such as events and properties. Listing 26-1 is the label bean, which we call MyLabel.

Listing 26-1: **The MyLabel Bean**

```
package event;
import java.awt.*;
import java.awt.event.*;
import java.io.Serializable;

public class MyLabel extends java.applet.Applet
                     implements ActionListener, Serializable
{
    private int value = 0;
    public MyLabel()
    {
    }
    public synchronized void paint(Graphics g)
    {
        String valueText = "" + value;
        FontMetrics fm = g.getFontMetrics();
        g.setColor(getBackground());
        g.setColor(getForeground());
        g.drawString(valTxt, 0, 0);
    }

    public synchronized void update(Graphics g)
    {   Image hidden = createImage(getSize().width,
            getSize().height);
        paint(hidden.getGraphics());
        g.drawImage(hidden, 0, 0, null);
    }
// event handler
    public void actionDone(ActionEvent evt)
    {   value = value + 1;
        repaint();
    }
}
```

Note that the bean is an applet with a null constructor (per the bean specification). It implements Serializable, which is again part of the requirement. An event handler (listener) exists in the label bean; the event handler simply increments the value of the label by 1 and then redraws the content. This is the Listener method that must be registered with the event source.

Listing 26-2 shows the event source, which is the button bean.

Listing 26-2: **The Button Bean**

```java
package event;
import java.awt.*;
import java.awt.event.*;
import java.io.Serializable;
import java.util.Vector;

public class Button extends Canvas
                    implements MouseListener, Serializable
{
    private transient Vector actionListeners;
    private String     label = "Increment";
    private boolean    depressed;
    public Button() {
        addMouseListener(this);
    }
    public synchronized void paint(Graphics g){
        FontMetrics fm = g.getFontMetrics();
        int asc = fm.getMaxAscent();
        int siz = asc + fm.getMaxDescent();
        int wdth = getSize().width;
        int hght = getSize().height;
        int txtWdth = fm.stringWidth(label);
        g.setColor(getBackground());
        g.fillRect(0, 0, wdth, hght);
        g.draw3DRect(0, 0, wdth-1, hght-1, !depressed);
        g.setColor(getForeground());
        g.drawString(label, (wdth-txtWdth)/2, (hght-siz)/2
            + asc);
    }
     public synchronized void update(Graphics g)
    {   Image hidden = createImage(getSize().width,
            getSize().height);
        paint(hidden.getGraphics());
        g.drawImage(hidden, 0, 0, null);
    }

    public Dimension getMinimumSize()
    {   FontMetrics fm = getFontMetrics(getFont());
        return new Dimension(10 + fm.stringWidth(label),
                             10 + fm.getMaxAscent() +
                             fm.getMaxDescent()
);
    }
    public Dimension getPreferredSize()
    {   return getMinimumSize();
    }

    public void mouseClicked(MouseEvent e)
    {
```

(continued)

Listing 26-2 *(continued)*

```java
    }
// this is the event we really care about
    public void mousePressed(MouseEvent e)
    {   depressed = true;
        repaint();
    }
// another event we care about
    public void mouseReleased(MouseEvent e)
    {   depressed = false;
        fireEvent();
        repaint();
    }
    public void mouseEntered(MouseEvent e)
    {
    }
    public void mouseExited(MouseEvent e)
    {
    }
// registration for new listeners
    public synchronized void addActionListener
        (ActionListener lis)
    {   if (actionListeners == null)
            actionListeners = new Vector();
        actionListeners.addElement(lis);
    }
// removes a registered listener
    public synchronized void
removeActionListener(ActionListener lis)
    {   if (actionListeners != null)
            actionListeners.removeElement(lis);
    }
// the actual firing of the event
    private void fireEvent()
    {   if (actionListeners != null)
// vector is used to keep track of listeners
        {   Vector listeners;
            ActionEvent evt = new ActionEvent (this,
                ActionEvent.ACTION_PERFORMED, null);
            synchronized(this) {    listeners = (Vector)
                actionListeners.clone(); }
// go through each listener one by one and invoke the event
// handler
            for (int i = 0; i < listeners.size(); i ++ )
            {   ActionListener lis =
                    (ActionListener)listeners.elementAt(i);
                lis.actionDone(evt);
            }
        }
    }
}
```

Again, note how the applet implements `Serializable` and has a null constructor. An adapter class is used to keep track of the events generated by the mouse. When the `MouseRelease` event occurs, we go through each of the listeners registered and invoke their `actionDone` method, passing it the current event object. Also note that we are using a utility class to register (add) listeners and remove them. The code skeleton is the foundation for complex event handling in JavaBeans, so study it closely until you feel comfortable with the flow.

You can import and use the preceding two beans with the BeanBox. First, you must store the beans in a JAR file (JAR files are discussed in detail in Chapter 11), and then you can import them into the BeanBox. In fact, if you place the JAR file in the appropriate directory, the beans automatically show up in the BeanBox window.

Going the Distance

Beans are an important part of Java. Its initial success prompted several new developments, which are all based on the software component model. "Glasgow" is the code name for the next release of JavaBeans (the current JavaBeans release is version 1.0). It adds several capabilities to JavaBeans and the bean framework. Let's take a quick look at each one.

Tip

The Beans Development Kit comes with a comprehensive tutorial, which is an excellent step-by-step guide to working with the BDK. In addition, the tutorial teaches you how to create and use your own beans—so it's the perfect thing to read when you're done with this chapter. Although simple in concept, JavaBeans is worthy of its own book. In fact, plenty of books dedicate themselves to JavaBeans programming. But before you rush out and buy one, be sure to check out the tutorial that comes with the BDK first; you'll likely find that it contains exactly what you need to kick your beans habit into high gear without having to plunk down more cash.

Extensible Runtime Containment and Services protocol

This specification is an effort to provide a more effective method for integration of beans into their container environment. A component resides inside a container. However, the JavaBeans specification has not defined a mechanism by which the bean can get information about the services available to it from the container. In addition, the hierarchy of beans inside a container is not well defined. The Extensible Runtime Containment and Services protocol addresses these shortcomings. With this protocol, beans will be executed under different containers. For example, the same bean could be executed inside an applet container or a Webtop (Web browser) container. It is important for the bean to be able to find information about its container at runtime. Associating each bean with its container creates a hierarchy, which is useful under any component model. Almost all GUI implementations employ such a hierarchy. For example, if you close the main window of an application, all of its child windows close as well.

Activation Framework specification

When you download a file using your Web browser, the browser looks at the file's MIME type to determine what application/plug-in to launch so that you can view that file. The Activation Framework specification provides a somewhat similar service for beans. One of the services that the framework offers is determination of the type of arbitrary data. Other services include discovery of the operations available on the data and encapsulation of data access methods.

Native-platform-capable Drag-and-Drop specification

AWT JDK 1.1 underwent some major changes. Most of the changes were geared toward providing a more powerful foundation for developing quality graphical user interfaces. JDK 1.1 introduced the Uniform Data Transfer Mechanism and the Clipboard protocol, both of which are essential for providing user interfaces. The Drag-and-Drop specification builds on that foundation and completes the last piece of the puzzle. This specification will enable interaction among beans (Java software components) and components already available on the particular platform.

Enterprise JavaBeans specification

Another important development on the bean front is the Enterprise JavaBeans specification. This is an attempt to transfer the advantages of JavaBeans, which are mostly visual components on the client side, to the server. Components on the server are fundamentally different from visual components. For one thing, they are most likely not visual. Their functions are typically database connectivity, transaction processing, and communication to remote objects. In a way, server components are more challenging to develop, but the effort is ongoing and Enterprise JavaBeans will be available by the time you read this book.

Summary

In this chapter, we have taken a look at one of the most exciting and growing aspects of the Java programming language. The JavaBeans specification takes Java to the next level by creating a standard software component model for the language. Important points to remember about this chapter include the following:

✦ With components, software development becomes more consistent and systematic.

✦ A *bean* is an object created based on the bean specification. It has a null constructor, a set of properties, a set of accessor methods for accessing those properties, and it interacts with other beans using events.

✦ Serialization is used to add persistence to beans and introspection to find information about beans at runtime and at the time of design.

✦ Beans are customizable via the BeanBox, which is distributed as part of the Bean Development Kit.

✦　　✦　　✦

Networking

The Java language comes from Sun Microsystems. Also from Sun, we get the motto *The network is the computer.* From this line of reasoning, you could assume that Java would have something to do with networking—and it does.

Java was built from the ground up with networking in mind, giving us the ability to write network-savvy programs with relative ease from day one. Today, Java's networking capabilities continue to grow by leaps and bounds as new features are layered on top of an already substantial foundation and research projects focused on Java networking make their way from JavaSoft's labs to our personal computers.

In this chapter, we'll explore the various elements that give Java a leg up over traditional programming languages when it comes to developing network-aware programs. In doing so, we'll dive into the "core" classes that together form Java's solid networking infrastructure.

Stacking Data with Addresses and Ports

The technology of the Internet is based on the TCP/IP stack. This stack—a piece of software that connects your applications to the Internet—can work with a number of protocols that wrap and unwrap data, and has some special addressing tricks that make the Internet work. Any number of computers can be connected; it works perfectly connecting two computers across the room from each other, or millions of computers scattered all over the world.

What's in an address?

The most fundamental thing you need to know when sending data over the Internet is where the data should go. Like dialing a phone or addressing an envelope, you need to know some magic incantation that will direct your message. There is a computer out there that deserves to receive the data you want to send—all you have to do is make sure your data gets to the right program inside the right computer. To do this, there are just three things you need to know:

✦ The IP address of the target computer

✦ The protocol that will be used to package the data

✦ The port number specifying a specific application to receive the data

That's it. Using these three pieces of information you can send any data to any program inside any computer in the world. For example, if you want your Web browser to send a request to the Web server program at IDG Books Worldwide, you need to know that the IP address is 206.80.51.140, the protocol is TCP, and the port number is 80.

The IP address

The IP address (IP stands for Internet Protocol) is simply a 32-bit number. Every computer on the Internet is assigned one of these numbers. If you use a dial-up connection, your Internet provider has a whole bunch of these numbers and, when you make a connection, it assigns one to your computer for the duration of your connection. Computers that are always connected to the Internet, such as Web servers, are assigned numbers that they keep. That's how we can find them; we send out the URL (`www.idgbooks.com`, for example) and get the IP number back. We discuss URLs further in the "URL Operations" section later in this chapter.

The IP address is a 32-bit number. That means there are 4,294,967,694 of them. There need to be a lot of them because every computer on the Internet has to have one. They are not normally written as a one big number, but rather as four little numbers—one representing the numeric value of each of the four bytes of the complete number. An IP address written in this way, which is sometimes called the dot format, looks like this:

```
206.80.51.140
```

The actual numeric value is 3,461,362,572, but we never write it that way.

The protocol

The TCP/IP stack uses two protocols: TCP (Transmission Control Protocol) and UDP (User Datagram Protocol). (Actually, the stack uses other special-purpose protocols as well, but you don't need to know more about them to send data across the Internet.) The TCP protocol is the most robust of the two and is what makes the Internet work so well. This is not to minimize the value of UDP because there are some places where it really comes in handy. The real name of the stack should probably be TCP/UDP/IP, but that begins to get a bit unwieldy.

The reason the protocol can be considered part of the address is that a process that is expecting a message in one protocol will never receive a message that is sent in a different protocol. That is, if you write a program that receives messages in TCP protocol, a UDP message will never be delivered to it.

The port number

Once an Internet message arrives at a computer and works its way up to the top of the stack, the stack then looks at the port number and protocol (TCP or UDP) of the message to determine which of the programs waiting for messages should be awarded this particular message. The application is handed the message, usually through a socket connection, and the communication is complete.

Protocols can share port numbers without conflict. For example, if you write an application that receives TCP messages on port 2012, there can be another process, running simultaneously, that receives UDP messages on port 2012.

As you can see, the port number is a crucial part of the addressing scheme. If a port number is incorrect, messages will become scrambled among the applications. You need to make sure when choosing your own port number that you don't pick one that is already used for something. Generally, if you pick a number above 1024, you should be safe (unless you just happen to run into someone else that is experimenting). The port number is an unsigned 16-bit number, so it can go on up to 32,767.

There are certain pre-assigned port numbers used throughout the Internet. These are called *well-known ports*. They handle e-mail, file transfers, the World Wide Web, and all of the other services available on the Internet. Table 27-1 lists some examples.

Table 27-1 A Few Commonly Used Port Numbers		
Port Number	**Keyword**	**Description**
5	ECHO	Message returned to sender
9	DISCARD	Message received and ignored
17	QUOTE	Returns the quote of the day
20	FTP-DATA	File Transfer Protocol port for data transfer
21	FTP	File Transfer Protocol port for control messages

(continued)

Table 27-1 *(continued)*		
Port Number	**Keyword**	**Description**
23	TELNET	Remote terminal login
25	SMTP	Simple Mail Transfer Protocol
80	HTTP	The Web server
53	DOMAIN	Domain Name Server
101	HOSTNAME	The InterNIC host name server
103	X400	X.400 mail service
111	SUNRPC	Sun remote procedure call
117	UUCP-PATH	UUCP path service

From network to internetwork

All Internet communication is made possible by the TCP/IP stack. This stack is the software that resides inside each and every computer connected to the Internet. It operates like a two-way bucket brigade passing the message from one hand to another until it reaches the destination. At the top of the stack are the user's application programs. At the bottom is the physical communications link. Messages flow up and down in the stack, all the while being appropriately packaged, unpackaged, and addressed along the way.

This software is called a stack because it is made of pieces that conceptually sit one on top of the other like the layers of a cake. Think of a network as a huge silver platter with a bunch of computers sitting on it like cakes, and think of the Internet as the connections among the platters. Some platters only hold one cake, and some hold hundreds. The icing on the top of each cake is the programmer's interface.

A message from an application program will proceed from the icing down through all the layers to the platter. The message will then move to the bottom of another cake—on another platter if need be—and then up through the layers of the other cake to the icing at the top and the application that is waiting for it. There are times when a message rising up through the layers will only go part of the way, be re-addressed, and then sent back down to the platter to be moved on to another cake—this is the action of an Internet router, which can send a message from any platter to any other platter. This type of communication forms an internetwork.

The TCP/IP stack

The TCP/IP stack is a collection of protocols that fit together in a software stack in such a way that data inserted at one end will be converted, according to the rules of some protocol, and come out the other end. In the simplest terms, the conversion is in the form of wrapping the package for delivery and unwrapping it on receipt. There can also be some other juggling for sizing and data verification and such.

The structure of a pair of TCP/IP stacks is diagrammed in Figure 27-1. An application is at one end of the stack (the top) while the network hardware and its drivers are at the other end (the bottom). For communications to occur, data passes from the application down through each layer of the stack and right out the bottom, where it is transmitted over some kind of data link. After being transmitted across the link, the data arrives at the bottom layer of another stack and works its way up until it arrives at some other application.

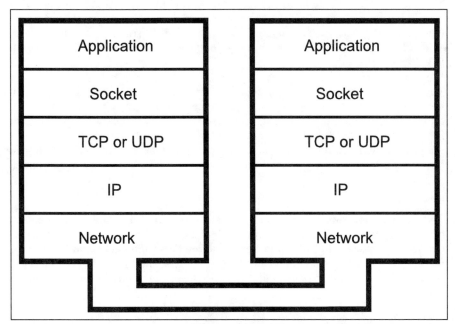

Figure 27-1: A pair of applications connected through a pair of TCP/IP stacks.

Sockets

Strictly speaking, the socket layer is not a part of the traditional TCP/IP stack, but sockets are so useful that everyone who programs Internet communications uses them. It is possible to talk directly from an application to the TCP/UDP layer of the stack without using sockets, and things were done this way for several years, but sockets make life so much easier. Besides, there are sockets built into the Java API, so why go elsewhere when everything you need is at your fingertips? If you would like to hear a programmer rant on for a while, find one who programmed Internet communications before the days of sockets.

In Java, all you need to do is create an object from the `java.net.Socket` class and start reading and writing over the Internet. However, just like making a phone call or sending a letter, you need to know the address of the recipient, or know how to get it.

TCP or UDP

These two protocols differ in the way they carry out the action of communicating. The TCP protocol establishes a two-way connection between a pair of computers, while the UDP protocol is a one-way message sender. The common analogy is that TCP is like making a phone call and carrying on a two-way conversation, while UDP is like mailing a letter.

The basic actions of the two protocols are very similar. They both pack data in headers and footers before sending it, and they both unpack it on reception. The difference comes in the relationship between sender and receiver. With TCP, the receiver converses with the sender as necessary to verify the valid transmission of the data (which could have been divided into several packets). With UDP, the sender never expects to hear a response, and the receiver doesn't bother to send one.

IP

This layer adds a new header to data being sent. Any human-readable names and addresses are encapsulated into binary blocks that are sent over the Internet. The IP address, the 32-bit binary number, is included in the header and is used to guide the data on its way. On receipt of data at this level, the binary headers are stripped off and what remains is passed up to the appropriate protocol on the level above.

Network

This is where the rubber hits the road (or the hits hit the highway). This is the connection to a dial-up modem, fiber link, LAN, cable modem, or whatever. What actually happens here will vary from one type of network to another, but the end result is that a binary stream is sent over some physical link to another computer. It then becomes the problem of the stack on the target computer to figure out what to do with it.

URL Operations

If you are going to work with the Internet and the World Wide Web, you need to create and manipulate URLs. Java has a handy little class for doing just that. The class `java.net.URL` is a wrapper for the standard URL string and has some methods that you can use to find out about the string and to fiddle with it. It can even make the connection for you. These methods are listed in Table 27-2.

<table>
<tr><td colspan="2" align="center">Table 27-2
java.net.URL Methods</td></tr>
<tr><td>*Method*</td><td>*Description*</td></tr>
<tr><td>`equals(Object)`</td><td>Determines whether two URL objects represent the same resource in the same way.</td></tr>
<tr><td>`getContent()`</td><td>Makes a connection and reads addressed contents.</td></tr>
<tr><td>`getFile()`</td><td>Returns the filename portion of the URL.</td></tr>
<tr><td>`getHost()`</td><td>Returns the host name portion of the URL.</td></tr>
<tr><td>`getPort()`</td><td>Returns the port number from the URL.</td></tr>
<tr><td>`getProtocol()`</td><td>Returns the name of the protocol of the URL.</td></tr>
<tr><td>`getRef()`</td><td>Returns the anchor reference portion of the URL.</td></tr>
<tr><td>`openConnection()`</td><td>Establishes a connection and returns the `URLConnection` object for it.</td></tr>
<tr><td>`openStream()`</td><td>Establishes a connection and returns a stream for reading it.</td></tr>
<tr><td>`sameFile(URL)`</td><td>Determines whether two URL objects address the same resource (ignoring references).</td></tr>
<tr><td>`setURLStreamHandlerFactory()`</td><td>Specifies the factory to be used to create any streams to establish connections.</td></tr>
<tr><td>`toExternalForm()`</td><td>Returns the URL in the string form used by Web browsers.</td></tr>
</table>

As you can see, the URL class supplies you with just about everything you need to read files and other resource data across an internet. There are several ways to get an object of this class. You can use a constructor to create one, or you can call a method to return one to you. The constructors listed in Table 27-3 construct URL objects from String objects and from other URLs.

Table 27-3
Class java.net.URL Constructors

Constructor	Description
URL(String,String, int,String)	The first String is the protocol, such as *http*. The second String is the host, such as *www.idgbooks.com*. The int is the port number. The final String is the name of the file, such as *index.html*.
URL(String,String, String)	The first String is the protocol, such as *http*. The second String is the host, such as *www.idgbooks.com*. The final String is the name of the file, such as *index.html*.
URL(URL,String)	The URL argument is the basis on which to build the new one. The String is an incomplete form used to modify the settings found in the original URL.
URL(String)	The String.

These are not the only ways you can get a URL object. If you are programming an applet, you can call the method getCodeBase() to get the URL of the directory containing the applet's class file, or you can call the method getDocumentBase() to get the URL of the directory containing the HTML file that invoked the applet. And, while this technique is not necessarily involved directly with networking, you can also get a URL object by calling the getResource() method of either Class or ClassLoader.

There is one other way. The method openConnection(), listed in Table 27-2, returns a URLConnection object for the URL, and a URLConnection object has a method named getURL() that returns a URLConnection. See the "Sockets" section later in this chapter for more information about the connections.

Basic URL manipulations

Just to show that it really works, here is a simple program that accepts your input string and uses it to construct a URL object from scratch:

```
import java.net.*;
public class ShowURL {
    public static void main(String[] arg) {
        try {
            URL url = new URL(arg[0]);
            System.out.println("File: " + url.getFile());
            System.out.println("Host: " + url.getHost());
            System.out.println("Port: " + url.getPort());
            System.out.println("Protocol: " + url.getProtocol());
```

```
            System.out.println("Ref: " + url.getRef());
            System.out.println(url.toExternalForm());
        } catch(MalformedURLException e) {
            System.out.println(e);
        }
    }
}
```

It is necessary to catch the `MalformedURLException` that could be thrown from the constructor of the `URL` object. If the exception is not thrown, it doesn't mean that the URL is valid—it only means that the input string is syntactically correct. This program allows you to enter the name of a URL and prints out its various parts. For example, typing this line:

```
java ShowURL http://www.xyz.com:80/poo.html#raul
```

results in this output:

```
File: /poo.html
Host: www.xyz.com
Port: 80
Protocol: http
Ref: raul
http://www.xyz.com:80/poo.html#raul
```

You most likely know the general format of a URL string, but you may not be familiar with a couple of parts. You can optionally include the port number in the string, but it isn't necessary to do so because the HTTP protocol causes a default to port 80. There are some rare instances in which you might want to specify the port number. For example, if you are experimenting with a new protocol that has no pre-defined default, or if you want to work with a Web server but don't want it to be publicly available, you can have it read from another port number and there will be no conflicts.

The *reference* is the location in the HTML where search engines look for inquiry strings and Web browsers look for the names of tags to automatically scroll to another portion of the page—that is, a link to a specific location within a page.

The great Web-page snatch

Reading a Web page from across an Internet connection is almost as easy as calling it by name. Here is an example that will list the entire text of any Web page on the Internet:

```
import java.net.*;
import java.io.*;
public class Snatch {
    public static void main(String[] arg) {
```

```
        int character;
        BufferedInputStream bin;
        try {
            URL url = new URL(arg[0]);
            bin = (BufferedInputStream)url.getContent();
            while((character = bin.read()) > 0)
                System.out.print((char)character);
            System.out.println();
        } catch(MalformedURLException e) {
            System.out.println(e);
        } catch(IOException e) {
            System.out.println(e);
        }
    }
}
```

All you need to do is type the URL string of a Web page, and the entire thing will be listed on the screen. Making a call to `getContent()` is the same as making a call to `openConnection()` to get a `URLConnection` object, and then calling its `getConnect()` method. The `getContent()` method returns an `Object` object that must be cast to the correct type before it can be used—there is more about this in the "URLConnection operations" section later in this chapter.

You have to catch the `MalFormedURLException`, which is thrown on a syntax error in the construction of the URL object. Also, you need to catch the `IOException` that could be thrown from the `getContent()` method or from reading from the `BufferedInputStream` object.

Encoding the URL string

Certain characters have special meanings and, if you want to include them, you need to insert them in such a way that they will not have an undesired effect. Say, for example, you want to include spaces, colons, slashes, or some other character that is used in the structure of a URL. To do this, take the URL string you would like to send and pass it through the `encode()` method of `java.net.URLEncoder`. Anything that might cause a problem is encoded so that it won't. Because this originated as a MIME process, it is known as MIME encoding.

This simple program accepts a string as a command-line argument and then displays the MIME encoded form of it.

The command line

```
java Encode "In character math 'a'+1 == 'b'"
```

resulted in this output:

```
In+character+math+%27a%27%2B1+%3D%3D+%27b%27
```

The encoding scheme converts all spaces to + characters. The characters A-Z and a-z, as well as 0-9, are left unchanged. All other characters are converted to a three-character sequence beginning with % and ending with a two-digit hexadecimal representation of the ASCII value of the character (which also happens to be the Unicode value).

URLConnection operations

It is possible to use a URL object to create a URLConnection object. In fact, you can create several URLConnection objects from a single URL and maintain more than one simultaneous connection, although this is almost never necessary. The URLConnection constructor is protected, so to create a URLConnection, you need to make a call to openConnection() of a URL object.

Several default settings are established when a URLConnection object is created. Static methods in the class allow the defaults to be modified. In addition, you can use a number of methods to query and modify the current settings for a URLConnection object. Most of the fields listed in Table 27-4 are protected, which means they can only be accessed through the methods.

Table 27-4
The Configuration Fields of the URLConnection

Field	Description
allowUserInteraction	Set this boolean field to true if there is some sort of human reaction involved with the resource (such as a data entry form on a Web page). The default setting is false.
connected	This boolean becomes true when a connection is established.
doInput	This boolean is true if the URLConnection can be used to read the resource.
doOutput	This boolean is true if the URLConnection can be used to write to the resource.
fileNameMap	The public static FileNameMap class can be used to convert the name of a file into MIME format.
ifModifiedSince	This long holds a date. A request to retrieve a remote resource will use the one in local cache instead if the remote version is older than the date.
url	This field is a reference to the URL from which this URLConnection was constructed.
useCaches	Setting this boolean to false forces the URLConnection to never use a cache—it will always get a new copy of the resource.

Table 27-5 is a list of the methods available in the URLConnection class. Several of them can be used to set the values of the internal fields. The defaults were designed to handle the most common situations, so unless you are doing something special, just leave them as they are. A number of them can be used to deal with the data.

Table 27-5 java.net.URLConnection Methods	
Method	Description
connect()	Opens a communications link.
getAllowUserInteraction()	Returns the setting of the allowUser InteractionFlag.
getContent()	Retrieves the object addressed by the URL. The actual type of object returned depends on the type of resource addressed by the URL.
getContentEncoding()	Returns the value of the content-encoding header field. Could be null.
getContentLength()	Returns the content length. Returns -1 if it is not known.
getContentType	Returns the value of the content-type header field. Could be null.
getDate()	Returns the value of the date header field as a long. Could be zero.
getDefaultAllowUserInteraction()	Returns the default setting of allowUserInteraction.
getDefaultRequestProperty (String)	Returns the default value of a request property.
getDefaultUseCaches()	Returns the default setting of the useCaches flag.
getDoInput()	Returns the current value of the doInput flag.
getDoOutput()	Returns the value of the doOutput flag.
getExpiration()	Returns the expiration date of the URL as a long. Could be zero.
getHeaderField(String)	Returns the value of the header field specified by its name.
getHeaderField(int)	Returns the header number (counting from the top).

Method	Description
getHeaderFieldDate(String,long)	The header field named as the String is taken to be a date and its long value is returned. If it is not found, the supplied default is returned.
getHeaderFieldInt(String,int)	The header field named as the String is taken to be an integer and its value is returned. If it is not found, the supplied default is returned.
getHeaderFieldKey(int)	Returns the key value specified by the number. Could be null.
getIfModifiedSince()	Returns the value of the date ifModifiedSince.
getInputStream()	Returns an InputStream that can be used to read the resource.
getLastModified()	Returns, as a long, the date found in the last-modified header field. Could be zero.
getOutputStream()	Returns an OutputStream that can be used to write to the location addressed by the URL.
getRequestPoperty(String)	Returns the string value of the named property.
getURL()	Returns the URL used to establish this connection.
getUseCaches()	Returns the value of the useCaches flag.
guessContentTypeFromName (String)	Looks at the name passed to it and returns a string identifying the type of resources. For example, a name ending with *.html* would be assumed to be a Web page.
guessContentTypeFromStream (InputStream)	Reads the InputStream passed to it and attempts to determine the type of resource by reading from it and analyzing what it finds.
setAllowUserInteraction (boolean)	Sets the value of the allowUser Interaction flag.

(continued)

	Table 27-5 *(continued)*
Method	*Description*
setContentHandlerFactory (ContentHandlerFactory)	Specifies the ContentHandlerFactory to be used by all URLConnection objects.
setDefaultRequestProperty (String,String)	Uses the first String as the key and the second as the general-request property. These properties are then used in the creation of every URLConnection.
setDefaultUsesCaches(boolean)	Sets the value of defaultUsesCaches.
setDoInput(boolean)	Sets the value of doInput.
setDoOutput(boolean)	Sets the value of doOutput.
setIfModifiedSince(long)	Sets the value of ifModifiedSince.
setRequestProperty(String, String)	Uses the first String as the key and the second as the value and sets the general-request property. These properties are then used only for this URLConnection.
setUsesCaches(boolean)	Sets the value of usesCaches.

The incoming headers

This is a simple program that, when given a URL string, opens a connection to the URL and displays all the header information:

```
import java.net.*;
import java.io.*;
public class WhatIsIt {
    public static void main(String[] arg) {
        int i = 1;
        BufferedInputStream bin;
        try {
            URL url = new URL(arg[0]);
            URLConnection con = url.openConnection();
            String header = con.getHeaderField(i);
            String key = con.getHeaderFieldKey(i);
            while(header != null) {
                System.out.println("H" + i + ": " +
                    key + "=" + header);
                i++;
                header = con.getHeaderField(i);
```

```
              key = con.getHeaderFieldKey(i);
          }
      } catch(MalformedURLException e) {
          System.out.println(e);
      } catch(IOException e) {
          System.out.println(e);
      }
    }
  }
```

This example uses the URL object to establish a connection and then retrieves all the headers from it. This command supplies the URL for the home page of an ISP:

```
java WhatIsIt http://www.xyz.net
```

The output is the complete list of headers and the values at the time the query was made:

```
H1: Date=Thu, 26 Feb 1998 20:28:05 GMT
H2: Server=Apache/1.1.3
H3: Content-type=text/html
H4: Content-length=1659
H5: Last-modified=Thu, 26 Feb 1998 04:24:27 GMT
H6: Connection=Keep-Alive
H7: Keep-Alive=timeout=15, max=5
```

The methods used, getHeaderField() and getHeaderKey(), retrieve the names of the fields and their values according to their positions in the file. Different locations on the Internet will supply different levels of detail—the number and content of the headers will vary—but you should always be able to determine content type.

Sockets

If you need to get closer to things than you can with the URL classes described in the previous section, you can use the sockets that are built into the Java core classes. Sockets are certainly no more difficult to use than URLs, and, with sockets, you have a lot more control over your communications. The drawback is that you will have to handle more of the details yourself. With the URL classes, we're only able to work with the client side of the client/server architecture—with sockets, we can work both sides of the street.

Finding an address

The Internet makes finding addresses quite simple really. You supply the name and the address will come right back for you. The class InetAddress will do this. Here is a simple program showing how it works:

```
import java.net.*;
public class GetAddresses {
    public static void main(String[] argv) {
        InetAddress ia;
        try {
            ia = InetAddress.getLocalHost();
            System.out.println("Local host: " + ia);
            ia = InetAddress.getByName(null);
            System.out.println("Null host: " + ia);
            ia = InetAddress.getByName("www.idgbooks.com");
            System.out.println("IDG host: " + ia);
        } catch(UnknownHostException e) {
            System.out.println(e);
        }
    }
}
```

This program retrieves three addresses—two of them are local and one is from the Internet. The output looks like this:

```
Local host: default/206.66.1.79
Null host: localhost/127.0.0.1
IDG host: www.idgbooks.com/206.80.51.140
```

This program was run from a computer with a dial-up connection, and the address 206.66.1.79 is the one that was assigned to the connection by the Internet service provider. That is the address returned from getLocalHost().

The second address, 127.0.0.1, is kind of special. This address is on every computer and is designed to not go anywhere. Whenever an application sends a message down the TCP/IP stack to this address, the message will simply reverse itself and return right back up the stack. You might find it handy if you have a couple of local applications that need to talk to one another—or if you want to test a client server connection by using a single computer.

The third address was retrieved from over the Internet. It is the address of the computer hosting the main Web page for IDG Books Worldwide. You now know how I found the address of IDB Books Worldwide in the "What's in an address?" section earlier in this chapter.

Setting up a simple socket server

This program sets itself up as a server and waits for a client connection to occur. Whenever a connection is made, the server spawns a new copy of itself (that is, it starts a new thread) and this copy is used to field requests and return responses. Any number of these threads can run at any one time, and they each remain active until the corresponding client — the program that initiated the connection — either requests a disconnect or drops its own connection.

This server doesn't do much. It simply receives character strings from the client and displays them:

```java
import java.net.*;
import java.io.*;
public class Server implements Runnable {
    Socket socket;
    int ID;
    public static void main(String[] arg) {
        int port = 9999;
        int count = 0;
        try {
            ServerSocket s = new ServerSocket(port);
            System.out.println("Waiting on port " + port);
            while(true) {
                Socket socket = s.accept();
                System.out.println("Connect! ID=" + ++count);
                Server server = new Server(socket,count);
                Thread thread = new Thread(server);
                thread.start();
            }
        } catch (Exception e) {
            System.err.println("Server error");
            System.err.println(e);
        }
    }
    Server(Socket socket,int ID) {
        this.socket = socket;
        this.ID = ID;
    }
    public void run() {
        try {
            InputStream is = socket.getInputStream();
            InputStreamReader isr = new InputStreamReader(is);
            BufferedReader br = new BufferedReader(isr);
            while(true) {
                String str = br.readLine();
                if(str.trim().equals("quit"))
                    break;
                System.out.println("ID " + ID + ": " + str);
```

```
            }
        } catch (Exception e) {
            System.err.println(e);
        } finally {
            System.out.println("Disconnect! ID=" + ID);
            try {
                socket.close();
            } catch(IOException e) {
                System.out.println(e);
            }
        }
    }
}
```

This socket server program waits on port number 9999 for a connection request. It does this by creating a new ServerSocket object and then going into an infinite loop calling the accept() method. Whenever accept() returns, it is with a Socket object representing a connection that has just been made.

Whenever a new connection is made, a new thread is created to handle communications. This thread is assigned the newly connected Socket, and it is assigned a unique number. The loop then continues by calling accept(), again waiting for another thread. This architecture enables Java to handle as many sockets as the underlying operating system will allow.

Once the thread comes into existence, the run() method is called. The thread will remain alive until run() returns. The run() method establishes input from the socket by calling getInputStream(). This is a raw input stream that you can interpret any way you like, but for the example here we are assuming that the only input will be character strings. To handle them, an InputStreamReader is attached to the raw input stream and, in turn, a BufferedReader is attached to it. This allows us to use the readLine() method in the BufferedReader to interpret the incoming stream of bytes as character strings.

The reading is done in a continuous loop until the word *quit* is received to break the connection. Note that only the one connection is broken (by making a call to the close() method of the socket); this has no effect on any other active connections, nor on the ServerSocket being used to establish connections.

Sending from a simple socket client

Now that we have a server ready to go, we need a client to send messages to it. This very simple client reads lines of text from the keyboard and sends it to the server:

```
import java.io.*;
import java.net.*;
public class Client {
    public static void main(String[] args ) {
        int port = 9999;
        String inString;
        InputStreamReader isr = new InputStreamReader(System.in);
        BufferedReader br = new BufferedReader(isr);
        try {
            InetAddress address = InetAddress.getByName(null);
            Socket socket = new Socket(address,port);
            OutputStream os = socket.getOutputStream();
            OutputStreamWriter osw = new OutputStreamWriter(os);
            PrintWriter pw = new PrintWriter(osw);
            while((inString = br.readLine()) != null) {
                pw.println(inString);
                pw.flush();
                if(inString.trim().equals("quit"))
                    System.exit(0);
            }
        } catch (IOException e) {
            System.err.println(e);
        }
    }
}
```

A BufferedReader is created to read lines of text from the keyboard. A socket is created with the same port number as the server. The number 9999 was chosen arbitrarily. The other end of the socket could be anywhere on the Internet, but for this example, a call is made to InetAddress.getByName(null) to get the address of the local host. Once the socket is created, the getOutputStream() method is called to get the writeable stream. This stream, along with an OutputStreamWriter, is then used to construct a PrintWriter that will be used to send strings through the socket connection.

The loop reads one string after the other and sends it to the server. After each string is sent, it is tested to see if it's the termination command. If the string is *quit*, the server will have recognized it on receipt and closed the other end of the socket. This application exits, causing the socket to close on this end.

These two simple programs—the server and the client—demonstrate the power of the Internet. Two simple programs like this can be anywhere in the world and, as long as the Internet address of the server is known to the client, they can hook up and communicate.

RMI Operations

The idea behind RMI is very simple. A program running on a computer somewhere on the Internet can invoke a method that is resident in a program running somewhere else on the Internet. To make this happen, several things need to be done, and all of them are built in to the `java.rmi` package.

The best way to learn about RMI is to go through a step-by-step explanation of what it takes to set things up for an RMI invocation.

The package

Create a directory that has the name of the package you would like to use. This directory can be inside other directories as long as the `CLASSPATH` variable is set correctly and the package names are included in the source files. This example uses the package name `rmitest`, which means that the `CLASSPATH` list of names includes the name of the directory immediately above the directory named rmitest.

The interface

For one program to invoke the method of another, they have to agree on the name and arguments of the method. Java has a built-in way of handling this. If an interface is defined and they both use it, then the name and arguments are bound to match. So, the first thing to do is define the interface. For our example, the interface is a very simple one with a single method:

```
package rmitest;
public interface StringTag extends java.rmi.Remote {
    public String appendX(String instring)
        throws java.rmi.RemoteException;
}
```

This interface defines the single method `appendX()`. It takes a `String` object as an argument and supplies a `String` as its return value. For our example, all the method is going to do is append `XXX` onto the end of any string it receives.

The arguments and return values must be serializable. To do this, they must implement the `Serializable` interface. Most of the Java API implements this interface, but if you are going to write any classes to pass as remote arguments, you need to write them so that they can be written to a stream.

The implementation

You need to write a class that implements the interface. For this example, it is called `StringTagImpl`:

```
package rmitest;
import java.rmi.*;
import java.rmi.server.UnicastRemoteObject;
public class StringTagImpl extends UnicastRemoteObject
            implements StringTag {
    public StringTagImpl() throws RemoteException {
        super();
    }
    public String appendX(String s) throws RemoteException {
        return(s + "XXX");
    }
    public static void main(String[] arg) {
        System.setSecurityManager(new RMISecurityManager());
        try {
            StringTagImpl sm = new StringTagImpl();
            Naming.rebind("StringTag",sm);
            System.out.println("StringTag bound in registry");
        } catch(Exception e) {
            System.out.println("StringTagImpl: " + e);
        }
    }
}
```

This is the server side of the rmi call—this is the class that holds the method that will actually be called. Not only does it implement the interface we described in the previous section, but it also extends the UnicastRemoveObject class, thus making it capable of receiving remote method calls.

There is always a default constructor. This one doesn't do anything, but it is included here to point out that if you need to have a constructor, you have to define it as throwing a RemoteException. The exception is actually thrown from the constructor of the superclass.

The body of the method is defined. This example is very simple—it simply creates a return string by combining the one passed in with the three characters XXX.

This program is to be executed on the server, so it must have a main(). The RMISecurityManager() must be defined so it will be in place to control access requested from remote locations. Without the security manager in place, no RMI is possible. The fact that you can design and install your own security manager gives you a great deal of control over security.

This object has to register itself with the Naming registry. When a remote request arrives at this computer, there is a search in the registry for the name. If a match is found, the appropriate method is called.

The stubs and the skeletons

Once the above pieces are defined, they can be compiled into class files with the Java compiler, like this:

```
javac StringTag.java
javac StringTagImpl.java
```

But there is one more step. The caller of the method will need a stub, and the method being called will need a skeleton. These are both class files, and you get both of them with this single command:

```
rmic rmitest.StringTagImpl
```

The output takes the form of these two files:

```
StringTagImpl_Skel.class
StringTagImpl_Stub.class
```

Then when the client calls the method, it actual calls the stub. The stub gathers up the necessary information and transmits it over the Internet to the machine that holds the server—the actual method. On the server side, there is a search in the registry for the name and, if found, the data that came over the Internet is turned over to the skeleton. The job of the skeleton is to unwrap the data and make the actual method call. When the method returns, the skeleton wraps up the answer and transmits it back to the stub. The stub then unwraps the returned data and passes the result to the original caller of the method.

This process of stubs and skeletons wrapping and unwrapping data is called *marshalling* and *unmarshalling*.

Starting the registry

Before any calls can be made, the host system needs to have a registry. The registry is the program that resolves the name requests that come in across the Internet. It is the one that holds the information that is passed in the Naming calls.

To start the registry on Window 95 or NT, enter

```
start registry
```

To start the registry on a UNIX system, enter

```
registry &
```

Starting the server

If a stub is not already on a local machine, it will be downloaded from the remote machine. To make this possible, when the server is started you have to specify the codebase so that the stub can be found. The codebase is defined this way on the command line that starts the server running:

```
java -Djava.rmi.server.codebase=http:/q/rmitest/
rmitest/StringTagImpl
```

The applet that makes the call

The remote call can be made from an applet or an application. For this example, we have an applet that calls the method:

```
package rmitest;
import java.awt.*;
import java.rmi.*;
public class StringTagApplet extends java.applet.Applet {
    String tagged;
    public void init() {
        try {
            StringTag st = (StringTag)Naming.lookup(
                "//" + getCodeBase().getHost() + "/StringTag");
            tagged = st.appendX("The string ");
        } catch(Exception e) {
            System.out.println(e);
            e.printStackTrace();
        }
    }
    public void paint(Graphics g) {
        g.drawString(tagged,25,30);
    }
}
```

This applet uses the `Naming.lookup()` method to get a reference to the local stub for the remote class. Once the stub has been retrieved, the methods can all be called just as if the stub were a local object. In our example, there is only one method, and it is called to make modifications to the character string.

The HTML

To run an applet, you need a browser and the HTML that controls it. Here is the HTML from this example:

```
<HTML>
<title>String appending</title>
<center><h1>Append X and Y</h1></title>
The result of appending to the strings is:
<p>
<applet codebase=".." code="rmitest.StringTagApplet"
    width=500 height=120>
</applet>
</HTML>
```

This HTML executes the applet. The setting of the codebase string depends on where the class files are located on your system. Note that the applet calls getCodeBase() to get a URL object representing the directory holding the class files.

Entering the command

```
appletviewer StringTag.html
```

pops up a window that displays the string that was modified by a remote procedure call.

Summary

Java takes the flexibility of the Internet and makes it easy. You should now understand how to add networking support to your own applications. Important points to remember abut this chapter include these:

✦ The most fundamental thing you need to know when sending data over the Internet is where the data should go. To do this, there are just three things you need to know: the IP address of the target computer; the protocol that will be used to package the data; and the port number specifying a specific application to receive the data.

✦ Sockets have been around several years now, and they really simplified things, but with the Java Sockets class it has even become simpler. Beyond that, if you are working with URL addressing, the URL classes, which rest on top of the sockets, make that kind of work easier than it has ever been.

✦ The RMI system is quite unique, and it has some very interesting implications. Local applications will no longer need regular upgrades because critical methods actually reside on other machines. A programmer can write code to access database information without caring what machine holds the actual data—in fact, the data can be moved at will without affecting any of the programs or system configurations.

✦   ✦   ✦

JDBC: Java API for Database Connectivity

This chapter covers the Java Database Connectivity Application Programming Interface (JDBC API), defined by JavaSoft, Inc. as part of the Core Java API. JDBC allows any applet or application written in Java to access remote databases and retrieve or update information stored in such databases. After an introduction to JDBC, the chapter discusses how to connect to databases and perform queries and updates. The subsequent section is a reference that lists the contents of the whole API, and finally we discuss more advanced issues such as stored procedures, transactions, and three-tier partitioning.

Introduction to JDBC

JDBC, the Java Database Connectivity API, is one of the key players in making Java an appropriate language and platform for building world-class applications. In this introduction, you learn the fundamentals of JDBC:

- ✦ Universal database connectivity
- ✦ Traditional client/server architectures
- ✦ SQL
- ✦ Database drivers
- ✦ The JDBC API

Universal database connectivity from Java

The Java Database Connectivity API allows Java applets, *servlets* (Web-server-side applets), and standalone applications to access data stored in relational database management systems (DBMS) in a universal way. The industry standard for accessing data is SQL (Structured Query Language), which permits maximum interoperability. Of course, SQL is the language used with JDBC. You build the connectivity itself using a single, standard API no matter what the DBMS: the JDBC API.

Relational databases are the most common kind of DBMS today and they impose absolute separation between physical and logical data. By accessing data through the logical model associated with it, you avoid the limitations of supplying information about physical storage locations. Relational databases let you define relationship and integrity rules among data sets organized in tables.

Using one query language (SQL) and one API (JDBC) lets you provide universal database connectivity from Java.

Last but not least, JDBC will work independently of the network environment. It is well suited for the intranet as well as for the Internet.

Basic characteristics of JDBC

To understand JDBC, you need to get acquainted with its most important characteristics. If you already have some knowledge of ODBC (Open Database Connectivity) under Microsoft Windows, you will probably see that JDBC and ODBC are similar in many ways:

✦ **Call-level SQL interface:** JDBC is a *call-level* SQL interface for Java used at the client side. It is totally independent of the various database management systems. It is a low-level application programming interface that allows Java programs to issue SQL statements and retrieve their results. It also provides methods for managing errors and warning messages. Figure 28-1 shows where JDBC is usually used.

✦ **SQL conformance:** JDBC does not set any restrictions on the type of queries that can be sent to an underlying DBMS driver. An application may use as much SQL functionality as desired. The underlying drivers are authorized to claim JDBC compliance if they fully support ANSI SQL-92 Entry Level, which is widely supported today and guarantees a wide level of portability.

✦ **Convenient implementation:** JDBC can be implemented on top of common SQL-level APIs, in particular, on top of ODBC.

Note

JDBC is usually implemented using native or nonnative drivers instead of being used on top of ODBC.

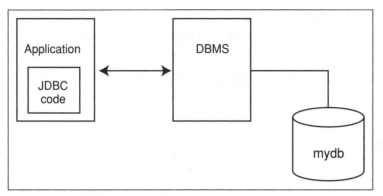

Figure 28-1: JDBC is used at the client side.

✦ **Consistent API:** JDBC provides a Java interface that stays consistent with the rest of Java. There are no conflicts due to opposed philosophies.

✦ **KISS paradigm:** The JDBC mechanisms are simple to understand and use, although there are little restrictions on specific database functionalities. (KISS means "Keep it simple, stupid.")

✦ **Strong, static typing:** JDBC uses strong, static typing wherever possible. This allows for more error checking to be performed at compile time.

✦ **One functionality, one method:** JDBC, unlike many other complex DBMS SQL-level APIs, is simple enough for a beginner to use, yet powerful enough for an experienced programmer.

JDBC components

A typical architecture involving JDBC to connect to databases usually involves four essential components: the application itself, the JDBC driver manager, specific drivers for the databases, and finally the database management systems.

Application

The user application invokes JDBC methods to send SQL statements to the database and retrieve results. It performs the following tasks:

✦ Requests a connection with a data source

✦ Sends SQL statements to the data source

✦ Defines storage areas and data types for the resultsets

✦ Requests results

✦ Processes errors

✦ Controls transactions—requests commit or rollback operations

✦ Closes the connection

Driver manager

The primary role of the JDBC driver manager is to load specific drivers on behalf of the user application. It may also perform the following tasks:

✦ Locate a driver for a particular database

✦ Process JDBC initialization calls

✦ Provide entry points to JDBC functions for each specific driver

✦ Perform parameter and sequence validation for JDBC calls

Driver

The driver processes JDBC method invocations, sends SQL statements to a specific data source, and returns results back to the application. When necessary, the driver translates and/or optimizes requests so that the request conforms to the syntax supported by the specific DBMS. The driver can handle these tasks:

✦ Establish a connection to a data source

✦ Send requests to the data source

✦ Perform translations when requested by the user application

✦ Return results to the user application

✦ Format errors in standard JDBC error codes

✦ Manage cursors if necessary

✦ Initiate transactions if it is explicitly required

Data Source

The data source consists of the data the user application wants to access and its parameters (in other words, the type of DBMS and network layer, if any, used to access the DBMS).

The JDBC API defines the possible interactions between the user application and the driver manager; the JDBC Driver API defines interactions among the driver manager and all JDBC drivers. Figure 28-2 shows the relationship among the four JDBC components.

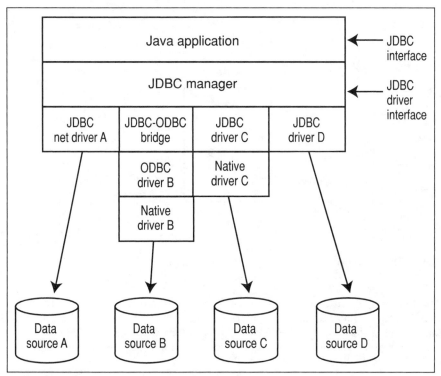

Figure 28-2: The complete JDBC architecture

Ready for client/server

The first generation of client/server architectures is *two-tiered*. It contains two active components: the client, which requests or sends data, and the server, which can be a DBMS. This type of system processes database queries and updates separately from those associated with user interface logic and presentation. In this respect, such a system differs from old-fashioned, mainframe-style user applications that handled gigabyte-long sequential files. Figure 28-3 depicts a typical client/server architecture.

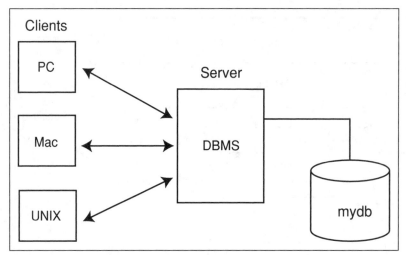

Figure 28-3: Typical client/server architecture with a DBMS

The two components usually run on different platforms, and in the Internet context, there may be numerous instances of client applications running at the same time. In the middle, the network serves as a transport mechanism for SQL messages containing database queries and rows of data resulting from these queries. This is illustrated in Figure 28-4.

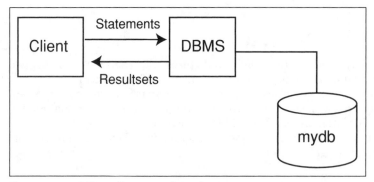

Figure 28-4: SQL messages and resultsets

JDBC conforms to the traditional client/server architecture. As we will see later, however, alternatives to the two-tiered client/server have emerged: three-tiered and multi-tiered. These approaches are basically an extension of the two-tiered client/server, so JDBC also has a place in such advanced architectures.

Data definition and manipulation using SQL

In contrast to the complete programming languages used to build complex applications, SQL is commonly used *within* a host language (which in turn offers the specific features for building complete applications). Nevertheless, SQL is an industry standard for database access. It enables data definition, manipulation and management, as well as access protection and transaction control.

SQL originated from the concept of relational databases; it handles many database objects for RDBMS purposes, including tables, indexes, keys, rows, and columns. First standardized by the American National Standards Institute (ANSI) in 1986, SQL was designed to be independent of any programming language or DBMS.

The ANSI 1989 standard defines three programmatic interfaces to SQL:

✦ **Modules:** These procedures may be defined within separate compiled modules and then called from a traditional programming language.

✦ **Embedded SQL:** This specification defines embedded statements for a few traditional programming languages. It allows static SQL statements to be embedded within complete programs.

✦ **Direct invocation:** Here access is *implementation-defined* — it can be different for every platform.

Although embedded SQL was quite popular a few years ago, it is not the best answer to the problem of querying databases in client/server environments. It is static in all senses of the term, and this limitation makes it unsuitable for newer software architectures.

The newer ANSI specification, SQL-92, addresses the needs of modern environments. It contains many new features, including support for dynamic SQL — as well as support for *scrollable cursors,* an advanced technique for accessing resultsets. Although dynamic SQL is not as efficient as static SQL, it does allow SQL statements to be prepared, to include parameters, and to be generated at runtime. (If you are using prepared statements, system performance may actually improve.) Dynamic SQL allows the database to prepare an access plan before execution, and to reuse the access plan each time the statement is called.

The SQL language may be used for various purposes, including these:

✦ Querying a database, as interactive language used by humans

✦ Querying a database within a program

✦ Defining data organization

✦ Administering data

✦ Accessing multiple data servers

✦ Managing transactions

The SQL language supports a set of verbs used to define, store, manipulate, and retrieve data. These keywords include CREATE TABLE, SELECT, INSERT, DELETE, UPDATE, and so on.

The following examples illustrate the most common actions you can perform with SQL:

✦ Creating a table:

```
CREATE TABLE employees
(
  id         int PRIMARY KEY,
  name       char(25) NOT NULL,
  address    char(25) NOT NULL,
  city       char(25) NOT NULL,
  zip        char(25) NOT NULL,
  dept       int,
  phone      char(12),
  salary     int
)
```

✦ Removing a table:

```
DROP TABLE employees
```

✦ Supplying new data:

```
INSERT INTO employees VALUES
(
  1,
  "John Doe",
  "10725 Java Drive",
  "Mountain View",
  "CA 94040",
  1,
  "415-960-1300",
  60000
)
```

✦ Removing rows of data:

```
DELETE FROM employees
WHERE dept = 0
```

✦ Retrieving data:

```
SELECT * FROM employees
WHERE dept = 1
ORDER BY salary DESC, name
```

✦ Modifying data:

```
UPDATE employees SET salary = 70000
WHERE name = "John Doe"
```

✦ Creating an index:

```
CREATE INDEX employees_idx
ON employees (name)
```

✦ Creating a stored procedure:

```
CREATE PROCEDURE getMaxSalary (@themax int OUT)
AS SELECT @themax = MAX(salary)
    FROM employees
```

 Tip SQL is a rich language. Various options and parameters are available for these keywords. You can (for example) nest statements for database queries, join tables, and define transactions.

JDBC drivers

As mentioned before, JDBC is independent of the various database management systems. Almost all of them use proprietary (non- or poorly documented) protocols to communicate with clients, so JDBC uses database drivers specific to these database engines.

Database vendors and third parties offer three types of JDBC drivers:

Native database drivers

These drivers process JDBC calls and send SQL statements to the data source. They may be *native-API/partly-Java* or *native-protocol/all-Java*. A native-API partly-Java driver forwards the calls to a locally installed library, usually developed in C and provided by the database vendor. It may be a DLL or a UNIX shared library, for example. Figure 28-5 shows the Java and non-Java sides of such a driver.

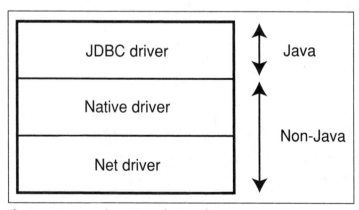

Figure 28-5: A native-API partly-Java driver

A native-protocol, all-Java driver implements in Java all the layers necessary to communicate with the database. These drivers are obviously fully portable, because they do not use local libraries or other native code. This type of driver is illustrated in Figure 28-6.

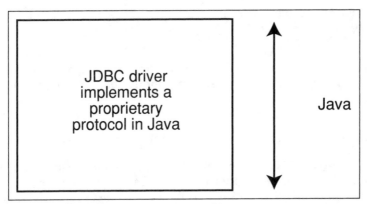

Figure 28-6: A native-protocol all-Java driver

Bridge drivers

A *bridge driver* acts as a bridge between JDBC and another CLI (Call-level Interface). For example, the JDBC-ODBC bridge is a bridge driver. It processes JDBC calls, and in its turn calls ODBC functions that send SQL statements to the ODBC data source. Figure 28-7 shows the Java and non-Java sides of such a driver.

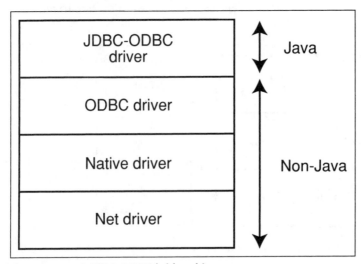

Figure 28-7: A JDBC-ODBC bridge driver

DBMS-independent, all-Java Net drivers

These drivers use a DBMS-independent, published network protocol. They are obviously very portable because they are 100-percent Java. Figure 28-8 depicts such a driver.

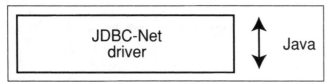

Figure 28-8: A Net driver

Overview of the API

The two major components of JDBC are the JDBC API and the JDBC Driver API. The JDBC API is a programming interface for database application developers; the JDBC Driver API is a lower-level programming interface for developers of specific drivers. We will focus on the JDBC API. Figure 28-9 clearly indicates the role of both APIs.

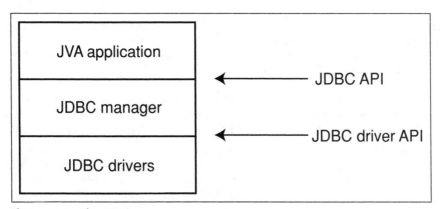

Figure 28-9: The APIs

Database application developers use these interfaces and classes:

✦ `java.sql.DriverManager`: This class provides methods to load drivers and to support the creation of database connections using methods expressed in the `java.sql.Driver` interface.

✦ `java.sql.Connection`: Represents a particular connection on which further action is performed.

✦ `java.sql.Statement`: Associated to a connection, this package is used to send SQL statements to the database.

✦ `java.sql.CallableStatement`: Same role, but in the context of database stored procedures.

✦ `java.sql.PreparedStatement`: Same role, but in the context of pre-compiled SQL.

✦ `java.sql.ResultSet`: Allows access to the resulting rows of a statement.

✦ `java.sql.ResultSetMetaData`: Gives information such as the column type and column properties of the resultset.

✦ `java.sql.DatabaseMetaData`: Provides information about the database as a whole.

Typical uses

You can use JDBC to connect Java to databases, send SQL statements from a Java client, and then retrieve the results, if any, off the database. This is true for standalone Java applications, as well as for Java applets running in Web browsers (if a 100-percent Java JDBC driver is used) and Java servlets running at the side of Web servers.

However, you need to consider a few things when running JDBC in a client applet. As long as an applet is unsigned, it is considered *untrusted*. There are some differences, however, between untrusted applets on the Internet (or on an intranet) and traditional standalone applications:

✦ Untrusted applets cannot access local files or open arbitrary network connections to remote hosts. In contrast, an application can access the local file system in accordance with the permissions that were granted to the user.

✦ Untrusted applets cannot rely on specific facilities provided by the underlying operating system—such as a local registry—to locate a database. Applications often rely on such facilities. For example, ODBC uses an INI file or the registry, and most proprietary APIs use specific property and configuration files.

✦ Response times of untrusted applets may be arbitrary when sporadic traffic peaks arise on the Internet; connections may be interrupted in the middle of a transaction because of network failure.

✦ Estimating the maximum number of simultaneous users of an untrusted applet is difficult in the Internet scenario.

Despite these differences, JDBC is still a good option for letting applets communicate with a database located on the Web server side. There are many situations in which you might want to use JDBC. To give you some examples, JDBC and 100-percent-Java JDBC drivers are easier to use than HTML solutions in the following cases:

✦ Lookups of online catalogs, using multiple search criteria, that return complex types such as text, images, compound documents, sounds, binary files, and so on.

✦ Any transactional Web application. JDBC allows you to group statements in one atomic transaction. This is mandatory when (for example) debit and credit have to happen at the same time on different tables.

✦ Replacement of any traditional database client software for a larger audience, on an intranet, an extranet, or the Internet using off-the-shelf Web browsers.

✦ Building decision-support tools that often rely on existing relationships among data entities, without any prior knowledge of these relationships.

✦ Simple, webtop-oriented administration tools for DBAs and DBOs (database administrators and database owners).

Connecting to a remote database

Java and your database can talk to each other, and they may as well start doing so. In this section, you will learn how to load a database driver, how to locate the database management system, and how to establish a connection to it.

A connection must be established to enable access to a database. Such a connection is a Java object, containing methods and data members that access the database and also hold and manage connection state. Various connection parameters are necessary to locate important elements of the database system—the database itself, specific drivers and protocols, user accounts and passwords in the DBMS, and so on. (You'll learn the format to use for such parameters later in this chapter.)

The first general step is to establish a connection. The last step will, of course, be to terminate (or *close*) the connection. Opening and closing the connection will create and release user resources within the driver manager, the driver, and the database management system.

Choosing an appropriate driver

Databases talk with clients by using various—but incompatible—protocols. As a result, for every specific database connection you establish, you have to provide an appropriate driver to JDBC to let it manage the connection. Methods that load a driver and handle driver properties are provided within the `DriverManager` and `Driver` objects. To tell JDBC what drivers are available, you provide the needed information through a `jdbc.drivers` system property. You can do so from the `java` interpreter command line or by means of a property file.

The following code shows how to use the command line for standalone programs and applets:

```
% java -Djdbc.drivers=foobar MyProgram
% java -Djdbc.drivers=foobar sun.applet.AppletViewer
  MyApplet.html
```

The following code shows how to use a file, which you might want to do when you use the Applet Viewer or the HotJava Web browser, for example:

```
# on unix, this is ~/.hotjava/properties
jdbc.drivers=vendor1.driver1
```

As explained later in the chapter, you can also specify the drivers programmatically.

Note The exact driver name is set by the driver manufacturer. Refer to your driver's documentation for more details about its package name and class name.

Tip Although the database URL specifies a specific database and protocol to be used, it may sometimes be useful to let the JDBC choose among two or more drivers — especially when you're using multiple databases. If you want to do so, just specify a list of drivers in the `jdbc.drivers` property, separating the driver class names with colons:

```
'vendor1.dbdrv:vendor2.sql.foodriver:vendor3.db.connectdrv'
```

JDBC will then try to use each of the drivers listed in `jdbc.drivers` until it finds one that can successfully connect to the given URL. Drivers that are considered untrusted code are skipped. The driver will register itself with the driver manager to allow connections to be established.

In case the `jdbc.drivers` system property is unavailable, you might want to use a programmatic technique to force a particular driver to be loaded. For example, the following line of Java code loads a JDBC-ODBC bridge driver:

```
Class.forName("sun.jdbc.odbc.JdbcOdbcDriver");
```

Another method is to use the following statements:

```
java.sql.Driver myDriver = new sun.jdbc.odbc.JdbcOdbcDriver();
java.sql.DriverManager.registerDriver(myDriver);
```

These statements explicitly instantiate the `JdbcOdbcDriver` class and register it with the driver manager.

Locating the database

JDBC uses a particular syntax for naming a database. The JDBC designers wanted to adopt a syntax widely used in the Internet context: the URL (Universal Resource Locator) syntax. The URL for JDBC data sources has this form:

```
jdbc:<subprotocol>:<subname>
```

In this syntax, `jdbc` indicates that the protocol is JDBC, the subprotocol field is the name of the JDBC driver to be used, and the subname is a parameter string that depends on the subprotocol. This mechanism is depicted in Figure 28-10.

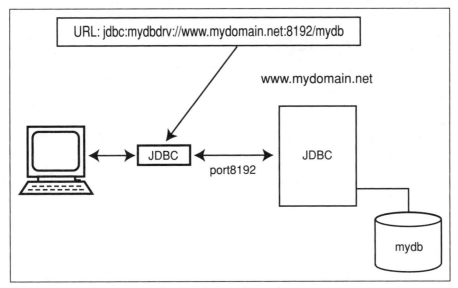

Figure 28-10: The JDBC mechanism for naming a data source

These two examples show you how you can use database URLs:

```
jdbc:odbc:sampledb;UID=javauser;PWD=hotjava
```

In this example, a JDBC-ODBC bridge is used, and the ODBC DSN (data source name) is `sampledb`. The database user name is `javauser`, and the password is `hotjava`.

```
jdbc:mydbdrv://www.mydomain.net:8192/mydb
```

In this case, the subprotocol is called `mydbdrv`, the database engine is running on the `www.mydomain.net` host (the subname field), the TCP/IP port used is 8192, and `mydb` is the name of the database to be accessed. The meaning of these parameters is somewhat arbitrary: For example, if the subprotocol (the driver) always uses the same port number, you don't have to provide it in the URL. You could also interpret `mydb`, which is a "subsubname," as anything else as well.

The ODBC subprotocol URL should always conform to this syntax:

```
jdbc:odbc:<dsn>[;<attribute-name>=<attribute-value>]*
```

As you can see, the JDBC URL syntax is flexible enough to allow specific drivers to interpret their own syntax.

Creating a connection

This URL string is used to create connections to the database. For this purpose, the `getConnection()` method on the driver manager is used to request a `Connection` object:

```
...
Connection connection;
String url = "jdbc:odbc:datasource";
Class.forName("sun.jdbc.odbc.JdbcOdbcDriver");
Connection = DriverManager.getConnection(url, "javauser",
"hotjava");
...
```

This example shows how to pass the URL string to the driver manager and specific parameters to the driver itself. Here is some further explanation of the code:

- ✦ The protocol is JDBC.
- ✦ The driver is a JDBC-ODBC bridge.
- ✦ The ODBC DSN (data source name) is `mysource`.
- ✦ A username is provided: `javauser`.
- ✦ A password is provided: `hotjava`.

The driver manager will try to find a registered JDBC driver that is allowed to reach the data source specified in the URL. Note that there are other methods that allow you to make a connection to the database. They have the same name, but they accept different parameters:

```
Connection getConnection(String url);
Connection getConnection(String url, String user, String
   password);
Connection getConnection(String url, java.util.Properties
info);
```

A connection will not last forever, so there is a method to terminate it: close().
This method releases driver and database resources of the connection. Listing 28-1
illustrates how to open and close a connection to a database using a JDBC-ODBC
bridge.

Listing 28-1: Opening and Closing a Connection

```java
// opening and closing a connection

import java.sql.*;

class SimpleExample
{
    public static void main(String args[])
    {
        String url = "jdbc:odbc:mysource";

        try {
            Class.forName("sun.jdbc.odbc.JdbcOdbcDriver");
            Connection connection =
                DriverManager.getConnection(url,
                "javauser", "hotjava");

            // ...
            connection.close();
        } catch (Exception ex) {
            System.out.println("A problem occurred during the
                establishment of the connection: " + ex);
        }
    }
}
```

In case of problems during the creation of the Connection object, the
getConnection() method throws a java.sql.SQLException. You should catch
such exceptions and write appropriate code to handle them, at least to warn the
user that there was a problem.

Performing database queries and updates

You are now ready to surf your database management system and perform queries
and updates from Java. This section teaches you these techniques through
comprehensive examples.

Database queries and updates

You use the Connection object to send SQL statements to the database engine. You can use different methods for doing this depending on the kind of operation needed. In this chapter, we will focus on sending normal SQL statements. Unlike prepared statements or calls to stored procedures, (discussed later), normal SQL statements are usually built, sent, and executed only once. This is the case, for example, within an interactive query tool where the user is allowed to build his or her own queries on the fly. Normal statements include both statements to query data from the database and statements to update the data.

Immediately after creating the connection, you have to create a SQL statement. This is not to say that you can't build a SQL query string before opening the connection. You are free to do so. A JDBC statement is an object associated with a connection, and it is used later to execute the SQL statement string within this connection environment on the DBMS.

This is the method used to create a Statement object:

```
Statement createStatement();
```

You obtain the Statement object by invoking this method on the Connection instance, as shown in the following example:

```
...
Connection connection = DriverManager.getConnection(url,
    "javauser", "hotjava");

Statement statement = connection.createStatement();

myConnection.close();
...
```

The SQL statement will finally be sent to the DBMS, where it is parsed, optimized, and then executed. But we have not built the statement text yet. Indeed, the SQL string is passed to the database at the time the call for execution of the statement is issued. Figure 28-11 illustrates this mechanism.

This SQL string may be converted into the DBMS native SQL grammar by the driver. It is possible to see the converted string without sending it to the database. You will normally not use this facility, but in some cases you might want to know what the native translation of a query is prior to sending it.

This method requires the Connection object because it is DBMS-dependent. Indeed, a connection is associated to one and only one DBMS through its driver:

```
String nativeSQL(String sql);
```

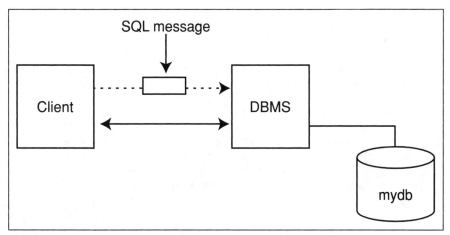

Figure 28-11: Sending an SQL statement

The string passed as an argument is the "user" SQL statement; `nativeSQL()` returns the native form of this statement.

Opening a connection and creating a statement are necessary before executing a query. They are required in all your JDBC-based applications.

SQL statements that return an integer, such as `DELETE`, `UPDATE`, and `INSERT`, do not need additional processing. The method to send them returns the integer, which usually is interpreted as a counter. Other SQL statements do not return rows of data or a counter.

This is not the case with queries that return normal rows of data; the resultset is composed of zero, one, or multiple rows coming from the database. Consequently, the next step is to scan this resultset, row by row, until all the rows of data have been fetched. You perform this operation within a loop. We will see later how to analyze the data that composes rows.

You create the `ResultSet` object when you send the statement to the DBMS. You do so by executing the `Statement` object. Closing the resultset releases all data associated with it.

You can use different methods to send a SQL statement to the database. They vary depending on the type of statement and the type of data they return. They apply to the newly created `Statement` object:

```
ResultSet executeQuery(String sql);
```

If the query returns normal rows of data, then you should use the `executeQuery()` method. In this case, the query is typically a static SQL `SELECT` statement. The SQL text is simply passed as a `String` argument.

Note

The text does not have to be translated to the native form, which otherwise you could do by using `nativeSQL()`.

This method returns a `ResultSet` object, which is discussed in the next section of this chapter, "Retrieving the results."

```
int executeUpdate(String sql);
```

In case the SQL statement returns nothing (returning nothing is different than returning 0 rows) or an integer value, as it is the case with SQL `INSERT`, `UPDATE`, or `DELETE` clauses, you should use the `executeUpdate` method. The call returns the integer value or 0 for statements that return nothing:

```
boolean execute(String sql);
```

When a SQL statement returns more than one result, you have to use `execute()` to request execution of the statement, as shown in Listing 28-2.

Listing 28-2: **Querying the Database**

```
// querying the database

import java.sql.*;

class SimpleExample
{
    public static void main(String args[])
{
    String url = "jdbc:odbc:mysource";

    try {
        Class.forName("sun.jdbc.odbc.JdbcOdbcDriver");
        Connection connection =
            DriverManager.getConnection(url,
            "javauser", "hotjava");

        String sql = "SELECT * FROM employees";
        System.out.println("native form: " +
            connection.nativeSQL(sql));

        Statement statement = connection.createStatement();

        ResultSet rs = statement.executeQuery(sql);

        connection.close();
        } catch (Exception ex) {
```

```
            System.out.println("A problem occurred: " + ex);
        }
    }
}
```

Retrieving the results

Resultsets are composed of rows of data. You use the `resultSet.next()` method in a loop to access and retrieve all these rows, row by row. Figure 28-12 illustrates the mechanism used to scan the rows contained in the resultset.

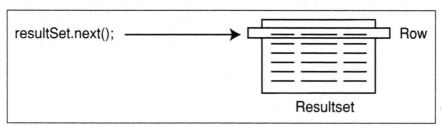

Figure 28-12: The `next()` method used to scan a resultset

Note that a resultset is initially positioned before its first row. You need to call the method first to access the first row. After the first call, the first row becomes the current row, and it is ready to be processed. Successive calls to `next()` will make the subsequent rows current, row by row. The method returns false when there are no more rows available in the resultset.

Getting the number and label of columns

A row is usually composed of table data that may be organized in columns of different types. You may want to obtain the properties of the resultset's rows — their number, type, and so on — at runtime. You can use the metadata methods on resultsets to obtain column and type information for your dataset. Only the column number and column labels are in the following examples.

The `getMetaData()` method returns a `ResultSetMetaData` object, which you can use to call `getColumnCount()`:

```
int getMetaData().getColumnCount();
```

The return type is integer. It is the number of columns contained in the rows composing this resultset:

```
String getMetaData().getColumnLabel(int i);
```

The parameter is the column index, where a value of 1 indicates the first column. The method obviously returns the label for the column at this index. Needless to say, the index range is 1 to getColumnCount().

Note It may be more efficient to store the ResultSetMetaData object once instead of calling the getMetaData() method to create it each time you need to access a property. The driver may provide caching, but it is a good idea not to use features such as caching unless they're really necessary. Because the JDBC allows you to access a wide variety of data sources, it's a good idea not to rely on any inherent driver behavior if you expect your applications to be portable.

Accessing columns

Columns must be fetched until there are no more to be fetched. You can do so in a loop using the column indexes or column names that you obtained with the ResultSetMetaData object. This is illustrated in Figure 28-13.

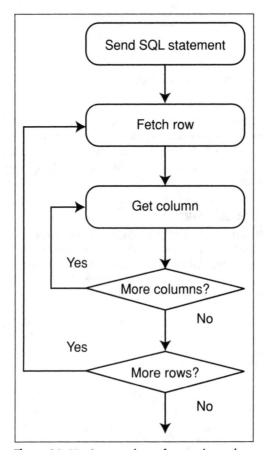

Figure 28-13: An overview of accessing columns

The rows' contents are accessible via getXXX() methods that allow extraction of values from the columns of rows contained in the resultset.

You can access columns in two ways: by column index or by column name. Accessing a column by name is more convenient, but certainly less efficient. Certain SQL statements return tables without column names or with multiple identical column names. It is absolutely necessary to use column numbers in these cases. Figure 28-14 shows how to access the columns of a resultset.

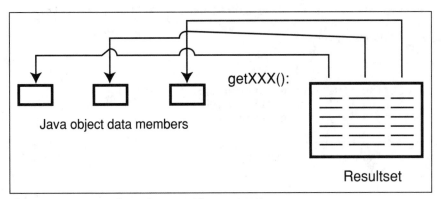

Figure 28-14: Accessing columns with getXXX()

All the columns within a row must be read in left-to-right order, and each column must be read only once. This rule may not be true with some DBMSs, but observing it ensures maximum portability.

Accessing columns by column indexes

These are the getXXX() methods available to fetch columns in a row:

```
String getString(int columnIndex);
boolean getBoolean(int columnIndex);
byte getByte(int columnIndex);
short getShort(int columnIndex);
int getInt(int columnIndex);
long getLong(int columnIndex);
float getFloat(int columnIndex);
double getDouble(int columnIndex);
java.math.BigDecimal getBigDecimal(int columnIndex, int scale);
byte[] getBytes(int columnIndex);
java.sql.Date getDate(int columnIndex);
java.sql.Time getTime(int columnIndex);
java.sql.Timestamp getTimestamp(int columnIndex);
java.io.InputStream getAsciiStream(int columnIndex);
java.io.InputStream getUnicodeStream(int columnIndex);
java.io.InputStream getBinaryStream(int columnIndex);
Object getObject(int columnIndex);
```

All these methods return the column value of the current row. Column indexes are integers.

The following code snippet shows how to execute a SQL statement and retrieve the results using column indexes. The rows are always read from left to right; columns are only read once:

```
...
java.sql.Statement statement = connection.createStatement();

ResultSet rs = statement.executeQuery("SELECT name, title,
salary
    FROM employees");

while (rs.next()) {
    // print the columns of the row that was retrieved
    String name = rs.getString(1);
    String title = rs.getString(2);
    long salary = rs.getLong(3);

    System.out.println("Employee " + name + " is " + title + "
        and earns $" + salary);
}
...
```

Accessing columns by column names

Column names may be more convenient to use as a means of access; the following getXXX() methods support column names:

```
String getString(String columnName);
boolean getBoolean(String columnName);
byte getByte(String columnName);
short getShort(String columnName);
int getInt(String columnName);
long getLong(String columnName);
float getFloat(String columnName);
double getDouble(String columnName);
java.math.BigDecimal getBigDecimal(String columnName, int
scale);
byte[] getBytes(String columnName);
java.sql.Date getDate(String columnName);
java.sql.Time getTime(String columnName);
java.sql.Timestamp getTimestamp(String columnName);
java.io.InputStream getAsciiStream(String columnName);
java.io.InputStream getUnicodeStream(String columnName);
java.io.InputStream getBinaryStream(String columnName);
Object getObject(String columnName);
```

The parameter you use should match exactly the column name of the row that you want to access.

The following code shows the same example as before, this time using column names:

```
...
java.sql.Statement statement = connection.createStatement();

ResultSet rs = statement.executeQuery("SELECT name, title,
salary
    FROM employees");

while (rs.next()) {
    // print the columns of the row that was retrieved
    String name = rs.getString("name");
    String title = rs.getString("title");
    long salary = rs.getLong("salary");

    System.out.println("Employee " + name + " is " + title + "
and
        earns $" + salary);
}
...
```

Putting the JDBC to Work

Listing 28-3 illustrates the previous techniques we learned for sending and executing database queries as well as for retrieving the results. It is as Interactive SQL program written using the JDBC; it allows SQL statements to be sent interactively using the keyboard. The program parses the keyboard input and sends the statements to the database if the input is not a keyword such as go or exit. The results are then displayed on the screen. Note how we handled statements that return multiple resultsets and/or update counts.

Listing 28-3: **The Interactive SQL Application**

```
import java.sql.*;
import java.io.*;
import java.util.*;

public class isql {

    static DataInputStream kbd = new
        DataInputStream(System.in);

    static String url = "jdbc:odbc:netbank";
    static String driver = "sun.jdbc.odbc.JdbcOdbcDriver";
    static String login = "dba";
    static String passwd = "javabank";
```

(continued)

Listing 28-3 *(continued)*

```java
static Connection curConn = null;

public static void main(String argv[]) throws IOException
{
    String temp = "";

    System.out.println("Simple Java Isql.\n");
    System.out.print("Enter the url or [ENTER] for " + url +
        " : ");
    System.out.flush();
    temp = kbd.readLine();
    if (!temp.equals("")) url = temp;
    System.out.print("Enter the login or [ENTER] for " +
        login + " : ");
    System.out.flush();
    temp = kbd.readLine();
    if (!temp.equals("")) login = temp;
    System.out.print("Enter the passwd or [ENTER] for
        default: ");
    System.out.flush();
    temp = kbd.readLine();
    if (!temp.equals("")) passwd = temp;

    isql session = new isql();
}

public isql() throws IOException
{
    try {
        Class.forName(driver);
        curConn = DriverManager.getConnection(url, login,
            passwd);
        checkForWarnings(curConn.getWarnings ());
    }
    catch(java.lang.Exception ex) {
        System.out.println("url     : " + url);
        System.out.println("login   : " + login);
        System.out.println("passwd : " + passwd);
        ex.printStackTrace();
        return;
    }
    processQueries();
    finalize();
}

protected void finalize()
{
    try {
```

```
            curConn.close();
        }
    catch (SQLException ex) { }
}

private void processQueries() throws IOException
{
    int i = 1;
    String temp = "";
    String query = "";
    String results = "";

    System.out.println("Type 'quit' on a blank line to
        exit, or 'go' to execute the query.");
    do {
        System.out.print(i + "> ");
        System.out.flush();
        temp = kbd.readLine();
        if (temp.equals("quit"))
            break;
        if (temp.equals("go")) {
            executeThisQuery(query);
            i = 1;
            query = "";
        }
        else {
            query = query + " " + temp;
            i++;
        }
    } while (true);
}

private void executeThisQuery(String sqlText)
{
    boolean resultSetIsAvailable;
    boolean moreResultsAvailable;
    int i = 0;
    int res=0;
    try {
        Statement curStmt = curConn.createStatement();
        resultSetIsAvailable = curStmt.execute(sqlText);
        ResultSet rs = null;
         for (moreResultsAvailable = true;
            moreResultsAvailable;  )
        {
            checkForWarnings(curConn.getWarnings());
             if (resultSetIsAvailable)
            {
                if ((rs = curStmt.getResultSet()) != null)
```

(continued)

Listing 28-3 *(continued)*

```java
            {
                // we have a resultset
                checkForWarnings(
                    curStmt.getWarnings());
                ResultSetMetaData rsmd =
                    rs.getMetaData();
                int numCols = rsmd.getColumnCount();

                // display column headers
                for (i = 1; i <= numCols; i++)
                {
                    if (i > 1) System.out.print(", ");
                    System.out.print
                        (rsmd.getColumnLabel(i));
                }
                System.out.println("");

                // step through the rows
                while (rs.next())
                {
                    // process the columns
                    for (i = 1; i <= numCols; i++)
                    {
                        if (i > 1)
                            System.out.print(", ");
                        System.out.print
                          (rs.getString(i));
                    }
                    System.out.println("");
                }
            }
        else
        {
            if ((res = curStmt.getUpdateCount())
                != -1)
            {
                // we have an updatecount
                System.out.println(res + " row(s)
                    affected.");
            }
            // else no more results
            else
            {
                moreResultsAvailable = false;
            }
        }
    if (moreResultsAvailable)
```

```
                {
                    resultSetIsAvailable =
                        curStmt.getMoreResults();
                }
            }
            if (rs != null) rs.close();
            curStmt.close();
        }
        catch (SQLException ex) {

            // Unexpected SQL exception.
            ex.printStackTrace ();
        }
        catch (java.lang.Exception ex) {

            // Got some other type of exception.  Dump it.
            ex.printStackTrace ();
        }
    }

    private static void checkForWarnings (SQLWarning warn)
        throws SQLException
    {
        while (warn != null) {
            System.out.println(warn);
            warn = warn.getNextWarning();
        }
    }
}
```

The JDBC API

This is a reference to the JDBC interfaces and classes. All these interfaces and classes are available in the `java.sql` package, which has been part of the JDK since JDK 1.1: They are the "application" side API of JDBC. The "driver" side API is not covered here because it is only useful for writers of JDBC drivers. Note that the `java.sql.DatabaseMetaData` interface is not covered here.

Interface java.sql.CallableStatement

```
public interface CallableStatement
extends Object
extends PreparedStatement

Methods:
public abstract BigDecimal getBigDecimal(int parameterIndex,
    int scale) throws SQLException
```

```
public abstract boolean getBoolean(int parameterIndex) throws
    SQLException
public abstract byte getByte(int parameterIndex) throws
    SQLException
public abstract byte[] getBytes(int parameterIndex) throws
    SQLException
public abstract Date getDate(int parameterIndex) throws
    SQLException
public abstract double getDouble(int parameterIndex) throws
    SQLException
public abstract float getFloat(int parameterIndex) throws
    SQLException
public abstract int getInt(int parameterIndex) throws
    SQLException
public abstract long getLong(int parameterIndex) throws
    SQLException
public abstract Object getObject(int parameterIndex) throws
    SQLException
public abstract short getShort(int parameterIndex) throws
    SQLException
public abstract String getString(int parameterIndex) throws
    SQLException
public abstract Time getTime(int parameterIndex)  throws
    SQLException
public abstract Timestamp getTimestamp(int parameterIndex)
    throws SQLException
public abstract void registerOutParameter(int parameterIndex,
    int sqlType) throws SQLException
public abstract void registerOutParameter(int parameterIndex,
    int sqlType, int scale) throws SQLException
public abstract boolean wasNull() throws SQLException
```

Interface java.sql.Connection

```
public interface Connection
extends Object
```

Variables:

```
public final static int TRANSACTION_NONE
public final static int TRANSACTION_READ_COMMITTED
public final static int TRANSACTION_READ_UNCOMMITTED
public final static int TRANSACTION_REPEATABLE_READ
public final static int TRANSACTION_SERIALIZABLE
```

Methods:

```
public abstract void clearWarnings() throws SQLException
public abstract void close() throws SQLException
public abstract void commit() throws SQLException
public abstract Statement createStatement()throws SQLException
```

```
public abstract boolean getAutoClose() throws SQLException
public abstract boolean getAutoCommit() throws SQLException
public abstract String getCatalog() throws SQLException
public abstract DatabaseMetaData getMetaData() throws
    SQLException
public abstract int getTransactionIsolation()  throws
    SQLException
public abstract SQLWarning getWarnings() throws SQLException
public abstract boolean isClosed() throws SQLException
public abstract boolean isReadOnly() throws SQLException
public abstract String nativeSQL(String sql) throws
    SQLException
public abstract CallableStatement prepareCall(String sql)
    throws SQLException
public abstract PreparedStatement prepareStatement(String sql)
    throws SQLException
public abstract void rollback() throws SQLException
public abstract void setAutoClose(boolean autoClose) throws
    SQLException
public abstract void setAutoCommit(boolean autoCommit) throws
    SQLException
public abstract void setCatalog(String catalog) throws
    SQLException
public abstract void setReadOnly(boolean readOnly) throws
    SQLException
public abstract void setTransactionIsolation(int level) throws
    SQLException
```

Interface java.sql.Driver

```
public interface Driver
extends Object
```

Methods:

```
public abstract boolean acceptsURL(String url)  throws
    SQLException
public abstract Connection connect(String url, Properties
    info) throws SQLException
public abstract int getMajorVersion()
public abstract int getMinorVersion()
public abstract DriverPropertyInfo[] getPropertyInfo(String
    url, Properties info) throws SQLException
public abstract boolean jdbcCompliant()
```

Interface java.sql.PreparedStatement

```
public interface PreparedStatement
extends Object
extends Statement
```

Methods:

```
public abstract void clearParameters() throws SQLException
public abstract boolean execute() throws SQLException
public abstract ResultSet executeQuery() throws SQLException
public abstract int executeUpdate() throws SQLException
public abstract void setAsciiStream(int parameterIndex,
    InputStream x, int length) throws SQLException
public abstract void setBigDecimal(int parameterIndex,
    BigDecimal x) throws SQLException
public abstract void setBinaryStream(int parameterIndex,
    InputStream x, int length) throws SQLException
public abstract void setBoolean(int parameterIndex, boolean x)
    throws SQLException
public abstract void setByte(int parameterIndex, byte x)
    throws SQLException
public abstract void setBytes(int parameterIndex, byte x[])
    throws SQLException
public abstract void setDate(int parameterIndex, Date x)
    throws SQLException
public abstract void setDouble(int parameterIndex, double x)
    throws SQLException
public abstract void setFloat(int parameterIndex, float x)
    throws SQLException
public abstract void setInt(int parameterIndex, int x) throws
    SQLException
public abstract void setLong(int parameterIndex, long x)
    throws SQLException
public abstract void setNull(int parameterIndex, int sqlType)
    throws SQLException
public abstract void setObject(int parameterIndex, Object x,
    int targetSqlType, int scale) throws SQLException
public abstract void setObject(int parameterIndex, Object x,
    int targetSqlType) throws SQLException
public abstract void setObject(int parameterIndex, Object x)
    throws SQLException
public abstract void setShort(int parameterIndex, short x)
    throws SQLException
public abstract void setString(int parameterIndex, String x)
    throws SQLException
public abstract void setTime(int parameterIndex, Time x)
    throws SQLException
public abstract void setTimestamp(int parameterIndex,
    Timestamp x) throws SQLException
public abstract void setUnicodeStream(int parameterIndex,
    InputStream x, int length) throws SQLException
```

Interface java.sql.ResultSet

```
public interface ResultSet
extends Object
```

Methods:

```
public abstract void clearWarnings() throws SQLException
public abstract void close() throws SQLException
public abstract int findColumn(String columnName) throws
    SQLException
public abstract InputStream getAsciiStream(int columnIndex)
   throws SQLException
public abstract InputStream getAsciiStream(String columnName)
    throws SQLException
public abstract BigDecimal getBigDecimal(int columnIndex, int
    scale) throws SQLException
public abstract BigDecimal getBigDecimal(String columnName,
    int scale) throws SQLException
public abstract InputStream getBinaryStream(int columnIndex)
    throws SQLException
public abstract InputStream getBinaryStream(String columnName)
    throws SQLException
public abstract boolean getBoolean(int columnIndex) throws
    SQLException
public abstract boolean getBoolean(String columnName) throws
    SQLException
public abstract byte getByte(int columnIndex) throws
    SQLException
public abstract byte getByte(String columnName) throws
    SQLException
public abstract byte[] getBytes(int columnIndex) throws
    SQLException
public abstract byte[] getBytes(String columnName) throws
    SQLException
public abstract String getCursorName() throws SQLException
public abstract Date getDate(int columnIndex) throws
    SQLException
public abstract Date getDate(String columnName)  throws
    SQLException
public abstract double getDouble(int columnIndex) throws
    SQLException
public abstract double getDouble(String columnName) throws
    SQLException
public abstract float getFloat(int columnIndex) throws
    SQLException
public abstract float getFloat(String columnName) throws
    SQLException
public abstract int getInt(int columnIndex) throws
    SQLException
public abstract int getInt(String columnName) throws
    SQLException
public abstract long getLong(int columnIndex) throws
    SQLException
public abstract long getLong(String columnName) throws
    SQLException
public abstract short getShort(int columnIndex) throws
    SQLException
```

```
public abstract short getShort(String columnName) throws
    SQLException
public abstract String getString(int columnIndex) throws
    SQLException
public abstract String getString(String columnName) throws
    SQLException
public abstract Time getTime(int columnIndex) throws
    SQLException
public abstract Time getTime(String columnName)  throws
    SQLException
public abstract Timestamp getTimestamp(int columnIndex) throws
    SQLException
public abstract Timestamp getTimestamp(String columnName)
    throws SQLException
public abstract InputStream getUnicodeStream(int columnIndex)
    throws SQLException
public abstract InputStream getUnicodeStream(String
    columnName) throws SQLException
public abstract ResultSetMetaData getMetaData() throws
    SQLException
public abstract Object getObject(int columnIndex) throws
    SQLException
public abstract Object getObject(String columnName) throws
    SQLException
public abstract SQLWarning getWarnings() throws SQLException
public abstract boolean next() throws SQLException
public abstract boolean wasNull() throws SQLException
```

Interface java.sql.ResultSetMetaData

```
public interface ResultSetMetaData
extends Object
```

Variables:

```
public final static int columnNoNulls
public final static int columnNullable
public final static int columnNullableUnknown
```

Methods:

```
public abstract String getCatalogName(int column) throws
    SQLException
public abstract int getColumnCount() throws SQLException
public abstract int getColumnDisplaySize(int column) throws
    SQLException
public abstract String getColumnLabel(int column) throws
    SQLException
public abstract String getColumnName(int column) throws
    SQLException
public abstract int getColumnType(int column) throws
    SQLException
```

```
public abstract String getColumnTypeName(int column) throws
   SQLException
public abstract int getPrecision(int column)  throws
   SQLException
public abstract int getScale(int column)  throws SQLException
public abstract String getSchemaName(int column) throws
   SQLException
public abstract String getTableName(int column) throws
   SQLException
public abstract boolean isAutoIncrement(int column) throws
   SQLException
public abstract boolean isCaseSensitive(int column) throws
   SQLException
public abstract boolean isCurrency(int column) throws
   SQLException
public abstract boolean isDefinitelyWritable(int column)
   throws SQLException
public abstract int isNullable(int column)  throws
   SQLException
public abstract boolean isReadOnly(int column) throws
   SQLException
public abstract boolean isSearchable(int column) throws
   SQLException
public abstract boolean isSigned(int column)  throws
   SQLException
public abstract boolean isWritable(int column) throws
   SQLException
```

Interface java.sql.Statement

```
public interface Statement
extends Object
```

Methods:

```
public abstract void cancel() throws SQLException
public abstract void clearWarnings() throws SQLException
public abstract void close() throws SQLException
public abstract boolean execute(String sql)  throws
   SQLException
public abstract ResultSet executeQuery(String sql) throws
   SQLException
public abstract int executeUpdate(String sql) throws
   SQLException
public abstract ResultSet getResultSet() throws SQLException
public abstract int getUpdateCount() throws SQLException
public abstract int getMaxFieldSize() throws SQLException
public abstract int getMaxRows() throws SQLException
public abstract boolean getMoreResults() throws SQLException
public abstract int getQueryTimeout() throws SQLException
public abstract SQLWarning getWarnings() throws SQLException
public abstract void setCursorName(String name) throws
```

```
            SQLException
public abstract void setEscapeProcessing(boolean enable)
    throws SQLException
public abstract void setMaxFieldSize(int max) throws
    SQLException
public abstract void setMaxRows(int max) throws SQLException
public abstract void setQueryTimeout(int seconds) throws
    SQLException
```

Class java.sql.Date

```
java.lang.Object
    |
    +----java.util.Date
            |
            +----java.sql.Date

public class Date
extends Date
```

Constructors:

```
public Date(int year, int month, int day)
public Date(long date)
```

Methods:

```
public String toString()
public static Date valueOf(String s)
```

Class java.sql.DriverManager

```
java.lang.Object
    |
    +----java.sql.DriverManager

public class DriverManager
extends Object
```

Methods:

```
public static void deregisterDriver(Driver driver) throws
    SQLException
public static synchronized Connection getConnection(String
    url, Properties info) throws SQLException
public static synchronized Connection getConnection(String
    url, String user, String password) throws SQLException
public static synchronized Connection getConnection(String
    url) throws SQLException
```

```
public static Driver getDriver(String url) throws SQLException
public static Enumeration getDrivers()
public static int getLoginTimeout()
public static PrintStream getLogStream()
public static void println(Stringmessage)
public static synchronized void registerDriver(Driverdriver)
    throws SQLException
public static void setLoginTimeout(int seconds)
public static void setLogStream(PrintStreamout)
```

Class java.sql.DriverPropertyInfo

```
java.lang.Object
    |
    +----java.sql.DriverPropertyInfo

public class DriverPropertyInfo
extends Object
```

Variables:

```
public String choices[]
public String description
public String name
public boolean required
public String value
```

Constructors:

```
public DriverPropertyInfo(String name, String value)
```

Class java.sql.Time

```
java.lang.Object
    |
    +----java.util.Date
             |
             +----java.sql.Time

public class Time
extends Date
```

Constructors:

```
public Time(int hour, int minute, int second)
public Time(long time)
```

Methods:

```
public String toString()
public static Time valueOf(String s)
```

Class java.sql.Timestamp

```
java.lang.Object
    |
    +----java.util.Date
              |
              +----java.sql.Timestamp
```

```
public class Timestamp
extends Date
```

Constructors:

```
public Timestamp(int year, int month, int date, int hour, int
    minute, int second, int nano)
public Timestamp(long time)
```

Methods:

```
public boolean equals(Timestamp ts)
public int getNanos()
public void setNanos(int n)
public String toString()
public static Timestamp valueOf(String s)
```

Class java.sql.Types

```
java.lang.Object
    |
    +----java.sql.Types
```

```
public class Types
extends Object
```

Variables:

```
public final static int BIGINT = -5
public final static int BINARY = -2
public final static int BIT = -7
public final static int CHAR = 1
public final static int DATE = 91
public final static int DECIMAL = 3
public final static int DOUBLE = 8
public final static int FLOAT = 6
public final static int INTEGER = 4
public final static int LONGVARCHAR = -4
```

```
public final static int LONGVARBINARY = -1
public final static int NULL = 0
public final static int NUMERIC = 2
public final static int OTHER
public final static int REAL = 7
public final static int SMALLINT = 5
public final static int TIME = 92
public final static int TIMESTAMP = 93
public final static int TINYINT = -6
public final static int VARBINARY = -3
public final static int VARCHAR = 12
```

Class java.sql.DataTruncation

```
java.lang.Object
    |
    +----java.lang.Throwable
            |
            +----java.lang.Exception
                    |
                    +----java.sql.SQLException
                            |
                            +----java.sql.SQLWarning
                                    |
                                    +----java.sql.DataTruncation

public class DataTruncation
extends SQLWarning
```

Constructors:

```
public DataTruncation(int index, boolean parameter, boolean
read,
    int dataSize, int transferSize)
```

Methods:

```
public int getDataSize()
public int getIndex()
public boolean getParameter()
public boolean getRead()
public int getTransferSize()
```

Class java.sql.SQLException

```
java.lang.Object
    |
    +----java.lang.Throwable
            |
            +----java.lang.Exception
                    |
```

```
                        +----java.sql.SQLException
```

```
public class SQLException
extends Exception
```

Constructors:

```
public SQLException(String reason, String SQLState, int
    vendorCode)
public SQLException(String reason, String SQLState)
public SQLException(String reason)
public SQLException()
```

Methods:

```
public int getErrorCode()
public SQLException getNextException()
public String getSQLState()
public synchronized void setNextException(SQLException ex)
```

Class java.sql.SQLWarning

```
java.lang.Object
    |
    +----java.lang.Throwable
            |
            +----java.lang.Exception
                    |
                    +----java.sql.SQLException
                            |
                            +----java.sql.SQLWarning
```

```
public class SQLWarning
extends SQLException
```

Constructors:

```
public SQLWarning(String reason, String SQLstate, int
    vendorCode)
public SQLWarning(String reason, String SQLstate)
public SQLWarning(String reason)
public SQLWarning()
```

Methods:

```
public SQLWarning getNextWarning()
public void setNextWarning(SQLWarning w)
```

Advanced Techniques

JDBC also has some nice features that allow developers to program enterprise-class applets and applications. This section focuses on prepared statements, stored procedures, database transactions, and three-tier software design.

Database prepared statements

A *prepared statement* is a SQL statement sent to the database prior to its execution. Unlike stored procedures, prepared statements do not remain in the database after the resources associated with them are freed. They may be called a number of times with different parameter values. Figures 28-15 and 28-16 illustrate some differences between the execution of simple SQL statements and the execution of prepared statements.

In the first case, the SQL text is sent to the database along with specific values and literals. Figure 28-15 illustrates an INSERT.

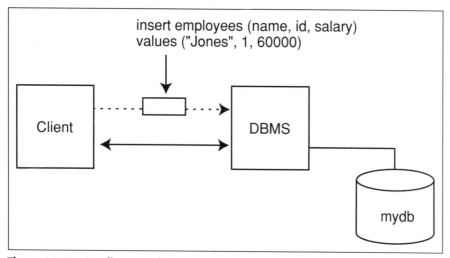

insert employees (name, id, salary)
values ("Jones", 1, 60000)

Client

DBMS

mydb

Figure 28-15: Sending a static statement

When executing a prepared statement, the SQL statement is already at the database side. It has been sent there using a specific mechanism. Only parameter values are passed; the call may be issued many times with different parameter values. Depending on the DBMS, the SQL statement may or may not have been optimized and precompiled at the database side, shown in Figure 28-16.

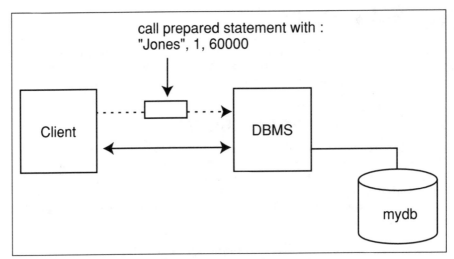

Figure 28-16: Sending parameters to a prepared statement

To summarize this procedure, you must follow these steps to use prepared statements with JDBC:

1. Prepare the SQL statement.

2. Set IN parameters.

3. Execute the statement.

4. Get the results, if any.

5. If necessary, set new IN parameter values and re-execute this statement:

```
PreparedStatement prepareStatement(String sql);
```

This method is used to get a PreparedStatement object that will later be executed. Parameters are symbolized by ? characters.

Passing IN parameters

When you use callable statements, IN parameters must be set individually. The following methods are available for this purpose:

```
void setNull(int parameterIndex, int sqlType);
void setBoolean(int parameterIndex, boolean x);
void setByte(int parameterIndex, byte x);
void setShort(int parameterIndex, short x);
void setInt(int parameterIndex, int x);
void setLong(int parameterIndex, long x);
```

```
void setFloat(int parameterIndex, float x);
void setDouble(int parameterIndex, double x);
void setBigDecimal(int parameterIndex, java.math.BigDecimal x);
void setString(int parameterIndex, String x);
void setBytes(int parameterIndex, byte x[]);
void setDate(int parameterIndex, java.sql.Date x);
void setTime(int parameterIndex, java.sql.Time x);
void setTimestamp(int parameterIndex, java.sql.Timestamp x);
void setAsciiStream(int parameterIndex, java.io.InputStream x,
    int length);
void setUnicodeStream(int parameterIndex, java.io.InputStream x,
    int length);
void setBinaryStream(int parameterIndex, java.io.InputStream x,
    int length);
void setObject(int parameterIndex, Object x);
void setObject(int parameterIndex, Object x, int targetSqlType);
void setObject(int parameterIndex, Object x, int targetSqlType,
    int scale);
void clearParameters();
```

Note

The setObject() and clearParameters() methods have the same meaning as they do for callable statements.

Executing the query and retrieving results

Once all IN parameters have been set, you execute a prepared statement as you do a normal one. A prepared statement may return a count value as well as a resultset. The following code shows all these steps put together:

```
...
Connection connection = DriverManager.getConnection(url,
    "javauser", "hotjava");

PreparedStatement stmt = connection.prepareStatement
    (   "UPDATE employees SET salary = ? WHERE name = ?");

stmt.setInt(1, 100000);
stmt.setString(2, "Jones");

int res = stmt.executeUpdate();

stmt.close();
connection.close();
...
```

Stored procedures

Basically, a *stored procedure* is a SQL statement sent once to the database. The DBMS will pre-compile it and store it in the database. Stored procedures are often used to store and perform some processing on the data that would be irrelevant if done within the clients. Database vendors claim it is the place to put the core business logic (as far as relational data is concerned). Figure 28-17 illustrates this statement.

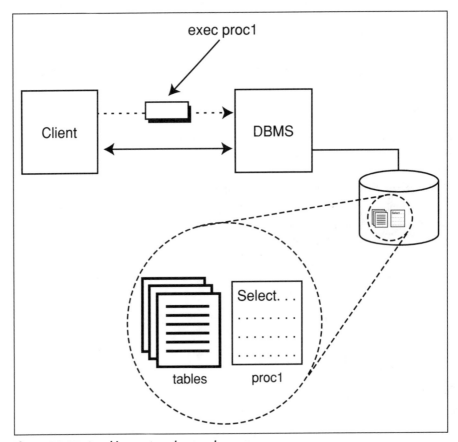

Figure 28-17: Invoking a stored procedure

Statements that invoke stored procedures should use the JDBC CallableStatement class. You must call a dedicated method to prepare the callable statement. You then use the usual methods to execute the statement:

```
CallableStatement prepareCall(String sql);
    where the argument is of the form:
    "{? =call stored_procedure_name ?, ?, ...}"
```

This is the method used to prepare a callable statement. It returns a CallableStatement object. You will discover the reason we need something more elaborate than a simple Statement object soon.

Stored procedures may, of course, return multiple result types, because they may be composed of SQL statements that return diverse result types. You use the usual methods to retrieve these results. If results such as resultsets are returned by a procedure, they must be retrieved first before accessing other kinds of return values from the procedure. Indeed, stored procedures may also have parameters.

Stored procedures may be called with parameters. They provide maximum flexibility by allowing values to be passed from and to the user's application. Such parameters are of two types: IN and/or OUT. IN parameters are used to pass data to the stored procedure and OUT parameters are values returned by the procedure code. Special JDBC methods let you set and access these parameters. Once the statement has been executed, you can explore all its OUT parameters one by one, in left-to-right order. If your stored procedure returns a resultset, you would simply add a loop to fetch the resultset *before* accessing the OUT parameters.

Setting IN parameters

IN parameters receive a value from the user's application. They are set via setXXX() methods that take two arguments: the parameter index, beginning at 1, and the value to set. The following methods are used to set values corresponding to their parameter's specific type:

```
void setNull(int parameterIndex, int sqlType);
void setBoolean(int parameterIndex, boolean x);
void setByte(int parameterIndex, byte x);
void setShort(int parameterIndex, short x);
void setInt(int parameterIndex, int x);
void setLong(int parameterIndex, long x);
void setFloat(int parameterIndex, float x);
void setDouble(int parameterIndex, double x);
void set BigDecimal(int parameterIndex, java.math.BigDecimal x);
void setString(int parameterIndex, String x);
void setBytes(int parameterIndex, byte x[]);
void setDate(int parameterIndex, java.sql.Date x);
void setTime(int parameterIndex, java.sql.Time x);
void setTimestamp(int parameterIndex, java.sql.Timestamp x);
void setAsciiStream(int parameterIndex, java.io.InputStream x,
    int length);
void setUnicodeStream(int parameterIndex, java.io.InputStream x,
    int length);
void setBinaryStream(int parameterIndex, java.io.InputStream x,
    int length);
void setObject(int parameterIndex, Object x);
void setObject(int parameterIndex, Object x, int targetSqlType);
void setObject(int parameterIndex, Object x, int targetSqlType,
    int scale);
void clearParameters();
```

The `setObject(...)` methods belong to advanced JDBC features. They allow given Java objects to be stored in the database. However, they are converted to the database target SQL data type before they are actually sent to the database. Note that it is possible to pass database-specific abstract data types by using a driver-specific Java type and using a `targetSqlType` of `java.sql.types.OTHER` with the `setObject(int parameterIndex, Object x, int targetSqlType)` and the `setObject(int parameterIndex, Object x, int targetSqlType, int scale)` methods.

Setting OUT parameters

OUT parameters must be registered prior to executing the callable statement. This is the way to specify their type. You can use the following methods to register these OUT parameters:

```
void registerOutParameter(int parameterIndex, int sqlType);
```

The first argument is the parameter index, beginning at 1. The `type` argument must be defined in `java.sql.Types`.

```
void registerOutParameter(int parameterIndex, int sqlType, int
    scale);
```

This method is used to register OUT parameters of type `SQL Numeric` or `Decimal`. The `scale` argument represents the desired number of digits to the right of the decimal point.

Accessing parameters

You must access parameters in left-to-right order with the appropriate method that matches their type. The following methods are provided for this purpose:

```
boolean wasNull();
String getString(int parameterIndex);
boolean getBoolean(int parameterIndex);
byte getByte(int parameterIndex);
short getShort(int parameterIndex);
int getInt(int parameterIndex);
long getLong(int parameterIndex);
float getFloat(int parameterIndex);
double getDouble(int parameterIndex);
java.math.BigDecimal getBigDecimal(int parameterIndex, int
    scale);
byte[] getBytes(int parameterIndex);
java.sql.Date getDate(int parameterIndex);
java.sql.Time getTime(int parameterIndex);
java.sql.Timestamp getTimestamp(int parameterIndex);
Object getObject(int parameterIndex);
```

If an OUT parameter has a null value, `wasNull()` returns true. Note that you must call the corresponding `getXXX()` method *before* calling `wasNull()`.

The following code snippet illustrates how to prepare a callable statement, set IN parameters, register OUT parameters, execute the statement, and access the OUT parameters:

```
...
Connection connection = DriverManager.getConnection(url,
    "javauser", "hotjava");

CallableStatement stmt = connection.prepareCall(
    "{call my_stored_procedure ?, ?}");

stmt.setString(1, "Hotjava");
stmt.registerOutParameter(2, java.sql.types.VARCHAR);

int res = myStmt.executeUpdate();

String outParam = stmt.getString(2);

stmt.close();
connection.close();
...
```

Database transactions

JDBC supports database transaction management. Transactions provide a way to group SQL statements so that they are treated as a whole: Either all statements in the group are executed or no statements are executed. All statements within a transaction are treated as a work unit. Transactions are thus useful to guarantee, among other things, data consistency.

Completing a transaction is referred to as *committing the transaction*, while aborting it is referred to as *rolling back the transaction*. A rollback undoes the whole transaction. Therefore, a transaction's boundaries are the beginning of its block and the commit or rollback. Once a commit has been issued, the transaction cannot be rolled back. Note that some DBMSs support nested transactions as well as intermediate markers within a transaction to indicate the point to which the transaction can be rolled back.

Transaction modes

Two transaction modes are usually supported by commercial DBMSs: unchained mode and ANSI-compatible chained mode. You should check your documentation to find out which one is the default.

✦ The unchained mode requires explicit statements to identify the beginning of a transaction block and its end, which will always be a commit or rollback statement. The transaction block may be composed of any SQL statements.

✦ The chained mode does not require explicit statements to delimit the transaction statements, because it implicitly begins a transaction before any SQL statement that retrieves or modifies data. The transaction must still be explicitly ended with a transaction commit or rollback.

Be aware that stored procedures that use the unchained transaction mode may be incompatible with other chained-mode transactions.

Transaction isolation levels

The ANSI defines three standard levels of transaction isolation. Transaction isolation makes sense when concurrent transactions execute simultaneously. The ANSI specification defines restrictions on the kind of actions permitted in this context of concurrent transactions to prevent *dirty reads, non-repeatable reads,* and *phantoms.*

✦ **Level 1: No dirty reads.** Dirty reads occur when a transaction updates a row, and then a second transaction reads that row before the first transaction commits. If the first transaction then rolls back the change, the information read by the second transaction becomes invalid.

✦ **Level 2: No non-repeatable reads.** Non-repeatable reads occur when a transaction reads a row, and then another transaction updates the same row. If the second transaction commits, subsequent reads by the first transaction get different values than the original read.

✦ **Level 3: No phantoms.** Phantoms occur when a transaction reads a set of rows that satisfy a search condition, and then another transaction updates, inserts, or deletes one or more rows that satisfy the first transaction's search condition. In this situation, if the first transaction performs subsequent reads with the same search condition, it obtains a different set of rows.

Note that the higher levels include restrictions imposed by all the lower levels. In practice, you achieve compatibility with all the transaction isolation levels by using locking techniques. You should check your database documentation for information on these techniques, and see how they can affect performances in a multiuser environment. As a general rule, remember that the higher the transaction isolation level, the longer locks are held.

Managing transactions with JDBC

JDBC always opens connections in *auto-commit mode.* This means that each statement is executed as a separate transaction without the need for supplying commit or rollback commands. In this default mode, it is not possible to perform rollbacks.

JDBC provides methods to turn off auto-commit mode, to set the transaction isolation level, and to commit or roll back transactions. JDBC transactions begin as soon as the auto-commit mode is disabled. In this case, an implicit transaction is associated with the connection, and it is completed or aborted with commit and rollback methods. The commit or rollback will then start a new implicit transaction. Note that the commit and rollback makes JDBC close all `PreparedStatements`, `CallableStatements`, and `ResultSets` opened during the transaction. Simple `Statement` objects stay open. This is the default behavior, and it may be disabled.

These are the JDBC methods to manage transactions:

```
void setTransactionIsolation(int isolationlevel);
int getTransactionIsolation();
void setAutoCommit(boolean autocommit);
boolean getAutoCommit();
void commit();
void rollback();
void setAutoClose(boolean autoClose);
boolean getAutoClose();
```

Table 28-1 lists the possible JDBC transaction isolation levels for `setTransaction Isolation()`.

Table 28-1
JDBC Transaction Isolation Levels for setTransactionIsolation()

Transaction Isolation Level	Description
TRANSACTION_READ_UNCOMMITTED	Dirty reads are done.
TRANSACTION_READ_COMMITTED	Only reads on the current row are repeatable.
TRANSACTION_REPEATABLE_READ	Reads on all rows of a result are repeatable.
TRANSACTION_SERIALIZABLE	Reads on all rows of a transaction are repeatable.
TRANSACTION_NONE	Transactions are not supported.

Note that this method cannot be called while in the middle of a transaction:

```
int setTransactionIsolation();
```

It returns the current transaction isolation levels. Note that a value of zero means that transactions are not supported. Compare

```
void setAutoCommit(boolean autocommit);
```

where `setAutoCommit(false)` will implicitly begin a new transaction. You have to use either `commit()` or `rollback()` to terminate the transaction. Again, compare

```
boolean getAutoCommit();
```

which returns the current auto-commit state. False means that user transactions are in use. Next, consider

```
void commit();
```

This method completes the transaction. All changes made since the previous transaction termination (committed or rolled back) are made permanent. All transaction locks are released. By contrast, in

```
void rollback();
```

all changes made since the previous transaction termination (committed or rolled back) are dropped. This method "undoes" the current transaction statements. All transaction locks are released. Finally, consider

```
void setAutoClose(boolean autoClose);
```

When the connection is in auto-close mode, all its `PreparedStatements`, `CallableStatements` and `ResultSets` are closed when the transaction is committed or rolled back. This is the default behavior, but you can disable it by passing `false` as the parameter. Note that some databases allow these objects to remain open across commits, whereas other databases close them. One more method,

```
boolean getAutoClose();
```

returns the current auto-close state for this connection.

Three-tiered design

Although the two-tiered architecture is widespread today, another design is becoming more common. To avoid embedding the application's logic at both the database side and the client side, a third software tier may be inserted, as shown in Figure 28-18.

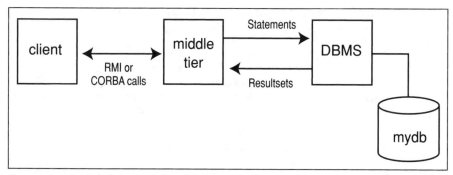

Figure 28-18: The three-tiered architecture

In three-tiered architectures, most of the business logic is located in the middle tier. One of the reasons for doing this is simple: It is easier to implement light changes in the logic whenever the business activity or business rules change because only the middle tier must be adapted.

A complete study of three-tiered architectures involving a database management system is beyond the scope of this chapter. However, we can mention the primary directions in which this architecture is headed:

The middle tier will show a number of functionalities to the clients using a well-defined API. These functionalities may be defined after the business services that the client has to access to perform its role. Methods such as `getAverageSalary()`, `getListOfEmployees()`, `setNewEmployee()`, and `getEmployeesByDepartment()` are examples of such business-oriented services. These methods will return business objects—Java objects defining an `Employee`, a `SetOfEmployees`, a `Department`, a `Company`, a `Product`, a `ProductCatalog`, a `PriceList`, and so on. Clients will then simply invoke these methods to send or retrieve these business objects, or to perform some processing irrelevant to them, but encapsulated in a business service. Speaking of processing which is irrelevant to clients, consider the following business service: `ProductCatalog.sendToCustomerByEmail()`. It can easily be written once, and then reused everywhere!

The middleware of choice for such an architecture is a simple, lightweight remote method invocation protocol such as RMI or CORBA on top of IIOP. These protocols are extremely simple to use from Java, but that's a whole other story!

The Future of Java Database Connectivity - Java Blend

Java Blend provides mappings between Java classes and relational tables. Developers can choose a mapping optimized for the expected kinds of queries, which better represent the underlying design of the database. Java Blend includes a mapping tool, which performs the mapping, uses schema information such as foreign keys to determine a default mapping that can be enhanced by the user. Java Blend includes the following abilities:

✦ Handle one-to-one, one-to-many, and many-to-many relationships. Foreign keys in the database are mapped to references in Java.

✦ Automatically infer inheritance relationships among tables, or create them for Java subclasses.

✦ Map one class to multiple tables, or multiple classes to one table, through various partitioning algorithms.

✦ Easy to port between DBMS products. Because the Java Blend programmer's interface is specifically designed to conform to the ODMG standard for Object/Relational mappings and object databases, it is easy to port to various DBMS products. (See www.odmg.org for more information on ODMG standards.)

✦ Use any DBMS for which JDBC- or ODBC-compliant drivers have been defined. Java Blend implements ODMG on top of JDBC, bridging these higher-level and lower-level standards.

For more information on Java Blend, refer to the Sun's Java Web site at http://sun.java.com

Summary

This chapter covered the Java Database Connectivity API, part of the Core Java API. We have introduced JDBC and explained how to connect to databases and perform queries and updates. Important points to remember when you use the JDBC include these:

✦ The Java Database Connectivity API is the universal way to connect to a database from Java, and is a key enabler for real client-server capabilities using Java.

✦ We learned how to connect to relational databases using specific JDBC drivers and JDBC Uniform Resource Locators to locate these databases.

✦ Database queries and updates require diverse approaches to the retrieval of resultsets, using column indexes and column names.

✦ The JDBC API reference section listed the API briefly.

✦ Advanced techniques such as prepared statements, stored procedures, and database transaction management can help you build more robust database client applications.

✦ The three-tiered design can easily be implemented by using JDBC behind your servers.

Note

For further information about JDBC, IDG Books Worldwide also publishes *JDBC, Java Database Connectivity,* by Bernard Van Haecke, ISBN 0-7645-3144-1. It contains a comprehensive tutorial, numerous examples, as well as a complete reference for the JDBC API.

Multimedia

One of the most exciting features of Java is its capability to help developers create sophisticated multimedia software products with relatively little effort. With built-in support for graphics, sound, and networking, Java opens the door for a new wave of multimedia technology.

Thanks to increased horsepower on the desktop, multimedia is used more today than ever before. Although users now take for granted the ways multimedia improves and enriches the computing experience, such as browsing the World Wide Web, it's also the cornerstone of emerging, futuristic technologies that are rapidly making their way into mainstream computing. Data visualization, complex simulations, realistic interactive games, and virtual reality are but a few of the areas in which multimedia is making an impact.

Today, doctors can practice "cybersurgery" without actually donning scrubs, pilots can hone their skills in difficult military situations without having to strap into a fighter jet, and scientists can watch a deadly virus ravage a host's immune system from the comfort of a reclining chair. Although these high-end systems are out of reach for the average user at the moment, the multimedia technology they employ is rocketing out of the research labs and into our homes even as you read this. Tomorrow you'll be able to take the controls and participate in these amazing experiences yourself.

Perhaps most important today, however, is multimedia for the masses. By combining text, sound, and graphics in creative ways, multimedia makes computers easier to use, more intuitive, and more accessible to the average user. Toss in a dash of interactivity, enabling users to actually participate in the experience, and multimedia delivers on its promise of revolutionizing personal computing as you know it. For proof, look no further than today's Java-savvy Web browser.

Much of the initial hype surrounding Java was due to its built-in multimedia capabilities, although only recently has any work been done with advanced multimedia features. Before Java, creating a networked, multimedia software project for multiple platforms was nothing short of horrifying.

Thanks to Java, this kind of nightmarish experience is quickly becoming a thing of the past. In this chapter you explore the basics of Java multimedia, starting with simple techniques for animating images and playing sound clips. Then you move into more complex territory as I discuss advanced multimedia topics such as double-buffered animations, sprites, parallax scrolling, and other cool topics. Hold on to your keyboard!

3 . . . 2 . . . 1 . . . Action!

Computer animation is similar to more traditional forms of animation—flipbooks, television, and movies. These forms all play a series of still images, each slightly different from one another, in quick succession. Our eyes fill in the "blanks" between still frames, tricking us into seeing motion where there is none. With this in mind, animation in Java is simple: Just load up a bunch of images, and draw each in quick succession. It's simple, at least in theory.

Practically, however, there are other issues you need to concern yourself with when moving from static display to animation. Most significantly, you need to keep track of the various images used in the animation, keeping in mind that these images will most likely reside on the network and require downloading prior to use. As you learned in Chapter 17, an array can be used to store the images used in an animation, but that approach isn't very flexible. For starters, you must know in advance how many images the animation contains in order to create the array in the first place. And, to make matters worse, you have to create a unique array for each animation, meaning your program will be overrun with array-management code if more than a few animations are required. Finally, there's no good, clean way to deal with incremental downloading of images as they come across the wire (or are loaded from the hard drive)—perhaps the biggest drawback to using arrays. What you need is a solid solution for dealing with multiple animation sequences. Thankfully, Java delivers one: `MediaTracker`.

You start with loading and displaying images and eventually move to animation. You also learn about audio in Java. Along the way I illustrate points by developing an intro-screen application, a complete animated sprite library, and a sound-event model, all suitable for high-octane multimedia applications.

MediaTracker (java.awt.MediaTracker)

Before you delve deep into graphics and sound, it's important to tackle the issue of managing these elements in Java using the `MediaTracker` class. Because your images and sounds are often located somewhere on the network, and not on the machine on which the Java program is actually running, you don't have any guarantee that these elements will be immediately available when you need them. Instead, it often takes time for images and sounds to be downloaded over the network, although your program is raring to go.

You've probably already noticed this when dealing with images in your applets. Because an image coming over the wire downloads a little at a time, it appears onscreen incrementally as more and more of it becomes available for drawing. This is because the image is still being downloaded when the applet tries to draw it; the applet draws what it can and waits for more to arrive. This situation may be fine when drawing individual images to the screen, but what about animations? In an animation, it's critical that all images in the sequence are completely loaded in order to create the illusion of motion. What good does flipping through a bunch of partially loaded images do, aside from convincing the user that something bizarre is going on with his or her display?

Understanding this, the good folks who gave us Java also gave us `MediaTracker`, a class specifically designed to manage images. Although it doesn't support sound, `MediaTracker` is indispensable when it comes to multimedia animations. With `MediaTracker`, you can load images over the network and assign each image an ID number to group them logically for later retrieval, enabling you to manage multiple animations with a single `MediaTracker` object. Even more importantly, `MediaTracker` enables you to quickly and easily ensure that all images for a particular group are completely loaded before using them.

Using `MediaTracker` is easy—it works just the way you might want it to. First, instantiate a new `MediaTracker` object, add to it the images you want to "track," and then ask it to wait until all those images are loaded. `MediaTracker` is so easy to use, there's no reason not to when it comes to animations. In fact, it's even worth considering when you're only using a single image. As a testimony to its simplicity, here is an applet that loads a single image but doesn't display it until `MediaTracker` has determined that it's completely finished loading:

```java
import java.awt.*;

public class MediaTrackTest extends java.applet.Applet {
  private MediaTracker tracker;
  private Image picture;

  public void init() {
    getAppletContext().showStatus("Image now loading...");
    tracker = new MediaTracker(this);
    picture = getImage("anyimage.gif");
    tracker.addImage(picture, 1);
  }


  public void paint(Graphics g) {
    try {
      tracker.waitForID(1, 5000);
    } catch (InterruptedException e) {
    // Set status bar to error message...
    getAppletContext().showStatus(e.toString());
    }
```

```
    if(tracker.isErrorID(1)) {
    getAppletContext().showStatus("Error loading image.");
    } else {
    g.drawImage(picture, 0, 0, this);
    }
    }
    }
```

This applet's `init()` method contains the code that creates the `MediaTracker` object and adds to it an image (loaded using the `getImage()` method you've been using all along). In this example, an ID of one (1) is assigned to the image. Because only one image is being dealt with in this example, the ID code isn't really crucial, as you'll see in a moment. But if multiple images were loaded, they could be logically grouped together by ID for later retrieval. In this way, you can use a single `MediaTracker` object to keep track of any number of unique animations.

When it's time to draw your image onscreen, as in the `paint()` method, the `MediaTracker` object is sent the `waitForID` message. In this example, you tell your `MediaTracker` object to give all images with the ID of one (1) up to 5000 milliseconds to load. Because this method can potentially be interrupted by another thread, you should call it from within a `try-catch` clause:

```
try {
    tracker.waitForID(1, 5000);
    } catch (InterruptedException e) {
    // Set status bar to error message...
    getAppletContext().showStatus(e.toString());
    }
```

This `try-catch` clause catches only a potential exception that is thrown when a thread interrupts the process of waiting for the image to load. It doesn't help you find out if the image was successfully loaded. To do that, you could have either checked the `boolean` value returned by this `waitForID()` method or explicitly asked the `MediaTracker` if any errors were encountered for images of this ID:

```
if(tracker.isErrorID(1)) {
    getAppletContext().showStatus("Error loading image.");
    } else {
    g.drawImage(picture, 0, 0, this);
    }
```

If an error has occurred, the user is alerted with a message on the browser's status bar. If not, you can safely assume the image has been completely loaded and so draw it on the screen.

Of course, this is just a simplistic example of using MediaTracker. Later in this chapter you really put this class to work. In the meantime, it's worth knowing that MediaTracker provides a few variations on the methods it supports. For example, you could have told MediaTracker to wait as long as necessary for the image to load, instead of the 5000 milliseconds specified in this example. However, because this version of the waitForID() method doesn't return a boolean value indicating the success or failure of the operation, you have no choice but to explicitly test for errors using any one of the various methods provided, as outlined in Listing 29-1. Listing 29-2 demonstrates how to catch MediaTracker error events.

Listing 29-1: **The Error-Handling Methods Provided by the MediaTracker Object**

```
public class java.awt.MediaTracker extends java.lang.Object
// Fields
public final static int ABORTED;
public final static int COMPLETE;
public final static int ERRORED;
public final static int LOADING;

// Constructors
public MediaTracker(Component comp);
 // Methods
public void addImage(Image image, int id);
public void addImage(Image image, int id, int w, int h);
public boolean checkAll();
public boolean checkAll(boolean load);
public boolean checkID(int id);
public boolean checkID(int id, boolean load);
public Object[] getErrorsAny();
public Object[] getErrorsID(int id);
public boolean isErrorAny();
public boolean isErrorID(int id);
public int statusAll(boolean load);
public int statusID(int id, boolean load);
public void waitForAll();
public boolean waitForAll(long ms);
public void waitForID(int id);
public boolean waitForID(int id, long ms);
```

Listing 29-2: **How to Catch MediaTracker Errors**

```
try {
  tracker.waitForID(1);
  } catch (InterruptedException e) {
  ...
  }

if(tracker.isErrorAny()) { // test for errors with ANY images!
  getAppletContext().showStatus("Error loading image.");
  } else {
  g.drawImage(picture, 0, 0, this);
  }
```

When it comes to waiting for images to load, you could have told MediaTracker to wait for *all* of them instead of just the ones with a specific ID (this would make sense, because the preceding code snippet indicates that you can check for errors occurring with any images loaded, not just those of a specific ID). Just like using ID codes, you can wait either indefinitely or for a specific amount of time (specified in milliseconds):

```
public void waitForAll();
public boolean waitForAll(long ms);
```

Of course, the real power of MediaTracker lies in its capability to keep track of multiple groups of images. We might, for example, load a bunch of images for one animation and assign each the ID zero (0), and then add an entirely new group of images for a completely different animation, and give them a different ID, such as one (1). Then, we could wait for all regardless of ID using one of the waitForAll() methods, or explicitly specify both in our try-catch clause:

```
try {
  tracker.waitForID(0);
  tracker.waitForID(1);
  } catch (InterruptedException e) {
  ...
  }
```

Although the MediaTracker class is a great way to manage your images, it does have shortcomings. Most significantly, it doesn't support sound. If it was only meant for images, you would think a name like ImageTracker would have been more appropriate, no? Although you can always override MediaTracker yourself and add support for sound that way, it sure would be nice if it lived up to its name by supporting other media types. Nevertheless, for the rest of this chapter you'll use MediaTracker in all your code to ensure smooth, professional-looking animation—it's just too useful to ignore!

Adding that professional splash

Although simple code examples are a nice way to learn about `MediaTracker`, it's time to put your newfound knowledge to good use and develop something worthwhile. How about a nifty splash screen that you can use with all your Java programs? By *splash screen* I mean the catchy product or company logo that most traditional applications display during the first few moments of execution (like the yellow cup o' Joe displayed when Symantec's Café development environment loads). Although such splash screens may seem merely decorative, they're usually displayed to give the user something snazzy to look at while the program prepares itself for use.

Write one of these splash screens for Java, not only to look cool but also to "hide" the process of image loading from the end user. If you need to load images anyway, why not do it while the splash screen is displayed instead of tossing up a boring message such as "Images loading, please wait..."?

In this example you create a class called, not surprisingly, `SplashScreen`. `SplashScreen` takes two parameters: one telling the class what image to display to the user, the other a vector (growable array) of images that must be loaded before the splash screen terminates. `SplashScreen` uses `MediaTracker` to wait for the display image to load and then draws it centered on the screen. `SplashScreen` waits for all the images referenced in the vector to load. (The display image remains onscreen to give the user something to look at as the vector's images load.) When each of the vector's images has been loaded, `SplashScreen` knows it's time to go away—it terminates and cleans up after itself. When all is said and done, the host application is able to use the images it requires without worrying about poky image loading.

You already know how to deal with image loading using `MediaTracker`, but how do you display the splash image on the screen for the user to see without painting directly on the applet's (or application's) drawing surface? You just want a drawing surface separate from the program itself, so `SplashScreen` can do what it needs without any knowledge of the code that calls it.

There's a way to do just that. As you may recall from Chapter 20, Java's AWT provides exactly the functionality you need in its `Window` class. We simply extend the `Window` class and override its `paint()` method to get our hands on a drawing surface that is completely independent of any program that will use `SplashScreen`.

When you have a drawing surface on which to display your splash image, the rest is just as easy—the `SplashScreen()` constructor and the `loadAndShow()` method do most of the work. Start by taking a look at the constructor. Because you want to make `SplashScreen` as simple and painless to use as possible, the constructor is also simple: It takes a `String` parameter, specifying the `SplashScreen` image itself, and a vector of images to load. (Because `SplashScreen` will typically be called from a full-featured program, the caller should already have references to the images it uses, meaning the image vector should be relatively simple for the caller to create.)

SplashScreen uses two MediaTracker objects, one to track the SplashScreen image itself, and the other to track the images to be used by the host application. The constructor mainly prepares you for image tracking. Listing 29-3 shows the code, along with another constructor for convenience that takes a vector of image filenames:

Listing 29-3: **Tracking the SplashScreen Images**

```
public class SplashScreen extends Window {
  private MediaTracker LogoTracker, ImagesTracker;
  private Image intro;

  public SplashScreen(String i, MediaTracker m, Frame parent) {
    super(parent);
    ImagesTracker = m;
    intro = getToolkit().getImage(i);
    LogoTracker = new MediaTracker(this);
    LogoTracker.addImage(intro, 1);
  }

  public SplashScreen(String i, Vector v, Frame parent) {
    super(parent);
    intro = getToolkit().getImage(i);
    ImagesTracker = new MediaTracker(this);
    for(int j=0;j<v.size();j++) {
     ImagesTracker.addImage(getToolkit().getImage((String)
       (v.elementAt(j))), 0);
    }
    LogoTracker = new MediaTracker(this);
    LogoTracker.addImage(intro, 1);
  }
}
```

Now you're ready to roll (or, more accurately, wait!). The loadAndShow() method sets everything off. It waits for the SplashScreen logo to load, centers the splash screen window and resizes it to fit the logo image exactly, and then displays it. The logo is displayed only long enough to load all the host images passed in by the constructor, and then it hides and disposes itself. As usual, you need to catch exceptions thrown by MediaTracker. Listing 29-4 shows the code:

Listing 29-4: **Completing SplashScreen with LoadAndShow**

```
import java.awt.*;
import java.util.Vector;

public class SplashScreen extends Window {
```

```
private MediaTracker LogoTracker, ImagesTracker;
private Image intro;

public SplashScreen(String i, MediaTracker m, Frame parent) {
 super(parent);
 ImagesTracker = m;
 intro = getToolkit().getImage(i);
 LogoTracker = new MediaTracker(this);
 LogoTracker.addImage(intro, 1);
}

public SplashScreen(String i, Vector v, Frame parent) {
 super(parent);
 intro = getToolkit().getImage(i);
 ImagesTracker = new MediaTracker(this);
 for(int j=0;j<v.size();j++) {
  ImagesTracker.addImage(getToolkit().getImage((String)
   (v.elementAt(j))), 0);
 }
 LogoTracker = new MediaTracker(this);
 LogoTracker.addImage(intro, 1);
}

public void loadAndShow() {
 try {
  LogoTracker.waitForAll(8000);
 } catch(InterruptedException e) {
  System.out.println("Error loading intro: "+e.toString());
 }

 // Our image is loaded, display our splash screen
 this.show();

 // Now center the window
 Dimension screenSize = getToolkit().getScreenSize();
 this.move((screenSize.width - intro.getWidth(this))/2,
  (screenSize.height - intro.getHeight(this))/2);
 this.resize(intro.getWidth(this), intro.getHeight(this));
 this.getGraphics().drawImage(intro, 0, 0, this);

 try {
  ImagesTracker.waitForAll(8000);
 } catch (InterruptedException e) {
  System.out.println("Error loading images: "+e.toString());
 };

 // Hide and clean up our splash screen
 hide();
 dispose();
}
```

(continued)

Listing 29-4 *(continued)*

```
// Let's override this just in case the window
// needs to be redrawn public void paint(Graphics g) {
  this.resize(intro.getWidth(this), intro.getHeight(this));
  g.drawImage(intro, 0, 0, this);
  }
}
```

If you've read most of this book so far, the majority of code shown here will seem self-explanatory, with the possible exception of the centering code. This bit of code gets the current screen width and height in pixels, subtracts the dimensions of the logo image (which is available immediately because you have waited for it to load), and divides what's left in half. This gives you the upper-left corner in which to draw your centered logo. Now you can add a professional touch to your Java applications with a few extra lines of code.

Flicker-free animation: double-buffering

Before you get going with a killer animation example, there is one more administrative detail to worry about when painting images to the screen in quick succession: screen flicker. When your rendering code draws repeatedly to a visible graphics context, synchronization problems lead to visual degradation. In graphics and game programming, this problem is typically avoided by drawing to a hidden offscreen buffer in memory. Then, when all rendering for the current frame is completed and in the buffer, the whole buffer is copied to the onscreen visible display area. This end-of-frame-copying process is known in graphics circles as *blitting*, and the entire process that takes place in offscreen memory is known as *double-buffering*.

Note

The word *frame* refers to the individual sequences of an animation, which, when drawn rapidly in sequence, produce the illusion of motion. By rendering each frame offscreen, in memory, the entire frame is guaranteed to be complete before it is painted on the physical screen where the user can see it. Although not a tremendous issue when dealing with small images, as you've been doing so far, animations with more complex frames (such as sprites, discussed later in this chapter) or larger, full-screen images, generate more flicker if you don't use double-buffering to transfer them from offscreen memory to the screen.

Double-buffering in Java isn't altogether different from any other language. In Java, the technique is achieved by using the createImage() method (java.awt. createImage) to create a fresh, new image from which an offscreen graphics content will be created (the "buffer"). Instead of drawing directly to the screen, the images in your animations (each image is a "frame") are instead drawn into the buffer. When the frame in the buffer is ready, meaning the entire current image has been drawn into the buffer, the whole kit and caboodle is transferred directly onto the screen—the frame is blitted from offscreen memory into display-screen memory using the drawImage() method.

Although it's probably confusing the first time around, double-buffering in Java is actually simple compared to other languages. With Java, you don't have to deal directly with memory allocation and memory copying. Instead, you can simply use the methods provided in Java's AWT to get the same results with a fraction of the hassle. The whole process is pretty simple and follows the chain of events described earlier. Check it out in Listing 29-5:

Listing 29-5: **Double-Buffering**

```
Image buffer;
Graphics offscreen;

Dimension d = this.size();
screenWidth = d.width;
screenHeight = d.height;

// Create offscreen buffer the size of our applet window
buffer = createImage(d.width, d.height);
offscreen = buffer.getGraphics();

// Render graphics using offscreen here
offscreen.fillRect...
offscreen.drawImage...

// Now copy everything from offscreen buffer to
// onscreen display area
getGraphics().drawImage(buffer, 0, 0, this);
```

As with `MediaTracker`, you will incorporate double-buffering from now on to keep your output looking sharp and professional. Although you've explored the essentials of Java's multimedia capabilities so far, it's just the beginning. But fret not—the groundwork has been laid for producing extremely slick and professional Java animations, the kind you'd expect with world-class multimedia products. The basics are already behind you: loading, managing, and drawing flicker-free animations. Now you just have to put what you've learned to good use.

Putting It All Together: A Sprite Engine

You will now use all of your hard-earned knowledge to build something useful: a sprite engine. A *sprite* is the term used in graphics programming to describe an image displayed in an animation, like the images typically used in video games. Although sprites have been around for years in arcade-style video games and, more recently, in desktop computer games, they are now commonly used to spice up Web sites. A *sprite engine* is a nice way to encapsulate many of the details of sprite animation, which can get hairy at times if you're new to sprite programming.

To take advantage of what you've learned so for, you're going to build a basic Java sprite engine—a clean, versatile, and reusable framework suitable for general-purpose multimedia applications.

In time, you'll find that it's easy to inadvertently "over-objectify" your code, turning everything possible into an object. Although objects are indeed the focal point of object-oriented programming, too much of a good thing can be dangerous. If you go nuts and turn everything in your program into an object, you'll likely find that even the most simple programs become incredibly complex.

Worse still, the overhead associated with managing so many objects (when it comes to applets, the overhead of loading classes over the network when needed, each of which requires a separate network connection) can greatly impact the overall speed of your program. As a result, your now overly complex program is also unnecessarily slow! For these reasons, the sprite engine discussed here is intentionally simple; objects are kept to a minimum, both to make the code easy for you to understand and efficient when running.

A sprite for thought

Start with the basic concepts behind a sprite and a sprite engine. Think of the `Sprite` class as the graphical information needed to display a sprite on the screen —nothing more, nothing less. You will treat sprites created using one image and sprites created using multiple images as similarly as possible, encompassing both in the `Sprite` class.

The core functionality you need is the capability to draw an image, or series of images (an animation), centered at any arbitrary point on the screen. To do so, you need to perform these three tasks:

✦ Load and store one or more images using `MediaTracker`.

✦ Keep track of the center point where the drawing will occur.

✦ Provide logic to flip between successive images for animated sprites.

To start, use a `Vector` object called `imageList` to store your image(s), because you don't want to limit yourself with the amount of images allowed per `Sprite`. For animated sprites, you want to be able to flip between each image that makes up the animation (and not limit yourself to one image per frame), so add a `speed` variable to dictate how many frames must pass before you display the next image in an animated sprite.

In addition to this basic behavior, it's also nice to be able to make sprites visible and invisible at will, so also add a `boolean visible` variable. Your sprite engine will use these variables to display your sprites properly, but it's just the beginning. Take a look at what you have so far:

```
public class Sprite extends Object {
  protected Vector imageList;
  protected int currentImage;
  protected int currentSpeed;

  public boolean visible = true;
  public int xPos, yPos;
  public int speed = 1;
  public int width, height;
}
```

You have two variables for internal use: currentImage and currentSpeed. Always have currentImage set to the offset into your vector containing the image number to draw for this frame. Use currentSpeed to loop from 0 to speed; when it resets, it increments your currentImage by one, providing the animation.

There are a few other things to note here. You are inheriting Sprite from Object so that you can later make a vector of Sprites in your sprite engine. This is a little hokey, but it is specific to Vectors and we purists just need to live with it. Also, note that your normally private variables are protected instead, so you can easily extend other classes from it. If you felt like building a particle system or video game later, this would be the way to do it. You want to make this as easy to use and extend as possible.

You then declare two internal variables for tracking your current image and current speed, which will be used for sprites with multiple images. You also keep track of the sprite's center point with xPos, yPos, whether it should currently be drawn with the boolean visible, the speed to loop through its images (if it has more than one), and two convenience variables for the sprite's image width and height. Now you'll add some methods.

There are two ways to instantiate a Sprite. You can have one image or multiple images. For example, consider

```
public Sprite(Applet a, String imgName);
public Sprite(Applet a, String imgName, int numImages);
```

If you have only one image to use, you can call the first constructor; if you want an animated sprite, you can use the second constructor. The imgName parameter is a filename relative to the applet and should be specified in the standard filename format. Either way, you need to pass a reference to your current applet so the sprite can locate the images using getDocumentBase(). If you use the animated sprite constructor, use the imgName as the filename without any numbers in it, and use numImages as the number of images to read in, starting with 1:

```
Sprite firstSprite = new Sprite(this, "image/test.gif", 3);
```

This builds a new animated sprite using images `test1.gif`, `test2.gif`, and `test3.gif` from the image subdirectory of the directory from which the applet was launched. Now you have a basic `Sprite` class. You can directly change its position and speed and make it visible or invisible. You want to encapsulate loading and waiting for images, so use the `MediaTracker` internally, as in Listing 29-6:

Listing 29-6: How to Encapsulate Loading and Waiting

```
public Sprite(Applet a, String imgName) {
 imageList = new Vector();
 a.getAppletContext().showStatus("Fetching image: "+imgName);
 imageList.addElement(a.getImage(a.getDocumentBase(),
imgName));
 waitForImages(a);
 a.getAppletContext().showStatus("Sprite loaded
successfully.");
 width = ((Image)imageList.elementAt(0)).getWidth(a);
 height = ((Image)imageList.elementAt(0)).getHeight(a);
 xPos = width/2;
 yPos = height/2;
}

public Sprite(Applet a, String imgName, int numImages) {
 imageList = new Vector();
 for(int i=0;i<numImages;i++) {
  try {
   String prefix = new String(imgName.substring(0,
    imgName.length() - 4));
   String ext = imgName.substring(imgName.length() - 4);
   a.getAppletContext().showStatus("Fetching image:
    "+prefix+(i+1)+ext);
   imageList.addElement(a.getImage(a.getDocumentBase(),
    prefix+(i+1)+ext));
  } catch(StringIndexOutOfBoundsException e) {
   System.out.println("Error reading sprite: "+e.toString());
  }
 }
 waitForImages(a);
 a.getAppletContext().showStatus("Sprite loaded
  successfully.");
 width = ((Image)imageList.elementAt(0)).getWidth(a);
 height = ((Image)imageList.elementAt(0)).getHeight(a);
 xPos = width/2;
 yPos = height/2;
}
```

This code fetches the image or images passed to it, adding each one to the Sprite's internal vector of images called imageList. You have to do some string parsing to resolve the image names nicely, but a little work here will make it that much easier to use later. Each time the Sprite fetches an image, it sets the applet's status bar to "Fetching *<image name>*." Then it calls the internal function waitForImages(). This sets your applet's status bar to "Waiting for images to load . . ." and uses a MediaTracker to wait for all images in imageList to load.

The Sprite constructor then sets the internal variables width and height to the width and height of the first image in imageList (it assumes that all images are the same size), and it initializes the center point to the middle of the image. As a result, the default sprite will be drawn in the upper-left corner of your applet if you don't change its position.

A few more small details: CurrentImage() returns the image at the offset currentImage into imageList. The advance() function advances the animated sprites' current images according to their speed. It increments the sprite's currentSpeed, incrementing the sprite's current image every speed frames. If an animated sprite's speed is three, then every three times advance() is called, the sprite's current image advances by one. This also loops back to the first image when it exceeds the number of images loaded. Whew! Okay, now get those sprites moving.

Start your sprite engine

Now that you have a nice, functional Sprite class, you need a sprite engine to manipulate it. The sprite engine handles standard graphical operations such as managing the graphics context and double-buffering, and it provides support for a background image or color. It also keeps a running calculation of the frames displayed per second. After you write the sprite engine, you will have offloaded all the graphics operations from the programmer to the engine, freeing yourself to work on the motion behind the sprites and your program logic. You need a Vector to maintain a list of Sprites to track, and you need internal variables for double-buffering and for drawing a background color or image. Here's the first try:

```
public class SpriteEngine extends Applet {
  // List of all Sprites we are keeping track of
  private Vector spriteList;

  // Accessible to child for game purposes
  protected int screenWidth, screenHeight;

  // For double buffering
  private Image buffer;
  private Graphics offscreen;

  // For color or image background support
  private Color bgcolor;
  private Image bgImage;
```

```
// For frame counting
private long startTime, stopTime;
private int frameCounter;
...
}
```

Notice that you are inheriting your `SpriteEngine` class from `Applet`. This is because you are designing the `SpriteEngine` to be inherited from, not contained in, applications that use it. Now start writing the functions. I like to design using the simplest interface I can imagine—the dream API. For example, this one comes close:

```
public class GraphicalApplication extends SpriteEngine {
...
Sprite s = new Sprite...
Sprite s1 = new Sprite...

addSprite(s);
addSprite(s2);

while(!done) {
 advance();
 blit();
}
...
}
```

The users of your sprite engine build a new class that inherits from `SpriteEngine`. In the main code, typically in the body of `run()`, users instantiate the `Sprites` they want to display and then add them to the `SpriteEngine` so it now tracks and displays them. Users can then simply call `advance()` to have animated sprites advance their images and `blit()` to draw everything to the screen as fast as possible. Double-buffering and a background image or color are taken care of automatically, and sprites are drawn centered over their `xPos`, `yPos` coordinates, in the order in which they are added to the engine. Sound good? I think so, so here goes. Start with an easy one, `addSprite()`:

```
public void addSprite(Sprite s) {
 spriteList.addElement(s);
}
```

Here the process simply adds the sprite passed as a parameter to the internal vector of sprites, called `spriteList`. Now try `advance()`:

```
public void advance() {
 for(int i=0;i<spriteList.size();i++) {
  ((Sprite)spriteList.elementAt(i)).advance();
 }
}
```

This process also is pretty simple. It runs through the current list of sprites being tracked by the engine and calls their individual advance() functions. This is where the power of OOP comes in. If a specific subclass of Sprite wants to define its own behavior here, it can do so with no change to the sprite engine. Particles can move with gravity, bullets can gain or lose acceleration, or Tumbling Duke can jitter like he's had four cups of coffee—just by adding functionality to a specific Sprite's advance() method.

There are a few helper functions to cover before you get to blit(), namely setSize(), setBackground(), and getFPS(). First, blit() needs to perform automatic double-buffering. You have already seen the code for this, but you haven't seen it in action. Here is the same basic code, but now it also checks to see whether the window has been resized since your last call. Put this in a separate function, called setSize():

```
private void setSize() {
  Dimension d = this.size();
  screenWidth = d.width;
  screenHeight = d.height;

  // Recreate offscreen double buffer
  buffer = createImage(d.width, d.height);
  offscreen = buffer.getGraphics();
  done = false;
}
```

This refreshingly straightforward function is called whenever the engine notices that the window has changed size. It does this by comparing the values of screenWidth and screenHeight with the applet's dimensions. Now look at setBackground(). There are two versions of this function; one version takes a Color as a parameter, and the other takes a String. If a Color is passed, the animation's background is set to this color. If a String is passed, it is assumed to be an image filename relative to the code base, and it is loaded and stretched to fit the applet's output window. This could be used to display a starry night background for a space animation, or maybe a test tube filled with green gunk for your elusive particle system. The color version is trivial; the image background version is a little more complex, mostly because it needs to wait for the image to load:

```
public void setBackground(Color c) {
  bgcolor = c;
}

public void setBackground(String imagename) {
  bgImage = getImage(getDocumentBase(), imagename);
  MediaTracker m = new MediaTracker(this);
  m.addImage(bgImage, 0);
  getAppletContext().showStatus("Waiting for background image
    to load...");
```

```
try {
 m.waitForAll(8000);
} catch (InterruptedException e) {
 // Set status bar to error message...
 getAppletContext().showStatus("Error loading background
  image: "+e.toString());
}
getAppletContext().showStatus("Image loaded.");
bgcolor = null;
}
```

The last function to examine before you write `blit()` is `getFPS()`. It's a performance statistic that calculates how many frames per second you are currently displaying, and it will appear in your applet's status window while you are animating. It uses the `getTime()` method of `Date` to find out how many seconds have elapsed, and it divides the number of frames you have displayed so far by the result to get your current frames per second:

```
public float getFPS() {
 Date d = new Date();
 stopTime = d.getTime();
 // Divide by 1000 because start and stop time in milliseconds
 float time = (stopTime-startTime)/((float)1000);
 float fps = ((float)frameCounter)/time;
 startTime = stopTime;
 frameCounter = 0;
 return fps;
}
```

Now, on to your `blit()` function. I have covered all of the functions it uses, so there isn't much else to explore. The `blit()` function first calls `setSize()` if it sees that your applet window has changed size since the last frame, recreating the double buffer if necessary. It then either fills the background with a color or scales an image to fit, or does neither, depending on whether either version of `setBackground()` was previously called. The `blit()` function then runs through the list of `Sprites` in `spriteList` and draws all visible `Sprites` centered over its internal position as given by `xPos,yPos`. All background and sprite drawing happens in the offscreen buffer. That buffer is copied to your onscreen applet window, displaying your updated animation frame. Every 15 frames, your applet status window is set to the current frames per second:

```
// Draw background, draws all sprites at specified size,
// then copies the whole thing to the graphics context
// passed to it (usually the applet gc). This handles
// double buffering automatically.
public void blit() {
 if(startTime == 0) {
  Date d = new Date();
```

```
  startTime = d.getTime();
}

// First check if window has changed in size...
Dimension d = this.size();
if((d.width != screenWidth) || (d.height != screenHeight)) {
  setSize();
}

// First draw background color or image...
if(bgcolor != null) {
  offscreen.setColor(bgcolor);
  offscreen.fillRect(0, 0, screenWidth, screenHeight);
} else if(bgImage != null) {
  offscreen.drawImage(bgImage, 0, 0, screenWidth,
    screenHeight, this);
}

// Now run through list of sprites and draw them
// at their current point at their current scaling
for(int j=0;j<spriteList.size();j++) {
  Sprite s = (Sprite)(spriteList.elementAt(j));
  if(s.visible) {
    offscreen.drawImage(s.currentImage(), s.xPos -
      ((int)(((float)s.width)/((float)2))), s.yPos -
      ((int)(((float)s.height)/((float)2))), this);
  }
}

// Now draw buffer to screen...
getGraphics().drawImage(buffer, 0, 0, this);

// Now update our frames per second...
frameCounter++;
if(frameCounter % 15 == 0) {
  getAppletContext().showStatus("Average fps: "+getFPS());
}
}
```

A couple more details and you'll be done. Notice that the `boolean` variable `done` is always set to `false` until the sprite engine is destroyed. This prevents synchronization problems when the engine is destroyed while it is still drawing. There is also the `init` variable that should be set by the host application after all the sprites have been added and loaded. The host application typically enters a `while(!done)` loop, each time changing sprite positions and program variables and then calling `advance()` and `blit()`. The final version of your sprite engine looks like Listing 29-7:

Listing 29-7: **The Sprite Engine**

```java
import java.applet.Applet;
import java.util.Vector;
import java.awt.Graphics;
import java.awt.Image;
import java.awt.Dimension;
import java.awt.Color;
import java.awt.MediaTracker;
import java.util.Date;

public class SpriteEngine extends Applet {
 // List of all Sprites we are keeping track of
 private Vector spriteList;

 // Accessible to child for game purposes
 protected int screenWidth, screenHeight;

 // For double buffering
 private Image buffer;
 private Graphics offscreen;

 // For color or image background support
 private Color bgcolor;
 private Image bgImage;

 // For happy cleanup
 protected boolean init = false, done = false;

 // For frame counting
 private long startTime, stopTime;
 private int frameCounter;

 public SpriteEngine() {
  spriteList = new Vector();
 }

 public void addSprite(Sprite s) {
  spriteList.addElement(s);
 }

 public void advance() {
  for(int i=0;i<spriteList.size();i++) {
   ((Sprite)spriteList.elementAt(i)).advance();
  }
 }

 private void setSize() {
  Dimension d = this.size();
  screenWidth = d.width;
  screenHeight = d.height;
```

```
 // Recreate offscreen double buffer
 buffer = createImage(d.width, d.height);
 offscreen = buffer.getGraphics();
 done = false;
 }

public void setBackground(Color c) {
 bgcolor = c;
}

public void setBackground(String imagename) {
 bgImage = getImage(getDocumentBase(), imagename);
 MediaTracker m = new MediaTracker(this);
 m.addImage(bgImage, 0);
 getAppletContext().showStatus("Waiting for background image
  to load...");
 try {
  m.waitForAll(8000);
 } catch (InterruptedException e) {
  // Set status bar to error message...
  getAppletContext().showStatus("Error loading background
   image: " + e.toString());
 }
 getAppletContext().showStatus("Image loaded.");
 bgcolor = null;
}

public float getFPS() {
 Date d = new Date();
 stopTime = d.getTime();
 // Divide by 1000 because start and stop time in milliseconds
 float time = (stopTime-startTime)/((float)1000);
 float fps = ((float)frameCounter)/time;
 startTime = stopTime;
 frameCounter = 0;
 return fps;
}

// Draw background, draws all sprites at specified size,
// then copies the whole thing to the graphics context
// passed to it (usually the applet gc). This handles
// double buffering automatically.
public void blit() {
 if(startTime == 0) {
  Date d = new Date();
  startTime = d.getTime();
 }

 // First check if window has changed in size...
 Dimension d = this.size();
```

(continued)

Listing 29-7 *(continued)*

```
 if((d.width != screenWidth) || (d.height != screenHeight)) {
  setSize();
 }

 // First draw background color or image...
 if(bgcolor != null) {
  offscreen.setColor(bgcolor);
  offscreen.fillRect(0, 0, screenWidth, screenHeight);
 } else if(bgImage != null) {
  offscreen.drawImage(bgImage, 0, 0, screenWidth,
   screenHeight, this);
 }

 // Now run through list of sprites and draw them
 // at their current point at their current scaling
 for(int j=0;j<spriteList.size();j++) {
  Sprite s = (Sprite)(spriteList.elementAt(j));
  if(s.visible) {
   offscreen.drawImage(s.currentImage(), s.xPos -
    ((int)(((float)s.width)/((float)2))), s.yPos -
    ((int)(((float)s.height)/((float)2))), this);
  }
 }

 // Now draw buffer to screen...
 getGraphics().drawImage(buffer, 0, 0, this);

 // Now update our frames per second...
 frameCounter++;
 if(frameCounter % 15 == 0) {
  getAppletContext().showStatus("Average fps: "+getFPS());
 }
}

public void paint(Graphics g) {
 // Init set to true by application when ready to
 // start main loop to prevent synchronization problems
 if(init) {
  blit();
 }
}

public void destroy() {
 done = true;
}
}
```

Lightweight sprites: SpriteShadows

Now, how about that particle system I keep blabbing about? If you run any of the examples, you'll notice that much time is spent waiting for the sprite images to load. No one wants to wait. This is especially true over the Web, where the average webber's attention span is rivaled by that of an average two-year old. If you wanted to have an animation with, for example, 200 sprites with the same image, think how long that would take to load and how much memory would be wasted with redundant image data. Now imagine if each sprite had ten frames of animation. Am I painting a dismal enough picture yet?

The solution is remarkably simple, and it's so easy to implement that you'll add it right now with just a few lines of code. I call them SpriteShadows. A SpriteShadow is a subclass of Sprite that takes only another Sprite (or a SpriteShadow) as a parameter. It sets all its internal variables—including x and y position, visible attribute, and speed—to the Sprite parameter. It then sets all the images in its imageList equal to the image *references* in the Sprite parameter's list. Notice that it doesn't re-read any images—it depends on the Sprite parameter having done that already. A SpriteShadow just sets its image references to point to the already loaded image(s).

The net result is that both Sprites use the same image or set of images, so there is only the additional overhead associated with having another Sprite to draw. Listing 29-8 shows the code:

Listing 29-8: **SpriteShadow**

```
import java.util.Vector;

public class SpriteShadow extends Sprite {
  public SpriteShadow(Sprite s) {
    visible = s.visible;
    xPos = s.xPos;
    yPos = s.yPos;
    imageList = new Vector();
    for(int i=0;i<s.imageList.size();i++) {
      imageList.addElement((s.imageList.elementAt(i)));
    }
    currentImage = s.currentImage;
    speed = s.speed;
    currentSpeed = s.currentSpeed;
    width = s.width;
    height = s.height;
  }
}
```

How about that particle system? Start with one particle—it moves randomly, bouncing off the walls of your applet (this behavior is controlled by its `advance()` method). For every frame, your applet creates a `SpriteShadow` using the original `Sprite` as the parameter to its constructor; they are then added to your `SpriteEngine`. You end up with a screen full of particles in no time, with minimal memory usage and almost no loading time! If your original `Sprite` was animated with multiple images, you could even have the individual `SpriteShadow`s running through the animation at different speeds because they each track their own `speed` and `currentImage` independently. Not bad. After all is said and done, your `Sprite`, `SpriteEngine`, and `SpriteShadow` total fewer than 300 lines of code.

Clipping and parallax scrolling

Now that you have all the low-level graphics details out of the way, how do you realistically manipulate your sprites? You could increment a sprite's coordinates by a constant every frame, but that looks about as realistic as Pong.

One technique for moving sprites realistically is called *parallax scrolling*. This is a graphics term for describing the way close-up objects appear to move faster than far-away objects. For example, if you look out to one side when you're driving down the highway, you see the grass (or billboards, depending where you live) on the side of the road rushing by you while the far-off mountains (or skyscrapers) appear to be moving slowly or not at all.

Parallax scrolling is really a special case of simulated perspective, and it is much easier to implement. You can implement it by incrementing all sprites' horizontal coordinates according to the supposed distance from the viewer. In your highway example, you might increment the grass four pixels every frame and the mountains only one pixel per frame because they are supposed to be much farther off. The difference fools your eyes into believing that the mountains are farther away from the grass, although they are both represented on the same flat screen. You will see an example of this in a moment.

Another detail to attend to is the subject of *clipping*. Clipping is the process of making sure you don't draw sprites or parts of sprites to an area offscreen. If the aforementioned grass is scrolled off one edge of the screen, normally you would have to adjust the grass size so that you don't write to an illegal memory address. Luckily for you, however, Java handles clipping automatically. It even provides an extra function called `clipToRect()` if you want to clip to a specific region. Of course, you do lose some performance as Java adjusts all drawing operations to valid boundaries before drawing them, causing a slowdown. Who knows, maybe the Java team decided on the easier brute-force approach of checking every *pixel* before writing it. At any rate, you know you don't have to worry about it.

A mystic temple and Jane on Mars

Now that you have a working sprite library and know how to put some realistic motion behind your sprites, you have all the tools to create a realistic animation. In this section is a little demo of all these components in action. I asked my friend, Scott Downey (reindeer@together.net), to create some artwork for me, and a couple of hours later he gave me this—don't complain if it's a little surreal. This example uses the sprite library and all the topics I've covered so far. Although the code is simple, I think you'll be impressed by the output.

With the actual graphics part of the code weighing in at only about 50 lines, this is a good indication that you designed your sprite engine well. You still have full control over your sprites, but you passed off all the drawing duties to the engine. Notice that you start by deriving a new class from SpriteEngine, agreeing to make it multithreaded by implementing Runnable. Now you simply have to write two methods: init() and run(). The init() method just starts a new thread in standard fashion; you've seen this many times before, so I won't cover it further. The run() method contains the actual sprite's animation code and starts by initializing the Jane sprite, the background sprite, and four parallax sprite layers. This is accomplished with the following lines:

```
Sprite s = new Sprite(this, "img/jane.gif", 18);
Sprite l1 = new Sprite(this, "img/level1.gif");
Sprite l2 = new Sprite(this, "img/level2.gif");
Sprite l3 = new Sprite(this, "img/level3.gif");
Sprite l4 = new Sprite(this, "img/level4.gif");
setBackground("img/bg.gif");
```

Two cheers for putting so much work into the Sprite constructors! This code reads the images jane1.gif through jane18.gif into one animated sprite, reads layer1.gif through layer4.gif into four static sprite layers, and reads bg.gif as your background. Because of your extensive MediaTracker usage, all images are loaded completely before the code returns. The layer images serve as your four parallax scrolling layers. You then add these to the sprite engine in back-to-front drawing order so that the engine can track and draw them. You only need one more line to get these images onscreen, and that's blit(). As you recall, this method actually draws all the sprites at their current x, y coordinates, double-buffering automatically.

The rest of the code in this example shows parallax scrolling and hard-coded numbers to make the animation look right. After setting everything up, run through your main loop, which scrolls each layer by a certain amount. Then call advance(), and then call blit(), which draws the new frame. advance() calls each sprite in the engine's own advance() function. This lets animated sprites track and change their currently displayed image independently. Sprites can also optionally keep track of other variables according to frame rate. For example, if the sprite was an enemy in a game you were writing, you could add functionality here that would determine its lifespan and direction, perhaps adjusting both randomly every frame. The only sprite that actually does anything in its advance() function in this case is Jane, which advances its current image by one, providing animation.

Here's the final code in Listing 29-9 (try to ignore the hard-coded mess):

Listing 29-9: **Jane on Mars: Animation Using Sprites**

```java
import java.lang.Thread;
import java.awt.Color;
import java.awt.Dimension;
import java.awt.Event;

public class Jane extends SpriteEngine implements Runnable {
 private Thread t;

 public void init() {
  super.init();

  t = new Thread(this);
  t.start();
 }

 public void run() {
  init = true;
  int mountainCounter = 0;

  Sprite s = new Sprite(this, "img/jane.gif", 18);
  Sprite l1 = new Sprite(this, "img/level1.gif");
  Sprite l2 = new Sprite(this, "img/level2.gif");
  Sprite l3 = new Sprite(this, "img/level3.gif");
  Sprite l4 = new Sprite(this, "img/level4.gif");
  setBackground("img/bg.gif");

  // Add to engine in back to front order:
  addSprite(l4);
  addSprite(l3);
  addSprite(l2);
  addSprite(l1);
  addSprite(s);

  s.xPos = 380; s.yPos = 228;
  l1.xPos = 75; l1.yPos = 175;
  l2.xPos = 110; l2.yPos = 150;
  l3.xPos = 130; l3.yPos = 170;
  l4.xPos = 180; l4.yPos = 100;

  while(!done) {
   s.xPos-=2;
   l1.xPos+=3;
   l2.xPos+=2;
   l3.xPos++;
   if(++mountainCounter > 2) {
    mountainCounter = 0;
    l4.xPos++;
   }
```

```
     // Reset our animation
     if((s.xPos > screenWidth) || (s.xPos < 0)) {
      s.xPos = 380; s.yPos = 228;
      l1.xPos = 75; l1.yPos = 175;
      l2.xPos = 110; l2.yPos = 150;
      l3.xPos = 130; l3.yPos = 170;
      l4.xPos = 180; l4.yPos = 100;
      mountainCounter = 0;
      }
     advance();
     blit();
    }
   }
  }
```

Now take a look at the applet, if you haven't already. Notice the parallax scrolling? The ground is scrolling along at three pixels per frame, the rocks behind it are scrolling at two pixels per frame, and the temple and mountain range are creeping along at one pixel per frame. This gives the illusion of depth and distance and is much more visually interesting than a flat scrolling rate. Also notice that Java is clipping all the images to your visible applet area automatically, so you don't have to worry about your images scrolling off the edge of the screen with disastrous results. There you have it! Congratulations, you've come a long way. Now move on to audio in Java.

Bright lights, loud city

So far, we have touched upon the visual side of things, but what about sound? What good is a spaceship flying through space without the satisfying whirs and clicks of alien technology? Where there's animation, there should be sound. Once again, the Java API for playing sound is almost insultingly easy:

```
AudioClip a = getAudioClip(getCodeBase(), "sounds/sound.au");
a.play();
```

All sound types are encapsulated by the class AudioClip, just as all image types are covered by Image. Like drawing images, before we can play a sound we have to fetch it first with the getAudioClip() function. This returns an AudioClip reference that we can use to call the play() method.

Although the Java JDK 1.1 can only support the audio (.au) sound file format, the Java JDK 1.2 can also support Wave (.wav) sound file format.

I can already hear you saying, *What about audio-clip loading latency?* `MediaTracker` *doesn't work for sounds.* The `getAudioClip()` function actually waits until the sound is loaded before it returns, providing the sound resource functionality that the `MediaTracker` is missing. The other useful functions for playing sounds are the `stop()` and `loop()` sound methods, which behave as you might expect. The only loophole (so to speak) when you play sounds is that there is currently no way to tell what sounds are playing—or when a sound has stopped playing. Listing 29-10 shows a sample applet that demonstrates Java audio in all its playing, stopping, and looping glory:

Listing 29-10: **A Sample Java Audio Applet**

```
import java.applet.*;
import java.util.Vector;

public class SoundsTest extends Applet implements Runnable {
  private Vector soundList;
  private Thread t;

  public void init() {
    getAppletContext().showStatus("Getting audio clips...(this
      may sound funky!)");
    soundList = new Vector();
    AudioClip a;
    a = getAudioClip(getCodeBase(), "sounds/intro.au");
    soundList.addElement(a);
    a = getAudioClip(getCodeBase(), "sounds/bullet.au");
    soundList.addElement(a);
    a = getAudioClip(getCodeBase(), "sounds/warp.au");
    soundList.addElement(a);
    a = getAudioClip(getCodeBase(), "sounds/explode2.au");
    soundList.addElement(a);

    try {
      t.sleep(4000);
    } catch(InterruptedException e) {
      System.out.println("Thread sleep failed: "+e.toString());
    }
  }

  public void start() {
    t = new Thread(this);
    t.start();
  }

  public void run() {
    getAppletContext().showStatus("Playing 4 simultaneous
      sounds...");
    for(int i=0;i<soundList.size();i++) {
      ((AudioClip)soundList.elementAt(i)).play();
    }
```

```
  try {
   t.sleep(16000);
  } catch(InterruptedException e) {
   System.out.println("Thread sleep failed: "+e.toString());
  }

  getAppletContext().showStatus("Playing and stopping
   sounds...");

  // Play all sounds
  for(int i=0;i<soundList.size();i++) {
   ((AudioClip)soundList.elementAt(i)).play();
  }

  // Pause 2 seconds
  try {
   t.sleep(2000);
  } catch(InterruptedException e) {
   System.out.println("Thread sleep failed: "+e.toString());
  }

  // Stop all sounds
  for(int i=0;i<soundList.size();i++) {
   ((AudioClip)soundList.elementAt(i)).stop();
  }

  try {
   t.sleep(1000);
  } catch(InterruptedException e) {
   System.out.println("Thread sleep failed: "+e.toString());
  }
   getAppletContext().showStatus("Looping sounds...(annoying,
    huh?)");
  for(int i=0;i<soundList.size();i++) {
   ((AudioClip)soundList.elementAt(i)).loop();
  }
 }

 // Important! Otherwise the sound could potentially keep
 // after applet closes!
 public void stop() {
  for(int i=0;i<soundList.size();i++) {
   ((AudioClip)soundList.elementAt(i)).stop();
  }
 }
}
```

There isn't much more to know about playing sounds in Java—it's just too easy. Incorporating it nicely into a time-critical application is a different matter, but we'll do that next.

A sound-event model

There isn't a whole lot left to the imagination with Java audio. The only hard part is using it in a real application, such as a game or another real-time application. Implementing a sound-event model, suitable for a more comprehensive multimedia application, demonstrates the point.

In this small example, it seems strange to post our sound messages to our event queue instead of just playing them, but think of the example in a larger context. Any function that can send your applet a message can play a sound according to your applet's context. This means we can consolidate all our sound code into one section. For a game, this might mean that we can keep track of, say, the sound for our player's current weapon so we don't need this logic everywhere we want to play a sound. For a multiplayer game, this would mean that you could send sound events to another player's applet. And because specific sounds aren't decided by the function that posts the message, program logic only has to be included in the handleEvent method.

If this is just case-statement-type logic, it doesn't help us too much, but what if we use a complex algorithm for determining which sound to play? Without a sound-event model, we would have to distribute this code everywhere from which a sound might be played—not a very maintainable or practical approach. Even more important, we don't want to have our sound data everywhere we need to be able to trigger a sound from, especially in a networked environment where latency times are a problem. A sound-event model provides that extra layer of abstraction for creating a robust and responsive sound environment.

The only tricky part is posting a message to the component's event queue, and that's not tough. We use the postEvent() method, which takes an Event as a parameter. So before we can call it, we need to build an Event that our handleEvent() method will recognize as an event signaling a sound trigger. There are a few constructors for Event(). Not surprisingly, I'll opt for the easiest one: public Event(Object target, int id, Object arg). For this simple example, we'll pass our applet as the target an arbitrary sound event constant that distinguishes this event as a sound event, and an actual audioClip as our argument.

Here's the code to post the event from within the applet that is receiving the sound:

```
static final int SOUND_EVENT = -1;
public void playSound() {
 this.postEvent(new Event(this, SOUND_EVENT, sound));
 }
```

Here's how we could detect the sound event from within handleEvent():

```
public boolean handleEvent(Event evt) {
  if(evt.id == SOUND_EVENT) {
  ((AudioClip)evt.arg).play();
  return true;
  }
  return false;
}
```

When playSound() is called, it creates a new Event type, SOUND_EVENT, and an argument, sound, that is a fictitious AudioClip. The next time handleEvent is called and that event is read from the event queue, we notice that it is of type SOUND_EVENT so we know the argument is the AudioClip to play. In a bigger system, we probably wouldn't want to pass an AudioClip as a parameter; rather, we would pass a constant such as PLAYER1_CURRENT_WEAPON_SND. That way, our handleEvent could apply logic to this identifier and resolve it to an AudioClip by itself. This also means code that signals a sound to be played doesn't actually have to load the sound itself. Let's try a bigger example that actually runs. This applet plays different sounds depending on mouse events. Try it out with Listing 29-11:

Listing 29-11: **Playing Sounds with Mouse Events**

```
import java.applet.*;
import java.awt.Event;

public class SoundEventModelTest extends Applet {
  // Hopefully we're not clobbering a different event enum
  static final int SOUND_EVENT = -1;
  AudioClip mouseDownSound, mouseUpSound, mouseDragSound;

  // Load sound clips so we'll be all ready to
  // play them at a moment's notice
  public void init() {
  mouseDownSound = getAudioClip(getCodeBase(),
    "sounds/smack.au");
  mouseUpSound = getAudioClip(getCodeBase(), "sounds/pop.au");
  mouseDragSound = getAudioClip(getCodeBase(),
    "sounds/bullet.au");
  }

  // We override the handleEvent method to implement two
  // functions. Posting sounds to the event queue when
  // necessary and reading sounds from the event queue
  // and then playing them.
  public boolean handleEvent(Event evt) {
```

(continued)

Listing 29-11 *(continued)*

```
      // We received a sound event that we posted!
      if(evt.id == SOUND_EVENT) {
       ((AudioClip)evt.arg).play();
       return true;
      }

      // User pressed down on a mouse button, post an event
      // to play the mouse down sound...
      if(evt.id == Event.MOUSE_DOWN) {
       getAppletContext().showStatus("MouseDown");
       this.postEvent(new Event(this, SOUND_EVENT,
        mouseDownSound));
       return true;
      }

      // User released a mouse button, post an event to play
      // the mouse up sound...
      if(evt.id == Event.MOUSE_UP) {
       getAppletContext().showStatus("MouseUp");
       this.postEvent(new Event(this, SOUND_EVENT, mouseUpSound));
       return true;
      }

      // User is dragging the mouse, post an event to play the
      // mouse drag sound...
      if(evt.id == Event.MOUSE_DRAG) {
       getAppletContext().showStatus("MouseDrag");
       this.postEvent(new Event(this, SOUND_EVENT,
        mouseDragSound));
       return true;
      }
      return false;
     }
   }
```

Although slightly annoying, this example starts to showcase the event model in action. Remember, those events could be posted from other applets or applications using InterApplet Communication.

The only other feature that would be useful to add to our sound-event model is the capability to track sounds that are currently playing. This could be done by the programmer registering a play duration for each sound to be played. The sound model would track the time when a sound was started and could provide simple functions to query whether a specified sound's duration had passed yet. This wouldn't be perfect, as playing sounds is largely system dependent, but it would probably work reasonably well for most applications.

Summary

Adding multimedia to your applications can bring new and dynamic life to your Java applications. There are a number of standard animation techniques, such as double-buffering and sprites, which can dramatically enhance your Java-based multimedia applications. Key points to remember about this chapter include the following:

✦ One of the most exciting features of Java is its capability to help developers create sophisticated multimedia software products with relatively little effort. With built-in support for graphics, sound, and networking, Java opens the door for a new wave of multimedia technology.

✦ MediaTracker is indispensable when it comes to multimedia animations. With it, we can load images over the network and assign each an "ID number" to group them logically for later retrieval, allowing us to manage multiple animations with a single MediaTracker object. And, even more importantly, MediaTracker allows us to quickly and easily ensure that all images for a particular group are completely loaded before using them.

✦ When your rendering code draws repeatedly to a visible graphics context, synchronization problems lead to visual degradation. Avoid this problem by blitting—drawing to a hidden offscreen buffer in memory; when all rendering for the current frame is completed and in the buffer, the whole buffer is copied to the onscreen visible display area. This entire *double-buffering* process takes place in offscreen memory.

✦ A *sprite* is the term used in graphics programming to describe an image displayed in an animation, like the images typically used in video games. Although they've been around for years in arcade-style video games (and, more recently, in desktop computer games), sprites are now commonly used to spice up Web sites.

✦ Parallax scrolling, a technique for moving sprites realistically, is a special case of simulated perspective (and a lot easier to implement). Implement it by incrementing all sprites' horizontal coordinates according to their supposed distance from the viewer.

✦ Clipping is the process of making sure we don't draw sprites or parts of sprites to an area off-screen. If the aforementioned grass is scrolled off one edge of the screen, normally we would have to adjust the grass size so that we don't write to an illegal memory address.

✦   ✦   ✦

The Future of Java

Although Java is unquestionably one of the most significant software developments of our time, the question inevitably comes around to *What next?* After all, we're dealing with the most explosive area ever: network computing in general, and the World Wide Web in particular. Innovations on the Web are being made by the bucketload, with previously unseen technology appearing on the ether every day. We're accustomed to new and exciting Web technology hurtling towards us at Mach 9. So what's in store for Java, and will it keep pace?

Although it's impossible to answer these questions with absolute confidence, it's a sure bet that Java is here to stay. In the short time since it's been available, Java has sparked a revolution on the World Wide Web as well as on computer desktops around the world, thanks to the relative ease with which you can use Java to build cross-platform, network-savvy programs.

But the buzz doesn't stop there. Java is well on its way to revolutionizing the entire consumer-electronics market as well—the very area for which it was originally developed, but which it failed to penetrate at the time. Today, however, it's clear that Java will soon invade home appliances and hand-held gizmos almost as fast as it invaded the Web and our personal computer systems. Gird thyself, my friend.

Thanks to a flurry of advanced Java technologies soon to be released by Sun Microsystems and their many partners, we can expect the Java invasion to continue at a blistering pace. From chips, cards, and international standards, to lightning-fast Just In Time (JIT) compilers, brand new APIs, fully distributed computing capabilities, and Java Network Computer—Java promises to grow by leaps and bounds in just about every way you can imagine.

The question really isn't *Will Java survive?* so much as it is *How in the world can I keep up with Java?* Fortunately, there's an easy way to do just that. As a *Java Bible* reader, you're granted special access to a "living" online article called "The Future of Java." Simply point your Web browser to the following Web site whenever you feel out of touch with the rapidly changing world of Java, and drink it all in:

```
http://www.mantiscorp.com/java/future/
```

As a regularly updated extension of this book, "The Future of Java" is published online to keep you abreast of important Java developments on the horizon. It's my way of saying "thanks" to you for reading the *Java Bible*. I hope you've enjoyed the book, and look forward to hearing from you. Please write to me at aaron@mantiscorp.com.

✦   ✦   ✦

Java Language Reference

You can shape your Java source code by using a versatile set of comments, separators, keywords, literals, data types, variables, and operators. This appendix provides a list of such basic tools, as well as the classes, methods, constructors, interfaces, and variables you can use to create Java objects, packages (groups of classes), strings, and arrays.

Comments

Java supports three different comment styles:

//	This comment can't span more than one line.
/*	This type of comment can, and often does, span multiple lines.
/**	This *Doc Comment* is used to generate documentation automatically from source code. Doc Comments can also span more than one line.

Separators

Separators are characters used to group and arrange Java source code. The following characters are valid Java separators:

( ) { } [ ], .

Keywords

A number of words are *reserved* in Java; you can't use them to name your classes, methods, or variables because each one has a specific purpose, and can be used only for that purpose. These reserved words are also known as *keywords* (see Table A-1).

Table A-1 Java Keywords			
abstract	boolean	break	byte
case	catch	char	class
const	continue	default	do
double	else	extends	false
final	finally	float	for
goto	if	implements	import
instanceof	int	interface	long
native	new	null	package
private	protected	public	return
short	static	super	switch
synchronized	this	throw	throws
true	transient	try	void
volatile	while		

Using a strict definition, the words true, false, and null are not keywords—they are literal constant values—but they are included in this table because they are reserved by Java and cannot be used for any other purpose.

The words const and goto are not defined as part of the Java language, but they are reserved for possible future use.

Literals

Java supports the following types of literals:

✦ Numeric (integer and floating-point)

✦ Character (character and string)

✦ Boolean

✦ The null literal

Numeric literals

The following are *integer literals*. The default is `int` (32 bits). The letter *L* (upper- or lowercase) specifies 64 bits:

```
545 43L 7632 4367 2346 57
```

These next examples are *floating-point literals*. The letter *D* (upper- or lowercase) specifies `double`. The letter *F* (upper- or lowercase) specifies `float`. The default is `double`:

```
5.34 .366 3e-6 5.34F 2.f .366F 3.03e+6f
```

Numeric integer literals can take one of three forms:

✦ Decimal form (representing positive integer values)

✦ Hexadecimal form (representing positive, zero, or negative values)

✦ Octal form (representing positive, zero, or negative values)

The following are numeric literals in decimal form. They consist of an initial digit ranging from 1 to 9, that may be followed by one or more digits ranging from 0 to 9:

```
935467L 534643 63036 2 2L
```

The following are a few examples of hexadecimal literals. They consist of a leading `0x` or `0X`, followed by one or more hexadecimal digits:

```
0xA8870X20C15E0 0xFFFA9B12 0x5AD6 0x63036 0X2 0x2L
```

And here are some octal literals, which consist of a leading 0 optionally followed by one or more digits, ranging from 0 to 7:

```
023505323434 0000 035674L 000235
```

Table A-2 shows the range of decimal, hexadecimal, and octal literals that are legal in Java programming.

Table A-2 Legal Range of Decimal, Hexadecimal, and Octal Literals			
Literal	*Decimal*	*Hexadecimal*	*Octal*
Max Positive (2^{31-1}) int	2147483647	0x7fffffff	017777777777
Max Negative (-2^{31}) int	-2147483648	0x80000000	020000000000
Max Positive (2^{63-1}) long	9223372036854775807L	0x7fffffffffffffffL	0777777777777777777777L
Max Negative (-2^{63}) long	-9223372036854775807L	0x8000000000000000L	0400000000000000000000L

Character literals

Java supports both single-character literals and string literals.

Single-character literals

Single-character literals are expressed either as a single character or as an escape sequence beginning with the backslash character, enclosed in single quotes ('\'). Consider these examples:

```
'a''A' 'z' 'Z' '\t' '\b' '\u012d' '\\'
```

Any character literal can be used as a Unicode escape if you specify the letter *u* and follow it with exactly four hexadecimal digits. A *leading-zero escape* is an octal escape that can be used to express the values '\0' through '\0377' (see Table A-3).

Table A-3
Character Literal Escape Codes

Escape Sequence	Unicode Escape	What They Represent
\b	\u0008	backspace (BS)
\t	\u0009	horizontal tab (HT)
\n	\u000a	linefeed (LF)
\f	\u000c	form feed (FF)
\r	\u000d	carriage return (CR)
\"	\u0022	double quote (")
\'	\u0027	single quote (')
\\	\u005c	backslash (\)

String literals

String literals are comprised of zero or more characters enclosed in double quotes, and may use the same escape sequences as single-character literals.

Following are examples of valid string literals:

`"Hello World!"`	(basic string)
`"Are you looking at me?"`	(your basic string, with an attitude)
`""`	(an empty string)
`" "`	(a string containing a blank)
`"\""`	(a string containing only ")

`"This string is " +`
`"too long to fit " +`
`"on one line!"`
	(three strings concatenated into one using the + operator)

Boolean literals

As with boolean data types generally, boolean literals can hold only one of two possible values: *true* or *false*. You can assign boolean variables to either of these two literals, and use them in expressions:

```
boolean myBoolean = false
while (true) { // infinite loop
}
```

Data Types and Variables

Java supports four categories of data types:

- ✦ Primitive types
- ✦ Class types
- ✦ Interface types
- ✦ Array types

Every variable in a Java program has an associated data type, which is often called its compile-time type since the compiler can always determine the type before a program is executed.

Java also supports two kinds of data values:

- ✦ Primitive values
- ✦ References (references to objects or arrays)

These can be stored in variables, passed to methods as arguments, returned as values, and be operated upon.

Table A-4 shows the primitive data types that are usable in Java.

Table A-4 Primitive Data Types		
Type	**Category**	**Values**
byte	integral arithmetic	8-bit signed twos complement integers
short	integral arithmetic	16-bit signed twos complement integers
int	integral arithmetic	32-bit signed twos complement integers
long	integral arithmetic	64-bit signed twos complement integers
float	floating-point arithmetic	32-bit IEEE 754 floating-point numbers
double	floating-point arithmetic	64-bit IEEE 754 floating-point numbers
char	character	16-bit Unicode characters which are 16-bit unsigned integers
boolean	boolean	true and false

Table A-5 shows the legal value ranges Java allows for integral data types.

Table A-5
Legal Value Ranges for Integral Types

Type	Legal Range
byte	-128 to 127, inclusive
short	-32768 to 32767, inclusive
int	-2147483648 to 2147483647, inclusive
long	-9223372036854775808 to 9223372036854775807, inclusive

Table A-6 shows the legal value ranges Java allows for floating-point data types.

Table A-6
Legal Value Ranges for Floating-Point Types

Type	Legal Range (from smallest to largest)
float	negative infinity, negative finite values, negative zero, positive zero, positive finite values, and positive infinity
double	negative infinity, negative finite values, negative zero, positive zero, positive finite values, and positive infinity

Table A-7 shows Java's default data-type values.

Table A-7
Default Data-Type Values

Type	Default
byte	zero: (byte)0
short	zero: (short)0
int	zero: 0
long	zero: 0L
float	positive zero: 0.0f
double	positive zero: 0.0d
char	null character: '\u0000'
boolean	false
reference (objects)	null

NaN: Not-a-Number

Floating-point data types support a special value known as Not-a-Number (NaN). NaN is used to represent the result of operations such as dividing zero by zero, where an actual number isn't produced. Most operations that have NaN as an operand will produce NaN as a result. A NaN value will never test as equal to any other number, not even itself.

Operators

Operators are used to perform operations on one or more variables or objects. They include arithmetic and boolean operators, as well as a specific set of Java operators.

Java operators

The operators specific to Java are as follows:

=	>	<	!	~	?	:	==
<=	>=	!=	&&	||	++	—	+
-	*	/	&	|	^	%	<<
>>	>>>	+=	-=	*=	/=	&=	|=
^=	%=	<<=	>>=	>>>=			

Table A-8 shows the distinctive order of preference that applies to Java operators.

Table A-8
Java Operator Precedence

Precedence	Operators
First	. ( ) (grouping)
Second	++ — +unary -unary ! ~
Third	new (casting)
Fourth	* / %
Fifth	+binary -binary
Sixth	<< >> >>>
Seventh	< > <= >= instanceof

Precedence	Operators
Eighth	== !=
Ninth	&
Tenth	^
Eleventh	|
Twelfth	&&
Thirteenth	||
Fourteenth	? :
Fifteenth	= += -= *= /= &= |= ^= %= >>= <<= >>>=
Last	,

As noted in Table A-8, some unary and binary arithmetic operators are also Java operators; as such they have specific operations they can perform, as shown in Table A-9.

Table A-9
Arithmetic Operators in Java

Type	Operator	Operation	Notes
Unary	-	negation	
	~	bitwise complement	
	++	increment	Postfix and prefix
	--	decrement	Postfix and prefix
Binary	+	addition	
	+=	addition	(a=a+b) is equivalent to (a+=b)
	-	subtraction	
	-=	subtraction	(a=a-b) is equivalent to (a-=b)
	*	multiplication	
	*=	multiplication	(a=a*b) is equivalent to (a*=b)
	/	division	Rounds toward zero. Division by zero throws `ArithmeticException`.
	/=	division	(a=a/b) is equivalent to (a/=b)
	%	modulo	%0 throws `ArithmeticException`.

(continued)

Table A-9 *(continued)*

Type	Operator	Operation	Notes
	%=	modulo	(a=a%b) is equivalent to (a%=b)
	>>=	right shift(propagate sign)	(a=a>b) is equivalent to(a>=b)
	<<	left shift	
	>>	right shift	Sign is propagated
	>>>	zero-fill right shift	Pads with zeros on left

Java's boolean operators can be unary, binary, or ternary; each type has specific operations and characteristics available to it in Java (as shown in Table A-10).

Table A-10
Boolean Operators in Java

Type	Operator	Operation	Notes
Unary	!	negation	
Binary	&	logical AND	Evaluates both operands
	&=	logical AND	(a=a&b) is equivalent to (a&=b)
	|	logical OR	Evaluates both operands
	|=	logical OR	(a=a|b) is equivalent to (a|=b)
	^	logical XOR	Evaluates both operands
	^=	logical XOR	(a=a^b) is equivalent to (a^=b)
	&&	logical AND	Short-circuit evaluation of operands
	||	logical OR	Short-circuit evaluation of operands
	>	greater than	
	<	less than	
	>=	greater than or equal	
	<=	less than or equal	
	==	equality	
	!=	inequality	
Ternary	?:	if, then	(if a then b else c) is equivalent to (a?b:c)

Classes, Methods, Constructors, Interfaces, and Variables

Classes are the code templates, or blueprints, from which objects are created (instantiated). The body of a class is typically made of variables, which maintain an object's state, and methods that produce the behavior of an object. Special methods known as constructors are used in the instantiation of objects.

Defining classes

Class declaration is especially vital in Java programming. When you declare a class, you can specify (for example):

✦ The name of the class

✦ What type of access other objects will have to it (an access level is specified using a class modifier)

✦ What superclass it inherits state and behavior from (default is `java.lang.Object`)

✦ What interfaces it implements (if any)

Following is the structure of a class definition (items in brackets are optional):

```
[ClassModifier] class className [extends superClass] [implements
interfaces] {
...
/* class body (typically variables and methods) */
...
}
```

Table A-11 shows the `ClassModifier` keywords you can use to custom-tailor a Java class to meet the needs of your application.

Table A-11
ClassModifier keywords

ClassModifier	Description
`<blank>`	When no class modifier is specified, the class or interface is accessible to objects within the current package.
`public`	Specifies that the class or interface is accessible to objects outside the package it is part of. Only one public class is permitted per source code file, and that file must have the same name as the class and a `.java` extension (example: `HelloWorldApplet.java`).

Table A-11 *(continued)*	
ClassModifier	**Description**
final	Specifies that the class or interface can not be subclassed. The Array class, for example, is final. As a result, you can't create an Array subclass.
abstract	Specifies the class cannot be instantiated. It may contain one or more abstract methods (methods defined without an implementation body). All interfaces are abstract.

Inner classes

One class can be defined inside another class. The inner class is only available to the class that contains it. In this example, Tpoint is an *inner class,* available for use only inside Triangle:

```
class Triangle {
    Tpoint p1;
    Tpoint p2
    Tpoint p3;
    public Triangle() {
        p1 = new Tpoint(5,10);
        p2 = new Tpoint(7,21);
        p3 = new Tpoint(30,8);
    }
    class Tpoint {
        int x;
        int y;
        Tpoint(int x,int y) {
            this.x = x;
            this.y = y;
        }
    }
}
```

Anonymous classes

An *anonymous class* is declared without a name. To define an instance of an anonymous class, you would use the new keyword with the name of a particular class you want the anonymous class to extend. In this example, the WindowAdapter class is instantiated with its windowClosing() method overloaded to exit the application:

```
public class Anon extends Frame {
    public Anon() {
        addWindowListener(new WindowAdapter()) {
```

```
public void windowClosing(WindowEvent e) {
    System.exit(0);
}
        }
    }
}
```

This code will exit the application whenever a user closes the window with the mouse.

Defining methods

Methods are the code routines that form the behavior of an object, and are analogous to functions in procedural programming languages. In order to define a method, you must write a method declaration and then implement the body of it. At the very least, a method is made up of:

✦ A return type

✦ The method name

✦ A method body

All three are shown in this piece of code:

```
returnType name() {
...
/* method body */
...
}
```

The example above is a very simple skeleton of a method declaration, which has many optional parts. In the following method declaration summary, each of the items in brackets is optional:

```
[accessSpecifier] [static] [abstract] [final] [native]
    [synchronized] returnType methodName ([paramlist]) [throws
    exceptionsList] {
...
/* method body */
...
}
```

If a method doesn't return a value, use the void keyword in place of a return type:

```
void theMethod() {
}
```

However, if a method does specify a return type, it must return a value of that type:

```
int theMethod() {
... method body ...
return aValue // aValue must be an int!
}
```

Table A-12 shows modifiers for methods, constructors, and member variables.

Table A-12
Modifiers for Methods, Constructors, and Member Variables

Modifier	Description
public	A public class or interface is accessible by any entity that can access the package.
	A public variable, method, or constructor can be accessed by any entity that can access the defining class or interface. It can be accessed from a subclass without qualification. If overridden, it can be accessed from a subclass by using super.
private	A private class or interface can only be accessed from within its defining compilation unit.
	A private variable or method can only be accessed from within its defining class.
	A method can be both private and protected.
protected	A protected constructor can be accessed by code within the same package, or from the constructor of a subclass by using super.
	A protected variable or method can be accessed directly from a subclass without qualification. If it has been overridden, it can be addressed by using super.
	A method can be both private and protected.
<default>	(This is the default when none of public, private, or protected is specified.)
	A default class can be accessed only within its own package.
	A default method is the same as public.
	A default constructor can be addressed from a subclass by using super only if the subclass is in the same package.
	A default variable or method is inherited only by subclasses defined in the same package.
final	A final method or variable cannot be overridden.
	A final class cannot be extended.

Modifier	Description
static	A static field is part of the class and all instances of the class share the same field and its values.
	A static method is part of the class. It can be called normally, as the method of an object, and it can also be called by using the name of the class. Non-static members of the class can refer to it, but it cannot refer to non-static members of the class.
abstract	An abstract class cannot be instantiated—it can only be extended. It may contain one or more abstract methods.
	All interfaces are abstract whether specified so or not.
synchronized	Used when more than one thread is executing. Specifies that the method, constructor, or field will be locked when being used by a thread to prevent simultaneous access by more than one thread.
native	Indicates the method's actual implementation is in another language, commonly C.

Constructors

Constructors are methods having the same name as their class, and are used to perform special initialization of objects when they are created.

Unlike standard methods, constructors cannot have a return type because they default to returning an object of the type being instantiated. They may optionally, however, accept parameters and specify an access level:

```
[accessSpecifier] className([paramlist]) {
}
```

Method and constructor parameters

Methods and constructors may optionally accept one or more parameters. In the case of multiple parameters, a comma is used to separate them. Each parameter is declared as follows:

```
dataType name
```

For example, the following method accepts three parameters:

```
void myMethod (String lastName, int age, float weight) {

   ...
}
```

When a method requires no parameters, the parentheses alone are provided:

```
void myMethod () {
   ...
}
```

Interfaces

An interface is an entirely abstract class. All methods in an interface are abstract, and must be supplied a method body by any class that implements the interface.

The syntax for declaring an interface follows (items in brackets are optional):

```
[public] [abstract] interface name [extends interface1,
    interface2, ...] {
... all methods must be public and abstract ...
... all variables will be treated as public, static, and final
...
}
```

To use an interface, a class need only follow the keyword implements with the name(s) of the interface(s) it plans to use. Although a class may only extend, or subclass, a single superclass, any number of interfaces may be implemented by one class:

```
class myClass implements interface1, interface2, ... {
}
```

Variables

Java classes may contain two types of variables:

   ✦ Member variables: Ones directly associated with the class and objects made from it. (They are declared inside the class but outside of any method.)

   ✦ Non-member variables: Ones not associated with the class. (They are variables declared inside methods, and variables passed in as parameters to methods.)

Variables are used to store either primitive data values, or references to classes (including interfaces), or arrays, and are declared using the following format:

```
dataType variableName
```

More that one variable name may be supplied for a given data type, provided each one is separated from the others by a comma. Variables may optionally be set to a value, or initialized, at the time they are declared. The following are a few variable declarations:

```
byte myByte = 5;
short count = 1234;
int age, miles;
long millimeters, nanoSeconds;
float weight = 2035;
double pi;
char theChar = 'z';
boolean critical = false, webBased = true;
Button okButton = new Button("OK");
AudioClip welcomeSound;
int myArrayOfIntegers[];
```

Member variables

All *member variables* are declared within the body of the class, not inside a method or as a parameter to a method. Member variables come in two flavors: class variables and instance variables. Following is a summary of the possible member variable declarations (items in brackets are optional):

```
[accessSpecifier] [static] [final] [transient] [volatile]
    dataType variableName
```

Note

The `transient` keyword is currently ignored in Java, but is expected to be implemented in a future release of the language. It has to do with values being stored or not being stored for object persistence.

Class variables—those declared using the `static` keyword—occur only once per class, no matter how many instances of that class are created. Memory for class variables is allocated by the Java runtime system the first time a class is encountered, and only then. All instances (objects) of a class share class variables they all see; all access exactly the same value associated with a class variable.

In contrast, instance variables—those declared not using the `static` keyword—are allocated once for every instance of a class. Whenever an instance of a class is created, the system allocates memory for all instance variables in that class. As a result, each object has its own copy of the instance variables defined in a class.

Class variables are distinguished from instance variables using the `static` keyword, as shown in the following example:

```
class Bogus {

static int myClassVar // declare class variable of type int
```

```
int myInstanceVar // declare instance variable of type
int

...

/* Method Declarations would follow... */

...

}
```

The `volatile` keyword can be used to notify the Java compiler that a field is to be accessed by separate threads, and that any thread could change the value. The JVM, then, will not keep local copies of the value but, instead, will access the field itself whenever the value is needed or is to be changed.

Constant variables

Class and instance variables can be declared as `final`, meaning they can never be changed. You can think of final variables as constants: once they're set, which must be done when declared, they can't be altered. To attempt such value modification will invoke an error message from the compiler or the Java runtime.

By convention, constant names in Java are in all capital letters. Thus, you might declare the value of pi using a constant as follows:

```
final double PI = 3.14159265359
```

Non-member variables

Variables that are part of a method parameter list, or are declared inside a class method, are not considered member variables. Although they may be critical to the object, they aren't considered part of the object's formal state. They come into existence when the method is called and disappear when it returns.

Unlike member variables, non-member variables cannot be specified as public, private, protected, final, static, volatile, or even transient. As a result, they have a very simple declaration format:

```
dataType variableName
```

this and *super* variables

In order to allow convenient access to the current object and its superclass, Java provides two special variables: `this` (references the current object) and `super` (references the object's superclass). These variables may be used anywhere in the body of the class, and are often seen inside methods and constructors.

`super` is typically used to invoke a method or constructor in the superclass:

```
super.methodName() // invoke superclass method
super([parameterList]) // invoke superclass constructor
```

`this` can be used to invoke the current object's constructor, although typically isn't used to invoke methods, since the method name alone will do the trick:

```
this([parameterList]) // invoke current object's constructor
this.methodName() // functional equivalent to methodName()
```

`this` is most often used to qualify references to field names. In this example it allows the class to have a variable with the same name as that on the method's argument list:

```
setApCount(int apCount) {
    this.apCount = apCount;
}
```

Objects

Objects are created, or instantiated, from class definitions using the `new` keyword:

```
new className() // instantiates an object from class
```

When a constructor is used in the instantiation of an object, parameters are often required:

```
new className(param1, param2, param3, ...)
```

Typically, the objects you create will be assigned to a variable. To do this, you must declare the variable as being of the same data type as the class itself (or of a data type compatible with the class):

```
className myObject = new className() // set variable equal to
new object
```

Methods in an object are invoked by using dot notation. The invocation includes the name of the method and a list of parameter values:

```
myObject.methodName() // invoke method requiring no parameters
myObject.methodName(param1, param2, param3, ...) // parameters
may be required
```

Variables inside an object may, or may not, be made available by using dot notation. Typically, variables are accessible only though special accessor methods:

```
myObject.variableName // direct access
myObject.getVariableMethod() // access via method
```

Class variables may be directly accessed without having to first instantiate an object, by providing the name of the class in dot notation:

```
className.classVariable /* class variable access without
                              instantiation */
```

Likewise, class methods may be accessed without first requiring object instantiation:

```
className.classMethod() /* class method access without
                             instantiation */
```

Duplicating objects

An object can be duplicated by using the `clone()` method, assuming they are of the same data type (or are compatible) and the class supports cloning. For an object to be cloned, its class must implement the `Clonable` interface, otherwise a `CloneNotSupportedException` will the thrown. Here is an example of cloning:

```
newObjectVariable = anObjectVariable.clone()
```

Determining an object's class

You can find out what class an object was created from by cascading the `getClass()` and `getName()` methods as follows:

```
anyObject.getClass().getName() /* retrieve the class name
                                     (a String) */
```

The above returns a `String` object, and so you might assign it to a string variable for future use:

```
String theClassName = anyObject.getClass().getName()
```

You can also use the `instanceof` operator to determine if an object was created from a specific class. To do so, provide the object on the left of `instanceof` and the class name on the right:

```
anyObject instanceof name
```

The `boolean` value `true` is returned if the object is an instance of the `name` class, has the `name` class as a superclass, or implements the `name` interface. Otherwise `false` is returned.

Comparing objects

Object references can be tested to see whether they refer to the same object in memory by testing for equality this way:

```
anyObject == anotherObject
```

The `boolean` value `true` is returned if the two object references point to the same object, otherwise `false` is returned.

Note

Two different objects can contain the same values, and be identical in all other respects, but this equality test will still result in `false`.

To test two different objects for equality, use the `equals()` method:

```
anyObject.equals(anotherObject)
```

The `boolean` value `true` is returned if the two objects are equal (contain the same values) otherwise `false` is returned. The default `equals()` method inherited from `Object` is a simple test for equality of the contents of the fields in the object, but some classes override `equals()` changing the comparison technique.

Object references

Whenever you assign an object to a variable or pass an object as a parameter to a method or class, it's done by reference. That is, instead of using a copy of the object, a reference—which is much like a pointer in C—is used. You can use the `=` operator to specify which object is being referred to:

```
objectVariable1 = objectVariable2
```

In this example, we don't copy `objectVariable2` into `objectVariable1`. Instead, `objectVariable1` now merely references (or points to) the same thing as `objectVariable2`. Whenever the object referred to by `objectVariable2` is altered, `objectVariable1` sees the result.

This way of treating an object is different from copying the object because both variables point to the same instance rather than maintaining separate copies. The most straightforward way to copy, or duplicate, an object is to *clone* it, as described earlier.

Null references

The null reference is a place holder used to specify that there is currently no instance of an object. That is, we can set object references to null, and then test them to see whether they are null or whether an actual instance is being referred to:

```
anyObject = null // set an object to null

if (anyObject == null) { // test for null

...

}
```

Type wrappers

Java's primitive data types are not objects, and, in many cases, must be "wrapped" inside one before they can be passed as a parameter. To facilitate this process, Java provides these wrapper classes:

```
Boolean (java.lang.Boolean)
Byte (java.lang.Byte)
Character (java.lang.Character)
Integer (java.lang.Integer)
Float (java.lang.Float)
Double (java.lang.Double)
Long (java.lang.Long)
Short (java.lang.Short)
Void (java.lang.Void)
```

Each of these has a TYPE reference that refers to its Class object. The Void wrapper does nothing except hold a type specifier, but it can be used as a convenient placeholder much like null.

Packages

Java classes can be organized into packages, allowing classes to be conceptually grouped with similar classes. Packages allow code to be easily reused, since you can import entire groups of classes (or specific classes in a package) into your own programs without having to manage the whereabouts of the class files.

Placing classes in packages

To specify a class as being part of a particular package, you need only supply the keyword package, followed by the name of the package at the top of the source file (before import statements or class definitions):

```
package packageName; /* makes class(es) in file part of
                        this package */
```

Packages can be nested inside one another by using dot references to qualify the names like

```
package java.awt;
```

and

```
package java.awt.event;
```

Using packages

Classes that are part of a package can be accessed in one of four ways:

1. By importing an entire package using the asterisk (*) wildcard, making all public classes in the package available to your program. When importing packages, you must supply the import statement before the class definition:

   ```
   import java.awt.event.*
   ```

   All that is needed is to refer to the class name:

   ```
   ActionEvent actionEvent = new ActionEvent();
   ```

2. By importing a specific class in a package and referring to the class by name. When importing packages, you must supply the import statement before the class definition:

   ```
   import java.awt.event.ActionEvent;
   ```

   All you need refer to is the class name:

   ```
   ActionEvent actionEvent = new ActionEvent();
   ```

3. By specifying the complete package name without the asterisk as a wildcard:

   ```
   import java.awt.event;
   ```

   It is then necessary to only specify the last part of the package name when referring to the class:

   ```
   event.ActionEvent actionEvent = new event.ActionEvent();
   ```

4. By specifying a class by its full name, including the package it is part of, directly in your code. In this case, you don't use the import statement at all and so may specify the class anywhere in the body of your source code:

   ```
   java.awt.event.ActionEvent actionEvent =
       new java.awt.event.ActionEvent();
   ```

Standard Java packages

Java comes with a large library of classes you'll use in your programs. These classes are organized into eight Application Programming Interface (API) packages and one debugging package. (See Table A-14.)

Table A-14 Standard Java Packages: General Description	
API Packages	**Description**
java.applet	Applet classes and interfaces
java.awt	Abstract Windowing Toolkit (AWT) classes and interfaces
java.beans	Platform-neutral component architecture
java.io	Input/output classes and interfaces
java.lang	Core Java language classes and interfaces
java.math	Extended precision arithmetic
java.net	Network classes and interfaces
java.awt.peer	Interface to machine-dependent GUI
java.rmi	Remote Method Invocation
java.security	Encryption and decryption of data
java.sql	Relational database interface definition (JDBC)
java.text	String and text manipulation
java.util	Utility classes and interfaces
org.omg	CORBA
Other Packages	**Description**
javax.servlet	Server-side Java servlets
sun.tools.debug	Debugging classes and interfaces

Table A-15 shows standard Java packages specifying their interfaces and classes.

Table A-15

Standard Java Packages: Interfaces and Classes

Package	Interface(s)	Class(es)
java.applet	AppletContext AppletStub AudioClip	Applet
java.awt	ActiveEvent Adjustable Composite CompositeContext ItemSelectable LayoutManager LayoutManager2 MenuContainer Paint PaintContext PrintGraphics Shape Stroke Transparency	AWTEvent AWTEventMulticaster AWTPermission AlphaComposite BasicStroke BorderLayout Button Canvas CardLayout Checkbox CheckboxGroup CheckboxMenuItem Choice Color Component Container Cursor Dialog Dimension Event EventQueue FileDialog FlowLayout Font FontMetrics Frame GradientPaint Graphics Graphics2D GraphicsConfiguration GraphicsDevice GraphicsEnvironment GridBagConstraints GridBagLayout GridLayout Image Insets Label List MediaTracker Menu MenuBar MenuComponent MenuItem MenuShortcut Panel Point Polygon PopupMenu PrintJob PrintJob2D Rectangle ScrollPane Scrollbar SystemColor TextArea TextComponent TextField TexturePaint Toolkit Window
java.awt.accessibility	Accessible AccessibleLayout AccessibleText	AbstractAccessible AccessibleEnumeration AccessibleResourceBundle AccessibleRole AccessibleState AccessibleStateSet
java.awt.color	ColorSpace ICC_ColorSpace ICC_Profile ICC_ProfileGray ICC_ProfileRGB	CMMException ProfileDataException
java.awt.datatransfer	ClipboardOwner Transferable	Clipboard DataFlavor StringSelection

(continued)

Table A-15 (continued)

Package	Interface(s)	Class(es)
java.awt.dnd	DragSourceListener DropTargetListener FlavorMap	DnDConstants DragSource DragSourceContext DragSourceDragEvent DragSourceDropEvent DragSourceEvent DropTarget DropTargetContext DropTargetContext.TransferableProxy DropTargetDragEvent DropTargetDropEvent DropTargetEvent
java.awt.event	ActionListener AdjustmentListener ComponentListener ContainerListener FocusListener InputMethodListener ItemListener KeyListener MouseListener MouseMotionListener TextListener WindowListener	ActionEvent AdjustmentEvent ComponentAdapter ComponentEvent ContainerAdapter ContainerEvent FocusAdapter FocusEvent InputEvent InputMethodEvent ItemEvent KeyAdapter KeyEvent MouseAdapter MouseEvent MouseMotionAdapter PaintEvent TextEvent WindowAdapter WindowEvent
java.awt.font	MultipleMaster OpenType	GlyphJustificationInfo GlyphMetrics GlyphSet StyledString StyledStringIterator TextAttributeSet TextHitInfo TextLayout
java.awt.geom	PathIterator	AffineTransform Arc2D Arc2D.Float Area CubicCurve2D CubicCurve2D.Float Dimension2D Ellipse2D Ellipse2D.Float FlatteningPathIterator GeneralPath GeneralPathIterator Line2D Line2D.Float Point2D Point2D.Double Point2D.Float QuadCurve2D QuadCurve2D.Float Rectangle2D Rectangle2D.Double Rectangle2D.Float RectangularShape RoundRectangle2D RoundRectangle2D.Float

Package	Interface(s)	Class(es)
	InputMethodRequests	InputContext InputMethodHighlight
java.awt.im		
java.awt.image	BufferedImageOp ImageConsumer	AffineTransformOp
	ImageObserver ImageProducer	AreaAveragingScaleFilter BandCombineOp
	ImagingLib RasterImageConsumer	BandedSampleModel
	RasterOp RenderedImage	BilinearAffineTransformOp BufferedImage
	TileChangeListener	BufferedImageFilter ByteLookupTable
	WritableRenderedImage	ColorConvertOp ColorModel
		ComponentColorModel ComponentSampleModel
		ConvolveOp CropImageFilter DataBuffer
		DataBufferByte DataBufferInt
		DataBufferShort DirectColorModel
		FilteredImageSource ImageFilter
		IndexColorModel Kernel LookupOp
		LookupTable MemoryImageSource
		MultiBandPackedSampleModel
		NearestNeighborAffineTransformOp
		PackedColorModel PixelGrabber
		RGBImageFilter Raster ReplicateScaleFilter
		RescaleOp SampleModel ShortLookupTable
		SingleBandPackedSampleModel ThresholdOp
		TileChangeMulticaster WritableRaster
java.awt.peer	ButtonPeer.java	(none)
	CanvasPeer.java	
	CheckboxMenuItemPeer.java	
	CheckboxPeer.java	
	ChoicePeer.java	
	ComponentPeer.java	
	ContainerPeer.java	
	DialogPeer.java	
	FileDialogPeer.java	

(continued)

Table A-15 (continued)

Package	Interface(s)	Class(es)
	FontPeer.java	
	FramePeer.java	
	LabelPeer.java	
	LightweightPeer.java	
	ListPeer.java	
	MenuBarPeer.java	
	MenuComponentPeer.java	
	MenuItemPeer.java	
	MenuPeer.java	
	PanelPeer.java	
	PopupMenuPeer.java	
	ScrollbarPeer.java	
	ScrollPanePeer.java	
	TextAreaPeer.java	
	TextComponentPeer.java	
	TextFieldPeer.java	
	WindowPeer.java	
java.awt.print	Printable	Book Book.PageAndPainter PageFormat Paper
java.awt.swing	Action BoundedRangeModel	AbstractAction AbstractButton
	ButtonModel CellEditor	AbstractButton.ButtonChangeListener
	CellEditorListener	AbstractListModel AbstractLookAndFeel
	ComboBoxEditor	BorderFactory Box Box.Filler BoxLayout
	ComboBoxModel	ButtonGroup CellRendererPane
	DesktopManager	DebugGraphics DefaultBoundedRangeModel
	FileType Icon	DefaultButtonModel DefaultCellEditor
	JComboBox.KeySelectionMana	DefaultCellEditor.EditorDelegate
	llRenderer ListModel	DefaultCellRenderer
	ListSelectionModel Renderer	DefaultCellRenderer.ValueProperty
	ScrollPaneConstants	DefaultDesktopManager
	Scrollable	DefaultFocusManager DefaultListModel
	SingleSelectionModel	DefaultListSelectionModel
	SwingConstants	DefaultSingleSelectionModel

Package	Interface(s)	Class(es)
	UIDefaults.ActiveValue UIDefaults.LazyValue WindowConstants	DiretoryModel DirectoryModel.WindowsRootDir FileType.Computer FileType.ExtensionBased FileType.FloppyDrive FileType.Folder FileType.GenericFile FileType.HardDrive FileType.Hidden FocusManager GrayFilter ImageIcon JApplet JButton JCheckBox JCheckBoxMenuItem JColorChooser JComboBox JComponent JDesktopIcon JDesktopPane JDialog JDirectoryPane JDirectoryPane.DefaultActionListener JDirectoryPane.GoUpAction JDirectoryPane.Redirector JDirectoryPane.SelListener JEditorPane JFileChooser JFileChooser.ModalListener JFrame JInternalFrame JLabel JLayeredPane JList JMenu JMenu.WinListener JMenuBar JMenuItem JOptionPane JPanel JPasswordField JPopupMenu JPopupMenu.ComponentListener JPopupMenu.WinListener JProgressBar JProgressBar.ModelListener JRadioButton JRadioButtonMenuItem JRootPane JRootPane.RootLayout JScrollBar JScrollPane JScrollPane.ScrollBar JSeparator JSlider JSlider.ModelListener JSplitPane JTabbedPane JTabbedPane.ModelListener JTable JTextArea JTextField JTextPane JToggleButton JToggleButton.ToggleButtonModel JToolBar JToolBar.Separator JToolTip JTree *(continued)*

Table A-15 (continued)

Package	Interface(s)	Class(es)
		JTree.DynamicUtilTreeNode JTree.EmptySelectionModel JTree.TreeSelectionRedirector JViewport JViewport.ViewListener JWindow KeyStroke OverlayLayout ProgressMonitor ProgressMonitorInputStream RepaintManager ScrollPaneLayout SizeRequirements SpringLayout SpringLayout.SpringValues SwingUtilities SyntheticImage Timer ToolTipManager ToolTipManager.insideTimerAction ToolTipManager.outsideTimerAction ToolTipManager.stillInsideTimerAction TypedFile UIDefaults UIManager ViewportLayout
java.awt.swing.basic	(none)	AbstractOptionPaneUI AbstractOptionPaneUI.SyncingLayoutManager AbstractTreeUI BasicArrowButton BasicButtonBorder BasicButtonListener BasicButtonUI BasicCheckBoxMenuItemUI BasicCheckBoxMenuItemUI.CheckBoxMenuItemLi stener BasicCheckBoxUI BasicComboBoxEditor BasicComboBoxEditor.UIResource BasicComboBoxRenderer BasicComboBoxRenderer.UIResource BasicComboBoxUI BasicDesktopIconUI BasicDesktopPaneUI BasicDirectoryPaneUI BasicDirectoryPaneUI.Listener BasicEditorPaneUI BasicEditorPaneUI.EditorController BasicFieldBorder BasicFileChooserUI

Package	Interface(s)	Class(es)
		BasicFileChooserUI.CancelAction
		BasicFileChooserUI.GoHomeAction
		BasicFileChooserUI.Listener
		BasicFileChooserUI.MkdirAction
		BasicFileChooserUI.NoFocusButton
		BasicFileChooserUI.OkayAction
		BasicFileChooserUI.TypeRenderer
		BasicFileChooserUI.TypesComboBoxModel
		BasicGraphicsUtils BasicIconFactory
		BasicInternalFrameUI
		BasicInternalFrameUI.BorderListener
		BasicLabelUI BasicListCellRenderer
		BasicListCellRenderer.UIResource
		BasicListUI BasicListUI.DataListener
		BasicListUI.PropertyListener
		BasicListUI.SelectionListener
		BasicLookAndFeel BasicMarginBorder
		BasicMenuBarBorder BasicMenuBarUI
		BasicMenuBarUI.ContaineeListener
		BasicMenuBarUI.ContaineeMenuListener
		BasicMenuBarUI.ContainerListener
		BasicMenuBarUI.DragListener
		BasicMenuBarUI.MenuSelectionListener
		BasicMenuItemUI
		BasicMenuItemUI.MenuItemListener
		BasicMenuUI BasicMenuUI.DragListener
		BasicMenuUI.MenuChangeListener
		BasicMenuUI.MenuMouseListener
		BasicMenuUtilities BasicOptionPaneUI
		BasicPasswordFieldUI BasicPopupMenuUI
		BasicPopupMenuUI.ComponentListener
		BasicPopupMenuUI.DragListener

(continued)

Table A-15 *(continued)*

Package	Interface(s)	Class(es)
		BasicPopupMenuUI.MenuSelectionListener
		BasicPopupMenuUI.PopupContainerListener
		BasicPopupMenuUI.PopupContainerListener
		.ContaineeListener
		BasicPopupMenuUI.PopupListener
		BasicProgressBarUI
		BasicRadioButtonMenuItemUI
		BasicRadioButtonMenuItemUI.RadioButtonMenu
		ItemListener BasicRadioButtonUI
		BasicScrollBarUI
		BasicScrollBarUI.ArrowButtonListener
		BasicScrollBarUI.ModelListener
		BasicScrollBarUI.ScrollListener
		BasicScrollBarUI.TrackListener
		BasicScrollPaneUI
		BasicScrollPaneUI.BasicScrollPaneLayout
		BasicScrollPaneUI.HSBListener
		BasicScrollPaneUI.VSBListener
		BasicScrollPaneUI.ViewportListener
		BasicSeparatorUI BasicSliderUI
		BasicSliderUI.ActionScroller
		BasicSliderUI.FListener
		BasicSliderUI.ModelListener
		BasicSliderUI.ScrollListener
		BasicSliderUI.SizingListener
		BasicSliderUI.TrackListener BasicSpinnerUI
		BasicSplitPaneDivider
		BasicSplitPaneDivider.DividerLayout
		BasicSplitPaneDivider.DragController
		BasicSplitPaneDivider.MouseHandler
		BasicSplitPaneDivider
		.VerticalDragController BasicSplitPaneUI

Package	Interface(s)	Class(es)
		BasicSplitPaneUI.BasicHorizontalLayout Manager
		BasicSplitPaneUI.BasicSplitPaneBorder
		BasicSplitPaneUI.
		BasicVerticalLayoutManager
		BasicTabbedPaneUI
		BasicTableHeaderUI BasicTableUI
		BasicTextAreaUI BasicTextFieldUI
		BasicTextPaneUI BasicTextUI
		BasicToggleButtonUI BasicToolBarUI
		BasicToolTipUI BasicTreeCellEditor
		BasicTreeCellEditorContainer
		BasicTreeCellRenderer BasicTreeUI
		BasicTreeUI.BasicTreeMouseListener
		BasicTreeUI.BasicTreeUIPaintInfo
		BasicTreeUI.CollapsedIcon
		BasicTreeUI.ExpandedIcon
		BasicVisibleTreeNode LargeTreeModelNode
		Spinner StringSpinner VisibleTreeNode
java.awt.swing.beaninfo **(none)**		AbstractButtonBeanInfo JButtonBeanInfo
		JCheckBoxBeanInfo JComboBoxBeanInfo
		JComponentBeanInfo JInternalFrameBeanInfo
		JLabelBeanInfo JMenuBeanInfo
		JMenuItemBeanInfo JOptionPaneBeanInfo
		JPopupMenuBeanInfo JRadioButtonBeanInfo
		JSplitPaneBeanInfo JToggleButtonBeanInfo
		JTreeBeanInfo SwingBeanInfo
java.swing.border	Border	AbstractBorder BevelBorder CompoundBorder
		EmptyBorder EtchedBorder LineBorder
		MatteBorder SoftBevelBorder TitledBorder

(continued)

Table A-15 (continued)

Package	Interface(s)	Class(es)
java.swing.event	AncestorListener ChangeListener DocumentEvent DocumentEvent.ElementChange DocumentListener ListDataListener ListSelectionListener MenuListener TableColumnModelListener TableModelListener TreeExpansionListener TreeModelListener TreeSelectionListener	AncestorEvent ChangeEvent DragEvent EventListenerList ListDataEvent ListSelectionEvent MenuEvent TableColumnModelEvent TableModelEvent TreeExpansionEvent TreeModelEvent TreeSelectionEvent
java.awt.swing.jlf	(none)	JFillSlider JLFArrowIcon JLFButtonBorder JLFButtonListener JLFButtonUI JLFButtonUI.JLFButtonMargin JLFCheckBoxMenuItemUI JLFCheckBoxUI JLFComboBoxEditor JLFComboBoxEditor.UIResource JLFComboBoxIcon JLFComboBoxListCellRenderer JLFComboBoxListCellRenderer.UIResource JLFComboBoxUI JLFDesktopIconUI JLFDesktopManager JLFDesktopMenu JLFDesktopPaneUI JLFDirectoryPaneUI JLFFileChooserUI JLFFileChooserUI.JLFTypeRenderer JLFFrameBorder JLFIconFactory JLFInternalFrameButton JLFInternalFrameUI JLFLabelUI JLFListCellRenderer JLFListUI JLFLookAndFeel JLFMenuBarBorder JLFMenuBarUI JLFMenuItemBorder JLFMenuItemUI JLFMenuUI JLFOldSliderUI

Package	Interface(s)	Class(es)
		JLFOldTabbedPaneUI JLFPasswordFieldUI
		JLFPopupMenuBorder JLFPopupMenuUI
		JLFProgressBarUI JLFRadioButtonMenuItemUI
		JLFRadioButtonUI JLFRolloverButtonBorder
		JLFScrollBarUI JLFScrollButton
		JLFScrollPaneUI JLFSeparatorUI JLFSliderUI
		JLFSpinnerUI JLFSplitPaneDivider
		JLFSplitPaneUI JLFTabbedPaneUI
		JLFTableHeaderUI JLFTableUI JLFTextAreaUI
		JLFTextBorder JLFTextFieldUI JLFTextPaneUI
		JLFToggleButtonUI JLFToolBarUI
		JLFToolTipUI JLFTreeCellRenderer JLFTreeUI
		JLFUtilities
java.awt.swing.motif	(none)	MotifBorderFactory MotifButtonListener
		MotifButtonUI MotifCheckBoxMenuItemUI
		MotifCheckBoxMenuItemUI
		.CheckboxMenuItemListener MotifCheckBoxUI
		MotifComboBoxRenderer
		MotifComboBoxRenderer.UIResource
		MotifComboBoxUI MotifDesktopIconUI
		MotifDesktopPaneUI MotifEditorPaneUI
		MotifFrameBorder MotifGraphicsUtils
		MotifInternalFrameBorder
		MotifInternalFrameUI MotifLabelUI
		MotifLookAndFeel MotifMenuBarUI
		MotifMenuBarUI.ContaineeListener
		MotifMenuBarUI.ContaineeMenuListener
		MotifMenuItemUI
		MotifMenuItemUI.MenuItemListener
		MotifMenuUI MotifMenuUI.MenuMouseListener
		MotifOptionPaneUI MotifPasswordFieldUI
		MotifPopupMenuUI

(continued)

Table A-15 (continued)

Package	Interface(s)	Class(es)
		MotifPopupMenuUI.MenuSelectionListener
		MotifProgressBarUI
		MotifRadioButtonMenuItemUI
		MotifRadioButtonMenuItemUI.RadioButtonMenu
		ItemListener MotifRadioButtonUI
		MotifScrollBarButton MotifScrollBarUI
		MotifScrollBarUI MotifScrollPaneUI MotifSeparatorUI
		MotifSliderUI MotifSplitPaneDivider
		MotifSplitPaneUI MotifTabbedPaneUI
		MotifTextAreaUI MotifTextFieldUI
		MotifTextFieldUI.MotifFieldController
		MotifTextPaneUI MotifTextUI
		MotifTextUI.MotifCaret
		MotifTextUI.MotifController
		MotifToggleButtonUI MotifToolTipUI
		MotifTreeCellRenderer
		MotifTreeCellRenderer.TreeLeafIcon
		MotifTreeUI MotifTreeUI.MotifCollapsedIcon
		MotifTreeUI.MotifExpandedIcon
java.awt.swing.multi	(none)	MultiButtonUI MultiCheckBoxMenuItemUI
		MultiComboBoxUI MultiDesktopIconUI
		MultiDesktopPaneUI MultiDirectoryPaneUI
		MultiInternalFrameUI MultiLabelUI
		MultiListUI MultiLookAndFeel
		MultiMenuBarUI MultiMenuItemUI MultiMenuUI
		MultiOptionPaneUI MultiPopupMenuUI
		MultiProgressBarUI
		MultiRadioButtonMenuItemUI
		MultiScrollBarUI MultiScrollPaneUI
		MultiSeparatorUI MultiSliderUI
		MultiSpinnerUI MultiSplitPaneUI
		MultiTabbedPaneUI MultiTableHeaderUI

Package	Interface(s)	Class(es)
		MultiTableUI MultiTextUI MultiToggleButtonUI MultiToolBarUI MultiToolTipUI MultiTreeUI
java.awt.swign.plaf	UIResource	BorderUIResource ButtonUI CheckBoxMenuItemUI ColorUIResource ComboBoxUI ComponentUI DesktopIconUI DesktopPaneUI DimensionUIResource DirectoryPaneUI FileChooserUI FontUIResource IconUIResource InsetsUIResource InternalFrameUI LabelUI ListUI MenuBarUI MenuItemUI MenuUI OptionPaneUI PopupMenuUI ProgressBarUI RadioButtonMenuItemUI ScrollBarUI ScrollPaneUI SeparatorUI SliderUI SpinnerUI SplitPaneUI TabbedPaneUI TableHeaderUI TableUI TextUI ToggleButtonUI ToolBarUI ToolTipUI TreeUI
java.awt.swing.table	TableCellEditor TableCellRenderer TableColumnModel TableModel	AbstractTableModel DefaultTableColumnModel DefaultTableModel JTableHeader TableColumn
java.awt.swing.target	Iterator Target TargetManager Trigger	TargetManager.Abstract TargetManager.Dummy TargetManager.Implementation TargetManager.Util Trigger.Abstract TriggerAction
java.awt.swing.text	AbstractDocument. AttributeContext AbstractDocument. Content AttributeSet Caret Document Element	AbstractDocument AbstractDocument.AbstractElement AbstractDocument.BranchElement AbstractDocument.LeafElement BoxView ComponentView CompositeView DefaultCaret

(continued)

Table A-15 (continued)

Package	Interface(s)	Class(es)
	Highlighter Highlighter. Highlight Highlighter. HighlightPainter Keymap MutableAttributeSet Position Style StyledDocument TabExpander TextController ViewFactory	DefaultDocumentEvent DefaultDocumentEvent.ElementEdit DefaultEditorKit DefaultHighlighter DefaultHighlighter.DefaultHighlightPainter DefaultStyledDocument DefaultStyledDocument.ElementBuffer DefaultStyledDocument.ElementSpec DefaultStyledDocument.SectionElement DefaultTextController DefaultTextController.KeyBinding DefaultTextUI EditorKit FieldView IconView JTextComponent LabelView ParagraphView PasswordView PlainDocument PlainView Segment SimpleAttributeSet StringContent StyleConstants StyleContext StyleContext.NamedStyle StyledEditorKit StyledEditorKit.AlignmentAction StyledEditorKit.BoldAction StyledEditorKit.FontFamilyAction StyledEditorKit.FontSizeAction StyledEditorKit.ForegroundAction StyledEditorKit.ItalicAction TextAction Utilities View
java.awt.swing.undo	StateEditable UndoableEdit UndoableEditListener	AbstractUndoableEdit CompoundEdit StateEdit UndoManager UndoableEditEvent UndoableEditSupport

Package	Interface(s)	Class(es)
java.beans	Aggregate AppletInitializer BeanInfo Customizer Delegate DesignMode PropertyChangeListener PropertyEditor VetoableChangeListener Visibility VisibilityState	AggregateObject BeanDescriptor Beans EventSetDescriptor FeatureDescriptor IndexedPropertyDescriptor Introspector MethodDescriptor ParameterDescriptor PropertyChangeEvent PropertyChangeSupport PropertyDescriptor PropertyEditorManager PropertyEditorSupport SimpleBeanInfo VetoableChangeSupport
java.beans.beancontext	BeanContext BeanContextChild BeanContextMembershipListener	BeanContextAddedEvent BeanContextEvent BeanContextMembershipEvent BeanContextRemovedEvent BeanContextSupport BeanContextSupport.BCSChildInfo
java.io	DataInput DataOutput Externalizable FilenameFilter ObjectInput ObjectInputValidation ObjectOutput Replaceable Resolvable Serializable	BufferedInputStream BufferedOutputStream BufferedReader BufferedWriter ByteArrayInputStream ByteArrayOutputStream CharArrayReader CharArrayWriter DataInputStream DataOutputStream File FileDescriptor FileInputStream FileOutputStream FilePermission FileReader FileWriter FilterInputStream FilterOutputStream FilterReader FilterWriter InputStream InputStreamReader LineNumberInputStream LineNumberReader ObjectInputStream ObjectInputStream.GetField ObjectOutputStream ObjectOutputStream.PutField ObjectStreamClass ObjectStreamField OutputStream OutputStreamWriter

(continued)

Table A-15 (continued)

Package	Interface(s)	Class(es)
java.lang		PipedInputStream PipedOutputStream PipedReader PipedWriter PrintStream PrintWriter PushbackInputStream PushbackReader RandomAccessFile Reader SequenceInputStream SerializablePermission StreamTokenizer StringBufferInputStream StringReader StringWriter Writer
java.lang	Cloneable Comparable Runnable Runtime.MemoryAdvice	Boolean Byte Character Class ClassLoader Compiler Double Float Integer Long Math Number Object Package Process Runtime RuntimePermission SecurityManager Short String StringBuffer System Thread ThreadGroup ThreadLocal Throwable Void
java.lang.ref	(none)	CachedReference GuardedReference PhantomReference Reference ReferenceQueue WeakReference
java.lang.reflect	Member	AccessibleObject Array Constructor Field Method Modifier ReflectPermission
java.math	(none)	BigDecimal BigInteger
java.net	ContentHandlerFactory FileNameMap SocketImplFactory URLStreamHandlerFactory	Authenticator ContentHandler DatagramPacket DatagramSocket DatagramSocketImpl HttpURLConnection InetAddress JarURLConnection MulticastSocket NetPermission PasswordAuthentication ServerSocket Socket SocketImpl SocketPermission URL URLClassLoader URLConnection URLEncoder URLStreamHandler

Package	Interface(s)	Class(es)
java.rmi	Remote	MarshalledObject Naming RMISecurityManager
java.rmi.activation	ActivationInstantiator ActivationMonitor ActivationSystem Activator	Activatable ActivationDesc ActivationGroup ActivationGroupDesc ActivationGroupID ActivationID
java.rmi.dgc	DGC	Lease VMID
java.rmi.registry	Registry RegistryHandler	LocateRegistry
java.rmi.server	LoaderHandler RMIFailureHandler RemoteCall RemoteRef ServerRef Skeleton Unreferenced	LogStream ObjID Operation RMIClassLoader RMISocketFactory RemoteObject RemoteServer RemoteStub SocketType UID UnicastRemoteObject
java.security	Certificate Guard Key Principal PrivateKey PublicKey	AccessControlContext AccessController AlgorithmParameterGenerator AlgorithmParameterGeneratorSpi AlgorithmParameters AlgorithmParametersSpi BasicPermission CodeSource DigestInputStream DigestOutputStream GuardedObject Identity IdentityScope KeyFactory KeyFactorySpi KeyPair KeyPairGenerator KeyPairGeneratorSpi KeyStore MessageDigest MessageDigestSpi Permission PermissionCollection Permissions Policy Provider SecureClassLoader SecureRandom Security SecurityPermission Signature SignatureSpi SignedObject Signer
java.security.acl	Acl AclEntry Group Owner Permission	AclNotFoundException LastOwnerException NotOwnerException

(continued)

Table A-15 (continued)

Package	Interface(s)	Class(es)
java.security.cert	X509Extension	Certificate RevokedCertificate X509CRL X509Certificate
java.security.interfaces	DSAKey DSAKeyPairGenerator DSAParams DSAPrivateKey DSAPublicKey	(none)
java.security.spec	AlgorithmParameterSpec KeySpec	DSAParameterSpec DSAPrivateKeySpec DSAPublicKeySpec EncodedKeySpec PKCS8EncodedKeySpec X509EncodedKeySpec
java.sql	CallableStatement Connection DatabaseMetaData Driver PreparedStatement ResultSet ResultSetMetaData Statement	Date DriverManager DriverPropertyInfo Time Timestamp Types
java.text	AttributeSet AttributedCharacterIterator CharacterIterator MutableAttributeSet	Annotation AttributedString BreakIterator ChoiceFormat CollationElementIterator CollationKey Collator DateFormat DateFormatSymbols DecimalFormat DecimalFormatSymbols FieldPosition Format MessageFormat NumberFormat ParsePosition RuleBasedCollator SimpleDateFormat StringCharacterIterator
java.util	Collection Comparator Enumeration EventListener Iterator List ListIterator Map Map.Entry Observer Set	AbstractCollection AbstractList AbstractMap AbstractSequentialList AbstractSet ArrayList ArrayMap ArraySet Arrays BitSet Calendar Collections Date Dictionary EventObject GregorianCalendar HashMap HashSet Hashtable LinkedList ListResourceBundle Locale Observable Properties PropertyPermission PropertyResourceBundle Random ResourceBundle SimpleTimeZone Stack StringTokenizer TimeZone TreeMap Vector

Package	Interface(s)	Class(es)
java.util.jar	(none)	Attributes Attributes.Name JarEntry JarFile JarInputStream JarOutputStream Manifest
java.util.mime	(none)	MimeType MimeTypeParameterList
java.util.zip	Checksum	Adler32 CRC32 CheckedInputStream CheckedOutputStream Deflater DeflaterOutputStream GZIPInputStream GZIPOutputStream Inflater InflaterInputStream ZipEntry ZipFile ZipInputStream ZipOutputStream
javax.servlet	Servlet ServletConfig ServletContext ServletRequest ServletResponse SingleThreadModel	GenericServlet ServletInputStream ServletOutputStream
javax.servlet.http	HttpServletRequest HttpServletResponse HttpSession HttpSessionBindingListener HttpSessionContext	Cookie HttpServlet HttpSessionBindingEvent HttpUtils
org.omg.CORBA	ARG_IN ARG_INOUT ARG_OUT AliasDef ArrayDef AttributeDef CTX_RESTRICT_SCOPE ConstantDef Contained Container EnumDef ExceptionDef IDLType IRObject ImplementationDef InterfaceDef ModuleDef Object OperationDef PrimitiveDef Repository SequenceDef	Any AnyHolder AttributeDescription AttributeMode BooleanHolder ByteHolder CharHolder CompletionStatus ConstantDescription Context ContextList Current DefinitionKind DoubleHolder DynamicImplementation Environment ExceptionDescription ExceptionList FloatHolder IntHolder InterfaceDescription LongHolder ModuleDescription NVList NamedValue ORB ObjectHolder OperationDescription OperationMode

(continued)

Table A-15 (continued)

Package	Interface(s)	Class(es)
	StringDef StructDef TypedefDef UnionDef	ParameterDescription ParameterMode PrimitiveKind Principal PrincipalHolder Request ServerRequest ShortHolder StringHolder StructMember TCKind TypeCode TypeCodeHolder TypeDescription UnionMember
org.omg.CORBA.ContainedPackage	(none)	Description
org.omg.CORBA.ContainerPackage	(none)	Description
org.omg.CORBA.ORBPackage	(none)	(none)
org.omg.CORBA.TypeCodePackage	(none)	(none)
org.omg.CORBA.portable	Streamable	Delegate InputStream ObjectImpl OutputStream
org.omg.CosNaming	BindingIterator NamingContext _BindingIteratorOperations _NamingContextOperations	Binding BindingHelper BindingHolder BindingIteratorHelper BindingIteratorHolder BindingListHelper BindingListHolder BindingType BindingTypeHelper BindingTypeHolder IstringHelper NameComponent NameComponentHelper NameComponentHolder NameHelper NameHolder NamingContextHelper NamingContextHolder _BindingIteratorImplBase _BindingIteratorStub _BindingIteratorTie _NamingContextImplBase _NamingContextStub _NamingContextTie

Package	Interface(s)	Class(es)
`org.omg.CosNaming.NamingContextPackage`	(none)	`AlreadyBoundHelper AlreadyBoundHolder CannotProceedHelper CannotProceedHolder InvalidNameHelper InvalidNameHolder NotEmptyHelper NotEmptyHolder NotFoundHelper NotFoundHolder NotFoundReason NotFoundReasonHelper NotFoundReasonHolder`

Table A-16 shows the exceptions and errors relevant to specific standard Java packages.

Table A-16
Standard Java Packages: Exceptions and Errors

Package	Exceptions	Errors
`java.awt`	`AWTException IllegalComponentStateException`	`AWTError`
`java.awt.color`	`CMMException ProfileDataException`	(none)
`java.awt.datatransfer`	`UnsupportedFlavorException`	(none)
`java.awt.dnd`	`InvalidDnDOperationException`	(none)
`java.awt.geom`	`IllegalPathStateException NoninvertibleTransformException`	(none)
`java.awt.image`	`ImagingOpException RasterFormatException`	(none)
`java.awt.swing.text`	`BadLocationException`	(none)

(continued)

Table A-16 *(continued)*

Package	Exceptions	Errors
java.awt.swing.undo	CannotRedoException CannotUndoException	(none)
java.beans	IntrospectionException PropertyVetoException	(none)
java.io	CharConversionException EOFException FileNotFoundException IOException InterruptedIOException InvalidClassException InvalidObjectException NotActiveException NotSerializableException ObjectStreamException OptionalDataException StreamCorruptedException SyncFailedException UTFDataFormatException UnsupportedEncodingException WriteAbortedException	(none)
java.lang	ArithmeticException ArrayIndexOutOfBoundsException ArrayStoreException ClassCastException ClassNotFoundException CloneNotSupportedException Exception IllegalAccessException IllegalArgumentException IllegalMonitorStateException IllegalStateException IllegalThreadStateException	AbstractMethodError ClassCircularityError ClassFormatError Error ExceptionInInitializerError IllegalAccessError IncompatibleClassChangeError InstantiationError InternalError LinkageError NoClassDefFoundError NoSuchFieldError NoSuchMethodError OutOfMemoryError StackOverflowError ThreadDeath UnknownError UnsatisfiedLinkError VerifyError

Package	Exceptions	Errors
	IndexOutOfBoundsException InstantiationException InterruptedException NegativeArraySizeException NoSuchFieldException NoSuchMethodException NullPointerException NumberFormatException RuntimeException SecurityException StringIndexOutOfBoundsException UnsupportedOperationException	VirtualMachineError
java.lang.ref	EnqueuedReferenceException	(none)
java.lang.reflect	InvocationTargetException	(none)
java.net	BindException ConnectException MalformedURLException NoRouteToHostException ProtocolException SocketException UnknownHostException UnknownServiceException	(none)
java.rmi	AccessException AlreadyBoundException ConnectException ConnectIOException MarshalException NoSuchObjectException NotBoundException RMISecurityException	(none)

(continued)

Table A-16 (continued)

Package	Exceptions	Errors
	RemoteException ServerError ServerException ServerRuntimeException StubNotFoundException UnexpectedException UnknownHostException UnmarshalException	
`java.rmi.activation`	ActivationException UnknownGroupException UnknownObjectException	(none)
`java.rmi.server`	ExportException ServerCloneException ServerNotActiveException SkeletonMismatchException SkeletonNotFoundException SocketSecurityException	(none)
`java.security`	AccessControlException DigestException GeneralSecurityException InvalidAlgorithmParameter Exception InvalidKeyException InvalidParameterException KeyException KeyManagementException KeyStoreException NoSuchAlgorithmException NoSuchProviderException ProviderException	(none)

Package	Exceptions	Errors
	SignatureException UnrecoverableKeyException	
java.security.acl	AclNotFoundException LastOwnerException NotOwnerException	(none)
java.security.cert	CRLException CertificateEncodingException CertificateException CertificateExpiredException CertificateNotYetValidException CertificateParsingException X509ExtensionException	(none)
java.security.spec	InvalidKeySpecException InvalidParameterSpecException	(none)
java.sql	DataTruncation SQLException SQLWarning	(none)
java.text	ParseException	(none)
java.util	ConcurrentModificationException EmptyStackException MissingResourceException NoSuchElementException TooManyListenersException	(none)
java.util.jar	JarException	(none)
java.util.mime	MimeTypeParseException	(none)
java.util.zip	DataFormatException ZipException	(none)
javax.servlet	ServletException UnavailableException	(none)

(continued)

Table A-16 *(continued)*

Package	Exceptions	Errors
`org.omg.CORBA`	BAD_CONTEXT BAD_INV_ORDER BAD_OPERATION BAD_PARAM BAD_TYPECODE Bounds COMM_FAILURE DATA_CONVERSION FREE_MEM IMP_LIMIT INITIALIZE INTERNAL INTF_REPOS INVALID_TRANSACTION INV_FLAG INV_IDENT INV_OBJREF MARSHAL NO_IMPLEMENT NO_MEMORY NO_PERMISSION NO_RESOURCES NO_RESPONSE OBJECT_NOT_EXIST OBJ_ADAPTER PERSIST_STORE SystemException TRANSACTION_REQUIRED TRANSACTION_ROLLEDBACK TRANSIENT UNKNOWN UnknownUserException UserException WrongTransaction	(none)
`orb.omg.CORBA.ORBPackage`	InvalidName	(none)
`orb.omg.CORBA.` `TypeCodePackage`	BadKind Bounds	(none)
`orb.omg.CosNaming.` `NamingContextPackage`	AlreadyBound CannotProceed InvalidName NotEmpty NotFound	(none)

Control Flow

Java supports several execution-control flow structures, which will be familiar to C and C++ programmers. Tables A-17 through A-19 provide examples of such structures: `if` statements, `switch` statements, `while`, and `do-while` loops, and `label`, `break`, and `continue` statements.

Table A-17
if Statements in Java Control Flow

Syntax	*Example*
```if (boolean expression) { ... code block ... }```	```if (x < 100) { System.out.println("x is LESS than 100") }```
```if (boolean expression) { ... "if" code block ... } else { ... "else" code block ... }```	```if (x < 100) { System.out.println("x is LESS than 100") } else { System.out.println("x is 100 or GREATER") }```
```if (boolean expression) { ... if code block ... } else if (boolean expression){ ... "else if" code block ... } else { ... "else" code block ...```	```if (x < 100) { System.out.println("x is LESS than 100") } else if (x == 100){ System.out.println("x is EXACTLY 100")} } else { System.out.println("x is GREATER than 100")}```

Table A-18
switch Statements in Java Control Flow

Syntax	Example
```switch (expression) { case Constant1: … break case Constant2: … break case Constant3: … break . . . default: … break }```	```switch (x) { case 25: System.out.println("x is twenty- five.") System.out.println("Twenty-five is a good number.") break case 100: System.out.println("x is one hundred.") System.out.println("There are 100 pennies in a dollar.") break case 111: System.out.println("x is one-hundred and eleven.") break case 3396: System.out.println("x is 3,396") System.out.print("3,396 is a big number, ") System.out.println("and important as well...") break default: System.out.println("x is something I didn't anticipate!") break }```

Table A-19
while and *do-while* Loops in Java Control Flow

Syntax	Example

`while (boolean expression) {`
`   … loop body …`
`}`
	`while (x++ < 100) {`
	`   System.out.println("x is: " + x)`
	`}`

`do {`
`   … loop body …`
`} while (boolean expression)`
	`do {`
	`   System.out.println("x is: " + x)`
	`} while (x++ < 100)`

Table A-20
for Loop

Syntax	Example

`for (expression boolean expression`
`expression){`
`   … loop body …`
`}`
	`for (int x=0 x<10 x++) {`
	`   System.out.println("x is: " + x)`
	`}`

Table A-21
label, *break*, and *continue* Statements in Java Control Flow

Syntax[1]	Example

label:
break [label]
	```enterLoop:```
	```int x=0```
	```enterLoop:```
	```while (x++<10) {```
	```System.out.println ("Inside the while loop,```
	```iteration:" + x)```
	``` switch (x) {```
	``` case 0: System.out.println ("Inside```
	``` switch, x equals: " + x)```
	``` break```
	``` case 1: System.out.println ("Inside```
	``` switch, x equals: " + x)```
	``` break```
	``` case 2: System.out.println ("Inside```
	``` switch, x equals: " + x)```
	``` break```
	``` default:```
	``` if (x==5) {```
	``` System.out.println ("Break out of```
	``` switch and while loop.")```
	``` break enterLoop /* break to enterLoop```
	``` label */```
	``` }```
	``` break```
	``` }```
	```System.out.println ("Out of switch, back in```
	``` while loop.")```
	```}```

continue [label]	```int x=0```
	```enterLoop:```
	```while (x++<5) {```
	```System.out.println ("Inside the while loop,```
	```iteration:" + x)```
	``` for (int i=0 i<10i++) {```
	``` System.out.println ("Inside the for loop,```
	``` iteration:" + i)```
	``` if (i == 5) {```
	``` System.out.println ("Transferring flow```
	``` out of for loop!")```
	``` continue enterLoop /* jump to enterLoop```
	``` label when i is 5 */```

Syntax[1]	Example
	``` } } System.out.println ("Out of for loop, back in while.") } ```

[1] Items in brackets are optional.

Strings and Arrays

Java strings and arrays are first-class objects with their own methods. However, the `String` class is declared `final` in Java, and so can't be subclassed. Arrays are instances of a special "invisible" array class which can not be subclassed, either.

String versus StringBuffer

Two Java classes deal with strings— `String` and `StringBuffer`, which allow us to create objects containing character data.

Unlike `String` and `StringBuffer` objects, which can contain only character data, *arrays* can hold any type of data we need, even other arrays—the only restriction is that each element in the array must be of the same type. You can't, for example, have an `int` in one element of an array, and a `char` in another.

Unlike C and C++ strings, which are simply an array of null-terminated characters, Java strings are actually objects. The `String` class is used to create `String` objects, which are immutable (meaning their contents can't be altered after characters have been stored in them). `StringBuffer`, on the other hand, is specifically for strings that are mutable (meaning they can be changed even after we've stored characters in them).

To declare a `String` object, we provide a variable name and the proper data type:

```
String myString
```

We can also initialize a `String` at the time it's declared:

```
String myString = "There once was a woman who lived in a shoe"
```

We can optionally instantiate a `String` object, as we would any other object (although the above technique works just fine):

```
String myString = new String ("There once was a woman who lived in a shoe ")
```

StringBuffer **objects, on the other hand, must be instantiated using the** new **keyword:**

```
StringBuffer myBuffer = new StringBuffer() // empty
// create empty, 50 characters in length:
StringBuffer myBuff2 = new StringBuffer(50)

StringBuffer myBuff3 = new StringBuffer("Hello") /* using
                                               String */
```

Once created, you can add items to a StringBuffer using one of a number of append() methods:

```
myBuffer.append("There once was a woman who lived in a shoe")
```

Since StringBuffer objects can be altered, appending to and changing their content is permitted.

Arrays

In Java, arrays are truly first-class objects. Not only are they impossible to subclass, you won't even find a class definition for them.

To declare an array, we need only specify a variable, through which we'll access the array and the data type of the elements that the array will contain. To differentiate between arrays and standard variables, square brackets ([ ]) are used. Array brackets can appear either directly after the data type or following the variable name:

```
dataType[] variableName;
dataType variableName[];
```

The following are a few array declarations:

```
int myIntegers[]; // declare an array of integers
char[] myCharacters; // declare an array of characters
float myFloats[]; // declare an array of floating-point numbers
String[] myStrings; // declare an array of String objects
StringBuffer myStringBuffs[]; // declare an array of
StringBuffer objects;
```

Before an array can be used, we must instantiate an object. In addition, a dimension for the array must be specified:

```
int myIntegers[] = new int[25]; // declare and instantiate
```

To access the elements in an array, an index (or subscript) must be provided:

```
array[index]
```

Array indexing begins at zero (0), meaning the first element in an array is accessed using an index value of zero:

```
array[0] // access first element in an array
```

As a result of zero-based indexing, the last element in an array is accessed by providing the number of dimensions minus one. For example, in the previous example we supplied a dimension of 25 to the `int` array. To access the last element in this array, we'd supply an index of 24:

```
myIntegers[24] // access last element in array of 25 elements
```

So, to find out how many elements are contained in an array, access the length variable:

```
int len = myIntegers.length; // get length of array
```

Multidimensional arrays

Although Java doesn't support truly multidimensional arrays, you can create arrays of arrays to achieve the same functionality:

```
int grid[][] = new int[10][10]
```

Exceptions

Java features a general-purpose error processing system known as an exception mechanism. Exceptions provide a uniform approach to signaling, and also processing errors, removing much of the burden of traditional error processing. (See Table A-22.)

Table A-22 Throwing an Exception	
Syntax	**Example**

`throw new AnyExceptionObject()`	`public static int myDivide(int x, int y) throws ArithmeticException {`
	 `if (y==0)`
	 `   throw new ArithmeticException()`
	 `      else`
	 `      return (x/y)`
	 `}`

Table A-23 shows the provisions Java makes for catching an exception.

<table>
<tr><td colspan="2" align="center">Table A-23
Catching an Exception</td></tr>
<tr><td>Syntax[1]</td><td>Example</td></tr>
</table>

Syntax[1]	Example

```try {```
```... try body ...```
```} catch (ThrowableClassName```
```variable) {```
```... catch body ...```
```} finally {```
```... finally body ...```
```}```
	```try {```
	```int y = myDivide(10,0)```
	```} catch (ArithmeticException e) {```
	```System.out.println("Arithmetic```
	```exception has been caught.")```
	```} catch (BogusException e) {```
	```System.out.println("XYZ exception```
	```has been caught.")```
	```} finally {```
	```System.out.println("cleaning```
	```up...")```
	```// do any clean-up work here```
	```}```

[1] Multiple *catch* clauses are supported; either the *catch* or *finally* clauses can be omitted, but not both. Both can be present, however.

Threads

In Java, threads of execution can be implemented in one of two ways:

✦ By extending the Thread class.

✦ By implementing the Runnable interface.

Extending the Thread class

```
class AnyClass extends Thread {
...
}
```

Implementing the Runnable interface

```
public class AnyClass extends java.applet.Applet implements
Runnable {
Thread myThread // a variable to hold our thread
public void start() {
if (myThread == null) {
myThread = new Thread(this) // create Thread
object
```

```
myThread.start() // start it
}
}
public void run() {
while (myThread != null) {
.... // what used to be in the start() method goes here
}
}

public void stop() {
myThread.stop() // stop it
myThread = null // prepare for garbage collection
}
}
```

Synchronized methods

To prevent multiple threads from accessing the same method at once, the synchronized keyword may be used to identify the body of that method as a critical section. As a result, only one thread at a time will be allowed to invoke the method. All other threads must wait until the current thread has finished:

```
public synchronized int anyMethod () {

... method body (now a critical section of code that can
...
... only be accessed by one thread at a time) ...

}
```

Although any block of code may be specified as synchronized, it's considered bad programming style to apply this keyword to any code other than a method.

✦   ✦   ✦

What's on the CD-ROM

The CD-ROM that accompanies this book includes a wealth of programs and files to help you become a master Java developer.

Directory Structure

The CD-ROM is organized into the following directory structure:

+ Applets
+ Book
+ JavaWorld
+ Mantis
+ UNIX
+ Win95NT

Applets

The **Applets** directory is packed with Java applets and the source code for each. Here, you'll find a wide range of applets, including many of the Web's top-rated, award-winning programs—over 100 in all! The source code for every one of them is supplied to give you a wide, deep base of Java programs to choose from as you learn Java. These applets can be used in your own Web pages "out of the box," as the basis for your own programs, or simply as a tool to help you learn the language. They have been organized for easy access using a Web browser. Simply open the **index.html** file in this directory, and away you go!

Book

The **Book** directory contains a selection of the Java programs that are developed in the text. Look in the appropriate chapter's directory for the program you're looking for. Use these files to save yourself the effort of typing in the code listings.

JavaWorld

The **JavaWorld** directory contains a collection of articles from back issues of JavaWorld, IDG's Web-based Java magazine that serves as the premier source of online information about Java development. As a valuable supplement to the *Java 1.2 Bible*, its articles contain step-by-step examples and source code; they cover a wide range of Java topics: threads, JFC, database access, inter-applet communication, JavaBeans, tips and tricks, and more.

The articles in this collection have been selected by the editors of JavaWorld to provide the most lasting value to the reader — you! To access the collection, simply open the file **index.html** and follow the links. Don't forget to use the Search function too. It searches the entire archive of back issues on the JavaWorld Web site: http://www.JavaWorld.com.

Mantis

The **Mantis** directory contains archives for Mantis Corporation's LivingLinks, a very powerful Java applet for enlivening Web pages with sound, animation, and multiple hyperlinks. Simply unzip each of the two archives to your hard disk and then open the files **index.html** (in the LivingLinks SDK directory) and **LivingLinks.html** (in the LivingLinks directory) to learn how to use this powerful Web development tool.

UNIX

The **UNIX** directory contains directories for Sun's Java™ JDK, version 1.1.5 and Sun's Beans Development Kit, version 1.0, for Solaris (both SPARC and x86). For the latest JDKs, BDKs, and info, visit Sun's Java Web site at http://java.sun.com. The **UNIX** directory also contains the JDesPro directory, which contains a JAR archive of BulletProof Corporation's JDesigner Pro, a leading development environment for Java intranet and Internet applications.

See the README and installation files in each JDK subdirectory for notes and installation instructions. To install JDesigner Pro, follow these steps:

1. Create a directory on your computer called JDesignerPro.

2. Copy the JAR archive into that directory.

3. Expand the JAR archive using the following command:

   ```
   /jdk1.1.5./bin/jar xvf Jdp2_5.jar
   ```

4. Open the file **index.htm** in your Web browser and click the Installation link for instructions on starting the software.

Win95NT

The **Win95NT** directory contains the following subdirectories:

✦ **BDK:** Sun's Beans Development Kit, version 1.0.

✦ **Explorer:** Microsoft Internet Explorer, version 4.0; simply double-click **setup.exe** to install.

✦ **JDesignerPro:** BulletProof Corporation's JDesigner Pro Java IDE. Simply double-click to install.

✦ **JDK:** Sun's Java™ JDK, version 1.1.5.

✦ **Navigator:** Netscape Navigator, version 4.04 (double-click to install).

✦ **Tools:** Contains archives of GoldWave 3.24, a fully functional digital audio editor; and WinZip 6.3, the ubiquitous Windows archiving utility. To install WinZip, simply double-click the file **wz32v63.exe**; then you can install GoldWave by extracting the Zip archive **gwave324.zip**.

✦   ✦   ✦

Index

(continued)

(continued)

(continued)

(continued)

(continued)

(continued)

Java™ Developer's Kit Version 1.1.5 Binary Code License

This binary code license ("License") contains rights and restrictions associated with use of the accompanying software and documentation ("Software"). Read the License carefully before installing the Software. By installing the Software you agree to the terms and conditions of this License.

1. **Limited License Grant.** Sun grants to you ("Licensee") a non-exclusive, non-transferable limited license to use the Software without fee for evaluation of the Software and for development of Java™ compatible applets and applications. Licensee may make one archival copy of the Software and may re-distribute complete, unmodified copies of the Software to software developers within Licensee's organization to avoid unnecessary download time, provided that this License conspicuously appear with all copies of the Software. Except for the foregoing, Licensee may not re-distribute the Software in whole or in part, either separately or included with a product. Refer to the Java Runtime Environment Version 1.1.5 binary code license (http://java.sun.com/products/JDK/1.1/index.html) for the availability of runtime code which may be distributed with Java compatible applets and applications.

2. **Java Platform Interface.** Licensee may not modify the Java Platform Interface ("JPI", identified as classes contained within the "java" package or any subpackages of the "java" package), by creating additional classes within the JPI or otherwise causing the addition to or modification of the classes in the JPI. In the event that Licensee creates any Java-related API and distributes such API to others for applet or application development, Licensee must promptly publish an accurate specification for such API for free use by all developers of Java-based software.

3. **Restrictions.** Software is confidential copyrighted information of Sun and title to all copies is retained by Sun and/or its licensors. Licensee shall not modify, decompile, disassemble, decrypt, extract, or otherwise reverse engineer Software. Software may not be leased, assigned, or sublicensed, in whole or in part. Software is not designed or intended for use in on-line control of aircraft, air traffic, aircraft navigation or aircraft communications; or in the design, construction, operation or maintenance of any nuclear facility. Licensee warrants that it will not use or redistribute the Software for such purposes.

4. **Trademarks and Logos.** This License does not authorize Licensee to use any Sun name, trademark or logo. Licensee acknowledges that Sun owns the Java trademark and all Java-related trademarks, logos and icons including the Coffee Cup and Duke ("Java Marks") and agrees to: (i) to comply with the Java Trademark Guidelines at http://java.sun.com/trademarks.html; (ii) not do anything harmful to or inconsistent with Sun's rights in the Java Marks; and (iii) assist Sun in protecting those rights, including assigning to Sun any rights acquired by Licensee in any Java Mark.

5. **Disclaimer of Warranty.** Software is provided "AS IS," without a warranty of any kind. ALL EXPRESS OR IMPLIED REPRESENTATIONS AND WARRANTIES, INCLUDING ANY IMPLIED WARRANTY OF MERCHANTABILITY, FITNESS FOR A PARTICULAR PURPOSE OR NON-INFRINGEMENT, ARE HEREBY EXCLUDED.

6. **Limitation of Liability.** SUN AND ITS LICENSORS SHALL NOT BE LIABLE FOR ANY DAMAGES SUFFERED BY LICENSEE OR ANY THIRD PARTY AS A RESULT OF USING OR DISTRIBUTING SOFTWARE. IN NO EVENT WILL SUN OR ITS LICENSORS BE LIABLE FOR ANY LOST REVENUE, PROFIT OR DATA, OR FOR DIRECT, INDIRECT, SPECIAL, CONSEQUENTIAL, INCIDENTAL OR PUNITIVE DAMAGES, HOWEVER CAUSED AND REGARDLESS OF THE THEORY OF LIABILITY, ARISING OUT OF THE USE OF OR INABILITY TO USE SOFTWARE, EVEN IF SUN HAS BEEN ADVISED OF THE POSSIBILITY OF SUCH DAMAGES.

7. **Termination.** Licensee may terminate this License at any time by destroying all copies of Software. This License will terminate immediately without notice from Sun if Licensee fails to comply with any provision of this License. Upon such termination, Licensee must destroy all copies of Software.

8. **Export Regulations.** Software, including technical data, is subject to U.S. export control laws, including the U.S. Export Administration Act and its associated regulations, and may be subject to export or import regulations in other countries. Licensee agrees to comply strictly with all such regulations and acknowledges that it has the responsibility to obtain licenses to export, re-export, or import Software. Software may not be downloaded, or otherwise exported or re-exported (i) into, or to a national or resident of, Cuba, Iraq, Iran, North Korea, Libya, Sudan, Syria or any country to which the U.S. has embargoed goods; or (ii) to anyone on the U.S. Treasury Department's list of Specially Designated Nations or the U.S. Commerce Department's Table of Denial Orders.

9. **Restricted Rights.** Use, duplication or disclosure by the United States government is subject to the restrictions as set forth in the Rights in Technical Data and Computer Software Clauses in DFARS 252.227-7013(c) (1) (ii) and FAR 52.227-19(c) (2) as applicable.

10. **Governing Law.** Any action related to this License will be governed by California law and controlling U.S. federal law. No choice of law rules of any jurisdiction will apply.

11. **Severability.** If any of the above provisions are held to be in violation of applicable law, void, or unenforceable in any jurisdiction, then such provisions are herewith waived to the extent necessary for the License to be otherwise enforceable in such jurisdiction. However, if in Sun's opinion deletion of any provisions of the License by operation of this paragraph unreasonably compromises the rights or increase the liabilities of Sun or its licensors, Sun reserves the right to terminate the License and refund the fee paid by Licensee, if any, as Licensee's sole and exclusive remedy.

Beans Development Kit (BDK) Version 1.0 License

This license ("License") contains rights and restrictions associated with use of the accompanying software.

1. **Limited License Grant.** Sun grants to you ("Licensee") a nonexclusive, nontransferable, worldwide, royalty-free license to use this release of Beans Development Kit Version 1.0 (the "Software"). Licensee agrees that except as provided in Section 2 below, it shall use the Software provided hereunder solely for Licensee's internal evaluation purposes and not for computer operations of any critical nature. This Software is subject to change, which may cause applications developed using the Software to be incompatible with subsequent versions.

2. **Redistribution of Demonstration Files.** Sun grants Licensee the right to use, modify and redistribute the Beans example and demonstration code, including the Bean Box ("Demos"), in both source and binary code form provided that (i) Licensee does not utilize the Demos in a manner which is disparaging to Sun; and (ii) Licensee indemnifies and holds Sun harmless from all claims relating to any such use or distribution of the Demos. Such distribution is limited to the source and binary code of the Demos and specifically excludes any rights to modify or distribute any graphical images contained in the demos.

3. **Restrictions.** The Software is confidential, copyrighted proprietary information of Sun and title to all copies is retained by Sun and/or its licensors. Licensee shall not make copies of Software, other than a single copy of Software in machine-readable format for back-up or archival purposes and, if applicable, Licensee may print one copy of on-line documentation, in which event all proprietary rights notices on Software and on-line documentation shall be reproduced and applied to all copies. Licensee shall not decompile, disassemble, decrypt, extract, or otherwise reverse-engineer Software. Except as provided in Section 2 above, Software may not be transferred, leased, assigned, or sublicensed, in whole or in part. No right, title or interest in and to any trademarks or trade names of Sun or Sun's licensors is granted hereunder. Software is not designed or intended for use in on-line control of aircraft, air traffic, aircraft navigation or aircraft communications; or in the design, construction, operation or maintenance of any nuclear facility. Licensee represents and warrants that it will not use or redistribute the Software for such purposes.

4. **Trademarks and Logos.** Licensee acknowledges that Sun owns the Java trademark and all Java-related trademarks, logos, and icons, including the Coffee Cup and Duke ("Java Marks"), and agrees : (i) to comply with the Java Trademark Guidelines at http://java.sun.com/trademarks.html; (ii) not do anything harmful to or inconsistent with Sun's rights in the Java Marks; and (iii) to assist Sun in protecting those rights, including assigning to Sun any rights acquired by Licensee in any Java Mark.

5. **Disclaimer of Warranty.** Software is provided "AS IS," without a warranty of any kind. ALL EXPRESS OR IMPLIED REPRESENTATIONS AND WARRANTIES, INCLUDING ANY IMPLIED WARRANTY OF MERCHANTABILITY, FITNESS FOR A PARTICULAR PURPOSE OR NON-INFRINGEMENT, ARE HEREBY EXCLUDED.

6. **Limitation of Liability.** SUN AND ITS LICENSORS SHALL NOT BE LIABLE FOR ANY DAMAGES SUFFERED BY LICENSEE OR ANY THIRD PARTY AS A RESULT OF USING OR DISTRIBUTING SOFTWARE. IN NO EVENT WILL SUN OR ITS LICENSORS BE LIABLE FOR ANY LOST REVENUE, PROFIT OR DATA, OR FOR DIRECT, INDIRECT, SPECIAL, CONSEQUENTIAL, INCIDENTAL OR PUNITIVE DAMAGES, HOWEVER CAUSED AND REGARDLESS OF THE THEORY OF LIABILITY, ARISING OUT OF THE USE OF OR INABILITY TO USE SOFTWARE, EVEN IF SUN HAS BEEN ADVISED OF THE POSSIBILITY OF SUCH DAMAGES.

7. **Termination.** Licensee may terminate this License at any time by destroying all copies of Software. This License will terminate immediately without notice from Sun if Licensee fails to comply with any provision of this License. Upon such termination, Licensee must destroy all copies of Software.

8. **Export Regulations.** Software, including technical data, is subject to U.S. export control laws, including the U.S. Export Administration Act and its associated regulations, and may be subject to export or import regulations in other countries. Licensee agrees to comply strictly with all such regulations and acknowledges that it has the responsibility to obtain licenses to export, re-export, or import Software. Software may not be downloaded, or otherwise exported or re-exported (i) into, or to a national or resident of, Cuba, Iraq, Iran, North Korea, Libya, Sudan, Syria or any country to which the U.S. has embargoed goods; or (ii) to anyone on the U.S. Treasury Department's list of Specially Designated Nations or the U.S. Commerce Department's Table of Denial Orders.

9. **Restricted Rights.** Use, duplication, or disclosure by the United States government is subject to the restrictions as set forth in the Rights in Technical Data and Computer Software Clauses in DFARS 252.227-7013(c) (1) (ii) and FAR 52.227-19(c) (2) as applicable.

10. **Governing Law.** Any action related to this License will be governed by California law and controlling U.S. federal law. No choice of law rules of any jurisdiction will apply.

Java, JavaBeans, and JavaSoft are trademarks of Sun Microsystems Inc.

IDG BOOKS WORLDWIDE, INC. END-USER LICENSE AGREEMENT

READ THIS. You should carefully read these terms and conditions before opening the software packet included with this book ("Book"). This is a license agreement ("Agreement") between you and IDG Books Worldwide, Inc. ("IDGB"). By opening the accompanying software packet, you acknowledge that you have read and accept the following terms and conditions. If you do not agree and do not want to be bound by such terms and conditions, promptly return the Book and the unopened software packet to the place you obtained them for a full refund.

1. **License Grant.** IDGB grants to you (either an individual or entity) a nonexclusive license to use one copy of the enclosed software programs (collectively, the "Software") solely for your own personal or business purposes on a single computer (whether a standard computer or a workstation component of a multiuser network). The Software is in use on a computer when it is loaded into temporary memory (RAM) or installed into permanent memory (hard disk, CD-ROM, or other storage device). IDGB reserves all rights not expressly granted herein.

2. **Ownership.** IDGB is the owner of all right, title, and interest, including copyright, in and to the compilation of the Software recorded on the CD-ROM ("Software Media"). Copyright to the individual programs recorded on the Software Media is owned by the author or other authorized copyright owner of each program. Ownership of the Software and all proprietary rights relating thereto remain with IDGB and its licensers.

3. **Restrictions on Use and Transfer.**

   (a) You may only (i) make one copy of the Software for backup or archival purposes, or (ii) transfer the Software to a single hard disk, provided that you keep the original for backup or archival purposes. You may not (i) rent or lease the Software, (ii) copy or reproduce the Software through a LAN or other network system or through any computer subscriber system or bulletin-board system, or (iii) modify, adapt, or create derivative works based on the Software.

   (b) You may not reverse engineer, decompile, or disassemble the Software. You may transfer the Software and user documentation on a permanent basis, provided that the transferee agrees to accept the terms and conditions of this Agreement and you retain no copies. If the Software is an update or has been updated, any transfer must include the most recent update and all prior versions.

4. **Restrictions on Use of Individual Programs.** You must follow the individual requirements and restrictions detailed for each individual program in Appendix B of this Book. These limitations are also contained in the individual license agreements recorded on the Software Media. These limitations may include a requirement that after using the program for a specified period of time, the user must pay a registration fee or discontinue use. By opening the Software packet, you will be agreeing to abide by the licenses and restrictions for these individual programs that are detailed in Appendix B and on the Software Media. None of the material on this Software Media or listed in this Book may ever be redistributed, in original or modified form, for commercial purposes.

5. **Limited Warranty.**

   (a) IDGB warrants that the Software and Software Media are free from defects in materials and workmanship under normal use for a period of sixty (60) days from the date of purchase of this Book. If IDGB receives notification within the warranty period of defects in materials or workmanship, IDGB will replace the defective Software Media.

   (b) **IDGB AND THE AUTHOR OF THE BOOK DISCLAIM ALL OTHER WARRANTIES, EXPRESS OR IMPLIED, INCLUDING WITHOUT LIMITATION IMPLIED WARRANTIES OF MERCHANTABILITY AND FITNESS FOR A PARTICULAR PURPOSE, WITH RESPECT TO THE SOFTWARE, THE PROGRAMS, THE SOURCE CODE CONTAINED THEREIN, AND/OR THE TECHNIQUES DESCRIBED IN THIS BOOK. IDGB DOES NOT WARRANT THAT THE FUNCTIONS CONTAINED IN THE SOFTWARE WILL MEET YOUR REQUIREMENTS OR THAT THE OPERATION OF THE SOFTWARE WILL BE ERROR-FREE.**

   (c) This limited warranty gives you specific legal rights, and you may have other rights that vary from jurisdiction to jurisdiction.

6. **Remedies.**

   (a) IDGB's entire liability and your exclusive remedy for defects in materials and workmanship shall be limited to replacement of the Software Media, which may be returned to IDGB with a copy of your receipt at the following address: Software Media Fulfillment Department, Attn.: *Java Bible*, IDG Books Worldwide, Inc., 7260 Shadeland Station, Ste. 100, Indianapolis, IN 46256, or call 1-800-762-2974. Please allow three to four weeks for delivery. This Limited Warranty is void if failure of the Software Media has resulted from accident, abuse, or misapplication. Any replacement Software Media will be warranted for the remainder of the original warranty period or thirty (30) days, whichever is longer.

   (b) In no event shall IDGB or the author be liable for any damages whatsoever (including without limitation damages for loss of business profits, business interruption, loss of business information, or any other pecuniary loss) arising from the use of or inability to use the Book or the Software, even if IDGB has been advised of the possibility of such damages.

   (c) Because some jurisdictions do not allow the exclusion or limitation of liability for consequential or incidental damages, the above limitation or exclusion may not apply to you.

7. **U.S. Government Restricted Rights.** Use, duplication, or disclosure of the Software by the U.S. Government is subject to restrictions stated in paragraph (c)(1)(ii) of the Rights in Technical Data and Computer Software clause of DFARS 252.227-7013, and in subparagraphs (a) through (d) of the Commercial Computer—Restricted Rights clause at FAR 52.227-19, and in similar clauses in the NASA FAR supplement, when applicable.

8. **General.** This Agreement constitutes the entire understanding of the parties and revokes and supersedes all prior agreements, oral or written, between them and may not be modified or amended except in a writing signed by both parties hereto that specifically refers to this Agreement. This Agreement shall take precedence over any other documents that may be in conflict herewith. If any one or more provisions contained in this Agreement are held by any court or tribunal to be invalid, illegal, or otherwise unenforceable, each and every other provision shall remain in full force and effect.

CD-ROM General Installation Instructions

Before you install the JDK or the BDK, please read the licensing agreements included in *Java 1.2 Bible*. The CD-ROM that accompanies this book contains Sun Microsystems Java™ Development Kits (JDKs) for Windows 95/NT, Solaris, and MacOS, as well as the Beans Development Kit (BDK). In addition, the disc contains Internet Explorer, Netscape Navigator, an archive of selected articles from the Web-based magazine JavaWorld; and a host of useful programs and files.

JDK installation requires a different procedure for each platform; refer to Appendix B for full details on the contents of the CD-ROM and how to install its components on your particular system.